CONSTITUTIONAL THEORY

ARGUMENTS AND PERSPECTIVES

By

Michael J. Gerhardt
Professor of Law
William and Mary Law School

Thomas D. Rowe, Jr.
Elvin R. Latty Professor of Law
Duke University School of Law

Rebecca L. Brown
Professor of Law
Vanderbilt University Law School

Girardeau A. Spann
Professor of Law
Georgetown University Law Center

LEXIS Publishing™

LEXIS®·NEXIS®· MARTINDALE-HUBBELL®
MATTHEW BENDER®· MICHIE™· SHEPARD'S®

Library of Congress Cataloging-in-Publication Data

Constitutional theory : arguments and perspectives / by Michael J. Gerhardt . . . [et al.].— 2nd ed.

   p. cm.

   Rev. ed. of: Constitutional theory / Michael J. Gerhardt, Thomas D. Rowe, Jr. c1993.

   Includes bibliographical references and index.

   ISBN 0-8205-4604-6

   1. Constitutional law—United States. I. Gerhardt, Michael J., 1956- II. Gerhardt, Michael J., 1956- Constitutional theory.

KF4550 .G467 2000
342.73—dc21

00-022066

Editorial Offices
2 Park Avenue, New York, NY 10016-5675 (212) 448-2000
201 Mission Street, San Francisco, CA 94105-1831 (415) 908-3200
701 East Water Street, Charlottesville, VA 22902-7587 (804) 972-7600
www.lexis.com

DEDICATION

For our families.

PREFACE

Preface to the Second Edition

Arguments about interpreting the United States Constitution take place on several levels. On the United States Supreme Court, the Justices debate and publish controversial opinions on how the Constitution should be interpreted. These opinions frequently become the focal point of public disputes about constitutional interpretation. In the political arena, the arguments reflect the high stakes that are involved when government tries to interpret the Constitution. These stakes may include the future role of the Supreme Court, as in the confirmation battles over the nominations of Robert Bork and Clarence Thomas as Associate Justices; the degree to which the Constitution without explicitly saying so protects individual liberties from state regulation, as reflected during the past two decades in controversies over abortion; or the standard for removing a president, as in the debates in Congress during the impeachment proceedings against President Clinton.

On yet another level, legal academicians heatedly debate the meaning and coherence of (1) constitutional doctrine—the Supreme Court's pronouncements on different constitutional issues and the frameworks for approaching particular areas—and (2) constitutional theory—the different ways scholars (as well as judges and lawyers) attempt to organize, explain, justify, and argue about constitutional decisionmaking. These controversies obviously interest the participants, who have, however, often done an inadequate job of explaining to students the relevance and significance of their academic disputes to the study and development of constitutional law.

For students in constitutional law classes, it is far from self-evident that theoretical debates about constitutional adjudication are as old as the Constitution itself, that they draw from and may at times inform the disputes among Supreme Court Justices about proper constitutional interpretation, and that they provide the intellectual justifications for the directions in constitutional law that different political forces or interest groups advocate. In short, the connection between judicial, political, and academic disputes over proper constitutional interpretation is real and substantial, and sometimes overlooked in books currently used in classes on the Constitution or American government.

The second edition of this book, like the first, aims to demystify constitutional theory both for those uninitiated in the study of constitutional law and for those with a grounding in constitutional doctrine. It brings together in one volume comprehensive materials, including Supreme Court decisions and scholarly commentary, across the spectrum of constitutional theory. The book fills a gap in the existing literature on constitutional law by providing in-depth surveys of and commentaries on different theoretical approaches to constitutional interpretation. This approach gives students, practitioners, and academics a better foundation for understanding the nature of different interpretive theories, as well as future events in which we can expect constitutional theory to play a significant role—events including confirmation proceedings, separation-of-powers conflicts such as impeachment trials, and constitutional disputes regarding civil liberties. This focus also clarifies the important connection between theory and judicial, political, and academic debates over the direction of constitutional law.

Part I provides important background material for the study of the relevance and significance of theory to constitutional adjudication in general. Part II examines in detail major sources and methods in constitutional interpretation, such as the text, framers' intent, structure, precedent, and moral reasoning, and presents controversies and difficulties concerning their use. Part III surveys major schools of thought about constitutional theory, presenting and critiquing liberal, conservative, feminist, and critical race perspectives. And Part IV concludes with some prominent alternatives in interpreting the Constitution if other available theories (particularly those built around or designed to effectuate a single unifying concept) have flaws or limits. Throughout, selections present opposing views to make readers better aware of existing conflicts and to facilitate debate. We have also attached at the end of each chapter a bibliography on the topics covered in order to assist professors interested in making assignments beyond the selections provided and to enable others to do more reading on their own. The bibliography lists references in addition to those excerpted or mentioned in the text of each chapter.

Professors using this book in courses or seminars on constitutional theory may find it valuable to begin with a class session on a prominent, current controversy that raises constitutional theory issues. Over the past few decades, such controversies have included the argument of and reaction to Raoul Berger's criticism of *Brown v. Board of Education*;[1] the exchange between Attorney General Edwin Meese and Associate Justice William Brennan on original intent and constitutional interpretation;[2] the debates over the Bork and Thomas nominations; the Supreme Court's treatment of precedent and the abortion issue in *Planned Parenthood v. Casey*;[3] and the impeachment and trial of President William Jefferson Clinton. We have included no such chapter in this book because it would rapidly become outdated.

Finally, we have omitted most footnotes from the materials presented, but the original numbering is used for those footnotes that we have retained. We have enclosed the latter numbers in brackets to distinguish them from our own footnotes. All omissions from or insertions within cases and excerpts of articles and books, except for some omitted citations, are indicated by ellipses or brackets.

---

[1] 347 U.S. 483 (1954). *See* RAOUL BERGER GOVERNMENT BY JUDICIARY: THE TRANSFORMATION OF THE FOURTEENTH AMENDMENT 117–33 (1977).

[2] *See, e.g.,* Addresses, *Construing the Constitution* (William J. Brennan, Jr., John Paul Stevens, and Edwin Meese III), 19 U.C. DAVIS L. REV. 1 (1985).

[3] 505 U.S. 833 (1992).

ACKNOWLEDGMENTS

We are grateful to Alexander Aleinikoff, Richard Chused, John Goldberg, Leslie Griffin, Carrie Menkel-Meadow, Gary Peller, Bob Rasmussen, Louis M. Seidman, Robin West, and Wendy Williams for their help and comments during the preparation of this book. In addition, we are grateful for the diligent research assistance and support provided by Derreck Brown, Felicia Burton, Dana Fitzsimons, Amanda Frazier, Matthew Gardner, Jeanne Gordon, Della Harris, Ian Morse, Gina Rudeira, and especially Mary Meek.

TABLE OF CONTENTS

Part IV
Conclusion

PART I

Why Theory?

Chapter 1

A Brief Historical Overview of the Development of American Constitutional Theory

§ 1.01 Introduction

A colleague likes to say that "the trouble with constitutional law is that nobody knows what counts as an argument." It may be more accurate to say that plenty of people think they know what does or should count, and that they often disagree. The divisions go much deeper than interpretation of particular constitutional language or application of precedent; underlying them are issues of fundamental approach and basic theory in constitutional adjudication. These themes have attracted much attention from commentators, judges, and elected officials—along with significant public notice, as during recent controversies over abortion, flag-burning, affirmative action, the nominations of Robert Bork and Clarence Thomas to the Supreme Court, the constitutionality of the Independent Counsel Act, and the impeachment proceedings against President Clinton.

It would be an exaggeration to say that these disagreements are total, because widespread consensus does exist that the constitutional text, history, structure, and precedent are valid sources for constitutional advocacy and judicial decisionmaking. Even with these conventional sources, however, deep divisions arise over their use and their very nature. Further controversy centers around whether such agreed sources are exclusive or whether other factors—for example, notions of fairness and social desirability, judicial perceptions of social mores when they are not reflected in positive law enacted by the legislature, and ideas of "natural law"—can properly play any role in constitutional decisionmaking (as some of them do with less controversy in common-law adjudication). These issues are far from abstract, for they reach both fundamental questions of the judicial role in a democratic society and vital substantive decisions affecting how we live: Should state-imposed racial segregation—or race-conscious affirmative action measures—be permitted? Should abortions be allowed—and should the overall decisions whether and when they are legal be made by judges or legislators?

In some democratic nations, these problems rarely arise. For example, the principle of parliamentary supremacy has been so firmly established in Great Britain that even a measure as controversial as muzzling media coverage of statements by Irish Republican Army supporters was not subject to serious

1

challenge in Her Majesty's courts. In the United States, however, three characteristics of the American governmental structure assure that questions of the judicial role in constitutional decisionmaking are likely to remain both endlessly debatable and politically charged: (1) the well-established practice of judicial review of the constitutionality of federal and state laws; (2) the institution of an unelected, life-tenured federal judiciary in a representative democracy; and (3) the presence in the Constitution of many broadly phrased clauses, such as "freedom of speech," "privileges or immunities," "due process of law," and "equal protection," with indefinite sweep and potential for significant substantive applications. The relationship among these three characteristics helps to explain the development of American constitutional theory.

§ 1.02 The Relationship Between Theory and Constitutional Structure

The historical justifications for judicial review as an institution of American government are widely (though not universally) regarded as beyond dispute.[1] Most legal scholars accept that the framers and ratifiers constructed the Constitution with the expectation that the federal judiciary would interpret the Constitution and, in doing so, review the constitutionality of certain majoritarian decisions. As Alexander Hamilton explained in Federalist Number 78, his classic early statement on the role of the federal judiciary under the Constitution, limitations on the power of the legislature "can be preserved in practice no other way than through the medium of the courts of justice, whose duty it must be to declare all acts contrary to the tenor of the Constitution void. Without this, all the reservations of particular rights or privileges would amount to nothing."[2] For purposes of the study of constitutional theory,

---

[1] For surveys of the historical justifications of judicial review, including the framers' expectations and subsequent generations' widespread acceptance of judicial review as part of the structure of American government, see ROBERT L. CLINTON, MARBURY V. MADISON AND JUDICIAL REVIEW (1989); LAURENCE H. TRIBE, AMERICAN CONSTITUTIONAL LAW: PART ONE 18–29, 207–310 (3d ed. 2000); RICHARD H. FALLON, DANIEL J. MELTZER, & DAVID L. SHAPIRO, HART & WECHSLER'S THE FEDERAL COURTS AND THE FEDERAL SYSTEM 11–13 (4th ed. 1996); RAOUL BERGER, CONGRESS V. THE SUPREME COURT (1969); LEONARD LEVY, JUDICIAL REVIEW AND THE SUPREME COURT (1967); ALEXANDER BICKEL, THE LEAST DANGEROUS BRANCH: THE SUPREME COURT AT THE BAR OF POLITICS 15–16 (2d ed. 1986); David Currie, The Constitution and the Supreme Court, 1801–1835, 49 U. CHI. L. REV. 646 (1982). For arguments that the power of judicial review may be plainly inferred from the structure of the Constitution, see OLIVER WENDELL HOLMES, Law and the Court, in COLLECTED LEGAL PAPERS 295 (1920); Charles Black, STRUCTURE AND RELATIONSHIP IN CONSTITUTIONAL LAW 74 (1969); Paul Freund, Umpiring the Federal System, 54 COLUM. L. REV. 561 (1954). For a contrary historical view, see 2 W. CROSSKEY, POLITICS AND THE CONSTITUTION IN THE HISTORY OF THE UNITED STATES 1008–46 (1953) (arguing that the framers did not intend judicial review). See also MARK V. TUSHNET, TAKING THE CONSTITUTION AWAY FROM THE COURTS (1999) (arguing that judicial review should be abandoned in favor of constitutional interpretation undertaken primarily by the people and their elected representatives); SYLVIA SNOWISS, JUDICIAL REVIEW AND THE LAW OF THE CONSTITUTION (1990) (arguing that Chief Justice Marshall transformed a more limited preexisting approach to judicial review). For differences of opinion on the political and theoretical justifications for judicial review, see infra note 3.

[2] THE FEDERALIST No. 78, at 491 (A. Hamilton) (B. Wright ed. 1961).

judicial review is, for all practical purposes, a given in the structure of American government.[3]

Also, in the United States the life tenure of federal judges, guaranteed in addition to undiminished compensation in Article III of the Constitution, protects judicial independence and places many controversial uses of judicial power beyond immediate political reprisal. The Supreme Court can overturn (or sustain) acts of the people's representatives, suffer nothing worse than criticism, and mostly have its decisions stick, at least for a considerable time. The means that the political branches can use to try to undo the Court's constitutional rulings are difficult to effect and time-consuming.[4] Our Constitution and system of federalism thus combine broad authorization for majoritarian political power with judicially enforced checks on its exercise, such as those in the Bill of Rights. This combination can give the federal judiciary itself a considerable measure of effective political power, and the people cannot vote the judges out as they can their elected leaders and representatives.

Much of constitutional theory responds to a felt need to justify, and at the same time to try to set bounds for the exercise of, this otherwise frequently unchecked nonmajoritarian power. Theories attempt to provide the judiciary a set of arguments or overarching principles to be used in deciding constitutional issues. Often debates over theory are cast in terms of whether the Court does and should exercise its authority in constitutional cases more or less according to strictly "legal" canons, or whether it can appropriately include any measure of judgment based on ideas of desirable policy. Other theorists question to what extent the distinction between "law" and "policy" or "politics" can be maintained, especially under the vaguer clauses of the Constitution and in the difficult cases that reach the pinnacle of our judicial system.

§ 1.03   Theory and the Countermajoritarian Difficulty in Early American History

Tracing the historical development of debates over sources and methods in American constitutional adjudication shows that many such disputes are

---

[3] Legal scholars and political scientists still debate the legitimacy and utility of judicial review, at least as matters of political theory. *See, e.g.,* M. TUSHNET, *supra* note 1, *passim*; RICHARD PARKER, "HERE THE PEOPLE RULE": A CONSTITUTIONAL POPULIST MANIFESTO (1994); Richard Posner, *Appeal and Consent,* THE NEW REPUBLIC, Aug. 16, 1999, at 36; Sanford Levinson, *A Constitutional Convention: Does the Left Fear Popular Sovereignty?,* DISSENT, Winter 1996, at 27. *See also* SANFORD LEVINSON, CONSTITUTIONAL FAITH (1988); ALBERT P. MELONE & GEORGE MACE, JUDICIAL REVIEW AND AMERICAN DEMOCRACY (1988); David Bryden, *Politics, the Constitution, and the New Formalism,* 3 CONST. COMMENTARY 415 (1986); Larry Simon, *The Authority of the Constitution and*

Its Meaning: A Preface to a Theory of Constitutional Interpretation, 58 S. CAL. L. REV. 603 (1985). For a detailed description of the classic debate between Judge Learned Hand and Columbia law professor Herbert Wechsler on the legitimacy of judicial review, *see* GERALD GUNTHER & KATHLEEN SULLIVAN, CONSTITUTIONAL LAW 17–18 (13th ed. 1997).

[4] The different ways that Supreme Court decisions may be modified or overruled are (1) the restaffing of the bench over many years (with significant input on the part of the President, who nominates judges, and the Senate, which must advise and consent to such nominations); (2) persuading Justices to change their minds about prior opinions; (3) congressional modifications of the Court's jurisdiction; (4) constitutional amendment; and (5) impeachment.

perennial, and that constitutional theories have often emerged as sophisticated reactions to (or even influences on) important political or social events.
During the ratification campaign, Alexander Hamilton explained that "[t]he
interpretation of the laws is the proper and peculiar province of the courts.
A constitution is . . . and must be regarded by the judges as, a fundamental
law. It therefore belongs to them to ascertain its meaning as well as the
meaning of any particular act proceeding from the legislative body."[5] Hamilton acknowledged but offered no solution to the possible problem that if, in
interpreting the Constitution, the judiciary "should be disposed to exercise
WILL instead of JUDGMENT, the consequence would be . . . the substitution
of their pleasure to that of the legislative body."[6]

Hamilton's recognition of the possibility of unprincipled or self-interested
judicial interference with the decisions of the people's duly elected representatives—raising what subsequently has been referred to as "the countermajoritarian difficulty"[7] —coexisted, in a tension that continues to the present day,
with another theme: the propriety, indeed the necessity, of the federal courts'
nonmajoritarian power as a critical component of the Constitution's system
of checks and balances. As Hamilton explained, "the courts were designed to
be an intermediate body between the people and the legislature in order . . .
to keep the latter within limits assigned to their authority."[8] Given this tension, it is not surprising that intense debates have erupted over the justifications for the Court's ensuing invalidations of majoritarian decisions.

For example, in *Marbury v. Madison*,[9] the Supreme Court for the first time
invalidated part of a congressional enactment—the Judiciary Act of 1789—as
impermissibly expanding the Constitution's allocation of original jurisdiction
to the Court in Article III. The *Marbury* opinion, sparing the Court from
having to order the President and the Secretary of State to recognize certain
people as federal judges, avoided a confrontation with the executive while
defining in broad terms the Court's power and duty to invalidate unconstitutional acts of the political branches. Subsequent generations still debate
Marshall's justifications for judicial review—the Constitution as written law;
the judiciary's special province to interpret federal law, including the Constitution; Article VI's supremacy clause making the Constitution the supreme
law of the land; and judges' oaths mandated by Article VI to support and
defend the Constitution in the discharge of their duties.[10]

There was even greater controversy the second time the Court invalidated
a congressional enactment, shortly before the Civil War in *Dred Scott v.*

---

[5] THE FEDERALIST No. 78, *supra* note 2, at
492 (A. Hamilton).

[6] *Id.* at 493.

[7] A. BICKEL, *supra* note 1, at 16. For the first
in a provocative series of articles tracing the
history of and challenging the conventional
concept of countermajoritarian difficulty, *see*
Barry Friedman, *The History of the Countermajoritarian Difficulty, Part One: The Road to
Judicial Supremacy*, 73 N.Y.U. L. REV. 333
(1998).

[8] THE FEDERALIST No. 78, *supra* note 2, at
492 (A. Hamilton).

[9] 5 U.S. (1 Cranch) 137, 180, 2 L. Ed. 60 (1803).

[10] *Marbury* was followed not long after by
Martin v. Hunter's Lessee, 14 U.S. (1 Wheat.)
304, 4 L. Ed. 97 (1816), in which the Court in
an opinion by Justice Joseph Story ruled that
both structurally and textually the Constitution authorized Supreme Court review of state
court judgments involving the federal Constitution.

Sandford.[11] John Marshall's successor as Chief Justice, Roger Taney, secured an infamous place in American history by arguing that neither slaves nor their descendants were (or could be) citizens of the United States but instead were property that could not be taken away from their masters, as might have been the effect of what Congress had done in the Missouri Compromise. Consequently, the Court struck down part of the Missouri Compromise based to some extent on Taney's reading of the historical record on slavery.[12] Among the dissenters, Justice Benjamin Curtis read the same historical record but reached the opposite conclusion that freedmen and slaves' descendants could be United States citizens.[13]

Dred Scott raised questions about the role of the judiciary that people still debate. By holding that the federal government could not legislatively limit the states' discretion over perpetuating slavery, the Supreme Court sparked a firestorm of criticism and aggravated sectional divisions on the eve of the Civil War. Some modern critics of recent liberal judicial activism see in *Dred Scott* an object lesson in the evils of departing from original intent to read one's own policy preferences into the Constitution,[14] or of judicial initiatives to address social issues when other organs of government have failed to act.[15]

The Court in *Dred Scott* helped to set the stage for the Civil War as well as the subsequent drafting and adoption of the Reconstruction Amendments. While it is clear that those amendments were designed to overrule *Dred Scott* and to guarantee equal status for the newly freed slaves and their descendants, the extent to which the broad language of those amendments, particularly the Fourteenth, did something more, such as insulating certain fundamental aspects of individual liberty from state regulation, remains a perennial subject of judicial, political, and academic controversy.[16]

§ 1.04   Theory in the Twentieth Century

After the Civil War, judicial review increasingly became a fact of American life, raising the issue of the courts' role in relation to the majoritarian branches also established by the Constitution. For modern readers, three crucial events in the 20th century can serve as points of departure in debates about constitutional theory: the crisis over the Supreme Court's striking down of many New Deal measures in the 1930s, and problems posed by two more recent landmark Supreme Court decisions—*Brown v. Board of Education,*[17]

---

[11] 60 U.S. (19 How.) 393, 15 L. Ed. 691 (1857).

[12] *Id.* at 406–27.

[13] *Id.* at 571–76 (Curtis, J., dissenting).

[14] *See* ROBERT BORK, THE TEMPTING OF AMERICA: THE POLITICAL SEDUCTION OF THE LAW 28–34 (1990).

[15] *See* William H. Rehnquist, *The Notion of a Living Constitution,* 54 TEX. L. REV. 693, 700–02 (1976).

[16] *See, e.g.,* AKHIL REED AMAR, THE BILL OF RIGHTS: CREATION AND RECONSTRUCTION (1998); WILLIAM NELSON, THE FOURTEENTH AMENDMENT: FROM POLITICAL PRINCIPLE TO JUDICIAL DOCTRINE (1988); MICHAEL KENT CURTIS, NO STATE SHALL ABRIDGE: THE FOURTEENTH AMENDMENT AND THE BILL OF RIGHTS (1985); RAOUL BERGER, GOVERNMENT BY JUDICIARY: THE TRANSFORMATION OF THE FOURTEENTH AMENDMENT (2d. ed. 1997); Robert Kaczorowski, *Revolutionary Constitutionalism in the Era of the Civil War and Reconstruction,* 61 N.Y.U. L. REV. 863 (1986); Charles Fairman, *Does the Fourteenth Amendment Incorporate the Bill of Rights? The Original Understanding,* 2 STAN. L. REV. 5 (1949).

[17] 347 U.S. 483, 74 S. Ct. 686, 98 L. Ed. 2d 873 (1954).

overturning public school segregation in 1954, and *Roe v. Wade*,[18] invalidating most proscriptions on abortion in 1973. A brief sketch of the events and the theoretical overtones of these controversies provides background to the deeper study of different theories later in the book.

The activism of the conservative Supreme Court majority before 1937, often protecting economic rights of business from government intervention in markets for goods and labor, raised questions of the legitimacy of the Court's role in the face of strong electoral support and overwhelming legislative majorities for liberal enactments. One of the first academicians to address these questions was Harvard law professor James Bradley Thayer. In an essay written in 1893 on the eve of an era of judicial activism on behalf of economic liberties, Thayer argued that under the American system, judicial interference with the decisionmaking of democratically elected officials sapped the other branches of government of initiative and responsibility. He suggested that legislators rather than judges are the primary arbiters of the constitutionality of laws and that as a reflection of their respect for this important legislative function courts should strike down only those laws predicated on clearly erroneous interpretations of the Constitution.[19] Thayer's arguments influenced a generation of Harvard Law School faculty and students, including but not limited to Justices Holmes, Brandeis, and Frankfurter. Because of this impact, Thayer's essay has been described as "the most influential essay ever written on American constitutional law."[20]

If Thayer sought to forestall a decisional trend, his efforts initially failed because little more than a decade later the Court in 1905 decided the case that came in the early 20th century to symbolize the controversy over the legitimacy of active judicial interference with democratic decisionmaking—*Lochner v. New York*.[21] There the Court ruled that a New York law regulating the hours of bakery workers violated a fundamental right to contract derived from the term "liberty" in the Fourteenth Amendment due process clause. Although *Lochner* was only one of almost 200 instances near the turn of the century (most occurring in the 1920s and 1930s) in which the Court struck down state laws as violating economic rights derived from and protected by due process,[22] the decision became a symbol of a controversial reading of the due process clauses of the Fifth and Fourteenth Amendments as insulating from regulation economic liberties not specifically mentioned therein.

---

[18] 410 U.S. 113, 93 S. Ct. 705, 35 L. Ed. 2d 147 (1973).

[19] James Bradley Thayer, *The Origin and Scope of the American Doctrine of Constitutional Law*, 7 HARV. L. REV. 129 (1893).

[20] Henry P. Monaghan, *Marbury and the Administrative State*, 83 COLUM. L. REV. 1, 7 (1983). For a comprehensive examination of the motivations for and significance of Thayer's essay, *see* Thayer Centennial Symposium, 88 Nw. U. L. REV. 1 (1993).

[21] 198 U.S. 45, 25 S. Ct. 539, 49 L. Ed. 937 (1905).

[22] For a comprehensive summary of the Court's decisions during this era, see N. SMALL (ED), THE CONSTITUTION OF THE UNITED STATES 1392–99, 1427–87 (1964 ed.). For discussions of this period of constitutional history, see E. LEWIS, HISTORY OF AMERICAN POLITICAL THOUGHT FROM THE CIVIL WAR TO THE WORLD WAR 101–07 (1937); P. MURPHY, THE CONSTITUTION IN CRISIS TIMES 1918–1969, at 18–37 (1972); A. MASON & W. BEANEY, THE SUPREME COURT IN A FREE SOCIETY 198–99 (1968). The effective end of *Lochner* came in Nebbia v. New York, 291 U.S. 502, 54 S. Ct. 505, 78 L. Ed. 940 (1934), and West Coast Hotel Co. v. Parrish, 300 U.S. 379, 392, 57 S. Ct. 578, 81 L. Ed. 703 (1937).

For many political liberals of the post-*Lochner* era, such as Justice Felix Frankfurter, a lesson of the thirties was the importance of judicial restraint to assure a considerable measure of deference to most policy decisions of the people and their elected leaders and representatives. For others, such as Justice William O. Douglas—who had been prominent in the movement known as legal realism—judicial decisions were not fully explicable through reference to the terms of the decisions themselves.[23] Legal realists tended to agree that the personal preferences of judges rather than precedent impelled or explained judicial decisions. They differed, however, over the extent of such influences and which of the various tools for understanding and criticizing decisions— judges' preferences, the social and economic effects of court rulings, etc.— should be used beyond academic analysis, and whether such factors ought actually to influence judicial treatment of the cases. In any event, the crisis precipitated by the Supreme Court's interference with majoritarian legislation on economic issues faded—without enactment of President Franklin D. Roosevelt's "Court-packing" plan to add more Justices—after an apparent change in the course of decisions and the filling of several Supreme Court vacancies.

Brown cut the other way and represents the dilemma posed by many of the rulings of the Warren Court. *Brown* was an activist decision striking down legislative action, with what many believed was questionable justification in conventional legal terms but with social and moral import that found wide approval in liberal and other communities. The *Brown* case presents in microcosm several of the themes that remain important in controversies over constitutional theory to this day—the use of the text, the binding force of history and the intent of the framers, the weight of precedent, the role of social facts beyond those of the individual case, the motives behind a legislative measure, and the place of moral reasoning in constitutional adjudication.

Liberal commentators split over *Brown.* For example, Professor Herbert Wechsler of Columbia Law School criticized the Court with regret, despite his sympathy for its holding. He insisted that "the main constituent of the judicial process is precisely that it must be genuinely principled. . . . A principled decision . . . rests on reasons with respect to all issues in the case, reasons that in their generality and their neutrality transcend any immediate result that is involved."[24] Wechsler could find no such "neutral principles" transcending the result of *Brown:* "Given a situation where the state must practically choose between denying [interracial] association to those individuals who wish it or imposing it on those who would avoid it, is there a basis in neutral principles for holding that the Constitution demands that the claims for association should prevail? I should like to think there is, but I confess that I have not yet [found it.]"[25]

---

[23] *See generally* LAURA KALMAN, THE STRANGE CAREER OF LEGAL LIBERALISM (1996); LAURA KALMAN, LEGAL REALISM AT YALE: 1927–1960 (1986).

[24] Herbert J. Wechsler, *Toward Neutral Principles of Constitutional Law,* 73 HARV. L. REV. 1, 19 (1959).

[25] *Id.* Wechsler's "neutral principles" theory was designed to define the appropriate performance of the judicial function and was only part of a larger school of thought—legal process—that tried to assign appropriate tasks to the different institutions of government. *See* HENRY M. HART, JR. & ALBERT M. SACKS, THE LEGAL PROCESS: BASIC PROBLEMS IN THE MAKING AND APPLICATION OF LAW (William N. Eskridge, Jr. & Philip C. Frickey eds., 1994).

Other liberals, such as Professor Charles Black of Yale Law School, found *Brown* defensible and the legal case for it even compelling. Black argued that the equal protection clause "should be read as saying that the Negro race, as such, is not to be significantly disadvantaged by the laws of the states," and that "segregation is a massive intentional disadvantaging of the Negro race, as such, by state law."[26]

Brown has now gained extremely wide acceptance in the legal community and in American society as a whole for its result, if not, among commentators, for the legal justifications given in the opinion.[27] But many other Warren Court decisions, including those that required population-based reapportionment of state legislative districts and those that subjected state criminal procedures to the standards of most of the federal Bill of Rights,[28] appeared to push further and drew fire on methodological grounds. Supporters of Warren Court decisions often found grounds for activism in the service of individual rights and liberties that they argued were lacking in the area of economic claims. It is probably accurate, however, to say that the dominant view in much of the legal academy in the 1950s and 1960s was hostile to the Court's expansive role, whatever the perceived desirability of its results. For many, the Court was engaging in politics masquerading as law, an illegitimate enterprise that could reduce respect for law and leave core constitutional protections too subject to changes in political climate.[29]

One of the leading constitutional theorists of the period, Professor Alexander Bickel of Yale Law School, began as a defender of *Brown* but became more

---

[26] Charles Black, *The Lawfulness of the Segregation Decisions*, 69 YALE L.J. 421, 421 (1960).

[27] To be sure, the significance of *Brown* is still debated. Some scholars argue that *Brown* never achieved its full promise, *see, e.g.*, Chapter Ten: Critical Race Theory, while others maintain that the importance of *Brown* as a watershed event in constitutional law has been exaggerated or misunderstood. The latter argue, for instance, that the Warren Court's striking down of segregation in public schools was an inevitable step to take in light of the early stirrings of the civil rights movement, the socio-economic and educational backgrounds of the justices, and other governmental decisions (such as President Truman's order in the late 1940s to desegregate the armed forces). *See, e.g.*, GERALD ROSENBERG, HOLLOW HOPE: CAN COURTS BRING ABOUT SOCIAL CHANGE? (1991); Michael Klarman, Brown, *Racial Change, and the Civil Rights Movement*, 80 VA. L. REV. 7 (1994). Other scholars question *Brown*'s significance on the ground that there is no solid evidence that it led to an improvement in the education of African-Americans or even to substantial public-school integration. *See, e.g.*, Sonia R. Jarvis, Brown *and the Afrocentric Curriculum*, 101 YALE L.J. 1285, 1289–91 (1992) (explaining that there has been minimal

progress in equalization of educational opportunity for black children, and that efforts to integrate schools—predominantly through busing— have been met with widespread resistance, white flight, and ultimate resegregation); Steven Spiegel, *Race, Education, and the Equal Protection Clause in the 1990s: The Meaning of* Brown v. Board of Education *in Light of Milwaukee's Schools of African-American Immersion*, 74 MARQ. L. REV. 501, 503–07 (1991) (finding principles articulated in *Brown* problematic when applied to Milwaukee's attempt to create special programs for African-American school children).

[28] For two sources on the development of the application of the Bill of Rights to the states through the Fourteenth Amendment due process clause, including the Warren Court's contributions to this procedure known as incorporation, *see* JOHN E. NOWAK & RONALD D. ROTUNDA, CONSTITUTIONAL LAW 339–42 (5th ed. 1995); and Michael J. Gerhardt, *The Ripple Effects of* Slaughter-House: *A Critique of a Negative Rights View of the Constitution*, 43 VAND. L. REV. 409, 420, 420 n.46 (1990). For a recent comprehensive reexamination of the historical support for incorporation of the Bill of Rights, *see* A. Amar, *supra* note 16.

[29] *See infra* Chapter 9, Conservative Constitutional Theory.

equivocal about the general course of Warren Court methods and decisions in his major 1962 book, *The Least Dangerous Branch: The Supreme Court at the Bar of Politics*. Even though Bickel argued that "judicial review is a deviant institution in the American democracy,"[30] he defended the Court's role as an educator in the enduring social values embodied in the broad phrases of the Constitution. However, he cautioned that, because of the Court's limited political capital, the legitimacy of judicial review depended to a significant degree on the Court's use of the "passive virtues" of avoiding precipitate or unnecessary decisions on constitutional flashpoints by using the discretionary and doctrinal avoidance devices available to the Justices.[31]

Bickel was more critical of the Warren Court in a series of lectures given at the end of the Warren era in 1969.[32] He argued that the Warren Court might have placed too much "confident reliance on the intuitive judicial capacity to identify the course of progress."[33] As a result, he feared that some of the Warren Court's landmark efforts were "heading toward obsolescence, and in large measure abandonment."[34]

Several new Court appointments, and some change in the pattern of decisions in the early 1970s, brought continuing controversy over the legitimacy of the Court's approaches and rulings. In some areas though, the Burger Court went even further than its predecessor—and with what seemed like less justification in conventional sources.[35]

Already in 1971 then-Professor Robert Bork of Yale Law School had prominently criticized the Warren Court for abandoning judicial fidelity to the "neutral principles" underlying and derived from the original understanding of the Constitution—what the public could have understood particular constitutional language to mean at the time it was drafted and ratified.[36] Bork focused on the Warren Court's First Amendment jurisprudence that gave broad protection to more than purely political speech and on its privacy decisions, particularly the 1965 ruling in *Griswold v. Connecticut*,[37] striking down a state ban on the use of contraceptives by married couples as violating a constitutionally protected zone of privacy. Bork argued that the Warren Court had gone well beyond the identification and application of the proper "neutral principle" embodied in the First Amendment that would protect only political speech not directed at "the forcible overthrow of the government or violation of law."[38] He also argued that *Griswold* was unprincipled because, without a foundation derived from the Constitution, the Court could favor the claims of "a minority claiming freedom" and "a majority claiming power to regulate" only on the basis of "its own value preferences."[39] For Bork, *Griswold* typified the Warren Court's efforts to aggrandize itself at the

---

[30] A. Bickel, *supra* note 1, at 18.

[31] *See generally id.* at 111–98.

[32] ALEXANDER BICKEL, THE SUPREME COURT AND THE IDEA OF PROGRESS (1969).

[33] *Id.* at 173–74.

[34] *Id.* at 173.

[35] *See generally* THE BURGER COURT: THE COUNTER-REVOLUTION THAT WASN'T (V. Blasi ed., 1983).

[36] Robert Bork, *Neutral Principles and Some First Amendment Problems,* 47 IND. L.J. 1 (1971).

[37] 381 U.S. 479, 485–486, 85 S. Ct. 1678, 14 L. Ed. 2d 510 (1965).

[38] Bork, *supra* note 36, at 30.

[39] *Id.* at 9.

expense of the legitimate majoritarian decisionmaking processes of the federal and state governments.

Yet in 1973 in *Roe v. Wade*, the Burger Court, relying in part on *Griswold*, overturned virtually all state abortion laws. *Roe v. Wade* posed even more acutely, for some, the *Brown* dilemma of politically desirable results without adequate foundation in principled legal reasoning. For many, *Roe v. Wade* was the quintessential example of judges illegitimately writing their personal preferences into constitutional doctrine. Whatever *Roe*'s justifiability, it does seem a less strained step from the equal protection clause to a ban on state-imposed segregation than from the due process clause to a fundamental right to an abortion. The contrast between *Brown* and *Roe v. Wade* also illustrates the importance of social consensus in keeping the fires of theoretical (not to mention political) controversy burning. After initial massive Southern resistance, *Brown* eventually achieved a degree of acceptance that *Roe* seems unlikely to gain—whether the latter stays on the books or is eventually overruled.

In the latter half of the 1970s, debate over the theoretical justifications for *Brown* and, particularly, *Roe v. Wade* continued. In 1975, Professor Thomas Grey of Stanford Law School helped to crystalize the debate by arguing that it is necessary to acknowledge that we have a partially "unwritten Constitution," based on a modern analog to earlier theories of natural law, in order to justify many of the fundamental decisions with which he sympathized.[40] Archibald Cox, a political liberal and professor at the Harvard Law School, argued in 1976 that the Burger Court had failed in *Roe v. Wade* "to establish the legitimacy of the decision by not articulating a precept of sufficient abstractness to lift the ruling above the level of a political judgment based upon the evidence currently available from the medical, physical, and social sciences."[41] For Cox, an appropriate principle should have been capable of developing "roots throughout the community and continuing over significant periods of time."[42] In 1977, Raoul Berger sharpened criticism of *Brown* with a detailed attack based on his reading of the history surrounding the adoption of the Fourteenth Amendment.[43]

In a series of articles culminating in his 1980 book, *Democracy and Distrust: A Theory of Judicial Review,* Professor John Hart Ely, now of the University of Miami Law School, defended *Brown* and the Warren Court generally as

---

[40] *See* Thomas Grey, *Do We Have an Unwritten Constitution?*, 27 STAN. L. REV. 703 (1975). This article is often credited with having coined terms to describe what were, at least for a time, major strains in contemporary debates over constitutional interpretation: interpretivism (arguing for limiting sources in constitutional adjudication to traditional ones such as the text and the framers' intent) and noninterpretivism (permitting judges to draw as well on sources outside of the constitutional text, such as moral philosophy or ideas of social desirability). By the 1980s, however, Professor Grey rethought and seemingly abandoned this view in favor of

what he regarded as a more realistic one. *See* Thomas Grey, *The Constitution as Scripture,* 37 STAN. L. REV. 1, 1 (1984) ("We are all interpretivists; the real arguments are not over whether judges should stick to interpreting, but over what they should interpret and what interpretive attitudes they should adopt.").

[41] ARCHIBALD COX, THE ROLE OF THE SUPREME COURT IN AMERICAN GOVERNMENT 113 (1976).

[42] *Id.* at 114.

[43] RAOUL BERGER, GOVERNMENT BY THE JUDICIARY 117–33, 286–87, 328–29, 342–43, 348 (1st ed. 1977).

having pursued a "representation-reinforcing" theory of judicial review, which justified judicial interference with legislative decisions in order to eliminate structural or procedural obstacles that prevent popular majorities from attaining control of legislatures, or that keep powerless or unrepresented minority segments of our society from fully participating in the political process producing those decisions. But he found less justification for some approaches, even those producing results congenial to political liberals, taken by the Burger Court. In particular, Ely—like Cox a political liberal—argued that *Roe v. Wade* could not be defended in process terms "for the obvious reason that the genuine source of trouble in the abortion context is not that the issue is peculiarly unsuited to democratic decision but rather that democratic decision quite often consistently generates value choices with which many of us, myself included, rather fervently disagree."[44] Professor Laurence Tribe of Harvard Law School prominently criticized Ely's "representation-reinforcing" theory. Tribe argued that Ely had ignored both the substantive character of numerous constitutional commitments and the indeterminacy of many supposedly process-oriented protections without an underlying substantive theory.[45]

The 1980s saw intensification of the debate and broadening—as well as some redefining—of its terms. With the Reagan era came added strength for conservative voices both on the bench[46] and in academia. These voices emphasized fidelity to the text of the Constitution and the framers' original understanding—two points of reference that may conflict surprisingly often. At the same time, some who came of age in the protest movements of the late sixties and early seventies, now legal academics, criticized liberal judicial methodology from the left and questioned whether law can ever be something other than raw politics in disguise.[47] The increasingly interdisciplinary nature of legal scholarship brought into the debate such themes as economic analysis[48] and the use of interpretive concepts from literary and theological studies.[49] The addition of significant numbers of women to the legal profession and law teaching added feminist perspectives to constitutional theory.[50] Additionally, an increasing number of minority scholars, loosely organized around a movement known as "critical race theory," offered their critiques of conventional or liberal approaches to legal analysis.[51]

---

[44] JOHN HART ELY, DEMOCRACY AND DISTRUST: A THEORY OF JUDICIAL REVIEW 248 n.52 (1980).

[45] Laurence Tribe, *The Puzzling Persistence of Process-Based Constitutional Theories,* 89 YALE L.J. 1063 (1980).

[46] For example, President Reagan appointed many conservative law professors to the federal bench, including Antonin Scalia to the Supreme Court and Richard Posner, Robert Bork, Ralph Winter, Stephen Williams, Frank Easterbrook, John Noonan, J. Harvie Wilkinson, Douglas Ginsburg, Pasco Bowman, and Kenneth Ripple to the federal courts of appeals.

[47] See *infra* Chapter 8, Liberal Constitutional Theory.

[48] See *infra* Chapter 9, Conservative Constitutional Theory.

[49] See *infra* Chapter 12, Interpretation Theory and Postmodernism.

[50] See *infra* Chapter 10, Feminist Legal Theory.

[51] See *infra* Chapter 11, Critical Race Theory.

§ 1.05 The Relevance of Theory to Recent Events

Throughout the 1980s and 1990s, it has been clear that, with the exception of conservative viewpoints, these added perspectives have not yet seemed to exert much overt influence on Supreme Court (or, for that matter, other governmental institutions') constitutional decisionmaking, perhaps because of an arguably widening division between the legal academy and the legal profession. Nevertheless, in this period legal scholars have been integrally involved as counsel, consultants, and expert witnesses in several major constitutional conflicts. Indeed, the intense controversy and large public mobilization over the nominations of Robert Bork and Clarence Thomas to the Supreme Court, and over the impeachment and trial of President Clinton, show how concerns about proper constitutional adjudication and interpretation are far from being merely academic. For example, the battle over Bork centered on two questions of critical importance to constitutional theory.[52] The first, sometimes referred to as the debate over the existence of a "living Constitution," focused on whether constitutional *interpreters* should largely attempt to determine the meaning and intent of the framers, or whether they may legitimately draw on contemporary perspectives (as constitution-*amenders* may do) beyond those available to the framers. The second question was whether the Constitution guarantees unenumerated (or implicit) rights such as protection from government intrusion upon intimate associations and procreative decisions.

Only four years later, the Senate faced another set of troubling issues involving constitutional theory in the Supreme Court confirmation proceedings for then-Circuit Judge Clarence Thomas. One issue in the controversy over his confirmation was the coherence and justifiability of his view of the role of "natural law" in constitutional adjudication. The question arose from articles he had written arguing, *inter alia,* that slavery violated certain judicially enforceable principles of natural law expressed in the Declaration of Independence.[53] Many Senators also vigorously questioned Judge Thomas about whether a speech he had given before he became a federal court of appeals judge showed that he might vote to overturn *Roe v. Wade* on the ground that it conflicted with a constitutionally protected fundamental right to life for fetuses that derived from natural law.[54] Although such positions deriving from conservative perspectives have been points of departure for the theoretical overtones in much recent adjudication and confirmation debate, as today's students become tomorrow's law clerks, lawyers, policymakers, executive officers, and judges, the courts (as well as the elected branches) will deal with many of the ideas now prominent across the spectrum of theoretical scholarship.

---

[52] *See generally* Morton Horwitz, *The Meaning of the Bork Nomination in American Constitutional History,* 50 U. PITT. L. REV. 655, 656–57 (1989).

[53] *See, e.g.,* Clarence Thomas, *The Higher Law Background of the Privileges and Immunities Clause of the Fourteenth Amendment,* 12 HARV. J.L. & PUB. POL'Y 63 (1989); Clarence Thomas, *Toward a "Plain Reading" of the Constitution—The Declaration of Independence in* *Constitutional Interpretation,* 30 HOW. L.J. 983 (1987).

[54] Clarence Thomas, *Why Black Americans Should Look to Conservative Policies,* Heritage Foundation Reports: The Heritage Lectures, June 18, 1987 (describing Lewis Lehrman's article, *The Declaration of Independence and the Right to Life,* THE AMERICAN SPECTATOR, April 1987, at 21, as a "splendid example" of the application of natural law to a constitutional issue).

Even within today's camps pronounced divisions already are evident. For instance, disagreement among conservatives is sometimes highly visible on the Supreme Court. Indeed, President Reagan's appointments of William Rehnquist as Chief Justice and Sandra Day O'Connor, Antonin Scalia, and Anthony Kennedy as Associate Justices, and President Bush's appointment of Clarence Thomas as Associate Justice, have consolidated a conservative majority that has frequently disagreed on the appropriate degrees of deference to, as well as on the prioritizing of, different sources of constitutional decision. These sources include text, structure, original understanding, historical practices, and precedent (particularly "liberal" precedent).[55] Moreover, some political conservatives favor fairly general judicial restraint, while others find justification in constitutional text and structure and in economic theory for a degree of federalist or market-oriented judicial activism.[56]

Just as divisions among the conservative justices of the Supreme Court have become increasingly evident and pronounced, so too have differences of opinion among political liberals and leftists about the role of the Supreme Court and methods of constitutional interpretation. At one extreme, leftist critics from the critical legal studies movement have strongly argued the incoherence and indeterminacy of conventional liberal constitutional doctrine, while only rarely producing prominent alternative theories of their own—which perhaps should not be expected from scholars whose work is often fundamentally critical of the existing legal order and hence unlikely to suggest modes of working within it.[57]

One prominent CLS scholar, Professor Mark Tushnet of the Georgetown University Law Center, proposed an alternative approach: using critical analysis to expose the competing and contradictory traditions in American constitutional history, to tear down the dominant liberal constitutional theory and doctrine, and to synthesize through the dialectical process elements of the liberal tradition with the subjugated tradition of republicanism. This tradition stresses that human beings are essentially political animals who can fulfill their natures only by participating in self-government, and that the most important aim of the political community should be to promote the common good.[58] Other liberal scholars outside or on the fringe of the critical legal studies movement, including Professors Frank Michelman of Harvard Law School and Cass Sunstein of the University of Chicago Law School, also argued for the resurgence of the republican tradition, advocating that constitutional decisionmaking by courts and other institutions should be approached with reference to public values that are informed by, if not directly linked to, republicanism.[59] While Tushnet's critique has also led him to urge the

---

[55] These disagreements cover a wide range of vital constitutional issues, including but not limited to criminal procedure, abortion rights, and freedom of expression. *See generally infra* Chapter 9: Conservative Constitutional Theory.

[56] *See id.*

[57] See *infra* Chapter 8, Liberal Constitutional Theory.

[58] *See* MARK V. TUSHNET, RED, WHITE, AND BLUE: A CRITICAL ANALYSIS OF CONSTITU-

TIONAL LAW (1988).

[59] *See, e.g.,* Frank Michelman, *The Supreme Court, 1985 Term—Foreword: Traces of Self-Government,* 100 HARV. L. REV. 4 (1986); Frank Michelman, *Law's Republic,* 97 YALE L.J. 1493 (1988); Cass Sunstein, *Beyond the Republican Revival,* 97 YALE L.J. 1539 (1988); Cass Sunstein, *Interest Groups in American Public Law,* 38 STAN. L. REV. 29 (1985). *See also* Symposium, *Roads Not Taken: Undercurrents of Republican Thinking in Modern Constitutional Theory,* 84 Nw. U. L. REV. 1 (1989).

abandonment of the institution of judicial review in favor of vesting primary responsibility for constitutional interpretation in the public themselves and their popularly elected representatives,[60] other liberal scholars have urged less radical solutions to the persistence of the countermajoritarian difficulty. For instance, Professor Sunstein has advocated judicial minimalism, an approach to judging that eschews broad grounds that will reduce the magnitude of the judges' inevitable errors while preserving a significant "space for democratic reflection from Congress and the states."[61]

Feminist legal scholars too have experienced divisions. Feminism has liberal and more radical wings that debate the degree to which liberal constitutional jurisprudence sees and treats women as men see and treat them, thereby requiring substantial, if not fundamental, restructuring of legal thought (if not the legal system) to achieve true equality for women.[62] These debates have helped to inspire movements in favor of anti-pornography and pro-choice legislation. Another group of modern feminists agrees with liberal feminists' insistence on gender-neutral laws for most issues, but maintains that formal equality denies important social and biological differences between men and women.[63] They argue further that equal treatment requires treating women differently based on the ways in which women and men are different. Last but not least, another group of feminists emphasizes that there is no monolithic feminine experience but many experiences that vary according to a woman's race, class, ethnicity, and culture.[64] These feminists suggest femininity is socially constructed and knowledge, rather than being objective, is situational and constructed from a confluence of multiple perspectives.

In addition, critical race theorists have sharply criticized the post-1960s efforts of mainstream (particularly liberal) scholars, judges, and politicians on behalf of civil rights. Critical race scholars argue that the civil rights movement has not fulfilled its promise and that African-Americans and other racial and ethnic minorities are being treated unfairly by the legal system and by white-dominated social institutions. As an outgrowth of the critical legal studies movement, critical race theorists use various techniques to argue that there is a racial tilt built into the status quo and that the legal system affirmatively contributes to the social oppression of racial minorities.[65]

As the arguments over constitutional theory enter the twenty-first century, theorists increasingly debate the consequences of their demonstrations of the

---

[60] M. TUSHNET, *supra* note 1, *passim.* Tushnet and his Georgetown colleague Louis M. Seidman also have expressed their skepticism about the possibilities for a return to what they regard as the golden age of New Deal and Great Society liberalism, and its judicial embodiment—the Warren Court—which "restored the good name of judicial activism." LOUIS M. SEIDMAN & MARK V. TUSHNET, REMNANTS OF BELIEF 43 (1996). In addition, Tushnet and Seidman express concern about a decline in civility in constitutional discourse and urge other academics to be more candid about the sources of their thinking and respectful of contrary opin-

ions or viewpoints.

[61] CASS R. SUNSTEIN, ONE CASE AT A TIME: JUDICIAL MINIMALISM ON THE SUPREME COURT, (1999). *See also* CASS R. SUNSTEIN LEGAL REASONING AND POLITICAL CONFLICT 35–48 (1996); Cass R. Sunstein, *The Supreme Court, 1995 Term—Foreword: Leaving Things Undecided,* 110 HARV. L. REV. 4, 6–10 (1996).

[62] See *infra* Chapter 10, Feminist Legal Theory.

[63] *See id.*

[64] *See id.*

[65] *See infra* Chapter 11, Critical Race Theory.

failures or limitations of "grand" or "unitary" theories designed to restrict constitutional interpretation to a single overarching, unifying principle.[66] Perhaps most prominently, Associate Justice Antonin Scalia has acknowledged the imperfections of reliance on original understanding but has argued, nevertheless, that original understanding is still a better and more legitimate basis for constitutional decisionmaking than the available alternatives.[67] Many scholars who believe "unitary" or "grand" theories of constitutional interptetation are unworkable have suggested less ambitious, yet often value-laden, descriptions of constitutional interpretation and adjudication. While not all of their approaches prescribe specific methodologies for resolving constitutional controversies, one significant enterprise undertaken by such "anti-formalists"[68] is to look for the common elements or features of multiple areas of constitutional doctrine, i.e., to explain constitutional interpretation in terms of cross-cutting doctrinal concepts or theories. For example, Harvard Law School Professor Larry Lessig, a former law clerk to Justice Scalia, has argued that constitutional interpretation entails an exercise not unlike that of translating a text from one language to another. Hence, he suggests that just as a good translation is not necessarily a literal one, so keeping faith with the intended meaning of the Constitution's framers may require rulings that depart from the framers' literal meanings.[69]

Other scholars characterize judicial review as a "dialogue" among the justices, governmental officials, and/or the citizenry using the framework and language of the Constitution as the medium and subject of discourse;[70] still

---

[66] See generally Chapter 13, Theory and Its Discontents.

[67] See ANTONIN SCALIA, A MATTER OF INTERPRETATION: FEDERAL COURTS AND THE LAW (1997) (with commentaries by Gordon S. Wood, Laurence H. Tribe, Mary Ann Glendon, and Ronald Dworkin); Antonin Scalia, Originalism: The Lesser Evil, 57 U. CIN. L. REV. 849 (1989).

[68] The term "anti-formalists" is used to describe such theorists because they reject the idea that the countermajoritarian difficulty can be resolved only if judges interpret the Constitution pursuant to certain clearly defined or "formal" criteria (such as strict, unaltering adherence to the framers' original understanding).

[69] See, e.g., Lawrence Lessig, Fidelity and Constraint, 65 FORDHAM L. REV. 1365, 1371–76 (1997); Lawrence Lessig, Fidelity in Translation, 71 TEX. L. REV. 1165, 1166–73 (1993).

[70] A wide variety of constitutional theorists have viewed adjudication as a kind of dialogue, including but not limited to civic republicans, see, e.g., Frank Michelman, Law's Republic, 97 YALE L.J. 1493, 1503–05, 1524–32 (1988) (advocating republican vision of "dialogic constitutionalism"); feminists, see, e.g., Ruth Colker, Feminism, Theology, and Abortion: Toward Love, Compassion, and Wisdom, 77 CALIF. L.

REV. 1011, 1073 (1989) (suggesting that those advocating the overruling of Roe have the burden of "demonstrat[ing] that criminal anti-abortion legislation can be the product of successful legislative dialogue (that is, dialogue that carefully addresses women's well-being"); and liberals, see, e.g., RONALD DWORKIN, A MATTER OF PRINCIPLE 70–71 (1985) (advocating active use of judicial review as a way of generating public debate on matters of principle); BRUCE A. ACKERMAN, RECONSTRUCTING AMERICAN LAW 96–104 (1983) (emphasizing centrality of "liberal dialogue" in construction of legal values); BRUCE A. ACKERMAN, SOCIAL JUSTICE IN THE LIBERAL STATE 4–5 (1980) (proposing "comprehensive insistence on dialogue" as basic method for resolving issues of justice and politics); Owen Fiss, The Supreme Court, 1978 Term—Foreword: The Forms of Justice, 93 HARV. L. REV. 1, 13 (1979) ("The judge is entitled to exercise power only after he has participated in a dialogue about the meaning of public values."). For a classic description of judicial review as a special form of dialogue, see ALEXANDER BICKEL, THE MORALITY OF CONSENT 11 (1975) (arguing that courts are part of an "endlessly renewed educational conversation" between the judges and the public that must decide whether to obey their edicts). See also Barry Friedman, Dialogue and Judicial

others regard judicial review as entailing either the balancing of competing interests of individuals and the government.[71] In addition, some constitutional scholars propose the use or combination of different theories or arguments from different sources of decision to explain or clarify constitutional issues or approaches. For instance, the liberal but eclectic Professor Richard Fallon of Harvard Law School has attempted to identify the conventional modalities of constitutional argumentation and to rank (or coordinate) sources and methods for constitutional decisionmaking.[72] In a manner somewhat similar to Fallon's, University of Texas Law Professor Philip Bobbitt identified the modalities of constitutional argumentation and the different ideologies with which those arguments could be paired.[73] Subsequently, Bobbitt has argued that judges must rely on their consciences or moral values to make choices on which modalities to use for their constitutional decisions.[74]

Moreover, over the past two decades Yale Law School Professor Bruce Ackerman has undertaken an ambitious effort to explain constitutional change in the absence of formal constitutional amendment, culminating in the publication of the first two volumes in a projected three-volume series.[75] In particular, Ackerman has suggested that constitutional law can be explained in terms of (1) a "dualist" conception of ordinary lawmaking (the outcomes of periods of "normal" politics) and enduring higher lawmaking (the outcomes

---

Review, 91 MICH. L. REV. 577, 580–81 (1993) ("Our Constitution is interpreted on a daily basis through an elaborate dialogue as to its meaning. All segments of society participate in this constitutional interpretive dialogue, but courts play their own unique role. Courts serve to facilitate and mold the national dialogue concerning the meaning of the Constitution, particularly but not exclusively with regard to the meaning of our fundamental rights.").

[71] *See, e.g.,* STEPHEN H. SHIFFRIN, DISSENT, INJUSTICE, AND THE MEANINGS OF AMERICA xi (1999) (suggesting that "[f]ree speech protection should depend on a balancing of its values and harms in particular contexts. Because those contexts are so numerous and undifferentiated, I believe that a general theory of the First Amendment is impossible. Nonetheless, free speech rightly plays an important part in our culture, and the balancing of free speech values requires a sense of what is particularly important and what is not."). *See also* Stephen Shiffrin, *Liberalism, Radicalism, and Legal Scholarship,* 30 UCLA L. REV. 1103, 1112 (1983) (defending balancing as one of the virtues of his preferred view of constitutional interpretation, which he calls "eclectic liberalism"); Stephen Shiffrin, *The First Amendment and Economic Regulation: Away from a General Theory of the First Amendment,* 78 NW. U. L. REV. 1212, 1251–55 (1983) (defending balancing as the appropriate methodology for deciding First Amendment cases); Gerald Gun-

ther, *In Search of Judicial Quality on a Changing Court: The Case of Justice Powell,* 24 STAN. L. REV. 1001, 1005–10, 1013–14 (1972) (commending Justice Harlan's balancing of competing interests in general and in freedom of speech cases in particular as a model of judicial decisionmaking to which the then-newly appointed Justice Powell should aspire).

[72] *See* Richard Fallon, *A Constructivist Coherence Theory of Constitutional Interpretation,* 100 HARV. L. REV. 1189 (1987).

[73] *See* PHILIP BOBBITT, CONSTITUTIONAL FATE: THEORY OF THE CONSTITUTION (1982). From a different political perspective but with a similar objective as Bobbitt's, Professor Richard Kay of the University of Connecticut Law School has argued that scholars need to redirect their energies from crafting complex theories that account (imperfectly) for every major aspect of constitutional law to more productive and meaningful activities. In particular, Kay, a conservative originalist, has argued that we should try to understand and to disclose the rules we postulate as the starting points for constitutional interpretation. *See* Richard Kay, *The Illegality of the Constitution,* 4 CONST. COMMENTARY 57 (1987); *Preconstitutional Rules,* 42 OHIO STATE L.J. 187 (1981).

[74] *See* PHILIP BOBBITT, CONSTITUTIONAL INTERPRETATION (1991).

[75] *See* BRUCE A. ACKERMAN, WE THE PEOPLE: VOLUME I, FOUNDATIONS (1991); VOLUME II, TRANSFORMATIONS (1998).

of rare periods of "constitutional" politics); (2) three transformative "constitutional moments" in the framing of the original Constitution, the adoption of the Reconstruction Amendments, and the New Deal; and (3) the Court's subsequent treatment and synthesis of these "constitutional moments."

In yet another antiformalist approach to constitutional interpretation, Judge Richard Posner of the U.S. Court of Appeals for the Seventh Circuit has proposed abandoning all efforts to develop theories to explain or guide constitutional interpretation and adjudication, because such theories pay insufficient attention to the practical demands of judging and "the details of public policy."[76] Instead, he suggests scholars and judges should adopt an eclectic "legal pragmatism," which requires "exploring the operation and consequences of constitutionalism."[77] The latter task entails applying the "methods of scientific theory and empirical inquiry to constitutional law," which should lead to "the eventual accumulation of enough knowledge to enable judges at least to deal sensibly with their uncertainty about the consequences of their decisions."[78]

Virtually every major constitutional scholar as well as leading intellectuals from other fields has weighed in on the meaning, significance, and legitimacy of the most significant constitutional conflict to occur on the eve of the millennium—the impeachment, trial, and acquittal of President William Jefferson Clinton. Indeed, more than 400 law professors signed a petition urging the House Judiciary Committee not to go forward with impeachment proceedings against President Clinton based on his testimony and other actions to conceal a romantic relationship with former White House intern Monica Lewinsky.[79] In addition, more than 20 law professors participated in the hearings as witnesses, congressional staffers, and informal consultants, while dozens of law professors commented on the proceedings for the media.

The President's impeachment, trial, and acquittal have raised at least three major constitutional issues of enduring concern to legal scholars. The first

---

[76] Richard Posner, *Against Constitutional Theory*, 73 N.Y.U. L. Rev. 1, 7 (1998). *See also* Richard Posner, The Problems of Jurisprudence *passim* (1990).

[77] Posner, *Against Constitutional Theory*, *supra* note 76, at 11. This task would require scholars to answer a wide range of practical questions about the benefits and harms of various exercises of judicial review, including but not limited to "How influenced are judges in constitutional cases by public opinion? How influenced is public opinion by constitutional decisions? Are constitutional issues becoming more complex, and if so, what are the courts doing to keep abreast of the complexities? Does intrusive judicial review breed constitutionally dubious statutes by enabling legislators to shift hot potatoes to the courts?" *Id.* Another strong proponent of legal pragmatism is University of Minnesota Law Professor Dan Farber. *See* Daniel A. Farber, *Legal Pragmatism and the Constitution*, 72 Minn. L. Rev. 1331, 1332

(1988) (explaining that legal pragmatism "essentially means solving legal problems using every tool that comes to hand, including precedent, tradition, legal text, and social policy.").

[78] Posner, *Against Constitutional Theory*, *supra* note 76, at 22. *See also id.* at 12 (suggesting he "would like to see the legal professoriat redirect its research and teaching efforts toward fuller participation in the enterprise of social science, and by doing this make social science a better aid to judges' understanding of the social problems that get thrust at them in the form of constitutional issues.").

[79] More than 400 historians also submitted a similar petition urging the House Judiciary Committee not to regard the President's misconduct as impeachable and therefore not to proceed with impeachment proceedings against the President. More than 90 other professors from various disciplines, however, signed a letter encouraging the House Judiciary Committee to find that the President's misconduct constituted impeachable offenses.

question was whether the President's misconduct qualified as an impeachable offense, which required clarifying the meaning of the constitutional phrase "other high Crimes and Misdemeanors."[80] This task called upon law profes-sors and others to put their money where their mouths are by choosing a methodology for resolving the interpretive question and thus demonstrating the extent to which they would rely for guidance on original understanding and inferences from the constitutional structure and historical practices. The second question involved assessing whether the Court properly decided two important constitutional cases (which in the views of many scholars paved the way for the impeachment proceedings against President Clinton)— *Morrison v. Olson*[81] and *Clinton v. Jones*.[82] Though one could have doubts about the two decisions yet still regard the information about the President's behavior that came to light because of them as grounds for impeachment, reassessing these decisions has required focus on the methodology for resolv-ing separation of powers disputes. The third question has been whether members of Congress are capable of making principled decisions in the course of impeachment proceedings. This question is in many respects the most pro-vocative, because such deliberations (as was true for President Clinton's trial) occur generally without any likelihood of judicial review.[83] If one were to answer this question in the affirmative, then one needs to consider why Congress can be trusted more in this context than others by the other branches (whose leaders are vulnerable to the impeachment process) or why judicial review is needed in other contexts.

The debates over constitutional theory have helped to shape the future direction of constitutional decisionmaking as well as the meanings and significance constitutional scholars and others assign to its past. We can see this no more clearly than in the fates of both *Lochner,* which has been all but formally overruled, and *Roe v. Wade*, which has been substantially weakened and came one vote short of being overruled.[84] Constitutional theory is an indispensable aid to students, lawyers, judges, and politicians who try to interpret the Constitution as well as argue over the direction of constitutional law. Consequently, one can fully expect that the debates over constitutional theory should endure at least as long as the Constitution they have helped to shape and illumine.

---

[80] U.S. Const., art. II, section 4.

[81] 487 U.S. 654, 108 S. Ct. 2597, 101 L. Ed. 2d 569 (1988) (upholding the constitutionality of the Independent Counsel Act).

[82] 520 U.S. 681, 117 S. Ct. 1636, 137 L. Ed. 2d 945 (1997) (holding that a sitting President is not entitled to delay indefinitely or even temporarily a civil lawsuit based on his unoffi-cial conduct).

[83] Although law professors do not agree on whether or the extent to which judicial review of impeachment proceedings is legitimate, the Supreme Court in 1993 rejected as nonjusticia-ble a challenge to the constitutionality of the procedures employed by the Senate in a federal judge's impeachment trial. *See* Nixon v. United States, 506 U.S. 224, 236–238, 113 S. Ct. 732, 122 L. Ed. 2d 1 (1993).

[84] *See* Planned Parenthood v. Casey, 505 U.S. 833, 944, 112 S. Ct. 2791, 120 L. Ed. 2d 674 (1992) (Rehnquist, C.J., concurring in the judgment in part and dissenting in part) ("*Roe* . . . should be overruled") (joined by White, Scalia, and Thomas, JJ.).

§ 1.06 Bibliography

[A] Commentaries on the Countermajoritarian Difficulty

Bruce Ackerman, *Constitutional Politics/Constitutional Law,* 99 YALE L.J. 453 (1989)

Dean Alfange, Jr., Marbury v. Madison *and the Original Understandings of Judicial Review: In Defense of Traditional Wisdom,* 1993 SUP. CT. REV. 329

Akhil Reed Amar, *The Consent of the Governed: Constitutional Amendment Outside of Article V,* 94 COLUM. L. REV. 457 (1994)

William Bishin, *Judicial Review in Democratic Theory,* 50 S. CAL. L. REV. 1099 (1977)

Charles L. Black, Jr., THE PEOPLE AND THE CONSTITUTION (1960); *The Supreme Court and Democracy,* 50 YALE L.J. 188 (1961)

Robert Burt, THE CONSTITUTION IN CONFLICT (1992)

Stephen J. Croley, *The Majoritarian Difficulty: Elective Judiciaries and the Rule of Law,* 62 U. CHI. L. REV. 689 (1995)

Stephen Carter, *The Right Questions in the Creation of Constitutional Meaning,* 66 B.U. L. REV. 71 (1986)

Erwin Chemerinsky, INTERPRETING THE CONSTITUTION (1987); *The Price of Asking the Wrong Question: An Essay on Constitutional Scholarship and Judicial Review,* 62 TEX. L. REV. 1207 (1984)

Jesse Choper, JUDICIAL REVIEW AND THE NATIONAL POLITICAL PROCESS (1980)

Henry Steele Commager, *Judicial Review and Democracy,* 19 VA. Q. REV. 417 (1943)

Robert A. Dahl, DEMOCRACY AND ITS CRITICS (1989); *Decision-Making in a Democracy: The Supreme Court as a National Policymaker,* 6 J. PUBL. L. 279 (1957)

Barry Friedman & Scott B. Smith, *The Sedimentary Constitution,* 147 U. PA. L. REV. 1 (1998)

Mark A. Graber, *The Nonmajoritarian Difficulty: Legislative Deference to the Judiciary,* 7 STUD. AM. POL. DEV. 35 (1993)

Morton J. Horwitz, *The Supreme Court, 1992 Term—Foreword: The Constitution of Change: Legal Fundamentality without Fundamentalism,* 107 HARV. L. REV. 30 (1993)

Michael Klarman, *Majoritarian Judicial Review: The Entrenchment Problem,* 85 GEO. L.J. 491 (1997); *Rethinking the Civil Rights and Civil Liberties Revolutions,* 82 VA. L. REV. 1 (1996)

Robert G. McCloskey & Sanford Levinson, THE AMERICAN SUPREME COURT (2d ed. 1994)

Eugene Rostow, *The Democratic Character of Judicial Review,* 66 HARV. L. REV. 193 (1952)

Girardeau A. Spann, RACE AGAINST THE COURT (1993)

Symposium, *Constitutional Adjudication and Democratic Theory*, 56 N.Y.U. L. REV. 259 (1981) (with articles by John J. Gibbons, Michael J. Perry, Henry P. Monaghan, John Hart Ely, Frank I. Michelman, Lawrence G. Sager, Terrance Sandalow, Ronald Dworkin, and Thomas Nagel)

Symposium, *Construing the Constitution*, 19 U.C. DAVIS L. REV. 1 (1985) (reprinting addresses by Justices William Brennan and John Paul Stevens and Attorney General Edwin Meese)

Symposium, *Judicial Review Versus Democracy*, 42 OHIO ST. L.J. 1 (1981) (with articles by Larry A. Alexander, Michael Les Benedict, Raoul Berger, Paul Brest, Thomas Gerety, Joseph D. Grano, Richard S. Kay, Earl M. Maltz, Richard D. Parker, Michael J. Perry, David A.J. Richards, Richard B. Saphire, Aviam Soifer, Mark Tushnet, and Harry H. Wellington)

Mark V. Tushnet, *Policy Distortion and Democratic Debilitation: Comparative Illumination of the Countermajoritarian Difficulty*, 94 MICH. L. REV. 245 (1995)

Harry Hillel Wellington, INTERPRETING THE CONSTITUTION: THE SUPREME COURT AND THE PROCESS OF ADJUDICATION (1990); *The Nature of Judicial Review*, 91 YALE L.J. 486 (1982); *Common Law Rules and Constitutional Double Standards: Some Notes on Adjudication*, 83 YALE L.J. 221 (1973)

J. Skelly Wright, *The Role of the Supreme Court in a Democratic Society*, 54 CORNELL L. REV. 1 (1968)

[B] Some Perspectives on the Status and Direction of Constitutional Theory

Akhil Reed Amar, *Intratextualism*, 112 HARV. L. REV. 747 (1999)

J.M. Balkin, *What Is a Postmodern Constitutionalism?*, 90 MICH. L. REV. 1966 (1992)

Richard H. Fallon, Jr., *How to Choose a Constitutional Theory*, 87 CALIF. L. REV. 535 (1999) (with commentaries by David A. Strauss and Michael C. Dorf)

David M. Golove, *Against Free-Form Formalism*, 73 N.Y.U. L. REV. 1791 (1998)

Robert Nagel, CONSTITUTIONAL CULTURES: THE MENTALITY AND CONSEQUENCES OF JUDICIAL REVIEW (1989)

Michael J. Perry, *Why Constitutional Theory Matters to Constitutional Practice (and Vice Versa)*, 6 CONST. COMMENTARY 231 (1989)

Jed Rubenfeld, *Reading the Constitution as Spoken*, 104 YALE L. J. 1119 (1995)

Lawrence Sager, *The Incorrigible Constitution*, 65 N.Y.U. L. REV. 893 (1990)

Symposium, *Fidelity in Constitutional Theory*, 65 FORDHAM L. REV. 1247 (1997) (with articles by Ronald Dworkin, Bruce Ackerman, Lawrence Lessig, Jack N. Rakove, and J.M. Balkin; and responses by Michael W. McConnell, Frederick Schauer, Robin West, James E. Fleming, Steven G. Calabresi, Sanford Levinson, Jed Rubenfeld, Abner S. Greene, Frank I. Michelman, Lawrence Sager, Mark Tushnet, Martin S. Flaherty, Christoper L. Eisgruber, Larry Kramer, Akhil Reed Amar, Robert J. Kaczorowski, Michael J. Klarman, Sotirios A. Barber, Dorothy E. Roberts, Catherine A. MacKinnon, and William Michael Treanor)

Symposium, *Moments of Change: Transformation in American Constitutionalism*, 108 YALE L.J. 1917 (1999) (with articles by William E. Forbath, Jack N. Rakove, Joanne B. Freeman, Joyce Appleby, Eric Foner, Michael Les Benedict, Rogers M. Smith, William E. Leuchtenberg, Stephen M. Griffin, Laura Kalman, Sanford Levinson, Walter Dean Burnham, and Bruce A. Ackerman)

Symposium, *Textualism and the Constitution*, 66 GEO. WASH. L. REV. 1081 (1998) (with articles by Jed Rubenfeld, Akhil Reed Amar, Lawrence Lessig, Jeffrey Rosen, William N. Eskridge, Jr., and Steven G. Calabresi; and commentaries by Lillian R. BeVier, Judge Frank H. Easterbrook, Michael W. McConnell, Suzanna Sherry, David A. Strauss, Bradford R. Clark, Gregory E. Maggs, Deborah Jones Merritt, Michael Kent Curtis, Walter Dellinger, Ira C. Lupu, John F. Manning, and Judge Stephen F. Williams)

Laurence Tribe, CONSTITUTIONAL CHOICES (1985); *Taking Text and Structure Seriously: Reflections on Free-Form Method in Constitutional Interpretation*, 108 HARV. L. REV. 1221 (1995)

Mark Tushnet, *Does Constitutional Theory Matter?: A Comment*, 65 TEX. L. REV. 777 (1987)

William Van Alstyne, *Notes on a Bicentennial Constitution*, 72 IOWA L. REV. 1281 (1987); *Interpreting* This *Constitution: The Unhelpful Contributions of Special Theories of Judicial Review*, 35 U. FLA. L. REV. 209 (1983)

Chapter 2

The Judicial Function and the Idea of
Principled Decisionmaking

§ 2.01 Introduction

As background for many of the issues to come, it is important to be familiar with some basic ideas on how courts work and how they should work (and with challenges to these ideas as well). Concerns about principled decision-making and reasoned justification lie behind many of the debates on the Supreme Court's role and on the appropriateness of particular decisions. The purpose of this chapter is to bring these concerns into the foreground. Part of the significance of these ideas is that, to the extent a judge accepts and operates in accordance with them, the judge is (or may be, depending on your views about judicial psychology and how manipulable or determinate legal rules are) constrained in both the results that can be reached and the rationales that can be given for them.

Martin Golding, professor of philosophy and law at Duke University, introduced these themes in his book, LEGAL REASONING 2–4 (1984):[1]

> It is sometimes said that judges do not always reveal the real reasons for their decisions, and that the reasons they do present are no more than *rationalizations* for the results they reach. This claim presumably is intended to suggest that in order to explain why a case is decided in a certain way, it is necessary to take into account factors that lie outside the explicitly given reasons. However, even if the claim is true, it in no way undermines the significance of an inquiry into the nature and logical force of judicial reasoning. A discussion of three points will reinforce this statement: discovery and justification in science and law, explanatory and justifying reasons, and reasoned decisions.

> The process of scientific discovery often involves hunches, intuitions, and flashes of insight. These may be inspired by anything ranging from a scientist's religious beliefs to prior scientific knowledge to the stimulation of a drug. No history of scientific discovery would be complete if these factors were left out. However, what characterizes the process as *science* is not the hunch or its source but rather the attempt to subject the hunch, formulated as a hypothesis, to verification by carefully controlled experiment. The fact that the collection of evidence comes after the formulation of the hypothesis does not impugn the validity of the experiment. On completion of the experiment, the investigator can express the hypothesis as a *conclusion* inferred from the confirming data. It is obvious that the initial flash of insight, though undeniably important in the process of discovery, offers no grounds for accepting the hypothesis as true or probable. . . .

> Judicial decision making is analogous to the situation just described. The result in a case may be suggested to a judge in a flash of insight,

---

but its rightness or acceptability can be shown only by providing reasons for it. When the judge writes his opinion, the insight, which initiated the process of deliberation (legal reasoning in the broad sense), will appear as the conclusion of an argument. And the strength of the argument will determine the acceptability of the decision just as much as the strength of the scientist's argument determines the acceptability of his results. This is not to suggest that judges conduct controlled experiments or that their arguments verify their decisions as true or probable in exactly the same sense in which scientists verify hypotheses by appeals to confirming data. Nevertheless, in some respects the judge's argument serves one function that experiments perform in science. A judge may come to realize that an opinion "won't write"—that is, a defensible argument cannot be found for the result initially arrived at—so that he is led to decide the case differently.

The claim that a judge's explicitly given reasons are no more than rationalizations for a decision rests, in part, on a conflation of the process of discovery and the process of justification. . . . In attempting to understand what judges do, one can no more ignore the arguments they give than one can, in attempting to understand what scientists do, ignore the arguments scientists give.

At any rate, the claim is, at best, only a partial truth. It may rest on the correct observation that judges frequently do not explicitly state *all* the reasons (premises) on which decisions are grounded, as a logical analysis of judicial opinions shows. But this is no more a fault of judges than it is of everyone else, including scientists. Nevertheless, it is a point of great importance. In order to assess the force of a judge's argument it may be necessary to reconstruct it and bring out its tacit assumptions. Some of these assumptions, of course, will have been too trivial for the judge to mention; but others may prove to be quite substantial and debatable, yet the judge may not have been aware of them. It therefore is not surprising that someone should conclude that the explicitly given reasons are mere rationalizations. On the other hand, it is certainly false that the reasons judges give are never sincerely meant, or that judges are never persuaded by their own arguments. The objectivity and impartiality that are supposed to characterize the judicial process are features that derive in part from the logical requirements that control the process of justification.

Sometimes one wishes to explain why a certain event has occurred or why a certain general state of affairs exists. In these cases one seeks the causal conditions for the event or circumstance, and it is natural to call these conditions the reason (or reasons) for its occurrence. However, reasons of this sort, explanatory reasons, are not the only kind of reason. One also seeks the reasons for asserting a given judgment or statement to be true or correct. In this case one wants to know what the justifying reasons are. Because of the ambiguity of the expression "a reason for," it is easy to be misled into thinking that one kind of reason can be substituted for the other. Each type serves a function, has a use, that cannot be provided by the other.

Richard Wasserstrom, professor emeritus of philosophy at the University of California at Santa Cruz, further described the distinction between types of reasons in THE JUDICIAL DECISION: TOWARD A THEORY OF LEGAL JUSTIFICATION 28–29 (1961):[2]

---

2 Reprinted with permission of the publishers, Stanford University Press. © 1961 by the Board of Trustees of the Leland Stanford Junior University.

[I]t is, I think, chimerical to suppose that most judicial opinions purport to describe the process of discovery. Surely the kind of reasoning process that is evidenced by the usual judicial opinion is more suggestive of a typical justificatory procedure. Turning by way of analogy to the example of the scientist—it is one thing to read a judicial opinion as a report of why or how the judge "hit upon" the decision and quite another thing to read the opinion as an account of the procedure he employed in "testing" it. To insist—as many legal philosophers appear to have done—that a judicial opinion is an accurate description of the decision process there employed if and only if it faithfully describes the procedure of discovery is to help to *guarantee* that the opinion will be found wanting. But if the opinion is construed to be a report of the justificatory procedure employed by the judge, then the not infrequent reliance upon such things as rules of law and rules of logic seems more plausible. For conceivably, at least, some judges have felt that before they render a decision in a case they must be able to justify that decision. They may have had a hunch that a particular decision would be "right," they may have had a grudge against a particular defendant or plaintiff, but they might also have felt that considerations of this kind do not count as justifications for rendering a binding judicial decision, and that unless they could justify the decision "they would like to give" by appealing to certain other criteria, the decision ought not to be handed down as binding upon the litigants. And it may just be that some judges have thought they must be able to establish a formally valid relationship between the decision and certain more general premises, and able also to give good reasons for the premises so selected. If this is so, then the attacks upon the deductive theory are not wrong; they are simply irrelevant.

Golding pointed out some of the functions and effects of judicial justifications (Golding, *supra,* at 6–10):[3]

Most people who are at the losing end of a case are not very happy with the outcome. The stakes at issue may have been high: years behind bars in a criminal case, a great deal of money in a civil case. Even if the issue in a civil case seems trivial to an outsider, it must have been important enough to the parties for them to have pursued their dispute in a court of law. So the loser may complain about the result. But is he *entitled* to complain? One of the important functions of the reasoned decision—a decision for which the judge or official articulates the (justifying) reasons—is to enable this question to be answered.

[T]he average case before a court deals with disputes over questions of fact (e.g., Was the traffic light red or green when Smith's car passed through?) rather than with questions of law. If a court (the judge or jury) gives wrong answers to the main questions of fact in a case, the outcome will be legally unjust. It is essential, therefore, that courts should employ fair and rational procedures for arriving at the correct (or the humanly best) answers to these factual questions. This means that the parties should be given adequate opportunity to prepare their cases, that they should be given a fair opportunity to present their evidence, and that each party should be given a fair chance to respond to the evidence presented by the opposing side.

. . .

In the average case, then, it is issues of fact that are in dispute. But what these issues of fact are depends on the relevant law. (The color of the traffic light is of concern only because there is a law prohibiting going

---

[3] Copyright © 1984 by Martin Golding. Reprinted with permission.

through red lights.) In the average case, the rules of law will be clear and not in dispute. But in some cases—usually the most interesting cases, philosophically—the parties are in agreement on the facts but disagree over what the law as applied to those facts is. And when a judge does have to rule on what the law is, it is also extremely important that rational procedures should be followed. The potential loser, and society at large too, has a strong interest that decisions on questions of law should not be made arbitrarily. (The adversary method also plays an important role when questions of law are at issue. Each party will bring to the court's attention all the statutes, precedents, and legal principles favorable to its position, so that no relevant consideration will be ignored.)

Strictly speaking, however, there is no sure-fire procedure for discovering correct answers to questions of law, any more than there is a sure-fire procedure for making significant discoveries in science. When faced with difficult questions of what the law is, judges naturally will go through a reasoning process of search and reflection—legal reasoning in the broad sense. But in order to ensure that their decisions are not arbitrary, they will have to articulate the reasons for their decisions—that is, justify them by giving arguments for them. Of course, it would be unfortunate if a judge's argument was a mere rationalization and if the judge did not sincerely hold the reasons he explicitly gives. But in an important respect this fact, whenever it is a fact, is irrelevant to the justifiability of the decision. The justifiability of the decision depends on how well the decision is reasoned.

It should be plain that judges do not engage in reason giving or opinion writing merely as an intellectual performance. . . . A judicial justification . . . is offered in order to *justify to* someone the decision or conclusion; a justification is directed to an audience. Perhaps the first person to whom the justification is directed is the losing litigant; and to this may be added all other people whose interests might be adversely affected by the result. These persons need to be assured that the administration of the law is not just a bald exercise of coercion, that it is not the might of the judge (the power of enforcement) that makes the decision right. Reasoned decisions, therefore, can be viewed as attempts at *rational persuasion;* and by means of such decisions, losing parties may be brought to accept the result as a legitimate exercise of authority. If this acceptance is achieved, the cause of social peace is also promoted, since every case has a loser. The system of administering justice through the courts is not likely to survive for very long if half the people whose disputes are resolved are convinced that judges arbitrarily decide questions of law.

In making an effort at rational persuasion, judges show respect for their audience by addressing its members as rational individuals, as it is clear that such individuals are not going to be persuaded by just *any* reasons a judge might give. The reasons will have to be regarded by them as *good reasons* for the decision. . . . If one regards the judge's reasons as good reasons for the decision and can find no countervailing considerations, then one ought to accept the judge's decision. Of course, the losing litigants will not be very happy with the outcome; but unless they can persuade one that the judge's reasons are not good or that there are countervailing considerations, one will not think them entitled to their complaint. In any case, even if the losers are not persuaded by the judge's argument, they may still be persuaded enough by it to acknowledge that the judge's ruling was one that a reasonable person could arrive at, and so, that the decision was not made arbitrarily.

The fact that rational individuals are not persuaded by just any reasons that a judge could conceivably give has an important consequence: the reasons have to be more than an expression of the judge's personal predilections. These reasons, therefore, operate as *controls* on the process of deliberation. Since judges are aware that they will have to supply a public justification of their rulings, any hunch, flash of insight, or "gut feeling" they initially had about a case before the court will be tested against the kinds of reasons that are likely to be appealing to their audience. The deliberation process, legal reasoning in the broad sense, need not be an entirely arational or irrational affair. Second, the judges' reasons will have an *objective* status in a significant degree. Ideally, a judge's reasons should be reasons that the losing litigant will recognize as good reasons; but in any event the judge will want his or her reasons to be reasons that independent observers, especially other judges and lawyers, will find acceptable. Of course, it is not necessarily the case that all independent observers will agree with the judge—as the history of American courts shows. Still, the fact that judges have to justify their decisions to an audience of rational persons is a highly significant feature of judicial argumentation.

Reasoned decisions serve other functions besides that of trying to convince people that judges do not act arbitrarily. A judge's decision in a case is also meant to supply *guidance* to other individuals on what the law is and on how their cases are likely to be decided should they end up in court, so that those individuals can adjust their conduct accordingly. But a decision can serve this function only if reasons are given, otherwise all one has is an unconnected series of raw facts. One has to know which facts are legally significant—which is what the reasons indicate. (The fact that the man who went through the red light was named Smith is not legally significant, but the fact that he was on his way to a hospital may be crucial.) Second, appellate courts are supposed to supply legal guidance to lower courts, and because of considerations similar to those just mentioned, their decisions will not be very helpful unless they lay out the reasons for their rulings. And third, in the American system many decisions are justified by reference to precedent—the decisions made in prior cases. Again, it is only because explicit reasons were given for these earlier decisions that they are of any use for later cases. Plainly, many of the functions that courts serve require reasoned decisions.

Enough has been said to dispose of the view that the study of legal reasoning, the explicit arguments judges give, is of no importance and also, perhaps, of the claim that judges' reasons are mere rationalizations. This chapter closes with a final comment on the idea that judges are not sincere about the reasons they give for their decisions. If this criticism is to have any force in undercutting the study of judicial reasoning, a clearer idea of its meaning is needed.

To say that a judge is not sincere is to say that he is not prepared to apply the same reasons that he gives in one case to the deciding of another case which involves a similar set of facts or which raises a similar legal issue; that is, that the judge feels no demand for *consistency* in the way he decides cases. The fact is that judges, since they may have to give a public justification of their rulings, are very much concerned with consistency. Plainly, a judge's decisions would offer no guidance for the future conduct of individuals if they could not count on judges to be consistent to a large extent. As to legal argument, judges frequently do test their reasoning by considering how they would decide other similar cases, actual and hypothetical.

[T]he notion of case-to-case consistency plays an important role in judicial reasoning. Still, judges' arguments are not always well articulated, and judges sometimes do fall into inconsistency, which in itself does not signify that judges are insincere. This is not to imply, though, that judges are never insincere or that judges are always honest and above-board in the way they make and defend their rulings.

§ 2.02 Principled Decisionmaking

The types of ideas just presented seem often to be summed up in a call for "principled decisionmaking." The arguments over what the concept entails can become elaborate, but the basic idea is one that takes no legal training to grasp; to put it colloquially, what's sauce for the goose is sauce for the gander. Slightly more formally, the concept calls for treating like cases alike and entails judicial consistency and impartiality as essential for fair treatment of litigants. As then-Judge Benjamin Cardozo put it in THE NATURE OF THE JUDICIAL PROCESS 33–34 (1921):[4]

> It will not do to decide the same question one way between one set of litigants and the opposite way between another. "If a group of cases involves the same point, the parties expect the same decision. It would be a gross injustice to decide alternate cases on opposite principles. If a case was decided against me yesterday when I was defendant, I shall look for the same judgment today if I am plaintiff. To decide differently would raise a feeling of resentment and wrong in my breast; it would be an infringement, material and moral, of my rights." Everyone feels the force of this sentiment when two cases are the same.

Decisions of the Warren Court reaching results that many scholars found laudable but which they found hard to justify on "principled" grounds led to expressions of concern over the Court's methods. Probably the most widely known was Columbia law professor Herbert Wechsler's Holmes Lecture at Harvard, the main theme of which is conveyed in the following brief excerpts. Herbert Wechsler, *Toward Neutral Principles of Constitutional Law,* 73 HARV. L. REV. 1, 11–12, 15, 19–20 (1959):[5]

> I revert then to the problem of criteria as it arises for both courts and critics—by which I mean criteria that can be framed and tested as an exercise of reason and not merely as an act of willfulness or will. Even to put the problem is, of course, to raise an issue no less old than our culture. Those who perceive in law only the element of fiat, in whose conception of the legal cosmos reason has no meaning or no place, will not join gladly in the search for standards of the kind I have in mind. I must, in short, expect dissent from . . . those . . . who, vouching no philosophy to warranty, frankly or covertly make the test of virtue in interpretation whether its result in the immediate decision seems to hinder or advance the interests or the values they support.
>
>   . . . The man who simply lets his judgment turn on the immediate result may not, however, realize that his position implies that the courts are free to function as a naked power organ, that it is an empty affirmation to regard them, as ambivalently he so often does, as courts of law. If he may know he disapproves of a decision when all he knows is that it has sustained a claim put forward by a labor union or a taxpayer, a Negro or a segregationist, a corporation or a Communist—he acquiesces in the proposition that a man of different sympathy but equal information may no less properly conclude that he approves.

---

[4] Copyright © 1921 by Yale University Press. Reprinted with permission.   [5] Copyright © 1959 by The Harvard Law Review Association. Reprinted with permission.

You will not charge me with exaggeration if I say that this type of *ad hoc* evaluation is, as it has always been, the deepest problem of our constitutionalism, not only with respect to judgments of the courts but also in the wider realm in which conflicting constitutional positions have played a part in our politics.

. . .

[W]hether you are tolerant, perhaps more tolerant than I, of the *ad hoc* in politics, with principle reduced to a manipulative tool, are you not also ready to agree that something else is called for from the courts? I put it to you that the main constituent of the judicial process is precisely that it must be genuinely principled, resting with respect to every step that is involved in reaching judgment on analysis and reasons quite transcending the immediate result that is achieved. To be sure, the courts decide, or should decide, only the case they have before them. But must they not decide on grounds of adequate neutrality and generality, tested not only by the instant application but by others that the principles imply? Is it not the very essence of judicial method to insist upon attending to such other cases, preferably those involving an opposing interest, in evaluating any principle avowed?

Here too I do not think that I am stating any novel or momentous insight. But now, as Holmes said long ago . . . we "need education in the obvious." We need it more particularly now respecting constitutional interpretation, since it has become a commonplace to grant what many for so long denied: that courts in constitutional determinations face issues that are inescapably "political" . . . in that they involve a choice among competing values or desires, a choice reflected in the legislative or executive action in question, which the court must either condemn or condone.

. . .

Let me repeat what I have thus far tried to say. The courts have both the title and the duty when a case is properly before them to review the actions of the other branches in the light of constitutional provisions, even though the action involves value choices, as invariably action does. In doing so, however, they are bound to function otherwise than as a naked power organ; they participate as courts of law. This calls for facing how determinations of this kind can be asserted to have any legal quality. The answer, I suggest, inheres primarily in that they are—or are obliged to be—entirely principled. A principled decision, in the sense I have in mind, is one that rests on reasons with respect to all the issues in the case, reasons that in their generality and their neutrality transcend any immediate result that is involved. When no sufficient reasons of this kind can be assigned for overturning value choices of the other branches of the Government or of a state, those choices must, of course, survive. Otherwise, as Holmes said in his first opinion for the Court, "a constitution, instead of embodying only relatively fundamental rules of right, as generally understood by all English-speaking communities, would become the partisan of a particular set of ethical or economical opinions . . ."

The virtue or demerit of a judgment turns, therefore, entirely on the reasons that support it and their adequacy to maintain any choice of values it decrees, or, it is vital that we add, to maintain the rejection of a claim that any given choice should be decreed.

The commentary evoked by Wechsler's lecture was voluminous. Martin Golding explored some of the implications of Wechsler's call for "neutral

principles" in *Principled Decision-Making and the Supreme Court,* 63 COLUM.
L. REV. 35, 40–43 (1963):[6]

A decision or judgment is principled only when it is guided by some
"external consideration," *i.e.,* a guiding principle that contributes to the
deliberation on the case. Such a principle is a *reason* (or part of the
reasons) for the decision. It cannot be a reason for the decision unless
it determines, at least to some extent, the outcome of the process of
deliberation. This means that a principle cannot be so flexible as to allow
for free-wheeling discretion. Furthermore, in applying a principle, the
instant case must be treated as an instance of a more inclusive class of
cases, *i.e.,* the case at hand is treated in a certain manner because it is
held to be proper to treat cases of its type in that manner. In this way
every principled judgment makes, or rests upon, a universal, or general,
claim. When the given case is treated differently from the way in which
it is held to be proper to treat cases of its type the decision-maker is
required to distinguish it from these cases. Here, too, such distinctions
must be drawn in a principled way: it is not sufficient to justify the
different treatment of persons or circumstances simply on the ground that
one is dealing with one person or circumstance rather than another. That
is to say, in principled decision-making one is permitted to make exceptions of this sort only insofar as they fall within a class of cases considered
appropriate for the different treatment.

Although the nature of distinction-making in principled decisionmaking is a complex topic deserving separate, detailed treatment, brief
discussion about it is in order here. First, it is obvious that in many cases
people disagree on whether there exist significant enough differences between apparently similar persons or circumstances to permit their being
treated in disparate ways. But this fact in no way affects the account of
principled decision I am presenting. This account does not assume or
require that people agree in their judgments. It is quite consistent with
it that two parties should be opposed in their judgments and yet both be
principled. Second, when such distinctions are made, the criteria for
determining which differences are significant or relevant must be drawn
in a principled way. Not just *any* distinction—which can always be found—
will do.

Briefly put, the requirements for principled decision are: (1) that a
reason for the disposition of the case be given; and (2) that the case be
so decided because it is held to be proper to decide cases of its type in
this way. It is in the meeting of the requirements for principled decision
that the qualities of neutrality and generality are achieved. . . .

It is important to recognize the fact that the above requirements constitute necessary conditions of a principled decision. I do not doubt that more
is required in order to explicate the notion of a *justified* decision. It is
especially important to recognize that I have been discussing the way one
ought to go about justifying a judgment, and not the psychological process
of reaching a judgment. One's decision is principled if one supports it by
reasons or reasoning of this kind. Of course, in situations in which people
are expected to make principled decisions it is expected that the psychological process will accord with the above procedures. . . . And it seems
to me that this does happen at least sometimes. On the other hand, even
when a decision is a so-called "guts reaction" it might be a mistake to
underrate the role of these procedures, for they may have been
"internalized."

---

[6] Copyright © 1963 by the Directors of the
Columbia Law Review Association, Inc. All
Rights Reserved. Reprinted by permission.

From the above delineation of principled decision-making it follows that the typical kind of argument that will be employed in both deliberation and criticism is that of *reductio ad absurdum*. One's judgment is "tested not only by the instant application but by others that the principles imply." When a principle is advanced in support of a decision and this principle would necessarily permit some given case to be treated in a manner different from the way in which by hypothesis it must be treated, one is forced either to distinguish the cases or, failing this, to reject the principle. Rationality, of which principled decision is an element, requires pragmatic consistency of this sort. Obviously, one's decisions lose their moral force when we indulge in inconsistency. Professor Wechsler quite correctly characterizes the criteria of principled decision as ones which we are "morally and intellectually obligated to support."

. . .

[P]rincipled judicial decision-making is both similar to and different from principled moral decision-making. The truth of the matter as I see it is that with two provisos principled judicial decision is formally congruent with principled moral decision. The two provisos are, first, that a legal system is able to stipulate in a large measure the principles that must be employed in deliberation and, second, a legal system may stipulate what grounds are and what grounds are not legitimate grounds for the different treatment of persons or circumstances. So, for example, a legal system may stipulate that mere racial difference is (or is not) an acceptable ground for the different treatment of individuals in certain types of cases.

Within the scope of these limitations it still remains possible to speak of principled judicial decision-making. Our legal system has no privileged status. Not only are systems possible that differ from ours in content, but so also can principled decisions occur within the framework of such systems. For in such systems courts can function as "courts of law" and may embody in their procedures "the main constituent of the judicial process . . . ." Thus, when a legal system does make racial (or other) differences relevant, it is still possible for principled judicial decision to exist, so long as the requirements for principled decision are met within the terms of the law that the system lays down. Principled legal judgment is not so much a matter of content as it is of form. Neutrality and generality are to be found not in the content of the law but in its application or administration. Principled judicial decision-making is possible in a tyranny. This is worth stressing, if only because Professor Wechsler's ideas move within a liberal democratic context. But I should also suppose that if we range states along a scale—"ideal" democracy at one end and "ideal" tyranny at the other—there is a point of no return, a point at which the form and content of the tyranny become inseparable, making it impossible to speak of principled judicial judgment.

A legal system, then, may broadly fix the starting-points of deliberation and the criteria of relevant distinctions. It is the lesson of American jurisprudence that this fixity has its limits and that a degree of discretion is inevitable. But we still demand that, so far as possible, courts be principled in their exercises of this discretion. This applies with greatest force to the Supreme Court when it has constitutional questions before it. . . .

Golding's generally friendly critique, though, pointed out what he regarded as a crucial problem in Wechsler's argument (pp. 48-49):

Is it possible to speak of principled judicial decision-making when more than one value is at stake, when it is impossible for a plurality of values to be fulfilled in equal measure? Certainly one would like to emphasize together with Professor Wechsler "the role of reason and of principle in the judicial, as distinguished from the legislative or executive, appraisal of conflicting values . . ." But what is that role? Certainly one would like to agree with him that the virtue or demerit in a judgment turns "entirely on the reasons that support it and their adequacy to maintain any choice of values it decrees. . . . But what is the test of adequacy? I cannot see much in the way of an answer to these questions in Professor Wechsler's lecture.

The above questions raise the most complicated problems in the analysis of legal reasoning. I fail to grasp Professor Wechsler's position if it consists in the statement that one ought to, or even can, supply "neutral principles" for "choosing" between competing values. I can, of course, choose between two competing values by reference to a third value which is more comprehensive or supreme, that is, when there is already an ordering of values. Assuming such an ordering, it seems to make sense to speak of "reasoned choice between competing values." Although I doubt it, perhaps this is precisely what Professor Wechsler is implying in his comment on the "preferred position" controversy when he says that it has virtue "insofar as it recognizes that some ordering of social values is essential; that all cannot be given equal weight, if the Bill of Rights is to be maintained." But it is difficult to see how the ordering itself is to be made on "neutral principles."

Far from all of Wechsler's critics were friendly. Arthur S. Miller, late professor of law at George Washington University, and political scientist Ronald F. Howell argued against Wechsler's basic thesis in *The Myth of Neutrality in Constitutional Adjudication,* 27 U. CHI. L. REV. 661, 690–91 (1960):[7]

[J]udicial decisions should be gauged by their results and not by either their coincidence with a set of allegedly consistent doctrinal principles or by an impossible reference to neutrality of principle. The effects, that is to say, of a decision should be weighed and the consequences assessed in terms of their social adequacy. Alternatives of choice are to be considered, not so much in terms of who the litigants are or what the issue is, but rather in terms of the realization or non-realization of stated societal values. What those values might be, we do not now set forth. Rather we contend that judges have always done this, in greater or lesser degree, overtly or covertly, consciously or unconsciously; and that now it should become a matter of conscious choice. The reports are replete with statements indicating that judges think in terms of effect, as well as of such other matters as precedent. The proposal here is that this should become recognized, on and off the bench, as the hallmark of the constitutional adjudicative process. Disputes are and should avowedly be settled in terms of the external consequences of their application—with those consequences spelled out in some degree of particularity.

The view Miller and Howell defended is sometimes labeled "result orientation," which those opposing it use as a pejorative contrast to "principled adjudication." But what, if anything, is wrong with being result-oriented? Does the call for "neutral principles" smell too much of the theorist's lamp, overlooking both social desirability and inescapable judicial reality? The late Judge J. Braxton Craven, Jr. of the United States Court of Appeals for the

Fourth Circuit had some reason to know and plainly thought so, as he wrote in *Paean to Pragmatism,* 50 N.C. L. REV. 977, 977 (1972):[8]

> In Perkins House at the Harvard Law School in the fall of 1939, it was possible to get up a serious discussion about whether judges decided cases and then figured out the reasons for the decisions or whether they were inevitably led to a decision by the reasons. I thought then and think now that the chicken generally comes first and lays down its reason to justify its existence. The opposite conclusion seems to me a bit naive, but some scholars of distinction apparently hold to the contrary and insist that there are neutral controlling principles brooding more or less omnipresently in the sky.
>
> I believe that there only two kinds of judges at all levels of courts: those who are admittedly (maybe not to the public) result-oriented, and those who are also result-oriented but either do not know it or decline for various purposes to admit it. Those who are unaware of their result-orientation have an advantage; they get where they want to go without the inhibition of a conscious awareness of how they got there. Those who know themselves well enough to recognize their result-orientation are inhibited by the knowledge that they may put into judicial decisions value judgments that may not have enduring validity and may even turn out to be wrong. A judge who is that introspective tends to be more flexible than his less perceptive brother who knows not what he does—if only because he is aware that he is constantly choosing, usually not between right and wrong but between two goods or two evils embraced within conflicting principles.

In the concluding chapter of his historical study of the transformation of American law from 1870 through 1960, Harvard Law School Professor Morton J. Horwitz criticizes the "neutral principles" idea for functioning, despite its purported impartiality, as a conservative defense of the sociolegal status quo. MORTON J. HORWITZ, THE TRANSFORMATION OF AMERICAN LAW 1870-1960: THE CRISIS OF LEGAL ORTHODOXY 266–68 (1992) (footnotes omitted) (emphasis in original):[9]

> [In his "Neutral Principles" lecture], Wechsler turned to recent Supreme Court decisions involving racial equality, "the decisions that for me provide the hardest test of my belief in principled adjudication." While these decisions, he wrote, "have the best chance of making an enduring contribution to the quality of our society of any that I know in recent years," they "are entitled to approval" only insofar as "they rest on neutral principles. . . ."
>
> First, he directed strong criticism against the cases that had outlawed the "white primary" and racially restrictive covenants, concluding that they were simply "*ad hoc* determinations of their narrow problems, yielding no neutral principles for their extension or support." Then he returned to *Brown v. Board of Education,* "which for one of my persuasion stirs the deepest conflict I experience in testing the thesis I propose." The judgment, he wrote,
>
> > must have rested on the view that racial segregation is, in principle, a denial of equality to the minority against whom it is directed: that is, the group that is not dominant politically and, therefore, does not make the choice involved. For many who support the Court's decision

---

this assuredly is the decisive ground. But this position also presents problems. Does it not involve an inquiry into the motive of the legislature, which is generally foreclosed by the courts? Is it alternatively defensible to make the measure of validity of legislation the way it is interpreted by those who are affected by it? In the context of a charge that segregation *with equal facilities* is a denial of equality, is there not a point in *Plessy* in the statement that if "enforced separation stamps the colored race with a badge of inferiority" it is solely because its members choose "to put that construction upon it"? Does enforced separation of the sexes discriminate against females merely because it may be the females who resent it and it is imposed by judgments predominantly male? Is a prohibition of miscegenation a discrimination against the colored member of the couple who would like to marry?

Why does Wechsler find inadequate "the view that racial segregation is, in principle, a denial of equality to the minority against whom it is directed [because] the group . . . is not dominant politically and, therefore, does not make the choice involved"? Why does he characterize the assertion of systematic white domination not as a statement of social reality but rather as an impermissible "inquiry into the motive of the legislature"? Indeed, does Wechsler show any real understanding of the bitter reality of racial domination when he declares that there is "a point" in the statement in *Plessy v. Ferguson* that if "enforced separation stamps the colored race with a badge of inferiority" it is because its members choose "to put that construction upon it"? Likewise, he finds it equally difficulty to imagine that "enforced separation of the sexes is discriminatory . . . merely because it may be the females who resent it and it is imposed by judgments predomin[an]tly male." And why should he have had any doubt about whether a prohibition against miscegenation discriminated "against the colored member of the couple who would like to marry"?

From the perspective of a generation later, Wechsler's difficulties in holding racially discriminatory statutes unconstitutional have that inaccessible quality of ancient structures of understanding derived from a time when a fundamentally different moral order seemed to prevail with assurance. Indeed, his conclusion that "the question posed by state-enforced segregation is not one of discrimination at all" seems positively astonishing. Was there something about neutral principles analysis that produced such a startling conclusion? If discrimination of whites against blacks did not provide a neutral principle for Wechsler, "freedom of association" might, he argued. "I think, and I hope not without foundation, that the Southern white also pays heavily for segregation, not only in the sense of guilt that he must carry but also in the benefits he is denied," Wechsler wrote. In other words, unless the Southern white "also pays heavily for segregation," there is no sufficiently general principle to condemn segregation. "But if the freedom of association is denied by segregation, integration forces an association upon those for whom it is unpleasant or repugnant. . . . Given a situation where the state must practically choose between denying the association to those who wish it or imposing it on those who would avoid it, is there a basis in neutral principles" for barring segregation? Wechsler asked. And he concluded: "I should like to think there is, but I confess that I have not yet written the opinion."

. . . Why did Wechsler find "freedom of association," not "discrimination," the appropriately neutral framework for evaluating the segregation cases? Though he was never entirely explicit, Wechsler seems to have believed that only something approaching unanimous agreement—that is, consensus—constituted a sufficiently general and neutral basis for making a value choice. Discrimination analysis entailed choosing between victims and victimizers—in other words, being forced to choose between conflicting moral positions. Yet freedom of association analysis also failed because it too could not be generalized, since it "forces an association upon those for whom it is unpleasant or repugnant." There was no basis for choosing on neutral grounds between denying or imposing freedom of association because Wechsler offered no basis for concluding that whites had been systematically wronging blacks. If there was a "point" in the *Plessy* view that blacks had chosen their "badge of inferiority," there could, of course, be no such basis. The moral claims of whites and blacks could only be prima facie equal.

[T]he neutral principles school sought to avoid ever having to decide whether one group was victimizing another, since that inevitably involved substantive evaluation of the justice of their respective claims. The emphasis on generality foreclosed any intervention to reform unjust social practices in precisely those cases in which the dominant groups had the greatest state in justifying the status quo. By abstracting the question of segregation from its concrete historical meaning in order to avoid being accused of having a result orientation, Wechsler achieved neutrality through formalism—that is, by simpl[y] assuming the equal legitimacy of both groups' desire to choose freely with whom to associate. In its unhistorical abstractness, neutral principles analysis combined with ethical positivism to produce a new conservative formulation in orthodox legal thought.

Lest the reader get the idea that the "neutral principles" versus "result orientation" disagreement nearly always coincides with right-left political divisions, it is worth noting the argument of Harvard law professor Archibald Cox against political, manipulative views of the Court. Cox, who was generally sympathetic with Warren Court decisions, said in THE ROLE OF THE SUPREME COURT IN AMERICAN GOVERNMENT 106–07 (1976):[10]

There is a school of political scientists in the United States that likens the Court to purely political agencies. The Court should do whatever it can—they say—to carry out the policies it deems desirable. Like other politicians the Court should consciously build a coalition of interest-groups, dependent upon judicial aid because they are under-represented elsewhere in government but strong enough collectively to sustain the Court against attacks. As the Court is a clientele agency, we should expect it to follow the pattern of other clientele agencies in acting to create and reinforce its own supporting interests. Part of the clientele is said to be the bench and bar, another part the 'interest-groups' naive enough to keep on believing the 'judicial myth' that judges are influenced by law and sincerely seek unbiased decisions referrable as often as possible to general and more or less objective standards. 'If the myth of the Court is destroyed in the law schools, the Court loses power', it is said; ' . . . the real problem is how the Supreme Court can pursue its policy goals without violating those popular and professional expectations of neutrality, which are an important factor in our legal tradition and a principal source of the Court's prestige.'[1]

Although it may fit the jargon of sociology to describe as an interest-group those who share a common belief in the integrity of the judicial process, surely there is for the judge himself as well as for the people a

---

[10] Copyright © 1976 by Oxford University Press, Inc. Used by permission of Oxford University Press, Inc.

[1] Shapiro, *Law and Politics in the Supreme Court* (1964), p. 31.

vast difference between, on the one hand, pursuing the goals of impartial justice *under law* to the satisfaction of those who share this aspiration and, on the other hand, arranging airline routes, highway subsidies, and television allotments to the satisfaction of those who enjoy the benefits. Nor is it possible to keep the 'myth of the Court' alive without living by it enough of the time to give it some reality. Law professors cannot keep a myth alive if political scientists are able to expose the fiction because of their greater candour or truer perception.

But the real vice in substituting a manipulative for a moral view of the judge's role lies much deeper. At the core of the Court's strength is [sic] impartiality and independence, and the Justices' freedom from every form of commitment or self-interest. I am not speaking only of freedom from the crasser forms of obligation and ambition, but of a cast of mind free so far as humanly possible from the ties of personal and group loyalties and implied commitments. Nothing can hurt the Court more than for a Justice to continue to maintain political or professional ties with members of the Executive or Legislative Branch or with private organizations. To seek to serve the interests of a clientele—the liberal press, the black, the poor, the extreme political groups, the American Civil Liberties Union, the Office of Economic Opportunity lawyers—is not the same as to seek to find and serve our society's long-range fundamental values appropriately expressed in constitutional law. Serving a clientele implies a degree of commitment apart from merit. Clientele interests and long-range societal values do not *always* overlap. Nor does one get near to describing a Holmes, a Brandeis, a Black, a Warren, or a Harlan by saying that he served a clientele of group-interests that reinforced the Court's position.

. . .

§ 2.03   "Pedigree Versus Policy" or Legitimism Versus Consequentialism as a Recurring Division in Constitutional Theory?

Chief Judge Richard Posner of the U.S. Court of Appeals for the Seventh Circuit uses the terms "pedigree" and "policy" as "warrants for judicial action" to articulate what he regards as a basic distinction in contemporary approaches to constitutional adjudication.[11] In his 1990 book, THE PROBLEMS

---

[11] Another way in which to phrase Judge Posner's distinction between "pedigree" and "policy" is through the terms "legitimism" and "consequentialism," respectively. The term in each pair reflects the stress that those who tend toward "pedigree" or "legitimism," on the one hand, place on conformity with canons of legal reasoning and appropriate institutional roles as criteria for evaluating judicial methods and results. In contrast, those with "consequentialist" or "policy" leanings emphasize their view of moral goodness, wisdom, social desirability, or likely effects of a judicial decision.

Readers may wish to consider how much the "pedigree-policy" or "legitimism-consequentialism" distinction is a useful tool for organizing and understanding many of the remaining materials in this book. First, the distinction

may help in part to bring to the surface some presumptions that underlie many disagreements about constitutional theory and the judicial role. It is not uncommon for commentators, students, and judges to speak from different premises without recognizing, articulating, and confronting the gulf that may separate their starting points. Nor is it unusual for those on each side of a debate—especially the most zealous advocates?—to assume rather than to seek to justify their fundamental premises.

Second, while of course the "pedigree-policy" or "legitimism-con-sequentialism" distinction falls short of explaining all the divisions in constitutional theory (and should not be taken to imply that such divisions are usually neat and polar), it may usefully capture a similarity among arguments that appear under what can be confusingly different labels. Readers going

OF JURISPRUDENCE, he discusses various aspects and implications of the division. First, judges who strongly disagree about fundamental premises may often agree about particular decisions: "In many cases the conventional materials will lean so strongly in one direction that it would be unreasonable for the judge to go in any other."[12] We can add that even in less determinate cases, disagreements over approach will usually not be total. Whatever the differences over *deriving* rules of decision, agreement would be widespread that they should be *articulated* rationally to attempt to cover like cases and *applied* impartially. This much accord leaves, to be sure, the key question of "the nature of the constraint [on judges] where the Constitution does not provide clear guidance."[13] Second, Posner argues that the legitimist or pedigree approach "needs to be justified, not just asserted."[14] To state the question "who has licensed judges to decide cases in accord with social vision?"[15] does not end the matter for Posner. Presuming the pedigree or legitimist answer that judges have no such license "appeal[s] covertly to a particular political theory, one that regards the judge as an agent" of other lawmakers and "thus insists that every judicial decision be fairly referable to a command by a principal."[16] The call for justification, of course, sounds alike for those drawn to "pedigree" or "policy" approaches, and it seems likely that what persuades each of us between the two tendencies will not be reasons internal to the legal system itself. Instead we may proceed from explicit or implicit judgments that are in some sense extra-legal ones, often provisional and subject to change, about the most likely institutional paths—mixes of majoritarian sovereignty, central versus dispersed power, and the scope of the umpiring and checking role of nonmajoritarian courts—to our vision of the good society.

In two articles, University of Connecticut Law School Professor Richard Kay has addressed the complex issues underlying choices of basic approach to constitutional decisionmaking and the judicial role. The "rules of recognition" by which we accept, qualify, or exclude types of constitutional arguments such as original intention or social desirability, he suggests, are "preconstitutional"—not amenable to "legally correct resolution" and subject to debate "only in terms external to the legal system."[17] We cannot, Kay maintains, "settle on a correct position" about the "fitness of one or another preconstitutional rule" "as a matter of law or logic."[18]

Kay argues that what "preconstitutional rule" is chosen and applied rests at bottom "on a social choice, and is desirable or undesirable only as a matter of judgment or taste concerning the proper relative roles of public and private

---

on to the debates over the interpretation of the constitutional text and the use of constitutional history may find it worth considering whether, for example, the "neutral principles," "interpretivist," and "originalist" positions all in essence stress "pedigree" or are forms of "legitimism." Similarly, can the advocates of "result orientation" and "noninterpretivism," and some critics of originalism, helpfully be understood as making arguments that proceed from "conse-quentialist" or "policy" premises?

[12] RICHARD POSNER, THE PROBLEMS OF JURISPRUDENCE 131 (1990).

[13] *Id.* at 138.

[14] *Id.* at 140.

[15] *Id.* at 135.

[16] *Id.*

[17] Richard Kay, *The Ilegality of the Constitution,* 4 CONST. COMMENTARY 57, 60 (1987).

[18] *Id.* at 80.

activity."[19] Thus, "in some cases our inability to agree on questions of constitutional law will be a result of our dispute on the proper characteristics of a preconstitutional rule." These differences are "in turn . . . traceable to fundamentally incompatible views concerning the proper role of government"[20] and of the allocation of powers between judicial and other organs of government. In short, fundamental differences like those between "pedigree" and "policy" as criteria for judicial decision and evaluating judicial method do not turn on "internal" legal arguments, and we should not expect easy or definitive resolutions.

Apart from these theoretical arguments over approaches to constitutional adjudication, there is the empirical question whether the Supreme Court's legitimacy in the eyes of the informed public turns more on its observance of Wechslerian canons or upon the popular acceptability of the results it reaches. Judge Posner, no liberal activist, thinks it is the latter: "[T]he Court's survival and flourishing are indeed more likely to depend on the political acceptability of its results than on its adherence to an esoteric philosophy of interpretation."[21] So does law professor David Bryden: "Among the general public, and even the educated elites, a decision's acceptability appears to be a function of its popularity as public policy rather than its fidelity to law, however one may define that term."[22]

A theoretical and empirical study by NYU psychology professor Tom R. Tyler and Boalt Hall law graduate Gregory Mitchell, *Legitimacy and the Empowerment of Discretionary Legal Authority: The United States Supreme Court and Abortion Rights,* 43 DUKE L.J. 703, 705–14, 780–81, 786–88, 798 (1994), challenges the Posner-Bryden view:[23]

> [The m]ost interesting [aspect of the Supreme Court's decision reaffirming *Roe v. Wade* in *Planned Parenthood v. Casey*] for our purposes . . . is the Court's exposition and endorsement of legitimacy theory,[12] or in the Court's terms, "principles of institutional integrity," as support for the decision that *Roe* could not be overruled.
>
> Essentially, the Court advances the proposition that unless its outcomes are viewed as principled, and not simply as the result of changes in Court personnel, its decisions will be viewed with skepticism by the public and will lose much of their obligatory force. Although the "underlying substance" of the Court's legitimacy lies "in the Constitution and the lesser sources of legal principle on which the Court draws[,] . . . a decision without principled justification [is] no judicial act at all." Thus, the perception of principled decisionmaking—and the avoidance of the perception of Court politics or political compromise—is the *sine qua non* of

---

[19] Richard Kay, *Preconstitutional Rules,* 42 OHIO ST. L.J. 187, 203 (1981).

[20] *Id.* at 204.

[21] Richard A. Posner, *Bork and Beethoven,* 42 STAN. L. REV. 1365, 1371 (1990).

[22] David Bryden, *Book Review,* 5 CONST. COMMENTARY 531, 538 (1988) (footnote omitted). For limited empirical confirmation of this view, see William Haltom & Mark Silverstein, *The Scholarly Tradition Revisited: Alexander Bickel, Herbert Wechsler, and the Legitimacy of Judicial Review,* 4 CONST. COMMENTARY 25 (1987) (surveying editorial reactions of major daily newspapers to landmark Supreme Court decisions).

[23] Copyright © 1994 by the Duke Law Journal. Reprinted with permission.

[12] The term "legitimacy theory" is used to describe the loose conglomeration of theories that all, in some form, ascribe importance to authorities' adherence to democratic principles as a means of creating obedience to or acceptance of these authorities and their directives. . . .

legitimate constitutional adjudication. The maintenance of such legitimacy is crucial because legitimacy is deemed necessary to the voluntary acceptance of Court decisions, voluntary acceptance being the only type of public acceptance of the decision on which the Court formally can rely. The Justices further argue that the legitimacy of the Court is especially at stake when confronting an "intensely divisive controversy" in which attention is great and stakes are high. A prior decision in this controversial area should be overruled, the joint opinion argues, only for "the most compelling reason." . . . Adherence to precedent provides one method for appearing principled and thus for maintaining legitimacy and obedience.

The Court's analysis is literally without citation (and, some would argue, without support,[19]), yet it closely parallels traditional legal and social science theories of legitimacy. Thus, in light of the Court's theorizing on legitimacy, we present this Article with two goals in mind: (1) to undertake the review of legitimacy theory and research that the Court fails to provide in its decision; and (2) to subject to empirical test the Court's own theses that legitimacy matters in the eyes of the public and that "principled" decisionmaking is most important to the maintenance of this legitimacy.

In recent years, the concept of legitimacy has been under attack within the legal community. A 1983 critique by Professor Alan Hyde has been especially widely cited. Professor Hyde argues that "[w]hatever the index chosen for its measurement . . . legitimacy cannot be shown to be as significant in explaining obedience as rational calculation, including evaluation of self-interest and sanctions." This argument has already been disproved in the case of everyday obedience to the law by studies showing that legitimacy not only influences obedience but that it has more influence on obedience than does "rational calculation."[21]

The present study expands the scope of these latter findings. Our study will show that, on a national level, in the case of the U.S. Supreme Court, institutional legitimacy relates significantly to empowerment. Further, that relationship is greater than any relationship between rational calculations and empowerment. If it was true in 1983 that "there appear to be no reported studies showing any significant behavioral correlation to belief in legitimacy," it is certainly no longer the case in 1994. Beyond influencing everyday obedience to the law, legitimacy shapes important feelings of empowerment and entitlement.

In this Article, we first present a review of literature on the relation of authorities' legitimacy to public willingness to defer to the decisions of these authorities. The most widely cited prior review of this literature, Professor Hyde's 1983 article arguing for abandonment of the concept of legitimacy, reached debatable conclusions and is now dated. Indeed, Professor Hyde's admonition notwithstanding, the concept of legitimacy and its role in the legal system is currently a topic of great debate. Given the considerable research advances and attention paid to the concept of legitimacy in recent years, and especially given the Supreme Court's exaltation of legitimacy as a rationale in *Casey,* a need exists for a new, thorough examination of this area.

[19] *See, e.g.,* Alan Hyde, *The Concept of Legitimation in the Sociology of Law,* 1983 Wis. L. Rev. 379, 395 n.31 ("In short, the hypothesis of an inherent tendency to obey the law because of a uniform attitude of 'legitimacy,' while perhaps provocative and exciting in the law reviews, turns out to be old hat, shopworn, and wrong in the political science and sociology journals.").

[21] *See* Tom R. Tyler, Why People Obey the Law 57–60 (1990) (presenting original data showing that legitimacy has more influence on obedience than deterrence and peer disapproval).

Second, we present original data investigating the link between perceptions of legitimacy, Court decisions, and public acceptance of those decisions. This data was garnered through survey interviews of an ethnically and socioeconomically diverse sample of the public conducted just prior to the *Casey* decision. This empirical analysis bolsters the conclusion of our literature review: legitimacy can be an effective tool of authorities and is largely premised, in the case of the Supreme Court, on perceptions of neutrality in decisionmaking.

We conclude by arguing that there is considerable support for the legitimacy model articulated in the *Casey* decision, yet we note that areas in need of further study do exist. We then place our findings in the context of jurisprudential writings (i.e., we contrast our empirical results with the theories of various legal scholars) and discuss the implications of legitimation for maintenance of the rule of law and the status quo.

In our examination of legitimacy theory, we will address three key questions. The first is whether the general legitimacy of the Supreme Court (i.e., the Court's institutional legitimacy) as an appropriate interpreter of the Constitution enhances the authoritativeness of the Supreme Court when it makes controversial decisions. In particular, are people more willing to empower the Court to make public policy in a controversial arena (here, abortion) if they regard the Court as a legitimate judicial institution? As noted above, we conclude that legitimacy is associated with empowerment, strongly supporting a basic premise of the joint opinion in *Casey*. The Court wisely attends to its legitimacy in the eyes of the public because the general institutional legitimacy of the Court is related to the public's willingness to defer to the claim in *Roe* that abortion is an issue of "legal rights" properly falling within the Supreme Court's jurisdiction.

The second question addressed is the basis of the Court's legitimacy. This question is addressed by examining the psychology underlying public views of the Court as a legitimate institution with the right to interpret the Constitution. [Yale Law School] Professor [Owen] Fiss has argued that "objectivity" is necessary to a legitimate functioning of judicial authority. This argument is consistent with [sociologist Max] Weber's discussions of rational authority in the law: to the extent the Court holds to certain "objective" standards or "disciplining rules" that constrain individual personal or political choices, the Court will be perceived as legitimate. The exercise of rational authority by judges with adherence to objective standards of interpretation involves the consistent application of clear legal rules by trained professionals who are unbiased, honest, and use facts and universal legal rules to make their decisions.

We analyze the perception of authority on two levels. First, we distinguish between self-interest-based and justice-based evaluations (i.e., evaluations of authority with reference to how it impacts personal gain or loss versus evaluations of the procedural and distributive fairness of authority). The results of our literature review and our empirical analysis indicate that procedural justice in decisionmaking is the key factor underlying views of authority.

In addition, we go to a deeper level and consider the elements that underlie a perception of procedural fairness in authoritative decisionmaking, with emphasis on the neutrality and trustworthiness of the decisionmaker, the respect accorded the public by the decisionmaker, and the extent to which the public may have control over how the decisionmaker decides. The data analyzed support the argument made by the Justices in *Casey* (as well as by legal scholars such as Fiss) that perceptions of political neutrality bear an important relationship to Court legitimacy.

However, these findings suggest that this argument captures only part of what leads to legitimacy of the Court in the public's eye. In particular, the model of Court legitimacy articulated by social scientists is elaborated and compared to the model presented in the *Casey* decision, and the original survey data presented here are dissected as well, to yield a more detailed picture of the psychology underlying a view of the Supreme Court as a legitimate institution of government. The addition of empirical data to this picture is crucial because to date very little empirical investigation of the bases of Court legitimacy has been undertaken.

The final question to be addressed is whether public views about legitimacy are shaped by current controversies involving the Court. Specifically, how did the Senate hearings over the confirmation of Clarence Thomas impact the perceived legitimacy of the Court? The *Casey* Court stated that legitimacy is difficult to acquire but easy to lose. Our data suggest that the Thomas hearings did have significant negative influence on perceptions of the Court's legitimacy and that legitimacy may indeed be a volatile property.

. . .

The findings of this study support other public opinion research in suggesting that the public generally regards the Supreme Court as a legitimate political institution. This legitimacy is clear, but not unqualified. The attitudes found are somewhat ambivalent, with many people feeling that the Court, although a legitimate institution, has taken on too much power.

The belief that the Court has taken on too much power is strongly endorsed in the case of abortion rights. A majority of respondents indicated that the Supreme Court should have less authority to determine public policy over the abortion issue. The Court is wise to be concerned about its public mandate. Much of the public is not supportive of the *Roe v. Wade* decision because the public believes that the availability of abortion is not an issue that the Supreme Court should handle.

Strikingly, neither agreement with past Court decisions about abortion nor views about the desirability of legalizing abortion influences attitudes about empowerment. People are not deciding whether to empower the Court to resolve the abortion question by evaluating whether they agree with past Court decisions. Instead, they are evaluating the processes by which the Court makes decisions (i.e., a more general attitude toward the Court, not attitudes about the Court's handling of specific cases, appears to have determined empowerment decisions).

. . .

The degree to which legitimacy influences the empowerment of legal authorities and compliance with legal rules has broad and important implications for our understanding of the nature of civic behavior. Rather than focus on the rewards and threats that are prominent under economic models of authority, legitimacy-based models direct attention to the justifications offered for authority and the manner in which this authority is carried out. Resources may be better spent maintaining perceptions of legitimacy than monitoring and sanctioning behavior.

. . .

What is it specifically that leads to a sense of procedural justice? The most significant component of judgments of procedural justice with regard to the Supreme Court involves perceptions of neutrality. Justices who are viewed as honest, impartial, and deliberative, basing their decisions on case-relevant information, rather than as driven by political pressures and personal opinion, are performing legitimately in the eyes of the public. Moreover, to the degree the Justices are viewed as respecting citizens' rights in general, they are viewed more positively. As with neutrality concerns, a perception of respect for people's rights denotes a confidence that the Court will act in good faith to resolve any dispute it hears. Under this theory, personal views and political agendas are irrelevant—the validity of legal claims predominates.

In this concern for neutrality and respect, citizens' views reflect the more impersonal nature of evaluations of national level authorities; people have greater direct contact with local level authorities, a fact represented in the more relational character of legitimacy evaluations at this level. Interestingly however, neutrality and general respect for rights do not provide a complete explanation for national level evaluations. People also are affected by the more relational concern of how Justices will treat them personally. Whether the Justices are seen as caring about personal concerns and likely to consider individuals' opinions when deciding a case is related to legitimacy. Thus, even in the context of the Supreme Court, people are still concerned with their personal relationship to the Court and its Justices.

These findings fit well into the framework of prior studies on legitimacy. The largely impersonal nature of the Court, with its exalted, removed, and even mysterious status, helps explain why neutrality was the most significant determinant of procedural justice judgments and, through them, judgments about the legitimacy of authority. These findings accord with the general focus on "rational" legal authority articulated by legal scholars. The honest, evenhanded application of universal legal rules legitimizes the exercise of legal authority.

The findings, however, also suggest support for a broader model of legal authoritativeness. In studies of legal, political, and managerial authorities with whom people have everyday contact, relational models of procedural justice receive strong support. These models indicate that people are strongly influenced by the nature of the social bond that arises between themselves and authorities. In the case of the U.S. Supreme Court, however, relational concerns—although present—are secondary. People do not have the opportunity to bond emotionally with the Court and so relational concerns do not dominate in this context; instead more general, context-independent, systemic concerns predominate. Apparently, people want to think of the Court as an objective decisionmaker doling out fair outcomes.

Although secondary, relational concerns are clearly important. That importance is most strikingly demonstrated by examining empowerment. Trust in the motives of the Justices was the key predictor of willingness to defer to legal authorities on the abortion issue. In fact, it was equal to neutrality in importance. Empowerment is of central concern because it represents the willingness to defer to legal authorities. Although evaluations of legitimacy were based on neutrality concerns, the key issue of empowerment had an important component of trust.

Although these findings support the emphasis on neutrality found in legal writings on authority, it is important to distinguish the neutrality concerns evinced here from those discussed by some legal scholars. "Neutrality" in jurisprudence often has a special meaning, namely, adherence to neutral principles in constitutional interpretation. This neutrality has been described more specifically by Judge Robert Bork as requiring as close an adherence to the textual and historical meaning of the Constitution as is possible and more generally by Professor Herbert Wechsler as requiring decisions that rest on reasons with respect to all the issues in a case, reasons that in their generality and their neutrality transcend any immediate result. This more specific conception of neutrality is distinct from that which we studied in that people were not asked their views on the propriety of any specific theory of constitutional interpretation. The more general conception, however, is similar in that it draws attention to the impartial conduct of adjudication, rather than to the specifics of any case. Moreover, all the authors arguing for neutrality in its various forms share at least one concern with our sample of Americans: that the law, not personal values and opinions, should drive outcomes. The degree to which this result is possible is debatable, nevertheless, the power of the perception of neutrality is great. A faith in neutrality "is deeply rooted in our history and in our shared principles of political legitimacy." The Justices in *Casey* thus appropriately seize on a conception of neutrality as crucial to the maintenance of Court legitimacy.

. . .

[T]he findings of this study suggest that the model of "objective" interpretation of the Constitution is very much alive in the minds of Americans. This model has been critiqued by a variety of "critical" legal scholars over recent years. Whatever the merits of these critiques, the Court remains a highly respected legal institution among the general public. Further, the public generally believes that the Court is a legitimate institution that uses fair decisionmaking procedures. These beliefs have very concrete implications: they serve as a basis for public willingness to empower the Court to resolve the controversial public policy issue of abortion.

Tyler and Mitchell's view that people have closer relationships with local authorities than with the Supreme Court raises an important question about what influences in society bind or influence the public beyond or besides the decisionmaking of national authorities such as the Supreme Court. Indeed, over the past decade, legal scholars have been exhaustively studying the ways in which community, family, and other norms can influence behavior more effectively than law and the ways in which law and social, communal, and other norms can influence each other. For an overview on this scholarship, see Lawrence Lessig, *The New Chicago School*, 27 J. Leg. Stud. 661 (1998). Professor Eric Posner has examined the complexity of the intervention of law (including constitutional law) into the domains of social, ethnic, and communal norms—i.e., how law can destroy the norm it seeks to support, or how norms can explain the success or failures of laws. See, e.g., Eric A. Posner, *Symbols, Signals, and Social Norms in Politics and the Law*, 27 J. Leg. Stud. 765 (1998); *The Regulation of Groups: The Influence of Legal and Nonlegal Sanctions on Collective Action*, 63 U. Chi. L. Rev. 133 (1996). For studies on the relative coercive power of a community's or smaller group's norms versus that of law, see James Q. Whitman, *What Is Wrong with Inflicting Shame Sanctions?*, 107 Yale L.J. 1055 (1998); Richard A. Posner, *Social Norms and the Law: An Economic Approach*, 87 Am. Econ. Rev. 365 (1997); Dan M. Kahan, *Social Influence, Social Meaning, and Deterrence*, 83 Va. L. Rev. 349 (1997); Cass R. Sunstein, *Social Norms and Social Roles*, 96 Colum. L. Rev. 903 (1996); Lawrence Lessig, *The Regulation of Social Meaning*, 62 U. Chi. L. Rev. 943 (1995).

§ 2.04 The Problem of Judicial Candor

Both the "principled adjudication" and "result-orientation" schools of thought face problems with the issue of judicial candor. Must a "principled" judge try to state *all* the grounds of a decision, or is it sometimes justifiable for judges to be less than fully candid? If a "result-oriented" judge thinks a particular decision is essential for some reason that does not seem to square with conventional judicial canons, such as its social desirability, can and should the judge say so? If judges regularly fail to be candid, are not the rest of us likely sooner or later to catch on and trust them less, with whatever effects would follow from that?

Professor David Shapiro of Harvard Law School carefully considered possible justifications for judicial dissembling in his article, *In Defense of Judicial Candor*, 100 HARV. L. REV. 731, 731–32, 736–39, 742–43, 747–50 (1987):[24]

> This idea—that judges at times may properly sacrifice openness and candor for the sake of other goals—has been expressed in many ways by a number of observers. Thus . . . it seems fitting . . . to consider the extent to which the judge's role may justify a departure from the principles of candor that are thought so indispensable to the scholar's function.
>
> . . .
>
> The case for honesty in all human relations, I believe, rests in part on the importance of treating others with respect: lack of candor often carries with it the implication that the listener is less capable of dealing with the truth, and thus less worthy of respect, than the speaker. The case also rests on a more instrumental ground: the need for trust in the carrying on of human affairs. In a society that placed no special value on truthfulness, all cooperative undertakings would be difficult or impossible. As one wise writer put it, "I cannot reasonably be expected to go over the edge of a cliff on a rope, for however vital an object, if I cannot trust you to keep hold of the other end of it." Indeed, even arguments for occasional deception depend for their effectiveness on a background of truthfulness, for the deception loses its point if it is not believed. . . .
>
> In my view, the case for candor in the crafting of judicial opinions and in other judicial acts draws special strength from the nature of the judicial process. I agree with Lon Fuller that reasoned response to reasoned argument is an essential aspect of that process. A requirement that judges give reasons for their decisions—grounds of decision that can be debated, attacked, and defended—serves a vital function in constraining the judiciary's exercise of power. In the absence of an obligation of candor, this constraint would be greatly diluted, since judges who regard themselves as free to distort or misstate the reasons for their actions can avoid the sanctions of criticism and condemnation that honest disclosure of their motivation may entail. In a sense, candor is the sine qua non of all other restraints on abuse of judicial power, for the limitations imposed by constitutions, statutes, and precedents count for little if judges feel free to believe one thing about them and to say another. Moreover, lack of candor seldom goes undetected for long, and its detection only serves to increase the level of cynicism about the nature of judging and of judges.
>
> I do not believe these arguments are weakened by the response that judges' reasons are at best post hoc rationalizations of results arrived at

---

[24] Copyright © 1987 by The Harvard Law Review Association. Reprinted with permission of Harvard Law Review Association and David Shapiro.

by instinct or hunch. Admittedly, judges themselves disagree about how decisions are reached. My own sense, based in part on my experience as an arbitrator and as a law clerk to a judge, is that the hunch theory falls desperately short of explaining the complex process of decisionmaking, in which reasoning plays an important role at every step. Yet even granting instinct more than its due, I think a great deal is lost in the process of debate if the reasons given by the judge to the public are inconsistent with those he would give in private, or to himself.[33]

Do these arguments demonstrate the need for candor as an unshakable rule of judicial behavior? Do they rebut the argument a utilitarian might make that judicial deception is warranted whenever it will yield a net gain? Surely not. But they do suggest that any utilitarian calculus must take account of the large institutional losses that would result from a lack of trust in the honesty of judges and from an inability to debate and to criticize the true reasons for their decisions. . . .

Some readers may think I have selected too easy a subject; who, after all, would be Grinch-like enough to argue for lack of candor? I would surely be hard-put to identify anyone who advocates deception across the board, but there are in the literature many eloquent statements of the need for some form of selective deception, or at least nondisclosure, in the plying of the judge's trade . . .

Defending Justice Holmes against a professor's charge that one of his opinions was question-begging, Justice Frankfurter said that Holmes had tried to deal with the issues but discovered after consulting with his fellow justices that "the boys wouldn't stand for" a good opinion. The result of the case, to uphold the constitutionality of an important regulatory statute over only one dissent, was, Justice Frankfurter said, "cheap at the price" of a critic's scorn.

This argument, or variants of it, is often used to justify the sacrifice of candor in order to maintain collegiality and to obtain a majority for a desirable result. In a multi-member court, it is said, a judge can only cause disruption and lose influence by insisting on a particular rationale or formulation.

Certainly, the art of compromise is not out of place in the halls of justice. An effective judge must have a sense of when to settle for less than his heart's desire, either in writing his own opinion or in joining someone else's. But I think the sticking point can and should be an unwillingness to make or join in a statement that does not represent the judge's views and that will mislead the opinion's readers as to what those views are. (Indeed, it is when a judge goes beyond this point that the term "result-oriented" seems an appropriate epithet.) Sometimes, the distinction may be only between a concurrence in an opinion and a concurrence in a judgment, but that distinction is not insubstantial. And though the alternative to dissembling may be a proliferation of separate opinions, I suspect the evils of that development have been overstated. . . .

. . . Barring the presence of a rare moral imperative, I simply do not think that the gain—often only an unstable coalition of judges whose disagreements are concealed from each other—is worth the inevitable loss of public regard and self-respect.

. . .

---

[33] . . . I do not think that a judge is obligated to search out and disclose the "deepest" explanation of his actions. But the reasons given for action should not be inconsistent with whatever additional motivation has risen to the level of the judge's consciousness, nor should they be mere pretexts.

In their study of "tragic choices" and in related writings, Guido Calabresi and Philip Bobbitt have argued that a certain amount of dishonesty may be desirable, if not inevitable, when life-and-death or other critical choices involve a clash of basic values. Although they suggest that lack of candor may be only a temporary expedient, often followed by a renewed effort to come to grips with the problem and perhaps a new subterfuge, they see these subterfuges as preferable to a clear choice of one value over another in the absence of a societal consensus in favor of that value. The subterfuge serves an important social purpose by enabling us to cling to both values without fully recognizing the conflict.

[A]n example may be helpful. Calabresi states that an archetypal case is presented by the problem of euthanasia. He believes that if we had a set of rules specifying in detail when a mercy killing was permissible, most people would find those rules intolerable because of the conflict with our commitment to the value of life. At the same time, we sympathize with the desire of relatives and physicians not to prolong suffering, and so the "solution" is to allow a jury, without explanation and perhaps for reasons not specified in its instructions, to acquit a person charged with mercy killing. Thus the "responsible" jury allows us to get out of the dilemma "without scandal."

As a description of what happens when a tragic choice is presented, this analysis (which is a good deal more complex than this brief summary would suggest) is brilliant. As a prescription, it enters far more debatable territory. Indeed, Calabresi and Bobbitt recognize this when they note that subterfuge can bring us peace only for a while; since we are "born to reason," honesty causes the tragic choice to reappear. . . .

Moreover, Calabresi has made it clear in his other work that his preference for candor is strong; that even in the presence of a clash of values, an intense search for accommodation must be made before the field is yielded to dissembling. I suspect that such an approach is always available, and that at least within the limits set by the inescapability of some self-deception, the scholar should always seek not only to recognize subterfuge but to urge its mitigation or abandonment. Take the mercy-killing case. Must we choose between jury nullification without guidance and a detailed set of rules laying out the permissible circumstances for ending suffering? In a prosecution involving a mercy-killing, is it unthinkable to make a move toward honesty by instructing the jury that if they find the defendant to have committed the acts charged, they still have a residual power to acquit—a power that should be used only in the extraordinary situation in which they are convinced that, measured against the community's sense of values, the conduct was not truly blameworthy? And is it not likely that, with the assistance of scientists and philosophers, we will develop guidelines effectively narrowing the range of cases in which the conflict of values is still sharply felt?

Indeed, there may be times when the only way to *preserve* one or both of the conflicting values is to abandon subterfuge. Paul Gewirtz, in a study of the gap between right and remedy in desegregation cases, argues forcefully that candid recognition of that gap is more likely to prevent erosion of the basic rights at stake than is the pretense that the remedies are adequate. Similarly, I wonder whether the value of human life is better served by a refusal to acknowledge and thus to afford some legitimacy to a growing practice of euthanasia, or by a more candid recognition of the tension between that value and the desire not to prolong suffering.

Ronald Dworkin has argued that when a judge is confronted with a conflict between legal and moral right, he may be compelled to lie. Consider, for example, a case in which a statute of the jurisdiction requires punishment for possessing certain racial characteristics, and in which there is no constitutional provision under which the statute may be held invalid. In such a case, a judge who decides that he has a moral duty to support the moral right, and that he cannot satisfy that duty by resigning, can fulfill his moral obligation in his official role only by lying—by saying that the governing legal rights are different from what he believes them to be.

I think that Dworkin is correct and that there is no escape from the obligation to lie in these circumstances. Of course, the interpretation and application of law is a dynamic process that is profoundly affected by questions of morality, and the significance of the judge's allegiance to both law and candor must be considered in determining his moral duty. Thus in a society that aspires to be just, the situation in which a judge might reasonably feel compelled to lie should be extremely rare. Simple disagreement with the applicable rule is plainly not enough. There is a vast difference, for example, between sending someone to the gas chamber because of his race or religion and holding that the statute of limitations has run before an injury was discovered. But, like Dworkin, I do not believe that the judge's predicament can be escaped by concluding that the legal right itself is a function of whatever morality requires. Of course the judge who does believe that, and acts accordingly, is not lacking in candor. Yet I fear that he is engaging in self-deception.

Professor Henry Monaghan of Columbia Law School seems generally to agree with Professor Shapiro on the importance of judicial candor, but in a 1979 article he confronted the difficulties of striving for full candor while trying to craft a coherent, useful opinion for a majority of the Justices. His resolution was to call on the Court for greater collegial effort so as not to abandon the disclosure of at least "all points of significance" on which collective agreement can be attained. He explained:[25]

Collective thought is more than an academic abstraction about the nature of a court; it is a mandatory goal. I view it as an intrinsic aspect of the "Supreme Court" established by article III. To say that each member of that Court takes an oath to support the Constitution as he sees it, not as others see it, does not detract from this point. For an appointment is to a Supreme *Court,* and that concept embodies something very different from viewing each Justice as a Leibnitzian monad colliding with eight other isolated, independent monads only at the point of voting.

The collegial conception of a Supreme Court carries with it specific normative consequences for its members. Professor Hart rightly insists that the votes taken after hearing argument should be viewed as far more tentative than they are in present practice now. And I believe substantially more effort should be made to reduce the volume of concurring opinions. This reduction can occur, of course, only if circulated drafts are taken seriously by the other members of the Court and if, in turn, the opinion writer seeks to accommodate the objections and suggestions of others. To what extent any of the foregoing in fact will occur is, of course, a function of docket size, as well as of personnel (the Justices) and occasion (the issues). Nonetheless, my study of the Court's work for the last fifteen years leaves me with a distinct impression that there is considerable unnecessary fragmentation within the Court—that the potential for unity has been insufficiently realized.

---

[25] Henry P. Monaghan, *Taking Supreme Court Decisions Seriously,* 39 MD. L. REV. 1, 22, 23–26   (1979). Copyright © 1979 by Henry Monaghan. Reprinted with permission.

In any event, it is reasonable to insist that the significant points in the "opinion of the Court" be understood as the result of a deliberate process which reflects the views of the members joining that opinion. Of course, some opinions will be insufficiently principled in the sense that they will contain obscurities. At times this will result from the necessity for compromise if the opinion writer truly seeks to issue a collective product. On other occasions, the obscurity will appear in hard cases—situations in which an acceptable controlling principle cannot be adequately perceived until fleshed out by a series of cases. Seeking the goal of an adequately principled opinion reflecting shared agreement is, after all, not a demand for impossible perfection. The premises of our legal system do assume that in practice an adequately principled opinion is a generally achievable goal, and in any event, a necessary aspirational feature of the judicial process. Accordingly, the inevitable imperfections in the opinion-making process do not support [the] contention that the opinion may properly omit factors in fact relied upon by the Justices. Although I recognize the pragmatic attractions of such a view, it seems to me wholly inconsistent with the root concepts of principled decisionmaking resulting in an opinion publicly exposed for criticism. To be meaningful, these concepts must govern the reality as well as the appearance of judicial opinions. If justifications cannot be stated in the opinion, they should not be relied upon in entering the judgment. A Justice who initially reached a decision on the basis of factors he is unwilling to assert publicly as a justification is, to my mind, under a duty to reconsider his decision with the impermissible factors excluded so far as is humanly possible . . . I would not permit even an "occasional sacrifice" of this principle in order to advance other "most compelling" goals.

Finally, Marquette law professor Scott C. Idleman challenges the conventional wisdom that he believes Professors Shapiro and Monaghan (and our earlier edition) have accepted—that judicial candor is a desirable objective—and examines several arguments that he contends can justify less candor than writers such as Shapiro and Monaghan seem to call for. In reading the following extracts from Professor Idleman's article, *A Prudential Theory of Judicial Candor,* 73 Tex. L. Rev. 1307, 1415–16, 1414–15 (1995), students should consider whether he calls for a degree of analysis that judges could not in practical work be expected to bother with:[26]

[T]here is something terribly familiar in . . . the characterization of judicial candor as a seemingly irresolvable problem. Lurking not far below the surface, in fact, is the conventional wisdom. For judicial candor is indeed a problem, and an unusually formidable one at that, whenever we begin with the notion that candor is presumptively desirable—that a "lack of candor is in itself always harmful"—only to realize the existence of certain circumstances which seem to call that desirability into question, but which are difficult to articulate or defend in light of the strong pro-candor presumption. If at the outset, however, we are able to deny the full authority of the conventional wisdom—if we are willing to expose the conventional wisdom as only partially defensible—then we are significantly freed from this confining and frustrating predicament. It is true, of course, that we still must decide whether and when the logic of the case for candor should be overridden, and by no means is this an easy task. However, upon realizing that the pro-candor rationales are subject to internal limitations, our focus shifts, or at least expands, to the vast realm of judicial discretion created by these limitations. And the largest

---

problem, then, is neither moral nor legal nor political as such, but rather conceptual. It is not the prospect of certain values in tension with the conventional wisdom, but the realization that the conventional wisdom itself—our very conceptual foundation—has turned out to be more apparent than real.

. . . The simple truth is that an ideal of full disclosure, even if entirely defensible in theory, simply cannot pass muster in the real world of law-where judges, lawyers, and the public are frequently less than rational; where courts are invariably subject to a host of complex political and institutional dynamics; where full cognizance, let alone perfect information, is not often to be had; and where the nature of law and the first principles of the social and political order are ever-shifting. The irony, of course, is that at some level, this is probably what many of us believe. Indeed, I suspect there is often a significant disparity between what we say in the abstract about how judges should act and how we actually believe judges should act based on the outcomes they can achieve by acting prudentially. This is, in many respects, nothing more than the basic tension between purism and prudentialism, and this Article has simply argued that in seeking to preserve the aspirational significance of the former, we not ignore the value and the reality of the latter.

Describing the approach that his position would prescribe for judges, Idleman gives the following sketch, *id.* at 1401–04:

[P]rudentialism is a mode of analysis characterized by a substantive emphasis on the political and institutional aspects or consequences associated with any given decisional situation, particularly those aspects or consequences concerning legitimacy. At the same time, it is characterized by a corresponding analytical emphasis on several interrelated factors: (1) the inherent complexity and uncertainty of the situation (coupled with a distrust of abstraction or absolutism), (2) the importance of discerning and maintaining continuity among the past, the future, and the resolution of the present dispute, (3) the practical constraints facing the decisionmaker as well as those facing other actors involved in the situation, (4) the need to be sensitive to the sovereignty of other institutions, (5) the probable desirability of compromise and accommodation and the virtues of incrementalism, and (6) the realization that, above all, governance is a human activity and thus is animated yet constrained by the aspirations and irrationalities of the human condition. And if all of this sounds quite similar to pragmatism, it is only because prudentialism is in many ways pragmatism of a more political and perhaps conservative variety—quite literally, political pragmatism.

As for the proper analytical role of prudential considerations, judges should use essentially a three-stage process for determining the propriety of candor within any particular situation. Stage 1 asks whether and to what extent one or more of the nine pro-candor rationales should apply, based on a comparison of the nature of the situation and the reasoning of each rationale. Assuming that one or more rationales do apply and assuming that their logical reach can be ascertained, stage 2 then asks whether any of the independent reasons for the avoidance of candor-the practical and normative constraints-ought also to apply and, if so, what the priority-based relationship of those reasons is to the relevant pro-candor rationales. Drawing from, among other things, various prudential considerations, the decisionmaker must then choose the appropriate level of candor. Finally, and depending partly on the outcome or applicability of stage 2, stage 3 asks whether prudential considerations would favor the use or avoidance of candor within the realm of discretion created by the logical limitations of the initial pro-candor rationales identified at stage 1. If the prudential analysis counsels in favor of candor, then the judge should probably exercise candor; conversely, if the prudential analysis counsels against candor, then the judge should probably decline to exercise candor. With this broad overview in mind, let us now examine each stage more closely.

The focus of stage 1 is the applicability and scope of the nine pro-candor rationales—accountability, limited power, improved decision-making, authoritativeness, duty to immediate parties, duty to all potential legal actors, judicial catharsis, long-term legal development, and moral duty. As demonstrated, the justificatory strength of a number of these supposed rationales is actually fairly weak, and a few contain serious logical or conceptual flaws that call into question even their most basic applicability. Nevertheless, to the extent that several of them remain capable of supporting some type of candor requirement, judges must look first to their relevance and scope. Thus, for example, if a judge is faced with the question of whether to disclose her growing dissatisfaction with a particular doctrine, she would first look to see if any of the rationales would support the disclosure. Assuming the most likely rationales are the duty to all potential legal actors and long-term legal development, the judge must then discern whether their logic and reasoning are of a sufficiently broad scope so as to require candor in the particular case.

That process of discernment should look something like the following. With regard to the duty-to-potential-actors rationale, for example, if several other judges are similarly dissatisfied, if together they have the power to alter the current doctrinal landscape, and if the disclosure would not create confusion in the state of the law (as opposed to clarification), then the disclosure would appear to be warranted. If, however, the judge is alone in her dissatisfaction, or if her dissatisfaction could not possibly affect current doctrine, or if the disclosure would in fact create confusion, then candor should not be compulsory. The same analysis would then be applied to the long-term-legal-development rationale. Thus, if the judge believes that the law should proceed in her favored direction (assuming that she has a proposal and not simply a protestation), if what she has to say has not already been said, and if her disclosure would neither run contrary to rules of restraint nor potentially create worse law through subsequent misappropriation, then candor would appear to be warranted. If, however, the judge either has no proposal or does not believe that it is best for her own position to be adopted, or if what she has to say has already been set forth adequately in the case law or legal literature, or if there is a significant risk that her disclosure could backfire or be misappropriated, then the long-term-legal-development rationale would not seem to compel candor after all. The same analysis could then be applied to any of the other seven rationales until the initial relevance and logical limits of each are determined.

Assuming for the moment that some measure of candor is logically warranted by one or both rationales, the judge would then proceed to stage 2. The critical question at this second stage is whether independent or extrinsic reasons exist that may counsel against candor despite the logical force of the pro-candor rationales. . . . I divided these reasons into two categories: practical constraints and normative constraints. The first category includes limited judicial foresight, inefficacy, and the dynamics of multimember courts, while the second category includes moral exigency, institutional legitimacy, and the need to employ legal phraseology. In terms of the judge who is dissatisfied with current doctrine, the most relevant extrinsic considerations would appear to be limited judicial foresight, inefficacy, and institutional legitimacy. Thus, if the judge's ability to discern the future impact of her candor is seriously limited, or if her candor would fall on deaf ears or could not possibly effect doctrinal change, or if her candor might cause damage to the legitimacy either of her court or of the judiciary in general, then indeed there is a conflict between the mandate of the pro-candor rationales and the concerns raised by these various practical and normative constraints.

In attempting to resolve this conflict—in attempting to discern the relative priority of each element on each half of the balance—the judge may properly look to, among other sources, prudential considerations. Because many of the practical and normative constraints themselves rest on prudential considerations, the judge should probably first attempt to isolate these considerations and to evaluate their comparative and independent importance. She should then look to each of the other prudential considerations set forth above—the institutional needs of the judiciary, including those of her own court and position, the demands of other governmental institutions and their relationship to the status of the judiciary, the uncertainty inherent in the decision she faces and the resultant need to proceed cautiously, the importance of continuity and public confidence in law, and so forth—as well as various other nonprudential considerations that she believes are relevant to the question of candor. Only upon an evaluation of all these factors, and of their relationship to the initial pro-candor rationales, should the judge reach her decision whether or not to make the disclosure. Indeed, because this decision effectively allows the judge to override an otherwise justifiable candor obligation and thus asks her to assume the persona of public fiduciary, she must approach it with due caution and with a full appreciation of the practical dangers of miscalculation.

Of course, the for[e]going analysis is necessary only if there exist applicable pro-candor rationales, as well as a conflict between those rationales and one or more of the practical or normative constraints. What if the judge, however, finds herself in a situation in which the pro-candor rationales are not applicable, either because they are inapplicable on their face or because their logical limits have been reached? In this situation, the judge would then enter stage 3 and proceed directly to a purely prudential analysis of the choice for or against candor. That analysis would essentially ask whether, on balance, the use of candor is favored or disfavored in light of the full range of prudential considerations and without regard to the pro-candor rationales. Once again, these considerations might include the need to maintain political legitimacy (of her own position, of her court, of the judiciary, or of the legal system as a whole), the need to preserve doctrinal and philosophical continuity in the law, the recognition of uncertainty and the need to proceed with moderation, and the importance of respecting the sovereignty of other institutions (as embodied, for example, in the principles of federalism and separation of powers). If candor is favored by this analysis, then the judge probably should employ candor. Conversely, if candor is disfavored, then the judge probably should forego candor. Again, this assessment is clearly a matter of context and degree—as prudential judgments by definition are—and therefore judges should necessarily proceed with a deliberate awareness of the likelihood and costs of misestimation. In contrast to considerations implicated in stage 2, however, the judge's decision in stage 3 cannot offend either the principles or the logic of the pro-candor rationales, for those rationales simply do not apply.

§ 2.05 Judicial Minimalism

In a book published in 1999, University of Chicago Law School Professor Cass Sunstein proposed a provocative model of the judicial function based on

the late Alexander Bickel's advocacy of judicial adherence to "passive virtues,"
which Bickel defined as the use of techniques of judicial avoidance to delay
decisions in important cases that might be further clarified by democratic
debate.[27] Professor Sunstein initially sketched his theory in a law review
article in which he defended judicial or decisional minimalism, which he
defined as "saying no more than necessary to justify an outcome and leaving
as much as possible undecided."[28] In the following extract from a review of
Professor Sunstein's book, Jeffrey Rosen, a law professor at George Washington University and legal affairs editor at *The New Republic*, summarizes
Sunstein's basic arguments, suggests that they cannot be reconciled with the
Court's traditional function, and defends the need for broader and deeper
analysis in some of the Supreme Court's major individual rights decisions over
the past decade. Jeffrey R. Rosen, *The Age of Mixed Results,* THE NEW
REPUBLIC, June 28, 1999, 44–51:[29]

> The fundamental characteristic of judicial minimalism, as Sunstein de-
> fines it, is a commitment to leaving important questions unresolved. As
> Sunstein puts it:

>> A minimalist court settles the case before it, but it leaves many things
>> undecided. It is alert to the existence of reasonable disagreement in
>> a heterogeneous society. It knows that there is much that it does not
>> know; it is intensely aware of its own limitations. It seeks to decide
>> cases on narrow grounds. It avoids clear rules and final resolutions.
>> Alert to the problem of unanticipated consequences, it sees itself as
>> part of a system of democratic deliberation; it attempts to promote
>> the democratic ideals of participation, deliberation, and responsive-
>> ness. It allows continued space for democratic reflection from Con-
>> gress and the states. It wants to accommodate new judgments about
>> facts and values. To the extent that it can, it seeks to provide rulings
>> that can attract support from people with diverse theoretical
>> commitments.

> Encouraging judges to preserve space for democratic deliberation, Sun-
> stein provides a series of distinctions. First, he argues that minimalist
> decisions should be narrow rather than broad—that is, minimalist justices
> should try to decide the case at hand without laying down a sweeping
> rule that will bind lower courts and legislatures in similar cases. By
> refusing to tie the hands of the political branches and the lower courts,
> Sunstein argues, the Supreme Court can preserve space for democratic
> disagreement.

> And Sunstein further argues that minimalist decisions should be
> shallow rather than deep. They should lay down a rule in the case at hand
> without giving an ambitious theoretical account of their reasons for doing
> so. By avoiding foundational questions, and converging on "incompletely
> theorized agreements," courts can "make it unnecessary for people to
> agree when agreement is impossible," again preserving space for demo-
> cratic debate.

> As an example of a decision that is narrow and deep, Sunstein points
> to the Virginia Military Institute case,[30] where the Court struck down

---

[27] Cass R. Sunstein, ONE CASE AT A TIME:
JUDICIAL MINIMALISM ON THE SUPREME COURT
(1999).

[28] Cass R. Sunstein, *The Supreme Court, 1995
Term—Foreword: Leaving Things Undecided,*
110 HARV. L. REV. 4, 6–8 (1995).

[29] Copyright © 1999 by The New Republic.
Reprinted with permission of The New Republic and the author.

[30] United States v. Virginia, 518 U.S. 515,
557–558, 116 S. Ct. 2264, 135 L. Ed. 2d 735
(1996).

the all-male admissions policy at VMI on the grounds that the Constitution prohibits gender-based stereotypes, while refusing to say whether or not single-sex education was or was not constitutional in other circumstances. As an example of a narrow but shallow decision, he points to *Romer v. Evans*,[31] where the Court invalidated an anti-gay rights amendment in Colorado without clearly explaining why it was doing so or what it thought about different forms of discrimination based on sexual orientation. (I am not sure that I have ever read another book in which "narrow" and "shallow" are terms of praise.) Sunstein contrasts these decisions with the decisions of the Warren Court that he considers wide and deep, such as *Brown v. Board of Education*,[32] invalidating school segregation, and *Reynolds v. Sims*,[33] declaring the constitutional principle of one-man-one-vote; and with a wide and shallow decision such as *Roe v. Wade*,[34] which struck down abortion restrictions in almost all circumstances without giving an intelligible reason why it was doing so.

Sunstein's matrix of categories is certainly provocative, but it seems just as malleable as the categories of activism and restraint that it wishes to usurp. Whether a decision is characterized as narrow or shallow, or deep or broad, seems entirely in the eye of the beholder. Sunstein lists *Brown* as an example of a wide and deep opinion, but it might just as well be seen as a narrow and shallow one. After all, the Court declared segregation in public schools unconstitutional without explaining very clearly why it was doing so, and without saying anything about the constitutionality of different forms of state-sponsored segregation (on public transportation, for example). The indeterminacy of Sunstein's categories calls their broader utility into question.

Read as a shallow decision, moreover, *Brown* is a good example of the chaos that can result when the Supreme Court refuses to lay down clear and easily understood rules. The result of the Court's refusal to explain whether its reasoning extended beyond schools was to create confusion in the lower courts and legislatures, which, in the years following *Brown*, were deeply divided about the constitutionality of segregation in public swimming pools, golf courses, and other public facilities. In a series of terse and unanimous opinions, unaccompanied by any reasons at all, the Supreme Court extended the narrow holding of *Brown*, striking down each of these further examples of public segregation one by one, but again without articulating a clear principle to justify its decisions.

Owing to the unreasoned quality of *Brown*, moreover, supporters of segregation were able to exploit its logical flaws. In 1963, for example, a Southern judge held a trial about the empirical validity of Kenneth Clark's studies of the self-esteem of African American children, as reflected in their reaction to white and black dolls. If, instead of focusing on the "feeling of inferiority" that segregation provoked in black children, the Court had issued an opinion that was genuinely deep—holding, say, that all state-sponsored racial segregation is unconstitutional because it is inherently caste-affirming—then lower courts and legislatures might have been less quick, in the wake of *Brown*, to take advantage of loopholes in the Court's terse commands, such as the requirement to implement desegregation "with all deliberate speed."

It is possible, of course, that no matter how broadly or deeply the *Brown* opinion had been written, it would have provoked the same resistance

---

[31] 517 U.S. 620, 635–636, 116 S. Ct. 1620, 134 L. Ed. 2d 855 (1996).

[32] 347 U.S. 483, 495–496, 74 S. Ct. 686, 98 L. Ed. 2d 873 (1954).

[33] 377 U.S. 533, 586, 84 S. Ct. 1362, 12 L. Ed. 2d 506 (1964).

[34] 410 U.S. 113, 166–167, 93 S. Ct. 705, 35 L. Ed. 2d 147 (1973).

from segregationists and the same support from integrationists. In his pathbreaking study THE HOLLOW HOPE,[35] Gerald Rosenberg has suggested that the *Brown* decision had little influence on the immediate progress of desegregation in America; it was not until political opinion against segregation had congealed during the civil rights movement of the 1960s that the public sphere was integrated in a meaningful way. If Rosenberg's thesis is correct, as Sunstein notes, then *Brown* might actually be seen not as a maximalist decision at all, but a "form of democracy-promoting minimalism," opening a dialogue with the political branches that remained unsettled for more than a decade. Yet Sunstein presents no empirical evidence about the degree to which legislatures or citizens may respond differently to shallow as opposed to deep decisions, and so it is hard to say with confidence whether or not a deep opinion can, in fact, provoke more democratic deliberation than an opaque one or a shallow one can.

Since the subset of lawyers who regularly read Supreme Court opinions after they have graduated from law school is tiny, and the subset of non-lawyers who read Supreme Court opinions at any point in their lives is far smaller, it would not be surprising if the shallowness or the depth of an opinion has little influence on the degree to which it influences political debate. (Most citizens get their knowledge of Supreme Court opinions from television, which suggests that Sunstein's central premise that the courts can participate in an informed dialogue with citizens may be idealistic.) Yet shallow opinions seem especially unlikely to provoke reasoned deliberation, because they give citizens and legislators so little to deliberate about, except to try to predict the future votes of the justices who produced them. Sunstein's strongest point about *Brown* is that it represented the culmination of decades of incremental victories in the lower courts; and that the Supreme Court would do well, in cases involving social issues about which there is profound division, to follow the opinions of lower courts and citizens rather than to lead them. Yet this is an argument for delaying important decisions, not for refusing to give coherent reasons in cases that the Court has finally agreed to decide.

If the Supreme Court were the only court in the nation, it might be able to embrace a highly personalized, "the law is what we say it is" jurisprudence, without worrying about giving very clear reasons for why it is doing so, and without tipping its hand about how it is likely to decide similar cases in the future. In the American system, however, the Supreme Court sits at the top of a pyramid of inferior federal courts, all of which are bound to apply its decisions uniformly throughout the nation. And lower courts, when faced with a narrow, shallow Supreme Court decision of the kind that Sunstein praises, may literally be at a loss about what the opinion means. This is more likely to promote chaos than reasoned deliberation.

Sunstein acknowledges that minimalism may shift the burden of making hard decisions from the Supreme Court to lower courts: "A court that economizes on decision costs for itself may in the process 'export' decision costs to other people, including litigants and judges in subsequent cases who must give content to the law," he writes. For this reason, he stresses that when "planning" by lower courts and citizens is important, minimalism may be inappropriate. But isn't "planning" important in every case that the Supreme Court agrees to hear? In an age in which the Supreme Court is deciding fewer and fewer cases, and selecting the

---

[35] GERALD ROSENBERG, THE HOLLOW HOPE:
CAN COURTS BRING ABOUT SOCIAL CHANGE?
(1991).

handful of cases that it agrees to hear by looking for areas of disagreement among the lower courts, it seems inefficient and even irresponsible for the justices to refuse to lay down clear rules in the few cases in which they have promised to do so.

Surely it is hard to argue that the legal questions in these cases would benefit from further debate in the lower courts, since it is the existence of vigorous disagreement in the lower courts that led the Supreme Court to agree to hear the case in the first place. When the Supreme Court issues terse opinions whose reasoning is hard to discern, it compounds the confusion of inferior courts in precisely those cases where the relevant actors are pleading for a clear resolution. The result is a national exercise in clairvoyance, as lower courts, citizens, and legislatures spend great energy and expense trying to puzzle through problems that the Supreme Court promised but then refused to resolve.

By embracing shallowness as a judicial virtue, Sunstein is advocating a version of the personalized jurisprudence of Sandra Day O'Connor; but O'Connorism is hardly a recipe for rich public debate. Consider the Voting Rights cases. In a series of opinions beginning with *Shaw v. Reno* in 1993,[36] O'Connor has cast tie-breaking votes to strike down a series of voting districts constructed on the basis of race. At the same time, O'Connor has taken care to stress that not all majority-minority districts are unconstitutional—going so far in one case as to write a separate concurrence to her own opinion that seemed to deny its logical implications.

Since O'Connor has refused to reveal the rules or the standards that, in her view, distinguish constitutional from unconstitutional districts, the process of redistricting in the wake of the 1990 census has largely become a[n] exercise in trying to read Justice O'Connor's mind. This has dramatically increased her power, but it has wreaked havoc on electoral maps across the country. Far from promoting reasoned deliberation, O'Connorism promotes its antithesis, entangling individual justices in the political process to the most minute and confusing degree. Justice Potter Stewart's famous test for obscenity—"I know it when I see it"—was based on the conviction that there was a social consensus about what is obscene, but that it reflected too many legal and moral permutations to be captured in a single judicial rule. O'Connor's focus on "oddly shaped districts" is far more self-aggrandizing, because it rests on no broader aesthetic than the sensibility of the individual justice herself.

Sunstein recognizes the democratic virtues of deep opinions as opposed to shallow ones—they help to promote the rule of law, by limiting judicial discretion and improving predictability—but still he defends shallow decisions, on the grounds that they permit citizens with "diverse theoretical commitments" to converge around outcomes when they are unable to converge around abstract principles. Yet the voting rights experiment calls even that modest claim into question. An incompletely theorized case such as *Shaw v. Reno* gives citizens no basis for knowing what, precisely, they are being asked to accept, beyond the unsatisfying claim that a voting district is unconstitutional if Justice O'Connor thinks it is. The broad and deep decisions of the Warren Court obviously thwarted democracy, by forbidding the legislature from acting in all sorts of spheres. But O'Connor's minimalism thwarts democracy in a different way: by personalizing constitutional interpretation in a way that is hardly consistent with reasoned argument.

The right-to-die cases offer another example of the hazards of O'Connorism. In 1997, all nine justices agreed that the Constitution does

---

[36] 509 U.S. 630, 113 S. Ct. 2816, 125 L. Ed. 2d 511 (1993).

not protect an open-ended right to physician-assisted suicide in all circumstances.[37] But the Court divided sharply on the question of whether a competent person experiencing great pain might have the right to hasten his imminent death. Four justices, led by Chief Justice Rehnquist, would have left this question entirely up to the representatives and the citizens of the states. In what Sunstein calls an "ambitious, emphatically nonminimalist opinion," Rehnquist would limit the Court's discretion to recognize new fundamental rights under the due process clause of the Constitution to those rights that are deeply rooted in longstanding traditions and practices.

But why is Rehnquist's opinion "emphatically nonminimalist"? The conventional tools of legal interpretation—text, history, tradition, constitutional structure, and judicial precedent—all fail to support the claim that there is a fundamental right to physician-assisted suicide, even to alleviate great pain when death is imminent. By recognizing the weakness of the argument for a judicially created right to die, and by removing the courts from the debate entirely, Rehnquist's approach would seem to preserve the largest space for democratic deliberation.

Yet Sunstein prefers the far more elusive approach of Justice O'Connor, who stressed that the Court had not decided whether or not a competent person experiencing great suffering might have a constitutional right to control the circumstances of imminent death. "O'Connor's opinion speaks for a group of justices who are not quite clear on how to handle fundamental rights under the due process clause and who want to leave the hardest and most contested issues for continuing democratic, and judicial, debate," Sunstein writes. But O'Connor characteristically gave no hints about what sort of constitutional arguments might persuade her to decide this question one way or another, and so it is impossible to say whether or not she was justified in refusing to tip her hand.

If O'Connor is waiting for further facts to illuminate some aspect of the constitutional debate, then her hesitation might be justified. In his own separate opinion, Justice Souter suggests that more empirical evidence, especially about the experience of the Netherlands, might cast light on the question of whether the line between assisted suicide and voluntary or involuntary euthanasia could become "porous" if the Court were to recognize a limited right to die for terminally ill people who are experiencing great pain. Still, empirical evidence is not the end of the matter. It may illuminate whether or not the state has a sufficiently strong interest in guarding against medical mistakes to override a fundamental right of terminally ill patients to end their suffering, but it casts little light on the question of whether or not the right exists in the first place. That is a question of judicial philosophy, of argument and interpretation.

Sunstein, like O'Connor, says that the Court should assume that the right to physician-assisted suicide is "presumptively protected" in medically hopeless cases, but should also hold that the state's interests are sufficiently strong to override it. Why is this opaque holding more "minimalist" than Rehnquist's far less intrusive alternative? Since neither Sunstein nor O'Connor explains the reasons that might persuade the Court to recognize a presumptive right to die under medically hopeless conditions, all this has the feel of a fiat, and it raises the specter that the Court might create other unenumerated rights in the future with similarly thin support in text, history, and precedent. Wasn't it precisely this threat of an untethered court inventing constitutional rights without

---

[37] *See* Washington v. Glucksberg, 521 U.S. 702, 735–736, 117 S. Ct. 2258, 138 L. Ed. 2d 772 (1997).

coherent explanations that the minimalist project was designed to avoid? Sunstein stresses that "there is a big difference between a refusal to give an ambitious argument for an outcome and a refusal to give any reasons at all," but the opinions that he praises sometimes seem to verge on reasonlessness in their refusal to reveal what the justices could be thinking.

In a powerful article called "Judges as Advicegivers," which appeared in the *Stanford Law Review* in 1998,[38] Neal Katyal argues that the best way for courts to achieve Sunstein's goal—avoiding interference with the political branches and encouraging legislators to settle constitutional issues politically rather than judicially—is to write narrow but deep opinions. That is, opinions explaining their carefully confined holdings with a generous reliance upon dicta, or non-binding advice, that provide clear guidance to legislators and citizens about the reasons and the assumptions behind a decision. The narrowness of the holding would ensure that democratic prerogatives are preserved across a range of issues, and the clear advice would permit the political branches to make informed decisions about the constitutional limits on their powers, rather than trying to read judicial tea leaves.

Thus Katyal argues, about *Clinton v. Jones*,[39] that the Court could have written a narrow opinion siding with Jones rather than a hyperbolic opinion declaring that text and history provide "no substantial support" for claims of presidential immunity. After acknowledging the closeness and uncertainty of the question, he continues, the Court could have declined to create the presidential immunity that Clinton requested, on the grounds that a constitutional solution to the problem would freeze the manner permanently. But the opinion could have included clarifying dicta, informing Congress about the potential constitutional problems, and strongly suggesting that a legislative grant of immunity would be the most appropriate way to address them.

With characteristic fair-mindedness, Sunstein acknowledges the arguments for judicial depth. By refusing to give intelligible reasons for their decisions, he notes, justices run the risk that litigants in similar cases will not receive equal treatment by lower courts. The main objection that he raises to a deep decision is that "judges may not be good at ambitious theorizing, and may hence blunder—a special problem when they are invalidating legislation." Still, it is not clear that judges are any better at less ambitious theorizing, which may require a subtlety and a complexity that more abstract arguments do not require. Consider the Court's opinion in *Romer v. Evans*,[40] the case striking down Colorado's anti-gay rights amendment. Justice Kennedy's opinion for the Court, Sunstein suggests, is narrow and shallow, cobbling together clashing theories without explaining very clearly the relationship between them. The most dramatic silence in the opinion is its failure to address the fate of *Bowers v. Hardwick*,[41] the decision a decade earlier that had upheld a Georgia anti-sodomy statute.

The most shallow way to read Kennedy's opinion is to say that *Romer* and *Bowers* can co-exist side by side. Even assuming, for the sake of

---

[38] See Neal Kumar Katyal, *Judges as Advicegivers*, 50 STAN. L. REV. 1709 (1998). For a response drawing on the author's experiences as a federal court of appeals judge, member of the U.S. House of Representatives, and Chief White House Counsel, see Abner J. Mikva, *Why Judges Should Not Be Advicegivers: A Response to Professor Neal Katyal*, 50 STAN. L. REV. 1825

(1998).

[39] 520 U.S. 681, 695, 117 S. Ct. 1636, 137 L. Ed. 2d 945 (1997).

[40] 517 U.S. 620, 635–636, 116 S. Ct. 1620, 134 L. Ed. 2d 855 (1996).

[41] 478 U.S. 186, 195–196, 106 S. Ct. 2841, 92 L. Ed. 2d 140 (1986).

argument, that it is permissible for a state to ban sodomy, so as to discourage conduct that citizens think is immoral, Kennedy seemed to suggest that prohibiting gays and lesbians from bringing any "claim of discrimination" against the state of Colorado was not a rational way of discouraging homosexual conduct. The sheer breadth of the amendment, as Kennedy put it, "seems inexplicable by anything but animus toward the class it effects." Under this shallow reading of Kennedy's opinion, the Constitution permits citizens to express their moral disapproval of homosexual behavior, as long as they do so rationally.

Sunstein acknowledges that Kennedy's opinion might be read in this limited way, but he rejects the shallow reading in favor of a deeper one. In Sunstein's view, Kennedy's opinion stands for the more ambitious proposition that the equal protection clause of the Constitution "requires that discrimination must be rational in the sense that it must be connected with a legitimate public purpose, rather than fear and prejudice or a bare desire to state public opposition to homosexuality as such." If the *Romer* Court had indeed embraced this plausible but deep principle, then the decision would seem to call into question not only the anti-gay rights amendment passed by the citizens of Colorado but also most laws expressing moral disapproval of homosexual behavior, including the ban on same-sex marriages. Sunstein acknowledges this possibility, but then he says that judges should resist the temptation to invalidate the ban on same-sex marriage, even if they believe that it violates the Constitution, because such a decision could "galvanize opposition," "weaken the antidiscrimination movement," "provoke more hostility and even violence against homosexuals" and "jeopardize the authority of the judiciary."

This exaltation of prudence over principle resurrects the vices of Frankfurterism. In the years after the Court decided *Brown v. Board of Education*, Frankfurter urged the Court to avoid hearing cases that would force it to strike down anti-miscegenation laws, on the grounds that such a decision would be fiercely resisted in the South. Yet there is no convincing evidence that *Loving v. Virginia*,[42] the decision that finally did strike down anti-miscegenation laws in 1968, would have been much more fiercely resisted if it had been handed down five years earlier; and it is hard to think of a good reason, aside from the self-protective instincts of the judiciary, for refusing to apply a constitutional principle to a similar case that it clearly encompasses. Sunstein rejects the notion that it is "too pragmatic and strategic, too obtusely unprincipled" for judges to exalt prudence over principle in highly controversial cases that are likely to provoke popular resistance; but since he fails to tell us what he thinks about the wisdom of deferring a decision in the miscegenation cases, or about the timing and substance of many other landmarks of the Warren era, it is hard to say whether his theory has more general application, or whether it is contrived for a particular group of justices at a particular time.

. . .

As the contrast between the gay rights opinion and the voting rights opinion shows, deep opinions may be as likely to preempt democracy as shallow ones, though for different reasons. This is a wrinkle that Sunstein's analysis is perfectly able to accommodate: he argues convincingly that the case for shallowness or depth may vary depending on the context in which a particular constitutional issue is being debated in the democratic sphere. A more fundamental criticism of Sunstein's judicial minimalism is that, when push comes to shove, he does not really trust

---

[42] 388 U.S. 1, 87 S. Ct. 1817, 18 L. Ed. 2d 1010 (1967).

democracy at all. He is committed to deliberation in the abstract, but he is willing to override the judgments of the actual citizens in actual debates when they do not coincide with his own intuitions about what a deliberative democracy should embrace. Democracy, Sunstein stresses repeatedly, should not be confused with simple majoritarianism: "There is a large difference between democracy, properly understood, and whatever it is that a certain majority has chosen to do at a certain time." But at times the outcomes that Sunstein is willing to credit as genuinely "deliberative," as opposed to "naked preferences" supported by "power but not reasons," look surprisingly like the outcomes with which Sunstein happens to agree.

Consider affirmative action. "I start with the suggestion that the issue of affirmative action should be settled democratically, not judicially," Sunstein writes. He then praises the Supreme Court's "meandering course, its refusal to issue rules, its minimalism" in the affirmative action cases, which "might be defended as performing a valuable catalytic function . . . to spur, but not to preempt, effective public debate." All this is entirely plausible. At the moment, the Court is closely divided between two wide, deep, and mutually inconsistent readings of the constitutional guarantee of equality. Four justices—Scalia, Thomas, Rehnquist, and a little more tentatively Kennedy—seem to believe that affirmative action is unconstitutional in nearly all circumstances because the Constitution is color-blind. Four justices—Stevens, Souter, Ginsburg, and Breyer—seem committed to the principle that affirmative action is permissible in most circumstances because the Constitution prohibits only racial classifications that promote racial castes. Sandra Day O'Connor, naturally, has not made up her mind.

The Court's inability to muster five votes for one alternative over the other has resulted in a series of fragmented opinions that have indeed provoked, as Sunstein suggests, a useful debate about the permissible scope of affirmative action in the public sphere. The affirmative action cases show O'Connorism at its most galvanizing: by offering a series of narrow and shallow distinctions—affirmative action may be permissible in universities but not in federal contracting; diversity is a more important goal in the classroom than on federal highway projects—the Court has provoked legislators and citizens to debate a complicated topic in sophisticated ways.

The most important of these debates took place in California and culminated in Proposition 209, which was adopted by the citizens of California on November 5, 1996. It says that "the state shall not discriminate against, or grant preferential treatment to, any individual or group on the basis of race, sex, color, ethnicity, or national origin in the operation of public employment, public education or public contracting." One would have expected Sunstein to praise Proposition 209 as a democratic settlement of our most hotly contested social question. In a remarkable passage, however, Sunstein suggests that Proposition 209 may not deserve to be considered democratic at all. "Political processes in California on this issue did not appear to be deliberative," he writes. The "American system is one of representative rather than direct democracy, partly because of a judgment that political deliberation can be best promoted through a representative system. If judicial decisions stimulate poorly functioning referenda processes, little will be gained."

Indeed, Sunstein goes so far as to suggest that the Court might have been justified in striking down Proposition 209 as unconstitutional when it was asked to do so: "It would have been an intriguing irony if the Court, committed to a minimalist path with respect to affirmative action, chose to strike down a referendum in part with the knowledge that it contained a ban that prevented the kind of careful analysis of particulars that has stood behind the Court's own decisions." But surely the point of minimalism is to allow citizens to converge around what they consider to be a deep principle of justice that removes some subjects from the judicial realm once and for all. Sunstein then backtracks, noting that "we can understand" the Court's refusal to hear a constitutional challenge to the California initiative on the grounds that "the judiciary ought not to disrupt ongoing processes of political debate over the status of affirmative action."

Sunstein's notion that Proposition 209 may not have been sufficiently "deliberative" calls his broader commitment to "deliberative democracy" into question. He offers no evidence about the character of the debate over Proposition 209, except to note casually that "in the context of affirmative action in particular, there is a danger that referendum outcomes will not be based on a careful assessment of facts and values, but instead on crude 'we-they' thinking." In fact, the debate over Proposition 209, like all political debates, was a messy combination of high principle and low politics: it contained appeals to clashing principles (its sponsors, two college professors, are earnest proponents of the view that the Constitution should be color-blind), factual predictions that turned out to be overly optimistic (affirmative action opponents didn't anticipate the political pressures to lower standards for all students across the board), as well as some crude racial appeals. But this is what real debates in real democracies look like.

. . .

The note on which Sunstein concludes his book seems exactly right. "I am speaking of a presumption, or perhaps of a mood, and not of a rule," he writes, indirectly evoking Learned Hand's famous definition of the spirit of liberty. "This is especially important for judges who are not too sure they are right." Adjudication in a pluralistic society, he suggests, calls for "a presumption in favor of theoretical modesty, especially when courts are asked to invalidate legislation." Sunstein's even-handed tone is exemplary in this regard; and if the Court followed Sunstein's model, with scrupulous acknowledgment of opposing arguments and of intellectual complexities, its opinions might be more convincing.

Still, Sunstein's indulgence of the Court's aversion to theory, and even to sophisticated legal argument, is based on a surprisingly dim view of the capacities of political or judicial actors to engage in a dialogue about controversial issues. He insists on deliberation in the abstract, but he has little faith in courts, legislatures, or the people themselves to persuade each other through reasoned debate. His tolerance of thinly reasoned, over-simplified judicial opinions is also hard to reconcile with the vision of democracy that he insists minimalist decisions are designed to serve. Democracy, he writes,

> embodies a commitment to . . . reason-giving in the public domain. For the deliberative democrat, political outcomes cannot be supported by self-interest or force. "Naked preferences," in the form of legislation supported by power but not reasons, are forbidden. Existing judgments and desires must be made to survive a process of reflection and debate; they are not to be taken as sacrosanct or automatically translated into law.

But how can we demand from the justices of the Supreme Court an even lower standard of deliberation, reflection, reason-giving, and intellectual accountability than we demand from the citizens of the United States?

. . .

. . . In an effort to avoid the grand style of Warrenism, the Rehnquist Court has swung so far in the other direction that legal scholars today are feeling a little like the man drinking at the bar on the Titanic. ("I asked for ice," he says, "but this is ridiculous.") What has been lost is the basic ingredient of principled decision-making, which is a commitment to judicial reason-giving. The problem with the most notoriously maximalist decisions of the Warren and Burger Courts—*Roe* is the paradigm case—was not that they were philosophically ambitious, it was that they were overly simplistic and thinly reasoned. And the minimalist decisions of the Rehnquist Court suffer from precisely the same flaw. Thus we have the spectacle of a Court exercising great power without offering publicly accountable reasons, which seems hard to reconcile with the vision of democracy that minimalism was designed to promote.

In judicial opinions, as in democracy, there are different ways of achieving consensus. One is to offer as few reasons as possible, so no one can possibly feel slighted. Another is to offer as many reasons as possible, none of which is dispositive, but each of which, like strands in a rope, bind together to strengthen the whole. A minimalist who took seriously the judicial duty of reason-giving might recognize that there are, in this pluralistic age, a range of plausible interpretive methodologies, and that judicial intervention seems most legitimate when it can be justified along as many different axes as possible. The conventional tools of legal interpretation—text, history, precedent, tradition, constitutional structure, and moral argument—often point in very different directions. A minimalist judge who took seriously her responsibility to persuade citizens of "diverse theoretical commitments," as Sunstein puts it, might be inclined to defer in the face of contestability, and to strike down laws only in those rare cases when the different methodological tools all point in the same direction. By giving more reasons, rather than fewer reasons, a decision to invalidate could be justified in ways that judges and citizens with clashing moral and political and constitutional commitments can accept and understand.

At this unexpected moment of legal consensus, as liberals and conservatives are converging around the ideal of theoretical humility, perhaps it is time to recover some of the faith in judges as reason-givers that we have spent the past forty years trying to overcome. I do not mean faith in the over-confident, democracy-thwarting opinions of the Warren era. I mean faith in the ability of chastened judges to justify their restrained decisions with intelligible, publicly accessible, well-reasoned and at times even deep arguments that provide clear guidance to citizens and legislators. Whether they (or we) like it or not, judges, and certainly justices of the Supreme Court, are, or should be, intellectuals. They exemplify, or they should exemplify, the indissoluble connection between law and reason.

Thanks largely to the transformation of legal culture that the reaction to Warrenism helped to precipitate, the federal bench in general, and the Supreme Court in particular, is now composed of an able group of Democrats and Republicans, whose similarities are more notable than their differences, and who agree more than they disagree about what distinguishes good legal arguments from bad ones. It is indeed passive-aggressive for this Court to hoard its enhanced authority by retreating into an elliptical and obscurantist unanimity. The philosophical silence of the Supreme Court is an anti-democratic silence. Have we all been so spooked by the ghost of Warrenism that we have inadvertently revived it in a different form?

§ 2.06 Conclusion

In reading the ensuing materials in Parts II and III, students should consider in what ways (or even whether it matters if) different theories of constitutional interpretation obstruct or facilitate the suggestions made by different theorists in this chapter for candor, prudence, and minimalism in judicial opinion writing.

§ 2.07 Bibliography

[A] The Judicial Function

Benjamin Cardozo, THE NATURE OF THE JUDICIAL PROCESS (1921)

Neal Devins, *The Democracy-Forcing Constitution,* 97 MICH. L. REV. 1971 (1999) (reviewing Cass R. Sunstein, ONE CASE AT A TIME: MINIMALISM ON THE SUPREME COURT (1999))

Harry T. Edwards, *The Judicial Function and the Elusive Goal of Principled Decisionmaking,* 1991 WIS. L. REV. 837

H.L.A. HART, THE CONCEPT OF LAW (1961)

Ken Kress, *Why No Judge Should Be a Dworkian Coherentist,* 77 TEX. L. REV. 1375 (1999).

Edward H. Levi, AN INTRODUCTION TO LEGAL REASONING (1949)

Richard Posner, *Appeal and Consent,* THE NEW REPUBLIC, August 16, 1999, at 36

Mark V. Tushnet, TAKING THE CONSTITUTION AWAY FROM THE COURTS (1999)

[B] Neutral Principles

Robert H. Bork, *Neutral Principles and Some First Amendment Problems,* 47 IND. L.J. 1 (1971)

Richard Fallon, *The Rule of Law as a Concept in Constitutional Discourse,* 97 COLUM. L. REV. 1 (1997)

Stanley Fish, THE TROUBLE WITH PRINCIPLE (1999)

Kent Greenawalt, *The Enduring Significance of Neutral Principles,* 78 COLUM. L. REV. 982 (1978)

Gary Peller, *Neutral Principles in the 1950s,* 21 U. MICH. J. L. REF. 561 (1988)

Cass R. Sunstein, *Neutrality in Constitutional Law,* 92 COLUM. L. REV. 1 (1992)

Mark V. Tushnet, RED, WHITE, AND BLUE: A CRITICAL ANALYSIS OF CONSTITUTIONAL LAW (1988)

[C] Judicial Candor

Scott Altman, *Beyond Candor,* 89 MICH. L. REV. 296 (1990)

Guido Calabresi, IDEALS, BELIEFS, ATTITUDES, AND THE LAW (1985)

Guidò Calabresi & Philip C. Bobbitt, TRAGIC CHOICES (1978)

Gail Herriott, *Way Beyond Candor,* 89 MICH. L. REV. 1945 (1991)

Robert A. Leflar, *Honest Judicial Opinions,* 74 NW. U. L. REV. 721 (1979)

Laura E. Little, *Hiding with Words: Obfuscation, Avoidance, and Federal Jurisdiction Opinions,* 46 UCLA L. REV. 75 (1998)

Bruce M. Selya, *Thoughts from the Bench: The Confidence Game: Public Perceptions of the Judiciary,* 30 NEW ENG. L. REV. 909 (1996)

PART II

Sources

Chapter 3

The Role of Constitutional Text

§ 3.01 Introduction

This Part explores some of the different sources of guidance to which judges may turn in interpreting constitutional provisions. Chapter 3 sets out the current debates over the role of the constitutional text itself. While nearly all theorists would agree that the text is the starting place for constitutional interpretation, and most even agree that text should be determinative if it clearly prescribes a certain result, there is a wide range of views on such questions as *when* the text is clear and *what* judges ought to do if it is not. Where one stands on these issues is closely related to one's understanding of the role of courts in the American democratic society.

The textualists tend to fall at one end of the spectrum, holding that the written text of the Constitution is the only legitimate source for judicial action. Those who hold this view are concerned that public policy not rest in the hands of unelected judges unconstrained by popular belief. The text of the original Constitution, even though ratified over two centuries ago, at least received popular support at the time of its adoption, and thus should be held to have priority over any other source. Although this reflects the "pure" textualist position, most textualists are willing to allow, in addition to the text, consideration of whatever historical evidence might be necessary to interpret the text according to the understanding of those who ratified it. This view has also borne the labels "interpretivist"[1] and "strict constructionist,"[2] terms that may carry different connotations with different authors.

---

[1] For example, in 1975, Professor Thomas Grey defined "interpretivists" as those who argue that "courts must rely [solely] on value judgments [found] within the four corners of the Constitution," while he suggested that "noninterpretivists" believe that the courts can also strike down legislation on the basis of "ideals . . . not expressed as a matter of positive law in the written Constitution." Thomas Grey, *Do We Have an Unwritten Constitution?*, 27 STAN. L. REV. 703, 706 (1975). Grey later rejected these labels as misleading and overly simplistic. *See* Thomas Grey, *The Constitution as Scripture*, 37 STAN. L. REV. 1, 1 (1984). —

[2] Professor Laurence Tribe has used the term "strict constructionist" to describe Justices or scholars whose "guiding principle" is "exclusive attention to the constitutional text." LAURENCE TRIBE, GOD SAVE THIS HONORABLE COURT: HOW THE CHOICE OF SUPREME COURT JUSTICES SHAPES OUR HISTORY 50 (1985). He explained that such people posit that the "justices must take the Constitution as they find it, and not make things up as they go along. Even if the Justices are appalled by the results this method produces, or believe the Constitution's literal commands are severely out of step with the

Those at the other end of the spectrum, in theory, would abandon text altogether and render constitutional decisions based solely on what was considered "best" by some extrinsic measure such as moral philosophy or political orientation. In truth, however, very few, if any, theorists profess an intention to abandon an effort at interpretation of the Constitution in favor of some admitted artifice of their own creation (even though some may be accused of this by their opponents). As Professor Thomas Grey of Stanford Law School has suggested, "[w]e are all interpretivists; the real arguments are not over whether judges should stick to interpreting [the Constitution], but over what they should interpret and what interpretive attitudes they should adopt."[3] By far the majority of judges and scholars fall between the two extremes, lying along a range of perspectives urging different degrees of what is sometimes called judicial "restraint" or "activism," reflecting their sense of the appropriate degree of judicial involvement in discretionary exercises of interpretation.[4] These theorists recognize the legitimacy of considerations supplemental to the text (and therefore are sometimes referred to as "supplementalists"), such as tradition, moral philosophy, efficiency, structural implications of the Constitution, or changes in societal values to adapt fundamental law to evolving social context. Several of these types of sources will be considered in more detail in subsequent chapters.

§ 3.02   What is Textualism?

If there is such widespread agreement among judges and scholars that the task of judges is interpretation and that in the process of interpretation the text matters, one might assume that the disagreement about interpretive theory is rare or mild. It is neither. Indeed, the debate about whether, when, and how to supplement the text with other considerations is as passionate and as longstanding as any question of constitutional theory. This debate cuts to the very heart of what it means to have a written Constitution, enforced by an independent judiciary, in a democratic state. In the excerpts reproduced below, the question of the legitimacy of a rights-enforcing, counter-majoritarian court in an otherwise majoritarian society lurks only slightly beneath the surface.

---

times, it is not their job to rewrite it. That prerogative belongs to the Congress and the President and ultimately to the people, who retain the power to amend the Constitution. The watchword of strict constructionism is 'restraint.'" *Id.*

[3] Thomas Grey, *The Constitution as Scripture,* 37 Stan. L. Rev. 1, 1 (1984). In making this statement, Grey abandoned his earlier distinction between "interpretivists" and "noninterpretivists." In his 1984 article, Grey opted for "the less misleading labels 'textualists' and 'supplementers' for, respectively, those who consider the text the sole legitimate source of operative norms in constitutional adjudication,

and those who accept supplementary sources of constitutional law." Grey, 37 Stan. L. Rev. at 1. *See also* Paul Brest, *The Misconceived Quest for the Original Understanding,* 60 B.U. L. Rev. 204, 204 n.1 (1980) (asserting that all sound theories are "interpretivist").

[4] Professor Sanford Levinson suggests that the dispute between textualists and those who accept supplementary sources of constitutional law closely resembles a parallel disagreement between Protestants, who have tended to believe that the Bible is the exclusive source of divine revelation, and Catholics, who have regarded tradition as a separate and supplementary source. *See* Sanford Levinson, Constitutional Faith 27–30 (1988).

When the ink was hardly dry on the constitutional text, two Justices of the Supreme Court openly disagreed on how exclusive that text should be in resolving constitutional questions. Responding in 1798 to Justice Chase's argument in support of natural law principles as a supplement to the written Constitution, Justice Iredell made the argument for what we now refer to as textualism, *Calder v. Bull*, 3 U.S. (3 Dall.) 386, 399 (1798) (opinion of Iredell, J.) (emphases omitted):

> [I]t has been the policy of all the American states . . . and of the people of the United States, . . . to define with precision the objects of the legislative power, and to restrain its exercise within marked and settled boundaries. If any act of Congress, or of the legislature of a state, violates those constitutional provisions, it is unquestionably void . . . . If, on the other hand, the legislature of the Union, or the legislature of any member of the Union, shall pass a law, within the general scope of their constitutional power, the Court cannot pronounce it to be void, merely because it is, in their judgment, contrary to the principles of natural justice. The ideas of natural justice are regulated by no fixed standard: the ablest and the purest men have differed upon the subject; and all that the Court could properly say, in such an event, would be, that the legislature (possessed of an equal right of opinion) had passed an act which, in the opinion of the judges, was inconsistent with the abstract principles of natural justice . . . . If the legislature pursue the authority delegated to them, their acts are valid. [Under such circumstances,] they exercise the discretion vested in them by the people, to whom alone they are responsible for the faithful discharge of their trust . . . .

Today, Justice Scalia is the most eloquent proponent of textualism. He set forth the affirmative case for his point of view in his book, Antonin Scalia, A Matter of Interpretation: Federal Courts and the Law 23 25, 37–47 (1997):[5]

> The philosophy of interpretation I [espouse] is known as textualism. In some sophisticated circles, it is considered simpleminded—"wooden," "unimaginative," "pedestrian." It is none of that. To be a textualist in good standing, one need not be too dull to perceive the broader social purposes that a statute is designed, or could be designed, to serve; or too hidebound to realize that new times require new laws. One need only hold the belief that judges have no authority to pursue those broader purposes or write those new laws.

> Textualism should not be confused with so-called strict constructionism, a degraded form of textualism that brings the whole philosophy into disrepute. I am not a strict constructionist, and no one ought to be—though better that, I suppose, than a nontextualist. A text should not be construed strictly, and it should not be construed leniently; it should be construed reasonably, to contain all that it fairly means. The difference between textualism and strict constructionism can be seen in a case my Court decided four terms ago. The statute at issue provided for an increased jail term if, "during and in relation to . . . [a] drug trafficking crime," the defendant "uses . . . a firearm." The defendant in this case had sought to purchase a quantity of cocaine; and what he had offered to give in exchange for the cocaine was an unloaded firearm, which he showed to the drug-seller. The Court held, I regret to say, that the defendant was subject to the increased penalty, because he had "used a firearm during

---

[5] Copyright © 1997 by Princeton University Press. Reprinted by permission of Princeton University Press.

and in relation to a drug trafficking crime." The vote was not even close (6-3). I dissented. Now I cannot say whether my colleagues in the majority voted the way they did because they are strict-construction textualists, or because they are not textualists at all. But a proper textualist, which is to say my kind of textualist, would surely have voted to acquit. The phrase "uses a gun" fairly connoted use of a gun for what guns are normally used for, that is, as a weapon. As I put the point in my dissent, when you ask someone, "Do you use a cane?" you are not inquiring whether he has hung his grandfather's antique cane as a decoration in the hallway.

But while the good textualist is not a literalist, neither is he a nihilist. Words do have a limited range of meaning, and no interpretation that goes beyond that range is permissible. My favorite example of a departure from text—and certainly the departure that has enabled judges to do more freewheeling lawmaking than any other—pertains to the Due Process Clause found in the Fifth and Fourteenth Amendments of the United States Constitution, which says that no person shall "be deprived of life, liberty, or property without due process of law." It has been interpreted to prevent the government from taking away certain liberties *beyond* those, such as freedom of speech and of religion, that are specifically named in the Constitution. (The first Supreme Court case to use the Due Process Clause in this fashion was, by the way, *Dred Scott*—not a desirable parentage.) Well, it may or may not be a good thing to guarantee additional liberties, but the Due Process Clause quite obviously does not bear that interpretation. By its inescapable terms, it guarantees only process. Property can be taken by the state; liberty can be taken; even life can be taken; but not without the *process* that our traditions require— notably, a validly enacted law and a fair trial. To say otherwise is to abandon textualism, and to render democratically adopted texts mere springboards for judicial lawmaking.

Of all the criticisms leveled against textualism, the most mindless is that it is "formalistic." The answer to that is, *of course it's formalistic!* The rule of law is *about* form. If, for example, a citizen performs an act— let us say the sale of certain technology to a foreign country—which is prohibited by a widely publicized bill proposed by the administration and passed by both houses of Congress, *but not yet signed by the President,* that sale is lawful. It is of no consequence that everyone knows both houses of Congress and the President wish to prevent that sale. Before the wish becomes a binding law, it must be embodied in a bill that passes both houses and is signed by the President. Is that not formalism? A murderer has been caught with blood on his hands, bending over the body of his victim; a neighbor with a video camera has filmed the crime; and the murderer has confessed in writing and on videotape. We nonetheless insist that before the state can punish this miscreant, it must conduct a full-dress criminal trial that results in a verdict of guilty. Is that not formalism? Long live formalism. It is what makes a government a government of laws and not of men.

. . .

. . . I wish to address a final subject: the distinctive problem of constitutional interpretation. The problem is distinctive, not because special principles of interpretation apply, but because the usual principles are being applied to an unusual text. Chief Justice Marshall put the point as well as it can be put in *McCulloch v. Maryland*:

A constitution, to contain an accurate detail of all the subdivisions of which its great powers will admit, and of all the means by which they may be carried into execution, would partake of the prolixity of a legal code, and could scarcely be embraced by the human mind. It would probably never be understood by the public. Its nature, therefore, requires, that only its great outlines should be marked, its important objects designated, and the minor ingredients which compose those objects be deduced from the nature of the objects themselves.

In textual interpretation, context is everything, and the context of the Constitution tells us not to expect nit-picking detail, and to give words and phrases an expansive rather than narrow interpretation—though not an interpretation that the language will not bear.

Take, for example, the provision of the First Amendment that forbids abridgment of "the freedom of speech, or of the press." That phrase does not list the full range of communicative expression. Handwritten letters, for example, are neither speech nor press. Yet surely there is no doubt they cannot be censored. In this constitutional context, speech and press, the two most common forms of communication, stand as a sort of synecdoche for the whole. That is not strict construction, but it is reasonable construction.

It is curious that most of those who insist that the drafter's intent gives meaning to a statute reject the drafter's intent as the criterion for interpretation of the Constitution. I reject it for both. I will consult the writings of some men who happened to be delegates to the Constitutional Convention—Hamilton's and Madison's writings in *The Federalist,* for example. I do so, however, not because they were Framers and therefore their intent is authoritative and must be the law; but rather because their writings, like those of other intelligent and informed people of the time, display how the text of the Constitution was originally understood. Thus I give equal weight to Jay's pieces in *The Federalist,* and to Jefferson's writings, even though neither of them was a Framer. What I look for in the Constitution is precisely what I look for in a statute: the original meaning of the text, not what the original draftsmen intended.

But the Great Divide with regard to constitutional interpretation is not that between Framers' intent and objective meaning, but rather that between *original* meaning (whether derived from Framers' intent or not) and *current* meaning. The ascendant school of constitutional interpretation affirms the existence of what is called The Living Constitution, a body of law that (unlike normal statutes) grows and changes from age to age, in order to meet the needs of a changing society. And it is the judges who determine those needs and "find" that changing law. Seems familiar, doesn't it? Yes, it is the common law returned, but infinitely more powerful than what the old common law ever pretended to be, for now it trumps even the statutes of democratic legislatures. Recall the words . . . "The judge makes law, by extorting from precedents something which they do not contain. He extends his precedents, which were themselves the extensions of others, till, by this accommodating principle, a whole system of law is built up without the authority or interference of the legislator." Substitute the word "people" for "legislator," and it is a perfect description of what modern American courts have done with the Constitution.

If you go into a constitutional law class, or study a constitutional law casebook, or read a brief filed in a constitutional law case, you will rarely find the discussion addressed to the text of the constitutional provision that is at issue, or to the question of what was the originally understood or even the originally intended meaning of that text. The starting point of the analysis will be Supreme Court cases, and the new issue will presumptively be decided according to the logic that those cases expressed, with no regard for how far that logic, thus extended, has distanced us from the original text and understanding. Worse still, however, it is known and understood that if that logic fails to produce what in the view of the current Supreme Court is the *desirable* result for the case at hand, then, like good common-law judges, the Court will distinguish its precedents, or narrow them, or if all else fails overrule them, in order that the Constitution might mean what it *ought* to mean. Should there be—to take one of the less controversial examples—a constitutional right to die? If so, there is. Should there be a constitutional right to reclaim a biological child put out for adoption by the other parent? Again, if so, there is. If it is good, it is so. Never mind the text that we are supposedly construing; we will smuggle these new rights in, if all else fails, under the Due Process Clause (which, as I have described, is textually incapable of containing them). Moreover, what the Constitution meant yesterday it does not necessarily mean today. As our opinions say in the context of our Eighth Amendment jurisprudence (the Cruel and Unusual Punishments Clause), its meaning changes to reflect "the evolving standards of decency that mark the progress of a maturing society."

This is preeminently a common-law way of making law, and not the way of construing a democratically adopted text . . . . The Constitution, . . . even though a democratically adopted text, we formally treat like the common law. What, it is fair to ask, is the justification for doing so?

One would suppose that the rule that a text does not change would apply a fortiori to a constitution. If courts felt too much bound by the democratic process to tinker with statutes, when their tinkering could be adjusted by the legislature, how much more should they feel bound not to tinker with a constitution, when their tinkering is virtually irreparable. It certainly cannot be said that a constitution naturally suggests changeability; to the contrary, its whole purpose is to prevent change—to embed certain rights in such a manner that future generations cannot readily take them away. A society that adopts a bill of rights is skeptical that "evolving standards of decency" always "mark progress," and that societies always "mature," as opposed to rot. Neither the text of such a document nor the intent of its framers (whichever you choose) can possibly lead to the conclusion that its only effect is to take the power of changing rights away from the legislature and give it to the courts.

The argument most frequently made in favor of The Living Constitution is a pragmatic one: Such an evolutionary approach is necessary in order to provide the "flexibility" that a changing society requires; the Constitution would have snapped if it had not been permitted to bend and grow. This might be a persuasive argument if most of the "growing" that the proponents of this approach have brought upon us in the past, and are determined to bring upon us in the future, were the *elimination* of restrictions upon democratic government. But just the opposite is true. Historically, and particularly in the past thirty-five years, the "evolving" Constitution has imposed a vast array of new constraints—new inflexibilities—on administrative, judicial, and legislative action. . . . And the future agenda of constitutional evolutionists is mostly more of the same—the creation of *new* restrictions upon democratic government, rather than the elimination of old ones. *Less* flexibility in government, not *more*. As things now stand, the state and federal governments may either apply capital punishment or abolish it, permit suicide or forbid it—all as the changing times and the changing sentiments of society may demand. But when capital punishment is held to violate the Eighth Amendment, and suicide is held to be protected by the Fourteenth Amendment, all flexibility with regard to those matters will be gone. No, the reality of the matter is that, generally speaking, devotees of The Living Constitution do not seek to facilitate social change but to prevent it.

There are, I must admit, a few exceptions to that—a few instances in which, historically, greater flexibility has been the result of the process. But those exceptions serve only to refute another argument of the proponents of an evolving Constitution, that evolution will always be in the direction of greater personal liberty. (They consider that a great advantage, for reasons that I do not entirely understand. All government represents a balance between individual freedom and social order, and it is not true that every alteration of that balance in the direction of greater individual freedom is necessarily good.) But in any case, the record of history refutes the proposition that the evolving Constitution will invariably enlarge individual rights. The most obvious refutation is the modern Court's limitation of the constitutional protections afforded to property. The provision prohibiting impairment of the obligation of contracts, for example, has been gutted. I am sure that We the People agree with that development; we value property rights less than the Founders did. So also, we value the right to bear arms less than did the Founders (who thought the right to self-defense to be absolutely fundamental), and there will be few tears shed if and when the Second Amendment is held to guarantee nothing more than the state National Guard. But this just shows that the Founders were right when they feared that some (in their view misguided) future generation might wish to abandon liberties that they considered essential, and so sought to protect those liberties in a Bill of Rights. We may *like* the abridgment of property rights and *like* the elimination of the right to bear arms; but let us not pretend that these are not *reductions of rights*.

Or if property rights are too cold to arouse enthusiasm, and the right to bear arms too dangerous, let me give another example: Several terms ago a case came before the Supreme Court involving a prosecution for sexual abuse of a young child. The trial court found that the child would be too frightened to testify in the presence of the (presumed) abuser, and so, pursuant to state law, she was permitted to testify with only the prosecutor and defense counsel present, with the defendant, the judge, and the jury watching over closed-circuit television. A reasonable enough procedure, and it was held to be constitutional by my Court. I dissented, because the Sixth Amendment provides that "[i]n *all* criminal prosecutions the accused shall enjoy the right . . . to be confronted with the witnesses against him" (emphasis added). There is no doubt what confrontation meant—or indeed means today. It means face-to-face, not watching from another room. And there is no doubt what one of the major purposes of that provision was: to induce *precisely* that pressure upon the witness which the little girl found it difficult to endure. It is difficult to accuse someone to his face, particularly when you are lying. Now no extrinsic factors have changed since that provision was adopted in 1791. Sexual abuse existed then, as it does now; little children were more easily upset than adults, then as now; a means of placing the defendant out of sight of the witness existed then as now (a screen could easily have been erected that would enable the defendant to see the witness, but not the witness the defendant). But the Sixth Amendment nonetheless gave *all* criminal defendants the right to *confront* the witnesses against them, because that was thought to be an important protection. The only significant things that have changed, I think, are the society's sensitivity to so-called psychic trauma (which is what we are told the child witness in such a situation suffers) and the society's assessment of where the proper balance ought to be struck between the two extremes of a procedure that assures convicting 100 percent of all child abusers, and a procedure that assures acquitting 100 percent of those falsely accused of child abuse. I have no doubt that the society is, as a whole, happy and pleased with what my Court decided. But we should not pretend that the decision did not *eliminate* a liberty that previously existed.

My pointing out that the American people may be satisfied with a reduction of their liberties should not be taken as a suggestion that the proponents of The Living Constitution *follow* the desires of the American people in determining how the Constitution should evolve. They follow nothing so precise; indeed, as a group they follow nothing at all. Perhaps the most glaring defect of Living Constitutionalism, next to its incompatibility with the whole antievolutionary purpose of a constitution, is that there is no agreement, and no chance of agreement, upon what is to be the guiding principle of the evolution . . . What is it that the judge must consult to determine when, and in what direction, evolution has occurred? Is it the will of the majority, discerned from newspapers, radio talk shows, public opinion polls, and chats at the country club? Is it the philosophy of Hume, or of John Rawls, or of John Stuart Mill, or of Aristotle? As soon as the discussion goes beyond the issue of whether the Constitution is static, the evolutionists divide into as many camps as there are individual views of the good, the true, and the beautiful. I think that is inevitably so, which means that evolutionism is simply not a practicable constitutional philosophy.

I do not suggest, mind you, that originalists always agree upon their answer. There is plenty of room for disagreement as to what original meaning was, and even more as to how that original meaning applies to the situation before the court. But the originalist at least knows what he is looking for: the original meaning of the text. Often—indeed, I dare say usually—that is easy to discern and simple to apply. Sometimes (though not very often) there will be disagreement regarding the original meaning; and sometimes there will be disagreement as to how that original meaning applies to new and unforeseen phenomena. How, for example, does the First Amendment guarantee of "the freedom of speech" apply to new technologies that did not exist when the guarantee was created—to sound trucks, or to government-licensed over-the-air television? In such new fields the Court must follow the trajectory of the First Amendment, so to speak, to determine what it requires—and assuredly that enterprise is not entirely cut-and-dried but requires the exercise of judgment.

But the difficulties and uncertainties of determining original meaning and applying it to modern circumstances are negligible compared with the difficulties and uncertainties of the philosophy which says that the Constitution *changes*; that the very act which it once prohibited it now permits, and which it once permitted it now forbids; and that the key to that change is unknown and unknowable. The originalist, if he does not have all the answers, has many of them. The Confrontation Clause, for example, requires confrontation. For the evolutionist, on the other hand, every question is an open question, every day a new day. No fewer than three of the Justices with whom I have served have maintained that the death penalty is unconstitutional, *even though its use is explicitly contemplated in the Constitution*. The Due Process Clause of the Fifth and Fourteenth Amendments says that no person shall be deprived of life without due process of law; and the Grand Jury Clause of the Fifth Amendment says that no person shall be held to answer for a capital crime without grand jury indictment. No matter. Under The Living Constitution the death penalty may have *become* unconstitutional. And it is up to each Justice to decide for himself (under no standard I can discern) when that occurs.

In the last analysis, however, it probably does not matter what principle, among the innumerable possibilities, the evolutionist proposes to determine in what direction The Living Constitution will grow. Whatever he might propose, at the end of the day an evolving constitution will evolve the way the majority wishes. The people will be willing to leave interpretation of the Constitution to lawyers and law courts so long as the people believe that it is (like the interpretation of a statute) essentially lawyers' work—requiring a close examination of text, history of the text, traditional understanding of the text, judicial precedent, and so forth. But if the people come to believe that the Constitution is *not* a text like other texts; that it means, not what it says or what it was understood to mean, but what it *should* mean, in light of the "evolving standards of decency that mark the progress of a maturing society"—well, then, they will look for qualifications other than impartiality, judgment, and lawyerly acumen in those whom they select to interpret it. More specifically, they will look for judges who agree with *them* as to what the evolving standards have evolved to; who agree with *them* as to what the Constitution *ought* to be.

It seems to me that this is where we are heading, or perhaps even where we have arrived. Seventy-five years ago, we believed firmly enough in a rock-solid, unchanging, Constitution that we felt it necessary to adopt the Nineteenth Amendment to give women the vote. The battle was not fought in the courts, and few thought that it could be, despite the constitutional guarantee of Equal Protection of the Laws; that provision did not, when it was adopted, and hence did not in 1920, guarantee equal access to the ballot but permitted distinctions on the basis not only of age but of property and of sex. Who can doubt that if the issue had been deferred until today, the Constitution would be (formally) unamended, and the courts would be the chosen instrumentality of change? The American people have been converted to belief in The Living Constitution, a "morphing" document that means, from age to age, what it ought to mean. And with that conversion has inevitably come the new phenomenon of selecting and confirming federal judges, at all levels, on the basis of their views regarding a whole series of proposals for constitutional evolution. If the courts are free to write the Constitution anew, they will, by God, write it the way the majority wants; the appointment and confirmation process will see to that. This, of course, is the end of the Bill of Rights, whose meaning will be committed to the very body it was meant to protect against: the majority. By trying to make the Constitution do everything that needs doing from age to age, we shall have caused it to do nothing at all.

§ 3.03 Some Critiques of Textualism

John Hart Ely wrote one of the most influential books on constitutional theory of his time, DEMOCRACY AND DISTRUST (1980). He is perhaps best known for his "representation-reinforcing" theory of judicial review, set forth in Chapter 5, which derives not strictly from the text of the Constitution, but more from its overall structure and purpose. Yet Ely also made a contribution with his distinction between different types of textual provisions in the Constitution: those he calls "specific" and those he terms "open-textured." The more specific text is amenable to a stricter interpretive approach, Ely suggests, while the more open-textured provisions may call for greater degrees of judgment and reliance on sources external to the text itself. In the passages below, Ely describes the allure of the interpretivist approach to constitutional law, but argues that it is ultimately unsatisfactory for several reasons. JOHN HART ELY, DEMOCRACY and DISTRUST: A THEORY OF JUDICIAL REVIEW 1–5, 7–8, 12–14, 22–80, 30 (1980):[6]

It would be a mistake to suppose that there is any necessary correlation between an interpretivist approach to constitutional adjudication and political conservatism or even what is commonly called judicial self-restraint. The language and legislative history of our Constitution seldom suggest an intent to invalidate only a small set of historically understood practices. (If that had been the point the practices could simply have been listed.) More often the Constitution proceeds by briefly indicating certain fundamental principles whose specific implications for each age must be determined in contemporary context. What distinguishes interpretivism from its opposite is its insistence that the work of the political branches is to be invalidated only in accord with an inference whose starting point, whose underlying premise, is fairly discoverable in the Constitution. That the complete inference will not be found there—because the situation is not likely to have been foreseen—is generally common ground.

. . .

Interpretivism is no mere passing fad . . . ; in fact the Court has always, when plausible, tended to talk an interpretivist line. And indeed two significant (and interrelated) comparative attractions of an interpretivist approach can be identified. [10] The first is that it better fits our usual conceptions of what law is and the way it works . . . .

The second comparative attraction of an interpretivist approach, one that is more fundamental, derives from the obvious difficulties its opposite number encounters in trying to reconcile itself with the underlying democratic theory of our government. . . . [M]ost of the important policy decisions are made by our elected representatives (or by people accountable to them). Judges, at least federal judges—while they obviously are not entirely oblivious to popular opinion—are not elected or reelected. "[N]othing can finally depreciate the central function that is assigned in democratic theory and practice to the electoral process; nor can it be denied that the policy-making power of representative institutions, born of the electoral process, is the distinguishing characteristic of the system. Judicial review works counter to this characteristic." Of course courts make law all the time, and in doing so they may purport to be drawing on the standard sources of the noninterpretivist—society's "fundamental principles" or whatever—but outside the area of constitutional adjudication, they are either filling in gaps the legislature has left in the laws it has passed or, perhaps, taking charge of an entire area the legislature has left to judicial development. There is obviously a critical difference: in nonconstitutional contexts, the court's decisions are subject to overrule or alteration by ordinary statute. The court is standing in for the legislature, and if it has done so in a way the legislature does not approve, it can soon be corrected. When a court invalidates an act of the political branches on constitutional grounds, however, it is overruling their judgment, and normally doing so in a way that is not subject to "correction" by the ordinary lawmaking process. Thus the central function, and it is at the same time the central problem, of judicial review: a body that is not elected or otherwise politically responsible in any significant way is

---

[10] It is also tempting to suppose that an interpretivist approach will generate a more predictable, less episodic set of decisions. This seems false in one sense but true in another. Once a dispute has been identified as appropriately constitutional, I doubt that the acceptance of an "interpretivist" philosophy by the decision-maker will render the outcome any more predictable, since constitutional language is characteristically delphic, its accompanying legislative history partial and inconsistent. (This is by no means interpretivism's problem alone. *Any* constitutional theory—aside, I suppose, from a total renunciation of review—will repeatedly generate debatable questions. My point is simply that interpretivism cannot convincingly claim any significant competitive edge in this regard.) . . . .

telling the people's elected representatives that they cannot govern as they'd like. That may be desirable or it may not, depending on the principles on the basis of which it is done. We will want to ask whether anything else is any better, but the usual brand of noninterpretivism, with its appeal to some notion to be found neither in the Constitution nor, obviously, in the judgment of the political branches, seems especially vulnerable to a charge of inconsistency with democratic theory.

This, in America, is a charge that matters. We have as a society from the beginning, and now almost instinctively, accepted the notion that a representative democracy must be our form of government. The very process of adopting the Constitution was designed to be, and in some respects it was, more democratic than any that had preceded it . . . . The document itself, providing for congressional elections and prescribing a republican form of government for the states, expresses its clear commitment to a system of representative democracy at both the federal and state levels.

. . .

Our constitutional development over the past century has . . . substantially strengthened the original commitment to control by a majority of the governed. Neither has there existed among theorists or among Americans generally any serious challenge to the general notion of a majoritarian control . . . . Thus the recurring embarrassment of the noninterpretivists: majoritarian democracy is, they know, the core of our entire system, and they hear in the charge that there is in their philosophy a fundamental inconsistency therewith something they are not sure they can deny.

All this belabors the obvious part [sic]: whatever the explanation, and granting the qualifications, rule in accord with the consent of a majority of those governed is the core of the American governmental system. Just as obviously, however, that cannot be the whole story, since a majority with untrammeled power to set governmental policy is in a position to deal itself benefits at the expense of the remaining minority even when there is no relevant difference between the two groups. This too has been understood from the beginning, and indeed the Constitution contains several sorts of devices . . . to combat it. The tricky task has been and remains that of devising a way or ways of protecting minorities from majority tyranny that is not a flagrant contradiction of the principle of majority rule: in law as in logical theory, anything can be inferred from a contradiction, and it will not do simply to say "the majority rules but the majority does not rule." The problem for a noninterpretivist approach has been convincingly to distinguish itself from just this sort of bald contradiction. There have been attempts to do so . . . but they have generally been halting and apologetic, with no one quite willing to accept anyone else's account of why democratic principles are not offended and indeed with the same commentator often hopping from one account to another. An untrammeled majority is indeed a dangerous thing, but it will require a heroic inference to get from that realization to the conclusion that the enforcement by unelected officials of an "unwritten constitution" is an appropriate response in a democratic republic.

Justice Black and the interpretivist school have an inference, one that seems to find acceptance with friend and foe alike. Of course, they would answer, the majority can tyrannize the minority, and that is precisely the reason that in the Bill of Rights and elsewhere the Constitution designates certain rights for protection. Of course side constraints on majority rule are necessary, but as the framers wisely decided, it is saner and safer to set them down in advance of particular controversies than to develop them as we go along, in the context of the particular political problem and its accompanying passion and paranoia. It is also, the argument continues, more democratic, since the side constraints the interpretivist would enforce have been imposed by the people themselves. The noninterpetivist would have politically unaccountable judges select and define the values to be placed beyond majority control, but the interpretivist takes his values from the Constitution, which means, since the Constitution itself was submitted for and received popular ratification, that they ultimately come from the people. Thus the judges do not check the people, the Constitution does, which means the people are ultimately checking themselves.

. . .

The amendments most frequently in issue in court, however—to the extent that they ever represented the "voice of the people"—represent the voice of people who have been dead for a century or two. There were those who worried about this even at the beginning. Noah Webster opined that "the very attempt to make perpetual constitutions, is the assumption of a right to control the opinions of future generations; and to legislate for those over whom we have as little authority as we have over a nation in Asia." . . . [And the Constitution] ordinarily requir[es] the concurrence of two-thirds of both Houses of Congress and ratification by the legislatures of three-quarters of the states to get rid of a constitutional provision or to add a new one. I am certainly not saying this is a bad thing, but it does fatally undercut the idea that in applying the Constitution—even the written Constitution of the interpretivist—judges are simply applying the people's will. Incompatability with democratic theory is a problem that seems to confront interpretivist and non-interpretivist alike.

Interpretivism does seem to retain the substantial virtue of fitting better our ordinary notion of how law works: if your job is to enforce the Constitution then the Constitution is what you should be enforcing, not whatever may happen to strike you as a good idea at the time. Thus stated, the conclusion possesses the unassailability of a truism, and if acceptance of *that* were all it took to make someone an interpretivist, no sane person could be anything else. But the debate over interpretivism is not an argument about the truth of a tautology, for interpretivism involves a further claim, that "enforcing the Constitution" necessarily means proceeding from premises that are explicit or clearly implicit in the document itself.

At this point it is helpful to clarify the concept in a way the literature to date has not, in particular to distinguish two possible versions of interpretivism. One might admit that a number of constitutional phrases cannot intelligibly be given content solely on the basis of their language and surrounding legislative history, indeed that certain of them seem on their face to call for an injection of content from some source beyond the provision, but hold nonetheless that the theory one employs to supply that content should be derived from the general themes of the entire constitutional document and not from some source entirely beyond its four corners. It might even be hoped that this broad form of interpretivism is capable of avoiding the pitfalls of a narrower (or "clause-bound") interpretivism and at the same time preserving those comparative advantages of an interpretivist approach that we canvassed [above] . . . . That position, however, will take some time to develop, and it is not what is generally recommended under the interpretivist flag. The suggestion instead is usually that the various provisions of the Constitution be approached essentially as self-contained units and interpreted on the basis of their language, with whatever interpretive help the legislative history can provide, without significant injection of content from outside the provision. We shall see, however, that this standard form of interpretivism runs into trouble—trouble precisely on its own terms, and so serious as to be dispositive. For the constitutional document itself, the interpretivist's Bible, contains several provisions whose invitation to look beyond their four corners—whose invitation, if you will, to become at least to that extent a noninterpretivist—cannot be construed away.

Constitutional provisions exist on a spectrum ranging from the relatively specific to the extremely open-textured. At one extreme—for example the requirement that the President "have attained to the Age of thirty five years"—the language is so clear that a conscious reference to purpose seems unnecessary. Other provisions, such as the one requiring that the President be a "natural born Citizen," may need a reference to historical usage so as to exclude certain alternative constructions— conceivably if improbably here, a requirement of legitimacy (or illegitimacy!) or non-Caesarian birth—but once that "dictionary function" is served, the provision becomes relatively easy to apply. Others, such as the First Amendment's prohibition of congressional laws "abridging the freedom of speech," seem to need more. For one thing, a phrase as terse as the others I have mentioned is here expected to govern a broader and more important range of problems. For another, and this may have something to do with the first, we somehow sense that a line of growth was intended, that the language was not intended to be restricted to its 1791 meaning. This realization would not faze Justice Black or most other interpretivists: the job of the person interpreting the provision, they would respond, is to identify the *sorts of evils* against which the provision was directed and to move against their contemporary counterparts. Obviously this will be difficult, but it will remain interpretivism—a determination of "the present scope and meaning of a decision that the nation, at an earlier time, articulated and enacted into the constitutional text."

Still other provisions, such as the Eighth Amendment's prohibition of "cruel and unusual punishments," seem even more insistently to call for a reference to sources beyond the document itself and a "framers' dictionary." It is possible to construe this prohibition as covering only those punishments that would have been regarded as "cruel and unusual" in 1791, but that construction seems untrue to the open-ended quality of the language. The interpretivist can respond as he did to the First Amendment, that even though it is true that the clause shouldn't be restricted to its 1791 meaning, it should be restricted to the general categories of evils at which the provision was aimed. If you pursue this mode of "interpretation" with regard to the Eighth Amendment, however—and the First Amendment case will come down to much the same thing—you'll soon find yourself, at worst, begging a lot of questions or, at best, attributing to the framers a theory that may be *consistent* with what they said but is hardly discoverable in their discussions or their dictionaries. But even admitting this, the disaster for the interpretivist remains less than complete. The Cruel and Unusual Punishment Clause does invite the person interpreting it to freelance to a degree, but the freelancing is bounded. The subject is punishments, not the entire range of government action, and even in that limited area the delegation to the interpreter is not entirely unguided: only those punishments that are in some way serious ("cruel") and susceptible to sporadic imposition ("unusual") are to be disallowed.

The Eighth Amendment does not mark the end of the spectrum, however. The Fourteenth Amendment—and I shall argue later that the Ninth Amendment is similar—contains provisions that are difficult to read responsibly as anything other than quite broad invitations to import into the constitutional decision process considerations that will not be found in the language of the amendment or the debates that led up to it.

Thus, Professor Ely provided a textual basis for imparting some degree of discretion to judges interpreting the more open-textured provisions. He also blurred somewhat the lines between "strict construction" and a more dynamic approach. These lines do not always coincide with the boundaries of political ideology. For example, Justice Black, often a hero to political liberals during the Warren Court years, stressed the literal text of the Constitution. Yet in the last years of the Warren Court, President Richard Nixon used the phrase "strict construction" to criticize some of that Court's decisions as too liberal. And from what may be a surprising source, Seventh Circuit Judge Richard Posner, has come an essay entitled, *What Am I? A Plotted Plant? The Case Against Strict Constructionism*:[7]

> Many people, not all of conservative bent, believe that modern American courts are too aggressive, too "activist," too prone to substitute their own policy preferences for those of the elected branches of government. This may well be true. But some who complain of judicial activism espouse a view of law that is too narrow. And a good cause will not hallow a bad argument.

> This point of view often is called "strict constructionism." A more precise term would be "legal formalism." A forceful polemic by Walter Berns . . . summarizes the formalist view well. Issues of the "public good" can "be decided legitimately only with the consent of the governed." Judges have no legitimate say about these issues. Their business is to address issues of private rights, that is, "to decide whether the right exists—in the Constitution or in a statute—and, if so, what it is; but at that point inquiry ceases." The judge may not use "discretion and the weighing of consequences" to arrive at his decisions and he may not create new rights. The Constitution is a source of rights, but only to the extent that it embodies "fundamental and clearly articulated principles of government." There must be no judicial creativity or "policy-making."

> In short, there is a political sphere, where the people rule, and there is a domain of fixed rights, administered but not created or altered by judges. The first is the sphere of discretion, the second of application. Legislators make the law; judges find and apply it.

> There has never been a time when the courts of the United States, state or federal, behaved consistently in accordance with this idea. Nor could they, for reasons rooted in the nature of law and legal institutions, in the limitations of human knowledge, and in the character of a political system.

> "Questions about the public good" and "questions about private rights" are inseparable. The private right is conferred in order to promote the public good. So in deciding how broadly the right shall be interpreted, the court must consider the implications of its interpretation for the public good. For example, should an heir who murders his benefactor have a right to inherit from his victim? The answer depends, in part anyway, on the public good that results from discouraging murders. Almost the whole of so-called private law, such as property, contract, and tort law, is instrumental to the public end of obtaining the social advantages of free markets. Furthermore, most private law is common law—that is, law

---

[7] Richard Posner, *What Am I? A Potted Plant?*, NEW REPUBLIC, Sept. 28, 1987, at 23–25. Copy- right © 1987 by The New Republic. Reprinted with permission.

made by judges rather than by legislators or by constitution-framers. Judges have been entrusted with making policy from the start.

. . .

A second problem is that when a constitutional convention, a legislature, or a court promulgates a rule of law, it necessarily does so without full knowledge of the circumstances in which the rule might be invoked in the future. When the unforeseen circumstance arises—it might be the advent of the motor vehicle or of electronic surveillance, or a change in attitudes toward religion, race, and sexual propriety—a court asked to apply the rule must decide, in light of information not available to the promulgators of the rule, what the rules should mean in its new setting. That is a creative decision, involving discretion, the weighing of consequences, and, in short, a kind of legislative judgment—though, properly, one more confined than if the decision were being made by a real legislature. . . .

[I]f a court decides (as the Supreme Court has done in one of its less controversial modern rulings) that the Fourth Amendment's prohibition against unreasonable searches and seizures shall apply to wiretapping, even though no trespass is committed by wiretapping and hence no property is invaded, the court is creating a new right and making policy. But in a situation not foreseen and expressly provided for by the Framers of the Constitution, a simple reading out of a policy judgment made by the Framers is impossible.

. . .

Opposite the unrealistic picture of judges who apply law but never make it, Walter Berns hangs an unrealistic picture of a populist legislature that acts only "with the consent of the governed." Speaking for myself, I find that many of the political candidates whom I have voted for have failed to be elected and that those who have been elected have then proceeded to enact much legislation that did not have my consent. Given the effectiveness of interest groups in the political process, much of this legislation probably didn't have the consent of a majority of citizens. Politically, I feel more governed than self-governing. In considering whether to reduce constitutional safeguards to slight dimensions, we should be sure to have a realistic, not an idealized, picture of the legislative and executive branches of government, which would thereby be made more powerful than they are today.

To banish all discretion from the judicial process would indeed reduce the scope of constitutional rights. The framers of a constitution who want to make it a charter of liberties and not just a set of constitutive rules face a difficult choice. They can write specific provisions, and thereby doom their work to rapid obsolescence or irrelevance; or they can write general provisions, thereby delegating substantial discretion to the authoritive interpreters, who in our system are the judges. The U.S. Constitution is a mixture of specific and general provisions. Many of the specific provisions have stood the test of time amazingly well or have been amended without any great fuss. . . . Most of the specific provisions creating rights, however, have fared poorly. Some have proved irksomely anachronistic—for example, the right to a jury trial in federal court in all cases at law if the stakes exceed $20. Others have become dangerously anachronistic, such as the right to bear arms. Some have been turned topsy-turvy, such as the provision for indictment by grand jury. The grand jury has become an instrument of prosecutorial investigation rather than a protection for the criminal suspect. If the Bill of Rights had consisted entirely of specific provisions, it would have aged very rapidly and would no longer be a significant constraint on the behavior of government officials.

Many provisions of the Constitution, however, are drafted in general terms. This creates flexibility in the face of unforeseen changes, but it also creates the possibility of multiple interpretations, and this possibility is an embarrassment for a theory of judicial legitimacy that denies that judges have any right to exercise discretion. A choice among semantically plausible interpretations of a text, in circumstances remote from those contemplated by its drafters, requires the exercise of discretion and the weighing of consequences. Reading is not a form of deduction; understanding requires a consideration of consequences. If I say, "Ill eat my hat," one reason that my listeners will "decode" this in non-literal fashion is that I couldn't eat a hat if I tried. The broader principle, which applies to the Constitution as much as to a spoken utterance, is that if one possible interpretation of an ambiguous statement would entail absurd or terrible results, that is a good reason to adopt an alternative interpretation.

Even the decision to read the Constitution narrowly, and thereby "restrain" judicial interpretation, is not a decision that can be read directly from the text. The Constitution does not say, "Read me broadly," or, "Read me narrowly." That decision must be made as a matter of political theory, and will depend on such things as one's view of the springs of judicial legitimacy and of the relative competence of courts and legislatures in dealing with particular types of issues.

. . .

. . . Everyone professionally connected with law knows that, in Oliver Wendell Holmes's famous expression, judges legislate "interstitially," which is to say they make law, only more cautiously, more slowly, and in more principled, less partisan, fashion than legislators. The attempt to deny this truism entangles "strict constructionists" in contradictions. Berns says both that judges can enforce only "clearly articulated principles" and that they may invalidate unconstitutional laws. But the power to do this is not "articulated" in the Constitution; it is merely implicit in it. . . .

The First Amendment also forbids Congress to make laws "respecting an establishment of religion." Berns says this doesn't mean that Congress "must be neutral between religion and irreligion." But the words will bear that meaning, so how does he decide they should be given a different meaning? By appealing to Tocqueville's opinion of the importance of religion in democratic society. In short, the correct basis for decision is the consequence of the decision for democracy. Yet consequences are not—in the strict constructionist view—a fit thing for courts to consider. . . .

The liberal judicial activists may be imprudent and misguided in their efforts to enact the liberal political agenda into constitutional law, but it is no use pretending that what they are doing is not interpretation but "deconstruction," not law but politics, because it involves the exercise of discretion and a concern with consequences and because it reaches results not foreseen 200 years ago. It may be bad law because it lacks firm moorings in constitutional text, or structure, or history, or consensus, or other legitimate sources of constitutional law, or because it is reckless of consequences, or because it oversimplifies difficult moral and political questions. But it is not bad law, or no law, just because it violates the tenets of strict construction.

Professor Lawrence Lessig of Harvard Law School expands on Ely's notion of open-textured language to argue that by making fidelity to text their highest priority, originalists may in fact sacrifice the actual meaning of that text. Fidelity to the original document is better served, he maintains, by translating the text from its original context to the changed context of the interpreter's world. For example, Lessig discusses the Fourth Amendment's protection of the right "of the people to be secure in their persons, houses, papers, and effects" against unreasonable "searches and seizures." He acknowledges that at the time the amendment was passed, it was understood to protect only against physical invasions. Thus, one way to interpret its scope today would be to hold, as the originalist would do, that the amendment still protects only against physical invasions, in accord with the founders' specific understanding. But the context has changed. While a constitutional provision protecting against physical invasions from government in the 18th century would have provided citizens protection against all or nearly all of the possible ways in which government could conceivably invade one's privacy, such a rule in the late 20th century would provide protection against only a very few of the possible ways in which the government could invade privacy:[8]

> "To protect against this new risk of invasion, to preserve the same amount of protection as originally afforded, Brandeis [in dissent in *Olmstead v. United States*, 277 U.S. 438, 471–485, 48 S. Ct. 564, 72 L. Ed. 944 (1928)] argued that the protections of the Fourth Amendment must be applied to acts that fall outside the literal scope of the text. If, counting eavesdropping, the amendment protected citizens against ninety percent of the practical means of governmental invasion when adopted, so too must it be applied to protect against ninety percent of those means today. Thus states the argument of translation."[9]

Professor David Strauss of the University of Chicago offers a different model for understanding the task of interpreting constitutional text, suggesting that the common-law process explains and justifies constitutional decisionmaking:[10]

> The Constitution of the United States is a document drafted in 1787, together with the amendments that have been adopted from time to time since then. But in practice the Constitution of the United States is much more than that, and often much different from that. There are settled principles of constitutional law that are difficult to square with the language of the document, and many other settled principles that are plainly inconsistent with the original understandings. More important, when people interpret the Constitution, they rely not just on the text but also on the elaborate body of law that has developed, mostly through judicial decisions, over the years. In fact, in the day-to-day practice of constitutional interpretation, in the courts and in general public discourse, the specific words of the text play at most a small role, compared to evolving understandings of what the Constitution requires.
>
> Despite this, the terms of debate in American constitutional law continue to be set by the view that principles of constitutional law must

---

[8] Lawrence Lessig, *Fidelity in Translation*, 71 Tex. L. Rev. 1165, 1268 (1993). Copyright © 1993 by the Texas Law Review Association. Reprinted with permission.

[9] *Id.*

[10] David A. Strauss, *Common Law Constitu-* *tional Interpretation*, 63 U. Chi. L. Rev. 877, 877–79, 880–93, 897–98, 906–08, 911, 925–30, 932–33, 934–35 (1996). Copyright © 1996 by the University of Chicago. Reprinted with permission.

ultimately be traced to the text of the Constitution, and by the allied view that when the text is unclear the original understandings must control. An air of illegitimacy surrounds any alleged departure from the text or the original understandings. In the great constitutional controversies of this century, for example, the contestants have repeatedly charged their opponents with usurpation on the ground that they were insufficiently attentive to the text or the original understandings. That was the claim made by the Justices of the so-called *Lochner* era; it was the claim made by Justice Black, first against the *Lochner* judges and then against other opponents; it was the claim made, during the last twenty years, by opponents of the Warren Court innovations. And today, textualism and originalism continue to be extraordinarily prominent on both sides of the principal debates in constitutional law.

But textualism and originalism remain inadequate models for understanding American constitutional law. They owe their preeminence not to their plausibility but to the lack of a coherently formulated competitor. The fear is that the alternative to some form of textualism or originalism is "anything goes"—that constitutional law, if cut loose from text and original understandings, will become nothing more than a reflection of judges' political views.

In fact, however, the alternative view is at hand, and has been for many centuries, in the common law. The common law approach restrains judges more effectively, is more justifiable in abstract terms than textualism or originalism, and provides a far better account of our practices. The emphasis on text, or on the original understanding, reflects an implicit adherence to the postulate that law must ultimately be connected to some authoritative source: either the Framers, or "we the people" of some crucial era. Historically the common law has been the great opponent of this authoritative approach. The common law tradition rejects the notion that law must be derived from some authoritative source and finds it instead in understandings that evolve over time. And it is the common law approach, not the approach that connects law to an authoritative text, or an authoritative decision by the Framers or by "we the people," that best explains, and best justifies, American constitutional law today.

. . .

The practice of following a written constitution, increasingly common throughout the world, is puzzling on at least two levels. First is what might be called the central problem of written constitutionalism. Following a written constitution means accepting the judgments of people who lived centuries ago in a society that was very different from ours. To adapt an argument that Noah Webster made in 1787, it would be bizarre if the current Canadian parliament asserted the power to govern the United States on such matters as, for example, race discrimination, criminal procedure, and religious freedom. But we have far more in common—demographically, culturally, morally, and in our historical experiences—with Canadians of the 1990s than we do with Americans of the 1780s or 1860s. Even if we pay no attention to specific intentions as revealed in the ratification debates and similar sources, the words of the Constitution reflect decisions made by those Americans. Why should we allow those decisions to govern our politics today?

Our practice is also puzzling on a less abstract level. There are a number of specific aspects of our practice of constitutional interpretation that are well settled, and that lie at the core of how constitutional law operates in our society, but that are difficult to justify under any theoretical approach now in circulation. These puzzles concern not just how the courts interpret the Constitution but how the Constitution is received in the society as a whole.

Everyone agrees that the text of the Constitution matters. Virtually everyone would agree that sometimes the text is decisive. But some constitutional provisions are interpreted in ways that are very difficult to reconcile with the text. And principles with no clear textual source are enforced. If we are cavalier with the text sometimes, why do we treat it somewhat seriously almost all the time, and extremely seriously sometimes?

Virtually everyone agrees that the specific intentions of the Framers count for something. In litigation over constitutional issues, evidence that the Framers' specific intentions favored one position is at least a strong argument. It is unusual for clear evidence of a specific intention to be disregarded, and occasionally specific intentions are decisive.

But sometimes, and on important issues, the Framers' specific intentions are overridden with only a little concern. Originalists urge that specific intentions must be taken more seriously; some critics reject the originalist position and suggest that specific intentions should count for little or nothing. In the meantime a practice somewhere in between— counting specific intentions for something but not everything—seems well settled. But that settled practice is not easy to rationalize.

A similar hard-to-rationalize equilibrium seems to hold on the question whether judges and other actors interpreting the Constitution may rely on their own judgments of right and wrong (generally phrased as judgments of fairness or good policy). It's hard to see how anyone could interpret the Constitution without relying on such judgments at least sometimes. But at the same time, the practice has an air of illegitimacy about it. It is often condemned as usurpation. And no one suggests that the interpreter's judgments of right and wrong are the only things that matter.

Not all constitutional provisions are equal; some are interpreted more expansively than others. For about the last half century, courts have narrowly interpreted the provisions of the Constitution that protect economic liberties, while interpreting other provisions, such as the guarantee of free speech, broadly. The legitimacy of this practice, by now well settled, has been one of the great issues of modern constitutional law. This is the issue to which the "preferred position" debate and the *Carolene Products* footnote were directed.[17] Here again there is a disjunction between settled practice and the theoretical debate, because a fully convincing theoretical justification for the practice still seems elusive.

Although everyone agrees that the text is in some sense controlling, in practice constitutional law generally has little to do with the text. Most of the time, in deciding a constitutional issue, the text plays only a nominal role. The issue is decided by reference to "doctrine"—an elaborate structure of precedents built up over time by the courts—and to considerations of morality and public policy.

This point is, I think, obvious for judicial decisions. It is the rare constitutional case in which the text plays any significant role. Mostly the courts decide cases by looking to what the precedents say. But the same is true for other political actors and for society as a whole. In public and political debates over the First Amendment, while the text is ritually incanted ("no law"), in fact the text matters very little (no one suggests that the First Amendment applies only to Congress), and instead the public debate invokes notions derived from precedents—clear and present

---

[17] United States v. Carolene Prods. Co., 304 U.S. 144, 152 n.4 (1938). . . . [For the text of the footnote, see Structural Reasoning, Chapter 5, *infra*.]

danger, prior restraint, obscenity, fighting words, viewpoint discrimination, subsidy versus prohibition, reckless disregard, incidental regulation,
the centrality of political speech. Debates over the Equal Protection
Clause invoke not the words of the Constitution but the supposed principles of *Brown v. Board of Education* and subsequent cases. The "requirement" of a search warrant is notoriously hard to square with the words
of the Fourth Amendment. Most informed nonlawyers would probably say
that the Constitution requires "the separation of church and state"—a
principle that is by no means a necessary implication of the words of the
Establishment Clause. Debates over criminal justice invoke such ideas
as reasonable doubt and the presumption of innocence that are not found
in the text.

The Constitution has changed a great deal over time, but—to overstate
the point only slightly—the written amendments have been a sidelight.
Most of the great revolutions in American constitutionalism have taken
place without any authorizing or triggering constitutional amendment.
This is true, for example, of the Marshall Court's consolidation of the role
of the federal government; the decline of property qualifications for voting
and the Jacksonian ascendance of popular democracy and political parties; the Taney Court's partial restoration of state sovereignty; the
unparalleled changes wrought by the Civil War (the war and its after-
math, not the resulting constitutional amendments, were the most
important agents of change); the rise and fall of a constitutional freedom
of contract; the great twentieth-century growth in the power of the executive (especially in foreign affairs) and the federal government generally;
the civil rights era that began in the mid-twentieth century; the reforma-
tion of the criminal justice system during the same decades; and the
movement toward gender equality in the last few decades. In some of
these instances—notably the expansion of the congressional commerce
power and the enforcement of gender equality—amendments bringing
about the changes were actually rejected, but the changes occurred
anyway.

There is, prominent in our legal tradition, a method—the method of the
common law—that both resolves the central puzzle of written constitutionalism and makes sense of these apparently problematic aspects of our
settled interpretive practices. The common law method has not gained
currency as a theoretical approach to constitutional interpretation because it is not an approach we usually associate with a written constitution, or indeed with codified law of any kind. But our written constitution
has, by now, become part of an evolutionary common law system, and the
common law—rather than any model based on the interpretation of
codified law—provides the best way to understand the practices of
American constitutional law.

The currently prevailing theories of constitutional interpretation are
rooted in a different tradition: implicitly or explicitly, they rest on the view
that the Constitution is binding because someone with authority adopted
it. This view derives from a tradition—that of Austin and Bentham, and
ultimately Hobbes—that historically has been the great opponent of the
common law tradition. This authoritative tradition sees the law as the
command of a sovereign. Most current theories of constitutional interpretation are of course vastly more refined than the reference to a "command"
would suggest. But they all in some way reflect the hold of the authoritative tradition rather than the tradition of the common law.

This point is perhaps most obvious in the case of straightforward forms
of originalism. In its simplest form, originalism treats the Framers of the
Constitution (or its ratifiers) as the authoritative entity, comparable to
Austin's sovereign. Originalism can, of course, be defended on other

grounds; but much of the intuitive plausibility of originalism stems from the notion that the Framers are a super-legislature. Just as our representatives in Congress have the power to tell us how to act, so do, in a more indirect way, the Framers.

The more sophisticated variants of originalism also belong to the Austinian tradition. Some of these variants emphasize the need to reinterpret or "translate" the Framers' commands in ways that take account of, for example, changes in factual knowledge and social understandings that have occurred since the Constitution was adopted. But the Framers' command is still the starting point, and still authoritative in significant ways. Perhaps the most important variant on originalism is what might be called the neo-Hamiltonian view, according to which judges should enforce not necessarily the intentions or understandings of those who adopted the original constitutional provisions but rather the decisions made by "we the people" at subsequent moments, when the population at large was intensely involved in politics. This approach, too, adheres to the command model; now, the authoritative entity is not the Framers but "we the people," appropriately defined.

My argument is that no version of a command theory, however refined, can account for our constitutional practices. Constitutional law in the United States today represents a flowering of the common law tradition and an implicit rejection of any command theory.

In a sense this should not be surprising. The common law is the most distinctive feature of our legal system and of the English system from which it is descended. We should expect that the common law would be the most natural model for understanding something as central to our legal and political culture as the Constitution. Other theories of constitutional interpretation struggle with the question why judges—and not historians, philosophers, political scientists, or literary critics—are the central actors in interpreting the American Constitution; the common law, more than any other institution, has been the province of judges. American constitutional law is preoccupied, perhaps to excess, with the question of how to restrain judges, while still allowing a degree of innovation; the common law has literally centuries of experience in the use of precedent to accomplish precisely these ends.

. . .

Properly understood, then, the common law provides the best model for both understanding and justifying how we interpret the Constitution. The common law approach captures the central features of our practices as a descriptive matter. At the same time, it justifies our current practices, in reflective equilibrium, to anyone who considers our current practices to be generally acceptable—either as an original matter or because they are the best practices that can be achieved for now in our society. The common law approach makes sense of our current practices in their broad outlines; but at the same time, it suggests some ways in which our practices might be modified. It also suggests other ways in which our practices should not be modified, for example in the direction of a greater emphasis on original intent.

Perhaps common law constitutionalism is not the best we could do if we were writing on a blank slate. But unless our current practices are to be rejected wholesale, the common law model is (I suggest) the best way to understand what we are doing; the best way to justify what we are doing; and the best guide to resolving issues that remain open.

At least two somewhat counterintuitive consequences follow from the common law approach to constitutional interpretation. The first is that the interpretation of the Constitution has less in common with the interpretation of statutes than we ordinarily suppose. Conventionally we think of legal reasoning as divided into common law reasoning by precedent on the one hand, and the interpretation of authoritative texts on the other. Constitutional and statutory interpretation, while of course different in many respects, are viewed as forms of the latter and fundamentally different from the former.

In fact, constitutional interpretation, as practiced today in this country, belongs on the other side of the line. The command view, although too simple, may make sense for many statutes: a recent statute enacted by the people's representatives is plausibly an authoritative command of the sovereign that should be followed for that reason. Of course this point must not be overstated. For many statutes, a common law approach to interpretation may again be both the best description of our practices and the best account of how we should proceed. But the usual reflex is to associate the interpretation of statutes with the interpretation of the Constitution, and to contrast both with the common law. To whatever extent the contrast with the common law is true of statutes, it is not true of an eighteenth-and nineteenth-century constitution. Some of the puzzling aspects of our current practices of constitutional interpretation appear problematic only because of the unreflective association of constitutional and statutory interpretation. Once we understand constitutional interpretation as an outgrowth of the common law, those practices are much less puzzling.

The second consequence of the common law approach to constitutional interpretation is of particular significance now, in a time of constitutional ferment in much of the world. It is that the conventional distinction between written and unwritten constitutions should be reconsidered. The important distinction is not between nations with written constitutions and those with unwritten constitutions, but rather between societies with mature, well established constitutional traditions and those with insecure traditions. The written constitutionalism of the United States has much more in common with the unwritten constitutionalism of Great Britain than it does with the written constitutionalism of a newly formed Eastern European state—or, for that matter, than it does with the written constitutionalism of, say, the postwar German Federal Republic or the Fifth French Republic in its first decade.

. . .

Common law constitutional interpretation has two components. Each of these components provides a partial explanation for why we should pay attention to the Constitution. Together they provide both the best available answer to that question and, I believe, the best account of our current practices of constitutional interpretation.

The first component is traditionalist. The central idea is that the Constitution should be followed because its provisions reflect judgments that have been accepted by many generations in a variety of circumstances. The second component is conventionalist. It emphasizes the role of constitutional provisions in reducing unproductive controversy by specifying ready-made solutions to problems that otherwise would be too costly to resolve. The traditionalism underlying the practice of constitutional interpretation is a rational traditionalism that acknowledges the claims of the past but also specifies the circumstances in which traditions must be rejected because they are unjust or obsolete. The conventionalist component helps explain why the text of the Constitution is important and how much flexibility judges should have in interpreting it.

Traditionalism in some realms of life is a matter of adhering to the practices of the past just because of their age. The traditionalist component of common law constitutional interpretation is different because it has a more rational basis. Its central notion is not reverence for the past either for its own sake or because the past is somehow constitutive of one's own or one's nation's "identity." Instead, the traditionalism that is central to common law constitutionalism is based on humility and, related, a distrust of the capacity of people to make abstract judgments not grounded in experience.

The central traditionalist idea is that one should be very careful about rejecting judgments made by people who were acting reflectively and in good faith, especially when those judgments have been reaffirmed or at least accepted over time. Judgments of this kind embody not just serious thought by one group of people, or even one generation, but the accumulated wisdom of many generations. They also reflect a kind of rough empiricism: they do not rest just on theoretical premises; rather, they have been tested over time, in a variety of circumstances, and have been found to be at least good enough.

Because, in this view of traditionalism, the age of a practice alone does not warrant its value, relatively new practices that have slowly evolved over time from earlier practices deserve acceptance more than practices that are older but that have not been subject to testing over time. That is why this form of traditionalism is associated with the common law and a system of precedent. New precedents, at least to the extent that they reflect a reaffirmation and evolution of the old, count for more than old precedents that have not been reconsidered.

The traditionalist argument for obeying the Constitution is that the Constitution reflects judgments that should be taken seriously for these reasons. . . . [T]raditionalism does not provide a completely solid justification for adhering to the text of the Constitution, but it is a start. The Framers do not have any right to rule us today, but their judgments were the judgments of people (the Framers and ratifiers) acting on the basis of serious deliberation. Moreover, the parts of the Constitution that have not been amended (the traditionalist argument says) have obtained at least the acquiescence, and sometimes the enthusiastic reaffirmation, of many subsequent generations. Consequently, these judgments should not be swept aside lightly. They should be changed only if there is very good reason to think them mistaken, or if they fail persistently.

Understood in this way, traditionalism is counsel of humility: no single individual or group of individuals should think that they are so much more able than previous generations. This form of traditionalism also subsumes the common-sense notion that one reason for following precedent is that it is simply too time consuming and difficult to reexamine everything from the ground up. The premise of that common-sense notion is that any radical reexamination of existing ways of doing things is likely to discard good practices, perhaps because it misunderstands them, and is unlikely to find very many better ones.

. . .

Although traditionalist ideas descend from the common law, to some degree they apply to the textual provisions of the Constitution as well. Except for the most recent amendments, the text of the Constitution has, by now, been validated by tradition. Subsequent generations have acquiesced in the judgments reflected in the provisions of the Constitution: they have not amended them, rebelled against them, insisted on judges who would refuse to enforce them, or repeatedly taken political actions that ignored them.

At the same time, however, as the association with the common law suggests, traditionalism is not unequivocal in its support for the text. The judgments to which deference is due are not just those embodied in the text. Nor is deference due to all the judgments in the text equally. If practices have grown up alongside the text, or as a matter of interpreting the text, or even in contradiction of the text, those practices too are entitled to deference if they have worked well for an extended time. An old precedent that has been accepted by subsequent generations is, under the traditionalist component of the common law approach, on a par with the text.

Marbury v. Madison and *McCulloch v. Maryland* are examples. Neither decision has a particularly clear textual basis. They are simply extremely well established precedents. But there is no sense in denying that both are every bit as much a part of the Constitution as the most explicit textual provision. The same is true of a well established practice that is neither explicit in the text nor embodied in a judicial precedent, such as the rule that a majority vote of the members of each house of Congress is necessary and sufficient to constitute "pass(age)" of a bill under Article I, Section 7. So far as traditionalism is concerned, provisions of the text are no more entitled to obedience than any other long standing practice.

By the same token, not every textual judgment is entitled to equal deference. All are perhaps entitled to a degree of respect, since they represent serious, good-faith efforts to address problems. But if some textual judgments have worked better than others, they are entitled to greater support. And, perhaps more strikingly, under the traditionalist view there is nothing wrong with sometimes deciding (in exceptional cases, to be sure) that a textual provision should be discarded—just as precedents can be overruled. In that respect traditionalism is quite clearly not consistent with our practices and must be modified in ways I will discuss below.

Traditionalism in this form provides at least a colorable answer to Noah Webster's question. We follow judgments made long ago by people living in a different society for two reasons—serious judgments made in good faith merit some deference; and, more important, those judgments have worked, at least well enough to enjoy continued acceptance in many subsequent, different circumstances. There is no need to apotheosize the Framers of the Constitution—only to recognize their seriousness and their good faith, and the fact that many of their arrangements have been at least reasonably successful for generations.

. . .

Traditionalism does fall short in at least one important respect: it cannot account for the deference that is given to the text. A strictly traditionalist approach would occasionally "overrule" textual provisions. But it is not acceptable, in our practice, to declare that a provision of the Constitution (for example, the provision requiring that the President be a natural-born citizen) has outlived its usefulness and therefore is no longer the law. Explicitly declaring that a provision was no longer part of the Constitution would be an act of civil disobedience or, if the provision were very important, revolution. In some way or another, however creative the interpretation, the text must be respected.

Moreover, where the text is relatively clear, it is often followed exactly. Simply as a descriptive matter, no one seriously suggests that the age limits specified in the Constitution for Presidents and members of Congress should be interpreted to refer to other than chronological (earth) years because life expectancies now are longer, that a President's term should be more than four years because a more complicated world requires greater continuity in office, or that states should have different numbers of Senators because they are no longer the distinctive sovereign entities they once were. The text is not always treated in this way: "Congress" in the First Amendment is taken, without controversy, to mean the entire federal government, even though elsewhere "Congress" certainly does not include the courts or the President. But sometimes the text is treated this way, and the traditionalist, Burkean account cannot explain why specific provisions are taken as seriously as they are, as often as they are.

Conventionalism, the second component of common law constitutional interpretation, takes care of this deficiency. Conventionalism is a generalization of the notion that it is more important that some things be settled than that they be settled right. The text of the Constitution is accepted . . . by an "overlapping consensus": whatever their disagreements, people can agree that the text of the Constitution is to be respected.

Left to their own devices, people disagree sharply about various questions, large and small, related to how the government should be organized and operated. In some cases, the text of the Constitution provides answers; in many other cases, the text limits the set of acceptable answers. People who disagree will often find that although few or none of them think the answer provided by the text of the Constitution—either the specific answer or the limit on the set of acceptable answers—is optimal, all of them can live with that answer. Moreover, not accepting that answer has costs—in time and energy spent on further disputation, in social division, and in the risk of a decision that (from the point of view of any given actor) will be even worse than the constitutional decision. In these circumstances, everyone might agree that the best course overall is to follow the admittedly less-than-perfect constitutional judgment.

In addition, conventionalism can be justified on the ground that it is a way for people to express respect for their fellow citizens. Even among people who disagree about an issue, it is a sign of respect to seek to justify one's position by referring to premises that are shared by the others. Moral argument in general has this structure (at least according to most modern conceptions). But appealing simply to shared abstract moral conceptions (such as a common abstract belief in human dignity) does less to establish bonds of mutual respect than appealing to more concrete notions that do more to narrow the range of disagreement—such as the appropriateness of adhering to the text of the Constitution.

. . .

Conventionalism, understood in this way—as an allegiance to the text of the Constitution, justified as a way of avoiding costly and risky disputes and of expressing respect for fellow citizens—helps explain the deference given to the text more fully than traditionalism standing alone. We do not "overrule" the text because any such overruling would jeopardize the ability of the text to serve as a generally accepted focal point. Once one textual provision was explicitly disregarded, others could be disregarded too, and the benefits of having a focus of agreement—imperfect but "there" and "good enough"—would be diminished. Conventionalism thus accounts for a prominent feature of our practices and provides the rest of the answer to the question of why we adhere to the text of the Constitution.

. . .

. . . A theory of constitutional interpretation for our society also ought to be able to explain how the institution of judicial review—judicial enforcement of the Constitution against the acts of popularly elected bodies—can be reconciled with democracy. It might be argued, in particular, that a theory of common law constitutional interpretation overlooks the crucial difference that common law judges can be overruled by the legislature but judges interpreting a constitution ordinarily cannot.

Neither the concern with judicial restraint nor the concern with democracy, however, undermines the justification of common law constitutionalism. If anything, with respect to both concerns, common law constitutionalism is superior to its competitors.

Textualism and originalism are sometimes defended as the best way of restraining judges and preventing them from abusing their authority. On the surface this may seem to be at least a plausible claim. But on closer examination I believe that it owes all of its plausibility to the unspoken assumption that some version of the common law approach to constitutional interpretation is operating in the background.

A judge who conscientiously tries to follow precedent is significantly limited in what she can do. But a judge who acknowledges only the text of the Constitution as a limit can, so to speak, go to town . . . . The notion that the text of the Constitution is an effective limit on judges is plausible only if one assumes a background of highly developed precedent. . . .

For similar reasons, it is implausible to say that adherence to the Framers' intentions, by itself (or together with adherence to text), limits judges more than precedent. The familiar problems—uncertainty about who counts as "the Framers," unclarity in the historical record (or no relevant record at all), difficulty in defining the level of generality on which to identify the intention, changing circumstances—all make the historical record a poor restraint on judges. In fact the strongest advocates of adherence to the Framers' intentions are often, at the same time, embroiled in controversies over what the Framers of particular provisions actually did intend. The existence of controversy in applying a method does not invalidate the method, of course, but it does mean that that method is a less sure way of preventing a judge from "finding" her own moral or political views in the Constitution.

By contrast, the common law method has a centuries-long record of restraining judges. Needless to say, precedents can be treated disingenuously, and judges can abuse the freedom that the common law approach gives them to make moral judgments about the way the law should develop. But no system is immune from abuse. A conscientious judge will find substantial guidance in a well developed body of precedent, like that interpreting the Constitution. Judges who might be tempted to overreach, but who are susceptible to criticism (by others or by themselves), can be evaluated by fairly well developed standards under the common law method. None of the competing views seems superior on this score, and most—including the various forms of originalism—seem decidedly worse.

Finally, common law constitutionalism has the advantage of confronting the question of judicial restraint—that is, the question of how concerned we should be about the danger that judges will implement their own moral and political views under the guise of following the law—more directly and candidly than other theories do. Under common law constitutionalism, the tension is between, on the one hand, the demands of tradition and the need to maintain the text as common ground, and, on the other hand, the perceived requirements of fairness, justice, and good policy. By facing that tension, the judge is forced to decide how restrained she should be. Approaches that emphasize the text or the Framers' intentions, by contrast, ordinarily insist on the supposed absolute priority of the text or the Framers' intentions over the judge's moral views. Those approaches have a tendency to suggest that it is a usurpation for a judge ever to consider the fairness or justice of the action she is being asked to take. In this way those approaches do not confront the issue of just how restrained a judge should be. Disputes that in fact concern matters of morality or policy masquerade as hermeneutic disputes about the "meaning" of the text, or historians' disputes about what the Framers did. By contrast, in common law constitutional interpretation, the difficult questions are on the surface and must be confronted forthrightly.

A crucial part of the argument for textualist or originalist approaches is not just that they restrain judges but that they are more consistent with democracy. The objective of constitutional interpretation, on these accounts, is to uncover and enforce the will of "we the people" as expressed in the Constitution. By contrast, the argument goes, common law approaches that rely on precedent exalt the views of "Judge & Co.," an elite segment of the population.

So far as the argument from democracy is concerned, the more simplistic forms of textualism and originalism are, of course, subject to Noah Webster's objection. It is difficult to understand why democracy requires us to enforce decisions made by people with whom the current population has so little in common. It is true that the Framers were Americans, and we are Americans. But it does not follow that adherence to their decisions is democratic self-rule in any remotely recognizable sense. The originalist notion that the decisions of the eighteenth-century Framers somehow reflect the views of a continuous "we the people" extending since that time is as mystical and implausible as the most remote reaches of the common law ideology.[116]

. . .

. . . [C]ommon law constitutionalism is democratic in an important sense: the principles developed through the common law method are not likely to stay out of line for long with views that are widely and durably held in the society. Indeed, by this standard the common law approach can plausibly claim to be as democratic as any of its competitors. Consider the most important principles that have emerged from constitutional common law in this century: expansive federal power; expansive presidential power, particularly in foreign affairs; the current contours of freedom of expression; the federalization of criminal procedure; a conception of racial equality that disapproves de jure distinctions and intentional discrimination; the rule of one person, one vote; a (somewhat formal) principle of gender equality; and reproductive freedom protected against criminalization. None of these important principles can be said to be rooted in original intent, and none has particularly strong textual roots. For most of them, it is hard to identify any "moment" at which a strong popular consensus crystallized behind them.

Instead, all of these principles were developed essentially by common law methods—the evolution of doctrine in response to the perceived demands of justice and the needs of society. All of these principles were once highly controversial. But it is plausible to say that all of them now rest on a broad democratic consensus. They are evidence that the common law approach is at least broadly consistent with the demands of democracy.

. . .

[Finally,] it may be a mistake to suppose that a *method* of constitutional interpretation should be democratic, at least when the courts have

---

[116] This problem is not cured by allowing "we the people" to amend the Constitution by some suitable vote . . . . The question remains why, in the absence of such an extraordinary action by "the people," decisions made generations ago should govern.

important responsibility for implementing it. Judicial review necessarily has a guild character in a sense, because by definition judges do it, and inevitably lawyers' norms will heavily influence it. This means that we have to address the tensions between democracy and judicial review on the level of substance, not on the level of method. That is, we should not try to find—because we cannot find—a wholly democratic method of constitutional interpretation. Instead, we should determine, as a matter of substantive constitutional law, when judges in a constitutional democracy must accept the decisions of the political branches and when the judges should oppose the political branches.

. . . [I]t may be more illuminating to recognize that judicial review, however practiced, has strongly undemocratic elements. The solution is to decide as a substantive matter when the democratic process should prevail and when it should be questioned. Common law constitutionalism focuses this question and forces us to answer it in the design of substantive doctrines. The other approaches (and the more mystical versions of the common law) obscure it by pretending that the method is sufficiently democratic to make it unnecessary to ask this question.

The objection that traditional common law decisions can be overruled by the legislature—and that the common law is therefore an inappropriate model for constitutional interpretation—can be met in the same fashion. This is, of course, an important difference between constitutional adjudication and common law adjudication, but it does not invalidate the common law model for constitutional interpretation. Instead it is a reason to adopt substantive principles of constitutional law that assign judges their proper role in constitutional adjudication. So, for example, we have adopted a principle that requires judges interpreting the Constitution to be deferential to legislative decisions in most circumstances. Similarly, the authority of constitutional judges to adopt innovative policies is much more sharply limited than that of traditional common law judges.

. . .

Our legal system is distinctive, perhaps unique, for the prominence it gives to judges. The distinctiveness is manifested in two practices in particular: judicial interpretation of the Constitution, and the common law. I have suggested that these two practices have much in common, and that American constitutionalism, over the years, has increasingly, and justifiably, taken on the character of a common law system. We sometimes say that the written Constitution is another distinctive aspect of our legal order. The written text does play a crucial role as a focal point for the conventionalism that is important to any political order. There are powerful reasons not to interpret the text in a way that would seem too contrived. But the Constitution is much more, and much richer, than the written document. When we apotheosize the Framers we understate the importance of the many subsequent generations of lawyers and judges, and nonlawyers and nonjudges, who have helped develop the principles of American constitutional law.

Today it is those principles, not just the document, that make up our Constitution. Originalist and textualist approaches often find themselves in the position of making exceptions for, or apologizing for, or simply being unable to account for, some of the most prominent features of our constitutional order. The common law approach greatly reduces the need to do any of that. It forthrightly accepts, without apology, that we depart from past understandings, and that we are often creative in interpreting the text. These practices, which are common and well settled, need not be carried on covertly or with a sense that they are somehow inappropriate. They are important parts of our system, and they can be justified on the basis of one of the oldest legal institutions, the common law.

Perhaps the most serious charge against the common law approach is that it is resistant to change. To some degree that is true. But properly understood the common law method does not immunize the past from sharp, critical challenges. Gradual innovation, in the hope of improvement, has always been a part of the common law tradition, as it has been a part of American constitutionalism. Even sudden changes are possible. They require a stronger justification, but the common law approach, unlike some other methods, allows judges to make them. Perhaps most important, the common law method identifies what is truly at stake: whether the arguments for change, in order to make the law fairer or more just, overcome the presumption that should operate in favor of the work of generations. Since we cannot avoid that question, we are perhaps better off with an approach that forces us to answer it.

§ 3.04   A Case In Point

The following excerpt from an article by Professors Jordan Steiker and Sanford Levinson of the University of Texas and J. M. Balkin of the Yale Law School, on the lighter side of textualism, explores the consequences of a strict reading of the Presidential Eligibility Clause:[11]

II. A Really Serious Reading of Article II, Or Why Zachary Taylor Was Our Last Constitutional President

. . . Read in the light of traditional craft values, the constitutional text, we think, demonstrates convincingly that there has been no legitimate president of the United States since Zachary Taylor. As we shall now explain, the constitutional text clearly limits presidential eligibility to those who were citizens of the United States at the time of the Constitution's adoption in 1788. No one else could (and can) serve in that office, at least without further amendment of the document. This discovery, we well recognize, considerably raises the constitutional stakes. We are no longer discussing the status of the long-terminated Washington presidency, but now we are grappling with the legitimacy of William Jefferson Clinton's current occupancy of the Oval Office. Nevertheless, we feel duty bound, as legal academics, to follow the truth wherever it may lead us. Fidelity to text and commitment to craft, we think, require no less.

Recall Article II's text once more: "No person except a natural born Citizen, or a Citizen of the United States, at the time of the Adoption of this Constitution, shall be eligible to the Office of President . . . ." A textual neophyte might think that the phrase "at the time of the Adoption of this Constitution" refers only to the immediately preceding language in Article II—"a Citizen of the United States"—so as to grandfather (or grandmother) johnny-come-latelies like Alexander Hamilton who entered the colonies after birth and only then became a citizen of one of the ratifying states. On this theory, citizens not "natural born" but naturalized at the time of ratification were allowed to attain the presidency, but those naturalized thereafter were forever barred from running for this august office. So understood, this clause of the Constitution has rightly and eloquently been denounced as the Constitution's stupidest provision by such eminent theorists as Randall Kennedy and Robert Post.

---

[11] Jordan Steiker, Sanford Levinson, & J.M. Balkin, *Taking Text and Structure Really Seriously: Constitutional Interpretation and the Crisis of Presidential Eligibility*, 74 Tex. L. Rev. 237, 243–248 (1995). Copyright © 1995 by the Texas Law Review Association. Reprinted with permission.

Nevertheless, this inequitable, albeit conventional, interpretation of the constitutional text is wholly inconsistent with the text and grammar of Article II. After all, the phrase "at the time of the Adoption of this Constitution" is separated by an all-important comma from the phrase that precedes it, thus suggesting, indeed requiring, that it modifies both "natural born Citizen" and "a Citizen of the United States." A rigorous textual interpretation of the clause thus avoids the vicious discrimination against non-natural-born citizens usually ascribed to it by routine interpretation. When the text is given its plain meaning, it suggests instead a far more profound discrimination against those who were not sufficiently part of the national community at the nation's birth.

Indeed, it seems clear enough that our reading of the text is absolutely required under a plain-meaning approach that pays due attention to the Constitution's words and its punctuation. To be sure, this interpretation requires some elaboration, but this is not fatal to plain-meaning arguments. After all, as Justice Scalia, the doyen of textualists, has pointed out, a patch of text may be "susceptible of only one meaning, although . . . that meaning is not immediately accessible" until one engages in a complex process of analysis.

Some benighted souls may dare to label our reading as "frivolous" because it seems to result in what they regard as a monumentally stupid—and therefore unacceptable—outcome. One might begin by noting that it is not at all clear that stupid outcomes are necessarily precluded by the standard norms of constitutional interpretation. It was, after all, James Madison himself who told his colleagues in the very first session of the House of Representatives that "[h]ad the power of making treaties... been omitted, however necessary it might have been, the defect could only have been lamented, or supplied by an amendment of the Constitution." One might lament that Bill Clinton is not truly eligible for the presidency (not having been a citizen of the United States in 1788); one might even suggest rectifying this obvious imperfection by quick passage of an amendment. But neither regret nor the need for reform would or should change the status of what the Constitution means. As Justice Thomas has recently reminded us, the Constitution means what it said when it left the hands of the Framers, and no amount of hand wringing or wishful thinking can change the unalterable meanings of the Founding Document.[51]

But, equally important, we think that the cavalier assumption that our reading is "stupid" or even "frivolous" begs the question. Instead, reflection on the plain meaning of the text, especially when coupled with reflection on some of the most prominent strands of the American political tradition, has led us to conclude that the Framers, in adopting the language they did, were sending an extraordinarily deep and profound message to later generations. As with Poe's purloined letter, we have failed to grasp this message only because we have refused to look at what was in front of us all the time.

Reserving the presidency to persons who were citizens at the time of the Founding is hardly shortsighted. To the contrary, it reflects the deeply held Jeffersonian impulse in American constitutionalism, with its emphasis on the need for periodic reconsideration and even revolution regarding our institutional structures. The Framers well understood, even if we do not, that the Constitution of 1787-1788 was a compact for the citizens of that generation and not for all time. This decision reflects an attractive

---

[51] McIntyre v. Ohio Elections Comm'n, 115 S. Ct. 1511, 1525 (1995). (Thomas, J., concur-   ring) (citing South Carolina v. United States, 199 U.S. 437, 448 (1905)).

modesty in the Founding Generation about the likelihood of their having achieved perfection in designing a radically new political system. More importantly, the limited term of eligibility is an overt acknowledgment of what is perhaps the greatest problem facing a revolutionary political regime like that constructed between 1776 and 1788: How does one maintain the warm zeal of the Founding Generation, which staked its own "lives, . . . fortunes, and . . . sacred Honor" on creating a new system of government? How does one pass this revolutionary spirit on to a new generation, born to a different set of experiences, reared in stability and relative comfort, who may see little glory in simply maintaining the work of their fathers?

Thus, the Framers may well have believed that it would be dangerous for the Republic to have a president whose republican spirit had not been born through baptism by total immersion in the holy spirit of 1775–1787. Could one really trust a leader whose own freedom was not fought for and earned through an audacious appeal to heaven, but who was instead handed his freedom routinely and unceremoniously as an expected birthright? Who among us will confidently answer "yes" to this question? For this reason, the fifth clause of Article II, section 1 placed a duty upon the later generations to grapple with their own fitness to rule, to confront the potential inadequacy of leaders who had not directly participated in the epic events of the Founding. It thus called upon Us the People to recognize the emergence of a true constitution-making moment. When the last embers of the Founding Generation died out, the nation was then rightly deprived of anyone legally eligible to rule as our president, because no one morally entitled to be president remained. A new generation must then take up the cause of the revolution—as did the generation of 1776. The members of this new generation must give their own free and willing consent to the basic institutional structures whose purpose is to secure the inalienable rights of "life, liberty, and the pursuit of happiness." These values may remain our beacon through all time, but there is certainly no reason to believe that the particular institutional means chosen in 1787 to achieve them will be similarly immortal. Instead, as Jefferson insisted, we must relentlessly scrutinize our institutions to make sure that they are still conducive to the purposes for which they were originally created. "Nothing," he rightly insisted, "is unchangeable but the inherent and unalienable rights of man." Whatever threatens these rights should be unsentimentally eliminated. "[L]aws and institutions must go hand in hand with the progress of the human mind. As that becomes more developed, . . . and manners and opinions change with the change of circumstances, institutions must advance also, and keep pace with the times." To paraphrase Jefferson, the tree of liberty often needs to be pruned of those branches whose rot threatens the survival of the tree itself.

The authors invite the reader to consider the idea of parody (perhaps or perhaps not as applied to their own work) in connection with the interpreter's consideration of authorial intent.

§ 3.05 Conclusion

Resort to textualism represents a prior determination about the role that a written constitution should play in a democracy. As Judge Posner pointed out in the excerpt reprinted above, the Constitution itself does not tell us whether to read its terms broadly or narrowly, except as necessarily implied by the choice of "open-textured" or more specific provisions. Thus, the battle over textualism is a battle about a much larger question regarding what it is that the polity expects from its constitution. As Professor James Fleming put it,

> the central question . . . , "What is the best conception of fidelity in constitutional interpretation?," ultimately poses the questions, *What* is the Constitution and *how* should it be interpreted?" The question of fidelity is not a narrower question about how to follow the original meaning of the text or how to interpret the Constitution so as to fit the historical materials surrounding its framing and ratification. Those narrower questions grow out of particular originalist answers to the question of fidelity. They are not the question of fidelity itself.[12]

In the chapters to come, the materials will address these questions in connection with the issue of what sources and methods a judge should employ in interpreting the constitutional text: "[T]he Constitution is merely words— deathless words, but words. And the future will not be ruled; it can only possibly be persuaded."[13]

§ 3.06   Bibliography

Akhil Reed Amar, *Textualism and the Bill of Rights*, 66 GEO. WASH. L. REV. 1143 (1998).

Christopher L. Eisgruber, *Justice and the Text: Rethinking the Constitutional Relation Between Principle and Prudence*, 43 DUKE L. J. 1 (1993).

Richard H. Fallon, Jr., *How to Choose a Constitutional Theory*, 87 CAL. L. REV. 535 (1999).

Michael J. Gerhardt, *A Tale of Two Textualists: A Critical Comparison of Justices Black and Scalia*, 74 B.U.L. REV. 25 (1994).

Thomas Grey, *Do We Have an Unwritten Constitution?*, 27 STAN. L. REV. 703, 706 (1975).

Gary Lawson, *On Reading Recipes . . . And Constitutions*, 85 GEO. L. J. 1823 (1997).

H. Jefferson Powell, *Parchment Matters: A Meditation on the Constitution as Text*, 71 IOWA L. REV. 1427 (1986).

Jed Rubenfeld, *Reading the Constitution as Spoken*, 104 YALE L. J. 1119 (1995).

Frederick Schauer, *Easy Cases*, 58 S. CAL. L. REV. 399 (1985).

Suzanna Sherry, *Textualism and Judgment*, 66 GEO. WASH. L. REV. 1148 (1998).

Suzanna Sherry, *The Founders' Unwritten Constitution*, 54 U. CHI. L. REV. 1127 (1987).

Symposium, *Textualism and the Constitution*, 66 GEO. WASH. L. REV. 1081 (1998).

---

[12] James E. Fleming, *Fidelity to our Imperfect Constitution*, 65 FORDHAM L. REV. 1335 (1997). Copyright © 1997 by the Fordham Law Review. Reprinted by permission.

[13] Alexander Bickel, *The Least Dangerous Branch: The Supreme Court at the Bar of Politics* 98 (1962).

Laurence H. Tribe, *Taking Text and Structure Seriously: Reflections on Free-Form Method in Constitutional Interpretation,* 108 HARV. L. REV. 1221 (1995).

Laurence Tribe & Michael Dorf, ON READING THE CONSTITUTION (1991).

Chapter 4

Constitutional History and the "Original Intention" Controversy

§ 4.01 Introduction and Overview

An area of constitutional theory that has received consistent attention in recent decades has been how much the courts should look to and be bound by the publicly expressed intentions of the framers and ratifiers of constitutional provisions. The uses of history and the relevance of the framers' intent cannot, of course, be neatly separated from the issues of interpretation of constitutional text surveyed in the preceding chapter; history can be a major source and aid for interpretation. The prominence of the original-intention controversy, however, warrants giving it a chapter of its own.

Many of the basic issues in originalism debates seem to remain little changed over the years. A 1989 article by Professor Daniel Farber of the University of Minnesota Law School still provides an excellent overview, and refers to leading treatments of the subject by others up to that time. After the Farber article we present some major recent works not reflected in his survey. Daniel A. Farber, *The Originalism Debate: A Guide for the Perplexed,* 49 OHIO ST. L.J. 1085, 1085–1103 (1989):[1]

I. INTRODUCTION

. . .

The role of historical evidence in constitutional law has always been of interest to scholars. Recently, however, it has become a matter of more pressing concern. Scholars began to question whether some crucial constitutional decisions could be justified on the basis of original intent. Those scholars who support the Court's rulings on abortion, integration, and reapportionment began to look for alternative constitutional theories.[1] This debate, as Professor Murray Dry explains, soon extended beyond academics to include judges and other government officials:

> This important debate came out of the academic closet in 1985, when Attorney General Edwin Meese gave public addresses on constitutional jurisprudence. In one, after noting that the new terms replaced the older ones of strict versus loose construction, he quipped, "Under the old system the question was *how* to read the Constitution; under the new approach, the question is *whether* to read the Constitution." He called for a return to a "jurisprudence of original intention," (a clearer term for interpretivism). Acting on that principle, he said the Justice Department stood prepared to challenge the incorporation doctrine, according to which nearly all of the provisions of the original

---

[1] Copyright © 1989 by the Ohio State Law Journal. Reprinted with permission.

[1] Dry, *Federalism and the Constitution: The Founders' Design and Contemporary Constitutional Law,* 4 CONST. COMMENTARY 233, 233–34 (1987).

Bill of Rights have been applied against the states under the fourteenth amendment. This drew from Justice Brennan a defense of an activist approach to individual rights and a twentieth-century reading of the Constitution. For Justice Brennan and his supporters, the choice is between being ruled by the dead hand of the past or the living present; for Attorney General Meese and his supporters, the choice is between courts that say what the law is, which is their job, and courts that make law and policy, which is the job of legislatures.

. . .

Before examining the arguments about originalism, it is useful to clarify some terms. Instead of using the term "interpretivism," I will call supporters of Meese's position "originalists." The latter term is found more frequently in current writings on the subject because it emphasizes that the issue is the role of *original* intent in constitutional interpretation. Most opponents of originalism also claim to be interpreting the Constitution; they simply have a different view of the appropriate methods of interpretation. I will call them "non-originalists" because they do not find original intent dispositive of contemporary constitutional questions.

. . .

Originalists have various shades of belief about the binding effect of original intent and about how to define "intent." The extreme view is that the *only* relevant factor is original intent; whichever side has the best historical evidence should always win. A moderate originalist might well view other factors as potentially important, particularly when the evidence of intent is unclear. At the very least, an originalist must believe that *clear* evidence of original intent is controlling on any "open" question of constitutional law; that is, any question that has not already been decisively resolved by the Supreme Court. [4] Originalists also differ about the level of generality at which they define original intent. Those who focus on the framers' general principles are quite different from those who emphasize the framers' views of particular governmental practices. Moderate originalists may be difficult to distinguish from non-originalists, as Dean Paul Brest explains:

> The only difference between moderate originalism and nonoriginalist adjudication is one of attitude toward the text and original understanding. For the moderate originalist, these sources are conclusive when they speak clearly. For the nonoriginalists, they are important but not determinative. Like an established line of precedent at common law, they create a strong presumption, but one which is defeasible in the light of changing public values. [6]

Similar divisions can be drawn among non-originalists based on the degree of deference they are inclined to give historical intent. Non-originalists share a rejection of the binding authority of original intent, but this leaves room for considerable disagreement about how much weight to give intent in comparison with other factors. Another important ground of distinction among non-originalists relates to how they supplement consideration of original intent. Some non-originalists trace their

---

[4] Originalists may give binding authority to Supreme Court precedent. *See* Monaghan, *Stare Decisis and Constitutional Adjudication,* 88 COLUM. L. REV. 723 (1988). An even looser use of the term "originalist" might include anyone who believes that the starting point of analysis should always be original intent but that original intent is not necessarily controlling even when it is clear. At this point, however, it becomes difficult to tell the difference between an originalist of this school and a non-originalist . . . .

[6] Brest, *The Misconceived Quest for the Original Understanding,* 60 B.U. L. REV. 204, 229 (1980).

intellectual lineage to Enlightenment rationalists. They seek general theories that will provide logical answers in particular cases. Others trace their lineage to Burke, placing their faith on evolving traditions and time-tested institutions rather than abstract theories. And some, of course, combine both approaches.

II. Is Originalism Workable?

Before we worry about whether originalism is *in principle* the right approach to constitutional interpretation, we have to consider a variety of arguments about whether it can work in practice. It may be, for example, that the original understanding of some or all of the Constitution is unknowable. Or perhaps originalism is inherently self-contradictory because the original intent was that judges would *not* use originalism. Or perhaps the Supreme Court has gone too far down the non-originalist path to make a return to originalism feasible. . . .

A. *Methodological Problems*

One initial problem is whether we can determine the original intent with any confidence. Various methodological problems may make it difficult to do so, and of course, if we cannot determine original intent, we cannot make it the basis for interpretation.

One problem is that the framers of various provisions often failed to discuss the issues in which we are interested today. Much time was spent discussing how the executive would be appointed, what the term of office would be, and so forth. Little thought was given to questions that today hold greater interest, such as the President's power to send troops into combat without congressional approval or his power to remove subordinate officers. Similarly, the debates about the fourteenth amendment focused on the now forgotten sections 2 and 3, which were of immediate concern in the context of Reconstruction but had no lasting importance. Section 1 of the amendment, which today looms larger in judicial application than any other provision of the Constitution, received only the most cursory attention. This is not to say that the record is wholly silent on these issues. Indeed, even the conspicuous lack of attention given to these questions may itself carry a message about the original understanding, although it may also indicate a failure to consider or contemplate particular issues. But the originalist task would certainly be easier if the framers had addressed these issues in detail.

Another question is whether the documentary evidence we do have is reliable. There have been recurring charges that Madison significantly altered his notes at a later date, perhaps to reflect his own changing views of the meaning of the Constitution. After a careful recent investigation, based on matters such as the watermarks on Madison's paper, James Hutson concludes that any alterations were not significant. But Hutson points out that Madison gave only a highly abbreviated account of the proceedings:

> Madison's notes, then, stand alone as the key to the Framers' intentions. If his notes on any given day are compared to the fragmentary records of debates left by other delegates that Farrand printed or that have been discovered more recently, a rough approximation between the accounts is evident—demonstrating that Madison was not inventing dialogue, but was trying to capture what was said. Still, there is an enigma about Madison's note-taking methods . . . .

> If read aloud Madison's notes for any particular day consume only a few minutes, suggesting that he may have recorded only a small

part of each day's proceedings . . . . Madison recorded only 600 of
a possible 8,400 words per hour, or seven percent of each hour's
proceedings. Even if the possible words per hour are reduced to 6,000,
Madison recorded only ten percent of each hour's proceedings. [7]

There is also some reason to be suspicious of Madison's accounts of his
own speeches; he may have improved them somewhat when he later
reduced them to written form.

Hutson points out even greater problems with other parts of the
documentary record. He concludes that the records of the ratification
debates are "too corrupt . . . [to] be relied upon to reveal the intentions
of the Framers." . . .

. . .

The potential unreliability of parts of the historical record do[es] not
mean that historical investigation is hopeless. If historians were reduced
to studying impeccably documented events, they would have little to do
with their time. But a significant part of a professional historian's training
consists of learning how to assess the validity of various documents.
Historians learn to make sophisticated credibility judgments based not
only on the documents themselves and their drafting, but also on a
knowledge of the culture and politics of the period. Credibility judgments
must also be made to determine which of various possible interpretations
of the historical record is the most plausible. But judges may be ill-prepared
to make such judgments:

> [J]udicial judgments about the credibility of various accounts of the
> constitutional past may be idiosyncratic and otherwise unsound.
> While judges have fulsome experience in regard to the behavioral
> patterns of the sorts of people who typically appear before them, they
> know little about how people behaved in the distant past. Thus they
> may reason anachronistically when they use their present-day behav-
> ioral assumptions to assess the accuracy of a particular interpretation
> of the past.

> After all, judges are not selected for office because they have special
> skill in reconstructing the intentions of individuals in the past . . . .
> [A] judge who decides constitutional cases on the basis of credibility
> is likely to mislead both himself and his audience as to the ultimate
> basis of his decisions. [11]

The difficulty of determining the plausibility of a historical interpretation is increased by the need to interpret the collective views of a diverse
group of individuals. These individuals may not have agreed with each
other on their interpretation of a provision. Some may have voted for a
package such as the Constitution or Bill of Rights because they approved
of some portions but had no particular view about the meaning or
desirability of other parts. How can we aggregate the varying views of
a diverse group in order to determine a collective intent? Of course, the
framers were not randomly drawn from different societies or even different segments of the same society. Their shared common culture should
be reflected in some degree of consensus about the meaning of texts. Even
where this is true, however, discerning that consensus may require a deep
knowledge of a historical period, which may be beyond the reach of anyone
but historians specializing in the period.

---

[7] Hutson, *The Creation of the Constitution:
The Integrity of the Documentary Record*, 65
TEX. L. REV. 1, 33–34 (1986).

[11] Nelson, *History and Neutrality in Constitutional Adjudication*, 72 VA. L. REV. 1237,
1250–51 (1986).

. . .

B. *Was Originalism the Original Understanding?*

The question of originalism can itself be approached from an originalist perspective, by asking whether the framers themselves expected their own intentions to control subsequent interpretation of the Constitution. Although earlier scholars had mentioned this problem, it is investigated in the greatest detail in an influential 1985 article by Professor H. Jefferson Powell.[12]

Professor Powell begins by exploring the common law's methods of interpreting various documents such as statutes, wills, and contracts. He argues that "intent" generally referred to the objective meaning of the language used in the document, not the subjective intentions of the authors:

> At common law, then, the "intent" of the maker of a legal document and the "intent" of the document itself were one and the same; "intent" did not depend upon the subjective purposes of the author. The late eighteenth century common lawyer conceived an instrument's "intent"—and therefore its meaning—not as what the drafters meant by their words but rather as what judges, employing the "artificial reason and judgment of law," understood "the reasonable and legal meaning" of those words to be.
>
> . . .
>
> The courts likewise looked to "rules of law" and to "common understanding" when interpreting statutes. The modern practice of interpreting a law by reference to its legislative history was almost wholly nonexistent, and English judges professed themselves bound to honor the true import of the "express words" of Parliament. The "intent of the act" and the "intent of the legislature" were interchangeable terms; neither term implied that the interpreter looked at any evidence concerning that "intent" other than the words of the text and the common law background of the statute. . . .
>
> The common law tradition did admit the propriety of looking beyond the statute's wording where the text was defective on its face. In such situations judges were free to substitute coherence for gibberish. A more serious interpretive problem occurred when the statute's wording was ambiguous, rather than clear but in conflict with its apparent intent. It was generally agreed that such *ambiguitas patens* could not be resolved by extrinsic evidence as to Parliament's purpose. . . .

Because the common law adopted somewhat different methods of interpretation for different kinds of documents, however, interpretation of the new Constitution posed something of a problem. To interpret it, the eighteenth-century lawyer first had to determine what kind of document it was. In the debates over ratification, according to Professor Powell, the Federalists took the position that the text would be interpreted like a statute, on the basis of the meaning of its words to a reasonable reader.

Even after the Constitution was in effect, according to Professor Powell, references to history were viewed with some suspicion as an innovation in methods of interpretation. A newer approach to interpretation, based

---

[12] Powell, *The Original Understanding of Original Intent*, 98 HARV. L. REV. 885 (1985).

on the understandings of the ratifiers, was ultimately crystallized by Madison:

> The text itself, of course, was the primary source from which that intention was to be gathered, but Madison's awareness of the imperfect nature of human communication led him to concede that the text's import would frequently be unclear. Madison thought it proper to engage in structural inference in the classic contractual mode of the Virginia and Kentucky Resolutions, and to consult the direct expressions of state intention available in the resolutions of the ratifying conventions. He regarded the debates in those conventions to be of real yet limited value for the interpreter: evidentiary problems with the surviving records and Madison's insistence on distinguishing the binding public intention of the state from the private opinions of any individual or group of individuals, including those gathered at a state convention, led him to conclude that the state debates could bear no more than indirect and corroborative witness to the meaning of the Constitution . . . . Last and least in value were the records of the Philadelphia convention.

Madison's objection to reliance on the convention debates was based on two factors: the possible defects in the historical record and the status of the ratifiers as the true sources of the Constitution's authority.

Professor Powell's historical evidence has been carefully examined by Professor Charles Lofgren. Professor Lofgren agrees with him about the nature of common law interpretative methods and about Madison's ultimate position. [15] The crux of the disagreement between these two scholars relates to timing. Professor Powell believes that the view of interpretation ultimately adopted by Madison did not become prevalent until well after ratification. Professor Lofgren argues, however, that this theory of interpretation based on the ratifiers' intent was adopted earlier, by the time the Constitution was ratified or soon thereafter. Both scholars agree that the convention debates themselves were not considered to have any authoritative status as a source of meaning because the Constitution took its authority from its adoption by the sovereign People: "We, the People" referred to the ratifiers, not the members of the Convention. Given this understanding, the Framers themselves were merely scriveners, drafting a document for possible use by others—little different from staff members in Congress who help draft legislation for Congress to consider. It seems somewhat unlikely that the intent of the scriveners was thought to be binding on the ratifiers, especially when the Framers were so careful to keep the proceedings of the Convention secret from the ratifiers themselves.

Of course, even if it is correct, this conclusion would not mean that the Convention debates should be disregarded. Besides their intrinsic interest, they are also strong evidence of the understanding of reasonable readers of the period. But even in the Framers' own views, the Convention debates were probably not considered authoritative.

Assuming, however, that only the intent of the ratifiers is dispositive, and taking into account the defective historical record concerning that intent, some area remains in which original intent might be decisive. For example, it might well be possible to establish that no intelligent eighteenth-century reader would have thought that the phrase "cruel and unusual punishment" included execution by hanging, or that no mid-nineteenth-century reader would have thought that "equal protection of

---

[15] Lofgren, *The Original Understanding of Original Intent?*, 5 CONST. COMMENTARY 77 (1988).

the laws" had anything to do with the right to vote. Thus, the problems with originalism considered above are not fatal to the originalist thesis that original intent controls where it can be determined.

C. Anti-Originalist Clauses

Another argument against originalism, which is related to that considered . . . previous[ly], is that the Framers anticipated that the courts would defend human rights beyond those expressly listed in the Bill of Rights. The basis for this enforcement of unwritten rights might either be natural law or certain "open-ended" clauses of the Constitution.

As one writer has recently explained, natural law was considered a legitimate basis for judicial decision in the period leading up to the framing of the Constitution:

> [F]or American judges in the late eighteenth century, the sources of fundamental law were as open-ended as they were in English opposition theory. The colonists inherited a tradition that provided not only a justification for judicial review but also guidelines for its exercise. As Bolingbroke proposed in theory and the new American states translated into action, judges were to look to natural law and the inherent rights of man, as well as to the written constitution, in determining the validity of a statute. Where the written constitution affirmatively addressed a problem—most often in governmental structure cases . . . but even in cases . . . where the constitution provided clear protection of individual rights—it was dispositive, but in other cases, judges looked outside the written constitution.[16]

The historical evidence suggests that natural rights theories persisted into the 1780s. Indeed, belief in the existence of an unwritten "higher law" continued until well into the nineteenth century. Some writers argue that the Framers accepted natural law as a judicially enforceable restriction on governmental power.[17]

The ninth amendment can easily be read as embodying unspecified natural rights. The privileges and immunities clause of the fourteenth amendment is another possible source of unenumerated rights. Perhaps the leading spokesman for this argument is Dean John Ely.[18] If Ely's

---

[16] Sherry, *The Founders' Unwritten Constitution,* 54 U. CHI. L. REV. 1127, 1145–46 (1987).

[17] *See id.;* Grey, *The Original Understanding and the Unwritten Constitution* (unpublished manuscript on file with the Ohio State Law Journal).

[18] Dean Ely argues that:

[T]he legislative history argument is one neither side can win. It really should not be critical, however. What is most important here, as it has to be everywhere, is the actual language of the provision that was proposed and ratified. On that score Justice Black surely has a point: "No State shall make or enforce any law which shall abridge the privileges or immunities of citizens of the United States" *does* seem an "eminently reasonable way of expressing the idea that henceforth the Bill of Rights shall apply to the States.". . . There is another edge to this, and that is that nothing in the material that has been discussed

supports Justice Black's *limitation* of the fourteenth amendment's privileges or immunities clause to the function of incorporating the Bill of Rights. There is some legislative history suggesting an intention to incorporate the Bill of Rights; there is none at all suggesting that was *all* the privileges or immunities clause was designed to do, and indeed Howard's speech, which is Black's strongest proof of incorporation, is quite explicitly against him on the limitation point. The words of the clause *are* an "eminently reasonable" way of applying the Bill of Rights to the states, but much more reasonable words could have been found had that been the *only* content intended. (emphasis in original).

J. ELY, DEMOCRACY AND DISTRUST: A THEORY OF JUDICIAL REVIEW 27–28 (1980). Ely's views are challenged in Berger, *Ely's "Theory of Judicial Review,"* 42 OHIO ST. L.J. 87, 98–110 (1981).

historical interpretation is correct, then at least some clauses of the Constitution seem to require judges to protect rights that are not themselves listed in the Constitution. Even if correct, however, that conclusion is not necessarily fatal to originalism. For it may still be possible to give an originalist reading to these unenumerated rights themselves. For example, we might look to the understandings of the times to find out precisely what rights were considered fundamental (and therefore presumably protected by the ninth amendment or the privileges and immunities clause).

Neither those who discussed the need for a bill of rights in the late eighteenth century, nor those who framed the fourteenth amendment seventy years later, seem to have spent much time worrying about whether unwritten fundamental rights were static or subject to change.[19] Thus, an originalist interpretation of these provisions might be limited to the specific fundamental rights of the time, or it might require an evolving list of rights. The original understanding of the "higher law" may be even more elusive than that of more specific constitutional language. Nevertheless, it might be possible to establish with some degree of confidence, for instance, that abortion was not considered a fundamental right in 1866 and that the list of fundamental rights was considered static. The question would then remain whether that historical understanding is binding today.

D. *The Ambiguity of Intent*

Determining the level of intent we are interested in is one difficulty inherent in implementing originalism. At its simplest level, we might consider the "original intent" to be a kind of multiple choice examination to be administered to the framers, in which all the questions look like this: "Constitutional provision X covers fact-pattern Y. True or false?"

One problem with this approach is that it may be very difficult to find out the answers, for the reasons discussed in the preceding sections. Moreover, some fact-patterns will involve situations that the framers could not directly consider. For example, the framers had no occasion to consider whether the fourth amendment applied to electronic eavesdropping, whether electrocution was cruel and unusual punishment, or whether the manufacture of computer chips is part of interstate commerce. If we seek to address these issues in terms of original intent, we will have to define our inquiry at a higher level of generality.

The view of original intent as a sort of checklist of specific prohibitions is also vulnerable to another sort of attack. Presumably, the checklist is not entirely arbitrary; it reflects some underlying beliefs or values of the framers. But this underlying belief system may be more complex than the checklist indicates, and in particular may contain some inner tensions or inconsistencies. Ignoring these complexities may fail to do justice to the original understanding. Yet, the more we understand the intellectual and cultural matrix in which a provision arose, the more difficult we may find the task of projecting its meaning into the contemporary world.[20]

---

[19] *See* Monaghan, *Our Perfect Constitution,* 56 N.Y.U. L. REV. 353, 367 (1981).

[20] In this hermeneutic approach to history, "[t]he historian must enter the minds of his or her subjects, see the world as they saw it, and understand it in their own terms." Tushnet, *Following the Rules Laid Down,* 96 HARV. L. REV. 781, 798 (1983). As Professor Tushnet explains, hermeneutics has potentially important implications for constitutional interpretation:

The intellectual world of the framers is one that bears some resemblance, which is more than merely genetic, to ours. A hermeneutic interpretivism would force us to think about the social contexts of the resemblances and dissimilarities. It would

The question of whether the death penalty is a form of cruel and unusual punishment exemplifies some of the problems. As Professor David Richards explains in criticizing the work of Raoul Berger, a leading originalist:

> The nature of the historiographical distortion in Berger's approach is brought out by comparing . . . Berger's *Death Penalties* [and] John McManners' *Death and the Enlightenment,* a study of changing attitudes toward death (including natural deaths, executions, and suicides) in eighteenth century France . . . . For McManners, the historiography of death in eighteenth-century France requires the broadest integration of diverse sources and perspectives bearing on deep shifts in the moral and human sensibilities surrounding death in its various forms. The consequence is remarkable: McManners, writing of France with no particular focus on legal issues, enables us to understand the moral norms implicit in the eighth amendment in exhaustive depth in a way that Berger does not remotely approximate. [21]

As Professor Richards explains, these different approaches to history have potential significance in terms of applying the eighth amendment today:

> If the Enlightenment thought the death penalty acceptable in certain cases, the period was more historically remarkable in its skepticism about the extent and forms of the penalty's use and in its special concern with abuse of the death penalty for terroristic degradation. Berger's "meaning" of the eighth amendment therefore is not the eighteenth century's meaning . . . . Why, then, should it be our meaning on the issue of the death penalty when many of the eighteenth century's grounds for skepticism, implicit in the principles of the eighth amendment, may, given the contemporary context with shifts in many relevant features (alternative ways of securing deterrence, the greater value of life, etc.), dictate a complete repudiation of the death penalty? Thus, seen at a higher level of generality, the Framers' views about what is cruel and unusual punishment might lead to a rejection of the death penalty today, while their more specific views are to the contrary.

Thus, as Dean Robert Bennett suggests, it may not be true "that knowing specific intentions allows one to project the intenders' values or process of decision over time, even as applied to phenomena very similar to the subjects of the specific intentions."[23]

A crucial question for originalists, then, is to determine the proper level of generality. Should we view the eighth amendment as requiring judges

---

lead us not to despair over the gulf that separates the framers' world from ours, but rather to the crafting of creative links between their ideals and our own. But in recognizing the magnitude of the creative component, we inevitably lose faith in the ability of interpretivism to provide the constraints on judges that liberal constitutional theory demands.

. . . We can gain an interpretive understanding of the past by working from commonalities in the use of large abstractions to reach the unfamiliar particulars of what those abstractions really meant in the past. The commonalities are what make the past

our past; they are the links between two segments of a single community that extends over time . . . . Interpretivism goes wrong in thinking that the commonalities are greater than they really are, but we would go equally wrong if we denied that they exist. (emphasis in original).

Id. at 803–04. . .

[21] Richards, *Interpretation and Historiography,* 58 S. CAL. L. REV. 489, 514–15 (1985).

[23] Bennett, *Objectivity in Constitutional Law,* 132 U. PA. L. REV. 445, 463 (1984). *See also* Bennett, *Originalist Theories of Constitutional Interpretation,* 73 CORNELL L. REV. 355 (1988).

to apply some general concept of what is "cruel and unusual"? Or should they ask only what specific punishments the framers meant to forbid? One possible answer is to try to determine the framers' own views on the appropriate level of generality. For example, we might investigate whether the framers expected judges to rely on the general concepts or the specific examples discussed in the debates. As Dean Paul Brest explains, the reality is that the framers probably would have intended that both their general principles and their specific examples be given some weight:

> A principle does not exist wholly independently of its author's subjective, or his society's conventional exemplary applications, and is always limited to some extent by the applications they found conceivable. Within these fairly broad limits, however, the adopters may have intended their examples to constrain more or less. To the intentionalist interpreter falls the unenviable task of ascertaining, for each provision, how much more or less.

The difficulties of this historical inquiry are obvious, since the framers are unlikely to have discussed the precise balance between general principles and specific examples.

Another possible originalist solution is to specify a nonhistorical rule for determining the proper level of abstraction. For example, Judge Robert Bork suggests that "the problem of levels of generality may be solved by choosing no level of generality higher than that which interpretation of the words, structure, and history of the Constitution fairly support."[25] His argument for adopting this rule is that higher levels of generality give judges increasing amounts of leeway in deciding cases, so the presumption should be in favor of specificity rather than generality. Unlike the approach discussed by Dean Brest, this approach does not look to the framers in order to establish their view about the proper level of generality. Rather than looking to history, Judge Bork looks to his own political theory to answer this question.

[S]ince the ultimate question before a court is the extent to which a constitutional provision limits majority rule, Judge Bork's test amounts to a presumption that all limits on governmental power should be read narrowly. But this is a rather far-reaching principle of interpretation for which Judge Bork provides no support, historical or otherwise, so his analysis at least must be considered somewhat incomplete.

E. *The Problem of Change*

Probably the most prevalent argument against originalism is that it is too static, and thereby disregards the need to keep the Constitution up to date with changing times. Originalism is unworkable, then, even if the original intent can be reliably determined, because originalism would make the Constitution itself unworkable. Thus, according to Justice William Brennan, the judicial approach to interpretation must be non-originalist:

> Current Justices read the Constitution in the only way we can: as twentieth-century Americans. We look to the history of the time of framing and to the intervening history of interpretation. But the ultimate question must be: What do the words of the text mean in our time? For the genius of the Constitution rests not in any static meaning it might have had in a world that is dead and gone, but in

---

[25] Bork, *The Constitution, Original Intent, and Economic Rights,* 23 SAN DIEGO L. REV. 823, 828 (1986).

the adaptability of its great principles to cope with current problems and current needs. What the constitutional fundamentals meant to the wisdom of other times cannot be the measure of the vision of our time. [26]

Non-originalists argue that the Supreme Court has always functioned this way, and that it is now too late to change the "rules of the game." For example, Professor Thomas Grey argues that there is only a shaky originalist basis for basic doctrines such as the application of the Bill of Rights to the states and the prohibition on racial discrimination by the federal government. [27] Indeed, Professor Grey suggests, the potential implications are even broader:

> [T]here is serious question how much of the law prohibiting state racial discrimination can survive honest application of the interpretive model. It is clear that the equal protection clause was meant to prohibit *some* forms of state racial discrimination, most obviously those enacted in the Black Codes. It is equally clear from the legislative history that the clause was *not* intended to guarantee equal political rights, such as the right to vote or to run for office, and perhaps including the right to serve on juries.

> It is at least doubtful whether the clause can fairly be read as intending to bar any form of state-imposed racial segregation, so long as equal facilities are made available . . .

> . . .

> While one might disagree with this rough catalogue on points of detail, it should be clear that an extraordinarily radical purge of established constitutional doctrine would be required if we candidly and consistently applied the pure interpretive model. Surely that makes out at least a prima facie practical case against the model.

Some originalists may be undismayed or even pleased by the thought of such a radical uprooting of current doctrine. Originalism need not, however, require such radical doctrinal change. First, for all the reasons we have explored previously in this article, history is rarely clear, and many of Professor Grey's specific conclusions are subject to dispute. So the originalist may be able in good conscience to uphold the correctness of many current constitutional doctrines.

Second, originalism may be tempered by an appreciation of the importance of stability in the law, so that an originalist who agrees with Professor Grey's list of mistaken doctrines might nonetheless oppose overruling them. Thus, Professor Henry Monaghan says:

> I accept as a premise that the illustrations cited are not consistent with original intent. . . . The expectations so long generated by this

---

[26] Brennan, *The Constitution of the United States: Contemporary Ratification,* 27 S. Tex. L.J. 433, 438 (1986). The primary line of response available to originalists is to agree that changing times must be accommodated somewhere in the system of government, but to ask why the courts' performance of constitutional review is the appropriate place. If people today have broader views of individual rights than those held by those who drafted the fourteenth amendment, they can prevail upon their legis-lators to recognize those rights. The Supreme Court's function, the originalist can maintain, is limited to enforcing the original understanding; social change simply must find its expression elsewhere. For a sophisticated discussion of the allocation of constitutional decision-making authority, see Komesar, *Back to the Future—An Institutional View of Making and Interpreting Constitutions,* 81 Nw. U.L. Rev. 191 (1987).

[27] Grey, *Do We Have an Unwritten Constitution?,* 27 Stan. L. Rev. 703, 712–13 (1975).

body of constitutional law render unacceptable a full return to original intent theory in any pure, unalloyed form. While original intent may constitute the starting point for constitutional interpretation, it cannot now be recognized as the only legitimate mode of constitutional reasoning. To my mind, some theory of *stare decisis* is necessary to confine its reach. Of course, this is to accord an authoritative status to tradition in "supplementing or derogating from" the constitutional text, at least if that "tradition" has worked its way into judicial opinions. But a *stare decisis* theory has its limits, at·least for those who take original intent seriously . . . . [T]his concession to reality would not be taken to entail, also in the name of reality, the further concession that our constitutional law now sanctions the general, nontextual mode of constitutional analysis
. . . .

Third, an originalist might take into account not only judicial precedents but also the changing views of those adopting later constitutional provisions. For example, those who ratified the fourteenth amendment's due process clause may have had a broader concept of the meaning of due process than their predecessors who adopted the fifth amendment's due process clause. Yet it would be incongruous to give the two due process clauses different interpretations today.

Even defeated constitutional amendments may count for something. For example, an amendment to allow Congress to regulate child labor failed to obtain ratification because it became clear that the Supreme Court had changed its mind on this issue. Or, to take another example, one argument against the proposed equal rights amendment was that it was unnecessary because the Supreme Court was already attacking sex discrimination by using the equal protection clause. After these amendments failed to obtain ratification, it seems dubious that the Court should feel free to abandon the positions on which the public relied. As with Professor Monaghan's treatment of precedent, however, these points could be conceded without abandoning originalism as a general principle.

III. The Normative Arguments For Originalism

Assuming that some form of originalism would be a feasible approach to constitutional interpretation, the question of whether it would be a desirable approach remains. There are three basic normative arguments in favor of originalism. The first is that legitimate authority in a democracy must be based on majority rule. Hence, a court is only justified in overruling one majority decision on the basis of another, even more authoritative, majority decision. In exercising judicial review, a judge is merely doing the will of the majority as contained in the Constitution, and the judge's job is simply to understand that majority will. The second argument is more general: that the job of the judge is to interpret legal documents like the Constitution, and that interpreting *any* document is simply a matter of determining the author's intentions. The third argument is that there is no principled alternative to originalism. I will discuss these arguments in turn.

A. *Majoritarianism*

As Attorney General Meese explained, majoritarianism is one of the fundamental underpinnings of originalism:

The Constitution represents the consent of the governed to the structures and powers of the government. The Constitution is the fundamental will of the people; that is the reason the Constitution is the fundamental law. To allow the courts to govern simply by what it views at the time as fair and decent, is a scheme of government no longer popular; the idea of democracy has suffered.[31]

Reduced to its essence, the argument is this: If judges get their authority from the Constitution, and the Constitution gets its authority from the majority vote of the ratifiers, then the rule of the judge is to carry out the will of the ratifiers.

Although Dean John Ely is not an originalist, he has given one of the best explanations of the majoritarian basis of originalism:

We have as a society from the beginning, and now almost instinctively, accepted the notion that a representative democracy must be our form of government. The very process of adopting the Constitution was designed to be, and in some respects was, more democratic than any that had preceded it . . . . All this belabors the obvious part: whatever the explanation, and granting the qualifications, rule in accord with the consent of a majority of those governed is the core of the American governmental system. Just as obviously, however, that cannot be the whole story, since a majority with untrammeled power to set governmental policy is in a position to deal itself benefits at the expense of the remaining minority . . . .

. . . Of course, [the originalists] would answer, the majority can tyrannize the minority, and that is precisely the reason that in the Bill of Rights and elsewhere the Constitution designates certain rules for protection . . . . Thus the judges do not check the people, the Constitution does, which means the people are ultimately checking themselves.

The majoritarian argument for originalism has three premises: that our society's "master norm" is democracy; that the Constitution gets its legitimacy solely from the majority will as expressed at the time of enactment; and that judicial decisions are less "democratic" than those of the elected branches of government.

1. *Democracy as a "Master Norm"*

A non-originalist might question the status of democracy as a uniquely fundamental norm of our society. . . . Why, one might ask, do we believe in democracy? Isn't it because of underlying beliefs in human dignity and equality, beliefs that are also the bases for judicial protection of individual rights? On this view, the individual rights should not be viewed as conflicting with democracy. Rather, majority rule and individual rights are both part of a harmonious vision of government.

Perhaps identifying democracy with unlimited majority rule is too simplistic. Instead, as one political theorist has put it, democracy may mean creating and maintaining "a society whose adult members are, and continue to be, equipped by their education and authorized by political structures to share in ruling."[33] Thus majority-approved policies that deprive some citizens of their right or ability to participate in governance are contrary to the ideal of democracy.

This structure of constrained majoritarianism is reflected in the Constitution itself (mostly in the Bill of Rights and other amendments). As

---

[31] Meese, *The Supreme Court of the United States: Bulwark of a Limited Constitution,* 27 S. TEX. L.J. 455, 465 (1986).

[33] A. GUTMAN, DEMOCRATIC EDUCATION xi (1987).

Justice Robert Jackson recognized: "The very purpose of a Bill of Rights was to withdraw certain subjects from the vicissitudes of political controversy, to place them beyond the reach of majorities and officials and to establish them as legal principles to be applied by the courts."[34] Those who recognize that the Constitution does not establish unmodified majoritarianism often talk about the "counter-majoritarian premise" of the Constitution.

Of course, the mere existence of a counter-majoritarian premise does not specify how it is to be applied, and originalists argue that it should be limited to the specific rights protected by the amendments. However, the existence of a counter-majoritarian premise, coupled with the political theory of democracy, suggests that the originalist reliance on "pure" majoritarianism as a reason for their position may not work.

2. *The Basis of Constitutional Legitimacy*

Non-originalists can also question the claim that majority ratification in the past is a valid source of majoritarian legitimacy in the present. After all, the adoption process had defects that today would be considered fatal to legitimacy:

> The drafting, adopting, or amending of the Constitution may itself have suffered from defects of democratic process which detract from its moral claims. To take an obvious example, the interests of black Americans were not adequately represented in the adoption of the Constitution of 1787 or the fourteenth amendment. Whatever moral consensus the Civil War Amendments embodied was among white male property-holders and not the populations as a whole.[35]

In addition, the ratifiers had no claim at all to represent those of us alive today, so it is unclear how their majority vote can override the will of current majorities: "We did not adopt the Constitution, and those who did are dead and gone."

Thus, in seeking a majoritarian source of legitimacy, we perhaps should look not to the vote of the drafters but rather to the popular support of the Constitution today. Since most people are not historians, that popular support may be based on the current legal understanding of the Constitution rather than on its original understanding. This assumes, of course, that the populace knows something about current constitutional judicial doctrines.

Even if part of the Constitution's legitimacy does rest on the fact that it was adopted by past majorities, this may not be the only source of its current authority. Individuals today may accept the Constitution partly because of its pedigree but partly because they think it is a *good* Constitution and therefore one worthy of continuing support. To the extent this is true, this additional source of legitimacy may not mandate abandonment of original intent, but it does support some degree of supplementation: we would want to give the Constitution a reading that is tied to its origins but that also makes it worthy of continuing allegiance.

3. *Majority Rule and the Judicial Branch*

The crux of the majoritarian argument is the incongruity in a democratic society of having major societal decisions made by non-elected

---

[34] West Virginia State Bd. of Educ. v. Barnette, 319 U.S. 624, 638 (1943).

[35] Brest, *supra* note 6, at 230.

officials like federal judges. In response, some non-originalists downplay the undemocratic nature of the judiciary. Federal judges, as a practical matter, are not removable from office, but they are subject to subtler influence by public opinion. Also, over time, new appointments tend to bring the courts into line with public opinion. As a last resort, there is the possibility of constitutional amendment. While these factors do tend to limit the divergence between public opinion and the courts, it is still clear that courts are less democratically responsive than other branches of government.

Non-originalists also point out special attributes of the judicial role that may give judges a comparative advantage in dealing with questions of principle. Among these traits are relative isolation from immediate public pressure, the requirement that all decisions be explained with reasoned opinions, and the utility of the adversary process in giving both sides a fair hearing. It is hard to assess the cumulative significance of these points, especially given the possibility that our elected officials would give more thought to matters of constitutional principle if they did not rely so much on judges to do so for them.

Although a great deal has been written about these issues, the conclusions seem fairly simple: federal courts are not as unresponsive to the public as they first appear, but they are still less democratic than other branches; and federal courts have some advantage as forums in which to decide matters of principle relating to individual rights, but perhaps not so much as many people believe. Whether the gain in principled decision-making is worth the cost in democratic responsiveness is a question not susceptible to proof one way or the other.

. . .

B. *Intentionalism*

Originalism can also be based on a broader theory of interpretation, one which has strong roots in our legal culture:

[Originalism] fits our usual conceptions of what law is and the way it works. In interpreting a statute, in order to decide whether certain private behavior is authorized or whether (and this is closer to the constitutional review situation) it conflicts with another statute, a court obviously will limit itself to a determination of the purposes and prohibitions expressed by or implicit in its language. Were a judge to announce in such a situation that he was not content with those references and intended additionally to enforce, in the name of the statute in question, those fundamental values he believed America had always stood for, we would conclude that he was not doing his job, and might even consider a call to the lunacy commission. [37]

Thus, originalism is closely linked to the Constitution's status as a legal text, and that status itself has been an important part of the argument for judicial review:

The Constitution is, among other things, a legal document, and it is on the Constitution's status as written law that justification of the practice of judicial review has largely rested. As Edwin Corwin once wrote, "The first and most obvious fact about the Constitution of the United States is that it is a document." Justice Black began his lectures on constitutional interpretation by saying, "It is of paramount

---

[37] J. Ely, *supra* note 18, at 3. *See also,* Berger, *Originalist Theories of Constitutional Interpretation,* 73 CORNELL L. REV. 350, 353 (1988) ("This is the essence of communication. It is for the writer to explain what his words mean . . . .").

importance to me that our country has a written constitution." With
words like these, contemporary constitutional interpreters hark back
to John Marshall's original argument for judicial review in *Marbury
v. Madison*, an argument permeated with reliance on the *"written-
ness"* of the Constitution. [38]

Since people often think of a document's meaning as consisting of the
author's intentions in writing it, this stress on the Constitution's status
as a written text provides strong support for originalism.

Still, while the Constitution is a text, it is a very special kind of text.
Unlike most texts, it was written by one group of people for adoption by
another, then amended over two centuries by yet other groups. Moreover,
its various authors and adopters may perhaps have intended that parts
of the text incorporate various norms outside of itself. All of this makes
it more difficult to identify a specific set of authors whose intent controls.
More fundamentally, the Constitution plays a unique role in our culture,
being not only a set of instructions but literally constitutive of our national
identity. Given that unique role, a special approach to interpretation could
well be appropriate.

Moreover, it is not clear that the meaning even of ordinary texts is to
be located in the author's intent as opposed to the reader's understanding.
Theories of interpretation are presently the subject of hot dispute among
philosophers and literary theorists, and to enter into this debate would
be far beyond my present purpose. Indeed, the complexity and subtlety
of the debate caution against any expectation that general theories of
interpretation will provide any simple means of resolving the dispute
about originalism.

As in many debates, one of the most difficult problems with assessing
originalism is deciding just what is in dispute. Some advocates of originalism make it clear that the original intent they have in mind does not
consist of a psychological state of the framers:

> Dworkin is scornful, and I think properly so, of the notion that in
> interpreting poetry or the Constitution we should seek to discern
> authorial intent as a mental fact of some sort. As to poetry, his argu-
> ment rightly holds that we would not consider an account of Shake-
> speare's mental state at the time he wrote a sonnet to be a more
> complete or better account of the sonnet than the sonnet itself.
> Dworkin would certainly disagree, as would I, with the notion that
> when we consider the Constitution we are really interested in the
> mental state of each of the persons who drew it up and ratified it.
> In this view, which we both reject, the texts of a sonnet or of the
> Constitution would be a kind of second-best; we would prefer to take
> the top off the heads of authors and framers—like soft-boiled eggs—to
> look inside for the truest account of their brain states at the moment
> that the texts were created. [40]

Yet, the author of this passage claims to champion the "attempt to
understand the Constitution according to the intention of those who
conceived it . . . ." But at this point, the precise meaning of originalism
becomes a bit murky.

On the whole, the earlier, majoritarian argument for originalism seems
stronger than the argument based on the primacy of authorial intent. The
problem is not just that the primacy of intent is disputable, but that even

[38] Grey, *The Constitution as Scripture*, 37
STAN. L. REV. 1, 14 (1984). . . .

[40] Fried, *Sonnet LXV and the "Black Ink"*

of the Framers' Intention, 100 HARV. L. REV.
751, 758–59 (1987).

attempting to define precisely what we mean by authorial intent is very difficult, even apart from the special problems of attributing a unified authorial intention to a document like the Constitution.

Moreover, even a successful theory of authorial intent might not be enough to justify originalism. After all, a general theory of interpretation must work equally well for interpreting a sonnet, the Constitution, the Bible, and a grocery list. It seems unlikely that such a theory would have decisive implications regarding the relatively subtle differences that separate originalism and anti-originalism. After all, the dispute between originalists and anti-originalists is not over the relevance of intent, on which both agree, but on specific rules for considering intent in deciding constitutional cases. There is no reason to think that the same specific rules about intent will apply to all written documents.

C. *Are There Principled Alternatives?*

One important normative argument in favor of originalism is the difficulty of specifying another principled basis for deciding cases . . . .

One suggested alternative looks to natural law or moral philosophy as a basis for judicial enforcement of individual rights. The difficulty is that our culture has no consensus on these matters:

"[A]ll theories of natural law have a singular vagueness which is both an advantage and disadvantage in the application of the theories." The advantage, one gathers, is that you can invoke natural law to support anything you want. The disadvantage is that everybody understands that.

. . .

The constitutional literature that has dominated the past thirty years has often insisted that judges, in seeking constitutional value judgments, should employ, in Alexander Bickel's words, "the method of reason familiar to the discourse of moral philosophy."

. . .

. . . The error here is one of assuming that something exists called "the method of moral philosophy" whose contours sensitive experts will agree on . . . . That is not the way things are. Some moral philosophers think utilitarianism is the answer; others feel just as strongly it is not. Some regard enforced economic redistribution as a moral imperative; others find it morally censurable . . . . There simply does not exist *a* method of moral philosophy.[42]

Similar attacks can be made on attempts to use tradition or consensus as the basis of decision-making. The American tradition is diverse, and contemporary American society contains an enormous variety of groups with strikingly different views of the world. Even the argument that the Constitution should be construed to promote the functioning of the democratic process falters in the light of the lack of agreement on any precise understanding of democracy.

As Dean Brest points out, these criticisms of non-originalist approaches are all rather similar, and all reminiscent of the attacks on originalism:

My point so far is not that any of these theories are untenable, but that all are vulnerable to similar criticisms based on their indeterminacy, manipulability, and, ultimately, their reliance on judicial value judgments that cannot be "objectively" derived from text, history,

---

[42] J. Ely, *supra* note 18, at 50–58.

consensus, natural rights, or any other source. No theory of constitutional adjudication can defend itself against self-scrutiny . . . .[43]

Thus, both originalists and anti-originalists seem to be highly effective in critiquing each others' theories. Perhaps the lesson is that the standards they set are inherently unattainable. The real problem may be that both sides have demanded too much. We may have to be content with an approach to constitutional law that leaves some room for judicial discretion while attempting to channel that discretion. In other words, the real problem may not be that originalism is less desirable than some other global theory of constitutional law, but that no global theory can work. If so, we might do better to abandon the attempt to create a theory of constitutional interpretation, and get on with the business of actually interpreting the Constitution. Perhaps, in other words, constitutional interpretation is best thought of as an activity that one can do well or poorly, rather than as an application of some explicit general theory.

Farber concludes with a brief statement of his own view, in which he rejects the strong originalist view "that all constitutional issues should be decided on the basis of original intent" because of several difficulties reflected in the earlier parts of the article, which make it "highly unlikely that original intent can provide an adequate basis for *all* constitutional decision."[2] He advocates instead drawing on multiple sources, including "judicial precedents, American traditions, and contemporary social values" as well as original intention,[3] an approach he describes as "pragmatic constitutionalism."[4] He suggests that the differences between his approach and moderate forms of originalism are not great, although he would not invariably treat original intent as binding in open cases—depending on the strength of other factors.[5]

Perhaps because it appeared not long before the publication of Farber's survey, a major article on originalism by University of Connecticut law professor Richard S. Kay received only brief mention in Farber's piece.[6] In that article, Kay attempted "not to make a complete affirmative case for original intentions adjudication,"[7] but to provide responses to three major reasons given for rejecting that approach. Those reasons are that adherence to the original intentions is (1) impossible either in the sense that the historical sources are inevitably indeterminate or in the sense that "it's too hard" to do well because of numerous practical difficulties;[8] (2) self-contradictory "because the enactors themselves did not want their intentions to govern judicial exposition on the lawfulness of certain governmental action";[9] or (3) wrong because it "makes for bad government and bad law."[10]

Kay defends originalism against these charges, concluding first that some difficulty and uncertainty do not add up to impossibility or complete indeterminacy, and that original intentions adjudication holds out the possibility of

---

[43] Brest, *The Fundamental Rights Controversy: The Essential Contradictions of Normative Constitutional Scholarship,* 90 YALE L.J. 1063, 1096 (1981).

[2] Daniel Farber, *The Originalism Debate: A Guide for the Perplexed,* 49 OHIO ST. L.J. 1085, 1104 (1989).

[3] *Id.*

[4] *Id.* at 1105.

[5] *Id.* at 1106.

[6] Richard Kay, *Adherence to the Original Intentions in Constitutional Adjudication: Three Objections and Responses,* 82 Nw. U. L. REV. 226 (1988).

[7] *Id.* at 229.

[8] *Id.* at 243.

[9] *Id.* at 259.

[10] *Id.* at 284.

more stable and impersonal rules. Second, dealing with the view that "the interpretive intentions of the enactors ought to control constitutional interpretation and that those intentions were that substantive intentions should not control,"[11] Kay finds the case made for that position so far to be unpersuasive in light of historical practices, the framers' care in choice of language, and the emphasis on written rules to "fix the limits of proper governmental action."[12]

Finally, regarding the "it's wrong" objection as "the most potent" of the three he treats,[13] Kay concedes that one's view "depends on personal judgments ultimately not susceptible to rational resolution."[14] He recognizes that the "choice of following or rejecting the original intentions is necessarily not a legal choice, but a moral and political one."[15] That choice, further, cannot be made in isolation but must involve a comparison of original intentions adjudication with other approaches. Kay argues that the originalism approach is "about as stable and objective as human beings can contrive while still working with a constitution sufficiently complex to be a workable instrument of government."[16] He defends it against the objection of excessive rigidity by pointing to the values of stability and clarity, and to the compatibility of originalist adjudication with change through democratic processes. He concludes that we are likely to continue to disagree about the desirability of adhering to original intentions because we give different weights to multiple conflicting values and differ "on the kinds of chances we are willing to take in living together in society."[17]

§ 4.02   The Appropriate Levels of Generality

A recurrent issue in the use of constitutional text and history, mentioned several times in Farber's article, deserves emphasis by treatment in a separate section here: In the currently most common terminology, at what "level (or levels) of generality" should courts frame a constitutional norm or the purposes that guide its interpretation? One can readily imagine questionably narrow or meaninglessly broad formulations, such as that the equal protection clause was meant solely to ban state discrimination against African Americans (even though its language is general and the framers were aware of other racial groups that were subject to discriminatory legislation) or that it was meant to promote the general welfare (which would let the courts read almost anything into the clause). Some formulations that span a broad intermediate range, from the clause's being meant to ban racial discrimination to its outlawing irrational or especially objectionable distinctions, are likely to seem more sensible—but even then may leave room for argument about the appropriate level(s) of generality at which a norm should be articulated as a key step in the process of deciding whether a law or practice violates it.

Over two decades ago Professor Ronald Dworkin, now of New York University and Oxford University, stated this issue in an early form. He distinguished between a constitution-framer's specific "conception" such as the

---

[11] *Id.*

[12] *Id.* at 281.

[13] *Id.* at 284.

[14] *Id.* at 229.

[15] *Id.* at 285.

[16] *Id.* at 287.

[17] *Id.* at 292.

unfairness of a particular practice and the broader "concept" of fairness (or equality, or whatever) that may fit best with the general language used in many constitutional clauses, such as "due process" and "cruel and unusual punishment."[18] He argued that, at least when framers chose general language, later generations are not limited to the framers' specific conceptions but may work out their own applications of the broader concepts the framers enacted—even if the applications might go beyond what the framers could have contemplated.[19]

This issue of the "level of generality" at which to articulate a constitutional norm has achieved prominence in some Supreme Court opinions, perhaps as an offshoot of debates over originalism and the judicial role. Justice Scalia, joined in this respect only by Chief Justice Rehnquist, argued for a narrow approach in a plurality opinion in *Michael H. v. Gerald D.*,[20] involving a challenge to the limits on rebuttability of a state law presumption of paternity of a child born to a married woman living with her husband:

> We refer to the most specific level at which a relevant tradition protecting, or denying protection to, the asserted right can be identified. If, for example, there were no societal tradition, either way, regarding the rights of the natural father of a child adulterously conceived, we would have to consult, and (if possible) reason from, the traditions regarding natural fathers in general. But there is such a more specific tradition, and it unqualifiedly denies protection to such a parent.[21]

In support of this view, Justice Scalia urged that reliance on general traditions provides guidance so imprecise as to "permit judges to dictate rather than discern the society's views."[22] Referring to disagreement in other opinions that took broader views over the proper result in the case, he spoke of the need "to adopt the most specific tradition as the point of reference" in order to avoid "arbitrary decisionmaking."[23] "Although assuredly having the virtue (if it be that) of leaving judges free to decide as they think best when the unanticipated occurs, a rule of law that binds neither by text nor by any particular, identifiable tradition is no rule of law at all."[24]

Justice O'Connor, joined by Justice Kennedy, concurred in all but the just-quoted footnote of Justice Scalia's opinion. She pointed to past decisions inconsistent with his approach,[25] and declined to "foreclose the unanticipated by the prior imposition of a single mode of historical analysis."[26]

In dissent, Justice Brennan argued:[27]

> Today's plurality . . . does not ask whether parenthood is an interest that historically has received our attention and protection; the answer to that question is too clear for dispute. Instead, the plurality asks whether the specific variety of parenthood under consideration—a natural father's relationship with a child whose mother is married to another man—has enjoyed such protection.

---

[18] RONALD DWORKIN, TAKING RIGHTS SERIOUSLY 134–35 (1977).

[19] *Id.* at 135–36.

[20] 491 U.S. 110, 109 S. Ct. 2333, 105 L. Ed. 2d 91 (1989).

[21] *Id.* at 127–128 n.6.

[22] *Id.*

[23] *Id.*

[24] *Id.*

[25] *Id.* at 132 (O'Connor, J., concurring in part).

[26] *Id.*

[27] *Id.* at 139–41 (Brennan, J., dissenting)

If we had looked to tradition with such specificity in past cases, many a decision would have reached a different result . . . .

The plurality's interpretive method . . . ignores the good reasons for limiting the role of "tradition" in interpreting the Constitution's deliberately capacious language. In the plurality's constitutional universe . . . our task is simply to identify a rule denying the asserted interest and not to ask whether the basis for that rule—which is the true reflection of the values undergirding it—has changed too often or too recently to call the rule embodying that rationale a "tradition." . . . [B]y suggesting that our sole function is to "*discern* the society's views," the plurality acts as if the only purpose of the Due Process Clause is to confirm the importance of interests already protected by a majority of the States. Transforming the protection afforded by the Due Process Clause into a redundancy mocks those who, with care and purpose, wrote the Fourteenth Amendment.

In construing the Fourteenth Amendment to offer shelter only to those interests specifically protected by historical practice, moreover, the plurality ignores the kind of society in which our Constitution exists. We are not an assimilative, homogeneous society, but a facilitative, pluralistic one, in which we must be willing to abide someone else's unfamiliar or even repellant practice because the same tolerant impulse protects our own idiosyncracies. Even if we can agree . . . that "family" and "parenthood" are part of the good life, it is absurd to assume that we can agree on the content of those terms and destructive to pretend that we do. In a community such as ours, "liberty" must include the freedom not to conform. The plurality today squashes this freedom by requiring specific approval from history before protecting anything in the name of liberty.

For Judge Bork's description of the views expressed in the case, and his argument that even Justice Scalia's position "assumes an illegitimate power," articulating a limitation that "will prove no restriction at all when there is only a general, unfocused tradition to be found," see ROBERT BORK, THE TEMPTING OF AMERICA: THE POLITICAL SEDUCTION OF THE LAW 235–40 (1989).

The most detailed response to the views of Justice Scalia and Judge Bork came in a book by Professor Laurence Tribe of Harvard Law School and Columbia law professor Michael Dorf. We quote here only their summary of their arguments. LAURENCE TRIBE & MICHAEL C. DORF, ON READING THE CONSTITUTION 98 (1991):[28]

[W]e argue that Justice Scalia's claim is false on [three] grounds: first, . . . the extraction of fundamental rights from societal traditions is no more value-neutral than is the extraction of fundamental rights from legal precedent; second, . . . there is no universal metric of specificity against which to measure an asserted right; and third, . . . even if Justice Scalia's program were workable, it would achieve a semblance of judicial neutrality only at the unacceptably high cost of near-complete abdication of the judicial responsibility to protect individual rights . . . .

§ 4.03   Originalism Debates in the 1990s

Professor Farber's survey provides an excellent overview of issues that remain basic to the continuing controversies over the role of history and original intent in constitutional interpretation. University of Virginia law professor

---

[28] Reprinted by permission of Harvard University Press, Cambridge, Mass. Copyright © 1991 by the President and Fellows of Harvard College.

Michael Klarman provides a similarly excellent summary of major contributions to these debates in the 1990s, along with his own view. Michael J. Klarman, *Antifidelity,* 70 S. CAL. L. REV. 381, 381–83, 387–93, 394–96, 398–99, 400–01, 402–03, 404–15 (1997):[29]

Constitutional scholars have devoted a great deal of attention in recent years to the question of how best to show fidelity to the Constitution. A more basic issue has elicited relatively little interest: Does the Constitution deserve our fidelity at all? The answer to that more fundamental question seems clear, if counterintuitive: Of course not. Why would one think, presumptively, that Framers who lived two hundred years ago, inhabited a radically different world, and possessed radically different ideas would have anything useful to say about how we should govern ourselves today? This is the famous dead-hand problem of constitutionalism: Why should today's generation be ruled from the grave?

Among constitutional originalists, who claim the purest form of fidelity to the Constitution, few even bother to confront this difficulty. Most originalists simply assert that since the Constitution is law, of course it must bind. Yet this argument is entirely circular; the question is whether we ought to treat the Constitution, with its attendant dead-hand difficulty, as binding law. As more thoughtful originalists and originalism's critics have observed, the decision to treat the Constitution as binding requires justification in the form of a "preconstitutional" rule—that is, a principle of political philosophy that justifies our obedience to the Constitution.[4] The document itself cannot, as a simple matter of logic, supply such a principle.

When originalists bother to offer a justification for their interpretive methodology, it tends to be a comparative one: Originalism is superior to its most plausible alternative, which is some form of relatively uncabined judicial value creation.[5] In other words, originalists often assert that it is antidemocratic for unelected, remotely accountable judges to invalidate democratically-enacted legislation on the basis of their own subjective value judgments.[6] But, one might retort, it is equally antidemocratic for a contemporary majority to be governed by values enshrined in the Constitution over two hundred years ago. That is, constitutional originalists have simply substituted a dead-hand problem for a judicial subjectivity problem. Both interpretive methodologies are susceptible to the charge of being antimajoritarian.

Are there any interpretive approaches that can avoid both the dead-hand problem and the judicial subjectivity problem? One solution might be simply to reject constitutionalism altogether. This approach does solve both problems simultaneously, by empowering contemporary majorities to govern themselves through the political process. But the anticonstitutionalist approach has obvious (or at least apparent) costs, which most scholars seem unwilling to bear. Those who believe either that judicial review is critical to the protection of individual rights or that legislatures are themselves pervasively antimajoritarian (for public choice reasons) are loath to embrace the anticonstitutionalist position. . . . In this essay I consider, and criticize, those scholarly strategies that seek intermediate

---

[29] Copyright © 1997 by the Southern California Law Review. Reprinted with permission.

[4] *See* Richard S. Kay, *Preconstitutional Rules,* 42 OHIO ST. L.J. 187, 194–95 (1981).

[5] *See, e.g.,* . . . Antonin Scalia, *Originalism: The Lesser Evil,* 57 U. CIN. L. REV. 849 (1989).

[6] . . . . *See also* David A. Strauss, *Common Law Constitutional Interpretation,* 63 U. CHI. L. REV. 877, 879 (1996) (suggesting that originalism owes its prominence as an interpretive theory not to its plausibility, but rather to the fear that the alternative is "anything goes").

solutions—that is, ameliorating the dead-hand problem while maintaining fidelity to the Constitution.

. . . As I already have noted, the Framers are not us. Indeed, in most ways the Framers do not even remotely resemble us, and it is not clear that they have a great deal of relevance to say about how we should govern ourselves today. . . .

. . . Given the vast gulf separating [the Framers] from us, is it clear that they have much of relevance to say about how we should govern ourselves today?

Nor does the possibility of securing constitutional amendments solve this enormous dead-hand problem, as some originalists have claimed. Article V of the Constitution specifies two paths for amendment, but both require supermajorities for success. Supermajority requirements necessarily privilege the status quo; they are antimajoritarian and difficult to reconcile with democratic premises. On numerous occasions in American history, the will of national majorities has been frustrated by their inability to satisfy the supermajority requirements of Article V. One thinks, for example, of the child labor amendment in the 1920s and 1930s, the school prayer amendment since the 1960s, the Equal Rights Amendment in the 1970s and 1980s, and the balanced budget and flag burning amendments in the 1990s. The dead-hand problem of constitutionalism is not solved by an amendment mechanism biased in favor of the status quo through supermajority requirements.

This essay will canvass, and criticize, the three leading scholarly "solutions" to the dead-hand problem of constitutionalism. These are the notions that (1) the Founding possesses some special normativity which justifies prioritizing that era's "constitutional politics" over the ordinary politics of today; (2) the Constitution has been amended in the twentieth century by non-Article V means, thus freeing us to a greater extent than is commonly supposed of dead-hand rule; and (3) the Constitution is a "living" document, fidelity to which requires "translating" Founding texts into the altered contexts of today.

. . . [T]he shared objective of all of these approaches is to avoid (or at least to ameliorate) dead-hand rule without simultaneously exacerbating the countermajoritarian problem posed by uncabined judicial review. That is, these solutions all seek, though in different ways, to locate intermediate points on the spectrum between dead-hand rule and judicial rule. None of them openly advocates entrusting constitutional decisionmaking to the unfettered discretion of unelected, remotely accountable judges. Rather, all three approaches would restrict courts to interpreting the Framers' values, though allowing for adjustments that putatively enable circumvention of the dead-hand problem of a strict originalist methodology.

The first solution is to ascribe some special normativity to the Founding (and any other "constitutional moments")—some quality that justifies privileging its values over those subscribed to by a contemporary popular majority. This is a very old strategy indeed; Alexander Hamilton deployed a version of it in FEDERALIST NO. 78, as did Chief Justice John Marshall in *Marbury v. Madison*. The leading candidates for this distinguishing normative criterion seem to be the Framers' greater wisdom, their greater virtue, and the unusual degree of popular mobilization that characterizes an exercise in "constitutional politics" (and, specifically, the Founding).

As to the Founders' greater wisdom, it may be conceded that James Madison, James Wilson, Alexander Hamilton, and company were an exceedingly talented bunch. Some might deny that their talents exceeded those of today's politicians, though I would not. But the real question is whether their greater wisdom offsets their ideological blinders, limited imaginations, and mistaken factual premises. No matter how smart the Framers were, they still held slaves and subordinated women; they could not dream of space travel, nuclear weapons, and computer technology; and they wrongly assumed basic demographic, political, and other facts about the world. Greater wisdom notwithstanding, it is hard to justify binding us to the Founders' constitutional commitments, given all the handicaps under which they operated.

Bruce Ackerman argues that the Founding and other "constitutional moments" warrant special deference because of the temporary suspension of self-interest that characterizes them. Only on these rare occasions, Ackerman suggests, do citizens temporarily subordinate their selfish interests to the "rights of citizens and the permanent interests of the community."[36] Ackerman's approach is subject to several objections. First, he offers no justification for privileging disinterest over self-interest. Since Ackerman rejects "rights foundationalism" (the notion of objective standards of right and wrong), it is unclear how he can justify this prioritization of values. Even if he could, however, it still would not be obvious how to balance the claims of (temporally distant) *constitutional* politics against the claims of *recent* (but "ordinary") political decisionmaking. Perhaps most significantly, Ackerman's account of the Founding bears little resemblance to historical reality. Ackerman accepts the Founders' (self-interested) pretensions to disinterestedness. Most historians, though, have been considerably more cynical, describing in rich detail the self-interested political horsetrading that characterized the constitutional convention. . . .

For Ackerman, constitutional politics is also characterized by the mass mobilization of popular opinion. One could quibble with Ackerman on the facts here as well—voter turnout in elections for the state ratifying conventions that approved the Constitution was not significantly higher than for ordinary elections. The more fundamental objection is conceptual: Ackerman is mistaken in thinking that special normativity flows from mass mobilization. The Nazi movement in Germany in the 1930s and the second Ku Klux Klan movement in America in the 1920s were characterized by mass popular mobilization as well. Did they thereby qualify as constitutional moments? Thus, even if Ackerman is right that the American citizenry was highly mobilized politically at the time of the Founding, it is unclear why we should be influenced by that fact today if we nonetheless believe that the Founders made wrong decisions.

A second proffered solution to the dead-hand problem is to show that the Constitution has been amended more often and more recently than we tend to think, thus significantly ameliorating the dead-hand problem of eighteenth-century rule in the late twentieth century. Specifically, it is plausible to believe that the largest of all dead-hand problems is the irreconcilability of the original Constitution and the modern welfare state. If the constitutionality of Franklin Roosevelt's New Deal is to be judged by a "horse and buggy" era's conception of interstate commerce, then the dead hand rules with a vengeance. Ackerman's solution is to show that Americans did in fact amend the Constitution in 1936–1937 to legitimize the modern regulatory state, though they did so without satisfying Article V's formal requirements for amendment.

While Ackerman is right that 1930s America should not be constrained by eighteenth-century conceptions of limited national power, his proffered

---

[36] *See* [Bruce Ackerman, WE THE PEOPLE 240 (1991)] . . . .

theory of non-Article V amendments (which is both descriptive and prescriptive) is fraught with difficulty. Most basically, Ackerman's account has a fictive quality to it. No contemporaries believed that the Constitution had actually been amended in 1936–1937; indeed President Roosevelt consciously rejected the idea of pursuing constitutional amendments because they were too time-consuming. Nor do the historical events of 1936–1937 neatly fit Ackerman's criteria for non-Article V amendments. In Ackerman's view, such amendments occur through a process that includes a proposal for constitutional change, an interbranch standoff when that proposal encounters resistance from defenders of the old order, a critical election at which the People choose between the crystallized constitutional alternatives, and subsequent acquiescence in the People's expressed will by the initially recalcitrant branch. Yet in the "critical election" of 1936, which Ackerman treats as the People's decisive verdict in favor of constitutional change, FDR consciously chose, against his advisors' recommendations, to say almost nothing about the Court issue. How can one derive a mandate on an issue from an election in which that issue went unaddressed? Moreover, it is debatable whether a "switch-in-time," which Ackerman treats as the initially recalcitrant Court's subsequent acquiescence in constitutional change, actually took place. Constitutional historians recently have raised credible doubts about the extent to which the swing justices, Hughes and Roberts, were influenced by political considerations in their 1937 votes.

More generally, the entire notion of non-Article V amendments is problematic for rule-of-recognition reasons. How is one to determine whether interbranch resistance is sufficient to crystallize the alternatives between which the electorate is to choose? What mandate is one to infer from a presidential election contested on a wide array of issues? How does one determine whether the initially resistant branch has subsequently acquiesced in the People's mandate? Finally, even setting aside these empirical and conceptual flaws in Ackerman's scheme, one still must wonder to what extent he has solved the dead-hand problem. If Ackerman is right, then the New Deal has been successfully constitutionalized, but in other areas of life the dead hand of the past continues to rule. While Ackerman's alternative amendment scheme does ameliorate the status-quo-biasing effect of Article V's supermajority requirements, he explicitly demands more than simple majority support for a non-Article V amendment. To that extent, Ackerman's regime still unjustifiably privileges the dead hand of the past.

. . .

Let us turn our attention now to the third, and most prevalent, proffered solution to the dead-hand problem. Most scholars and justices, searching for a middle ground between the polar positions of dead-hand rule and uncabined judicial subjectivity, have embraced some version of the living Constitution. The concept has been variously described as "a constitution intended to endure for ages to come, and, consequently, to be adapted to the various *crises* of human affairs," a "living Constitution," "evolving standards of decency," "multi-generational synthesis," "moderate originalism," or "soft originalism." Recently, Larry Lessig has given this old notion new currency and bestowed upon it a fancier title: "translation."[73] However labeled, the idea is that one can avoid the vices of both dead-hand control and uncabined judicial subjectivity by "translating" the Framers' concepts into modern circumstances. The obvious problem with the enterprise is one of indeterminacy—translating old

---

[73] Lawrence Lessig, *Fidelity in Translation*,
71 Tex. L. Rev. 1165, 1172 (1993) . . . .

concepts into modern contexts inevitably implicates the very sort of unconstrained judicial subjectivity that translation's proponents seek to avoid. In the remainder of this paper, I hope to demonstrate that this translation enterprise is quite hopeless. While translation reveals a good deal about the political preferences of the translator, it tells us nothing at all about how the Framers would have solved our problems had they shared our circumstances.

Interestingly, the first problem with translation is one of the dead hand revisited. If we are translating old constitutional concepts to accommodate new circumstances, the dead-hand problem persists because it is always possible for an unconstrained modern decisionmaker to simply conclude that the old concept has outlived its usefulness. One can put the same point another way: Translators have selected an arbitrarily low level of generality at which to translate. They adjust the Framers' constitutional commitments to reflect changed circumstances, but fail to ask whether the Framers would have remained committed to the same concepts had they been aware of future circumstances. Most translators criticize Justice Scalia and Judge Bork for selecting an arbitrarily low level of generality at which to describe the Framers' intentions—"conceptions" rather than "concepts," to use Dworkin's terminology—but they themselves are subject to precisely the same objection: Perhaps the Framers would not have remained committed to certain concepts had they foreseen relevant changed circumstances.

. . .

Now let us set aside this dead-hand objection to the translation of old concepts. Suppose instead there is agreement that an old concept warrants translation to reflect changed circumstances, rather than repudiation. For example, suppose that we have concluded that changed material circumstances justify an expansion of the national government's power, but not the abandonment of all federalism constraints. A second-order question immediately arises for the translator: Does the accommodation to changed circumstances in one context warrant making a responsive adjustment in another? Some have labeled this notion of compensating adjustments a constitutional theory of the "second best," or, alternatively, "constitutional damage control." It is really just another variation of the translation question: Would the Framers have intended that a compensating adjustment be made to reflect the initial accommodation to changed circumstances? [An] example[] should both make the issue concrete and reveal the debilitating indeterminacy problems that compensating adjustments raise.

[C]onsider Randy Barnett's response to the exponential growth in national government power during the twentieth century.[88] Barnett does not admire this development, but he grimly acknowledges the reality that there is no going back. . . . Barnett does not advocate judicial invalidation of the modern welfare state. Rather he asks courts to make a compensating adjustment for the relative demise of federalism constraints on the national government: Courts should expand individual rights protections by supplying a robust interpretation of the Bill of Rights, including the Ninth Amendment. Greater governmental regulatory power, in Barnett's view, warrants an expansion of individual rights guarantees to constrain that power.

. . .

---

[88] *See* [Randy Barnett, *Reconceiving the Ninth Amendment,* 74 CORNELL L. REV. 1, 25–26 (1988)].

All of this sounds very plausible indeed. The problem, though, is that one could argue precisely the opposite position from Barnett . . . with equal plausibility. . . . Presumably, American society and American courts grew increasingly tolerant of broad national power in the twentieth century because of a widely perceived need for such power. No doubt this had something to do with the expansion of national and international markets, the transportation and communications revolutions, the country's growing international role, the increased mobility of the American population, the bad name that states rights federalism acquired as a result of secession and civil war, and the reduced fear of distant national government felt by Americans as that government became less distant through advances in communication and transportation and as generations passed without that government foisting an oppressive monarchy upon the People (as many Anti-Federalists had predicted it would).

Yet, if national power expanded to meet changing reality, perhaps this is a good argument for *not* making any compensating adjustment. The creation of new individual rights guarantees to check expanded national power would be, to some extent, removing with one hand what had just been granted with the other. I do not mean to suggest that compensating adjustments are always a bad idea because they defeat the purpose of the initial accommodation. But sometimes they are. How one resolves this tension depends on one's evaluation of the competing virtues and vices of expanded national power, as well as the intensity of one's commitment to individual liberty. Barnett, because of his strong libertarian bent, is suspicious of a powerful national government and wishes to check it. Many of the Founders shared Barnett's concern that a distant government is potentially oppressive, but of course they did not share our circumstances (which arguably make expanded national power necessary). The translation question is whether the Framers, placed in our current circumstances, would continue to share Barnett's strong aversion to expansive national power. Since some of us do today, probably some of them would as well. But almost certainly some others would not, since some of us do not. There is absolutely no way to tell for sure. Indeed, when we ask the question in these terms we are misleading ourselves: What we really are asking is what do *we* think about expansive national power, not what would the Framers have thought given our circumstances.

. . .

The two difficulties with translation discussed thus far—the questions of whether to repudiate old concepts altogether and when to make compensating adjustments—are simply specific illustrations of the enterprise's two most daunting challenges. First, when translating, how do we know which circumstances to hold constant and which to vary—that is, when asking what the Framers would have done under modern circumstances, which aspects of their world do we vary and which do we leave in place? Second, assuming we can answer this question of which changed circumstances are relevant to the translation, how do we calculate what the Founders would have done in light of those changes? That is, in which direction and to what extent do changed circumstances cut?

Consider first the question of which changed circumstances to incorporate into the translation. A rather large problem immediately presents itself: If we treat *all* changed circumstances as relevant variables, then we simply will have converted the Framers into us, and asking how they would resolve a problem is no different from asking how we ourselves would resolve it. Yet a decision to treat some changed circumstances as variables and others as constants seems entirely arbitrary. For example, it is wholly uncontroversial to vary the existing state of technology when translating the congressional power to regulate interstate commerce. I am aware of nobody who argues that Congress cannot regulate airplanes because they did not exist when the Constitution was adopted; airplanes are the modern analogue of ships, so certainly Congress can regulate their interstate movement. Yet in translating Congress's Commerce Clause power, it is no less justifiable to treat as relevant variables all of the changed federalism circumstances noted above—for example, the modern proliferation of national and international markets, the transportation and communications revolutions, and so forth.

If we treat all of these changed circumstances as relevant variables, and ask how the Framers would have solved today's problems in light of today's circumstances, surely the answer is that they would have behaved pretty much as we do, which is to say that they would have disagreed among themselves about how to weigh the competing virtues and vices of broad national regulatory authority. The changed circumstances itemized above might have made the Framers more receptive toward expansive national power—after all, these changes have had precisely this effect on many persons in the twentieth century, which is why the Supreme Court until recently had essentially vacated the federalism field. On the other hand, these changed circumstances might not have greatly influenced the Framers' views about federalism—after all, many people today oppose expansive national power, notwithstanding these transformations. When we ask how the Framers would have regarded the vast accretions to national regulatory authority in light of *all* the changed circumstances, we're really just asking what do *we* think about the issue. We can derive a different answer than our own from the Framers only by ignoring some of the changed circumstances—treating them as constants rather than as variables. That choice, however, would be utterly lacking in principled justification.

. . .

Let us move on now to the next question: Even if we can agree upon which changed circumstances are relevant to a translation, how are we to know in which direction they cut? Consider Congress' power to raise armies and the question of whether this includes the power of conscription. A surprisingly strong argument can be made that the Framers in 1787 would not have understood the power to raise armies to include the power to conscript soldiers (as opposed to offering inducements to volunteers). There was still tremendous opposition to standing armies in 1787. The Framers successfully overcame that opposition, but only because of the perception that potentially oppressive congressional purposes would be checked by the implicit requirement that Congress hire volunteers, rather than conscripting unwilling citizens.

Of course, this original understanding of Congress' limited power to raise armies did not contemplate a world in which million-member forces would be required to meet America's vastly expanded international obligations (for example, the number of men in uniform during World War II was more than three times the *entire nation's population* at the time of the Founding). Nor could this restrictive original understanding foresee two hundred years of subsequent history in which the presence of a standing army had resulted in neither the institution of a monarchy nor any obvious suppression of the People's liberties (as the Anti-Federalists had predicted it would). In light of these changed circumstances, does fidelity to the Framers' intentions require that conscription now be permitted?

I submit that it is impossible to answer this question without taking a view on the underlying merits, since the relevant changed circumstances plausibly can be understood to cut in either direction. Specifically, the need to fight foreign wars on a large scale arguably renders military conscription essential. It also arguably renders conscription more problematic, since the success of foreign wars, which usually are less obviously essential to the nation's survival, is especially dependent upon popular support, the absence of which conscription may partially obscure. Similarly, reasonable people may disagree about whether contemporary society's reduced fear of standing armies counsels in favor of or against translating the Framers' original intentions to permit conscription. Conscription may seem to be less threatening where standing armies are thought to pose less of a danger, and thus perhaps the Framers' translated intentions would permit conscription today. On the other hand, reduced fear is likely to yield reduced vigilance; thus perhaps conscription should be forbidden in an era in which citizens are insufficiently zealous in safeguarding their liberties from an invasive government. One cannot hope to resolve this question without taking a view on the merits as to what international role the nation should play, how suspicious of the national government citizens should be, how substantial a violation of individual freedom conscription is, and so forth. This debate has nothing to do with translating the Framers' views and everything to do with our own substantive disagreements.

Yet even if we could agree on which changed circumstances are relevant and in which direction they cut, we still would need to figure out whether the extent of the change has been sufficient to justify a translation. For example, as we shall see momentarily, Michael McConnell argues that while education may not have been understood to be a civil right at the time of the Fourteenth Amendment's enactment, changed circumstances plainly had made it such by the time of *Brown,* and probably by the time of *Plessy v. Ferguson.* [110] Similarly, Larry Lessig argues that by the 1930s changed circumstances—both in conceptions of the nature of law and in political and social variables, the most notable of which was the Great Depression—justified the Supreme Court's repudiation of the *Lochner* era's commitment to laissez-faire economics and limited national government power.

Both McConnell's and Lessig's empirical claims about changed circumstances seem convincing. Education plainly occupies a very different place in American life in the twentieth century than it did in 1868, and the pathologies of a complex urban, industrial society plainly reduced the allure of laissez-faire economics and increased support for national government regulation by the 1930s. Yet a court charged with the complex task of translating the Framers' intentions needs to know more than the general direction of changing circumstances; it needs to identify with precision the point at which those changes have become sufficient to justify a translation. Thus, it is one thing for scholars engaged in positive constitutional theory to account for *West Coast Hotel Co. v. Parrish* and *NLRB v. Jones & Laughlin Steel Corp.* in terms of translation. It is quite another to *prescribe* such a task for courts exercising the judicial review power.

At any particular point in time, reasonable people will disagree about whether the change in circumstances has been sufficient to justify a translation of the Framers' intentions. As late as 1937, the Four Horsemen still had not spotted sufficient change in circumstances to justify a translation of laissez-faire and federalism concepts. On the other hand, as early as 1905–1910, some justices and scholars already had identified

---

[110] 163 U.S. 537 (1896). *See* [Michael W. McConnell, *Originalism and the Desegregation Decisions,* 81 VA. L. REV. 947, 1103–04 (1995)].

sufficient change to warrant a translation. Similarly, the Supreme Court in 1972 and 1973 probably calculated that changed circumstances were sufficient to justify translating Fourteenth Amendment concepts to prohibit the death penalty and most abortion restrictions. Subsequent history in these two areas would seem to confirm the difficulty of contemporaneously identifying the sufficiency and permanency of changed circumstances.

Furthermore, it is difficult to believe that one's view of the sufficiency of changed circumstances does not reflect, to a substantial degree, one's normative commitments. The Four Horsemen, for example, would have been unconvinced of the sufficiency of changed circumstances in 1937, largely because they liked things better the old way. Measuring the extent of changed circumstances and assessing whether they are sufficient to justify a translation are tasks certain to yield controverted answers. One can phrase this in terms of translation—would the Framers have considered the changed circumstances sufficient to justify altering their constitutional commitments? But since the answer to this question is so obviously indeterminate, it appears that the real ground of controversy is over what we think should be done, rather than over what the Framers would have done in our changed circumstances.

It may be useful at this point to reconsider, though from an opposite angle, the question of the relevance of changed circumstances—that is, which circumstances to treat as variables and which as constants in translating the Framers' intentions. I believe that determining the appropriate level of generality at which to describe the Framers' intentions with regard to a particular constitutional provision raises precisely the same question as assessing the relevancy of particular changed circumstances to a translation. This is because specifying a particular level of generality determines which changed circumstances are relevant to the translation (to be treated as variables) and which are not (to be treated as constants). Thus understood, the enterprise of translation is fundamentally about abstracting from the Framers' more specific intentions. Yet there are an infinite number of ways in which one can abstract from specific intentions. The intractable problem is knowing at which level of generality to stop. It turns out, unfortunately, that there exists no principled basis for choosing one resting point over another. Thus, the level of generality we choose tells us a great deal about ourselves, but nothing at all about the Framers.

Consider in this regard Michael McConnell's recent heroic effort to supply an originalist justification for the Supreme Court's decision in *Brown*. In general, McConnell argues that the Fourteenth Amendment's drafters intended to bar school segregation. Yet he concedes at one point that perhaps they only intended to guarantee equality—which they understood, McConnell argues, to require nonsegregation rather than separate but equal—with regard to civil rights, which public education arguably did not qualify as a civil right in 1866–1868. By 1954, though, public education plainly qualified as a civil right, given its increased importance in American life, its guaranteed status in most state constitutions, and its mandatory nature under compulsory attendance laws. Thus, McConnell concludes, the Court in *Brown* was right to bar state-mandated racial segregation in public schools as a denial of equality with regard to civil rights.

McConnell's strategy is essentially one of translation, although he proceeds from an opposite angle. Rather than beginning with changed circumstances and then assessing their relevance to translating the Framers' intentions, McConnell begins by identifying the appropriate level of generality at which to describe the Framers' intentions and then assesses the relevance of changed circumstances. In describing the intentions of the Fourteenth Amendment's drafters, McConnell rejects the most specific level of generality—that they intended to bar racial discrimination with regard to contract, property, court access, and so forth. Rather, he abstracts from these specific intentions to a general ban on racial discrimination with regard to civil rights.

There is nothing wrong with this argument; the Framers' intentions are accurately described at either level of generality. The problem is that McConnell has picked an arbitrary stopping point in this exercise of ratcheting up the level of generality at which one describes the Framers' intentions. If one describes their intentions with regard to rights at a general level, why not do the same with regard to groups or with regard to the meaning of equality? Concretely, just as one can accurately describe the intention of the Fourteenth Amendment's Framers specifically as protecting contract rights and generally as protecting civil rights, so can one accurately describe their intention as protecting the rights of blacks specifically and of an historically oppressed group generally. If the nature of "civil rights" is subject to translation over time, why not the nature of "oppressed groups"?

The same can be said about the notion of equality that the Framers intended to guarantee in the Fourteenth Amendment. If dominant understandings of "civil rights" and "oppressed groups" can change over time, why not notions of "equality"? It may be that McConnell is correct that "equality" in 1868 meant "nonsegregation" rather than "separate but equal." But perhaps by 1900 changed circumstances justified a translation of the concept that would permit a separate-but-equal doctrine. Is it possible that McConnell selects the level of abstraction he does because he admires *Brown,* abhors *Plessy,* and (one may infer) does not have much truck with either *United States v. Virginia* [125] or *Romer v. Evans?* [126] The level of abstraction he chooses tells us a good deal about Professor McConnell's political preferences, but nothing at all about how the Framers would have resolved difficult contemporary questions of sex discrimination and gay rights in light of today's changed circumstances.

. . .

The whole point of "translation," "the living Constitution," "soft originalism," or whatever snazzy term one wishes to affix to the enterprise, is to enable the Framers to supply solutions to our problems while avoiding the constricting dead hand of the past. Yet it turns out on reflection that translation accomplishes neither of these objectives: it does not eliminate the dead-hand problem (because it is *past* concepts that are being translated), nor does it supply the *Framers'* answers to our problems (since translation operates only as a cloak for the translator's contested view on the merits). In one sense, the failure of the translation enterprise is hardly a problem: We *should* be deciding current controversies for ourselves, rather than entrusting their resolution to Founding Fathers who inhabited a radically different world and embraced radically different ideas. Sensible people eschew this seemingly obvious solution to the dead-hand problem only because deciding things for ourselves means, under our current regime, *judicial* resolution through the guise of constitutional interpretation. So, in another sense, the failure of the translation enterprise is a huge problem: How do we justify delegating our most controversial social policy questions, through the guise of constitutional interpretation, to unelected, remotely accountable judges?

---

[125] 518 U.S. 515 (1996) (invalidating exclusion of women from the Virginia Military Institute).

[126] 517 U.S. 620 (1996) (invalidating a Colorado constitutional provision barring local gay rights ordinances).

If neither of the polar alternatives—dead-hand rule and uncabined judicial rule—[is] attractive, and splitting the difference through translation doesn't seem to work, are there any other alternatives available to us? I think there is one, though it sounds awfully radical: We can simply be anticonstitutionalists. That is, we can decide controverted policy questions for ourselves through political struggle (as much of the rest of the world does), rather than through the edicts of long-dead Framers or relatively unaccountable judges. In the brief space that remains, I hope to explain why this solution is a great deal less radical than it initially appears.

For starters, the Court for much of our constitutional history has, to a rather startling degree, embraced the anticonstitutionalist position, though never explicitly. (One might add that if it hadn't, we truly would have witnessed a revolution against the Court, as we very nearly did in 1937.) Think of all the constitutional constraints on legislative action that have fallen by the wayside over the years. Until recently, the Court had utterly abandoned the Founders' "horse and buggy" conception of interstate commerce in favor of unbridled congressional power (at least with regard to federalism constraints). The Contract Clause, a critical part of the Founders' original design, has been reduced to a virtual shadow of its former self, permitting state and federal governments to engage in wholesale retrospective impairments of contract. The Privileges or Immunities Clause of the Fourteenth Amendment—a potentially revolutionary constraint on the power of state legislatures—was nullified by the Court almost from its inception. The Ninth Amendment, another potentially drastic limitation on the power of Congress (and, if incorporated, on the power of state legislatures), has never been interpreted to impose any limits. The Constitution's tripartite division of powers, another core element of the original design, has been largely eviscerated in the twentieth century in order to accommodate the exponential growth of the modern administrative state. The Court has yet to invoke Congress' clearly designated power to declare war as a constraint on the ability of presidents to maneuver the nation into war without explicit congressional consent. On each of these issues, as well as on many others, the Court has declined to enforce the Constitution, preferring instead to entrust resolution to the political branches. In short, the Court frequently chooses to ignore the dead hand of constitutionalism and permit today's People to rule themselves as they see fit. And, one might add, properly so.

Of course this is not always the posture assumed by the Court. Indeed, very much to the contrary, one might plausibly argue that the Supreme Court over the last forty years (roughly since *Brown*) has constitutional ized a greater range of issues than ever before in its history, notwithstanding the countervailing examples noted in the last paragraph. The critical point for present purposes is that in none of these newly constitutionalized contexts has the Court's intervention been guided by anything remotely resembling the dead hand of the past. Rather, these recent interventions appear distillable into two general categories. In some settings, the Court has confronted an issue that rends the nation approximately in half and has awarded victory to one side or the other (or attempted to split the difference). I believe this is a fairly accurate description of *Brown v. Board of Education* (school segregation), *Furman v. Georgia* (death penalty), *Roe v. Wade* (abortion), *Regents of the University of California v. Bakke* (affirmative action), and *Romer v. Evans* (gay rights). In other constitutional contexts, the Court seizes upon a dominant national view, constitutionalizes it, and then deploys it against outlier states. This description fits leading cases such as *Griswold v. Connecticut* (right to use contraceptives); *Harper v. Virginia Board of Elections* (poll tax); *Moore v. City of East Cleveland* (familial relationships); *Coker v. Georgia* (proportionality requirement in the death penalty); *Plyler v. Doe* (right of children of illegal aliens to free public education); and *United States v. Virginia* (right of women to attend Virginia Military Institute). It is crucial to note that in neither of these two categories of cases—awarding victory to one side of a genuinely divisive public policy dispute or deploying a national consensus against resistant outliers—can the Court's intervention possibly be anything more than marginally countermajoritarian. While it is true that the Court in these settings has not repudiated constitutionalism, it has deployed majoritarian, or at least quasi-majoritarian, norms to guide its constitutional interpretations.

In sum, the anticonstitutionalist position may not be as radical as it sounds. In a significant number of areas, the Court already has adopted that position in everything but name, permitting legislatures free rein where the original Constitution would never have allowed it. In another large array of cases, the Court has not been anticonstitutionalist, but neither has it constrained contemporary society by the dead hand of the past. Rather, in these settings the Court, under the guise either of translation or of some other equally indeterminate theory of constitutional interpretation, has provided contemporary solutions to contemporary problems. Whether the Court is the appropriate institution in a democratic society to resolve such controverted policy issues is an interesting *normative* question. My only point here, though, is *positive*—that the anticonstitutionalist position is not all that radical a departure from where we are now. Whether one applauds or deplores the Court's countermajoritarianism, it should be possible to agree upon the significantly limited range within which it operates.

§ 4.04 Nothing New Under the Sun? A Voice from the Past

Given the vigor of originalism debates in recent decades, it may be valuable near the end of this chapter to consider a contention that the terms of the debate have not really changed in the past 100 years. Georgia State law professor Eric Segall recently unearthed a two-part article published in the *Harvard Law Review* in 1900 by University of Chicago law professor Arthur W. Machen[30] and argued that Machen said it all a hundred years ago. Eric J. Segall, *A Century Lost: The End of the Originalism Debate,* 15 CONST. COMM. 411 (1998):[31]

Machen explored the relationship between a fixed Constitution and an ever-changing society and advanced three propositions about originalism and constitutional interpretation. First, judges must attempt to ascertain the original meaning of the Constitution whenever they exercise judicial review. Second, a political practice determined by judges to be constitutional may later be invalidated by judges, and vice-versa, because the facts to which the original principles are applied are constantly changing. Third, the Framers might originally have believed that the meaning of vague constitutional provisions, like the Eighth Amendment's ban on "cruel and unusual punishments," would not be fixed as of the date of enactment, but should be fleshed out by judges over time according to the values of succeeding generations.

Professor Machen's article demonstrates that he was what modern scholars refer to as a "sophisticated" originalist. He believed the examination of original meaning is not the search for what the Framers specifically

---

[30] Arthur W. Machen, *The Elasticity of the Constitution* (pts. 1 & 2), 14 HARV. L. REV. 200, 273 (1900).

[31] Copyright © 1998 by Constitutional Commentary. Reprinted with permission.

had in mind when they drafted the text, but rather for the general and reasonable meaning of the language they used. Moreover, Professor Machen knew there would be many constitutional questions originalism cannot answer. In such cases, judges must turn to other "rules of construction" and "positive law," which inevitably provide them significant discretion to determine the proper results in difficult cases.

This essay argues that the academic debate over the legitimacy of originalist and non-originalist constitutional interpretation has not progressed materially since Professor Machen's article. Furthermore, a review of his work teaches us that originalism does not lead inevitably to active or passive judicial review; that questions about originalism as an interpretive tool are largely irrelevant to how judges decide real cases; and that there is little reason for scholars to continue to argue about the proper role of original meaning in constitutional interpretation. That role should be as clear to us as it was to Professor Machen—judges refer to the original meaning of the Constitution to provide an important link to our past culture and traditions, but the original meaning rarely dictates results in real cases because the context within which that meaning is applied is constantly changing.

After summarizing Machen's argument and comparing it with the views of modern commentators including Justice Antonin Scalia, NYU and Oxford professor Ronald Dworkin, Chicago law professor Cass Sunstein, Yale law professor Jed Rubenfeld, and Harvard law professor Lawrence Lessig, Segall concludes:

> [A] proper use of history in constitutional interpretation requires a study, not just of the original meaning of constitutional language, but of how that meaning has been applied over the full course of American history. Interpretations inevitably evolve because judges must apply vague constitutional norms to a society whose institutions and values are constantly changing. This point . . . was . . . made by Professor Machen almost one hundred years ago when he recognized that constitutional decisions depend as much upon the factual context at the time of the case as the applicable legal principle. Whether this is true because the Framers intended that the vague norms they established must be interpreted over time . . . or because the nature of judging does not allow us to be ruled by people who lived centuries ago, does not really matter. What separates us is not the question of the relevance of history to constitutional interpretation, but rather what our history, traditions, and reason teach us about fundamental values and which political institutions should define and enforce those values. It is upon those difficult issues, not the appropriate role of original meaning in constitutional interpretation, that legal scholars and judges should focus their considerable energies.

There have been numerous law review articles and books written in the last twenty years devoted to the subject of originalism and constitutional interpretation. This focus on a question largely irrelevant to how the Supreme Court decides cases is truly unfortunate. As Professor Machen told us a long time ago, an ever-changing society governed by a vague foundational document will require judicial decisions that apply new circumstances to old rules. History and custom will be important to that application, but not decisive. Judges do not have to choose between a Living Constitution and the dead hand, but they must inevitably make difficult judgments about competing institutional roles and fundamental rights and liberties. Those are the truly hard questions of constitutional law, and it is time that we face them without the baggage of an old and unhelpful debate about the relationship between original meaning and constitutional interpretation.

§ 4.05 Conclusion

Because lawyers and judges are not formally trained in doing historical research, one might wonder what tools would be appropriate for originalists. In trying to answer this question, one might also consider whether the historical research undertaken by a lawyer or judge should satisfy the standards applicable to professional historians. Cf., e.g., *Velasquez v. Frapwell*, 160 F.3d 389, 393 (7th Cir. 1998) (Posner, C.J.) (emphases in original), *vacated in part on other grounds*, 165 F.3d 593 (7th Cir. 1999): "[J]udges do not have either the leisure or the training to conduct *responsible* historical research or *competently* umpire historical controversies. . . . This is not to deny the relevance of history to adjudication. It is to question the relevance of *contested* history to adjudication." If Judge Posner is right, what does his argument imply for the uses of history and original intent in constitutional adjudication?[32]

§ 4.06 Bibliography

Commentaries on Original Understanding

J.M. Balkin, *Constitutional Interpretation and the Problem of History* (Review Essay), 63 N.Y.U. L. Rev. 911 (1988)

Randy E. Barnett, *The Relevance of the Framers' Intent*, 19 Harv. J.L. & Pub. Pol'y 403 (1996)

Raoul Berger, Federalism: The Framers' Design (1987); Government by Judiciary: The Transformation of the Fourteenth Amendment (2d ed. 1997); *Original Intent: Bittker v. Berger*, 1991 B.Y.U. L. Rev. 1201 (1991); *The Founders' Views—According to Jefferson Powell*, 67

---

[32] For earlier comments on the use and abuse of history in the Supreme Court, see Gerhard Casper, Jones v. Mayer: *Clio, Bemused and Confused Muse*, 1968 Sup. Ct. Rev. 89 (criticizing as manipulative the Court's treatment of statutory text, legislative history, and precedent in Jones v. Alfred H. Mayer Co., 392 U.S. 409, 88 S. Ct. 2186, 20 L. Ed. 2d 1189 (1968); Alfred H. Kelly, *Clio and the Court: An Illicit Love Affair*, 1965 Sup. Ct. Rev. 119 (attacking partisan "law-office" use of history in several Supreme Court opinions). For a recent argument that historical scholarship offers rich insights into American constitutional history but that theorists have made insufficient and somewhat one-sided uses of it, see Martin S. Flaherty, *History "Lite" in Modern American Constitutionalism*, 95 Colum. L. Rev. 523 (1995):

> [M]odern constitutional theory itself has yet to make full use of the opportunity that recent historical scholarship presents because it retains the earlier historians' habit of looking [to England and the Continent

to make sense of early American experience]. Specifically, "neo-liberals" such as Richard Epstein overplay the early American commitment to rights, and "neo-republicans" such as [Cass] Sunstein overemphasize the Founding commitment to civic virtue and political participation. . . . [A]ny theory opting for reductive simplicity, especially for the sake of either democratic process or individual liberty, is likely to forfeit its claim to historical credibility, at least to the extent it purports to rest on the nation's nascent constitutional experience. If early American constitutional development reveals anything, it reveals that neither those who would base their theories preeminently on rights and autonomy, nor those who would ground their paradigms exclusively on self-government and democracy, can lay easy claim to the traditions that the Constitution itself embodies—try though they might.

Id. at 529. Copyright © 1995 by the Columbia Law Review. Reprinted with permission.

TEX. L. REV. 1033 (1989); *The Activist Flight From the Constitution*, 47 OHIO ST. L.J. 1 (1986); *"Original Intention" in Historical Perspective*, 54 GEO. WASH. L. REV. 296 (1986)

Boris I. Bittker, *The Bicentennial of the Jurisprudence of Original Intent: The Recent Past*, 77 CALIF. L. REV. 235 (1989); *Interpreting the Constitution: Is the Intent of the Framers Controlling? If Not, What Is?*, 19 HARV. J.L. & PUB. POL'Y 9 (1995)

Rebecca L. Brown, *Tradition and Insight*, 103 YALE L.J. 177 (1993)

Michael C. Dorf, *Integrating Normative and Descriptive Constitutional Theory: The Case of Original Meaning*, 85 GEO. L.J. 1765 (1997) (with responses by Gary Lawson, Lawrence Lessig, and James G. Fleming, and reply by Dorf)

John J. Gibbons, *Intentionalism, History and Legitimacy*, 140 U. PA. L. REV. 613 (1991)

Mark D. Greenberg & Harry Litman, *The Meaning of Original Meaning*, 86 GEO. L.J. 569 (1998)

Leonard Levy, ORIGINAL INTENT AND THE FRAMING OF THE CONSTITUTION (1989)

Earl Maltz, RETHINKING CONSTITUTIONAL LAW: ORIGINALISM, INTERVENTIONISM, AND THE POLITICS OF JUDICIAL REVIEW (1994); *The Failure of Attacks on Constitutional Originalism*, 4 CONST. COMMENTARY 43 (1987); *Foreword: The Appeal of Originalism*, 1987 UTAH L. REV. 773; *Some New Thoughts on an Old Problem—The Role of the Intent of the Framers in Constitutional Theory*, 63 B.U. L. REV. 811 (1983)

Edwin Meese, *Toward a Jurisprudence of Original Intent*, 11 HARV. J. L. & PUB. POL'Y (1988)

Buckner F. Melton, Jr., *Clio at the Bar: A Guide to Historical Method for Legists and Jurists*, 83 MINN. L. REV. 377 (1998)

H. Jefferson Powell, LANGUAGES OF POWER: A SOURCE BOOK OF EARLY AMERICAN CONSTITUTIONAL HISTORY (1991); *Rules for Originalists*, 73 VA. L. REV. 659 (1987); *The Modern Misunderstanding of Original Intent* (Book Review), 54 U. CHI. L. REV. 1513 (1987)

Jack N. Rakove, *The Original Intention of Original Understanding*, 13 CONST. COMM. 159 (1996); ORIGINAL MEANINGS: POLITICS AND IDEAS IN THE MAKING OF THE CONSTITUTION (1996)

Glenn H. Reynolds, *Sex, Lies, and Jurisprudence: Robert Bork*, Griswold *and the Philosophy of Original Understanding*, 24 GA. L. REV. 1045 (1990)

Neil M. Richards, *Clio and the Court: A Reassessment of the Supreme Court's Uses of History*, 13 J.L. & POL. 809 (1997)

Pierre Schlag, *Framers' Intent: The Illegitimate Uses of History*, 8 U. PUGET SOUND L. REV. 283 (1985)

Larry Simon, *The Authority of the Framers of the Constitution: Can the Originalist Interpretation Be Justified?*, 73 CALIF. L. REV. 1482 (1985)

1 Laurence H. Tribe, AMERICAN CONSTITUTIONAL LAW 47–70 (3d ed. 2000)

Mark V. Tushnet, RED, WHITE, AND BLUE: A CRITICAL ANALYSIS OF CONSTITUTIONAL LAW 21–69 (1988)

Chapter 5

Structural Reasoning

§ 5.01 Introduction

In much of constitutional theory, the structure of government and the institutional relationships that the Constitution creates are as important to interpretation as any specific text. Even for those theorists who claim adherence to text primarily, an important piece of their argument rests on structural inference. For example, the argument that courts are less legitimate than legislatures as vehicles for creating social policy is itself an argument that rests on the structure of the constitutional government. Certain important concepts that are familiar to any student of constitutional law, such as "federalism" (referring to the relationship between the federal government and the state governments) and "separation of powers" (referring to the relationships among the three branches of the federal government) are terms that themselves never appear in the constitutional text. Instead, they are concepts that derive from the document understood as a whole. Even the notion of "majoritarianism" does not derive from any specific text in the Constitution, but rather rests on an understanding of how the entire governmental organism works. Thus, an understanding of constitutional theory and interpretation is not complete without consideration of the type of reasoning that comes from relationships created by the constitutional structures of government.

One of the leading early discussions of structural argument was written in 1969 by Professor Charles Black of the Yale Law School, in his book STRUCTURE AND RELATIONSHIP IN CONSTITUTIONAL LAW 10–15, 17–19, 22–27, 29–32 (1969):[1]

> What basic kinds of legal reasoning, broadly, does the ordinary, competent American judge see as being open to him when he has to ascertain and fix the right law for application to a case before him?
>
>   . . .
>
> Most fundamentally, there are two great headings, corresponding to two bodies of material conceived by the working lawyer as formal sources of law. One is the method of precedent, the finding of sound analogy in the past case or line of cases. Out of the development of such decisional reasoning, systematic concepts develop, but the *case* remains paramount in importance and in authority. This is the heart-method of Anglo-American legal reasoning. But legislative activity, administrative rule-making, the conceiving of treaties as municipal law, and the making of written constitutions have brought into being in highly developed form a second and seemingly quite different method—the searching of the written text for its *meaning* in application to the presented case.
>
>   . . .

---

[1] Copyright © 1969 by Charles Black.

It would be intellectually satisfying, though the fact would be far from satisfying, to be able to say that our legal culture *never* employs, for constitutional law, the method of inference from structure and relation, but always purports to move on the basis of the interpretation of particular constitutional texts. As we shall see, that is not true; the first of these styles of thought has played its part at least at one point of the very first importance in the development of our constitutional law, and at other points of somewhat less importance. What can be asserted is that our preference for the particular-text style has been a decided one, leading not only to the failure to develop a full-bodied case-law of inference from constitutional structure and relation but even to a preference, among texts, for those which are in form directive of official conduct, rather than for those that declare or create a relationship out of the existence of which inference could be drawn.

I should like to begin with the case of *Carrington v. Rash,* [380 U.S. 89, 85 S. Ct. 775, 13 L. Ed. 2d 675 (1965)], decided by the Supreme Court in 1965. [Professor Black summarized the facts and opinions in *Carrington,* which involved a challenge by a career Army serviceman—from Alabama, but stationed in Texas—to a Texas constitutional provision limiting him to voting in his county of residence as of the time he entered the service. The Court struck down Texas' refusal to let Carrington vote there as resting on an "unreasonable" classification, a ground Black finds shaky.]

Yet I agree with the decision in the case on grounds which may illustrate my theme for these lectures—on grounds, moreover, whose entire omission by both Court and counsel illustrates an interesting point about our American juristic style. Carrington, I should rather have said, was a federal soldier, recruited by the national government to perform a crucial national function. Conceding that in every other way he qualified to vote, Texas said that, solely upon the showing that he was in the performance of that function, he was not to vote. It makes little difference whether you call that a penalization of membership in the national Army. It is, in neutral terminology, the imposition, by a state, of a distinctive disadvantage based solely on membership in the Army. My thought would be that it ought to be held that no state may annex any disadvantage simply and solely to the performance of a federal duty.

Now the stylistic, or, if you like, methodological difference between the reason I would have given and the reason the Court gave goes to the essence of what I have to say. The Court (and counsel in the briefs) exhibited our standard preference for the ground that purports to proceed from interpretation of a particular text. The ground I would have preferred is one sounding in the structure of federal union, and in the relation of federal to state governments; it can point to no particular text as its authority. This is a mode of reasoning which tends to be rejected, or ignored as a possibility, by our legal culture.

I think it is very simple to show, however, that the logic of national structure, as distinguished from the topic of particular textual exegesis, has broad validity. One can do this with extreme cases. Suppose there were no Fourteenth Amendment. Could a state make it a crime to file suit in a federal court? Could a state provide that lifelong disqualification from voting or holding property was to result from even a short service in the United States Army? . . . As matters stand, we would prefer, I think, to point to texts, mostly in the Fourteenth Amendment, to establish the unconstitutionality of such extreme actions. But is it not clear that, if those texts were not there, we would point to other texts, so long as we adhered to the textual style? And is it not, further, clear that our real reasons would not be textual, and that if we had no text which by any stretch of its interpreter's will could apply, we would still decide these, and a host of other similarly extreme cases, in the same way, on the substantial ground that such state measures interfere with and impede relations which the national government has set up for its own purposes?

Now you may say these are indeed extreme cases, to the point of cartooning. But every legal method starts with such cases. One of the questions I would raise is why, as amongst different legal methods, equally available, we elect to pursue the textual method from the cartoon case on into the fine grain of real problems while leaving virtually unused the method of inference from political structure. The ground of my objection is well illustrated by *Carrington v. Rash*; it is simply that the textual method, in some cases, forces us to blur the focus and talk evasively, while the structural method frees us to talk sense. The action of Texas was not really "arbitrary" in that case; there *are* differences between military people and other people with respect to the meaning of their residence. Giving effect to those differences is well within the latitude we ordinarily allow to the state, in the general case, under the equal protection clause. The real question is whether we think Texas, reasonably or not, should be allowed to annex a disability solely to federal military service.

Early along in every course in constitutional law, one takes up the case of *McCulloch v. Maryland* [17 U.S. (4 Wheat.) 316, 4 L. Ed. 579 (1819)]. The great opinion of Mr. Chief Justice Marshall in that case addresses itself to two questions. First, there was the question whether the Congress might permissibly create a corporation to be called and to function as the Bank of the United States. It will be familiar learning to nearly all here that the strong preference of our legal culture for the holding based on the specific text is shown by the fact that later comment on the opinion has sometimes treated this part of it as though it rested solidly on the so-called "necessary and proper" clause. A reasonably careful reading shows that Marshall does not place principal reliance on this clause as a ground of decision; that before he reaches it he has already decided, on the basis of far more general implications, that Congress possesses the power, not expressly named, of establishing a bank and chartering corporations; that he addresses himself to the necessary and proper clause only in response to counsel's arguing its *restrictive* force; and that he never really commits himself to the proposition that the necessary and proper clause enlarges governmental power, but only to the propositions, first, that it does not restrict it, and, secondly, that it *may* have been inserted to remove doubt on questions of power which the rest of Article I, Section 8, without the necessary and proper clause, had not, in Marshall's view, really left doubtful.

The second question in the case was whether a state might tax the functioning of the Bank of the United States, admitting the latter to be a validly created national instrumentality. Here I find my students, each year, become rather puzzled. As laymen they have absorbed the layman's notions about constitutional law, and they think it consists, indeed that it must consist, in the interpretation of the commands embodied in particular texts. Yet Marshall's reasoning, on this branch of the case is, as I read it, essentially structural. It has to do in great part with what he conceives to be the warranted relational proprieties between the national government and the government of the states, with the structural corollaries of national supremacy—and, at one point, of the mode of formation of the Union. You can root the result, if you want to (and Marshall sometimes may seem to be doing this) in the supremacy clause of Article VI, but that seems not a very satisfying rationale, for Article VI declares the supremacy of whatever the national law may turn out

to be, and does not purport to give content to that law. In this, perhaps
the greatest of our constitutional cases, judgment is reached not fundamentally on the basis of that kind of textual exegesis which we tend to
regard as normal, but on the basis of reasoning from the total structure
which the text has created.

. . .

I am inclined to think well of the method of reasoning from structure
and relation. I think well of it, above all, because to succeed it has to make
sense—current, practical sense. The textual-explication method, operating on general language, may often—perhaps more often than not—be
made to make sense, by legitimate enough devices of interpretation. But
it contains within itself no guarantee that it will make sense, for a court
may always present itself or even see itself as being bound by the stated
intent, however nonsensical, of somebody else. In *Hoxie School District
[Brewer v. Hoxie School Dist*. No. 46, 238 F.2d 91 (8th Cir. 1956)], on the
other hand, the only way to justify the result was to argue that it was
implied, in the nature of the federal-state relationship, that people were
forbidden to interfere with state officials who were trying to implement
federal rights. I think this an eminently sensible implication. You may
not think so. If you do not, then we can and must begin to argue at once
about the practicalities and proprieties of the thing, without getting out
dictionaries whose entries will not really respond to the question we are
putting, or scanning utterances, contemporary with the text, of persons
who did not really face the question we are asking. We will have to deal
with policy and not with grammar. I am not suggesting that grammar
can be sidestepped, or that policy can legitimately be the whole of law.
I am only saying that where a fairly available method of legal reasoning,
by its very nature, leads directly to the discussion of practical rightness,
that method should be used whenever possible. It is the best wisdom of
every system of law to seek and to cleave unto such intellectual modes.

How might our federal constitutional law use the method of reasoning
from structure and relation? What relations and structures are soundly
enough established to furnish a basis for this kind of legal thought? Some
possibilities (in part, as we have seen, actualized in practice) suggest
themselves.

First, there is the national government itself, as a functioning structure
and as a party to relations. *McCulloch v. Maryland* started and well
illustrates the kind of thought to which this leads, but the development
on the whole has been rather meager. If lawyers were trained to think
constantly of this heading as a live and productive one, it is my view that
such an opinion as the Court uttered in *Carrington v. Rash* would never
have been written; instead, it would have been held—probably *per curiam*
by the Supreme Court of Texas—that the subjecting of a federal soldier,
strictly as such and on no other showing than that of his being a federal
soldier, to an adverse discrimination, so clearly tended to impede the
operation of the national government as to be forbidden quite without
regard to its violation of any specific textual guarantee. We would have
been spared what I cannot help regarding as an unsound opinion,
supporting a sound—indeed something like a necessary—holding.

. . .

The concept of interference with national governmental function shades
off into the concept of interference with rights created and protected by
the national government. These concepts are bound together by the fact
that the creation and protection of individual rights is the highest function
of any government. Even the carriage of the mails moves toward delivery

of the letter as its final cause, and therefore toward the right to receive it. The *Hoxie School District* case makes the point as to "state action." In that case, the action complained of was "private," in the technical sense. It is true that the school board plaintiff was a state agency, but it was very far from denying anybody equal protection of the laws. "No state," to quote the phrase which has given verbal underpinning to the state action doctrine, was doing anything in violation of a constitutional guarantee. Private individuals, acting on their own, were trying to coerce an agency of the state not to comply with the Constitution. I cannot see why it makes any difference whether this private action was aimed at a school board or at a private person resting under some federal obligation. Let us take the case of a restaurant owner who wants and tries to comply with the Civil Rights Act of 1964, by receiving Negroes freely in his restaurant, but who is threatened with or subjected to physical, social, or economic coercion by those who want him to violate the act by keeping his restaurant white. It is true that the restaurant owner, unlike the school board, has not taken an Article VI oath to support the Constitution. But he, no whit less than they, is under a definite obligation to obey national law. I can see no reason why, if a federal court may enjoin interference with their obedience, a federal court may not enjoin interference with his obedience. And there is in the one case no more reason than in the other to ask whether the action interfering with obedience is "state action" or "private action." The unhallowed "state action" doctrine takes its origin from operations performed, in the *Civil Rights Cases* of 1883, on particular texts; where the right at stake is not derived from those or any similar texts, the doctrine itself has no right to live [109 U.S. 3, 3 S. Ct. 18, 27 L. Ed. 835 (1883)].

Let me develop this idea in another direction by mentioning its aptness to dissolve many doubts as to congressional power, or at least to enable these to be placed on a basis, more closely adapted morally to the evils than is the commerce clause. It is hard nowadays to remember, for example, what the objections were to a federal anti-lynching bill. The sheriff who holds a prisoner holds him subject to a federally sanctioned rule that he shall not be deprived of life or liberty without due process of law. To take him out of the sheriff's custody for the purpose of frustrating the performance of this federal obligation would seem to me a federal wrong in strict analogy to the one enjoined in the *Hoxie School District* case. But even if you cannot go that far with me, how can it be thought that Congress may not prevent, by penalizing it, this kind of interference with processes commanded by federal law?

. . .

Let me finish . . . with two points. The first is that, in suggesting the possibility of a wider use of inference from relation and structure in the intellectual processes of constitutional law, I do not think I am suggesting that precision be supplanted by wide-open speculation. The precision of textual explication is nothing but specious in the areas that matter. . . . The question is not whether the text shall be respected, but rather how one goes about respecting a text of that high generality and consequent ambiguity which marks so many crucial constitutional texts. I submit that the generalities and ambiguities are no greater when one applies the method of reasoning from structure and relation. I submit that the opinion in *McCulloch v. Maryland* has just as satisfying a legal quality as the opinions in *Fletcher v. Peck* and the *Dartmouth College Case* [17 U.S. (4 Wheat.) 518, 624, 4 L. Ed. 629 (1819)], where the obligation of contracts clause was being interpreted, after the preferred mode of our legal culture.

Finally, I have learned so to fear the maxim *expressio unius* that I must timidly correct a doubtless nonexistent impression that what I have suggested is the total abandonment of the method of particular-text interpretation. It is entirely plain, on the contrary, that so long as we continue to look on our Constitution as a part of the law applicable in court, just so long the work of sheer textual interpretation will be a great part—probably the greatest part—of judicial work in constitutional law. There is, moreover, a close and perpetual interworking between the textual and the relational and structural modes of reasoning, for the structure and relations concerned are themselves created by the text, and inference drawn from them must surely be controlled by the text.

All I am suggesting is that a method not unknown in our constitutional law be brought more clearly into the conscious field of those who work in that law. I make this suggestion in the faith, fundamentally, that clarity about what we are doing, about the true or the truly acceptable grounds of judgment, is both a good in itself, and a means to sounder decision.

Black is sanguine about the possibilities for avoiding "wide-open speculation" with greater use of structural reasoning. In what follows the reader should consider whether Black's optimism seems warranted on the basis of examples from arguments over the separation of powers, federalism, and individual rights.

In their article, *Comfortably Penumbral*, 77 B.U. L. Rev. 1089 (1997), Yale Senior Fellow Brannon P. Denning and University of Tennessee Professor Glenn Harlan Reynolds show that the idea of structural reasoning has not gone away in the years since Black wrote his book. To the contrary, the Supreme Court appears to be resorting to structural inference with increasing frequency, not only in cases involving federal-state relations, but also in those involving individual rights:[2]

The emergence of a working conservative majority on the Supreme Court during the last five years has produced a number of interesting developments. Two are especially notable. The first is the apparent victory of conservative judges and scholars who stressed the primacy of text and history in constitutional interpretation. The second is the subject of this Essay: the Court's willingness to supplement text, precedent, and history with inferences derived from related constitutional provisions, the overall structure of the Constitution, and the principles that animated its framing.

The 1995–96 and 1996–97 Terms produced several decisions that illustrated the extent to which the "conservative" Rehnquist Court has adopted interpretive methodologies that, ten or twenty years ago, would have been anathema to self-respecting "strict constructionists." In short, conservatives on the Court have embraced what has been termed "penumbral reasoning," of the sort employed in *Griswold v. Connecticut* [381 U.S. 479, 85 S. Ct. 1678, 14 L. Ed. 2d 510 (1965)]. The "liberal" members of the Court and many commentators, meanwhile, have decried this trend, and are now posturing as defenders of the Constitution against "activist" attempts at its rewriting.

We, however, come not to bury penumbral reasoning, but to praise it. This Essay argues that neither conservatives nor liberals should characterize penumbral reasoning as a less legitimate method of constitutional

---

[2] Volume 77:5, Boston University Law Review (1997) 1089–1120. Reprinted with permission. Copyright © 1999 Trustees of Boston University, Forum of original publication. Boston University bears no responsibility for any errors which have occurred in reproducing this article.

explication than originalism, textualism, strict constructionism, or living constitutionalism. In many ways, penumbral reasoning, conscientiously employed, combines the best characteristics of these methods without suffering the defects that dogmatic adherence to one school of constitutional interpretation often entails. To confuse penumbral reasoning with judicial activism is thus a mistake or, more often, politically motivated sloganeering.

. . . [A]lthough *enthusiasm* for penumbral reasoning seems somewhat outcome-driven, the method itself is a sound tool for interpreting the Constitution and is sometimes superior to other methods of interpretation, like Borkian originalism. Moreover, penumbral reasoning provides a corrective to the exceedingly narrow "clause-bound" focus of past Supreme Courts. Additionally, penumbral reasoning can elevate constitutional interpretation above what Professor Charles Black, an eloquent advocate of penumbral reasoning and reasoning from structure, sardonically characterized as "Humpty-Dumpty textual manipulation." Now that penumbral reasoning has largely sloughed off its "liberal" connotations, proponents and opponents of its outcomes should focus instead on penumbral reasoning's *use*, that they can more credibly point out instances of its *abuse*.

I. Penumbral Reasoning: Past

Simply put, penumbral reasoning involves "reasoning-by-interpolation," drawing logical inferences by looking at relevant parts of the Constitution as a whole and their relationship to one another. In most judges' and scholars' minds, the premier contemporary example of penumbral reasoning is *Griswold*. In *Griswold* Justice Douglas looked at various provisions of the Bill of Rights, including those that protect assembly, freedom from self-incrimination, and the right not to have troops quartered in one's home. From his survey, he inferred that there was a common thread throughout that government could not intrude into the privacy of individuals absent fairly compelling circumstances.

As Justice Black's dissent made clear, there is nothing explicit about privacy in the text of the Bill of Rights. Justice Black's criticisms, however, were the result of his not being able to see the forest for the leaves. Black had a clause-bound vision of liberty in which government power was limited only by those specific clauses that prohibited it from acting. Douglas's method, in contrast, was closer to that of the Framers': loath to ascribe to a government unlimited power at the expense of individual liberty. Moreover, Douglas's method would have been readily recognizable to those of the Founding Era as well.

Griswold however, is neither the *alpha* nor the *omega* of penumbral reasoning. Consider briefly Justice Marshall's opinion in *McCulloch v. Maryland* [17 U.S. (4 Wheat.) 316, 400, 4 L. Ed. 579 (1819)], in many ways the quintessential example of penumbral reasoning. The issues in *McCulloch* echo today in the cases discussed below. Marshall, reasoning from the text and structure of the Constitution, and supplementing his citations to specific constitutional provisions with reference to overarching principles that bind—and illuminate—both text and structure, answered both questions presented: (1) whether Congress had the power to incorporate a bank; and (2) whether the state of Maryland could exercise its concurrent power to tax an instrumentality of the federal government. Though the literal text of the Constitution provided no definitive answer to either question, Marshall formulated a persuasive answer based on the whole structure of the Constitution, its text, the interrelatedness of its provisions, and constitutional "first principles." His approach in *McCulloch* is embodied in his oft-misquoted reminder that "it is a *constitution* we are expounding."

In answering the first question—whether the federal government could charter a bank—Marshall rejected the characterization of the Necessary and Proper Clause as a limitation on the power of Congress. He noted its inclusion in the section of the Constitution that granted power to Congress, and not in a subsequent section that restricted Congress's power. Marshall noted that as an additional grant of power, "necessary" could not thus mean "absolutely necessary." In addition, he cited for the proposition that the Congress was, within its enumerated powers, supreme, the language of the Supremacy Clause,[26] which emphasized both the preeminence of the Constitution and announced its authoritativeness as an act of a National People. Moreover, the text of the Constitution and the availability of judicial review served to prevent the clause from being construed as an endless grant of power to the Congress. After all, Congress could only exercise its discretion in the choice of means by reference to an enumerated power. Further, Marshall made it clear that the judiciary would be obligated to act should Congress exercise power *ultra vires* under the pretext of implied powers, or otherwise overstep the limits of its enumerated powers.

Thus, Marshall defended his construction of the Necessary and Proper Clause against charges of potential abuse with reference to the explicit enumeration of Congress's powers "herein granted" and to the Tenth Amendment, while holding that it allowed Congress flexibility within the parameters established by the Constitution itself. Marshall further offered examples of how his implied powers doctrine was reasonable in light of the specific powers given to Congress, and what authority Congress would by necessity have to have in order to execute those powers in any meaningful sense. He wrote that, "[t]he power being given, it is the interest of the nation to facilitate its execution. It can never be their interest, and cannot be presumed to have been their intention, to clog and embarrass its execution by withholding the most appropriate means."

The second question required even less effort than the first. Though the states clearly possessed the concurrent power to tax, they could not use that power to undermine the overarching federal principles embodied in the Constitution. Specifically, they could not use the state power to tax a federal instrumentality, lest it be empowered to tax it out of existence. To hold otherwise, Marshall believed, would endanger the whole constitutional enterprise. Moreover, such a holding would contravene the words of the Supremacy Clause that made explicit the supreme authority of the Constitution.

Although there was "no express provision" prohibiting Maryland from taxing the bank, Marshall wrote that "the claim has been sustained on a principle which so entirely pervades the constitution, is so intermixed with the materials which compose it, so interwoven with its web, so blended with its texture, as to be incapable of being separated from it, without rending it into shreds." Marshall acknowledged the strength of that argument and held that when the exercise of a concurrent power by a state conflicted with the legitimate goals of the federal government, the

---

[26] The Supremacy Clause states:

This Constitution, and the Laws of the United States which shall be made in Pursuance thereof; and all Treaties made, or which shall be made, under the Authority of the United States, shall be the supreme Law of the Land, and the Judges in every State shall be bound thereby, any Thing in the Constitution or Laws of any State to the Contrary notwithstanding. U.S. Const. art. VI, § 2.

Constitution, its provisions, and the principles animating its formation commanded that the states not exercise the power. In light of Marshall's logic, it would seem extremely literal to conclude that the absence of a textual provision on point would ever end a constitutional conversation, be it about the power of government, federalism, or the rights of individuals.

As has been duly noted, "advocacy scholarship" probably lies at the heart of conservative approval of *McCulloch*, and excoriation of *Griswold*, because the methodologies used in both cases are virtually indistinguishable. Perhaps general suspicion of penumbral reasoning also proceeds from what Professor Charles Black termed the "modern mode, and indeed the mode of choice in our legal style": textual explication, or less charitably, textual manipulation. Nevertheless, penumbral reasoning has always played a consistent, if peripheral, role in the formulation of constitutional doctrine, albeit in many constitutional areas less sexy than "privacy."

Moreover, conservatives no less than liberals have found it useful. Their embrace of penumbral reasoning is evident in opinions written during the two most recent Supreme Court Terms. Not surprisingly, conservatives' resort to penumbral reasoning in high profile cases involving controversial issues like federalism has drawn fire from other members of the Court and Court commentators, proving liberals are no less apt than conservatives to denounce cases based on their outcomes by invoking the "activism" shibboleth. In *Romer v. Evans*, however, members of the Court's conservative majority eager to embrace penumbral reasoning in other areas, expressly declined to join fellow conservative Anthony Kennedy in striking down Colorado's Amendment Two. The caustic dissent by Justice Scalia—in which he was joined by Chief Justice Rehnquist and Justice Thomas—criticized the majority for adopting the interpretive methodology that he later embraced in *Printz v. United States*. Thus, it appears that some members of the Court embrace penumbral reasoning only when it produces outcomes of which they approve. As predicted in a past article, conservative members of the Court sometimes morph from "defenders of principle" into "unprincipled noninterpretivists."

II. Penumbral Reasoning: Present

Principled or not, conservatives on the Court have found penumbral reasoning a useful tool to advance several favored causes in the [1995 and 1996] Terms. Recent decisions in the areas of federalism and sovereign immunity indicate a majority that has begun to roll back some of the New Deal jurisprudence and is willing to rely extensively on penumbral reasoning to do so. Moreover, though not yet a majority view, Justices Scalia and Thomas recently have championed a theory of the dormant Commerce Clause that, if ever able to command a majority of the Court, could rewrite vast portions of constitutional law. It, too, relies largely on penumbral reasoning, as does the Court's entire body of "negative" Commerce Clause doctrine.

One caveat: in examining the following cases for evidence of penumbral reasoning, overt or covert, we imply neither that resort to penumbral reasoning made the Court's holding inevitable, nor that a Court's particular opinion was a "good" application of penumbral reasoning. Nor do we suggest that we agree with all of the Court's decisions. These important considerations necessarily invite debate. This Essay, however, seeks only to provide a necessary foundation for that debate: recognition that the Court presently and properly engages in penumbral reasoning when it decides issues of constitutional law.

A. *Sovereign Immunity*

One of the more remarkable changes in the [1995 and 1996] Terms has been the emergence of a strong reaffirmation of sovereign immunity principles that extend far beyond the strict text of the Eleventh Amendment.[51] In two recent cases, Chief Justice Rehnquist's earlier dissents became the basis for a new majority view. In *Seminole Tribe v. Florida*, the Court, *per* Chief Justice Rehnquist, struck down a congressional statute that waived states' sovereign immunity under congressional authority to regulate "commerce with the Indian Tribes." Rehnquist wrote:

> Although the text of the [Eleventh Amendment] would appear to restrict only the Article III diversity jurisdiction of the federal courts, "we have understood the Eleventh Amendment to stand not so much for what it says, but for the presupposition . . . which it confirms." That presupposition, first observed over a century ago in [*Hans v. Louisiana,* 134 U.S. 1, 13, 10 S. Ct. 504, 33 L. Ed. 842 (1890)], has two parts: first, that each State is a sovereign entity in our federal system; and second, that "[i]t is inherent in the nature of sovereignty not to be amenable to the suit of an individual without its consent." . . . For over a century we have reaffirmed that federal jurisdiction over suits against unconsenting States "was not contemplated by the Constitution when establishing the judicial power of the United States."

Seminole Tribe overruled an earlier case, *Pennsylvania v. Union Gas Co.* [491 U.S. 1, 23, 109 S. Ct. 2273, 105 L. Ed. 2d 1 (1989)], in which the plurality opinion authorized Congress to abrogate state sovereignty on the strength of the Interstate Commerce Clause. Chief Justice Rehnquist wrote that the "plurality's rationale . . . deviated sharply from our established federalism jurisprudence and essentially eviscerated our decision in [*Hans v. Louisiana*]." *Union Gas* had ignored not only that part of the Eleventh Amendment that, to Rehnquist, seemed "clear enough" that "state sovereign immunity limited the federal courts' jurisdiction under Article III," but also that part of the Court's jurisprudence that is neither clear nor present in the text of the Amendment. "[O]ur decisions since *Hans* had been equally clear that the Eleventh Amendment reflects 'the fundamental principle of sovereign immunity [that] limits the grant of judicial authority in Article III.'"

Moreover, the Rehnquist opinion quoted approvingly an earlier opinion written by Chief Justice Charles Evans Hughes clearly stating that the principles in *Hans* and the Court's Eleventh Amendment jurisprudence went beyond the mere text of the Amendment:

> Manifestly, we cannot rest with a mere literal application of the words of § 2 of Article III, or assume that the letter of the Eleventh Amendment exhausts the restrictions upon suits against nonconsenting States. *Behind the words of the constitutional provisions are postulates which limit and control.* There is the essential postulate that the controversies, as contemplated, shall be found to be of a justiciable character. There is also the postulate that States of the Union, still possessing attributes of sovereignty, shall be immune from suits, without their consent, save where there has been a "surrender of this immunity in the plan of the convention."

---

[51] The Eleventh Amendment states: "The Judicial power of the United States shall not be construed to extend to any suit in law or equity, commenced or prosecuted against one of the United States by Citizens of another State, or by Citizens or Subjects of any Foreign State." U.S. CONST. amend. XI.

The Chief Justice further bolstered the Court's sovereign immunity analysis with an appeal to extra-constitutional sources of authority such as the law of nations: "[*Hans*] found its roots not solely in the common law of England, but in the much more fundamental " 'jurisprudence in all civilized nations.' "

Lest anyone miss the point, the Court, in its [1996] Term, reaffirmed its sovereign immunity jurisprudence summarized in *Seminole Tribe*.[3] Writing for the majority in *Idaho v. Coeur d'Alene* [521 U.S. 261, 267, 117 S. Ct. 2028, 138 L. Ed. 2d 438 (1997)] Justice Kennedy admitted that a literal reading of the text of the Eleventh Amendment "could suggest that [it], like the grant of Article III, § 2, jurisdiction, is cast in terms of reach or competence, so the federal courts are altogether disqualified from hearing certain suits brought against a State." However, he continued:

> This interpretation . . . has been neither our tradition, nor the accepted construction of the Amendment's text. Rather, a State can waive its Eleventh Amendment protection and allow a federal court to hear and decide a case commenced or prosecuted against it. The Amendment, in other words, enacts a sovereign immunity from suit, rather than a non-waivable limit on the federal judiciary's subject-matter jurisdiction.

> The Court's recognition of sovereign immunity has not been limited to the suits described in the text of the Eleventh Amendment. To respect the broader concept of immunity, implicit in the Constitution, which we have regarded the Eleventh Amendment as evidencing and exemplifying, we have extended a State's protection from suit to suits brought by the State's own citizens.

Needless to say, there are many critics of the Court's sovereign immunity jurisprudence. Even if the Framers intended to keep some form of it in place, it is certainly not apparent from either the Constitution or the text of the Eleventh Amendment, which speaks only to the ability of federal courts to hear suits in which a non-resident sues a state. Moreover, as critics like Akhil Reed Amar point out, the concept of sovereign immunity is at odds with a system like ours, where the people, not an individual or even the government itself, are sovereign. The goal here, however, is not to evaluate the substance of the Court's decisions—as many of commentators have already done—but to illustrate the *method* the Court uses to reach those decisions: penumbral reasoning.

B. *Federalism*

During the [1995 and 1996] Terms, the Court has also actively policed the boundaries of power between the state and federal governments. Specifically, the Court has worked to reinvigorate "Our Federalism" and to limit the degree of power that the federal government may constitutionally exercise over the states. The Court has accomplished this in part through the application of its sovereign immunity jurisprudence, but also

---

[3] In two more recent cases, the Court expanded the protection for states created by *Seminole Tribe*. In *Florida Prepaid Postsecondary Educ. Expense Bd. v. College Sav. Bank,* 527 U.S. 627, 119 S. Ct. 2199, 144 L. Ed. 2d 575 (1999), and *College Savings Bank v. Florida Prepaid Postsecondary Educ. Expense Bd.,* 527 U.S. 666, 119 S. Ct. 2219, 144 L. Ed. 2d 605 (1999), the Court held that Congress's power to abrogate the sovereign immunity of the states under its Fourteenth Amendment power is narrow and empowers Congress to subject states to suit only for actions that would violate the due process clause. The two federal statutory schemes at issue in the two cases, the Lanham Act and the patent laws, were held not to satisfy this standard.

by limiting the scope of congressional power exercised under color of the Commerce Clause. Finally, the Court has policed these boundaries through the application of penumbral reasoning. Its use guaranteed neither a "nationalist" nor a "states' rights" outcome: in one case the states benefited; in the other, the federal government was the beneficiary.

In *U.S. Term Limits, Inc. v. Thornton* [514 U.S. 779, 837-838, 115 S. Ct. 1842, 131 L. Ed. 2d 881 (1995)], the Court struck down an Arkansas referendum that imposed term limits on its officials elected to serve in Congress. Justice Stevens's majority opinion, as well as Justice Kennedy's concurrence in which Kennedy responded to Justice Thomas's provocative dissent, relied, among other things, on an interpretation of the Constitution that drew its authority from a constitutive act of a national people. In contrast, the dissent characterized the Constitution's ratification as an act of a people in their capacity as citizens of sovereign states delegating authority from those states to the federal government. In addition, the majority's opinion appealed to "basic principles of our democratic system": the right to stand for office and the right of the people to elect who they wish to represent them.

The majority explicitly rejected the argument that, absent a specific textual prohibition, states were free to add additional qualifications to the age, citizenship, and residency requirements present in the Constitution[78] because such power was "reserved" to states and their citizens under the Tenth Amendment.[79] The Court stated:

Petitioner's Tenth Amendment argument misconceives the nature of the right at issue because that Amendment could only "reserve" that which existed before. As Justice Story recognized, "the states can exercise no powers whatsoever, which exclusively spring out of the existence of the national government, which the constitution does not delegate to them. . . . No state can say, that it has reserved, what it never possessed."

Simply put, because the structure of the federal government was entirely new, and because there was no Congress of the sort created by the Constitution prior to its ratification, the states had no preexisting power regarding its representatives' qualifications to reserve.

Bolstering this historical analysis was the penumbral interplay among the sections of the Constitution that established the national government and provided for federal elections:

For example, Art. I, § 5, cl. 1 provides: Each House shall be the Judge of the Elections, Returns and Qualifications of its own Members. The text of the Constitution thus gives the representatives of all the people the final say in judging the qualifications of the representatives of any one State. . . .

Two other sections of the Constitution further support our view of the Framer's vision. First, . . . the Constitution provides that the salaries of representatives should "be ascertained by Law, and paid out of the Treasury of the United States," Art I., § 6, rather than by individual States. . . . Second, the provisions governing elections reveal the Framers' understanding that powers over the election of federal officers had to be delegated to, rather than reserved by, the

---

[78] See U.S. CONST. art. I, § 2, cl. 2 (stating that a Representative must be twenty-five years old, a seven-year U.S. citizen, and, when elected, an inhabitant of the state represented).

[79] "The powers not delegated to the United States by the Constitution, nor prohibited by it to the States, are reserved to the States respectively, or to the people." U.S. CONST. amend. X.

States. It is surely no coincidence that the context of federal elections provides one of the few areas in which the Constitution expressly requires action by the States . . . . This duty parallels the duty under Article II that "Each State shall appoint, in such Manner as the Legislature thereof may direct, a Number of Electors." Art. II, § 1, cl. 2.

Taken together, the Court argued, the Constitution's text and structure—informed by constitutional first principles regarding the nature of the Founding itself—refuted the dissent's assertion that the states could add qualifications for its citizens seeking federal office, despite textual silence. "In sum," it concluded, "the available historical and textual evidence, read in light of the basic principles of democracy underlying the Constitution . . . reveal the Framers' intent that neither Congress nor the States should possess the power to supplement the exclusive qualifications set forth in the text of the Constitution." It was the sort of inference drawn from the various textual provisions implementing the federal structure that would have made Professor Black—and John Marshall—proud.

Penumbral reasoning played an important role in *Thornton* despite its rejection by the dissent. It was even more successful in *Printz v. United States* [521 U.S. 898, 117 S. Ct. 2365, 138 L. Ed. 2d 914 (1997)]—in many ways the most penumbral decision of the . . . two Terms. Not surprisingly, critics of the Court conservatives have reserved their most intense criticism for *Printz*. In the most telling example, before reading his dissent from the bench, Justice John Paul Stevens "remarked spontaneously that Justice Scalia's opinion for the Court reminded him of Justice Douglas's opinion in the *Griswold* contraceptives case of 1965, which extrapolated a right to privacy from the Constitution's 'penumbras' and 'emanations.' "

Printz arose from the 1993 amendments to the Gun Control Act of 1968, popularly known as the "Brady Bill." Prior to the establishment of a nationwide network capable of performing an instant background check of persons wishing to purchase handguns, provisions of the Brady Bill required the chief law enforcement officer ("CLEO") in all states to perform these background checks to ascertain if the prospective purchaser had a criminal record, history of mental illness, or some other disqualifying factor that would prevent that person from purchasing a handgun. In short, "the Brady Act purport[ed] to direct state law enforcement officers to participate, albeit only temporarily, in the administration of a federally enacted regulatory scheme."

The Court, in an opinion by Justice Scalia, held that the statute unconstitutionally impressed state CLEOs into federal service, but admitted at the outset that "there is no constitutional text speaking to this precise question . . . ." In finding this provision of the Brady Bill unconstitutional, the Court consulted "historical understanding and practice, . . . the structure of the Constitution, and . . . the jurisprudence of this Court." For our purposes, we shall examine the Court's reliance on constitutional structure and the resulting penumbral inferences.

From the Constitution's structure, Scalia argued, one could discern "essential postulates" that included a system of dual sovereignty consisting of both a federal system of discrete and enumerated powers and a larger area of "[r]esidual state sovereignty." The Court first observed that "[t]his separation of the two spheres is one of the Constitution's structural protections of liberty." Scalia reasoned that the federalist system constructed by the Framers would suffer "if [the federal government] were able to impress into its service—and at no cost to itself—the police officers of the 50 States," because the federal government would be able to increase its own power at the expense of the states. Second, Scalia argued, the scheme in *Printz* transgressed another "essential postulate": the separation of power between the three branches of the federal government. He argued that the "Brady Act effectively transfers this responsibility to thousands of CLEOs in the 50 States, who are left to implement the program without meaningful Presidential control . . . ." The Brady Bill thus potentially undermined the "vigor and accountability" of the executive branch.

Finally, Scalia defended his method of arriving at the Court's decision, and took the dissenters to task for

> falsely presum[ing] that the Tenth Amendment is the exclusive textual source of protection for principles of federalism. Our system of dual sovereignty is reflected in numerous constitutional provisions . . . and not only those, like the Tenth Amendment, that speak to the point explicitly. *It is not at all unusual for our resolution of a significant constitutional question to rest upon reasonable implications.*

Justice Stevens, the author of the majority opinion in *Thornton* that had relied in part upon a textual "basic principles of our democratic system" to strike down Arkansas' term limits law, found the majority's arguments simply unpersuasive. In his dissent, Justice Stevens termed Scalia's argument "remarkably weak," resting as it did on a " 'principle of state sovereignty' mentioned nowhere in the constitutional text." Stevens wrote that there is "not a clause, sentence, or paragraph in the entire text of the Constitution of the United States that supports the proposition that a local police officer can ignore a command contained in a statute enacted by Congress pursuant to an express delegation of power enumerated in Article I."

The dissent then took issue with the substance of Justice Scalia's penumbral inferences. First, in response to Scalia's invocation of enumerated powers, Stevens criticized the majority for not deferring sufficiently to Congress's interpretation of its implicit power in passing the Brady Bill. Second, objecting to Scalia's citation of *INS v. Chadha* [462 U.S. 919, 103 S. Ct. 2764, 77 L. Ed. 2d 317 (1983)] in support of the nontextual "structural protection" provided by the separation of powers, Stevens wrote that unlike this case, *Chadha*

> rested on the Constitution's express bicameralism and presentment requirements, . . . not on judicial inferences drawn from a silent text and a historical record that surely favors the congressional understanding. Indeed, the majority's opinion consists almost entirely of arguments against the substantial evidence weighing in opposition to its view; the Court's ruling is strikingly lacking in affirmative support. Absent even a modicum of textual foundation for its judicially crafted constitutional rule, there should be a presumption that if the Framers had actually intended such a rule, at least one of them would have mentioned it.

Finally, he argued that the Framers' intent to preserve state sovereignty did not answer the question posed in *Printz*: whether Congress may require state employees to perform federal statutory obligations.

It is difficult to square Justice Stevens's dissent with his majority opinion in *Thornton*, except on grounds that the outcome in the latter was more acceptable to him than that in *Printz*. Stevens's dissent provides evidence for this conclusion. He argued that, taken to extremes, the majority's refashioned boundaries of "Our Federalism" "would undermine most of our post-New Deal Commerce Clause jurisprudence." Yet precisely the mode of reasoning Stevens rejects in *Printz* he adopts in a recent opinion on the dormant Commerce Clause.

C. *Separation of Powers*

The Court relied at least in part on penumbral reasoning . . . in deciding *Boerne v. Flores* [521 U.S. 507, 117 S. Ct. 2157, 138 L. Ed. 2d 624 (1997)]. At issue was whether Congress, through its power to enforce the provisions of the Fourteenth Amendment through "appropriate legislation," could pass the Religious Freedom Restoration Act of 1993 ("RFRA"). Among other things, RFRA had the practical effect of overruling an earlier Supreme Court decision. The Court struck down RFRA, in part relying on the principles it regarded as implicit in the separation of powers doctrine.

Justice Kennedy began the analytical portion of the opinion by quoting *Marbury v. Madison*: "The judicial authority to determine the constitutionality of laws, in cases and controversies, is based on the premise that the "powers of the legislature are defined and limited; and that those limits may not be mistaken, or forgotten, the constitution is written." Justice Kennedy's reliance on Marbury is certainly no coincidence. In fact, the reasoning of *Boerne* tracked that of Chief Justice Marshall.

In *Marbury*, before Chief Justice Marshall analyzed the question whether the Court had the power to nullify a law of Congress adjudged to be unconstitutional, he wrote that though the question was itself "deeply interesting," it was "not of an intricacy proportioned to its interest." He proceeded to deduce from the right of the people to establish a supreme authority, the power to separate and limit power in a written constitution, and the *inability* of the established branches to act outside the limits of that document. "It is a proposition too plain to be contested," Marshall wrote, "that the constitution controls any legislative act repugnant to it" and that a legislature may not "alter the constitution by an ordinary act." He then concluded that it was the judiciary's duty to resolve any alleged conflicts between the legislature and the Constitution. To hold otherwise, or to say that the judiciary must defer to Congress, "would subvert the very foundation of all written constitutions." Moreover, "[i]t would be giving to the legislature a practical and real omnipotence, with the same breath which professes to restrict their powers within narrow limits."

Like Marshall, Justice Kennedy quickly apprehended the consequences of a literal interpretation of Section 5, which arguably could be interpreted to grant Congress the authority to determine by normal legislation the substantive content of the Fourteenth Amendment—a position the Court nearly adopted in the 1960s. Kennedy wrote:

> If Congress could define its own powers by altering the Fourteenth Amendment's meaning, no longer would the Constitution be "superior paramount law, unchangeable by ordinary means." It would be "on a level with ordinary legislative acts, and like other acts, . . . alterable when the legislature shall please to alter it." *Marbury v. Madison* 1 Cranch, at 177. Under this approach, it is difficult to conceive of a principle that would limit congressional power . . . . Shifting legislative majorities could change the Constitution and effectively circumvent the difficult and detailed amendment process contained in Article V.

Such a holding would diminish the Court's power, and would subvert the ideal of a written constitution. In addition, as Kennedy noted, such a broad reading of Section 5 would provide a back door for Congress to amend the Constitution outside the Article V process. Kennedy's logic was sound—even the dissenters agreed with his analysis of Congress's Section 5 power—but the text does not specifically command it. Kennedy's conclusions rely on the very nature of a written constitution and the separation of powers doctrine inferred from other provisions and suggested by the Constitution's structure. These principles are *implicit*, not explicit. They are, in fact, penumbral.

. . .

E. Romer v. Evans: *Odd Man Out*

While the 1995 and 1996 Terms often provided the unusual spectacle of the Court's conservatives embracing penumbral reasoning, and its liberals rejecting it largely in disputes over congressional power and state sovereignty, one case from the 1995 Term demonstrated that penumbral reasoning still could be employed, as students of *Griswold* became accustomed, in defense of individual rights. The case is *Romer v. Evans* [517 U.S. 620, 116 S. Ct. 1620, 134 L. Ed. 2d 855 (1996)]. Justice Kennedy, author of the majority opinion and most likely the deciding vote in the case, again showed himself willing to rely on structure and penumbral reasoning. In contrast, the more conservative Justice Scalia—joined by Chief Justice Rehnquist and Justice Thomas—ridiculed and disparaged Kennedy's resort to structure apparently because they found the outcome unpalatable. Although Kennedy's decision was criticized as lacking citation to case law or legal text and as "conspicuously fail[ing] to articulate a principled justification" for its result, it is a clear—and convincing—example of penumbral reasoning. Viewed from this perspective, Kennedy's approach seems less like unprincipled usurpation and more like an articulation of inferences derived from a close reading of the Constitution and the Fourteenth Amendment.

Romer involved a challenge to the constitutionality of a Colorado amendment, popularly known as "Amendment Two," which forbade any state or local governmental entity from enacting any laws, ordinances, or regulations that prohibited discrimination against homosexuals on the basis of their sexual orientation. In rendering its decision, the Court affirmed the Colorado Supreme Court's grant of injunctive relief, but rejected the ground upon which it had relied: that Amendment Two infringed homosexuals' fundamental right to full participation in the political process. Rather, in an opinion influenced by an *amicus curiae* brief written by Laurence Tribe and signed by such constitutional law luminaries as Kathleen Sullivan, Gerald Gunther, and John Hart Ely, the Supreme Court adopted the position that Amendment Two was a per se violation of the Equal Protection Clause of the Fourteenth Amendment.

Kennedy's reasoning proceeded from the principles of the Fourteenth Amendment with which he began his opinion: "that the Constitution 'neither knows nor tolerates classes among citizens,'" and that it is committed to "the law's neutrality where the rights of persons are at stake." Justice Kennedy wrote that the Equal Protection Clause supports this principle and directed the Court's invalidation of Amendment Two. Though the Court dutifully discussed rational basis review, it departed from this traditional model and instead embraced what has been called "rationality with teeth." The animating spirit of this view was best captured by the late Justice William Brennan who wrote that, "if the constitutional conception of 'equal protection of the laws' means anything, it must at the very least mean that a bare . . . desire to harm a politically unpopular group cannot constitute a *legitimate* governmental interest."

Although critics were correct in observing that Kennedy's opinion lacked copious citation to precedent and discussion of original understanding, such focus missed the force of the opinion. A close reading of the Court's opinion shows that the majority avoided textual manipulation, and instead employed a structure-driven, common sense reasoning that was so simple that it almost escaped those of us reared on the exhaustive discussion of Court doctrine and the invocation of hydra-headed "balancing" tests that were a hallmark of the Burger Court. Justifying his return to first principles, Kennedy emphasized the unique nature of Amendment Two: "[i]t is not within our constitutional tradition to enact laws of this sort." He then articulated the theoretical basis for striking down the Colorado amendment:

> Central both to the idea of the rule of law and to our own Constitution's guarantee of equal protection is the principle that government and each of its parts remain open on impartial terms to all who seek its assistance. Equal protection of the laws is not achieved through indiscriminate imposition of inequalities. . . . Respect for this principle explains why laws singling out a certain class of citizens for disfavored legal status or general hardships are rare. A law declaring that in general it shall be more difficult for one group of citizens than for all others to seek aid from the government is itself a denial of equal protection of the laws in the most literal sense. The guaranty of equal protection of the laws is a pledge of the protection of equal laws.

Though Kennedy, like Chief Justice John Marshall, eschewed citations that might have obscured the underlying principle, one can, in retrospect, cite constitutional provisions that support the principles on which the Court relied in its opinion. For example, in support of Kennedy's first principle, that "government and each of its parts remain open on impartial terms," one need only look as far as Article I's requirement that House of Representatives elections occur every other year, and the requirement that states hold elections for federal offices, both of which provide individuals with access to the federal government. Recall, as well, the First Amendment's proscription against any congressional enactment "abridging . . . the right of the people . . . to petition the Government for a redress of grievances." Further, Article IV's guarantee of a "[r]epublican [f]orm of [g]overnment" arguably precludes state governmental policies that impose *de jure* discriminatory classifications on its citizens.

Other provisions of the Constitution support Kennedy's observation that "laws singling out a certain class of citizens for disfavored legal status or general hardships are rare." A glance at the Constitution reveals unqualified prohibitions against both congressional *and* state passage of ex post facto laws and bills of attainder. Even the Contracts Clause reveals the Framers' concern that state legislatures interested in pleasing their debtor-constituents not single out unpopular creditors for unfair treatment. These provisions give substance to the Federalist hope that the government would be of "laws, and not of men." Read with these provisions in mind, the majority's principle of legal equality seems to track the Framers' vision. In fact, the *Romer* decision represented a particularly appropriate use of penumbral reasoning, given the unique nature of Amendment Two. The Colorado referendum highlights one shortcoming of a strict "originalist" or "literalist" interpretation of the Constitution. One will often search a text in vain for answers to questions the Framers never asked themselves. Although laws of the type Colorado attempted to enact would have been unknown to the Framers, the closest analogies to laws extant in the Framers' era were prohibited by the Constitution.

Even more remarkable than the majority's embrace of penumbral reasoning, in which even Justice Stevens joined, was Justice Scalia's emphatic rejection of penumbral reasoning, especially in light of his decision in *Printz*. In his *Romer* dissent, Scalia derided the majority's "heavy reliance upon principles of righteousness rather than judicial holdings," and stated that "[s]ince the Constitution of the United States says nothing about this subject, it is left to be resolved by normal democratic means, including the democratic adoption of provisions in state constitutions." He characterized as "facially absurd" the majority's proposition that laws enacted through the democratic process can be unconstitutional, and concluded that the "opinion ha[d] no foundation in American constitutional law, and barely pretend[ed] to." However, Scalia's overstated, and arguably overheated, dissent was no improvement upon the majority opinion that he criticized.

As an example of penumbral reasoning, *Romer* is not as explicit as was *Griswold*; but a close reading of Kennedy's opinion clearly reveals that the majority reasoned from overarching constitutional inference. More interesting, in light of the cases from this most recent Term, is how outcome seemed to drive the degree to which the members of the Court embraced penumbral reasoning. Moreover, to the extent those dissenting Justices were dissatisfied with the outcomes generated by penumbral reasoning, they tended to attack the majority's interpretive method, seeking to tar it with the brush of illegitimacy. What should be apparent to those Justices, however, is that when they do so, they foul their own nest, leaving themselves open to charges of intellectual hypocrisy in future cases where penumbral reasoning proves useful, whether to achieve "liberal" results as in *Romer* or "conservative" results as in *Printz*.

III. Penumbral Reasoning: Future

As more issues involving federalism and separation of powers dominate the Court's agenda, it will have more opportunities to employ penumbral reasoning. Perhaps the increase in the Court's use of penumbral reasoning can help remove the taint that seems to have attached to its use since *Griswold*. Only by moving past the criticisms of penumbral reasoning as an illegitimate interpretive technique, which really mask dissatisfaction with particular outcomes, can its ultimate utility be analyzed. Viewed disinterestedly, penumbral reasoning has several virtues.

First, penumbral reasoning is perhaps *less* susceptible to abuse "because it ties the development of new principles to the overall structure and purposes of the Constitution . . . ." At the very least, by forcing the Court to place its decisions in the context of the words and structure of the Constitution and to render decisions based on reasonable inferences derived therefrom, penumbral reasoning offers ordinary citizens a better opportunity to participate in a constitutional dialogue than when the Court declares that *original intent* or *stare decisis* mandates a particular outcome. Should one, after all, need a Ph.D. in history, or be a professor of constitutional law to evaluate the Court's decisions? We think not, and suggest that penumbral reasoning provides the Court a way to articulate a logical position without clumsy textual manipulation or "law office history."

Second, because penumbral reasoning focuses on the text of the Constitution itself, and demands not only a close reading of its provisions and their relationship to one another, but also close attention to the Constitution as an enterprise, it is a useful educative tool, both for professionals and for the public. One of the unfortunate legacies of the Court's *Carolene Products* approach to the Constitution is that it seems to preclude any other method of interpretation than what John Hart Ely famously termed "clause bound interpretivism." While ostensibly a method of restraining the judiciary and minimizing the countermajoritarian difficulty, divorcing specific clauses from the overall structure of the Constitution and requiring them to bear the constitutional weight asked of them by the Warren and Burger Courts made for some unconvincing Supreme Court opinions in the 1960s and 1970s. Far from ensuring stability and legitimacy, this approach made constitutional law look like a parlor game—conservative scholars called for a return to "original intent," leftists responded with citations to Foucault, and the Great Interpretive Debate was on. Penumbral reasoning did not even get a fair hearing as the debate polarized around "strict constructionists" and "living Constitutionalists."

Yet its constant reemergence in spite of ridicule suggests that penumbral reasoning plays a vital role. Penumbral reasoning can mediate between the need to root constitutional decisions in the text of the Constitution, and the frank realization that the Framers did not—and could not—provide answers to all of our interpretive questions. As when one concentrates too closely on one part of a television screen or on an Impressionist painting, the Constitution, too, can dissolve into incomprehensibility if one fails to take account of the larger picture.

Additionally, by taking such a broad view, penumbral reasoning can help clean up the "inkblot" problem posed by puzzling constitutional provisions, like the Ninth and Tenth Amendments, the Necessary and Proper Clause, and the Equal Protection Clause. Unclear on their own, these provisions make sense when read alongside related provisions. Similarly, penumbral reasoning is often the only way to vindicate principles that "everyone knows" informed the Constitution, but are nowhere mentioned explicitly: judicial review, federalism, separation of powers, and popular sovereignty, to name a few. In so doing, penumbral reasoning holds the promise of reintroducing a coherence and an integrity too long absent from constitutional doctrine. Regular use might allow for the reintroduction of moribund, but important, constitutional doctrines like the nondelegation principle, once thought essential to guarantee liberty through limited government, or even the Guarantee Clause, which has never done significant constitutional work.

True to the authors' prediction, the Court has again explicitly relied on the notion of structural reasoning in a case decided after their article was published. In *Alden v. Maine,* 527 U.S. 706, 119 S. Ct. 2240, 2269, 144 L. Ed. 2d 636 (1999), the Court held that Congress cannot abrogate a state's immunity from suits in its own courts. The majority opinion, joined by the Court's more conservative justices (Kennedy, Rehnquist, O'Connor, Scalia and Thomas), is noteworthy in that it minimizes the importance of the text of the Eleventh Amendment—which by its terms clearly does not apply to suits in state courts—and relies instead on "history, precedent, and the structure of the Constitution."[4]

§ 5.02 Majoritarianism

During the middle part of the twentieth century, particularly focusing on the activist decisions of the Warren Court such as *Brown v. Board of Education,* 347 U.S. 483, 74 S. Ct. 686, 98 L. Ed. 873 (1954), scholars debated the proper role of judicial review in the constitutional structure—a debate that

---

[4] *Id.* at 2269.

continues to this day. An early participant who actually set the stage for much of what was to follow was Yale Law Professor Alexander Bickel, in his 1962 book, THE LEAST DANGEROUS BRANCH. In that book, Bickel set out to defend the notion of judicial review.[5] But his defense was a very lukewarm one:

The root difficulty is that judicial review is a counter-majoritarian force in our system. There are various ways of sliding over this ineluctable reality. Marshall did so when he spoke of enforcing, in behalf of "the people," the limits that they have ordained for the institutions of a limited government. And it has been done ever since in much the same fashion by all too many commentators. Marshall himself followed Hamilton, who in the 78th *Federalist* denied that judicial review implied a superiority of the judicial over the legislative power—denied, in other words, that judicial review constituted control by an unrepresentative minority of an elected majority. "It only supposes," Hamilton went on, "that the power of the people is superior to both; and that where the will of the legislature, declared in its statutes, stands in opposition to that of the people, declared in the Constitution, the judges ought to be governed by the latter rather than the former." But the word "people" so used is an abstraction. Not necessarily a meaningless or a pernicious one by any means; always charged with emotion, but nonrepresentational—an abstraction obscuring the reality that when the Supreme Court declares unconstitutional a legislative act or the action of an elected executive, it thwarts the will of representatives of the actual people of the here and now; it exercises control, not in behalf of the prevailing majority, but against it. That, without mystic overtones, is what actually happens. It is an altogether different kettle of fish, and it is the reason the charge can be made that judicial review is undemocratic.

Most assuredly, no democracy operates by taking continuous nose counts on the broad range of daily governmental activities. Representative democracies—that is to say, all working democracies—function by electing certain men for certain periods of time, then passing judgment periodically on their conduct of public office. It is a matter of a laying on of hands, followed in time by a process of holding to account—all through the exercise of the franchise. The elected officials, however, are expected to delegate some of their tasks to men of their own appointment, who are not directly accountable at the polls. The whole operates under public scrutiny and criticism—but not at all times or in all parts. What we mean by democracy, therefore, is much more sophisticated and complex than the making of decisions in town meeting by a show of hands. It is true also that even decisions that have been submitted to the electoral process in some fashion are not continually resubmitted, and they are certainly not continually unmade. Once run through the process, once rendered by "the people" (using the term now in its mystic sense, because the reference is to the people in the past), myriad decisions remain to govern the present and the future despite what may well be fluctuating majorities against them at any given time. A high value is put on stability, and that is also a counter-majoritarian factor. Nevertheless, although democracy does not mean constant reconsideration of decisions once made, it does mean that a representative majority has the power to accomplish a reversal. This power is of the essence, and no less so because it is often merely held in reserve.

I am aware that this timid assault on the complexities of the American democratic system has yet left us with a highly simplistic statement, and

---

I shall briefly rehearse some of the reasons. But nothing in the further complexities and perplexities of the system, which modern political science has explored with admirable and ingenious industry, and some of which it has tended to multiply with a fertility that passes the mere zeal of the discoverer—nothing in these complexities can alter the essential reality that judicial review is a deviant institution in the American democracy.

. . .

A further, crucial difficulty must also be faced. Besides being a counter-majoritarian check on the legislature and the executive, judicial review may, in a larger sense, have a tendency over time seriously to weaken the democratic process. Judicial review expresses, of course, a form of distrust of the legislature. . . . "The legislatures," wrote James Bradley Thayer at the turn of the century, . . . are growing accustomed to this distrust and more and more readily inclined to justify it, and to shed the considerations of constitutional restraints . . . turning that subject over to the courts; and what is worse, they insensibly fall into a habit of assuming that whatever they could constitutionally do they may do—as if honor and fair dealing and common honesty were not relevant to their inquiries. . . . The tendency of a common and easy resort to this great function [judicial review] . . . is to dwarf the political capacity of the people, and to deaden its sense of moral responsibility. . . ."

. . .

Such, in outline, are the chief doubts that must be met if the doctrine of judicial review is to be justified on principle. Of course, these doubts will apply with lesser or greater force to various forms of the exercise of the power. For the moment the discussion is at wholesale, and we are seeking a justification on principle, quite aside from supports in history and the continuity of practice. The search must be for a function which might (indeed, must) involve the making of policy, yet which differs from the legislative and executive functions; which is peculiarly suited to the capabilities of the courts; . . . and whose discharge by the courts will not lower the quality of the other departments' performance by denuding them of the dignity and burden of their own responsibility. . . .

. . . [M]any actions of government have two aspects: their immediate, necessarily intended, practical effects, and their perhaps unintended or unappreciated bearing on values we hold to have more general and permanent interest. It is a premise we deduce not merely from the fact of a written constitution but from the history of the race, and ultimately as a moral judgment of the good society, that government should serve not only what we conceive from time to time to be our immediate material needs but also certain enduring values. This in part is what is meant by government under law. But such values do not present themselves ready-made. They have a past always, to be sure, but they must be continually derived, enunciated, and seen in relevant application. And it remains to ask which institution of our government—if any single one in particular—should be the pronouncer and guardian of such values.

Men in all walks of public life are able occasionally to perceive this second aspect of public questions. Sometimes they are also able to base their decisions on it; that is one of the things we like to call acting on principle. Often they do not do so, however, particularly when they sit in legislative assemblies. There, when the pressure for immediate results is strong enough and emotions ride high enough, men will ordinarily prefer to act on expediency rather than take the long view. Possibly legislators—everything else being equal—are as capable as other men of

following the path of principle, where the path is clear or at any rate
discernible. Our system, however, like all secular systems, calls for the
evolution of principle in novel circumstances, rather than only for its
mechanical application. Not merely respect for the rule of established
principles but the creative establishment and renewal of a coherent body
of principled rules—that is what our legislatures have proven themselves
ill equipped to give us.

. . . Judges have or should have, the leisure, the training, and the
insulation to follow the ways of the scholar in pursuing the ends of
government. This is crucial in sorting out the enduring values of a society,
and it is not something that institutions can do well occasionally, while
operating for the most part with a different set of gears. It calls for a habit
of mind, and for undeviating institutional customs. Another advantage
that courts have is that questions of principle never carry the same aspect
for them as they did for the legislature or the executive. . . . The courts
are concerned with the flesh and blood of an actual case. This tends to
modify, perhaps to lengthen, everyone's view. It also provides an extremely
salutary proving ground for all abstractions; it is conducive, in a phrase
of Holmes, to thinking things, not words, and thus to the evolution of
principle by a process that tests as it creates.

Their insulation and the marvelous mystery of time give courts the
capacity to appeal to men's better natures, to call forth their aspirations,
which may have been forgotten in the moment's hue and cry. This is what
Justice Stone called the opportunity for "the sober second thought." Hence
it is that the courts, although they may somewhat dampen the people's
and the legislatures' efforts to educate themselves, are also a great and
highly effective educational institution. . . .

. . . This line of thought may perhaps blunt, if it does not meet, the
force of all the arguments on the other side. No doubt full consistency
with democratic theory has not been established. The heart of the
democratic faith is government by the consent of the governed. The
further premise is not incompatible that the good society not only will
want to satisfy the immediate needs of the greatest number but also will
strive to support and maintain enduring general values. I have followed
the view that the elected institutions are ill fitted, or not so well fitted
as the courts, to perform the latter task. This rests upon the assumption
that the people themselves, by direct action at the ballot box, are surely
incapable of sustaining a working system of general values specifically
applied. But that much we assume throughout, being a representative,
deliberative democracy. Matters of expediency are not generally submitted to direct referendum. Nor should matters of principle, which require
even more intensive deliberation be so submitted. Reference of specific
policies to the people for initial decision is, with few exceptions, the fallacy
of the misplaced mystics, or the way of those who would use the forms
of democracy to undemocratic ends. It is not the way in which working
democracies live. But democracies do live by the idea, central to the process of gaining the consent of the governed, that the majority has the
ultimate power to displace the decision-makers and to reject any part of
their policy. With that idea, judicial review must achieve some measure
of consonance.

[Bickel devotes the rest of his book to discussing ways in which the Court
can restrain itself, and thus assist in the reconciliation with democracy, by
using what he terms "the passive virtues." These are doctrines like standing,
ripeness, political question, certiorari jurisdiction, and the like, which the
Supreme Court can use to avoid deciding questions that are too much at odds
with the current political climate of the times. He continues:]

. . . At the root is the question—in the large—of the role of principle in democratic government. No attempt to lift the Court out of the Lincolnian tension [between expediency and principle] can be successful. The rule of the neutral principles merely distorts the tension, by placing the weight of the Court most often on the side of expediency; for that weight is felt whenever the Court legitimates legislative choices on the constitutional merits. The court is able to play its full role, as it did in the *School Segregation Cases* [Brown v. Board of Education], maintaining itself in the tension on which our society thrives, because it has available the many techniques and devices of the mediating way between the ultimates of legitimation and invalidation. . . .

It follows that the techniques and allied devices for staying the Court's hand, as is avowedly true at least of certiorari, cannot themselves be principled in the sense in which we have a right to expect adjudications on the merits to be principled. They mark the point at which the Court gives the electoral institutions their head and itself stays out of politics, and there is nothing paradoxical in finding that here is where the Court is a most political animal.

Subsequent articles have attempted to respond to Bickel's attack on judicial review in various ways. The following excerpt argues that Bickel's structural assumption about the deviance of judicial review is simply wrong. Rebecca L. Brown, *Accountability, Liberty, and the Constitution*, 98 COLUM. L. REV. 531, 531–38, 571–79 (1998):[6]

Honk if you are tired of constitutional theory. More than ever before thought, the blame lies with Alexander Bickel. At his instigation, contender after contender has stepped forward to try a hand at pulling the sword of judicial review from the stone of illegitimacy. Each suggests a different way to ease the discomfort of unaccountable decisionmaking in a democracy. Some have argued that judicial review is not *countermajoritarian*, but is more supramajoritarian[1] or paramajoritarian,[2] others that it is not *counter*majoritarian,[3] still others that it is not *countermajoritarian*.[4] The curious thing about these defenses of judicial review, however, is that they suggest not that unaccountable decisionmaking is legitimate, but only that it is not really unaccountable. The arguments take the form of a confession and avoidance, rather than a rebuttal, of Bickel's charge.

The vast majority of theorists have failed to challenge Bickel's basic assumption, that political accountability is the sine qua non of legitimacy in government action. As a consequence, that assumption for decades framed the debate in constitutional law. Even the most sympathetic theorists tended to assume the role of apologist for judicial review, while the unsympathetic made concerted efforts to exploit that widespread assumption in order to engender profound skepticism about judging itself.

---

[6] Copyright © 1998 by the Columbia Law Review. Reprinted with permission.

[1] See BRUCE ACKERMAN, WE THE PEOPLE: FOUNDATIONS 6–7 (1991) (setting forth dualist theory in which constitutional limitations are democratically justified by the fact that they were themselves agreed to by the people acting at a higher level of lawmaking).

[2] See JOHN HART ELY, DEMOCRACY AND DISTRUST 87–88 (1980) (setting forth "representation-reinforcing" approach to judicial review

which limits courts' involvement to policy the process of representation).

[3] See Barry Friedman, *Dialogue and Judicial Review*, 91 MICH. L. REV. 577, 590–607 (1993) (arguing that courts do not really act in opposition to majority will); . . . .

[4] See, e.g., Frank N. Easterbrook, *The Supreme Court, 1983 Term—Foreword: The Court and the Economic System*, 98 HARV. L. REV. 4, 15–18 (1984) (demonstrating nonmajoritarian aspects of modern lawmaking practice); . . . .

Judgment was no longer the proper and revered sphere of judges, but was recast as the unforgivable "value imposition." These attacks on the legitimacy of judgment in a democracy have left their mark not only on the academy, but also on the public understanding of the judicial role and on the Supreme Court's understanding of its own role. These effects, in turn, have had palpable implications for the recognition and enforcement of individual rights.

In this Article, I do not emulate Arthur. It seems to me that too much effort has been expended in the quest to solve Bickel's difficulty, especially since efforts to "solve" the difficulty serve rather to entrench the insidious assumption underlying it. Instead, I seek to contribute to the budding effort to resist the siren song of popular sovereignty as the foundation of constitutional thought. I do so by examining the character of accountability itself.

My claim is that political accountability—broadly, the requirement that public officials stand periodically for election—has been misunderstood. Almost universally, it has erroneously been cast as the servant of the constitutional value of majoritarianism. Readers of the Constitution routinely look to the various textual provisions establishing different types of accountability as compelling evidence of an overarching constitutional commitment to a *telos* of majority rule. This understanding contains two important errors: First, it wrongly identifies majoritarianism as the primary constitutional value, and second, it misconceives the purpose of political accountability.

Some scholarly effort has been devoted to attacking the first error. Powerful arguments have been launched to demonstrate that, whatever value a purely majoritarian system might have in the abstract, it surely is not the system that we have. It is not difficult to make the historical case that the Constitution envisions limitations on majority rule and the buffering of popular preference. Yet even those who have recognized that our democracy is not purely majoritarian appear to have succumbed to or ignored the second error, the assumption that the purpose of political accountability is to effectuate majority will. They are thus forced into a defensive position in trying to justify the clear strain of accountable decisionmaking that pervades the constitutional structure. If majority rule is not its purpose, why does the Constitution provide so emphatically for electoral accountability?

Many who have recognized before me that majoritarianism is not the goal of the Constitution have reasoned, essentially, that, because the Constitution contains several familiar departures from a strictly majoritarian system of government, we can safely conclude that it was not intended to establish a pure democracy. Accordingly, there is no theoretical difficulty in allowing an unelected, unaccountable judiciary to review the acts of the elected branches. The difficulty is solved.

This reasoning suffers from a logical fallacy: Even if the Constitution does not embody perfectly accountable government, that does not justify jettisoning accountability altogether for the sake of independent courts. There is quite a bit of ground lying between some ideal of maximum accountability or direct democracy, on the one hand, and life-tenured judges acting autonomously, on the other. In that middle ground lies much of what I see as the dangerous consequence of majoritarian-bound reasoning: If the only justification for courts is that Articles I and II and the Bill of Rights contain certain procedural and substantive limitations on pure majority rule, then those who advocate severe restrictions on courts' judgment have a strong case. "Don't give up on the ideal of majoritarianism altogether," they say, "just because it is tempered somewhat in the Constitution. Rather, adhere to it as closely as our imperfect system will allow." This means (assuming judicial review at all) maximum judicial deference to legislative judgments, narrow reading of the constitutional text, and parsimonious interpretations of the Bill of Rights. That is the interpretative legacy of the majoritarian paradigm.

What has been missing is a model for understanding constitutional government that makes sense of majority rule while still affirmatively boasting judgment—an activity peculiarly ill-suited to majority rule—as an element of the structure of our democracy. I believe such a theory depends on a critical examination of the principle underlying our commitment to majority rule—the principle of political accountability.

This Article posits that accountability is best understood, not as a utilitarian means to achieve maximum satisfaction of popular preferences, but as a structural feature of the constitutional architecture, the goal of which is to protect liberty. In this respect it is much like the other structural constitutional features such as separation of powers, checks and balances, and federalism—all of which are more comfortably accepted as devices for protecting individual rights. It may seem counterintuitive to consider that a system of electorally accountable government might also be designed to serve the end of individual liberty. We have been trained to view popular will as antithetical to the protection of rights. But it is counterintuitive only because we have not properly honed our intuitions about the Constitution that we have.

The resolution of this conundrum asks the reader to abandon the deeply entrenched prejudices that haunt a generation weaned on the countermajoritarian difficulty. It asks the reader to turn Bickel's difficulty on its head and wonder instead how one might justify a system of *majority rule* in a government whose final cause is the protection of *individual rights*. The resolution lies in the almost instinctive realization that unless a government is politically accountable, an independent judiciary that vigorously protects rights from government encroachment could not survive.

Imagine how one would proceed to design a government if one were committed to the principle that the primary goal of government is to protect the liberty of the people from government invasion. Accept with me for the purpose of argument that this was the Framers' commitment, and consider what kinds of structures would plausibly advance the newly formed polity toward that goal. One might well start by designing an institutional body whose job it is to ensure that the laws of the polity—however they may come to be created—are applied to individual cases in a way that preserves basic individual rights. The obvious question then is how to ensure that such a rights-protecting body could itself be sufficiently protected in its independent status to allow it to do that job effectively without being overcome by the very organs of government that the rights-protecting body is designed to cabin. It turns out that a very good answer to that question is the establishment and maintenance of a politically accountable government. Indeed, it may be that a politically accountable government is the *only* effective means of governing a polity while still enabling an independent judiciary to survive.

Thus, the structural feature of accountability for political actors can be understood, not as a means to maximize the preferences of the majority of the people on matters of routine governance, as it has been widely understood, which is a purpose always in tension with a commitment to individual rights, but rather as a means primarily to minimize the risk of tyranny in government, which is not. Accountability serves this goal in two ways: by allowing the people to check abuse of power at the polls if they detect a threat and wish to eradicate it (a traditionally majoritarian check on tyranny) and, more importantly, by involving the polity in standing behind a political structure which includes a judicial branch empowered to step in if the majority is itself carried away by an impulse to tyrannize (a countermajoritarian check).

So understood, majority rule becomes much more than just an article of faith. It gains an anchor of legitimacy that is otherwise elusive in a nation founded on the commitment to individual liberty. It serves, rather than strains, the cause of liberty. At the same time, this understanding frees us from the torment of condemning the protection of individual liberty as "deviant" in our nation.

I will show that there is considerable historical support for the notion of accountability that I urge here, enough to give not insubstantial grounding for the theoretical propositions I will espouse. And that is all I would hope to get from the dubious exercise of searching the founding documents.

The first Part of this Article asks where the fixation on accountability came from. It briefly traces the path of the current preoccupation with accountability and the possible philosophical roots of such a preoccupation. This history corresponds closely to the rise of what others have called the "majoritarian paradigm" in American law. But that history does more. It also demonstrates that a group that I will call the "modern majoritarian" theorists—those writing after 1960—have introduced a skepticism about the possibility of rights as exogenous limits on majority rule, an attitude that was not characteristic of those whom they claim to follow. Thus we can consider ourselves liberated from any ancestral legacy establishing accountability as the centerpiece of legitimate public law. The majoritarian paradigm as it persists today, with its concomitant belligerence toward judgment, was new with Bickel and his contemporaries.

. . . [The Article] goes on to inquire into what might be the more accurate understanding of accountability in the American brand of democracy. It explores the historical backdrop of representation against which the American Framers developed our representative system as expounded in a historical thesis of Edmund Morgan. A plausible reading of this history shows that the American Constitution rejected the English (and ancient Greek) understanding of representation, which connoted popular *participation* in government, and substituted an understanding of representation which retained for the people the means to *protect* themselves from government through the electoral process. This shift from "participation" to "protection" as a description of the people's role in government represents a fundamental change in the concept of liberty. Thus, when the modern majoritarians avow that "[t]he Constitution preserves our liberties by providing that all of those given the authority to make policy are directly accountable to the people through regular elections," they have invoked an understanding of "liberties" that conflicts with the evidence of this nation's history and comports much more with English tradition. That tradition suggests a "utility-maximizing" definition of accountability, while the structure of representation unique to the United States envisions a "tyranny-minimizing" purpose for accountability.

[T]his "protection" theory of representation suggests that an important purpose of elections under the Constitution is to supply an extrinsic check on the entire system of power delegated by the people to their representatives. Unlike the English and Greek models of representation that preceded it, the American system retained for the people the power to stand outside the government and enforce the terms of the delegation. The government so monitored includes an independent court charged with protecting individual rights. Thus, I suggest that democracy, with its commitment to popular sovereignty, is best understood as the hand-maiden of liberty.

. . .

If one's commitment is to liberty, then the theoretical starting point for government should be a body whose duty it is to protect the liberty of the people and whose inclination to infringe liberty is institutionally at its weakest. In Hamilton's view, the judiciary was indisputably the "weakest of the three departments of power . . . [I]t can never attack with success either of the other two; . . . and the general liberty of the people can never be endangered from that quarter . . . ." Thus, the judiciary was entrusted with the primary responsibility for guarding the value that underlay the entire constitutional structure: The courts were expected to commit to "inflexible and uniform adherence to the rights of the Constitution, and of individuals . . . ."

This body, entrusted with such an indispensable role, "must ultimately depend upon the aid of the executive arm even for the efficacy of its judgments." It is not enabled to go out and take life, liberty, or property from people, and, given its political insulation, would have very little reason to do so. Thus, the judiciary does not present a "difficulty," but is by far the easiest branch to reconcile with a government devoted to the preservation of liberty.

The more provocative question is how to justify a legislature, or an executive, in a government devoted to the preservation of liberty. They are the branches endowed with the powers that might well enable them to trespass upon the rights of the people, as well as being subject to influences that might motivate them to do so. These branches are checked by various means in the constitutional scheme to hamper their accomplishment of this nefarious end. But those checks operate only at the broadest levels; because the two elected branches—which do hold the daunting powers of sword and purse—are accountable to a majority vote of the electorate, ultimately they are not institutionally responsive to individual or minority interests, and might not be deterred from exercises of their substantial power which trampled those interests, assuming most of the people were supportive.

The question of how to justify the existence and nature of such branches, seemingly at odds with notions of liberty and individual rights, has two answers—an easy one and a hard one. The easy answer is that government power must be lodged somewhere to accomplish the more instrumental objectives of government, such as common defense and other measures needed to promote the public good. I do not mean to suggest that governance is a constitutional goal of negligible importance; the powers needed to govern must be placed in some repository other than the judiciary. But why place them in an elected, accountable government which has been shown to present a real threat to liberty, a primary objective of government itself? This requires the hard answer.

The judgments of the rights-protecting branch, the judiciary, must be enforced by someone if liberty is to be preserved. Moreover, the members of this judicial branch must be subject to some scheme for selection and removal. And most importantly, this branch must nonetheless remain truly independent of those whose exercises of power it reviews, or its value in protecting individual rights will be lost. Consider the possibility that, to support the independent, rights-protecting judiciary, the Constitution provided that the power to govern would be placed in the hands of a hereditary monarch or unaccountable despot. The despot's exercise of power would be reviewed by the independent courts for conformity with constitutional limitations. Quite quickly, one would expect to see the un-accountable government seeking to take over the independent court, to control its judgments, or at the very least to resist any unwanted orders issuing from the court. There would be no structural incentive for this government to enforce or support the independence of the court. It is unimaginable that such an unaccountable government would allow the court to survive as a truly independent reviewer of its actions, because there would be no external check to prevent the government from disre-garding the court's judgments. The stronger branch would simply canni-balize the weaker.

Historical anecdote bears out this prediction. It is no coincidence that, when accountable government has broken down in regimes of the past, the courts have been prime targets of the autocratic ruler. Two of Hitler's early acts—to ensure that the judiciary would erect no barrier to his goals—were suspending constitutional provisions protecting individual rights, and then pressuring the Prussian Supreme Court of Administra-tion to issue an edict expressly declaring that the orders and actions of the Gestapo were not subject to judicial review. This was a nominally accountable government acting to ensure its own insulation from indepen-dent scrutiny, with no extrinsic check to prevent that structural corrosion. And Pablo Escobar's efforts to undermine another nominally accountable government included a strike, quite literally, at the courts when he murdered half of the Supreme Court of Colombia to avoid being subjected to the powers of independent courts via extradition. These examples merely support the intuition that it would be extremely difficult for a truly independent court, committed to the preservation of individual rights through judicial review, to coexist with a government that had no external check through electoral accountability. "[L]iberty can have nothing to fear from the judiciary alone, but would have everything to fear from its union with either of the other departments . . . ."

Thus, it is essential to the security of the courts that government have a mechanism that keeps it within its proper bounds and forces it to resist the temptation to swallow up the judiciary in pursuit of its own ends. One way of achieving this security derives from the distinctively American conception of representation. One of the genuinely unique aspects of the Constitution was its dependence on a principle of representation "where all authority flows from and returns at stated periods to, the people." Representation, while having ancient roots, was redefined when it came to America as the pervasive principle on which the entire government rested, even as it comprised only a limited delegation of power. "All parts of the government were equally responsible but limited spokesmen for the people, *who remained as the absolute and perpetual sovereign, distrib-uting bits and pieces of power to their various agents.*" Thus, in America, it became obvious that there was no supreme power except what the people themselves held. "The powers of the people were thus never alien-ated or surrendered to a legislature. Representation, in other words, never eclipsed the people-at-large, as apparently it did in the English House of Commons." They delegated a portion of their power in whatever manner, and for whatever time, they chose.

This unique structure of American government, then, does not divide all power amongst the branches. It divides all *delegated* power amongst the branches, always retaining the role of the people as an overseer of the entire system. Thus, if the executive refused to enforce the orders of the court, or if the legislature tried to impeach the members of the court without warrant, the people would still stand outside of those actions and could pass judgment on them through their retained political powers by holding elected officials accountable for any such breach of trust. Thus, the encroachment into the independence of the judiciary that seemed inevitable under any form of autocratic government is subject to an extrinsic check by the people under their own Constitution. And this role for the people gives meaning to the Constitution's commitment to accountability, without making it necessary to jettison its equally clear commitment to liberty.

There lies the hard answer to the question why, in a system whose final cause is liberty, the powers of government should be housed in an accountable body, elected by the people: to support the existence of the judiciary and thus to allow for the continual protection of liberty. John Hart Ely's theory, discussed above, leads to the conclusion that the Bill of Rights exists to support majoritarian government. If he is right, the Constitution is a miserable failure. The government is not majoritarian and does not even come close to enabling pure majority preferences to prevail in the policymaking process. But Ely had it exactly backwards. A better understanding of the system we have is that *majoritarian government exists to support the Bill of Rights.*

All of the criticism, skepticism, and accusation that has been leveled at judicial review in this country notwithstanding, it appears that this nation has a strong commitment to the principle of judicial independence. There is clearly a tension here, perhaps even a schizophrenia. But in their capacity as overseers of the delegations of power they have collectively made, the people have tended to support judicial independence overwhelmingly at moments when that issue achieved salience. If my theory of accountability is defensible as a descriptive matter, one would expect to find moments in history when the people have had an opportunity to weigh in on the structural questions that define their government.

Moments of constitutional awareness and action, then, would mean times when the people have been called upon in some way to consider the issue of judicial independence and take a stand on it, perhaps not even explicitly. Much empirical work has been done to examine whether judicial independence is anything more than a myth in this country. Most conclude that it is not. But, for me, the important lesson to be learned from this body of work is that the vast majority of political efforts to interfere structurally with the independence of the judiciary have failed. There are many moments in history in which such efforts have been made, dating back to the beginning of the republic. Attempts typically employ the following tactics: use of the Senate's confirmation power; the enactment of constitutional amendments to change the Court or its decisions; impeachment of judges; withdrawing jurisdiction from the Court; altering the selection and removal process for judges; requiring supermajority votes within the Court for certain outcomes; allowing revision of Court decisions by more representative bodies; removing the power of judicial review; slashing the budget; and altering the size of the Court.

One notable example of such efforts [is] Franklin Roosevelt's infamous Court-packing plan, which did not succeed. All of the other Court-curbing bills that were prepared during the same period of conflict between the Court and the administration met a similar fate. Similarly, in the 1950s, despite vehement public passion on the issues of desegregation, suppression of political subversion, and criminal procedure, of over fifty Court-curbing bills introduced in Congress, only one very modest one was passed.

Another important period of congressional anger with the Court occurred in the early and mid-1960s, a period when the Court was often in the news. Several socially divisive issues such as prayer in public schools and apportionment had come to the Court, and its decisions had met with widespread criticism. The issue of curbing the Court became a prominent campaign issue in the contest between Goldwater and Johnson; with the election of Johnson, the attacks on the Court subsided. This is an example in which the question of the Court's independence was explicitly aired in the political arena, and was resolved at the ballot box in favor of judicial independence. A more recent example can be found in the issue of abortion. Although many, including Presidents Carter and Reagan and a substantial number of citizens, opposed the practice of abortion, no one translated that substantive position into a successful political campaign to erode the Court's independence with regard to its decision in *Roe v. Wade*. Many bills and constitutional amendments were proposed in Congress taking advantage of several of the above methods of controlling the judiciary. Despite bitter and well-aired opposition to *Roe v. Wade* itself, the separate position arguing for curbing the independence of the Court has so far never garnered enough political support to succeed.

A final example of salience for the question of judicial independence is the confirmation hearings for Judge Robert Bork to become an Associate Justice of the Supreme Court in 1987. In those hearings, the principal issue—widely publicized and politicized—can be understood as the degree to which Judge Bork would honor the independence of the judiciary as a member of the Court. His tenacious insistence on the primacy of majority rule and judicial deference to legislative decisions can fairly be seen in retrospect as a referendum on the people's desire to have their Court exercise judgment independent of current popular preference. The publicly accountable Senate ultimately resolved that issue in favor of a commitment to judicial independence.

There may be a hint of contradiction in the idea of testing the people's support for judicial independence by popular vote. If votes could be relied on to preserve the more enduring principles of the community, we would not need a constitution as a precommitment to those principles. Nor would we need independent courts to enforce them against our passing preferences. But there is something meaningful in asking whether the polity appears to be supporting the way that the government is carrying out its trust. That, I argue, is the core of accountability under the Constitution.

This understanding of accountability confronts the Bickelian vision of constitutional democracy—so absolutely integral to constitutional debate for over thirty years—head on. My effort has been to topple majoritarian government from its pedestal as the primary value in our constitutional government, and replace it with a different model of constitutional understanding. That model, I have argued, accords primacy to the value of liberty and views accountability as a structural means to achieve liberty. This model relieves judges of the need to apologize for the exercise of judgment in interpreting the Constitution, allowing them to realize that they serve in an institutional structure designed to provide a hospitable environment for that exercise–a structure ultimately supported by constitutional democracy.

It is not my aim in this Article to suggest particular interpretations of constitutional provisions, but rather to suggest that freeing judges from a Bickelian orientation would have consequences for those interpretations. Without a default rule that legislatures have some penumbral "right" to do as they please to individuals in the absence of clear judicial justification for interference, the courts could more responsibly bring to bear the various influences essential to constitutional judgment in striking a balance between majority preference and individual right. Perhaps we have had our fill of arguments about how judges are more accountable than we thought or legislatures less so. This model could free up academic debate for a more useful discussion about how to provide meaningful protection of individual rights in an increasingly heterogeneous society in which government is "representative" of fewer and fewer. In such a world, the assumptions underlying the countermajoritarian difficulty become more and more hazardous to liberty.

An accountable government with no independent judiciary is perfectly imaginable. It would lead to a majoritarian system in which individuals and political minorities would shoulder whatever burdens the political majority chose to impose upon them, with nothing but political remedies. An independent judiciary with no accountable government, however, is unimaginable.

The answer that accountability exists to serve the protection of people from their own representative government raises some questions of its own. One obvious retort is that this understanding of accountability, intended to free us from the yoke of majority rule, actually relegates the governmental system to popular sovereignty once again. In a broad sense, this is true. Ultimately, if the people go so far toward rights skepticism that they no longer believe in the Constitution and oppose the institution of the independent judiciary, then there is not much that a theory of constitutional interpretation can do to rescue judicial review or judgment. It would be as illegitimate to force a constitutional government down the throats of an unwilling populace as it would be to force an autocratic one. But as long as the Constitution persists in holding on to the loyalty of most Americans, we would be well advised to think about the principles that it purports to carry forward for this polity. It places a high premium on liberty, defined to mean the protection of citizens from government, which is promoted by both majoritarian and nonmajoritarian means. It places a high premium on judgment, that of representatives and that of judges, both of whom are entrusted with the duty to protect liberty.

This Article has been an effort to fill a void in the thinking about the role of the courts in the constitutional system. What has been missing from the literature is a way to understand electoral accountability so that it does not betray the Constitution's commitment to individual liberty. I am simply not content to brand the "citadel of the public justice" as "a deviant institution in the American democracy." Thus, I have used the concept of representation in its historical setting to create a model of the Constitution in which an accountable system of government is not irreconcilable with the idea of an independent judiciary. Conceived as interconnected essentials of a world in which liberty is the final cause, neither the accountable decisionmaker nor the unaccountable is illegitimate, neither is deviant. They are simply the yin and yang of American constitutionalism, tugging in opposite ways perhaps, but always interdependent, complementing one another in the joint enterprise of constituting a polity in which "[j]ustice is the end of government."

§ 5.03   Representation-Reinforcement

Structural argument can produce general theories as well as bearing on particular areas of law such as separation of powers and federalism. John Hart Ely's "representation-reinforcing" theory of judicial review is a product of structural reasoning that proceeds from ideas about the themes behind much of our scheme of government. Ely reads the Constitution as a whole to contain only, or primarily, values of process rather than substantive values. He starkly presents the question whether the courts should limit their role to that of enforcers of proper procedure (broadly defined), rather than having an important voice in the types of outcomes that the procedures produce. These materials reflect that controversy in excerpts from Ely's book and from an article in response by Professor Laurence Tribe of Harvard Law School.

First, JOHN HART ELY, DEMOCRACY AND DISTRUST: A THEORY OF JUDICIAL REVIEW 73–77, 86–88 (1980):[7]

An interpretivist approach—at least one that approaches constitutional provisions as self-contained units—proves on analysis incapable of keeping faith with the evident spirit of certain of the provisions. When we search for an external source of values with which to fill in the Constitution's open texture, however—one that will not simply end up constituting the Court a council of legislative revision—we search in vain. Despite the usual assumption that these are the only options, however, they are not, for value imposition is not the only possible response to the realization that we have a Constitution that needs filling in. A quite different approach is available, and to discern its outlines we need look no further than to the Warren Court.

That Court's reputation as "activist" or interventionist is deserved. A good deal of carping to the contrary notwithstanding, however, that is where its similarity to earlier interventionist Courts, in particular the early twentieth-century Court that decided *Lochner v. New York* and its progeny, ends. For all the while the commentators of the Warren era were talking about ways of discovering fundamental values, the Court itself was marching to a different drummer. The divergence wasn't entirely self-conscious, and the Court did lapse occasionally into the language of fundamental values: it would be surprising if the thinking of earlier Courts and the writings of the day's preeminent commentators hadn't taken some toll. The toll, however, was almost entirely rhetorical: the constitutional decisions of the Warren Court evidence a deep structure significantly different from the value-oriented approach favored by the academy.

Many of the Warren Court's most controversial decisions concerned criminal procedure or other questions of what judicial or administrative process is due before serious consequences may be visited upon individuals—process-oriented decisions in the most ordinary sense. But a concern with process in a broader sense—with the process by which the laws that govern society are made—animated its other decisions as well. Its unprecedented activism in the fields of political expression and association obviously fits this broader pattern. Other Courts had recognized the connection between such political activity and the proper functioning of the democratic process: the Warren Court was the first seriously to act upon it. That Court was also the first to move into, and once there seriously to occupy, the voter qualification and malapportionment areas. These were certainly interventionist decisions, but the interventionism was fueled not by a desire on the part of the Court to vindicate particular substantive values it had determined were important or fundamental, but rather by a desire to ensure that the political process—which is where such values *are* properly identified, weighed, and accommodated—was open to those of all viewpoints on something approaching an equal basis.

Finally there were the important decisions insisting on equal treatment for society's habitual unequals: notably racial minorities, but also aliens, "illegitimates," and poor people. But rather than announcing that good or value X was so important or fundamental it simply had to be provided

---

or protected, the Court's message here was that insofar as political officials had chosen to provide or protect X for some people (generally people
like themselves), they had better make sure that everyone was being
similarly accommodated or be prepared to explain pretty convincingly
why not. Whether these two broad concerns of the Warren Court—with
clearing the channels of political change on the one hand, and with
correcting certain kinds of discrimination against minorities on the
other—fit together to form a coherent theory of representative government, or whether, as is sometimes suggested, they are actually inconsistent impulses, is a question I shall take up presently. But however that
may be, it seems to be coming into focus that the pursuit of these "partici-
pational" goals of broadened access to the processes and bounty of
representative government, as opposed to the more traditional and
academically popular insistence upon the provision of a series of particular substantive goods or values deemed fundamental, was what marked
the work of the Warren Court. Some condemn and others praise, but at
least we're beginning to understand that something different from old-
fashioned value imposition was for a time the order of the day.

The Warren Court's approach was foreshadowed in a famous footnote
in *United States v. Carolene Products Co.*, decided in 1938. Justice Stone's
opinion for the Court upheld a federal statute prohibiting the interstate
shipment of filled milk, on the ground that all it had to be was "rational"
and it assuredly was that. Footnote four suggested, however, that mere
rationality might not always be enough:

> There may be narrower scope for operation of the presumption of
> constitutionality when legislation appears on its face to be within a
> specific prohibition of the Constitution, such as those of the first ten
> amendments, which are deemed equally specific when held to be
> embraced within the Fourteenth . . .

> It is unnecessary to consider now whether legislation which re-
> stricts those political processes which can ordinarily be expected to
> bring about repeal of undesirable legislation, is to be subjected to
> more exacting judicial scrutiny under the general prohibitions of the
> Fourteenth Amendment than are most other types of legislation . . .

> Nor need we enquire whether similar considerations enter into the
> review of statutes directed at particular religious . . . or national . . .
> or racial minorities . . . ; whether prejudice against discrete and
> insular minorities may be a special condition, which tends seriously
> to curtail the operation of those political processes ordinarily to be
> relied upon to protect minorities, and which may call for a correspond-
> ingly more searching judicial inquiry.

The first paragraph is pure interpretivism: it says the Court should
enforce the "specific" provisions of the Constitution. We've seen, though,
that interpretivism is incomplete: there are provisions in the Constitution
that call for more. The second and third paragraphs give us a version of
what that more might be. Paragraph two suggests that it is an appropriate function of the Court to keep the machinery of democratic government
running as it should, to make sure the channels of political participation
and communication are kept open. Paragraph three suggests that the
Court should also concern itself with what majorities do to minorities,
particularly mentioning laws "directed at" religious, national, and racial
minorities and those infected by prejudice against them.

For all its notoriety and influence, the *Carolene Products* footnote has
not been adequately elaborated. Paragraph one has always seemed to
some commentators not quite to go with the other two. Professor Lusky,

who as Stone's law clerk was substantially responsible for the footnote, has recently revealed that the first paragraph was added at the request of Chief Justice Hughes. Any implied substantive criticism seems misplaced: positive law has its claims, even when it doesn't fit some grander theory. It's true, though, that paragraphs two and three are more interesting, and it is the relationship between those two paragraphs that has not been adequately elaborated. Popular control and egalitarianism are surely both ancient American ideals; indeed dictionary definitions of "democracy" tend to incorporate both. Frequent conjunction is not the same thing as consistency, however, and at least on the surface a principle of popular control suggests an ability on the part of a majority simply to outvote a minority and thus deprive its members of goods they desire. . . . I have suggested that both *Carolene Products* themes are concerned with participation: they ask us to focus not on whether this or that substantive value is unusually important or fundamental, but rather on whether the opportunity to participate either in the political processes by which values are appropriately identified and accommodated, or in the accommodation those processes have reached, has been unduly constricted. But the fact that two concepts can fit under the same verbal umbrella isn't enough to render them consistent either, and a system of equal participation in the processes of government is by no means self-evidently linked to a system of presumptively equal participation in the benefits and costs that process generates; in many ways it seems calculated to produce just the opposite effect. . . .

. . .

. . . [Yet] what are sometimes characterized as two conflicting American ideals—the protection of popular government on the one hand, and the protection of minorities from denials of equal concern and respect on the other—in fact can be understood as arising from a common duty of representation. Once again, Madison said it early and well:

> I will add, as a fifth circumstance in the situation of the House of Representatives, restraining them from oppressive measures, that they can make no law which will not have its full operation on themselves and their friends, as well as on the great mass of society. . . . If it be asked, what is to restrain the House of Representatives from making legal discriminations in favor of themselves and a particular class of the society? I answer: the genius of the whole system; the nature of just and constitutional laws; and above all, the vigilant and manly spirit which actuates the people of America . . .

[Ely then summarizes his arguments to come, whose full development we omit here:]

The remainder of this chapter will comprise three arguments in favor of a participation-oriented, representation-reinforcing approach to judicial review. The first will take longer than the others, since it will necessitate a tour, albeit brisk, of the Constitution itself. What this tour will reveal, contrary to the standard characterization of the Constitution as "an enduring but evolving statement of general values," is that in fact the selection and accommodation of substantive values is left almost entirely to the political process and instead the document is overwhelmingly concerned, on the one hand, with procedural fairness in the resolution of individual disputes (process writ small), and on the other, with what might capaciously be designated process writ large—with ensuring broad participation in the processes and distributions of government. An argument by way of *ejusdem generis* seems particularly justified in this case, since the constitutional provisions for which we are attempting to identify modes of supplying content, such as the Ninth Amendment and the

Privileges or Immunities Clause, seem to have been included in a "we must have missed something here, so let's trust our successors to add what we missed" spirit. On my more expansive days, therefore, I am tempted to claim that the mode of review developed here represents the ultimate interpretivism. Our review will tell us something else that may be even more relevant to the issue before us—that the few attempts the various framers *have* made to freeze substantive values by designating them for special protection in the document have been ill-fated, normally resulting in repeal, either officially or by interpretative pretense. This suggests a conclusion with important implications for the task of giving content to the document's more open-ended provisions, that preserving fundamental values is not an appropriate constitutional task.

The other two arguments are susceptible to briefer statement but are not less important. The first is that a representation-reinforcing approach to judicial review, unlike its rival value-protecting approach, is not inconsistent with, but on the contrary (and quite by design) entirely supportive of, the underlying premises of the American system of representative democracy. The second is that such an approach, again in contradistinction to its rival, involves tasks that courts, as experts on process and (more important) as political outsiders, can sensibly claim to be better qualified and situated to perform than political officials.

[After Ely's detailed discussion of the arguments just summarized, he concludes, *id.* at 101–03:]

As I have tried to be scrupulous about indicating, the argument from the general contours of the Constitution is necessarily a qualified one. In fact the documentary dictation of particular substantive outcomes has been rare (and generally unsuccessful), but our Constitution is too complex a document to lie still for *any* pat characterization. Beyond that, the premise of the argument, that aids to construing the more open-ended provisions are appropriately found in the nature of the surrounding document, though it is a premise that seems to find acceptance on all sides, is not one with which it is impossible to disagree. Thus the two arguments that follow, each overtly normative, are if anything more important than the one I have just reviewed. The first is entirely obvious by now, that unlike an approach geared to the judicial imposition of "fundamental values," the representation-reinforcing orientation whose contours I have sketched and will develop further is not inconsistent with, but on the contrary is entirely supportive of, the American system of representative democracy. It recognizes the unacceptability of the claim that appointed and life-tenured judges are better reflectors of conventional values than elected representatives, devoting itself instead to policing the mechanisms by which the system seeks to ensure that our elected representatives will actually represent. There may be an illusion of circularity here: my approach is more consistent with representative democracy because that's the way it was planned. But of course it isn't any more circular than setting out to build an airplane and ending up with something that flies.

The final point worth serious mention is that (again unlike a fundamental-value approach) a representation-reinforcing approach assigns judges a role they are conspicuously well situated to fill. My reference here is not principally to expertise. Lawyers *are* experts on process writ small, the processes by which facts are found and contending parties are allowed to present their claims. And to a degree they are experts on process writ larger, the processes by which issues of public policy are fairly determined: lawyers do seem genuinely to have a feel, indeed it is hard to see what other special value they have, for ways of insuring that everyone gets his or her fair say. But too much shouldn't be made of this. Others, particularly the full-time participants, can also claim expertise on how the political process allocates voice and power. And of course many legislators are lawyers themselves. So the point isn't so much one of expertise as it is one of perspective.

The approach to constitutional adjudication recommended here is akin to what might be called an "antitrust" as opposed to a "regulatory" orientation to economic affairs—rather than dictate substantive results it intervenes only when the "market," in our case the political market, is systematically malfunctioning. (A referee analogy is also not far off: the referee is to intervene only when one team is gaining unfair advantage, not because the "wrong" team has scored.) Our government cannot fairly be said to be "malfunctioning" simply because it sometimes generates outcomes with which we disagree, however strongly (and claims that it is reaching results with which "the people" really disagree—or would "if they understood"—are likely to be little more than self-deluding projections). In a representative democracy value determinations are to be made by our elected representatives, and if in fact most of us disapprove we can vote them out of office. Malfunction occurs when the *process* is undeserving of trust, when (1) the ins are choking off the channels of political change to ensure that they will stay in and the outs will stay out, or (2) though no one is actually denied a voice or a vote, representatives beholden to an effective majority are systematically disadvantaging some minority out of simple hostility or a prejudiced refusal to recognize commonalities of interest, and thereby denying that minority the protection afforded other groups by a representative system.

Obviously our elected representatives are the last persons we should trust with identification of either of these situations. Appointed judges, however, are comparative outsiders in our governmental system, and need worry about continuance in office only very obliquely. This does not give them some special pipeline to the genuine values of the American people: in fact it goes far to ensure that they won't have one. It does, however, put them in a position objectively to assess claims—though no one could suppose the evaluation won't be full of judgment calls—that either by clogging the channels of change or by acting as accessories to majority tyranny, our elected representatives in fact are not representing the interests of those whom the system presupposes they are.

Harvard Law Professor Laurence Tribe's critique of Ely's approach is from *The Puzzling Persistence of Process-Based Constitutional Theories,* 89 YALE L.J. 1063, 1063–80 (1980):[8]

In deciding constitutional cases, the Supreme Court has often invoked a vision of how politics should work, justifying judicial intervention as a response to supposed gaps between that vision and political reality. Legislation or other governmental action is of constitutional concern, the Court suggests, when it seems to obstruct political representation and accountability—by blocking speech or voting, for example—or when it reveals the existence of past or present obstructions by distributing the law's benefits and burdens in ways that show a particular group to have been denied fair representation. By invalidating legislative or administrative acts of this sort, the Court can reason, it avoids controversial judgments about substantive issues left open by the Constitution's text and history, and safeguards the representative character of the political process.

[8] Reprinted by permission of the Yale Law Journal Company, Fred B. Rothman & Company, and Laurence Tribe.

It is easy to see why courts would be attracted to this way of describing the content and role of constitutional law. Such an account permits courts to perceive and portray themselves as servants of democracy even as they strike down the actions of supposedly democratic governments. But other constitutional theorists, unencumbered by the judiciary's rhetorical needs, also find the idea of perfecting process, and process alone, to be powerfully magnetic. In the most recent and lucid argument for a process-perfecting view of constitutional law, John Ely's *Democracy and Distrust,* the vision is boldly stated:

[C]ontrary to the standard characterization of the Constitution as "an enduring but evolving statement of general values," . . . in fact the selection and accommodation of substantive values is left almost entirely to the political process and instead the document is overwhelmingly concerned, on the one hand, with procedural fairness in the resolution of individual disputes (process writ small), and on the other, with what might capaciously be designated process writ large—with ensuring broad participation in the processes and distributions of government.

Yet it is not difficult to show that the constitutional theme of perfecting the processes of governmental decision is radically indeterminate and fundamentally incomplete. The process theme by itself determines almost nothing unless its presuppositions are specified, and its content supplemented, by a full theory of substantive rights and values—the very sort of theory the process-perfecters are at such pains to avoid. If that proposition, which this Article seeks to elaborate, is correct, it leaves us with a puzzle: why do thoughtful judges and scholars continue to put forth process-perfecting theories as though such theories could banish divisive controversies over substantive values from the realm of constitutional discourse by relegating those controversies to the unruly world of power?

One difficulty that immediately confronts process theories is the stubbornly substantive character of so many of the Constitution's most crucial commitments: commitments defining the values that we as a society, acting politically, must respect. Plainly, the First Amendment's guarantee of religious liberty and its prohibition of religious establishment are substantive in this sense. So, too, is the Thirteenth Amendment, in its abolition of slavery and repudiation of the Constitution's earlier, ostensibly procedural, protections of that institution.

In many of its parts, the Constitution also evinces a substantive commitment to the institution of private property and to the contractual expectations that surround it. The just compensation clause of the Fifth Amendment is an obvious example. The contracts clause of article I, section 10 is another. The old substantive due process, which is obviously an important part of our constitutional history and thus significant for our understanding of what the Constitution is about, also served to protect the transactions and expectations to which the institution of private property gives rise. Whatever our views of the substantive due process heyday, most of us would readily concede that the framers of the 1787 Constitution adopted a federal system of government in order to, among other goals, help secure the institution of private property. When Madison, in his theory of faction, suggested that shifting the legislative responsibility for certain problems from the state to the national level could help assure that majorities would not trample minority rights, the problems he had in mind were largely economic; the minority rights the federal system would protect were, for the most part, rights of property and contract.

Religious freedom, antislavery, private property: much of our constitutional history can be written by reference to just these social institutions and substantive values. That the Constitution has long addressed such matters, and often with beneficial effect, ought to surprise no one. What is puzzling is that anyone can say, in the face of this reality, that the Constitution is or should be predominantly concerned with *process* and *not* substance.

But our constitutional reality poses even deeper problems for process theorists. Even the Constitution's most procedural prescriptions cannot be adequately understood, much less applied, in the absence of a developed theory of fundamental rights that are secured to persons against the state—a theory whose derivation demands precisely the kinds of controversial substantive choices that the process proponents are so anxious to leave to the electorate and its representatives.

Much of the Constitution does indeed appear to address matters of procedure. Sometimes the subject is *adjudicative* process—the process due to individuals who become defendants in criminal or civil litigation or targets of administrative actions. Elsewhere, the Constitution focuses on *representative* process—including the process that governs the election of Congress, of the President, or of state representative bodies. That the *subject* in all these cases is procedure, however, is not to say that the *meaning* and *purpose* of the Constitution's prescriptions on each such subject are themselves merely procedural. There is no reason to suppose that "constitutive" rules—rules defining the basic structure of political and legal relations—can or should be essentially neutral on matters of substantive value.

The very dichotomy just drawn—between adjudicative and representative process—would prove incoherent without a substantive theory. How do we decide which *form* of participation the complaining individual may claim: the right to be heard as a litigant, or the right to be counted as a voter? The question whether individuals may insist on being heard by rulemakers, for whom they have already (directly or indirectly) voted, has bedeviled administrative law since the turn of the century. . . .

The question of whether adjudicative or representative process is required in a given context simply cannot be analyzed in terms of how fairly and accurately various participatory processes reflect the interests and inputs of those governed by them. Deciding what *kind* of participation the Constitution demands requires analysis not only of the efficacy of alternative processes but also of the character and importance of the interest at stake—its role in the life of the individual as an individual. That analysis, in turn, requires a theory of values and rights as plainly substantive as, and seemingly of a piece with, the theories of values and rights that underlie the Constitution's provisions addressing religion, slavery, and property.

Once one has decided whether the Constitution requires adjudicative or representative process in a particular setting, one must again rely on substantive values in elaborating the requirements of either procedural form. Consider first the problem of adjudicative process. Certainly the Fifth Amendment's self-incrimination and double jeopardy clauses embody concerns for protecting individual dignity in the criminal process. A substantive concern for individual "privacy" necessarily underpins the Fourth Amendment. Other superficially procedural provisions of the Constitution, such as the rights to counsel, confrontation, bail, and jury trial, echo similar themes; they function, often at some cost to the efficiency and accuracy of fact-finding, to prevent the government from treating individuals in the criminal process as though they were objects.

Even outside the criminal context, elaborating rights of adjudicative process requires recourse to a substantive theory. Procedural due process rights are not simply means of protecting whatever "entitlements" happen to be conferred by legislation or administrative regulation. Otherwise, the drafters of an entitlement could frame it in the procedural terms of their choice, and the constitutional guarantee would be reduced to a right to receive whatever process the drafters had defined as due. But that view has been repeatedly rejected by the Supreme Court, which has never fully embraced a purely positivist theory of procedural due process. The only alternative theories, however, are ones that posit a right to individual dignity, or some similarity substantive norm, as the base on which conceptions of procedural fairness are constructed.

If process is constitutionally valued, therefore, it must be valued not only as a means to some independent end, but for its intrinsic characteristics: being heard is part of what it means to be a person. Process itself, therefore, becomes substantive. . . .

The process theorist is similarly confounded by questions about the right to vote—the quintessential procedural right in the realm of politics. Voting-rights issues commonly take one of two forms. One set of issues concerns *who* votes. Is the electorate to include racial minorities, women, District of Columbia residents, eighteen-year-olds? Is it to include only property owners, only property owners and parents, only residents, only citizens? What of the disenfranchisement of children? Who votes, it turns out, is a profoundly substantive question. For *who* participates—who counts—in the electoral process is a question that must precede any inquiry into the fairness of the process itself. The issue goes not to fairness procedurally, but to our sense of who constitutes a political community, and of which relations in society must be horizontal rather than vertical, fraternal rather than hierarchical. And if *any* question is plainly substantive, that question is fundamentally so.

The second set of issues concerns how voting power is to be *allocated* among those who are included within an electoral constituency. Sometimes, in this context, the Supreme Court looks to whether the election is one that chooses representatives or one that resolves a one-shot issue, or whether voters are voting as individuals or as, say, property owners. But generally, the Court has enforced the famous rule announced in the reapportionment cases: one person, one vote. The obvious substantive underpinnings of this rule—its role as an expression of the equal respect in which we as a society aspire to hold each individual—all of this the theorists of perfecting process must ignore. They can defend the rule only hesitantly, claiming, for example, that it is merely a matter of administrative convenience. Again we observe the irony already revealed in the adjudicative process cases: because embracing process for its own sake means embracing process as substance—as an expression of the value in which we would hold individuals—theorists who would defend constitutional law as ultimately reducible to the quest for perfection of process cannot themselves treat process as primary. Again the puzzle deepens: as the next section will show, theorists of perfecting process are not only undercut by their inability affirmatively to advocate process as such, but their negative critique of obstructed process is stunted as well.

For those who would fill the gaps left by the Constitution's ambiguities and silences with representation-reinforcing principles, perhaps the core "process value" is the value of protecting certain minorities from perennial defeat in the political arena. The theme was anticipated by John Marshall; it assumed a central role for Harlan Fiske Stone; it signally motivated Earl Warren; and it has been elaborated by numerous scholars, most powerfully in the work of John Ely. The idea seems as simple as it sounds reasonable: governmental action that burdens groups effectively excluded

from the political process is constitutionally suspect. In its most sophisticated form, the resulting judicial scrutiny is seen as a way of invalidating
governmental classifications and distributions that turn out to have been
motivated either by prejudiced hostility or by self-serving stereotypes.

It all sounds pretty good—until we ask how we are supposed to
distinguish such "prejudice" from principled, if "wrong," disapproval.
Which groups are to count as "discrete and insular minorities"? Which
are instead to be deemed appropriate losers in the ongoing struggle for
political acceptance and ascendancy?

To begin with, of course, the theory must clearly distinguish itself from
its *reductio ad absurdum:* "whichever group happens to lose the political
struggle or fails to command the attention of the legislature . . . is—by
that fact alone—a discrete and insular minority." How about focusing on
immutability, discreteness, insularity? For the process theorist, all such
features might seem helpful in suggesting why a legislature would regard
some groups as "different" and thus fall prey to cruel or self-servingly
careless stereotyping. Or such features may signal why other groups
would fail to interact with a group considered "different," or to engage
in the usual protective logrolling.

But features like immutability are neither sufficient nor necessary. For
in looking at social attitudes toward groups, one cannot simply play
Linnaeus and engage in taxonomy. One cannot speak of "groups" as
though society were objectively subdivided along lines that are just there
to be discerned. Instead, people *draw* lines, attribute differences, as a way
of ordering social existence—of deciding who may occupy what place, play
what role, engage in what activity . . . .

The temptation to think of groups as simply given is exacerbated by
the complex interaction between social attitudes and those identified as
group members. Individuals who find themselves so identified may indeed
see themselves as group members; because they approve of the options
that society leaves them and want to protect those options, they identify
the options with themselves, the differentiated "group." Alternatively,
assertion of group status may be a form of internal exile, a way of
repudiating the limited possibilities for action that the larger social
structure would allow, a choice of "exit" rather than "voice."

This way of thinking about groups, I believe, captures not only much
of the dynamics of race, but also much of the social significance of religion,
alienage, gender, sexual preference, legitimacy, wealth—traits we as a
society commonly use in separating out groups. Views about the "differ-
entness"of groups generally, therefore, may reflect an interacting set of
judgments about activities or options or roles, expressed sometimes
harmoniously and sometimes dialectically by *both* "we" and "they." If so,
the conclusion that a legislative classification reveals prejudicial stereotypes must, at bottom, spring from *a disagreement with the judgments
that lie behind the stereotype:* judgments about the propriety of the options
left to individuals or the burdens imposed on them.

Consider several illustrations. Burglars are subject to widespread
hostility: indeed, the activity that defines the group is everywhere
legislatively prohibited. Are burglars therefore a "suspect class"? Of course
not. Suspect status is unthinkable—but only because of the substantive
value we attach to personal security, and the importance for us of the
system of private property and its rules of transfer, which the burglary
prohibition preserves. If we speak of burglars as a class, we do so as a
way of giving form to our view that burglary *is* a "different" activity,
different not so much because burglars visibly define a group as because
we disapprove of the activity, deny it any claim to protection as a right.

Homosexuals, too, are subject to widespread hostility; legislation penalizing homosexuals and homosexual practices is common. Homosexuals often do not identify themselves by sexual preference when acting politically, and generally do not "come out of the closet" to refute the traditional stereotypes. But even if they did, legislation might be unaltered. Coming out of the closet could dispel ignorance, but it may not alter belief. Legislators may see homosexuals as "different" not out of ignorance, but on principle—on the basis of a morality that treats certain sexual practices as repugnant to a particular view of humanity, and thus regards people who engage in those practices as "other." Such legislation can be rejected only on the basis of a principle that is equally substantive: a view of what it means to be a person, and to have a sexual identity. Process and prejudice thus seem profoundly beside the point. Any constitutional distinction between laws burdening homosexuals and laws burdening exhibitionists, between laws burdening Catholics and laws burdening pickpockets, must depend on a substantive theory of which groups are exercising fundamental rights and which are not.

Indeed, even laws putting blacks and women "in their place"—banning racial intermarriage, say, or excluding women from combat—are likely to reflect neither simple hostility nor self-serving blindness but *a substantive vision of proper conduct*—a vision that no amount of attention to flaws in the political process could condemn or correct. Accordingly, the idea of blacks or women as properly segregated beings can be rejected *only* by finding a constitutional basis for concluding that, in our society, such hierarchical visions are substantively out of bounds, at least as a justification for government action. And such a finding would in turn entail a theory of unenumerated substantive rights, rights at best *suggested* by constitutional text and history, rights whose necessarily controversial elaboration the process theorists seek to eschew.

The crux of any determination that a law unjustly discriminates against a group—blacks, or women, or even men—is not that the law emerges from a flawed process, or that the burden it imposes affects an independently fundamental right, but that the law is part of a pattern that denies those subject to it a meaningful opportunity to realize their humanity. Necessarily, such an approach must look beyond process to identify and proclaim fundamental substantive rights. Whatever difficulties this may entail, it seems plain that important aspects of constitutional law, including the determination of which groups deserve special protection, can be given significant content in no other way. Thus it is puzzling indeed that process-based approaches—designed to deny the need for, and legitimacy of, any such substantive theory—should nonetheless continue to find such articulate proponents and persist in attracting such perceptive adherents.

If protecting minorities requires a theory of substantive rights, might another value, that of "political openness"—of clearing the channels for change through speech and voting—be salvaged as a unifying theme for the process-minded? . . . [T]here are at least three fundamental difficulties with any effort to reduce substantive rights to mere mechanisms for channel-clearing. The first problem is the inherently incomplete nature of channel-clearing as an aim. Why *should* politics be open to equal participation by all? Doesn't that norm itself presuppose some substantive vision of human rights? Why wouldn't a vision rich enough to support a reasonably complete theory of political openness also suffice to generate a theory of which substantive claims individuals may make against the majority?

The second problem is the absence of any plausible stopping point for channel-clearing theories. If the system must be open to change through peaceful persuasion, how do we distinguish between example and advocacy or between demonstration and assertion as forms of persuasion? If we do not draw some such distinction, life-style choices that seek to convince by demonstration—communal living arrangements or homosexual marriage, for example—are entitled to constitutionally protected status. Surely that is not what process theorists have in mind! Efforts to draw the necessary distinctions, however, are inevitably unsatisfactory. To accord special protection to advocacy alone is to censor those messages that can be conveyed only by example. Moreover, dichotomies such as speech and conduct, expression and action, or persuasion and instruction, do not in truth separate.

If the acts of individuals may be demonstrations, and hence forms of persuasion, may not the same be said of the acts of government? The actions of government define expectations, confer legitimacy, establish a status quo, and thus necessarily shape the nature and distribution of interests and attitudes in society itself. The state shapes society almost as much as society shapes the state: this is the third problem that any channel-clearing theory must confront—but cannot surmount without losing its "procedural" status.

Government subsidies to "major" political parties, for example, or the failure of state governments to provide funds to compensate school districts lacking "rich" property tax bases, are government actions that affirm some aspects of the status quo as desirable, and others as inevitable. Such government actions are at present constitutional, as are governmental decisions that inculcate the young with the standard public virtues and defeat the self-defining, value-forming, and power-amassing efforts of all but the more standard social groupings. Unable to support a challenge to such exercises of power, a truly procedural channel-clearing theory seems doomed to irrelevance, for without such challenge government may well be able to shape the "will" of the governed in the image of those who govern, reducing consent and representation to all but empty ideals.

§ 5.04 Conclusion

An important question to ask, of those who offer structural inference as a way to claim greater fidelity to the Constitution, is whether they have succeeded in assuaging the concern about excessive judicial discretion. Are the structures and themes of the Constitution sufficiently clear that they constrain judges more than judges would be constrained if they were not reasoning from structure? Yet, even if the answer to that question is no, perhaps it might still be the case that responsible interpretation of the Constitution should include the drawing of inferences from the entire document. Perhaps penumbral or structural reasoning is an inevitable consequence of a true commitment to fidelity to the Constitution.

§ 5.05 Bibliography

Akhil Reed Amar, *Intratextualism*, 112 HARV. L. REV. 747 (1999).

Charles L. Black, A NEW BIRTH OF FREEDOM: HUMAN RIGHTS, NAMED AND UNNAMED (1997).

Vincent Blasi, *Creativity and Legitimacy in Constitutional Law*, 80 YALE L.J. 176 (1970) (reviewing CHARLES BLACK, STRUCTURE AND RELATIONSHIP IN CONSTITUTIONAL LAW (1969))

Rebecca L. Brown, *Separated Powers and Ordered Liberty*, 139 U. PA. L. REV. 1513 (1991).

John Hart Ely, *Another Such Victory: Constitutional Theory and Practice in a World Where Courts are no Different From Legislatures*, 77 VA. L. REV. 833 (1991).

James E. Fleming, *Constructing the Substantive Constitution*, 72 TEX. L. REV. 211 (1993).

James E. Fleming, *Securing Deliberative Autonomy*, 48 STAN. L. REV. 1 (1995).

Michael J. Klarman, *The Puzzling Resistance to Political Process Theory*, 77 VA. L. REV. 747 (1991).

John F. Manning, *Constitutional Structure and Judicial Deference to Agency Interpretations of Agency Rules*, 96 COLUM. L. REV. 612 (1996).

Daniel R. Ortiz, *Pursuing a Perfect Politics: The Allure and Failure of Process Theory*, 77 VA. L. REV. 721 (1991).

Michael J. Perry, *The Legitimacy of Particular Conceptions of Constitutional Interpretation*, 77 VA. L. REV. 669 (1991).

Martin H. Redish, THE CONSTITUTION AS POLITICAL STRUCTURE (1995)

Edward L. Rubin & Malcolm Feeley, *Federalism: Some Notes on a National Neurosis*, 41 UCLA L. REV. 903 (1994).

Lawrence Sager, *The Incorrigible Constitution*, 65 N.Y.U. L. R.EV 893 (1990).

Frederick Schauer, *The Calculus of Distrust*, 77 VA. L. REV. 653 (1991).

Girardeau A. Spann, RACE AGAINST THE COURT: THE SUPREME COURT AND MINORITIES IN CONTEMPORARY AMERICA (1993).

Cass R. Sunstein, THE PARTIAL CONSTITUTION (1993).

Symposium—*On Democracy and Distrust: Ten Years Later*, 77 VA. L. REV. (1991).

Laurence Tribe, *Structural Due Process*, 10 HARV. CIV. RTS.-CIV. LIB. L. REV. 269 (1975).

John C. Yoo, *The Judicial Safeguards of Federalism*, 70 S. CAL. L. REV. 1311 (1997).

Chapter 6

Moral Reasoning

§ 6.01 Introduction

The inscription above the front entrance to the Supreme Court declares, "Equal Justice Under Law." Yet some would claim that "justice" is not the concern of the Supreme Court; that, rather, justice is a value arising only from the laws and policies of the representative branches. Judge Robert Bork, for example, has said that "We administer justice according to law. Justice in a larger sense, justice according to morality, is for the Congress and the President to administer, if they see fit, through the creation of new law."[1]

The topic of this Chapter is the place of moral reasoning in the interpretation of the Constitution. Moral reasoning can be formal according to philosophical principle, or it can take the form of filling in gaps in the constitutional language based on what the judge deems to be the best, or right, answer under prevailing societal standards as the judge perceives them. Many scholars acknowledge that some degree of judgment is inevitable in the process of constitutional interpretation, and that judgment invariably calls for the making of some form of choices among competing societal values or principles. If one agrees that such choices are a necessary part of the task of interpretation, then it may be better for judges to do it explicitly rather than hiding behind any number of mechanical formulas that pretend to avoid value choices while still facilitating them. The call for moral reasoning according to a judge's honest assessment of the enduring principles of the society—as opposed to the judge's own preferences—is one approach to the question of how to give meaning to the open-textured provisions of the Constitution without simply resorting to personal preference.

Asking judges to make interpretive choices on the basis of their readings of social morality rather than their own value preferences might reduce the concern that many voice about allowing unelected judges to determine fundamental law. Yet it would still present the question of the propriety of supplementing constitutional law with judicial understandings of moral principle—and the feasibility of distinguishing those understandings from judges' own personal values.

---

[1] Hohri v. United States, 793 F.2d 304, 313 (D.C. Cir. 1986) (Bork, J., dissenting from denial of rehearing en banc), rev'd, 482 U.S. 64 (1987). Justice Holmes expressed what may be a similar sentiment in an exchange with Judge Learned Hand, in which Hand reportedly told Holmes to "do justice." Holmes replied, "That is not my job. It is my job to apply the law." See Michael Herz, "Do Justice!": Variations of a Thrice-Told Tale, 82 VA. L. REV. 111 (1996) (discussing different versions of the story and their implications).

§ 6.02   The Use of Moral Philosophy to Discover the Right Answers to Constitutional Questions

Ronald Dworkin is the leading constitutional theorist advocating a moral reading of the Constitution. He defends that view in his book, FREEDOM'S LAW: THE MORAL READING OF THE AMERICAN CONSTITUTION:[2]

This book . . . illustrates a particular way of reading and enforcing a political constitution, which I call the *moral* reading. Most contemporary constitutions declare individual rights against the government in very broad and abstract language, like the First Amendment of the United States Constitution, which provides that Congress shall make no law abridging "the freedom of speech." The moral reading proposes that we all—judges, lawyers, citizens—interpret and apply these abstract clauses on the understanding that they invoke moral principles about political decency and justice. The First Amendment, for example, recognizes a moral principle—that it is wrong for government to censor or control what individual citizens say or publish—and incorporates it into American law. So when some novel or controversial constitutional issue arises—about whether, for instance, the First Amendment permits laws against pornography—people who form an opinion must decide how an abstract moral principle is best understood. They must decide whether the true ground of the moral principle that condemns censorship, in the form in which this principle has been incorporated into American law, extends to the case of pornography.

The moral reading therefore brings political morality into the heart of constitutional law. But political morality is inherently uncertain and controversial, so any system of government that makes such principles part of its law must decide whose interpretation and understanding will be authoritative. In the American system judges—ultimately the justices of the Supreme Court—now have that authority, and the moral reading of the Constitution is therefore said by its critics to give judges absolute power to impose their own moral convictions on the public. I shall shortly try to explain why that crude charge is mistaken. I should make plain first, however, that there is nothing revolutionary about the moral reading in practice. So far as American lawyers and judges follow any coherent strategy of interpreting the Constitution at all, they already use the moral reading . . . .

That explains why both scholars and journalists find it reasonably easy to classify judges as "liberal" or "conservative": the best explanation of the differing patterns of their decisions lies in their different understandings of central moral values embedded in the Constitution's text. Judges whose political convictions are conservative will naturally interpret abstract constitutional principles in a conservative way, as they did in the early years of this century, when they wrongly supposed that certain rights over property and contract are fundamental to freedom. Judges whose convictions are more liberal will naturally interpret those principles in a liberal way, as they did in the halcyon days of the Warren Court. The moral reading is not, in itself, either a liberal or a conservative charter or strategy. It is true that in recent decades liberal judges have ruled more statutes or executive orders unconstitutional than conservative judges have. But that is because conservative political principles for

[2] RONALD DWORKIN, FREEDOM'S LAW: THE MORAL READING OF THE AMERICAN CONSTITUTION 2–17, 22–24, 81–83 (Harvard University Press 1996). Copyright © 1996 by Ronald Dworkin. Reprinted by permission of Ronald Dworkin and the Harvard University Press. Please note that portions of this excerpt are from different chapters of FREEDOM'S LAW; and some portions were originally published prior to their re-publication in FREEDOM'S LAW.

the most part either favored or did not strongly condemn the measures that could reasonably be challenged on constitutional grounds in those decades. There have been exceptions to that generalization. Conservatives strongly disapprove, on moral grounds, the affirmative action programs . . . , which give certain advantages to minority applicants for universities or jobs, and conservative justices have not hesitated to follow their understanding of what the moral reading required in such cases. That reading helps us to identify and explain not only these large-scale patterns, moreover, but also more fine-grained differences in constitutional interpretation that cut across the conventional liberal-conservative divide. Conservative judges who particularly value freedom of speech, or think it particularly important to democracy, are more likely than other conservatives to extend the First Amendment's protection to acts of political protest, even for causes that they despise, as the Supreme court's decision protecting flag-burners shows.

So, to repeat, the moral reading is not revolutionary in practice. Lawyers and judges, in their day-to-day work, instinctively treat the Constitution as expressing abstract moral requirements that can only be applied to concrete cases through fresh moral judgments. [T]hey have no real option but to do so. But it would indeed be revolutionary for a judge openly to recognize the moral reading, or to admit that it is his or her strategy of constitutional interpretation, and even scholars and judges who come close to recognizing it shrink back, and try to find other, usually metaphorical, descriptions of their own practice. There is therefore a striking mismatch between the role the moral reading actually plays in American constitutional life and its reputation. It has inspired all the greatest constitutional decisions of the Supreme Court, and also some of the worst. But it is almost never acknowledged as influential even by constitutional experts, and it is almost never openly endorsed even by judges whose arguments are incomprehensible on any other understanding of their responsibilities. On the contrary, the moral reading is often dismissed as an "extreme" view that no really sensible constitutional scholar would entertain. It is patent that judges' own views about political morality influence their constitutional decisions, and though they might easily explain that influence by insisting that the Constitution demands a moral reading, they never do. Instead, against all evidence, they deny the influence and try to explain their decisions in other—embarrassingly unsatisfactory—ways. They say they are just giving effect to obscure historical "intentions," for example, or just expressing an overall but unexplained constitutional "structure" that is supposedly explicable in nonmoral terms.

This mismatch between role and reputation is easily explained. The moral reading is so thoroughly embedded in constitutional practice, and is so much more attractive, on both legal and political grounds, than the only coherent alternatives that it cannot readily be abandoned, particularly when important constitutional issues are in play. But the moral reading nevertheless seems intellectually and politically discreditable. It seems to erode the crucial distinction between law and morality by making law only a matter of which moral principles happen to appeal to the judges of a particular era. It seems grotesquely to constrict the moral sovereignty of the people themselves—to take out of their hands, and remit to a professional elite, exactly the great and defining issues of political morality that the people have the right and the responsibility to decide for themselves.

That is the source of the paradoxical contrast between mainstream constitutional practice in the United States, which relies heavily on the moral reading of the Constitution, and mainstream constitutional theory, which wholly rejects that reading. The confusion has had serious political costs. Conservative politicians try to convince the public that the great constitutional cases turn not on deep issues of political principle, which they do, but on the simpler question of whether judges should change the Constitution by fiat or leave it alone. For a time this view of the constitutional argument was apparently accepted even by some liberals. They called the Constitution a "living" document and said that it must be "brought up to date" to match new circumstances and sensibilities. They said they took an "active" approach to the Constitution, which seemed to suggest reform, and they accepted John Ely's characterization of their position as a "noninterpretive" one, which seemed to suggest inventing a new document rather than interpreting the old one. In fact, as we shall see, this account of the argument was never accurate. The theoretical debate was never about whether judges should interpret the Constitution or change it—almost no one really thought the latter—but rather about how it should be interpreted. But conservative politicians exploited the simpler description, and they were not effectively answered.

The confusion engulfs the politicians as well, however. They promise to appoint and confirm judges who will respect the proper limits of their authority and leave the Constitution alone, but since this misrepresents the choices judges actually face, the politicians are often disappointed. When Dwight Eisenhower, who denounced what he called judicial activism, retired from office in 1961, he told a reporter that he had made only two mistakes as President—and that they were both on the Supreme Court. He meant Chief Justice Earl Warren, who had been a Republican politician when Eisenhower appointed him to head the Supreme Court, but who then presided over one of the most "activist" periods in the Court's history, and Justice William Brennan, another politician who had been a state court judge when Eisenhower appointed him, and who became one of the most liberal and explicit practitioners of the moral reading of the Constitution in modern times.

Presidents Ronald Reagan and George Bush were both profound in their outrage at the Supreme Court's "usurpation" of the people's privileges. They said they were determined to appoint judges who would respect rather than defy the people's will. In particular, they (and the platform on which they ran for the presidency) denounced the Court's 1973 *Roe v. Wade* decision protecting abortion rights, and promised that their appointees would reverse it. But . . . when the opportunity to do so came, three of the justices Reagan and Bush had appointed between them voted, surprisingly, not only to retain that decision in force, but to provide a new legal basis for it that more evidently adopted and relied on a moral reading of the Constitution. The expectations of politicians who appoint judges are often defeated in that way, because the politicians fail to appreciate how thoroughly the moral reading, which they say they deplore, is actually embedded in constitutional practice. Its role remains hidden when a judge's own convictions support the legislation whose constitutionality is in doubt—when a justice thinks it morally permissible for the majority to criminalize abortion, for example. But the ubiquity of the moral reading becomes evident when some judge's convictions of principle—identified, tested, and perhaps altered by experience and argument—bend in an opposite direction, because then enforcing the Constitution must mean, for that judge, telling the majority that it cannot have what it wants.

Senate hearings considering Supreme Court nominations tend toward the same confusion. These events are now thoroughly researched and widely reported by the media, and they are often televised. They offer a superb opportunity for the public to participate in the constitutional process. But the mismatch between actual practice and conventional theory cheats the occasion of much of its potential value. . . . Nominees and legislators all pretend that hard constitutional cases can be decided in a morally neutral way, by just keeping faith with the "text" of the document, so that it would be appropriate to ask the nominee any questions about his or her own political morality. (It is ironic that Justice Thomas, in the years before his nomination, gave more explicit support to the moral reading than almost any other well-known constitutional lawyer has; he insisted . . . that conservatives should embrace that interpretive strategy and harness it to a conservative morality.) Any endorsement of the moral reading—any sign of weakness for the view that constitutional clauses are moral principles that must be applied through the exercise of moral judgment—would be suicidal for the nominee and embarrassing for his questioners. In recent years, only the hearings that culminated in the defeat of Robert Bork . . . seriously explore issues of constitutional principle, and they did so only because Judge Bork's opinions about constitutional law were so obviously the product of a radical political morality that his convictions could not be ignored. In the confirmation proceedings of now Justices Anthony Kennedy, David Souter, [Clarence] Thomas, Ruth Bader Ginsburg, and Stephen Breyer, however, the old fiction was once again given shameful pride of place.

The most serious result of this confusion, however, lies in the American public's misunderstanding of the true character and importance of its constitutional system. As I have argued elsewhere, the American ideal of government not only under law but under principle as well is the most important contribution our history has given to political theory. Other nations and cultures realize this, and the American ideal has increasingly and self-consciously been adopted and imitated elsewhere. But we cannot acknowledge our own contribution, or take the pride in it, or care of it, that we should.

That judgment will appear extravagant, even perverse, to many lawyers and political scientists. They regard enthusiasm for the moral reading, within a political structure that gives final interpretive authority to judges, as elitist, antipopulist, antirepublican and antidemocratic. That view rests, as we shall see, on a popular but unexamined assumption about the connection between democracy and majority will, an assumption that American history has in fact consistently rejected. When we understand democracy better, we see that the moral reading of a political constitution is not antidemocratic but, on the contrary, is practically indispensable to democracy. I do not mean that there is no democracy unless judges have the power to set aside what a majority thinks is right and just. Many institutional arrangements are compatible with the moral reading, including some that do not give judges the power they have in the American structure. But none of these varied arrangements is in principle more democratic than others. Democracy does not insist on judges having the last word, but it does not insist that they must not have it. I am already too far ahead of my argument, however. I must say more about what the moral reading is before I can return to the question of why it has been so seriously misunderstood.

The Moral Reading

The clauses of the American Constitution that protect individuals and minorities from government are found mainly in the so-called Bill of Rights—the first several amendments to the documents—and the further amendments added after the Civil War. (I shall sometimes use the phrase "Bill of Rights," inaccurately, to refer to all the provisions of the Constitution that establish individual rights, including the Fourteenth Amendment's protection of citizens' privileges and immunities and its guarantee of due process and equal protection of the laws.) Many of these clauses are drafted in exceedingly abstract moral language. The First Amendment refers to the "right" of free speech, for example, the Fifth Amendment to the process that is "due" to citizens, and the Fourteenth to protection that is "equal." According to the moral reading, these clauses must be understood in the way their language most naturally suggests: they refer to abstract moral principles and incorporate these by reference, as limits on government's power.

There is of course room for disagreement about the right way to restate these abstract moral principles, so as to make their force clearer for us, and to help us to apply them to more concrete political controversies. I favor a particular way of stating the constitutional principles at the most general possible level. . . .I believe that the principles set out in the Bill of Rights, taken together, commit the United States to the following political and legal ideals: government must treat all those subject to its dominion as having equal moral and political status; it must attempt, in good faith, to treat them all with equal concern; and it must respect whatever individual freedoms are indispensable to those ends, including but not limited to the freedoms more specifically designated in the document, such as the freedoms of speech and religion. Other lawyers and scholars who also endorse the moral reading might well formulate the constitutional principles, even at a very general level, differently and less expansively than I just have however, and though this introductory chapter is meant to explain and defend the moral reading, not my own interpretations under it, I should say something about how the choice among competing formulations should be made.

Of course the moral reading is not appropriate to everything a constitution contains. The American Constitution includes a great many clauses that are neither particularly abstract nor drafted in the language of moral principle. Article II specifies, for example, that the President must be at least thirty-five years old, and the Third Amendment insists that government may not quarter soldiers in citizens' houses in peacetime. The latter may have been inspired by a moral principle: those who wrote and enacted it might have been anxious to give effect to some principle protecting citizens' rights to privacy, for example. But the Third Amendment is not itself a moral principle: its *content* is not a general principle of privacy. So the first challenge to my own interpretation of the abstract clauses might be put this way. What argument or evidence do I have that the equal protection clause of the Fourteenth Amendment (for example), which declares that no state may deny any person equal protection of the laws, has a moral principle as *its* content though the Third Amendment does not?

This is a question of interpretation or, if you prefer, translation. We must try to find language of our own that best captures, in terms we find clear, the content of what the "framers" intended it to say. (Constitutional scholars use the word "framers" to describe, somewhat ambiguously, the various people who drafted and enacted a constitutional provision.) History is crucial to that project, because we must know something about the circumstances in which a person spoke to have any good idea of what he meant to say in speaking as he did. We find nothing in history, however, to cause us any doubt about what the framers of the Third Amendment meant to say. Given the words they used, we cannot sensibly interpret them as laying down any moral principle at all, even if we believe they were inspired by one. They said what the words they used would normally be used to say: not that privacy must be protected, but that soldiers must not be quartered in houses in peacetime. The same process of reasoning—about what the framers presumably intended to say when they used the words they did—yields an opposite conclusion about the framers of the equal protection clause, however. Most of them no doubt had fairly clear expectations about what legal consequences the Fourteenth Amendment would have. They expected it to end certain of the most egregious Jim Crow practices of the Reconstruction period. They plainly did not expect it to outlaw official racial segregation in school—on the contrary, the Congress that adopted the equal protection clause itself maintained segregation in the District of Columbia school system. But they did not *say* anything about Jim Crow laws or school segregation or homosexuality or gender equality, one way or the other. They said that "equal protection of the laws" is required, which plainly describes a very general principle, not any concrete application of it.

The framers meant, then, to enact a general principle. But which general principle? That further question must be answered by constructing different elaborations of the phrase "equal protection of the laws," each of which we can recognize as a principle of political morality that might have won their respect, and then by asking which of these it makes most sense to attribute to them, given everything else we know. The qualification that each of these possibilities must be recognizable as a political *principle* is absolutely crucial. We cannot capture a statesman's efforts to lay down a general constitutional principle by attributing to him something neither he nor we could recognize as a candidate for that role. But the qualification will typically leave many possibilities open. It was once debated, for example, whether the framers intended to stipulate, in the equal protection clause, only the relatively weak political principle that laws must be enforced in accordance with their terms, so that legal benefits conferred on everyone, including blacks, must not be denied, in practice, to anyone.

History seems decisive that the framers of the Fourteenth Amendment did not mean to lay down only so weak a principle as that one, however, which would have left states free to discriminate against blacks in any way they wished so long as they did so openly. Congressmen of the victorious nation, trying to capture the achievements and lessons of a terrible war, would be very unlikely to settle for anything so limited and insipid, and we should not take them to have done so unless the language leaves no other interpretation plausible. In any case, constitutional interpretation must take into account past legal and political practice as well as what the framers themselves intended to say, and it has not been settled by unchallengeable precedent that the political principle incorporated in the Fourteenth Amendment is not that very weak one, but something more robust. Once that is conceded, however, then the principle must be something *much* more robust, because the only alternative, as a translation of what the framers actually *said* in the equal protection clause, is that they declared a principle of quite breathtaking scope and power: the principle that government must treat everyone as of an equal status and with equal concern.

. . . [T]his brief discussion has mentioned two important restraints that sharply limit the latitude the moral reading gives to individual judges. First, under that reading constitutional interpretation must begin in what the framers said, and, just as our judgment about what friends and strangers say relies on specific information about them and the context in which they speak, so does our understanding of what the framers said. History is therefore plainly relevant. But only in a particular way. We turn to history to answer the question of what they intended to *say*, not the different question of what *other* intentions they had. We have no need to decide what they expected to happen, or hoped would happen, in consequence of their having said what they did, for example; their purpose, in that sense, is not part of our study. That is a crucial distinction . . . . We are governed by what our lawmakers said—by the principles they laid down—not by any information we might have about how they themselves would have interpreted those principles or applied them in concrete cases.

Second, and equally important, constitutional interpretation is disciplined, under the moral reading, by the requirement of constitutional *integrity*. . . . Judges may not read their own convictions into the Constitution. They may not read the abstract moral clauses as expressing any particular moral judgment, no matter how much that judgment appeals to them, unless they find it consistent in principle with the structural design of the Constitution as a whole, and also with the dominant lines of past constitutional interpretation by other judges. They must regard themselves as partners with other officials, past and future, who together elaborate a coherent constitutional morality, and they must take care to see that what they contribute fits with the rest. (I have elsewhere said that judges are like authors jointly creating a chain novel in which each writes a chapter that makes sense as part of the story as a whole.) Even a judge who believes that abstract justice requires economic equality cannot interpret the equal protection clause as making equality of wealth, or collective ownership of productive resources, a constitutional requirement, because that interpretation simply does not fit American history or practice, or the rest of the Constitution.

Nor could a judge plausibly think that the constitutional structure commits any but basic, structural rights to his care. He might think that a society truly committed to equal concern would award people with handicaps special resources, or would secure convenient access to recreational parks for everyone, or would provide heroic and experimental medical treatment, no matter how expensive or speculative, for anyone whose life might possibly be saved. But it would violate constitutional integrity for a judge to treat these mandates as part of constitutional law. Judges must defer to general, settled understandings about the character of the power the Constitution assigns them. The moral reading asks them to find the best conception of constitutional moral principles—the best understanding of what equal moral status for men and women really requires, for example—that fits the broad story of America's historical record. It does not ask them to follow the whisperings of their own consciences or the traditions of their own class or sect if these cannot be seen as embedded in that record. Of course judges can abuse their power—they can pretend to observe the important restraint of integrity while really ignoring it. But generals and presidents and priests can abuse their powers, too. The moral reading is a strategy for lawyers and judges acting in good faith, which is all any interpretive strategy can be.

I emphasize these constraints of history and integrity, because they show how exaggerated is the common complaint that the moral reading gives judges absolute power to impose their own moral convictions on the rest of us. Macauley was wrong when he said that the American Constitution is all sail and no anchor, and so are the other critics who say that the moral readings turn judges into philosopher-kings. Our constitution is law, and like all law it is anchored in history, practice, and integrity. Most cases at law—even most constitutional cases—are not hard cases. The ordinary craft of a judge dictates an answer and leaves no room for the play of personal moral conviction. Still, we must not exaggerate the drag of that anchor. Very different, even contrary, conceptions of a constitutional principle—of what treating men and women as equals really means, for example—will often fit language, precedent, and practice well enough to pass these tests, and thoughtful judges must then decide on their own which conception does most credit to the nation. So though the familiar complaint that the moral reading gives judges unlimited power is hyperbolic, it contains enough truth to alarm those who believe that such judicial power is inconsistent with a republican form of government. The constitutional sail is a broad one, and many people do fear that it is too big for a democratic boat.

What Is the Alternative?

Constitutional lawyers and scholars have therefore been anxious to find other strategies for constitutional interpretation, strategies that give judges less power. They have explored two different possibilities . . . . The first, and most forthright concedes that the moral reading is right— that the Bill of Rights can only be understood as a set of moral principles. But it denies that judges should have the final authority themselves to conduct the moral reading—that they should have the last word about, for example, whether women have a constitutional right to choose abortion or whether affirmative action treats all races with equal concern. It reserves that interpretive authority to the people. That is by no means a contradictory combination of views. The moral reading, as I said, is a theory about what the Constitution means, not a theory about whose view of what it means must be accepted by the rest of us.

. . .

The first alternative strategy, as I have said, accepts the moral reading. The second alternative, which is called the "originalist" or "original intention" strategy, does not. The moral reading insists that the Constitution means what the framers intended to say. Originalism insists that it means what they expected their language to *do*, which as I said is a very different matter. (Though some originalists, including one of the most conservative justices now on the Supreme Court, Antonin Scalia, are unclear about the distinction.) According to originalism, the great clauses of the Bill of Rights should be interpreted not as laying down the abstract moral principles they actually describe, but instead as referring, in a kind of code or disguise, to the framers' own assumptions and expectations about the correct application of those principles. So the equal protection clause is to be understood as commanding not equal status but what the framers themselves thought was equal status, in spite of the fact that, as I said, the framers clearly meant to lay down the former standard not the latter one. The *Brown* decision I just mentioned crisply illustrates the distinction. The Court's decision was plainly required by the moral reading, because it is obvious now that official school segregation is not consistent with equal status and equal concern for all races. But the originalist strategy, consistently applied, would have demanded the opposite conclusion, because, as I said, the authors of the equal protection clause did not believe that school segregation, which they practiced themselves, was a denial of equal status, and did not expect that it would one day be deemed to be so. The moral reading insists that they misunderstood the moral principle that they themselves enacted into law. The originalist strategy would translate that mistake into enduring constitutional law.

That strategy, like the first alternative, would condemn not only the *Brown* decision but many other Supreme Court decisions that are now widely regarded as paradigms of good constitutional interpretation. For that reason, almost no one now embraces the originalist strategy in any thing like a pure form. Even Robert Bork, who remains one of its strongest defenders, qualified his support in the Senate hearings following his nomination to the Supreme Court—he conceded that the *Brown* decision was right, and said that even the Court's 1965 decision guaranteeing a right to use contraceptives, which we have no reason to think the authors of any pertinent constitutional clause either expected or would have approved, was right in its result. The originalist strategy is as indefensible in principle as it is unpalatable in result, moreover. It is as illegitimate to substitute a concrete, detailed provision for the abstract language of the equal protection clause as it would be to substitute some abstract principle of privacy for the concrete term of the Third Amendment, or to treat the clause imposing a minimum age for a President as enacting some general principle of disability for persons under that age.

So though many conservative politicians and judges have endorsed originalism, and some, like Hand, have been tempted to reconsider whether judges should have the last word about what the Constitution requires, there is in fact very little practical support for either of these strategies. Yet the moral reading is almost never explicitly endorsed, and is often explicitly condemned. If neither of the two alternatives I described is actually embraced by those who disparage the moral reading, what alternative do they have in mind? The surprising answer is: none. Constitutional scholars often say that we must avoid the mistakes of both the moral reading, which gives too much power to judges, and of original-ism, which makes the contemporary Constitution too much the dead hand of the past. The right method, they say, is something in between which strikes the right balance between protecting essential individual rights and deferring to popular will. But they do not indicate what the right balance is, or even what kind of scale we should use to find it. They say that constitutional interpretation must take both history and the general structure of the Constitution into account as well as moral or political philosophy. But they do not say why history or structure, both of which, as I said, figure in the moral reading, should figure in some further or different way, or what that different way is, or what general goal or standard of constitutional interpretation should guide us in seeking a different interpretive strategy.

So though the call for an intermediate constitutional strategy is often heard, it has not been answered, except in unhelpful metaphors about balance and structure. That is extraordinary, particularly given the enor-mous and growing literature of American constitutional theory. If it is so hard to produce an alternative to the moral reading, why struggle to do so? One distinguished constitutional lawyer who insists that there must be an interpretive strategy somewhere between originalism and the moral reading recently announced, at a conference, that although he had not discovered it, he would spend the rest of his life looking. Why?

I have already answered that question. Lawyers assume that the dis-abilities that a constitution imposes on majoritarian political processes are antidemocratic, at least if these disabilities are enforced by judges, and the moral reading seems to exacerbate the insult. If there is no genuine alternative to the moral reading in practice, however, and if efforts to find even a theoretical statement of an acceptable alternative have failed, we would do well to look again at that assumption. I shall argue, as I have already promised, that it is unfounded.

I said earlier that the theoretical argument among constitutional scholars and judges was never really about whether judges should change the Constitution or leave it alone. It was always about how the Constitu-tion should be interpreted. Happily, in spite of the politicians' rhetoric, that is now generally recognized by constitutional scholars, and it is also generally recognized that the question of interpretation turns on a political controversy, because the only substantial objection to the moral reading, which takes the text seriously, is that it offends democracy. So the academic argument is widely thought to be about how far democracy can properly be compromised in order to protect other values, including individual rights. One side declares itself passionate for democracy and anxious to protect it, while the other claims to be more sensitive to the injustices that democracy sometimes produces. In many ways, however, this new view of the debate is as confused as the older one. I shall try to convince you to see the constitutional argument in entirely different terms: as a debate not about how far democracy should yield to other values, but about what democracy, accurately understood, really is.

The Majoritarian Premise

Democracy means government by the people. But what does that mean? No explicit definition of democracy is settled among political theorists or in the dictionary. On the contrary, it is a matter of deep controversy what democracy really is. People disagree about which techniques of representation, which allocation of power among local, state, and national governments, which schedule and pattern of elections, and which other institutional arrangements provide the best available version of democracy. But beneath these familiar arguments over the structures of democracy there lies, I believe, a profound philosophical dispute about democracy's fundamental *value* or *point* and one abstract issue is crucial to that dispute, though this is not always recognized. Should we accept or reject what I shall call the majoritarian premise?

This is a thesis about the *outcomes* of a political process: it insists that political procedures should be designed so that, at least on important matters, the decision that is reached is the decision that a majority or plurality of citizens favors, or would favor if it had adequate information and enough time for reflection. That goal sounds very reasonable, and many people, perhaps without much reflection, have taken it to provide the very essence of democracy. They believe that the complex political arrangements that constitute the democratic process should be aimed at and tested by this goal: that the laws that the complex democratic process enacts and the policies that it pursues should be those, in the end, that the majority of citizens would approve.

. . .

In the United States, however, most people who assume that the majoritarian premise states the ultimate definition of and justification for democracy nevertheless accept that on some occasions the will of the majority should *not* govern. They agree that the majority should not always be the final judge of when its own power should be limited to protect individual rights, and they accept that at least some of the Supreme Court's decisions that overturned popular legislation, as the *Brown* decision did, were right. The majoritarian premise does not rule out exceptions of that kind, but it does insist that in such cases, even if some derogation from majoritarian government is overall justified, something morally regrettable has happened, a moral cost has been paid. The premise supposes, in other words, that it is *always* unfair when a political majority is not allowed to have its way, so that even when there are strong enough countervailing reasons to justify this, the unfairness remains.

If we reject the majoritarian premise, we need a different, better account of the value and point of democracy. Later I will defend an account— which I call the constitutional conception of democracy—that does reject the majoritarian premise. It denies that it is a defining goal of democracy that collective decisions always or normally be those that a majority or plurality of citizens would favor if fully informed and rational. It takes the defining aim of democracy to be a different one: that collective decisions be made by political institutions whose structure, composition, and practices treat all members of the community, as individuals, with equal concern and respect. This alternate account of the aim of democracy, it is true, demands much the same structure of government as the majoritarian premise does. It requires that day-to-day political decisions be made by officials who have been chosen in popular elections. But the constitutional conception requires these majoritarian procedures out of a concern for the equal status of citizens, and not out of any commitment to the goals of majority rule. So it offers no reason why some nonmajoritarian procedure should not be employed on special occasions when this would better protect or enhance the equal status that it declares to be the essence of democracy, and it does not accept that these exceptions are a cause of moral regret.

The constitutional conception of democracy, in short takes the following attitude to majoritarian government. Democracy means government subject to conditions—we might call these the "democratic" conditions—of equal status for all citizens. When majoritarian institutions provide and respect the democratic conditions, then the verdicts of these institutions should be accepted by everyone for that reason. But when they do not, or when their provision or respect is defective, there can be no objection, in the name of democracy, to other procedures that protect and respect them better. The democratic conditions plainly include, for example, a requirement that public offices must in principle be open to members of all races and groups on equal terms. If some law provided that only members of one race were eligible for public office, then there would be no moral cost—no matter for moral regret at all—if a court that enjoyed the power to do so under a valid constitution struck down that law as unconstitutional. That would presumably be an occasion on which the majoritarian premise was flouted, but though this is a matter of regret according to the majoritarian conception of democracy, it is not according to the constitutional conception. Of course, it may be controversial what the democratic conditions, in detail, really are, and whether a particular law does offend them. But, according to the constitutional conception, it would beg the question to object to a practice assigning those controversial questions for final decision to a court, on the ground that that practice is undemocratic, because that objection assumes that the laws in question respect the democratic conditions, and that is the very issue in controversy.

. . .

Does Constitutionalism Undermine Liberty?

The majoritarian premise insists that something of moral importance is lost or compromised whenever a political decision contradicts what the majority of citizens would prefer or judge right if they reflected on the basis of adequate information. We must try to identify that moral cost. What is lost or compromised? Many people think the answer is: equality. I shall consider that apparently natural answer shortly, but I begin with a different suggestion, which is that when constitutional disabling provisions, like those found in the Bill of Rights, limit what a majority can enact, the result is to compromise the community's freedom.

That suggestion plainly appeals to what Isaiah Berlin and others have called positive as distinct from negative liberty, and what Benjamin Constant described as the liberty of the ancients as distinct from that of the moderns. It is the kind of freedom that statesmen and revolutionaries and terrorists and humanitarians have in mind when they insist that freedom must include the right of "self-determination" or the right of the "people" to govern themselves. Since the suggestion that constitutional rights compromise freedom appeals to positive rather than negative liberty, it might be said to pit the two kinds of liberty against each other. Constitutionalism, on this view, protects "negative" liberties, like free speech and "privacy," at the cost of the "positive" freedoms of self-determination.

. . .

I discuss this defense of the majoritarian premise first because it is emotionally the most powerful. Self-determination is the most potent—and dangerous—political ideal of our time. People fervently want to be governed by a group not just to which they belong, but with which they identify in some particular way. They want to be governed by members of the same religion or race or nation or linguistic community or historical nation-state rather than by any other group, and they regard a political community that does not satisfy this demand as a tyranny, no matter how otherwise fair and satisfactory it is.

. . .

But powerful as the idea of democratic self-governance is, it is also deeply mysterious. Why am I *free*—how could I be thought to be governing *myself*—when I must obey what other people decide even if I think it wrong or unwise or unfair to me and my family? What difference can it make how many people must think the decision right and wise and fair if it is not necessary that *I* do? What kind of freedom is that? The answer to these enormously difficult questions begins in the communal conception of collective action. If I am a genuine member of a political community, its act is in some pertinent sense my act, even when I argued and voted against it, just as the victory or defeat of a team of which I am a member is my victory or defeat even if my own individual contribution made no difference either way. On no other assumption can we intelligibly think that as members of a flourishing democracy we are governing ourselves.

That explanation may seem only to deepen the mystery of collective self-government, however, because it appeals to two further ideas that seem dark themselves. What could *genuine* membership in a political community mean? And in what sense *can* a collective act of a group also be the act of each member? These are moral rather than metaphysical or psychological questions: they are not to be answered by counting the ultimate constituents of reality or discovering when people feel responsible for what some group that they belong to does. We must describe some connection between an individual and a group that makes it *fair* to treat him—and *sensible* that he treat himself—as responsible for what it does. Let us bring those ideas together in the concept of moral membership, by which we mean the kind of membership in a political community that engages self-government. If true democracy is government by the people, in the communal sense that provides self-government, then true democracy is based on moral membership.

In this section we are considering the argument that the moral cost incurred when the majoritarian premise is flouted is a cost in liberty. We have now clarified that argument: we must understand it to mean that the people govern themselves when the majoritarian premise is satisfied, and that any compromise of that premise compromises that self-government. But that majoritarianism does not guarantee self-government unless all the members of the community in question are moral members, and the majoritarian premise acknowledges no such qualification. German Jews were not moral members of the political community that tried to exterminate them, though they had votes in the elections that led to Hitler's Chancellorship, and the Holocaust was therefore not part of their self-government, even if a majority of Germans would have approved it. Catholics in Northern Ireland, nationalists in the Caucasus, and separatists in Quebec all believe they are not free because they are not moral members of the right political community. I do not mean that people who deny moral membership in their political community are always right. The test, as I said, is moral not psychological. But they are not wrong just because they have an equal vote with others in some standing majoritarian structure.

When I described the constitutional conception of democracy earlier, as a rival to the majoritarian conception that reflects the majoritarian premise, I said that the constitutional conception presupposes democratic conditions. These are the conditions that must be met before majoritarian decision-making can claim any automatic moral advantage over other procedures for collective decision. We have not identified the same idea through another route. The democratic conditions are the conditions of moral membership in a political community. So we can now state a strong conclusion: not just that positive liberty is not sacrificed whenever and just because the majoritarian premise is ignored, but that positive liberty is enhanced when that premise is rejected outright in favor of the constitutional conception of democracy. If it is true that self-government is possible only within a community that meets the conditions of moral membership, because only then are we entitled to refer to government by "the people" in a powerful communal rather than a barren statistical sense, we need a conception of democracy that insists that no democracy exists unless those conditions are met.

. . .

Law's Integrity

Where do we stand? The most natural interpretation of the Bill of Rights seems, as I said, to give judges great and frightening power. It is understandable that constitutional lawyers and teachers should strive to tame the Bill of Rights, to read it in a less frightening way, to change it from a systematic abstract conception of justice to a list of discrete clauses related to one another through pedigree rather than principle. These efforts fail, however, and are bound to fail, because the text and history of the Bill of Rights will not accept that transformation. They are found to fail, moreover, in a paradoxical and disastrous way. Because the semantic distinctions on which the efforts are based have no sense as they are used, they are powerless themselves to define any particular set of constitutional rights. As the recent history of the Court amply demonstrates, a judge who claims to rely on a speaker's meaning, "enumeration," or a preference for clause-by-clause interpretation must actually choose which constitutional rights to enforce on grounds that have nothing to do with these semantic devices, but that are hidden from view by his appeal to them. The search for limits on judicial power ends by allowing judges the undisciplined power of the arbitrary.

Posner's reply acknowledges that fact, with typical candor. He says that the semantic devices beloved of conservative lawyers "could end up with a document that gave answers only to questions that no one was asking any longer," and that judges who say they are constrained by those useless devices will necessarily decide according to their own "personal values"— according, he says, to what makes them "puke." His own personal values endorse "stretching" the due process clause to yield *Griswold* and, if I read correctly between the lines, *Roe v. Wade* as well. But he knows that other judges have stronger stomachs about society dictating sexual morality: their puke tests will flunk affirmative action programs instead. The idea that the Constitution cannot mean what it says ends in the unwelcome conclusion that it means nothing at all.

What is to be done? We can finally, after two hundred years, grow up and begin to take our actual Constitution seriously, as those many nations now hoping to imitate us have already done. We can accept that our Constitution commands, as a matter of fundamental law, that our judges do their best collectively to construct, reinspect, and revise, generation by generation, the skeleton of liberal equal concern that the great clauses, in their majestic abstraction, demand. We will then abandon the pointless search for mechanical or semantic constraints, and seek genuine constraints in the only place where they can actually be found: in good argument. We will accept that honest lawyers and judges and scholars will inevitably disagree, sometimes profoundly, about what equal concern requires, and about which rights are central and which only peripheral to liberty.

We will then acknowledge, in the political process of nomination and confirmation of federal judges, what is already evident to anyone who looks: that constitutional adjudicators cannot be neutral about these great questions, and that the Senate must decline to confirm nominees whose convictions are too idiosyncratic, or who refuse honestly to disclose what their convictions are. The second stage of the Thomas confirmation hearing was, as most people now agree, physically revolting. But the first stage was intellectually revolting, because candidate and senators conspired to pretend that philosophy had nothing to do with judging, that a nominee who said he had abandoned convictions the way a runner sheds clothing was fit for the office he sought.

The constitutional process of nomination and confirmation is an important part of the system of checks through which the actual Constitution disciplines the striking judicial power it declares. The main engines of discipline are intellectual rather than political, however, and the academic branch of the profession has a responsibility to protect that intellectual discipline, which is now threatened from several directions. Of course, we cannot find a formula which will guarantee that judges will all reach the same answer in complex or novel or crucial constitutional cases. No formula can protect us from a *Lochner* which Posner tells us stinks, or from a *Bowers v. Hardwick* which upheld a law making consensual homosexual sodomy a crime. The stench of those cases does not lie in any jurisdictional vice or judicial overreaching. After a near century of treating *Lochner* as a whipping boy, no one has produced a sound mechanical test that it fails. The vice of bad decisions is bad argument and bad conviction; all we can do about those bad decisions is to point out how and where the arguments are bad. Nor should we waste any more time on the silly indulgence of American legal academic life: the philosophically juvenile claim that, since no such formula exists, no one conception of constitutional equality and liberty is any better than another, and adjudication is only power or visceral response. We must insist, instead, on a principle of genuine power: the idea, instinct in the concept of law itself, that whatever their views of justice and fairness, judges must also accept an independent and superior constraint of integrity.

Integrity in law has several dimensions. First, it insists that judicial decisions be a matter of principle, not compromise or strategy or political accommodation. That apparent banality is often ignored: the Supreme

Court's present position on the politically sensitive issue of affirmative action, for example, cannot be justified on any coherent set of principles, however, conservative or unappealing. Second, integrity holds vertically: a judge who claims a particular right of liberty as fundamental must show that his claim is consistent with the bulk of precedent, and with the main structures of our constitutional arrangement. Third, integrity holds horizontally: a judge who adopts a principle must give full weight to that principle in other cases he decides or endorses.

Of course not even the most scrupulous attention to integrity, by all our judges in all our courts, will produce uniform judicial decisions, or guarantee decisions you approve of, or protect you from those you hate. Nothing can do that. The point of integrity is principle, not uniformity: We are governed not by a list but by an ideal, and controversy is therefore at the heart of our story. We are envied for our constitutional adventure, and increasingly imitated, through the democratic world: in Delhi and Strasbourg and Ottawa, even, perhaps, in the Palace of Westminster and, perhaps tomorrow or the day after, in Moscow and Johannesburg. In all those places people seem ready to accept the risk and high promise of government by ideal, a form of government we created in the Constitution. We have never fully trusted that form of government. But unless we abandon it altogether, which we will not do, we should stop pretending that it is not the form of government we have. The energy of our best academic lawyers would be better spent in making, testing, and evaluating different conceptions of liberal equality, to see which conception best fits our own history and practice. They should try to guide and constrain our judges by criticism, argument, and example. That is the only way to honor our great constitutional creation, to help it prosper.

Professor Michael Perry, now of Wake Forest University, offered a different route to a similar end. He viewed the Constitution as containing the aspirations of the community, leaving to judges the task of ascertaining just what those aspirations may be, as set forth in his book, MICHAEL J. PERRY, MORALITY, POLITICS, AND LAW: A BICENTENNIAL ESSAY 147, 149-51 (1988):[3]

By virtue of its political insularity, the federal judiciary has the institutional capacity to engage in the pursuit of political-moral knowledge—a search for answers to the various questions as to how we, the political community, given our basic aspirations, should live our collective life, our life in common in a relatively disinterested manner that has sometimes seemed to be beyond the reach of the electorally accountable branches of government, for many of whose members the cardinal value is "incumbency."

. . .

However, the fundamental aspirations signified by the Constitution . . . are highly indeterminate. And, so, different persons will have different views as to what an aspiration requires—in conjunction with all other relevant considerations—in a given case or conflict. On what beliefs as to what an aspiration requires in the case at hand should a judge rely? Conventional beliefs—beliefs as to which there is a consensus in the political community? Or at least majoritarian beliefs—beliefs that enjoy majoritarian support in the community? (If no beliefs as to what an aspiration requires enjoy ascertainable majoritarian support, then the beliefs implicit in, or presupposed by, the policy choice whose constitutionality is at issue can fill in for majoritarian beliefs.) Or, instead, should the judge rely on her own beliefs as to what the relevant aspiration requires in the case at hand?

Why should a judge rely on conventional or at least majoritarian beliefs as to what the relevant aspiration requires? (1) Because that's the "democratic"—in the sense of majoritarian—thing to do? But why should judicial review be majoritarian? For the nonoriginalist no less than for the originalist, judicial review is a deliberately countermajoritarian institution. (2) Because the majoritarian beliefs are correct? By hypothesis, the judge thinks them incorrect. (I'm assuming a difference between what the majority believes and what the judge believes. If there is no difference in a given case, then the judge need not decide whether to rely on what the majority believes or, instead, on what she believes, for in that case it and she believe the same thing.) Because the majoritarian beliefs might be correct, and the judge should humbly accept them? The virtue of humility may call for judicial self-restraint or self-limitation, . . . but surely it does not invariably require a judge to defer to majoritarian beliefs as to what the aspiration requires.

For the very reasons I gave [at the beginning of this extract] in support of a significant judicial role, the judge should rely on *her own beliefs* as to what the aspiration requires. Is that a worrisome proposition? The judge is almost certainly not a radical (of either the right or left). The real danger is not that the judge will go too far, against government, but that she will not go far enough. To say, as I have, that at their best judges can play a prophetic role in constitutional adjudication, is not to suppose that many real, live judges have either the capacity or inclination to be "prophets." But even if some judges are radicals, the beliefs of such a judge cannot, in the nature of things, be determinative. No belief can be determinative in constitutional adjudication unless it is widely shared among judges. A federal trial judge is subject to reversal by a federal appeals court. A federal appeals judge needs at least one ally, since federal appeals court panels typically consist of three judges. A federal appeals court panel is subject to reversal by the federal appeals court as a whole. Moreover, any federal appellate decision is subject to reversal by the Supreme Court, where, since there are nine Justices of the Court, a Justice needs at least four allies.

To say that the judge should rely on her own beliefs as to what the relevant aspiration requires in the case at hand is not to say that she should ignore original beliefs. She should not. The ratifiers, too, were participants in the tradition. In their day, they were among the stewards of the tradition. The ways in which they shaped and responded to the aspirations of the tradition may well shed important light on how we should shape and respond to those aspirations. Why assume we have nothing to learn from our past? The judge should consult original beliefs.

Nor am I suggesting that the judge should ignore the beliefs of past judges. She should not ignore those beliefs—including "precedent"—or, indeed, any other source that may shed light on the problem before the court. (She cannot be immune to precedent, even if she wanted to be, if "the interpretation of a work is invariably conditioned by the prior history of the effects of that work. Any prior interpretation will count as part of that history.") A thoughtful judge will rely on her own beliefs as to what the aspiration requires only after *forming* those beliefs, or at least *testing* them, in the crucible of dialogic encounter with the wisdom of the past, of the tradition, including original beliefs, precedent, and anything else relevant and helpful. As Bickel understood, "The function of the Justices . . . is to immerse themselves in the tradition of our society and of kindred societies that have gone before, in history and in the sediment of history which is law, and . . . in the thought and the vision of the philosophers and the poets. The Justices will then be fit to extract 'fundamental presuppositions' from their deepest selves, but in fact from the evolving morality of our tradition." Moreover, the thoughtful judge will rely on her own beliefs only after forming or testing them in the crucible of dialogic encounter with the beliefs of her contemporaries, in particular, other judges struggling with the same or similar problems.

Facing possible objections that his call for judges to rely on their own beliefs about what constitutional aspirations require was inconsistent with democratic preconceptions, Perry continued, *id.* at 165-66, 168-69:

> Any particular conception of democracy, of what the judicial role should be within the overall governmental apparatus, must be defended. To presuppose the authoritative status of a particular conception is to beg the question. One must *argue for* a particular conception. (To argue for a particular conception of democracy, of judicial role within the overall governmental apparatus, is to argue for a particular conception of constitutional text and interpretation, namely, the conception entailed by the prescribed judicial role.) How do we conduct that argument—by reference to what considerations? How else but by reference to the ways in which a particular conception of judicial role comports with (or fails to comport with) the constitutive purposes and projects—the central aspirations—of the political tradition? A lot turns, therefore, on how one understands those central, constitutive aspirations.

> One such aspiration, of course, is for governance that is both responsive, and, because it is not always responsive, accountable to the electorate. Electorally accountable government is plainly not the only constitutive aspiration of the American political tradition, however. The tradition has aspired to "liberty and justice for all" as well as to "popular sovereignty." . . .

> A central aspiration of the tradition has been to achieve justice, and justice has generally been seen to lie partly in the direction marked out by more particular aspirations signified by various constitutional provisions regarding human rights. Put another way, a central aspiration of the tradition has been to keep faith with the more particular aspirations regarding the form of life of the polity, the life in common. To say this is not to deny that at any given point in the course of the tradition there have been various competing visions of the requirements of justice, or that various considerations of self-interest have powerfully distorted the visions and pursuit of justice. Still, a constitutive aspiration of the American political tradition has been to achieve "liberty and justice for all."

>   . . .

>   . . . My suggestion, which concededly is speculative (but speculation is all we have to go on here), is that what the tradition is likely to gain, in terms of justice—in terms, that is, of the correct mediation of the past of the tradition with its present—from a judicial role of the nonoriginalist sort the Court has (often) played in the modern period, more than offsets what the tradition is likely to lose, in terms of "responsiveness" and "accountability."

> What is the tradition likely to lose? Certainly the electorate cannot exercise the comparatively direct and immediate political control (through its elected representatives) over the constitutional decisions of the Court that it can exercise over the Court's nonconstitutional decisions. But American history leaves little doubt that when a serious tension develops between the direction in which the Court is leading and the direction in

which the electorate, in the end, after deliberation, is determined to move, the electorate, not the Court, will prevail. The various mechanisms of political control or influence over the Court—in particular, the appointments power and, ultimately, the amendment power—have proven adequate in that regard.

Constitutional decisionmaking by the Court is responsive to the polity—not immediately, but it is responsive. Still, immediacy counts for something, and there is no denying that time can be lost. (Time is not always lost. In the course of the dialectical interplay between Court and polity I've discussed elsewhere, the political community may eventually come to see it as a good thing it did not get its way. When that happens, time is not lost. But, sometimes, time has been lost, as in the case of child labor legislation.) The significance one attaches to that occasional loss depends mainly on the significance one attaches to the actual or potential gain, in terms of justice. A black person is more likely to attach greater significance to, to value more highly, the gain, in the modern period, than a white person. Whose point of view is more likely distorted? . . .

Moreover, one who has a strong sense of herself, of her identity, as a participant in a living tradition, whether religious or political, is likely to be more concerned that institutional authority be allocated so that the tradition stands a better chance of getting it right—achieving justice—than that a majority of the community get its way *here and now*.

Does all this seem inconclusive? It *is* inconclusive—but for originalists no less than for nonoriginalists. One's decision to accept or reject, one's argument for or against, any conception of judicial role, including the originalist conception, is always *contingent, speculative,* and *provisional* and therefore *revisable.* The decision is contingent because it is rooted partly in one's sense or vision of justice—in one's view of the proper interpretation of the tradition, of the correct mediation of the past of the tradition with its present. The decision is speculative because it is grounded partly on our answers to counterfactual questions about the past and present ("Where would we be today had the Court not played a nonoriginalist role in the last thirty years?") and partly on our predictions of future governmental (both judicial and nonjudicial) behavior on the basis of past behavior. And the decision is provisional and therefore revisable because one's sense or vision of justice may change, one's predictions may prove wrong, or both.

Both Perry and Dworkin argue that their vision of constitutional interpretation is not antidemocratic. Consider whether they have persuaded you. Consider further whether the success of a constitutional theory should depend on whether it can be reconciled with some understanding of democratic processes.

§ 6.03   The Critique of Moral Reasoning

Among the many who have taken issue with Dworkin's vision of the judicial role, Professor Michael W. McConnell, of the University of Utah, is representative. The following is from his article, *The Importance of Humility in Judicial Review: A Comment on Ronald Dworkin's "Moral Reading" of the Constitution* 65 FORDHAM L. REV. 1269, 1269–81, 1284–87, 1289–91 (1997):[4]

Introduction

In recent writings, Professor Ronald Dworkin advocates what he calls "The Moral Reading of the Constitution." This approach, he says, cuts across the usual categories of "liberal" or "conservative" decisionmaking. Its distinguishing characteristic is that judges must decide cases on the basis of how the "abstract moral principles" of the Constitution are "best understood." This means that judges should decide, frankly, on the basis of their "own views about political morality" rather than purporting to decide on the basis of such "metaphorical" notions as "historical 'intentions'" or "constitutional 'structure.'"

Many arguments can be made, some more persuasive than others, that judges are superior to legislatures in making decisions of moral importance. It is easy to see why these arguments would appeal to law professors, who share with federal judges a common background, social class, and education. In other writings, I have questioned the validity of such arguments. But Dworkin does not make these arguments. Instead, Dworkin makes the claim that "The Moral Reading" is necessary if we are to show proper "fidelity" to the Constitution. In other words, he claims that his approach is the most faithful interpretation of the constitutional text. He claims that historical approaches to interpretation are "substitutes for fidelity," which "ignore the text of the Constitution." In this Response, I will explain why this claim is not convincing.

Before making the argument, it is necessary to achieve greater clarity about the nature of Dworkin's argument. Running through Dworkin's account is a profound ambivalence toward arguments based on history (text, history, practice, and precedent). It is not too much to say that there are two Dworkins, with two quite different versions of "The Moral Reading." I will call these "the Dworkin of Fit" and "the Dworkin of Right Answers." According to the Dworkin of Fit, judges are, and should be, seriously constrained by what has come before—by text, history, tradition, and precedent—and should exercise their moral-philosophical faculties only within the limits set by history. The Dworkin of Fit recognizes that the constraints of history are an indispensable part of the "principle" that governs judicial decision making. The Dworkin of Right Answers, by contrast, distinguishes sharply between "the party of history" (bad) and "the party of principle" (good). He insists that text, history, and unwelcome precedent must be interpreted at a sufficiently abstract level that they do not interfere with the judge's ability to make the Constitution "the best it can be." The "best reading" is the reading that, in the judge's own opinion, will produce the best answers, defined philosophically and not historically.

The relation between the Dworkin of Fit and the Dworkin of Right Answers is unclear at a theoretical level. One would expect the Dworkin of Fit to attack the Dworkin of Right Answers for the latter's lack of respect for the distinctive qualities of judging within the American tradition (what he calls elsewhere "integrity"), and the Dworkin of Right Answers to charge the Dworkin of Fit with sacrificing "principle" to "history." Each Dworkin seems to refute the other. But the two work together harmoniously at a practical level. The division of labor is as follows: The Dworkin of Right Answers decides all important contested cases, while the Dworkin of Fit defends against charges of judicial imperialism. The Dworkin of Fit is allowed to resolve hypothetical cases, but in all of Dworkin's writings I am unable to discover an actual, important, controversial case in which "fit" ever precluded the Dworkin of Right Answers from having his way.

Let us consider each of these versions of "The Moral Reading" on its own terms.

I. The Dworkin of Fit

The Dworkin of Fit sounds mainstream, even conservative. This Dworkin is attentive to the problem of judicial overreaching and respectful of the constraints of constitutional text and history. The essence of his position is that a judge is not writing on a blank slate, free to decide every question according to his own view of the best answer. Rather, he is seriously constrained by what has come before: by text, history, practice, and precedent. This is what he calls "fit." Only within the bounds set by text, history, practice, and precedent may the judge use the tools of moral philosophy to determine what is best.

Dworkin begins his argument by noting that a claim of right, in our system, is "not just a prediction about beneficial consequences" but is based on "a backward looking glance at a document which we take to record commitments." This means that the legal system has a necessary historical element. Moreover, he says he takes "fidelity to the text to mean deploying an argument . . . which is sound, because it correctly understands what commitments are embedded in the text." The difficulty, however, is that many provisions of the Constitution are written in broad and abstract language, permitting many different plausible interpretations. Thus, while text will rule out some possible wrong answers, it leaves room for more than one—perhaps many—plausible right answers.

Dworkin then consults the history surrounding the framing of the relevant constitutional provision. "History is crucial" to interpretation, he explains, "because we must know something about the circumstances in which a person spoke to have any good idea of what he meant to say in speaking as he did." Indeed, Dworkin acknowledges that his theory is one of authorial intent, which he calls "semantic intentions." But even after consulting the semantic intention of the Framers, as revealed in history, there still will remain multiple plausible interpretations. All this is mainstream. Indeed, there is not much difference, so far, between Dworkin and his *béte noire*, Robert Bork.

Dworkin's next step is also mainstream. He explains that "judges must defer to general, settled understandings about the character of the power the Constitution assigns them." The "moral reading" asks judges

> to find the best conception of constitutional moral principles . . . that fits the broad story of America's historical record. It does not ask them to follow the whisperings of their own consciences or the traditions of their own class or sect if these cannot be seen as embedded in that record.

For Dworkin, this deference to past practice follows from the very nature of law: "Our Constitution is law, and like all law it is anchored in history, practice, and integrity." Even after consulting history, practice, and tradition, however, it is likely that more than one conception of constitutional principles still will be available: "Very different, even contrary, conceptions of a constitutional principle . . . will often fit language, precedent, and practice well enough to pass these tests."

This approach can be seen as a three-stage filtering process. Out of the entire universe of moral principles, the text of the Constitution embraces some principles, and excludes others. The linguisitic intentions of the Framers provide a second filter, excluding some interpretations that are textually plausible but that do not fit the historical circumstances.

Practice and precedent provide a third filter, but even these leave the judge, in many cases, with a range of possible answers.

It is at this stage in the analysis that Dworkin departs from mainstream constitutional practice. When different conceptions of the constitutional principle satisfy the tests of "language, precedent, and practice," he says, *"thoughtful judges must then decide on their own which conception does most credit to the nation."* In other words, after the backward-looking process of examining text, history, practice, and precedent is completed, the judge decides among the remaining possible answers on philosophic, normative, non-interpretive grounds. Dworkin sometimes calls this stage in the process "justification." By contrast, mainstream practice treats any decision of the representative branches that survives the filters of text, history, practice, and precedent as constitutional. Indeed, properly enacted legislation enjoys a presumption of constitutionality, and can be overturned only when the alleged constitutional violation is tolerably clear. The notion that in unclear cases judges may substitute "their own views about political morality" for the considered judgments of representative bodies, turns settled constitutional practice—as articulated by such revered figures as Marshall, Brandeis, Holmes, Stone, and Harlan—on its head.

The theory underlying this more modest view of constitutional judicial review is that the Constitution is not designed to produce the one "best answer" to all questions, but to establish a framework for representative government and to set forth a few important substantive principles, commanding supramajority support, that legislatures are required to respect. The job of the judge is to ensure that representative institutions conform to the commitments made by the people in the past, and embodied in text, history, tradition, and precedent. Another way to express the point is: "Fit is everything." When the dictates of "fit" are satisfied, the judge's role is at an end. Within the range of discretion established by the various conceptions that are consistent with text, history, practice, and precedent, the people through their representative institutions—not the courts—have authority to decide which course of action "does most credit to the nation." There may be many different answers to that question, and none is constitutionally privileged. It is the right, privilege, and obligation of the people to deliberate about such questions through their elected representatives.

The contrast between Dworkin and mainstream practice becomes especially stark when we notice that Dworkin assigns *no weight whatsoever* to the decision of the representative branches of government in deciding the case. In examining the constitutionality of a law—the state law forbidding assisted suicide, for example—Dworkin advises that the judge examine the text of the Constitution, the semantic intentions of the Framers, past practice, and precedent. If those are inconclusive, "thoughtful judges must then decide on their own which conception does most credit to the nation." It does not seem to matter, one way or the other, that the legislature has passed a law. The legislative judgment, far from being entitled to a presumption of constitutionality, is formally irrelevant.

This point can be illustrated by reference to Dworkin's famous analogy to writing a chain novel. I have always considered this one of Dworkin's more perceptive suggestions because, as he says, it helps us understand that the process of judging is neither one of "total creative freedom" nor of "mechanical textual constraint." That seems right . . . .

My question to Professor Dworkin is: Why does he assign the role of "author" to the judge? In the context of law making subject to constitutional judicial review, it seems more accurate to view the various legislative, executive, and common law decision makers as the authors, and to view judges as editors or referees. The judges' task, it seems, is to ensure that that [sic] the author of each chapter conforms to the rules of chain novel writing, not to write the books themselves.

. . .

II. The Dworkin of Right Answers

In other recent writings, Dworkin draws a sharper dichotomy between the constraints of history and the search for "the right answer" to constitutional questions, arguing that fidelity to history is antithetical to principled decision making. The "party of history," he says, looks to whether a putative right has been historically recognized either through original understanding at the time of the framing or by past practice—whether it is "deeply rooted in this Nation's history and tradition." The "party of principle," by contrast, "argues that the abstract constitutional rights acknowledged for one group be extended to others if no moral ground distinguishes between them." The Dworkin of Right Answers criticizes judges who allow the apparent constraints of history and tradition to distract them from the most "principled" answer.

According to this view, the words of the Constitution should be read as abstractions having meaning independent of any meaning that the Framers and Ratifiers, or the people, may have intended to communicate. For example, in interpreting the Equal Protection Clause, Dworkin advises that we should not ask what the framers and ratifiers meant by "equal citizenship;" nor what "we think" about the issue. "I am interested in the *right answer* to the question, what is equal citizenship properly understood." Similarly, Dworkin gives the example of the Eighth Amendment:

> The Eighth Amendment of the Constitution forbids "cruel" and unusual punishment. Does that mean punishments that the authors thought were cruel or (what probably comes to the same thing) punishments that were judged cruel by the popular opinion of their day? Or does it mean punishments that are in fact—according to the *correct standards* for deciding such matters—cruel?

Unsurprisingly, Dworkin opts for the latter interpretation. "The Moral Reading," he says, is to understand the Constitution, or at least significant parts of it, as setting forth abstract moral principles, to which the interpreter should apply the "correct standards"—*meaning the interpreter's own standards*, even if they conflict with the standards of the framers, the nation over time, past precedents, or democratic institutions.

Especially revealing is Dworkin's depiction of Justice Scalia's affirmative action decisions as an example of a conservative "Moral Reading"—one with which he would disagree, but which is a "principled" interpretation nonetheless. Dworkin maintains—accurately or not—that Scalia's "color blind" interpretation of the Equal Protection Clause "is not to be found in history," but is, instead, the Justice's "emotional and moral reaction." One might think that would be a criticism, but it is not. In Dworkin's view, this establishes that Scalia is giving a "Moral Reading," even if it is one with which Dworkin would not agree. The defining characteristic of "The Moral Reading," as this example shows, is not that the interpretation is correct or well-reasoned, but simply that it *does not rest on historical authority*. If Scalia's view were, in fact, historically grounded, it would not be deemed a "Moral Reading." This suggests that "The Moral Reading" is nothing but a repudiation of "fit"—any reading is a "Moral Reading" so long as it is based on the judge's own "moral and emotional reaction" to the problem rather than on the nation's historical understanding of constitutional principle. Indeed, it suggests that by "The Moral Reading," Dworkin means nothing other than judicial willfulness.

That this is Dworkin's position is further evident from his conclusion that the death penalty is unconstitutional. There is no serious argument that the framers of either the Eighth or the Fourteenth Amendment deemed death, in all cases, a cruel and unusual punishment; indeed, the very language of the constitutional text belies this. Nor is there any serious argument that the tradition of the nation has judged capital punishment to be immoral. Nor do the precedents of the Supreme Court support that position. In a case where the democratically accountable branches have prescribed the death penalty, therefore, the only conceivable ground for Dworkin's legal conclusion is that the interpreter's own opinion of what is "cruel and unusual" is entitled to prevail. "Fit" counts for nothing. The same must be said of Dworkin's constitutional positions on euthanasia and abortion, at least at the time of *Roe v. Wade*. In neither of these cases can a persuasive argument be made that the constitutional text, history, practice, tradition, or precedent required invalidation of the state statutes in question. Nonetheless, on the basis of independent moral judgment, Dworkin contends that the courts should declare these statutes unconstitutional. This version of "The Moral Reading," then, is the argument that courts must read the language of the Constitution abstractly, in light of their own judgment of the best answer, with only slight constraint, if any, from text or history.

If I seem to belabor this point, it is solely because Dworkin declares "exaggerated" the "common complaint that the moral reading gives judges absolute power to impose their own moral convictions on the rest of us." The reason the complaint is exaggerated, Dworkin says, is because judges are bound by fit. If the constraints of fit are illusory, as they turn out to be, the complaint is not exaggerated.

III. "Fidelity" and "The Moral Reading"

As noted above, Dworkin defends his approach to constitutional interpretation not explicitly on the basis that courts are more virtuous decision makers, but on the ground that it is the only way to show "fidelity" to the constitutional text. "The Moral Reading," he contends, is simply faithful interpretation. Let us examine his argument, as it applies to text, history, precedent, and deference to representative institutions.

A. Text and Semantic Intention

Dworkin professes to deem text, interpreted in accordance with the semantic intention of its Framers, as authoritative and dispositive. Contrary to some of his admirers, he does not take the view that constitutional principles are independent of, or unaffected by, their particular expression in the document we call the Constitution. Rather, he says, judges must be faithful to the text, and judging must be understood as an interpretive enterprise, fundamentally distinct from legislation.

I wish Dworkin would elaborate on his reasons for taking this position. I suspect that if we knew the reason for treating the text, interpreted in light of the semantic intention of its Framers, as authoritative, we would find it difficult to account for Dworkin's readiness to depart from the Framers' understanding of constitutional principles. If the Framers' words have authority for us today, this is because, in Chief Justice Marshall's words, "the people have an original right to establish, for their future government, such principles as, in their opinion, shall most conduce to their own happiness." This, he said, "is the basis on which the whole American fabric has been erected." It would seem to follow that it is the principles to which the people assented, understood as nearly as is possible as they understood them, which should guide us today. There are good reasons not to follow the principles of people many generations ago, but I can think of no good reasons to pretend to adhere to their words, if those words are stripped of the principles they sought to express.

Instead of exploring the arguments underlying the idea of linguistic intent in greater detail, Dworkin argues by example. Hamlet's "hawk" must have meant a "renaissance tool" because otherwise the juxtaposition to a "handsaw" would be "silly." The Third Amendment is narrowly confined to the quartering of soldiers in private homes because nothing in the text or history suggests a broader meaning. More interestingly, Dworkin notes that Milton's reference in Paradise Lost to "Satan's gay hordes" could theoretically mean either that Satan's hordes are "jolly" or that they are "homosexual;" but, because the use of the term "gay" to mean "homosexual" came about several centuries after Milton wrote, it is an "easy job" to answer the question what he means. This, according to Dworkin, is an appropriate use of history, because it illuminates what the authors of the text "intended to say, not . . . what they expected to happen, or hoped would happen, in consequence of their having said what they did."

I believe Dworkin's embrace of "semantic intention" brings him closer to the mainstream originalist view than he realizes. In the context of directive or prohibitory language, what the authors intend to "say" is precisely what they intend to require, authorize, or prohibit; thus, what they intend to "say" is what they intend to have happen "in consequence of their having said what they did." It is not possible to isolate "semantic intentions" from the broader context of their purpose and political theory.

. . .

A genuine commitment to the semantic intentions of the Framers requires the interpreter to seek the level of generality at which the particular language was understood by its Framers. Just as the Ex Post Facto Clause should be read as confined to criminal laws, other provisions of the Constitution should be read in light of their intended scope. If "cruel and unusual punishment" was understood to mean something like "punishments that are widely regarded as excessively cruel and therefore have passed out of common accepted use," then the interpreter would apply *that* standard, rather than the interpreter's own moral judgment, to the issue of capital punishment. It is perfectly possible that, upon dispassionate historical investigation, the interpreter would discover that some provisions of the Constitution were understood at a high level of generality, or that judges would be expected to apply their own moral judgments. But such a conclusion must be based on a serious examination of the context, linguistic conventions, and historical purposes of the provision in question, and not on *a priori* preferences for abstract interpretations.

It is emblematic of Dworkin's ambiguity that I do not know whether he would agree or disagree with the preceding paragraph. To be sure, he "favors a particular way of stating the constitutional principles at the most general possible level." This is his rationale for increasing judicial discretion. But he claims to derive this high level of generality as a matter of "fidelity" to the constitutional text and the semantic intentions of the Framers. He thus tries to have it both ways: to liberate judges to achieve their own vision of the "best answers" to controversial questions without regard to the Framers' opinions, while simultaneously claiming to be faithfully carrying out the Framers' intentions. Let us see if he carries off this happy feat persuasively.

. . .

B. Originalism

Dworkin claims that the only serious alternative to "The Moral Reading" is the "originalist" or "original intention" position. Indeed, he states that he is unaware of any other alternative. By refuting the originalist position, therefore, he claims to have argued conclusively in favor of "The Moral Reading." Once again, we see the familiar fallacy of black and white reasoning at work.

Dworkin describes the originalist position as follows:

> According to originalism, the great clauses of the Bill of Rights should be interpreted not as laying down the abstract moral principles they actually describe, but instead as referring, in a kind of code or disguise, to the framers' own assumptions and expectations about the correct application of those principles.

The problem with this argument is that no reputable originalist, with the possible exception of Raoul Berger, takes the view that the Framers' "assumptions and expectation about the correct application" of their principles is controlling. Robert Bork, for example, wrote in 1986 that his position "is not the notion that judges may apply a constitutional provision only to circumstances specifically contemplated by the Framers. In such a narrow form the philosophy is useless." The position Dworkin describes is a straw man.

Mainstream originalists recognize that the Framers' analysis of particular applications could be wrong, or that circumstances could have changed and made them wrong. Like Dworkin, they believe that "we are governed by what our lawmakers said—by the principles they laid down—not by any information we might have about how they themselves would have interpreted those principles or applied them in concrete cases."

Thus, there are not two, but at least three alternative approaches:

(1) to read the Constitution in light of the Framers' expectations about specific applications;

(2) to read the Constitution in light of the moral and political principles they intended to express; and

(3) to read the Constitution in light of what we now think would be the best way to understand the abstract language.

I agree that Dworkin has effectively refuted the first alternative, but he has not refuted the second and therefore has not provided an argument for the third.

Let me offer an analogy to show the difference between these approaches, and to show why the second, rather than the third, is most consistent with ordinary notions of interpretive fidelity. Suppose that a scholar is writing a monograph on the political and moral thought of Aristotle. This requires interpretation; Aristotle uses a lot of abstract language about moral ideas, as well as providing numerous examples of how his reasoning applies. Under the first approach, the scholar would be limited to the specific examples; under the second approach the scholar would attempt to discover and explain the principles underlying Aristotle's arguments; under the third approach the scholar would interpret

Aristotle's abstract language in the way that the scholar thinks provides the best answer to the moral problems posed.

It is readily apparent that the first and third alternatives are flawed. Aristotle's examples should not be taken as fixed or sacrosanct. It may well be that some of them would require modification in light of current circumstances. For instance, an argument might be made that, on Aristotle's own principles, American chattel slavery was wrong, even though Aristotle defends slavery of a sort. It is even possible that Aristotle made a mistake or two, and that some of his examples should have come out the other way. (Though the more examples we reject, the more likely it is that we are making mistakes about Aristotle than it is that Aristotle made so many mistakes in applying his own principles.)

On the other hand, if every time the scholar sees abstract moral language, he makes Aristotle look like John Stuart Mill—or even worse, like the scholar himself, even if that scholar is Ronald Dworkin—then he has abandoned interpretive fidelity. It is not the job of the interpreter to "make Aristotle the best he can be" if that means substituting the interpreter's moral theory for Aristotle's. Ancient texts are not mirrors.

To be sure, I have not offered an argument that judges should read the Constitution in the same way that a scholar should read Aristotle. It may be that, for various reasons, law either cannot or should not be conducted on the basis of interpretive fidelity. I claim only that Dworkin's argument against originalism, which is really only an argument against specific intentionalism, does not follow from the premises of interpretive fidelity. Dworkin's refutation of specific intentionalism no more discredits originalism than a refutation of Lamarck would discredit evolution. In particular, Dworkin's inflammatory claim that originalism is a way "of ignoring the text of the Constitution" is as unfounded as it is uncharitable.

Let us move, then, from Aristotle to the Constitution. I will use the Due Process Clause as an example. Suppose that historical investigation revealed that the framers thought that any procedure that had been used by the states for a great period of time was "due process." In other words, assume that the purpose of the Clause was to limit the power of the government to depart from longstanding principles of procedural regularity. It would be an error, in a case in 1996, for the judge to ask whether a particular procedure was thought acceptable in 1789. Dworkin is right about that. Some procedures thought acceptable in 1789 have long since been abandoned, and their reinstitution would be indefensible; other procedures unheard of in 1789 are now an accepted part of our practice. But Dworkin claims that, having rejected that form of originalism, the only other alternative is the judge's own "Moral Reading"—that judges should decide what procedures really are "due" according to the "correct" standard, in the judge's independent judgment. But Dworkin has left out (not refuted) the possibility of interpreting the Constitution in light of the *Framers'* moral reading, which we have supposed to be that procedures that are long-established satisfy due process.

By the same token, suppose that the substantive aspect of due process (more plausibly understood to be an interpretation of the Privileges or Immunities Clause) was understood by the framers of the Fourteenth Amendment to protect rights that had been protected by most of the states for a significant period of time. In other words, the privileges and immunities of citizens of the United States were conceived against a common law backdrop, gradually evolving over time as circumstances and public mores change. Now we have to consider whether an action of government (for example, requiring all children to attend public schools, prohibiting married couples from using contraceptives, or prohibiting doctors from assisting in the suicide of their patients) is constitutional. Dworkin is right that we should not ask whether these putative rights were recognized in 1866. But he is wrong to suggest that, having rejected that alternative, the only remaining approach is for today's judge to decide the moral question independently. Nothing in Dworkin's argument refutes the plausible alternative that the judge should carry out the Framers' understanding, and examine the putative right in light of longstanding practice. Under such an approach, the right to send one's child to a private school would surely be protected, as would the right to use contraceptives; but the right to take a lethal poison would not.

As Dworkin demonstrates, it is unlikely that "careful statesmen" would tether future constitutional law to their own ideas about how specific cases should come out. But it is equally unlikely that they would delegate virtually unbridled authority to future courts, at the expense of future legislators. Their experience with courts—most recently, the Court that gave them *Dred Scott*—was not happy. It is more likely that statesmen immersed in the common law tradition (we should clarify: the pre-legal realist common law tradition) would understand words such as "liberty," "due process," or "privileges or immunities of citizens," as requiring reference to the settled judgment of the nation rather than the abstract theorizing of federal judges.

. . .

D. The Majoritarian Premise

For most judges, most of the time, the principal constraint on constitutional authority is not text, history, or even precedent, but deference to the decisions of representative institutions in close cases. Justice Brandeis provided the definitive account of this practice—the presumption of constitutionality—in his concurring opinion in *Ashwander v. TVA* [297 U.S. 288, 354, 56 S. Ct. 466, 80 L. Ed. 688 (1936)]. The reasons for this deference are many and subtle. In part, deference to representative bodies reflects the need for compromise and accommodation, which is more appropriate to legislatures than to principle-bound judges; in part it reflects the need for flexibility and experimentation in the face of uncertainty; in part it reflects the superior institutional capability of legislatures and executives to make the empirical assessments necessary to prudent decisionmaking; in part it reflects the concern that a judiciary that makes "political" judgments will be transformed and corrupted by politics; in part that aggressive judicial review will cause the legislature's own commitment to moral and constitutional reasoning to become impoverished; in part it reflects a distrust of a small and hierarchical institution; and in part it reflects a commitment to popular sovereignty.

Dworkin reductively attributes this longstanding tradition of deference to democratic decisionmaking to the "grip" of the "majoritarian premise." And this, he says, is a misconception. We should not value the right of the majority to make decisions. Rather, we should value a system in which "collective decisions . . . [are] made by political institutions whose structure, composition, and practices treat all members of the community, as individuals, with equal concern and respect." Because, for a variety of reasons, our actual system falls short and because "The Moral Reading" will bring us closer to the ideal of equal concern and respect, Dworkin maintains that we have no persuasive reason to cling to the empty forms of majoritarian democracy. As he states,

> When majoritarian institutions provide and respect the democratic conditions, then the verdicts of these institutions should be accepted

by everyone for that reason. But when they do not, or when their provision or respect is defective, there can be no objection, in the name of democracy, to other procedures that protect and respect them better.

Even if this were an attractive conception of democracy, it would fail as an argument for unconstrained judicial review, as I will explain below. But it is not an attractive conception. Indeed, it is not democracy at all. Democracy is not only government for the people, but of and by the people as well. Under Dworkin's view, the ideal form of government would be a benign and evenhanded trustee, who would make all decisions in our interest, showing each of us equal concern and respect, as a good trustee should. This vision leaves something out: self-government, or political liberty. The right to participate in self-government has been regarded as an essential part of liberty throughout our history. We are not wards. But Dworkin's conception is not only unattractive; it is also self-contradictory. Part of "equal concern and respect" is the understanding that each citizen's ideas about justice and the public good are entitled to an equal hearing. In a democracy of "equal concern and respect" there is no mandarin class whose views, by virtue of station or status or position, are thought to provide "the best answer" to questions about which we are divided—even if they are judges or law professors. That is the moral ground of the so-called "majoritarian premise." In the face of disagreements among the citizens about issues of justice and the public good, the only way to show equal concern and respect is to govern democratically, subject to constraints to which the people themselves have agreed.

Even putting aside these objections, however, Dworkin's argument is flawed. To be sure, American working democracy falls short of the utopian democratic ideal. So has every other form of government in the history of the world. To insist that a democracy must be perfect in order for the will of the people to be entitled to presumptive validity is to allow the best to be the enemy of the good.

It would be equally logical to make the opposite argument. Dworkin and his admirers, we might say, are in the "grip" of the "judicial premise"—the assumption that judges decide cases fairly and wisely. But in actuality, all judges fall short of the judicial ideal. Some are biased; some are unintelligent; most have trouble transcending the interests and opinions of their class. What should Dworkin say about this? Perhaps: "when judicial institutions provide and respect the ideals of fair and wise decision making, then the verdicts of these institutions should be accepted by everyone for that reason. But when they do not, or when their provision or respect is defective, there can be no objection, in the name of proper judicial authority, to other procedures that protect and respect these ideals better." This sounds like a justification for allowing legislatures to overrule courts.

Neither argument is sound. All human institutions fall short of the ideal. All are "defective," to use Dworkin's term. But that does not mean that our representative institutions should be disregarded any more than it means the judiciary should be divested of its proper role. Our representative institutions, despite their flaws, still represent the will of the people tolerably well, and better than any alternative that comes readily to mind. Judges do a tolerably good job of enforcing social norms fairly and equally, treating like cases alike—better, at least, than the alternatives. The so-called "majoritarian premise" is not the whole story of our constitutional system, but it is an important part, and it does not lose its legitimate place because our system fails to satisfy a utopian set of criteria. The people's representatives have a right to govern, so long as they do not transgress limits on their authority that are fairly traceable to the constitutional precommitments of the people themselves, as reflected directly through text and history, or indirectly through longstanding practice and precedent.

§ 6.04 Conclusion

The materials quoted in this chapter are reminiscent of Alexander Bickel's words when he said that the Supreme Court should be the guardian of society's "enduring values." Yet we saw that Bickel envisioned a very limited role for the Court. Consider how much common ground there may be between the guardian of enduring values as described by Bickel and the judicial role in achieving societal justice propounded by Dworkin, or the aspirations of the tradition described by Perry. Can a judiciary dispensing justice be constrained in any meaningful ways? Should it be?

§ 6.05 Bibliography

Raoul Berger, *Ronald Dworkin's The Moral Reading of the Constitution: A Critique,* 72 IND. L.J. 1099 (1997).

Philip C. Bobbitt, CONSTITUTIONAL INTERPRETATION (1991).

Michael C. Dorf, *Truth, Justice, and the American Constitution,* 97 COLUM. L. REV. 133 (1997).

Ronald Dworkin, *The Arduous Virtue of Fidelity: Originalism, Scalia, Tribe, and Nerve,* 65 FORDHAM L. REV. 1249 (1997).

Ronald Dworkin, LAW'S EMPIRE (1986); TAKING RIGHTS SERIOUSLY (1977); *Bork's Jurisprudence* (Book Review), 57 U. CHI. L. REV. 657 (1990).

Christopher L. Eisgruber, *Justice and the Text: Rethinking the Constitutional Relation Between Principle and Prudence,* 43 DUKE L.J. 1 (1993).

James Fleming, *Constructing the Substantive Constitution,* 72 TEX. L. REV. 211 (1993).

Michael W. McConnell, *The Role of Democratic Politics in Transforming Moral Convictions into Law* (Book Review), 98 YALE L.J. (1989).

Michael Moore, *A Natural Law Theory of Constitutional Interpretation,* 58 S. CAL. L. REV. 277 (1985).

Michael J. Perry, *The Authority of Text, Tradition, and Reason: A Theory of Constitutional Interpretation,* 58 S. CAL. L. REV. 551 (1985).

Richard Posner, *The Problematics of Moral and Legal Theory,* 111 HARV. L. REV. 1637 (1998).

Anthony J. Sebok, *The Insatiable Constitution,* 70 S. CAL. L. REV. 417 (1997).

Steven D. Smith, THE CONSTITUTION AND THE PRIDE OF REASON (1998).

Robin West, *Integrity and Universality: A Comment on Ronald Dworkin's Freedom's Law,* 65 FORDHAM L. REV. 1313 (1997).

Chapter 7

Precedent in Constitutional Adjudication

§ 7.01 Introduction

In constitutional cases, as in others, prior rulings in fact exert significant influence and in principle are generally accepted as one source for argument and grounds for decision. In theory, adherence to precedent not only constrains the discretion of judges acting in subsequent cases, but it also constrains the discretion of judges acting in the precedent-setting case itself by reminding those judges that they will be bound tomorrow by what they say today. In practice, *stare decisis* is often weighty, yet at the same time precedent is far from always controlling. In virtually any Supreme Court Term one can find instances of both adherence to precedents that the present Justices would not have reached were the questions ones of first impression, and overruling or limitation of precedents ancient and modern that earlier Justices would not have abandoned or narrowed. The stress on *stare decisis* in the majority opinion reaffirming the central holding of *Roe v. Wade*[1] in *Planned Parenthood v. Casey*[2] for example, and the judicial philosophies and some other opinions of its joint authors (Justices O'Connor, Kennedy, and Souter), make it seem unlikely that they all would have joined the original *Roe v. Wade* majority. At the same time, the prevailing opinion limits the sweep of *Roe* and approves some restrictions on abortion that would have been struck down as little as six years earlier.[3]

It is easy to state some highly general normative propositions about the role of *stare decisis* in constitutional adjudication that would probably draw wide agreement. First, the Court should ordinarily afford its constitutional precedents some weight, not treating them *ab initio* as if the issues they decided were matters of first impression. Second, however, precedents rarely, if ever, foreclose the possibility of their own reconsideration and possible overruling, limitation, or extension. Third, because it is far harder to amend the Constitution than to amend a statute, the Court should be readier to correct what it sees as an erroneous constitutional interpretation than to overrule a statutory interpretation.

Such statements, of course, illustrate Justice Holmes' remark that "[g]eneral propositions do not decide concrete cases."[4] They raise but do not

---

[1] 410 U.S. 113, 93 S. Ct. 705, 35 L. Ed. 2d 147 (1973).

[2] 505 U.S. 833, 112 S. Ct. 2791, 120 L. Ed. 2d 674 (1992).

[3] *See id.* at 882–83 (1992) (plurality opinion) (O'Connor, Kennedy, and Souter, JJ.) (overruling invalidation of informed consent requirements in Thornburgh v. American College of Obstetricians & Gynecologists, 476 U.S. 747, 762–65, 106 S. Ct. 2169, 90 L. Ed. 2d 779 (1986), and City of Akron v. Akron Center for Reproductive Health, 462 U.S. 416, 444–45, 103 S. Ct. 2481, 76 L. Ed. 687 (1983)).

[4] Lochner v. New York, 198 U.S. 45, 75, 25 S. Ct. 539, 49 L. Ed. 937 (1905) (Holmes, J., dissenting).

answer the question of the relative weight owing to precedent and such possibly conflicting sources as original intention. This sort of tension poses the further problem for an "originalist" of how to square the call for adherence to original intent with its apparent dilution if one leaves standing a precedent inconsistent with the perceived intent of the Framers. Issues of the relative weight owing to constitutional precedent take on special importance at times of major judicial transition, such as the peak years of the Warren Court and the present phase of a strengthened conservative majority on the Rehnquist Court. If one applauds the pathbreaking of the Warren Court, can one consistently level the charge of inappropriate activism at the Rehnquist Court majority when it overrules decisions it regards as having overstepped appropriate limits on the judicial role?

Apart from the potential tension between originalism and respect for precedent, it may be especially easy to see a place for individual Justices' judgment on values and social importance in deciding whether to let a questionable precedent stand. *Brown v. Board of Education*, at least in what has come to be taken as its core ruling that government-imposed racial segregation denies equal protection, seems certain to endure. It is almost equally certain that this holding does not square with the specific intention of at least a large majority of those who proposed and ratified the Fourteenth Amendment. Among the reasons for this permanence (debates about the relevant level of generality at which to treat the framers' intentions aside) must be the widely shared sense that the *Brown* principle is profoundly right and of highest social importance in modern America.

A good place to begin the consideration of the role of precedent in constitutional adjudication is with the concise listing, by then-Dean Geoffrey Stone of the University of Chicago Law School, of reasons commonly given for why the Court should follow or respect its prior decisions. Geoffrey R. Stone, *Precedent, the Amendment Process, and Evolution in Constitutional Doctrine*, 11 HARV. J. L. & PUB. POL'Y 67, 70 (1988):[5]

> Several justifications are commonly offered for the doctrine of precedent. First, we do not have unlimited judicial resources. If every issue in every case is a question of first impression, our judicial system would simply be overwhelmed with endless litigation. Second, we need a degree of predictability in our affairs. Interests of fairness, efficiency, and the enhancement of social interaction require that governments and citizens have a reasonably settled sense of what they may and may not do. Third, the doctrine of precedent raises the stakes. The Justice who knows that each decision governs not only the litigants to the particular case, but the rights of millions of individuals in the present and future, will approach the issue with less concern with the merits of the litigants as individuals and more concern with the merits of the underlying legal question to be decided. Fourth, the doctrine of precedent reflects a generally cautious approach to the resolution of legal issues. It reflects the view that change poses unknown risks, and that we generally should prefer the risks we know to those we cannot foresee. . . . Fifth, the doctrine of precedent reduces the potential politicization of the Court. It moderates ideological swings and thus preserves both the appearance and the reality of the Court as a legal rather than a purely political institution. And finally, from the

[5] Copyright © 1988 by the Harvard Society   permission of the Harvard Journal of Law and
for Law and Public Policy, Inc. Reprinted with   Public Policy.

perspective of the Justices themselves, the doctrine of precedent enhances the potential of the Justices to make lasting contributions. If a Justice disregards the judgments of those who preceded him, he invites the very same treatment from those who succeed him. A Justice who wants to preserve the value of his own coin must not devalue the coin of his predecessors.

Despite any consensus that there might be on the reasons why the Court in the abstract should follow its prior constitutional decisions, the following sections demonstrate that Justices and commentators frequently disagree over the standards the Court should actually follow in overruling prior decisions and over the application of any such standard in a given case. The second section examines some of the different standards and arguments the Justices have used over the years in determining the degree to which their decision-making should be constrained by precedent(s). The third section features a colloquy between Raoul Berger and Professor Boris Bittker of the Yale Law School on whether the incompatibility between original understanding and precedent is so extensive that originalism may be practically useless because the Court could not apply it without causing substantial havoc or without seriously modifying its unifying principle. The final set of extracts from a commentary by Harvard Law School Professor Charles Fried discusses constitutional precedent and doctrine from a philosophical viewpoint.

§ 7.02   Case Illustrations

The Supreme Court can overturn or otherwise weaken precedents through explicit overrulings, overrulings *sub silentio,* or subsequent decisionmaking that narrows or distinguishes precedents to the point of practical nullification. Explicit overrulings tend to be the best cases in which to examine attitudes regarding precedent, because they are relatively easy to identify and are the most likely occasion for disparate views on precedent to come into visible conflict. Explicit overrulings can result from various factors, including but not limited to changes in the Court's personnel, changed conditions, the lessons of experience (such as the apparent unworkability of a decision), and conflicting precedents. Indeed, one of the Court's earlier (and most dramatic) overrulings, in *The Legal Tender Cases*[6] offers a dramatic example of a turnabout traceable to a change in personnel. In 1870, the Court ruled 5-3 in *Hepburn v. Griswold*[7] that Congress did not have the authority to issue unbacked paper money. In the year following *Hepburn,* Justice Grier, who had been listed in the *Hepburn* majority, was replaced by Justice Strong, and Congress added a ninth seat to the Court, filled by Justice Bradley. In 1871, Justices Strong and Bradley joined the three *Hepburn* dissenters (Justices Miller, Swayne, and Davis) in overruling *Hepburn,* prompting a bitter dissent from Chief Justice Chase (the author of *Hepburn*). Chase charged, *inter alia,* that *Hepburn* was being overruled under the unprecedented circumstances in which none of the justices who had participated in *Hepburn* had been persuaded in the meantime to vote differently on the constitutionality of paper

---

[6] Knox v. Lee, 79 U.S. (12 Wall.) 457, 20 L. Ed. 287 (1871), *overruling* Hepburn v. Griswold, 75 U.S. (8 Wall.) 603, 19 L. Ed. 513 (1870).

[7] 75 U.S. (8 Wall.) 603, 19 L. Ed. 513 (1870).

money, and in which "the then majority find themselves in a minority on the court."[8]

Subsequently, the Court's overrulings of its prior decisions have become almost commonplace. Justice John Paul Stevens and former Justice Lewis Powell each suggested that the Court in this century has overruled itself two to three times each Term,[9] and Chief Justice Rehnquist cited 33 overrulings in the previous 20 Terms as support for his opinion at the end of the 1990 Term overturning two recent decisions.[10] In many of the Court's overrulings, the Justices have argued about the standards and the necessity for reversing precedent. For example, Justice Louis Brandeis gave the following classic statement on why the Court owed less than the usual deference to its own constitutional precedents. *Burnet v. Coronado Oil & Gas Co.* 285 U.S. 393, 406–08, 52 S. Ct. 443, 76 L. Ed. 815 (1932) (Brandeis, J., dissenting):

> *Stare decisis* is usually the wise policy, because in most matters it is more important that the applicable rule of law be settled than that it be settled right. . . . But in cases involving the Federal Constitution, where correction through legislative action is practically impossible, this Court has often overruled its earlier decisions. The Court bows to the lessons of experience and the force of better reasoning, recognizing that the process of trial and error, so fruitful in the physical sciences, is appropriate also in the judicial function.

Justice Owen Roberts expressed a less tolerant view of overturning constitutional precedents. He once criticized overruling a decision that overruled another reached nine years before as tending "to bring adjudications of this tribunal into the same class as a restricted railroad ticket, good for this day and train only. I have no assurance . . . that the opinion announced today

---

[8] *Knox,* 79 U.S. at 572 (Chase, C.J., *dissenting*).

[9] *See* Lewis Powell, *Stare Decisis and Judicial Restraint,* 47 WASH. & LEE L. REV. 281, 284 (1990); John Paul Stevens, *The Life Span of a Judge-Made Rule,* 58 N.Y.U. L. REV. 1, 4–5 (1983).

[10] *See* Payne v. Tennessee, 50 U.S. 808, 828–29 & n.1, 111 S. Ct. 2597, 115 L. Ed. 2d 720 (1991), *overruling* South Carolina v. Gathers, 490 U.S. 805, 109 S. Ct. 2207, 104 L. Ed. 2d 876 (1989), *and* Booth v. Maryland, 482 U.S. 496, 107 S. Ct. 2529, 96 L. Ed. 2d 440 (1987). By the end of the 1998 Term, the Supreme Court had overruled at least five more constitutional precedents. *See* College Savings Bank v. Florida Prepaid Postsecondary Education Expense Board, 527 U.S. 666, 119 S. Ct. 2219, 144 L. Ed. 2d 605 (1999) (*overruling* Parden v. Terminal Railway, 377 U.S. 184, 84 S. Ct. 1207, 12 L. Ed. 2d 233 (1964), which had held that a state implicitly or constructively waives its 11th amendment sovereign immunity by engaging in federally regulated commercial activities); Agostini v. Felton, 521 U.S. 203, 117 S. Ct. 1997, 138 L. Ed. 2d 391 (1997) (*overruling* Aguilar v. Felton, 473 U.S. 402, 105 S. Ct. 3232,

87 L. Ed. 2d 290 (1985), which had held that the First Amendment's Establishment Clause bars a state or city from sending public school teachers into parochial schools to provide remedial education to disadvantaged children); Seminole Tribe of Florida v. Florida, 517 U.S. 44, 116 S. Ct. 1114, 13 L. Ed. 2d 252 (1996) (*overruling* Pennsylvania v. Union Gas, 491 U.S. 1, 109 S. Ct. 2273, 105 L. Ed. 2d 1 (1989), in which a plurality had taken the position that pursuant to its commerce clause power Congress had the authority to abrogate states' sovereign immunity under the 11th amendment); Adarand Constructors, Inc. v. Pena, 515 U.S. 200, 115 S. Ct. 2097, 132 L. Ed. 2d 158 (1995) (*overruling* Metro Broadcasting, Inc. v. FCC, 497 U.S. 547, 110 S. Ct. 2997, 111 L. Ed. 2d 445 (1989), which had upheld under intermediate scrutiny certain FCC policies designed to increase the diversity of broadcast ownership); and United States v. Dixon, 509 U.S. 688, 113 S. Ct. 2849, 125 L. Ed. 2d 556 (1993) (*overruling* Grady v. Corbin, 495 U.S. 508, 110 S. Ct. 2084, 109 L. Ed. 2d 548 (1990), which had held that the Double Jeopardy Clause bars successive prosecutions based on the same set of facts but not charging the same offenses).

may not be shortly repudiated and overruled by justices who deem they have new light on the subject."[11]

Particularly in the 1960s, the Warren Court's aggressive overrulings often sparked sharp debates among its justices. One of the more heated exchanges occurred in *Mapp v. Ohio*.[12] In *Mapp*, a 5-4 majority overruled *Wolf v. Colorado*[13] which had held that "in a prosecution in a State court for a State crime the Fourteenth Amendment does not forbid the admission of evidence obtained by an unreasonable search and seizure."[14] *Mapp* was especially noteworthy in that the appellant had not raised the *Wolf* issue among the substantial federal questions tendered in her jurisdictional statement, nor even cited *Wolf* in her brief.[15] Writing for the *Mapp* majority, Justice Clark argued that *Wolf* needed to be overruled because it conflicted with a number of other recent precedents and because, 367 U.S. at 660,

> we can no longer permit [the Fourth Amendment] to be revocable at the whim of any police officer who, in the name of law enforcement itself, chooses to suspend its enjoyment. Our decision [that the Fourteenth Amendment makes the Fourth Amendment's exclusionary rule applicable to the states], founded on reason and truth, gives to the individual no more than that which the Constitution guarantees him, to the police officer no less than that to which honest law enforcement is entitled, and, to the courts, that judicial integrity so necessary in the true administration of justice.

In a separate concurrence, Justice Black explained the reasons for his joining the Court's decision to overrule *Wolf* (a decision in which he had concurred), *id.* at 666 (Black, J., concurring):

> [T]he continued existence of mutually inconsistent precedents together with the Court's [recent] inability to settle upon a [standard for determining when illegally seized evidence could not be admitted in state prosecutions] left the situation at least as uncertain as it had been before.

Justice Douglas also concurred on the ground that he "believ[ed] that this is an appropriate case in which to put an end to the asymmetry which *Wolf* imported into the law."[16]

In dissent, Justice Harlan took the majority to task for too lightly disregarding "the sense of judicial restraint which, with due regard for *stare decisis*, is one element that should enter into deciding whether a past decision of this Court should be overruled."[17] Given the presence in the case of a First Amendment privacy issue concerning mere possession of obscene material, which the parties had briefed and argued, he found it "fair to say that five members of this Court have simply 'reached out' to overrule *Wolf*."[18] He further pointed to the substantial reliance of state law enforcement authorities on *Wolf* as a reason against abandoning that precedent in a litigation that

---

[11] Smith v. Allwright, 321 U.S. 649, 669, 64 S. Ct. 757, 88 L. Ed. 987 (1944) (Roberts, J., dissenting), *overruling* Grovey v. Townsend, 295 U.S. 45, 55 S. Ct. 622, 79 L. Ed. 1292 (1935).

[12] 367 U.S. 643, 81 S. Ct. 1684, 6 L. Ed. 2d 1081 (1961).

[13] 338 U.S. 25, 69 S. Ct. 1359, 93 L. Ed. 1782 (1949).

[14] *Id.* at 25, 33.

[15] *See Mapp*, 367 U.S. at 673 & n.4–5 (Harlan, J., dissenting).

[16] *Id.* at 670 (Douglas, J., concurring).

[17] *Id.* at 672 (Harlan, J., dissenting).

[18] *Id.* at 674.

had barely touched on the question.[19] Justice Harlan argued that at least the Court should have called for reargument rather than, in effect, summarily overruling *Wolf* without argument.[20] He concluded that "what has been done is not likely to promote respect either for the Court's adjudicatory process or for the stability of its decisions."[21]

More recently, the Rehnquist Court's narrowing of abortion rights,[22] weakening or overruling of several criminal procedure precedents, steadfast opposition to affirmative action, and significant limitation of congressional authority to expand federal jurisdiction at the expense of state sovereignty, have prompted some sharp disagreements among the Justices, and subjected it to charges of activism like those leveled at the Warren Court. Examples of such decisions are *Payne v. Tennessee*;[23] *Planned Parenthood v. Casey;*[24] *Adarand Constructors, Inc. v. Pena*;[25] *Seminole Tribe v. Florida*;[26] and *College Savings Bank v. Florida.*[27] In *Payne,* the Court overruled two recent decisions[28] in which it had held that the Eighth Amendment prohibited the admission of victim impact statements in the sentencing phase of capital murder trials. But the six-member majority reflected some differing emphases on the appropriate criteria for overruling those precedents. Speaking for the majority (consisting of himself and Justices White, O'Connor, Scalia, Kennedy, and Souter), Chief Justice Rehnquist argued that the two decisions, *South Carolina v. Gathers*[29] and *Booth v. Maryland*[30] deserved less deference than constitutional decisions usually receive because they had been recently decided by 5-4 votes with vigorous dissents and had both been erroneously reasoned.[31]

Joined by Justices White and Kennedy, Justice O'Connor separately concurred on the ground that *Booth* and *Gathers* needed to be overruled because they "were wrongly decided."[32] In another separate concurrence, Justice Scalia, joined by Justices O'Connor and Kennedy, argued that, contrary to the assertions made in Justice Marshall's (final) dissent, the Court did not need to show any "special justification" for overruling *Booth* and *Gathers* and that those decisions did far more damage to the notion of *stare decisis* than *Payne* because they had violated the "general principle that the settled practices and expectations of a democratic society should generally not be disturbed by the courts."[33] In yet another separate concurrence, Justice Souter, joined by

---

[19] *See id.* at 676.

[20] *See id.* at 677.

[21] *Id.*

[22] *See, e.g.* Webster v. Reproductive Health Services, 492 U.S. 490, 109 S. Ct. 3040, 106 L. Ed. 2d 410 (1989).

[23] 501 U.S. 808, 112 S. Ct. 28, 115 L. Ed. 2d 1110 (1991).

[24] 505 U.S. 833, 112 S. Ct. 2791, 120 L. Ed. 2d 674 (1992).

[25] 515 U.S. 200, 115 S. Ct. 2097, 132 L. Ed. 2d 158 (1995).

[26] 517 U.S. 44, 116 S. Ct. 1114, 134 L. Ed. 2d 252 (1996).

[27] 527 U.S. 666, 119 S. Ct. 2219, 144 L. Ed. 2d 605 (1999).

[28] South Carolina v. Gathers, 490 U.S. 805, 109 S. Ct. 2207, 104 L. Ed. 2d 876 (1989); Booth v. Maryland, 482 U.S. 496, 107 S. Ct. 2529, 16 L. Ed. 2d 440 (1987).

[29] 490 U.S. 805, 109 S. Ct. 2207, 104 L. Ed. 2d 876 (1989).

[30] 482 U.S. 496, 107 S. Ct. 2529, 16 L. Ed. 2d 440 (1987).

[31] *See Payne,* 501 U.S. 808 at 827–30, 111 S. Ct. 2597, 115 L. Ed. 2d 720 (1991).

[32] *Id.* at 832 (O'Connor, J., concurring).

[33] *Id.* at 835 (Scalia, J., concurring).

Justice Kennedy, argued that *Booth* and *Gathers* should be overruled because they were erroneously reasoned and demonstrably unworkable.[34]

Justices Marshall and Stevens wrote separate dissents, each joined by Justice Blackmun, challenging, *inter alia,* the majority's approach to precedent. Justice Marshall castigated the new majority for making "[p]ower, not reason, . . . the new currency of th[e] Court's decisionmaking."[35] He argued that (1) these overrulings could be traced to recent changes in the Court's personnel;[36] (2) overrulings based on prior close votes and disagreements with precedents' reasoning already expressed in dissents would disrupt constitutional law significantly;[37] and (3) the majority had generally failed to "come forward with the type of extraordinary showing that this Court has historically demanded before overruling one of its precedents."[38] Justice Marshall argued further that the Chief Justice's position that 5-4 decisions with vigorous dissents deserve less than the usual deference owed to precedents threatened to "destroy" the Court's authority as the final decisionmaker on questions involving individual liberties, because it "invites" state actors to treat certain decisions as nonbinding and instead "to renew the very policies deemed unconstitutional in the hope that this Court may now reverse course, even if it has only recently reaffirmed the constitutional liberty in question."[39] In his dissent, Justice Stevens accused the majority of abandoning sound reasoning and *stare decisis* due to the " 'hydraulic pressure' of public opinion."[40]

A year after *Payne,* its six-Justice majority split 3-3 in *Planned Parenthood v. Casey*[41] over whether to overrule *Roe v. Wade.*[42] Justices O'Connor,

---

[34] *Id.* at 839–40 (Souter, J., concurring).

[35] *Id.* at 844 (Marshall, J., dissenting).

[36] *See id.*

[37] *Id.* at 845.

[38] *Id.* at 848.

[39] *Id.* at 854.

[40] *Id.* at 867 (Stevens, J., dissenting) (citation omitted). For another decision (decided the same day as *Payne*) reflecting disagreements among the Justices on the proper respect owed to precedent, *see* Harmelin v. Michigan, 501 U.S. 957, 111 S. Ct. 2680, 115 L. Ed. 2d 836 (1991). In *Harmelin,* the five-member majority upheld Michigan's imposition of a life sentence without parole for drug possession but split over the necessity and the criteria for overruling Solem v. Helm, 463 U.S. 277, 103 S. Ct. 3001, 77 L. Ed. 2d 637 (1983). In *Solem,* the Court had found that a mandatory life sentence without the possibility of parole for the commission of at least three felonies violated the principle that the Eighth Amendment prohibits imposition of a sentence that is disproportionate to the severity of a crime. On behalf of himself and the Chief Justice, Justice Scalia argued that *Solem* should be overruled because it was erroneously reasoned, articulated an

unworkable standard, and was inconsistent with the original understanding of the Eighth Amendment and other case law. *Harmelin,* 501 U.S. at 966–95. Justices O'Connor and Souter joined in Justice Kennedy's concurrence rejecting Justice Scalia's arguments for overruling *Solem.* Instead, Justice Kennedy maintained that even though *Solem* could have been better reasoned and could have articulated a more workable standard, the Court could remedy those problems by narrowing but not overruling *Solem. Id.* at 998–1001 (Kennedy, J., concurring in part and concurring in the judgment). In dissent, Justice White (joined by Justices Blackmun and Stevens) found that neither the history nor the case law regarding the Eighth Amendment supported Justice Scalia's conclusion that the Eighth Amendment contained no proportionality principle. As for Justice Kennedy's analysis, Justice White argued that it was "contradicted by the language of *Solem* and by our other cases interpreting the Eighth Amendment." *Id.* at 1009–10, 1018 (White, J., dissenting).

[41] 505 U.S. 833, 112 S. Ct. 2791, 120 L. Ed. 2d 674 (1992).

[42] 410 U.S. 113, 93 S. Ct. 705, 35 L. Ed. 2d 147 (1973).

Kennedy, and Souter, joined by *Payne* dissenters Blackmun and Stevens, made a bare majority to reaffirm the existence of a constitutional right to abortion that had been originally recognized in *Roe.* The three swing Justices made a controlling plurality to adopt a new "undue burden" standard for the validity of state abortion regulations. Chief Justice Rehnquist and Justices White and Scalia, joined by new Justice Clarence Thomas, would have overruled *Roe* and permitted state regulations and restrictions that are rationally related to a legitimate state interest.

In an extensive discussion of the doctrine of *stare decisis,* the majority framed its approach in these terms:

> [W]hen this Court reexamines a prior holding, its judgment is customarily informed by a series of prudential and pragmatic considerations designed to test the consistency of overruling a prior decision with the ideal of the rule of law, and to gauge the respective costs of reaffirming and overruling a prior case. Thus, for example, we may ask whether the rule has proved to be intolerable simply in defying practical workability; whether the rule is subject to a kind of reliance that would lend a special hardship to the consequences of overruling and add inequity to the cost of repudiation; whether related principles of law have so far developed as to have left the old rule no more than a remnant of abandoned doctrine; or whether facts have so changed or come to be seen so differently, as to have robbed the old rule of significant application or justification.[43]

The opinion dealt briefly with the workability question, finding that the determinations required under *Roe* "fall within judicial competence,"[44] and turned to the more difficult issue of reliance. "Since the classic case for weighing reliance heavily in favor of following the earlier rule occurs in the commercial context [citing *Payne*], where advance planning of great precision is most obviously a necessity, it is no cause for surprise that some would find no reliance worthy of consideration in support of *Roe.*"[45] "[C]ognizable reliance," however, goes beyond "specific instances of sexual activity":

> [F]or two decades of economic and social developments, people have organized intimate relationships and made choices that define their views of themselves and their places in society, in reliance on the availability of abortion in the event that contraception should fail. The ability of women to participate equally in the economic and social life of the Nation has been facilitated by their ability to control their reproductive lives.[46]

The majority considered *Roe* in the context of other decisions, finding its doctrine neither anomalous nor obsolete. And it saw supervening developments in medical knowledge and technology as requiring no more than flexibility in the application of *Roe*'s central holding, rather than its overruling.[47]

Recognizing that *Roe* is no ordinary precedent, the majority broadened its discussion to consider arguable parallels with two abandoned lines of cases, those identified with *Lochner v. New York*[48] and *Plessy v. Ferguson.*[49] It

---

[43] *Planned Parenthood,* 505 U.S. at 854–55 (citations omitted).

[44] *Id.* at 855.

[45] *Id.* at 855–56.

[46] *Id.* at 856.

[47] *See id.* at 859–61.

[48] 198 U.S. 45, 25 S. Ct. 539, 49 L. Ed. 937 (1905).

[49] 163 U.S. 537, 16 S. Ct. 1138, 41 L. Ed. 256 (1896).

viewed the abandonment of the constitutional doctrines of liberty of contract and separate but equal as resting on major changes in facts or in their understanding, beyond mere changes in Court membership or disagreement with the original holdings, that made reconsideration "not only justified but required."[50] With *Roe,* the majority saw not just a threat to the Court's legitimacy from too-frequent vacillation but an analogy to *Brown v. Board of Education*[51] in that there and in *Roe* the Court in interpreting the Constitution had called on "the contending sides of a national controversy to end their national division by accepting a common mandate rooted in the Constitution."[52]

> A decision to overrule *Roe*'s essential holding under the existing circumstances would address error, if error there was, at the cost of both profound and unnecessary damage to the Court's legitimacy, and to the Nation's commitment to the rule of law. It is therefore imperative to adhere to the essence of *Roe*'s original decision . . .[53]

The partial dissents of Chief Justice Rehnquist and Justice Scalia, each joined by the other and by Justices White and Thomas, would have found overruling of *Roe* fully consistent with the respect due to constitutional *stare decisis.* Both opinions strongly emphasized the gravity of what they viewed as the error of *Roe,* and Justice Scalia likened the case to the dishonor of *Dred Scott*[54] rather than to the abandonment of *Lochner* and *Plessy.*[55] Chief Justice Rehnquist's opinion contended that the prevailing opinion abandoned rather than adhered to *stare decisis* because of its modification of the *Roe* approach,[56] and disagreed point by point with its arguments on precedent and the plurality's reformulated "undue burden" standard.

> Strong and often misguided criticism of a decision should not render the decision immune from reconsideration, lest a fetish for legitimacy penalize freedom of expression.

> . . .

> The sum of the joint opinion's labors in the name of *stare decisis* and "legitimacy" is this: *Roe v. Wade* stands as a sort of judicial Potemkin Village, which may be pointed out to passers by as a monument to the importance of adhering to precedent. But behind the facade, an entirely new method of analysis, without any roots in constitutional law, is imported to decide the constitutionality of state laws regulating abortion. Neither *stare decisis* nor "legitimacy" [is] truly served by such an effort.[57]

Three years after *Casey,* its five-member majority split 2-2 in *Adarand* (with Justice Blackmun in the interim having been replaced by Justice Breyer) over whether to overrule the Court's 1989 decision in *Metro Broadcasting.* In the

---

[50] *Planned Parenthood,* 505 U.S. at 862.

[51] 347 U.S. 483, 74 S. Ct. 686, 98 L. Ed. 873 (1954).

[52] *Planned Parenthood,* 505 U.S. at 867.

[53] *Id.* at 869.

[54] Dred Scott v. Sandford, 60 U.S. (19 How.) 393, 15 L. Ed. 691 (1857).

[55] *See Planned Parenthood,* 505 U.S. at 998, 1001 (Scalia, J., concurring in the judgment in part and dissenting in part).

[56] *Id.* at 953–54 (Rehnquist, C.J., concurring in the judgment in part and dissenting in part).

[57] *Id.* at 964–66. For two opposing views on the role of precedent in *Casey,* see Earl Maltz, *Abortion, Precedent, and the Constitution: A Commentary on* Planned Parenthood of Southeastern Pennsylvania v. Casey, 68 NOTRE DAME L. REV. 11 (1992); Michael J. Gerhardt, *The Pressure of Precedent: A Critique of the Conservative Approaches to Stare Decisis in Abortion Cases* 10 CONST. COMM. 67 (1993).

latter case, the Court had upheld 5-4 the constitutionality of Federal Communications Commission policies allowing minority ownership to be taken into account in the awarding and transferring of broadcast licenses. In her opinion for the majority in *Adarand* (consisting of herself, Chief Justice Rehnquist, and Justices Kennedy, Scalia, and Thomas), Justice O'Connor quoted approvingly Justice Felix Frankfurter's admonition that " 'stare decisis is a principle of policy and not a mechanical formula of adherence to the latest decision, however recent and questionable, when such adherence involves collision with a prior doctrine more embracing in its scope, intrinsically sounder, and verified by experience.' "[58] Applying this principle to the case before her, Justice O'Connor found that *Metro Broadcasting* "undermined important principles of this Court's equal protection jurisprudence, established in a line of cases stretching back over 50 years. . . ."[59] The principles established in those cases, according to Justice O'Connor, "stood for an 'embracing' and 'intrinsically soun[d]' understanding of equal protection 'verified by experience,' namely, that the Constitution imposes upon federal, state, and local governmental actors the same obligation to respect the personal right to equal protection of the laws."[60] She concluded that *Adarand* "therefore presents precisely the situation described by Justice Frankfurter[:] We cannot adhere to our most recent decision without colliding with an accepted and established doctrine."[61] Moreover, she explained, the widespread scholarly criticism of *Metro Broadcasting* and the Court's "past practice in similar circumstances support[] our action today."[62]

Mindful that the Court's overruling of *Metro Broadcasting* might appear to be in conflict with the Court's re-affirmation of *Roe* in *Casey* just three years earlier, Justice O'Connor took pains to distinguish the Court's approaches to precedent in *Adarand* and in *Casey*. She argued that "*Casey* explained how considerations of *stare decisis* inform the decision whether to overrule a long-established precedent that has become integrated into the fabric of the law. Overruling precedent of that kind naturally may have consequences for 'the ideal rule of law' . . . In addition, such precedent is likely to have engendered substantial reliance . . ."[63] She suggested that whereas *Casey* had been consistent with a series of decisions reaffirming *Roe*'s core holding, "*Metro Broadcasting*. . . departed from our prior cases—and did so quite recently. . . . By refusing to follow *Metro Broadcasting* then, we do not depart from the fabric of the law; we restore it."[64]

In dissent (joined by Justices Breyer, Ginsburg, and Souter), Justice Stevens argued that *Metro Broadcasting* could hardly conflict with well established constitutional law because it had only been the Court's third opinion "consider-[ing] the constitutionality of a federal affirmative-action program."[65] The first such case had been *Fullilove v. Klutznick*, 448 U.S. 448, 100 S. Ct. 2758, 65 L. Ed. 2d 902 (1980), in which six justices had agreed to uphold (but without a majority agreeing on the reasons for upholding) a congressional enactment

---

[58] *Adarand*, 515 U.S. at 231 (quoting Helvering v. Hallock, 309 U.S. 106, 119, 60 S. Ct. 444, 84 L. Ed. 604 (1940)).

[59] *Id.* at 231.

[60] *Id.* at 231–32.

[61] *Id.* at 232.

[62] *Id.*

[63] *Id.* at 233.

[64] *Id.* at 234.

[65] *Id.* at 234.

providing that at least 10 percent of federal funds granted for local public works must be used to obtain services or supplies from minority-owned businesses. The second decision had been *City of Richmond v. J.A. Croson Co.*, 488 U.S. 469, 109 S. Ct. 706, 102 L. Ed. 2d 854 (1989), in which the Court 5-4 had struck down a city plan modeled on the federal program upheld in *Fullilove*. In *Adarand*, Justice Stevens explained, "*Metro Broadcasting* involved a federal program, whereas *Croson* involved a city ordinance. *Metro Broadcasting* thus drew support from *Fullilove* which predated *Croson* and which *Croson* [had] distinguished on the grounds of the federal-state dichotomy that the majority today discredits. . . . [T]he law at the time of [*Fullilove* had been] entirely open to the result that the Court reached. Today's decision is an unjustified departure from settled law."[66]

Departure from clearly settled law, including subsequent cases, served as the primary basis in the late 1990s for the Court's overrulings of two precedents raising fundamental questions about the scope of federal power to restrict state sovereignty under the 11th amendment. The 11th amendment provides, "The Judicial power of the United States shall not be construed to extend to any suit in law or equity, commenced or prosecuted against one of the United States by Citizens of another State, or by Citizens or Subjects of any foreign State." Though the text of the 11th amendment explicitly bars only suits brought against a state by citizens of another state, the Court held more than a century ago in *Hans v. Louisiana*[67] that the 11th amendment also bars suits brought against a state by its own citizens. In 1989, a plurality of the Court in *Pennsylvania v. Union Gas* joined in the outcome but not in the reasoning by Justice White—had found that the Interstate Commerce Clause granted Congress the power to abrogate state sovereign immunity under the 11th amendment. The plurality reasoned that the power to regulate interstate commerce would be "incomplete without the authority to render States liable in damages."[68] The other four justices—Chief Justice Rehnquist and Justices O'Connor, Kennedy, and Scalia—vigorously dissented on the grounds that the decision could not be squared with the original understanding of the 11th amendment or the Court's other precedents in the area, including *Hans*.

Seven years later, the Court in *Seminole Tribe* readdressed the issue in the course of adjudicating a challenge to a congressional enactment under the Indian Commerce Clause[69] permitting an Indian tribe to sue a state for failing

---

[66] *Id.* at 256–57.

[67] 134 U.S. 1, 10 S. Ct. 504, 33 L. Ed. 842 (1890).

[68] *Union Gas,* 491 U.S. at 19–20.

[69] Article I, section 8, clause 3 provides in pertinent part that "Congress shall have the power . . . [t]o regulate Commerce with foreign Nations, and among the several States, and with the Indian tribes." In *Seminole Tribe* the Court acknowledged that "the Indian Commerce Clause accomplishes a greater transfer of power from the States to the Federal Government than does the Interstate Commerce Clause. This is clear enough from the fact that the States still exercise some authority over interstate trade but have been divested of virtually all authority over Indian commerce and Indian tribes." *Seminole Tribe,* 517 U.S. at 62. Nevertheless, since the exercise of power under either clause raised a question about whether "the States' partial cession of authority over a particular area includes cession of the immunity from suit," the Court determined that "the plurality opinion in *Union Gas* allows no principled distinction in favor of the States to be drawn between the Indian Commerce Clause and the Interstate Commerce Clause." *Id.* at 63.

to perform its statutory duty to negotiate in good faith a compact with the tribe to provide gaming activities within the state. Split precisely along the same lines as it had been in *Adarand*, the *Seminole Tribe* Court overruled *Union Gas*. In a lengthy opinion for herself, Chief Justice Rehnquist and Justices Kennedy, Scalia, and Thomas, Justice O'Connor "conclude[d] that none of the policies underlying stare decisis require our continuing adherence to [the] holding [of *Union Gas*]."[70] First, she noted that the 5-4 decision in *Union Gas* lacked "an express rationale agreed upon by a majority of the Court."[71] Consequently, the decision, in her view, "ha[d] created confusion among the lower courts that have sought to understand and apply the deeply fractured decision."[72] Second, Justice O'Connor found that the "result in *Union Gas* and the plurality's rationale depart[ed] from our established understanding of the Eleventh Amendment and undermine the accepted function of Article III."[73] Relying instead on a rationale put forward by Justice Scalia in his dissent in *Union Gas*,[74] she explained that *Hans* and subsequent case law had made clear that Article III, as amended by the 11th amendment, defined the outer limits of federal-court jurisdiction. In her view, the case law clearly dictated that the Fourteenth Amendment was the only constitutional provision that conceivably allowed Congress to expand federal court jurisdiction under Article III. Thus, by upholding an attempt by Congress to use its commerce clause authority to expand federal jurisdiction, *Union Gas* "ha[d] proved to be a solitary departure from established law."[75]

In their respective dissents, Justice Stevens and Souter gave different reasons for opposing the majority's overruling of *Union Gas*. Writing only for himself, Justice Stevens denounced the majority's characterization of *Union Gas*' holding as a novel or incomprehensible " 'plurality decision.' "[76] He found "far more significant than the 'plurality' character of the . . . opinions supporting the holding in *Union Gas* [is] the fact that the issue confronted today has been squarely addressed by a total of 13 justices [in prior precedents], 8 of whom cast their votes with [the position of] the so-called 'plurality.' "[77]

Joined by Justices Stevens, Breyer, and Ginsburg, Justice Souter suggested in his dissent that the majority's extension of *Hans* did more damage to settled law than the plurality opinion in *Union Gas*. Justice Souter explained that federal jurisdiction could be based on diversity of citizenship between the parties to a lawsuit or the presence of a question of federal law. The major error in *Hans*, he suggested, was the Court's mistaken "assum[ption] that a State could plead sovereign immunity against a noncitizen suing under federal-question jurisdiction, and for that reason h[olding] that a State must enjoy the same protection in a suit by one of its citizens."[78] This assumption was mistaken because it transformed a pre-constitutional common law rule, which had recognized state sovereignty immunity in diversity cases, into a constitutional prohibition on Congress' power to expand federal-question

---

[70] 517 U.S. at 66.

[71] 517 U.S. at 63.

[72] *Id.* at 64 (citations omitted).

[73] *Id.* at 66.

[74] *Id.* at 65 (citation omitted).

[75] *Id.* at 66.

[76] *Id.* at 94 (citation omitted).

[77] *Id.* (citation omitted).

[78] *Id.* at 102.

jurisdiction in a case involving diverse parties. Thus, Justice Souter argued, *Hans* answered only the narrow question

> whether the Constitution, without more, permits a State to plead sovereign immunity to bar the exercise of federal-question jurisdiction. . . . Although the Court invoked a principle of sovereign immunity to cure what it took to be the Eleventh Amendment's anomaly of barring only those state suits brought by noncitizen plaintiffs, the *Hans* Court had no occasion to consider whether Congress could abrogate that background immunity by statute. Indeed (except in the special circumstance of Congress' power to enforce the Civil War Amendments), this question never came before our Court until *Union Gas* and any intimations of an answer in prior cases were dicta. In *Union Gas* the Court held that the immunity recognized in *Hans* had no constitutional status and was subject to congressional abrogation. Today the Court overrules *Union Gas* and holds just the opposite. In deciding how to choose between these two positions, the place to begin is with *Hans'* holding that a principle of sovereign immunity derived from the common law insulates a State from federal-question jurisdiction at the suit of its own citizen. A critical examination of that case will show that it was wrongly decided, as virtually every recent commentator has concluded.[79]

Justice Souter suggested that the transformation of a common law rule into a constitutional principle was reminiscent of the Court's widely criticized opinion in *Lochner*. He warned that in taking such a discredited and dangerous approach, the *Seminole Tribe* Court was "follow[ing] a course that has brought it to grief before in our history, and promises to do so again."[80] He explained,

> It was the defining characteristic of the *Lochner* era, and its characteristic vice, that the Court treated the common-law background (in those days, common-law property rights and contractual autonomy) as paramount, while regarding congressional legislation to abrogate the common law on these economic matters as constitutionally suspect. . . . And yet the superseding lesson that seemed clear after *West Coast Hotel Co. v. Parrish*, 300 U.S. 379 (1937), that action within the legislative power is not subject to greater scrutiny merely because it trenches upon the case law's ordering of economic and social relationships, seems to have been lost on the Court.[81]

If there were any difference between *Lochner* and *Seminole Tribe*, Justice Souter suggested, it was that *Lochner* had made

> an ostensible effort to give content to some other written provision of the Constitution, like the Due Process Clause, the very object of which is to limit the exercise of governmental power. . . . Some textual argument, at least, could be made that the Court was doing no more than defining one provision that happened to be at odds with another. Today, however, the Court is not struggling to fulfill a responsibility to reconcile two arguably conflicting and Delphic constitutional provisions, nor is it struggling with any Delphic text at all. For even the Court concedes that the Constitution's grant of plenary power over relations with Indian tribes at the expense of any state claim to the contrary is unmistakably clear, and this case does not even arguably implicate a textual trump to the grant of federal-question jurisdiction.[82]

---

[79] *Id.* at 117 (Souter, J., dissenting) (citations omitted).

[80] *Id.* at 102.

[81] *Id.* at 166.

[82] *Id.* at 167.

Justice Souter's protracted criticisms of *Hans* did not, however, lead him to call for the overruling of *Hans*. Just the opposite. He concluded that "for reasons of stare decisis I would not disturb the century-old precedent [of *Hans*]."[83] He acknowledged that

[t]he *Hans* decision was erroneous, but it has not previously proven to be unworkable or to conflict with later doctrine or to suffer from the effects of facts developed since its decision (apart from those indicating its original errors). I would therefore treat *Hans* as it has always been treated in fact until today, as a doctrine of federal common law. For, as so understood, it has formed one of the strands of the federal relationship for over a century now, and the stability of that relationship is itself a value that stare decisis aims to respect.[84]

Three years after *Seminole Tribe*, the Justices in *College Savings Bank* split again along exactly the same lines as they had in *Adarand* and *Seminole Tribe* to overturn another precedent dealing with the scope of federal power to limit state sovereign immunity under the 11th amendment. The precedent at issue was *Parden v. Terminal Railway Co. of Alabama.*[85] In *Parden* the Court unanimously had held that a state constructively or implicitly waives its 11th amendment sovereign immunity by engaging in commercial activity in a federally regulated marketplace. *College Savings Bank v. Florida* revisited this question in the context of a federal lawsuit brought against a state by a private business claiming that the state had engaged in commercial activities that constituted false and misleading advertising in violation of federal trademark law.

In his opinion for the Court, Justice Scalia described in detail the Court's long retreat from and persistent questioning of the validity of *Parden*. He noted, for instance, that in 1987 the Court in part of an opinion—the part that Justice Scalia had joined—had overruled *Parden* " 'to the extent [it] is inconsistent with the requirement that an abrogation of Eleventh Amendment immunity by Congress must be expressed in unmistakably clear language.' "[86] Justice Scalia then summarized the Court's reasons for overruling whatever remained of *Parden*:

We think that the constructive-waiver experiment of *Parden* was ill-conceived, and see no merit in attempting to salvage any remnant of it. . . . *Parden* broke sharply with prior cases, and is fundamentally incompatible with later ones. We have never applied the holding of *Parden* to another statute, and in fact have narrowed the case in every subsequent opinion in which it has been under consideration. In short, *Parden* stands as an anomaly in the jurisprudence of sovereign immunity, and indeed in the jurisprudence of constitutional law. Today, we drop the other shoe: Whatever may remain of our decision is expressly overruled.[87]

In a dissent joined by Justices Stevens, Souter, and Ginsburg, Justice Breyer initially disputed that *Parden* had "br[oken] 'sharply with prior

---

[83] *Id.* at 159.

[84] *Id.* at 183.

[85] 377 U.S. 184, 84 S. Ct. 1207, 12 L. Ed. 2d 233 (1964).

[86] Welch v. Texas Department of Highways and Public Transportation, 483 U.S. 468, 478,

107 S. Ct. 2941, 97 L. Ed. 2d 389 (1987), quoted in College Savings Bank v. Florida, 527 U.S. 666, 119 S. Ct. 2219, 2227, 144 L. Ed. 2d 605.

[87] College Savings Bank v. Florida, 527 U.S. 666, 119 S. Ct. 2219, 2228, 144 L. Ed. 2d 605 (1999).

cases.' "[88] *Parden* itself cited authority that found related "waivers in at least roughly comparable circumstances."[89] Moreover, *Parden* had support from both "[e]arlier" and "[l]ater case law."[90] Second, he argued that the case law claimed by the majority as supporting its abandonment of *Parden*, including *Seminole Tribe*, did no such thing. He claimed that *Seminole Tribe* rather than *Parden* was the anomaly in 11th amendment jurisprudence. After arguing that *Seminole Tribe* lacked support from constitutional text, history, and precedent, Justice Breyer suggested that the most serious problem with *Seminole Tribe* was that it marked a return to *Lochnerism*. He explained, "The similarity to *Lochner* lies in the risk that *Seminole Tribe* and the Court's subsequent cases will deprive Congress of necessary legislative flexibility . . . to achieve one of federalism's basic objectives . . . the protection of liberty."[91] He concluded with a call for overruling *Seminole Tribe*:

> Unfortunately, *Seminole Tribe* and today's related decisions, separate one formal strand from the federalist skein—a strand that has been understood as anti-Republican since the time of Cicero—and they elevate that strand to the level of an immutable constitutional principle more akin to the thought of James I than of James Madison. They do so when the role sovereign immunity once played in helping to assure the States that their political independence would remain even after joining the Union no longer holds center stage. . . . They do so when a federal court's ability to enforce its judgment against a State is no longer a major concern. . . . And they do so without adequate legal support grounded in either history or practical need. To the contrary, by making that doctrine immune from congressional Article I modification, the Court makes it more difficult for Congress to decentralize governmental decisionmaking and to provide individual citizens, or local communities, with a variety of enforcement powers. By diminishing congressional flexibility to do so, the Court makes it somewhat more difficult to satisfy modern federalism's more important liberty-protecting needs. In this sense, it is counterproductive.[92]

The 5-4 splits on the Court in *Adarand*, *Seminole Tribe* and *College Savings Bank*[93] raise a serious question about the likely stability of these decisions

---

[88] *Id.* at 2235 (Breyer, J., dissenting).

[89] *Id.*

[90] *Id.*

[91] *Id.* at 2238–39. In his majority opinion, Justice Scalia contested the dissent's likening of *Seminole Tribe* to *Lochner* as unfounded and irrational. He suggested *Seminole Tribe*

resembles *Lochner*, of course, in the respect that it rejects a novel assertion of governmental power which the legislature believed to be justified. But if that alone were enough to qualify as a mini-*Lochner*, the list of mini-*Lochners* would be endless. Most of our judgments invalidating state and federal laws fit that description. We had always thought that the distinctive feature of *Lochner* . . . was that it sought to impose a particular economic philosophy upon the Constitution. And we think that feature aptly characterizes, not our opin-

ion, but Justice Breyer's dissent, which believes that States should not enjoy the normal constitutional protections of sovereign immunity when they step out of their proper economic role to engage in . . . "ordinary commercial ventures" . . . Whatever happened to the need for "legislative flexibility"?

Id. at 2233 (citations omitted).

[92] *Id.* at 2240 (citations omitted).

[93] Besides Justice Souter's cataloguing of the evils likely to be engendered by the Court's extension of *Hans* in *Seminole Tribe* and Justice Breyer's call for the overruling of *Seminole Tribe* in *College Savings Bank*, Justice Stevens "note[d his] continuing dissent from the Court's aggressive sovereign immunity jurisprudence" in the companion case to *College Savings Bank*, Florida v. College Savings Bank, 527 U.S. 627, 119 S. Ct. 2199, 2219, 144 L. Ed. 2d 575 (1999)(Stevens, J., dissenting).

in the future. One cannot help but wonder whether the Court's jurisprudence in the areas covered by these decisions will turn out to be ones in which Chief Justice Rehnquist will be haunted by his suggestion in *Payne* that 5-4 constitutional decisions with vigorous dissents are not entitled to the same deference as other constitutional precedents. With the presidential election of 2000 just around the corner, the speculation has already begun about just how soon the next President will have a chance to replace any of the current Justices on the Court. And of course there are questions about the kinds of justices whom the next President will appoint. If the four dissenters in *Adarand, Seminole Tribe,* and *College Savings Bank* remain on the Court until that opportunity arises, then the next appointee is likely to determine not only the fates of these precedents but also the stability of the constitutional doctrine set forth in them.

§ 7.03   Constitutional Theory and the Problem of Nonconforming Precedent

At this juncture one might question how the interpretive theories thus far covered in this book would work in practice: Would their faithful application mean the overruling or abandonment of large numbers of Supreme Court precedents that do not conform to their methodology or reasoning? If so, is society prepared for the upheaval such decisions would produce? If not, by what standard(s) would the Court or theorists determine to accept nonconforming precedents, and are these criteria or conditions compatible with the interpretive theory being applied?

These questions have been most extensively considered in the debate over originalism. For example, Professors Henry Monaghan of Columbia Law School and Michael Perry of Wake Forest School of Law have argued that so much Supreme Court precedent has been based on a rejection of original understanding that a true originalist has only two choices.[94] The first choice is to strive to overrule the better part of constitutional doctrine and thereby thrust the world of constitutional law into turmoil; the second is to acquiesce in past abandonments of original understanding in numerous substantive areas in order to provide constitutional law with stability and continuity.

Professor Michael Gerhardt of the William and Mary School of Law argues that the tension that exists between precedent and original understanding is not unique, but rather is inevitable with respect to all other unitary constitutional theories, which seek to explain constitutional law in terms of a single unifying principle. Gerhardt contends, *inter alia,* that precedent and unitary theory are in perpetual, irreconcilable conflict because precedents are a product of "a dynamic (dialogic) process in which the Justices" debate the reasons for perpetuating the values the Court has previously endorsed for guiding the operation of government, while unitary theory "aims to perpetuate or reinforce itself but not to mediate (as the dialogic process does) among different constitutional visions."[95] He argues further that because the Justices

---

[94] *See* MICHAEL PERRY, THE CONSTITUTION, THE COURTS, AND HUMAN RIGHTS 64–67 (1982); Henry Monaghan, *Stare Decisis and Constitutional Adjudication,* 88 COLUM. L. REV. 723,

723–24 (1988).

[95] *See* Michael J. Gerhardt, *The Role of Precedent in Constitutional Decisionmaking and Theory,* 60 GEO. WASH. L. REV. 68, 73 (1991).

each typically reflect different backgrounds, training, and outlooks, it is practically impossible to guarantee that they will all think alike over time regarding interpretive questions, including the standards for interpreting the Constitution and for overruling precedent.[96]

Two prominent originalists have responded to the arguments that originalism conflicts with constitutional doctrine to such an extent that it cannot be practically applied in constitutional adjudication. First, former Judge Robert Bork has tried to reconcile this tension by proposing three guidelines for judicial reconsideration of precedent: (1) lower courts should respect precedent more rigorously than must the Court itself, (2) the Court should never overrule any decision unless it finds that the case was wrongly decided, and (3) the Court should not overrule prior erroneous decisions when that would seriously disrupt well-established government structures or practices.[97]

Second, Raoul Berger is notable for his opposition to the charge that an originalist judge would wreak havoc on constitutional law because he would feel compelled to overturn the substantial numbers of precedents that conflict with original understanding. In the following excerpt, Berger addresses not only this charge but also the more specific argument of Professor Emeritus Boris Bittker of the Yale Law School that originalists cannot provide principled review of nonoriginalist precedents because there is no original understanding on that problem.[98] Berger maintains in part that Bittker has mischaracterized the ways in which an originalist judge could live with nonoriginalist precedent and has discounted the need for the Court to get back on the right interpretive track with the appropriate originalist principles by which to decide cases. Berger argues that, with only a few practical limitations, it is still more important for the Court to answer constitutional questions correctly than to perpetuate its errors. Raoul Berger, *Original Intent and Boris Bittker,* 66 IND. L.J. 723, 747–54 (1991):[99]

> What should be the criteria for overruling prior unconstitutional decisions, Bittker asks. In considering this question we should separate legal from pragmatic considerations. On the legal issue, . . . "that which is wrong in the beginning cannot become right in the course of time." Usurpation is not legitimated by repetition. Faced in *Erie Railroad Co. v. Tompkins* with overruling *Swift v. Tyson,* around which a century of expectations had gathered, Justice Brandeis . . . quoted Justice Holmes, who had branded *Swift* as " 'an unconstitutional assumption of powers by courts of the United States which no lapse of time or respectable array of opinion should make us hesitate to correct.' "[181] Bittker likewise does not favor "systematically perpetuating earlier decisions that . . . were devoid of constitutional legitimacy."
>
> Convinced (by my study fourteen years ago of the history of the fourteenth amendment)[183] that *Brown v. Board of Education,* which

---

condemned segregated schools, was without constitutional warrant, I yet concluded, "It would . . . be utterly unrealistic and probably impossible to undo the past in the face of the expectations that the segregation decisions, for example, have aroused in our black citizenry. . . . But to accept thus far accomplished ends is not to condone the continued employment of the unlawful means."[185] A few years later I wrote, "But while decisions can be overruled, past events are not so easily undone. Like poured concrete, they have hardened, so that overruling decisions cannot restore the status quo ante."[186] The past, Chief Justice Marshall wrote, "cannot be recalled by the most absolute power."[187] But, I continued, "The practical difficulty of a rollback cannot excuse the *continuation,* the ever-expanding resort to such unconstitutional practices. 'Go and sin no more' does not signify the acceptance of illegitimate acts, but counsels, rather, do not continue to apply unconstitutional doctrine in ever-expanding fashion."[188] Concretely, Bittker and I agree that " 'blacks cannot be forced back into a ghetto,' " but I would halt " 'court-administered schools and prisons, affirmative action, busing, and the like.' " The passage of years has not shaken my confidence that these views represent sound sense.

Bittker rightly points out that there is "no evidence that *the framers* intended this result[,]" i.e., an "entirely discretionary doctrine in deciding whether to preserve or overrule erroneous constitutional decisions[.]" On ruthlessly logical grounds one may conclude "all or nothing." Nevertheless, I am prepared to let *Brown* stand under Henry Monaghan's test: overturn would trigger "massive destabilization . . . [that] would threaten the functioning of the federal government."[191] Does repudiation of the *Legal Tender Cases* [192] pose similar hazards? At issue was the constitutional authority for issuance of paper money. The youthful Holmes encapsulated the difficulty: the power to coin money implies metallic coin and does not extend to paper money. He "could not see 'how a limited power which is expressly given . . . can be enlarged as an incident to some other express power.' "[193] Possibly an overruling decision might be so cushioned as to sustain the further use of paper money until an amendment to authorize its use can be prepared and adopted. Whether or not overturn of the *Legal Tender Cases* may in terms of consequences be analogized to *Brown* is a matter of judgment on which I have no opinion.

The inclusion of corporations in the due process clause of the fourteenth amendment affords a similar example; it took place in 1886. The language of the clause is identical with that of the fifth amendment. Bittker convincingly demonstrates that the fifth's "person" was applicable only to man. Willard Hurst, the foremost historian of the "American law's adjustment to the business corporation" observed that the fourteenth's protection of "person" was "extended by fresh lawmaking." And he rejected the " 'conspiracy theory' of the fourteenth amendment . . . which asserted that wily lawyers smuggled corporations into the fourteenth amendment's due process clause[.]" My own study of the history of the amendment uncovered no hint that the framers were concerned with anything other than actual persons. In our time Justice Black, taking no account of

---

[185] R. BERGER, *supra* note [183], at 412–13.

[186] R. BERGER, [FEDERALISM: THE FRAMERS' DESIGN 179–80 (1987)].

[187] Fletcher v. Peck, 10 U.S. (6 Cranch) 87 (1810).

[188] R. BERGER, FEDERALISM, *supra* note [186], at 180 (emphasis in original) (footnotes omitted).

[191] Monaghan, *Stare Decisis and Constitutional Adjudication,* 88 COLUM. L. REV. 723, 750 (1988) (footnote omitted).

[192] 79 U.S. (12 Wall.) 457 (1870).

[193] *See* 6 C. FAIRMAN, HISTORY OF THE SUPREME COURT OF THE UNITED STATES 715 (1971) (quoting 4 AM. L. REV. 768 (letter by Holmes, J., to the editor)).

possible "massive destabilization," called on the Court to read corporations out of the fourteenth amendment on the ground that "the people were not told" that they were "granting new and revolutionary rights to corporations." Whatever consequences might follow should be weighed against the integrity of the Constitution and the unconstitutional revision of the instrument by the judiciary.

But I do not share Monaghan's view that reapportionment is " 'far too deeply embedded in the constitutional order to admit of reassessment.' " The reapportionment doctrine was born in *Baker v. Carr* [200] in 1962; it is only twenty-nine years old. Yet, Philip Kurland observed, "The list of opinions destroyed by the Warren Court reads like a table of contents from an old constitutional casebook." [201] Why is a twenty-nine-year-old "precedent" more sacrosanct than decisions that were 100 years old or older, and therefore nearer to the thinking of the drafters of the instrument? It is not as if reapportionment was the inescapable answer, as the split of the Court in *Baker v. Carr* attests.

In a response to Berger, Professor Bittker expands his earlier article (the subject of Berger's critique) in which Bittker wrote in the guise of a fictitious appellate court charged in the future with the task of applying original understanding in every constitutional case. [100] Below, in a mock opinion, Bittker considers the difficulties of trying to find originalist principles by which to review nonoriginalist precedents. Boris I. Bittker, *Observations on Raoul Berger's "Original Intent and Boris Bittker,"* 66 IND. L.J. 757, 768–71 (1991): [101]

> In our earlier opinion, we called attention to "the conventional theory that stare decisis rarely, if ever, protects earlier constitutional decisions from reexamination.". . . We went on, however, to recognize the pressures to preserve some long-entrenched or popular decisions even though they flout the framers' original intent, and we then asked: "If we are to eschew judicial lawmaking, a prime objective of the Jurisprudence of Original Intent, can we properly employ an inherently subjective and entirely discretionary doctrine [that is, stare decisis] in deciding whether to preserve or overrule erroneous constitutional decisions?"
>
> The issue, needless to say, is not confined to a handful of so-called Warren Court decisions. Important though they are, they are merely the tip of the Iceberg of Non-Interpret[i]vism. As Judge Bork has reminded us, [68] the threat of judicial activism can be found as early as Justice Chase's opinion in *Calder v. Bull*, [69] decided in 1798. While the future Chief Justice Warren was still in law school, his constitutional law course was undoubtedly awash with cases violating the original intent of the framers, but these were nevertheless viewed as the sources of fundamental constitutional principles. The *Legal Tender Cases* of 1870 and the pretwentieth century decisions applying the Interstate Commerce and Sherman Anti-Trust Laws are only two examples. Nor did the original intent of the framers receive full faith and credit when the Warren Court gave way to the Burger Court and it to the Rehnquist Court. Within a few months after Judge Bork described *Roe v. Wade* [71] as "the greatest

---

[200] 369 U.S. 186 (1962).

[201] P. KURLAND, POLITICS, THE CONSTITUTION AND THE WARREN COURT 90–91 (1970).

100 *See supra* note 98.

101 Copyright © 1991 by the Trustees of Indiana University. Reprinted by permission of

the Indiana Law Journal and the William S. Hein Co., Inc.

[68] R. BORK, THE TEMPTING OF AMERICA 19–20 (1990).

[69] 3 U.S. (3 Dall.) 386, 387–89 (1798).

[71] 410 U.S. 113 (1973).

example and symbol of the judicial usurpation of democratic prerogatives in this century,"[72] it acquired a rival: the right-to-die case.[73] To be sure, the majority opinion written by Chief Justice Rehnquist did not unequivocally endorse "[t]he principle that a competent person has a constitutionally protected liberty interest in refusing unwanted medical treatment" but instead hedged by saying that the principle "may be inferred from our prior decisions[,]" but our constitutional history is replete with tent flaps nudged aside by the noses of camels. Thus, Justice Scalia was not crying wolf when he said that "[t]o raise up a constitutional right here we would have to create out of nothing (for it exists neither in text nor tradition) some constitutional principle whereby, although the State may insist that an individual come in out of the cold and eat food, it may not insist that he take medicine. . . ." In short, our constitutional history is proof positive that "wide is the gate, and broad is the way, that leadeth to destruction, and many there be which go in thereat."

While Mr. Berger's head tells him that every violator of the Jurisprudence of Original Intent should be shot on sight, his heart tells him—and through him, us—to exercise mercy if this draconic penalty would trigger " 'massive destabilization. . . . [that] would threaten the functioning of the federal government.' " This is a surprising concession, given Mr. Berger's oft-repeated assertion that perceived deficiencies in the Constitution as originally intended should be cured by amendments under article V, especially because, as we noted in our earlier opinion, an erroneous constitutional decision that has indeed become indispensable to the orderly functioning of our society will almost certainly be promptly restored by a constitutional amendment if its illegitimate judicial prop is removed. Thus, we can have our cake and eat it too.

Be that as it may, Mr. Berger provides a sample inventory of the cases that, in his view, could be overruled without undue damage to the status quo. So far as it appears, the only decision inconsistent with the Jurisprudence of Original Intent that he would unequivocally nominate for preservation is *Brown v. Board of Education.* Thus, the best that Mr. Berger offers the *Legal Tender Cases,* which most if not all other devotees of the Jurisprudence of Original Intent would probably describe as illegitimate in origin but sanctified by usage, is that "[p]ossibly an overruling decision might be so cushioned as to sustain the further use of paper money until an amendment to authorize its use can be prepared and adopted." Since Mr. Berger is not a candidate for appointment to the federal judiciary, it would perhaps improperly invade his privacy to inquire about the fate, in his constitutional universe, of *Griswold v. Connecticut* and *Roe v. Wade.*

Mr. Berger's suggestion that a decision overruling the *Legal Tender Cases* might include a *temporary* "cushion" may imply that the offending doctrine should be eradicated root and branch if the Court's patience runs out before the amendment has been ratified. This suggestion reminds us that in dealing with erroneous constitutional decisions, the courts are not confined to a check list with two boxes marked "overrule" and "preserve." There is instead a spectrum of choices, whose breadth can be illustrated with a single example—preserving the erroneous decision but confining it to its "facts"—which invites, indeed requires, judicial micromanagement of the affected area of commercial, political or personal life. Recognizing that "[n]o one has a 'principled theory [of *stare decisis*] to offer,' " we expressed in our earlier opinion the fear that the employment of such an

---

[72] R. BORK, *supra* note [68], at 116.

[73] Cruzan v. Missouri Dep't of Health, 497 U.S. 261 (1990).

"inherently subjective and entirely discretionary doctrine in deciding whether to preserve or overrule erroneous constitutional decisions" would plunge us into judicial lawmaking, pure and simple. Mr. Berger, alas, gives us no shield against that peril of perils, perhaps because it is an unavoidable by-product of the Jurisprudence of Original Intent. We find cold comfort in the conclusion that the framers' intent to bind us to their intent included the intent to bind us to the painfully disillusioning Law of Unintended Consequences.

§ 7.04   Philosophical Commentary on Judges' Competing Obligations to Constitutional Doctrine and to the Constitution

In the following extracts, Professor Charles Fried, who served as Solicitor General in the Reagan administration and for a few years as a justice on the Massachusetts Supreme Judicial Court, ponders a question raised by some legal theorists (particularly adherents to critical legal studies) about whether constitutional doctrine, i.e., the "rules and principles of constitutional law" should "guide judgment in applying the Constitution."[102] Charles Fried, *Constitutional Doctrine,* 107 HARV. L. REV. 1140, 1140–1157 (1994):[103]

Doctrine is the work of judges and of those who comment on and rationalize their decisions. But our allegiance and that of the judges is ultimately owed to the Constitution itself. Because only the Constitution has the authority of a founding document, the question arises: is it not wrong to substitute the course of judgments in the Supreme Court for that authority authentically discerned? I put aside whether the authentic meaning is arrived at by reconstructing the intentions of those who wrote, debated, and ratified the text, or by discerning the meaning of the text, or by recurring directly to whatever fundamental truths of morality and justice the Constitution is believed to embody. Judges have occasionally reacted with exasperation at the maze of doctrine coming between the Constitution itself and their decisions in particular cases. And judges are not the only public officials who take the oath to support the Constitution required by Article VI—executive and legislative officials, in good causes and bad, have invoked that oath to justify actions based on their own, not some court's, best judgment of what the Constitution requires of them.

This attack on doctrine is related to the trouble some feel about the invocation of precedent in constitutional adjudication.[6] Doctrine and

---

[102] Charles Fried, *Constitutional Doctrine,* 107 HARV. L. REV. 1140, 1140 (1994).

[103] Copyright © 1994 by the Harvard Law Review Association. Reprinted with permission.

[6] *See, e.g.,* Tyler Pipe Indus. v. Washington State Dep't of Revenue, 483 U.S. 232, 265 (1987) (Scalia, J., dissenting) (criticizing the Court for extending precedents that were not constitutionally justified, but instead "acquired by a sort of intellectual adverse possession"); Gary S. Lawson, *An Interpretivist Agenda,* 15 HARV. J.L. & PUB. POL'Y 157, 161 (1992) (questioning whether federal courts have the power "to decide cases in accordance with prior decisions, even when those prior decisions contra-

dict the text of the Constitution"). [Professor Lawson argues that it is unconstitutional for the Supreme Court to grant any precedential weight to its own decisions, because its duty under *Marbury v. Madison* " 'to say what the law is' requires it to choose the Constitution over the prior decision." Lawson, 15 HARV. J.L. & PUB. POL'Y at 27 (citation omitted). Professor Frederick Schauer of the Kennedy School of Government at Harvard has responded, *inter alia* that precedent is most likely to be relevant in cases lacking clear constitutional answers, and judges who must in any event be persuaded at "retail" in an individual case can plausibly (and constitutionally) regard prior decisions as having a "wholesale" persuasive—but not bind-

precedent are related, not identical. In civil law countries, doctrine plays a great role in giving the law its substance and texture, but treatise writers and academic discourse, not the opinions nor even the decisions of courts, are the dominant organs of the growth and statement of doctrine there. Although doctrine does not entail respect for precedent, respect for precedent comes much closer to entailing doctrine. Reference to a prior decision to justify a present one requires identifying what it is about the prior decision that is being carried forward. A judge might, of course, say no more than that this new case seems similar to the old one and decline to explain what it is about the precedent that makes it controlling. If the citation is more than decoration, however, it implies that the prior decision explains and justifies the present result. Such an explanation is at least the germ of a doctrine; the invocation of a previous decision to justify a new one implies a general proposition by virtue of which the judgment on one state of the world bears on the judgment on another state of the world, which can be similar only in some respects.

Although any decision that explains itself implies some generalization, and to that extent a commitment to that generalization, some may object that this commitment cannot be taken to show the inevitability of doctrine in constitutional adjudication, much less to justify deference to prior decisions as elements or building blocks of doctrine, because the commitment need not extend beyond that occasion. This objection assumes that adjudication might go forward as a series of discrete decisions, each starting from the ground up, although of course the unencumbered judge might look to past decisions as a source of wisdom—as he might to the arguments of counsel or to law review articles. This "fresh start" conception is quite different from the notion that a decision need imply no commitment or generalization at all. Imagine that a court strikes down, as violating the First Amendment, a state statute that punishes speech disrespectful of the legislature. If the court then declined to invalidate a statute punishing speech disrespectful of the governor, it would either have to explain why such a statute is different (thus honoring the prior decision) or acknowledge, while disregarding, the similarity. When deciding for the governor, it may acknowledge that its decision against the legislature was incompatible and therefore wrong. Convinced of its prior error, why should the court not shift ground completely? In each case a responsible court would offer—or at least have in mind—a justification for its decision, a justification that should point to how this decision fits with, or criticizes, other decisions that have been or might be made. There would be doctrine in the first case, maybe even quite an elaborate doctrine, and contrary doctrine in the second—doctrine at every turn. Not only doctrine, but even commitment. It is just not a commitment that survives reevaluation in light of the acknowledged ultimate criterion of correctness. This way there is not a deficiency, but a surplus of doctrine—as much as one doctrine for each decision. What is lacking in such an account is not a place for doctrine, but for the persistence of doctrine— and persistence connects with precedent.

One argument that is supposed to justify the persistence of doctrine seems too weak and contingent: people may have come to rely on the prior doctrine, and in order to avoid disruption, we stay with a doctrine even

---

ing—effect. Schauer, *Precedent and the Necessary Externality of Constitutional Norms*, 17 HARV. J.L. & PUB. POL'Y 45, 54 (1994). He further ascribes to Lawson "the mistake of supposing that the norms of constitutional interpretation are or can be determined by the Constitution itself," rather than by norms that

"are logically prior to the Constitution." *Id.* (footnote omitted). For two other critical responses to Lawson's argument, *see* Charles Fried, *Reply to Lawson*, 17 HARV. J.L. & PUB. POL'Y 35 (1994); Akhil R. Amar, *On Lawson on Precedent*, 17 HARV. J.L. & PUB. POL'Y 39 (1994).]

when it no longer seems right. But the wish to avoid disruption fails to justify the degree and kind of persistence we have grown used to and now require, because a court could limit its adherence to doctrine it no longer believes correct to those cases in which the costs of disruption from changing would be too great. Thus, for instance, a court might apply its new doctrine only prospectively, or retrospectively only when persons have not relied or have not relied too much. Persistence in doctrine must be built on a firmer foundation than reliance. After all, if it were well known that courts felt free, even obliged, to revise their doctrines anew every time things looked different to them, rational expectations would take account of that and no one could claim disappointment. Indeed, if a court got the answer wrong the first time, the only proper expectation would be of an eventual right answer. No one would be entitled to rely on anything else.

The edifice of precedent in doctrine cannot be built upon the shifting sands of expectation, because to speak of expectation begs the question. I suspect that an intuition of this sort may account for the false note detected in the lengthy and somewhat extravagant protestations of fidelity to precedent in the controlling joint opinion in *Planned Parenthood v. Casey*, reaffirming while modifying *Roe v. Wade*. Justices O'Connor, Kennedy, and Souter were moved by the need for continuity and stability in constitutional law, yet paradoxically they seemed to give this factor undue prominence relative to their conviction of the rightness of the actual decision—almost as if the decision could not stand on its own and needed an apology. Properly seen, respect for precedent is an intrinsic part of what makes the decision right—it is not as if a decision that is dubious on the merits is carried over the top by precedent.

We require continuity in legal doctrine. Yet we also require each new decision to be more or less right on its merits, and not just because it accords with prior cases. The only way we can have both is for the new decision to be right, in part at least, because it accords with established doctrine—and right, as we have seen, not merely because of expectations that may have been invested in the prior regime. We encounter here an instance of what may seem a general paradox of rationality: a rational person is always in principle open to reason, yet any human pursuit—certainly the pursuit of reason—would be thwarted if those committed to it kept returning to first principles to make sure that the beginning was right. I call this a paradox because we try to have it both ways: to shut down argument after some reasonable point and yet to remain open to reason at all times. (We want to avoid being like the man who cannot get to work in the morning because he must keep returning home to make quite sure that he has turned off the gas.) The paradox appears in its most intimate form in the design of our own life plans—and it manifests itself in the law, even though the judge's plan is not her personal life plan, but a plan for the law. . . .

The solution to the paradox at every level begins by noticing that we are time-extended, not punctual, beings. The ends we pursue, the thoughts we entertain, the sentiments that grip us are all time-extended, not punctual. Think of a melody. It has a beginning, a continuation, and an end, and that end marks a distinct and desired resolution, say at a C-major chord. But it would be absurd to see the final chord as a goal in the sense that it would be preferable to move straight to it without first moving through the modulations of the melody. The same is true of the satisfaction of solving a puzzle, and of delights that are thought to be purely physical. Everything we desire, take pleasure in, or value exists for us extended in time. Indeed, every argument, however abstract, consists of a sequence of steps, and this sequence can only be gone through in time. To state the conclusion without having worked through the sequence is as unsatisfactory relative to the practice of argument as would be the final chord played alone out of the context of the sequence leading up to it. An argument, then, is more like a story than we may care to admit. . . . Doctrine is somewhere between story and argument.

I call the rationality implicit in all these structures constitutive, as opposed to instrumental or means-end, rationality. In instrumental rationality an end or value is posited, and all other elements in the argument are judged by whether they best lead to that end or maximize that value. Constitutive rationality proposes complex structures in which elements are related according to rules or principles, and it is the resultant whole that satisfies the conditions of this kind of rationality. An activity to which this concept applies I call rationally constituted. . . . It is the difference between removing your opponent's pieces from the board by capturing them and just putting them in your pocket.

Now move from this to our moral life. Our affections, commitments, and projects are also time-extended. Just as we could not whistle a tune if at every moment we started afresh, so we could be neither friend nor enemy, we could not keep promises, do acts of kindness, nor take revenge, if every momentary and discrete movement were the occasion of a fresh choice, encumbered only causally or teleologically by what proceeds and comes after it. What we intend is the gesture as a whole, the sequence of movements that make it up. Such gestures can even take the greater part of a lifetime to run their course. Steadiness and commitment are not just virtues that keep us unswervingly on course to some goal or endpoint: they make our lives more or less coherent; they allow us to understand and describe what it is that moves us at all. They give character. So when we speak of fulfilling an obligation, showing kindness, following a career, or living out relationships of family or friendships, we refer to rules and principles that apply to a rationally constituted activity (or set of activities). Even more grandly, it is not far-fetched to say that a satisfying life is one that has shape and consistency—that is, such a life is rationally constituted. . . .

The conduct of the many delightful, serious, or moving transactions of our lives has the structure of a story: a family meal, a visit to a sick or dying friend, the act of love, or more extensively, the trajectory of a parent's relations with a child from infancy to the parent's old age. . . . Constitutive rationality informs the purposes, events, and institutions of cities and nations, as much or more than those of individuals and families. It is what allows us to say of them too that they have a certain character. . . .

A criminal trial has a trajectory constitutive of public values: the formal equality of the parties before the law, the sovereignty of reason, of evidence, and of argument, the dramatic exclusion of extraneous influences, and judgment rendered by an assembly of ordinary citizens. Thus, in *Richmond Newspapers, Inc. v. Virginia*,[27] the Supreme Court held that criminal trials are presumptively open to the public, even if neither the state nor the accused desires it. The Court did not rest its decision squarely on the First Amendment, because it did not want to announce a constitutional right of media access to government information in general. Nor could it be said that a closed trial was unfair to a defendant who preferred it. Rather, openness was seen as an important condition for making the grave impositions of the criminal law acceptable in general. Open criminal trials were seen as an essential part of the

---

[27] 448 U.S. 555 (1980).

institutional event that might lead to the state's depriving persons of their liberty or their lives.

The mistaken view that all reason must be instrumental invites us to scorn this most operatic of our public functions. Even the much cooler progress of appellate procedure, say before the Supreme Court, shares these forms. It might be supposed that the ritual of oral argument before a bench so well briefed, staffed, and prepared as the Supreme Court is an empty formality. But it is not: this may be the one time in the course of the appeal that the parties must answer, cannot artfully evade, questions and difficulties, and the one time when anyone sitting in the courtroom can see that arguments are actually addressed to the persons of the Justices and that they appear to respond to them. This is legal reason as theater.

Doctrine is constitutive reason. Judges and publicists have regularly proclaimed some value or goal in the name of the law and sought to bend legal decisions to the service of that goal; this is legal decision according to instrumental rationality and, without more, hardly doctrine. It is only when a court moves beyond advancing some value on a particular occasion—by supplying a subsidy to a favored industry, redistributing wealth from a richer to a poorer individual—to ordering whole chunks of time-extended conduct, that we enter the realm of doctrine. Such ordering is designed to further some goal, but it reaches that goal by designating an integrated whole. So even if contract law is assigned the sole function of advancing economic efficiency, it can only do this if the inner structure of contract doctrine is allowed to have some integrity. When law just states a desirable, mandatory, or forbidden end, with the steps along the way no more than means for its attainment, then the law operates like a recipe—the whole proof of the pudding is in the eating. In an argument, on the other hand, the proof of the pudding is in the proof. Doctrine, unlike naked assertion or sheer command, moves like an argument. Doctrine orders a course of conduct not by commanding an external goal, but, like an argument, by developing from within that course of conduct, lending to or acknowledging in that conduct a structure whose statement is not exhausted by the statement of the goal to which it may be directed. In this it is more like a score than a recipe. Indeed, some goals cannot even be stated, do not exist, apart from that structure.

Arguments, stories, games, and doctrine are rationally constituted along the dimension of time. There are three degrees of doctrine as constitutive reason. Although I will distinguish the three degrees and consider them independently, any particular doctrine exists simultaneously at all three degrees. The three degrees I identify are the degrees to which time, and with it rationality, enter into the nature of doctrine. When we have run through all three, we get a fuller sense of how doctrine works in our world, and thus a fuller sense of what we may expect of constitutional doctrine. In the *first degree,* doctrine acts upon a particular rationally constituted, time-extended activity, like the score for playing a piece of music. Doctrine is constitutive reason in the first degree when it provides—if only for a single occasion—the plan, say, of a fair trial procedure that expresses the values of openness to argument and equality before the law.

In the first degree we identify one aspect of doctrine and its relation to time: doctrine as it applies to a course of events that unfolds over a period of time and takes account of this time-extendedness of its subject as it authorizes or condemns. The time-extendedness inheres more in the subject of the doctrine, and in the doctrine itself only insofar as the steps in an argument present an ordered sequence. The doctrine itself might even be seen as an infinitesimally brief burst of ordered, sequenced judgment about something that necessarily unfolds in real, not just abstract, time. . . .

This first degree of doctrine is obviously an abstraction. To fill out the picture, doctrine must be seen as time-extended in a more ample sense. Doctrine must be seen as itself taking place in real time, and not just applying to and judging actions that do. It must be seen as temporally extended, not just abstractly sequenced. This is the second degree of doctrine.

In the *second degree,* we mark this temporal duration of doctrine itself, not just of its subject. It is not only that, say, a particular trial is played out according to a plan that gives the event as a whole its significance. There is the further circumstance that trials in general follow this plan, and that they do so this way because of a doctrine that takes its origin in some text, has been elaborated by courts, refined perhaps by legislation, so that now trials at many times and places are played out according to this single score. The additional aspect I emphasize now is not the performance and its constituted rationality, but the constituted rationality of a more complex reflexive activity: the production of a score coupled with a whole set of first order activities, say trials, in accordance with that score. Without this second degree of constituted rationality, there would not be anything recognizable as doctrine, but only discrete, unconnected judgments on particular discrete (though time-extended) performances. The subjects to which the law is directed do not always improvise their performance, with law judging them after the fact, but often refer to a score that it is the function of the courts (and legislatures) to compose. It is this persisting scored activity that makes a kind of social coordination and coherence possible. It is the function of courts (or other composers in other settings) to devise and maintain the conditions necessary for this activity.

What I call the second degree of doctrine points to the constant cross-reference between the criteria for judgment and what is judged, the score and the performance. The actions coordinated according to the doctrinal score are not just a very complex action, a protracted performance with many players; that would still be doctrine in the first degree, with the sequenced but practically timeless burst of doctrine determining something more elaborate and protracted. The analogy had better switch to a conductor and orchestra. The conductor not only gives direction according to—enforces compliance with—the score on her desk; she adjusts her directions according to the playing of the musicians, and they in turn adjust their playing from the same score on their desks according to the directions they receive from the podium. In this way doctrine itself, not just its subject, is played out in real, not just abstract, time.

Doctrine provides the scores according to which a large number of social performances are played. Constitutional doctrine supplies a particular set of scores for a particular set of such performances at various levels: for instance, there are scores that govern the production of further scores, and as the Establishment and Takings Clauses illustrate, there are negative scores as well—do not play like that! Establishment Clause doctrine may be seen in part as precluding public displays of endorsement for religion—such a display being a type of complex, extended social performance; some of the Supreme Court's recent Takings Clause cases point to a typical sequence of prohibited events in which a parcel of land is transferred out of the control of a private owner to a public use. As doctrine in the second degree, these examples of doctrine do not merely judge a particular social performance or sequence of events, but order them generally. Takings and Establishment Clause doctrines may be exemplary narratives of what government may not do. The fact that doctrine tells a negative story, a cautionary tale, does not alter its role and structure as doctrine. If the government, in justifying its imposition, can tell an alternative tale, the prohibition might not hold. This is what happened in the Sunday Closing Cases,[34] in which the states successfully argued that, although Sunday closing laws took their origins in religious practice, their modern function was to provide a common day of rest, on which family and friends might come together. . . .

Doctrine must persist in order to constrain. Unless doctrine persists, unless doctrine itself is prolonged, it cannot sufficiently order social action: it is not just that this trial goes "by the book," but that it goes according to the same book as other trials. The Constitution promises that kind of persistence, and it can only deliver if its commands are instantiated in doctrines that persist. If what the Constitution meant were open to reinterpretation from the ground up (from the text, or original intention, or fundamental values up), if a new story could be started, a new argument made at each instance of its application—not just by the Supreme Court, but by lower courts, state courts, and officials at all levels— then, whatever might be said about the "correctness" of some of these interpretations, the ensemble of purportedly constitutional activities would exhibit an incoherence that must be much further from the reason for having a Constitution than the departure worked by any particular doctrine, no matter how far afield it may have wandered.

And so in the second degree, we see doctrine as itself extended in historical time, the time it takes the Court to tell the story in a series of decisions, the contents of which respond to the questions the audience implicitly or explicitly asks of the judicial narrator. But the time dimension enters into doctrine in another, still more intimate way, according to which doctrine is rationally constituted in the *third degree*. The public expects steadiness and commitment in the courts; the Supreme Court as an institution should have a character, as men and women have character. The Court should be like a careful, sober, and reliable trustee of someone else's assets. Imagine how such a person goes about some project. She is unlikely to conceive every detail and ramification at the first moment of action. Our important undertakings have a life-cycle. And so, too, there are the rhythms and sequences by which doctrine, like the doctrine about takings or the establishment of religion, is brought into being, elaborated, modified, and perhaps eventually abandoned. In fact, the great organizing doctrines of constitutional law have come into being in a variety of ways. Some, like judicial review or the decisions stating the relation between state and federal courts, did indeed seem to issue from early and sweeping decisions—*Marbury v. Madison, Martin v. Hunter's Lessee, Cohens v. Virginia, Osborn v. President, Directors, & Co. of the Bank of the United States*—with the whole course of later jurisprudence working out the implications instinct in their large generalizations. But others, like the First Amendment jurisprudence protecting expression, had a late and halting beginning, and only later, through an accumulation of distinctions, accretions, and expansions, did anything like a comprehensive principle emerge.

The case for constitutive reason displayed over time must take account not only of how commitments come into being, but also of changed plans and understandings. So far I have emphasized how a person, and analogously a social institution like Supreme Court adjudication, cannot lead

---

[34] *See* Braunfeld v. Brown, 366 U.S. 599 (1961); McGowan v. Maryland, 366 U.S. 420 (1961).

a punctual existence in which reason turns afresh at every moment to determine what is the best thing to do *NOW*. Large stretches of life and attention are taken up with moving according to a plan already set, playing according to a score already written, adhering to commitments already made. But just as a punctual existence is inhuman, so a life lived strictly according to plan is mad—and dangerous. Whole projects are cast aside as mistaken, and what follows can be liberating, thrilling, or full of promise. Those who don't get trapped have a kind of peripheral vision that allows them to notice the chance of a new departure even while they keep their eye on the ball. This is a manifestation of the paradox of rationality to which I referred earlier.

I cast this in terms of paradox, because although we cannot always return to first principles, neither will it do to pretend that every opportune shift is really according to plan after all, merely responsive to new circumstances as they bear on the same old plan. Now, this argument itself is subject to two different accounts. Take, for example, the Supreme Court's willingness after 1937 to acknowledge the widest variety of economic regulation as falling within Congress's power to regulate interstate commerce. Some might say that this represented a radical break with both the Constitution's plan to limit Congress's authority to matters of national concern and to limit the authority of all levels of government over economic activity. It seems to me, however, that the shift need not be seen as so radical and abrupt: the original plan could not help but expand to its modern proportions once the economy had become, and it was seen to have become, integrated, intricate, and national in scope. The project had not changed—only the circumstances in which it was applied. And the development may soon swing in another direction. In the mid-seventies, the Supreme Court for the first time acknowledged that commercial speech cannot, without violence to principle, be excluded from First Amendment protection. In recent years, it has become evident that information is becoming one of the most important items of commerce (or more broadly, of production, exchange, and consumption), so that constitutional protection for liberty of expression and information may be the route by which the Constitution is once again invoked to protect broad lines of economic activity from governmental regulation.

There are shifts; plans are abandoned altogether. When, why, on what principles? What kind of answer do you expect? Is a change of plan always only a change of direction in accordance with some master plan—a plan of plans? This is true only if the notion of plan is so general and accommodating as to offer no intellectual resistance. Why must there be a master plan? If there always had to be such a master plan, on what principles would it be chosen? But if there are just the plans we have, have had, and will have, then there need not be any plan-like account of why we abandon one and pick up another. For instance, a project can simply come to an end, run its course: the final chord has sounded, the piece is over. We have kept alert, alive; we launch another. In short, it is no part of my argument that we can have only one plan all our life long, or that we can never change tack altogether. Nor do I see why a community or a legal tradition may not simply lose interest in a topic because there is little of interest left in it. The development of a cheap, easy, and safe mode of self-administered abortion would deprive a whole line of doctrine of any relevance, just as the integration of the national economy deprived complicated doctrines like the original-package doctrine, used to distinguish matters of local from those of national concern, of any useful reference.

I certainly contend that a life without projects is inhuman, and so by implication is one in which projects are picked up and dropped at too frequent intervals. How frequent? There is no rule. Let me suggest, however, that there are different times in our lives when change is more or less appropriate. Early on, abandonments and radical changes of course seem more appropriate, as we come to know the world and ourselves. Much later it is not abandonment, but completions and endings, that make new departures appropriate—without regret for what has gone before. This suggests that a whole life does have, if not a plan, then at least a shape, that gradually emerges and becomes more definite, more constraining. Perhaps we often do not know quite what our plans will be until they are well underway—the ratio of forethought to improvisation will vary. The third degree of doctrine is like that: it is of great interest how doctrine gets started, how refined and elaborated, when abandoned and when left behind as completed, extinguished.

A judicial decision is both an intellectual and a moral act, and the commitment to the argument behind it correspondingly is made both to oneself and to others. A mathematician, a scientist could not pursue a line of reasoning (the very locution implies time extension) if at every moment thought returned to first principles. However carefully we reason, we must be willing to take a prior step as established before we can see where it leads. Of course, at some point, we recognize that we have moved down a blind alley, and then we have to unravel our thought, perhaps all the way to the first stitch—this is where the contradictory phenomenon of peripheral vision comes in. [53] But still, if we did not proceed with some considerable measure of confidence in our prior steps, we could not progress at all. Reasoning about the Constitution certainly requires at least that kind of commitment to one's own thought, and in this sense implies respect for precedent—that is, at least the Court's commitment to the prior steps in its own process of reasoning.

But the view of constitutional decision as free of precedent, as punctual at least in principle, misses another dimension of constitutive rationality that is salient in (if not special to) any act of public reasoning meant to justify the exercise of political power. Earlier I spoke of expectations and reliance, but those are just the instrumental correlates to another public need. If reasoning implies continuity for him who engages in it, all the more must it do so for those to whom it is addressed and who are asked to accept it.

To accept another's reasoning is to follow along with it. At the least, this requires that the reasoning exhibit the kind of steadiness and

---

[53] David Remnick, in LENIN'S TOMB, makes a subtle but profound argument that a new beginning is only possible when a people regains its history—that is, when the accretion of lies is removed:

After some initial hesitation at the beginning of his time in power, Gorbachev had decreed that the time had come to fill in the "blank spots" of history. There could be no more "rose-colored glasses," he said. At first, his rhetoric was guarded. He spoke of "thousands" instead of tens of millions of victims. He did not dare criticize Lenin, the demigod of the state. But despite Gorbachev's hesitation, the return of historical memory would be his most important decision, one that preceded all others, for without a full and ruthless assessment of the past—an admission of murder, repression, and bankruptcy—real change, much less democratic revolution, was impossible. The return of history to personal, intellectual, and political life was the start of the great reform of the twentieth century and, whether Gorbachev liked it or not, the collapse of the last empire on earth.

DAVID REMNICK, LENIN'S TOMB: THE LAST DAYS OF THE SOVIET EMPIRE 4 (1993). In the terms I have been developing here, this suggests that a new project can only be undertaken if its relation to prior projects and context is clarified. If it is built on lies it risks infection by, and continuity with, lies. A sharp break is not possible without acknowledging that it is taking place, and that means acknowledging what is being broken from.

commitment we aspire to in our own reasoning. In the sphere of public authority, this need is even more urgent. It is not just that we wish for evidence that the public reasoner is indeed reasoning, as we would if we were considering her for, say, a post as an editor, but we demand that she commit to reason for us, in a way that we are invited to follow as she goes along, and so the public manifestation, the rituals of reasoning are owed as much as the substance. In this sense, the judge's respect for precedent is of a piece with her attending at and to oral argument—as for instance by asking questions that demonstrate both that she is engaged with the subject matter and trying to give the advocate the chance to address the real doubts of a mind not yet made up. So it is correct, after all, to say that respect for precedent protects expectations, engenders reliance, and procures stability, but it does this first of all by assuring the public that it is ruled by law so conceived.

This assurance is the outside of doctrine—doctrine as it presents itself to the public that is ruled by it. To be convincing, the outside must correspond to an inside, which is the performance of the judges who develop and follow the doctrine. . . . In deciding a new case, a judge takes into account past decisions. She does not feel free to start from scratch. She will be drawn to maintain continuity, keep faith, with her own past decision, at least in order to conceive of herself as a person with projects and steadiness of reason. Then, because her reasoning will be part of her Court's reasoning, what she says must relate not only to what she has said and will say, but also to what the other judges can subscribe to, so that she can speak for them. In the same way, she must incorporate into her present thinking what other judges have previously said in her name. So her reasoning is public inside and out: its steadiness and coherence must not only be palpable to those who will be ruled by it; it must be steady and coherent to her. It must exhibit both forms of steadiness and coherence if it is to be part of a joint line of reasoning of a collegiate body of which she is just one member. ("The Chief Justice, with whom Justices O' Connor, Scalia, Kennedy, Souter, and Thomas join . . . .") And it is hardly a further step at all to see how she must be ready to incorporate lines of reasoning from which she dissented, or (more compellingly) which were started before she joined the Court.

Doctrine is like that. This explains why it can have a structure, be constraining, and yet be beside the point to ask for the general rules—the necessary and sufficient conditions—of that structure. Such a system of rules would, after all, itself be another course of reasoning, and what would the rules for that be? The looming infinite regress has prompted some to deny that we think and act according to reason at all. But that is unreasonable. So let us begin.

§ 7.05 Conclusion

In discussing when a Justice may properly vote to overrule a prior constitutional decision, then-Law School Dean Stone concluded as follows. Geoffrey Stone, *Precedent, the Amendment Process, and Evolution in Constitutional Doctrine,* 11 HARV. J. L. & PUB. POL'Y 67, 72–73 (1988):[104]

Except in the most extraordinary of circumstances, a prior interpretation can be said to be "wrong" not in any definitive sense, but only in the sense that the process of constitutional interpretation is a process of evolution. It is a dynamic process through which constitutional law comes,

---

[104] Copyright © 1988 by the Harvard Society of Law and Public Policy, Inc. Reprinted with permission of the Harvard Journal of Law and Public Policy.

as in Mr. Levi's words, "to express the ideas of the community."[14] Those who reject this vision of the Constitution and who insist on a definitive and static view of constitutional "right" and "wrong," ultimately must rely on power, rather than on principle, to effect their constitutional change.

The real truth is that within the bounds of reason—and I believe that there are bounds of reason—*Miranda v. Arizona* is no more definitely wrong than *Bowers v. Hardwick* is definitely right. These decisions are based on widely divergent theories of constitutional interpretation, but these theories are each held by persons possessing intellect, thoughtfulness, a commitment to the Constitution, and good will. We must never stop debating these questions, but we must also not lose our humility in the process. If we stop, and if we insist definitely on the ultimate "rightness" of our views, then we surely pose the greatest threat to our constitutional order.

Is it possible to ascertain from former Dean Stone's discussion the principle by which *he* would determine the precedents he would follow and those he would overrule? Is there a more appropriate basis on which to overrule a precedent than its "rightness" or "wrongness"? If not, why not? If so, is it possible to square this basis with constitutional theory?

§ 7.06   Bibliography

[A]   Commentaries on Constitutional Stare Decisis

Larry Alexander & Frederick Schauer, *On Extrajudicial Constitutional Interpretation*, 110 HARV. L. REV. 1359 (1997).

Christopher P. Banks, *The Supreme Court and Precedent: An Analysis of Natural Courts and Reversal Trends*, 75 JUDICATURE 262 (1992).

Robert W. Bennett, *A Dissent on Dissent*, 74 JUDICATURE 255 (1991).

Raoul Berger, *Original Intent: Bittker v. Berger*, 1991 B.Y.U. L. REV. 1201 (1991); Raoul Berger, *Original Intention in Historical Perspective*, 54 GEO. WASH. L. REV. 296 (1986); *The Activist Legacy of the New Deal Court*, 59 WASH. L. REV. 751 (1984).

Philip Bobbitt, CONSTITUTIONAL FATE: THEORY OF THE CONSTITUTION 39–58 (1982).

Henry J. Bourguignon, *The Second Mr. Justice Harlan: His Principles of Judicial Decisionmaking*, 1979 SUP. CT. REV. 251.

William J. Brennan, Jr., *In Defense of Dissents*, 37 HASTINGS L.J. 427 (1986).

Erwin Chemerinsky, *The Supreme Court, 1988 Term—Foreword: The Vanishing Constitution*, 103 HARV. L. REV. 43, 56–74 (1989).

William O. Douglas, *Stare Decisis*, 49 COLUM. L. REV. 735 (1949).

Frank Easterbrook, *Ways of Criticizing the Court*, 95 HARV. L. REV. 802 (1982).

Philip P. Frickey, *A Further Comment on Stare Decisis and the Overruling of* National League of Cities, 2 CONST. COMMENTARY 341 (1985); *Stare*

---

[14] E. LEVI, AN INTRODUCTION TO LEGAL REASONING 4 (1949).

Decisis in Constitutional Cases: Reconsidering National League of Cities, 2 CONST. COMMENTARY 123 (1985).

Jerrold H. Israel, Gideon v. Wainwright: *The Art of Overruling,* 1963 SUP. CT. REV. 211.

Andrew M. Jacobs, *God Save this Postmodern Court: The Death of Necessity and the Transformation of the Supreme Court's Overruling Rhetoric,* 63 U. CIN. L. REV. 1119 (1995).

Maurice Kelman, *The Forked Path of Dissent,* 1985 SUP. CT. REV. 227.

R. Randall Kelso & Charles D. Kelso, *How the Supreme Court Is Dealing with Precedents in Constitutional Cases,* 62 BROOK. L. REV. 973 (1996).

David W. Koehler, *Comment: Justice Souter's "Keep-What-You-Want-and-Throw-Away-the-Rest" Interpretation of Stare Decisis,* 42 BUFF. L. REV. 859 (1994).

Earl Maltz, *Some Thoughts on the Death of Stare Decisis,* 1980 WIS. L. REV. 467.

Note, *Constitutional Stare Decisis,* 103 HARV. L. REV. 1344 (1990).

Christopher J. Peters, *Foolish Consistency: On Equality, Integrity, and Justice in Stare Decisis,* 105 YALE L.J. 2031 (1996).

James C. Rehnquist, Note, *The Power That Shall Be Vested in a Precedent: Stare Decisis, The Constitution, and the Supreme Court,* 66 B.U. L. REV. 345 (1986).

Antonin Scalia, *The Rule of Law as a Law of Rules,* 56 U. CHI. L. REV. 1175 (1989).

Frederick Schauer, *Precedent,* 39 STAN. L. REV. 571 (1987).

Laurence Tribe, GOD SAVE THIS HONORABLE COURT: HOW THE CHOICE OF SUPREME COURT JUSTICES SHAPES OUR HISTORY 122–25 (1985).

Laurence Tribe & Michael C. Dorf, ON READING THE CONSTITUTION 31–33, 71–73, 93 (1991).

Richard A. Wasserstrom, THE JUDICIAL DECISION 56–84 (1961).

John Wallace, Comment, *Stare Decisis and the Rehnquist Court: The Collision of Activism, Passivism, and Politics in* Casey, 42 BUFF. L. REV. 187 (1994).

[B] Constitutional Theory and the Problem of Nonconforming Precedent

Charles J. Cooper, *Stare Decisis: Precedent and Principle in Constitutional Adjudication,* 73 CORNELL L. REV. 401 (1988).

Michael C. Dorf, *Integrating Normative and Descriptive Constitutional Theory: The Case of Original Meaning,* 85 GEO. L.J. 1765, 1772–74 (1997).

Frank Easterbrook, *Stability and Reliability in Judicial Decisions,* 73 CORNELL L. REV. 422 (1988).

Richard Fallon, *A Constructivist Coherence Theory of Constitutional Interpretation,* 100 HARV. L. REV. 1189, 1190–91, 1202–04, 1243–46, 1260–62, 1268–86 (1987).

Michael J. Gerhardt, *Interpreting Bork,* 75 CORNELL L. REV. 1358, 1383–85 (1990) (Book Review).

Anthony Kronman, *Precedent and Tradition,* 99 YALE L.J. 1029 (1990).

Michael Moore, *A Natural Law Theory of Constitutional Interpretation,* 58 S. CAL. L. REV. 277, 358–76 (1985).

Stephen R. Munzer & James W. Nickel, *Does the Constitution Mean What It Always Meant?,* 77 COLUM. L. REV. 1029 (1977).

PART III
Perspectives

Chapter 8
Liberal Constitutional Theory

§ 8.01 Introduction

For much of the past half century or so, liberalism in various forms has been a leading if not the dominant perspective in constitutional theory. Especially in recent years, liberal approaches to constitutional adjudication have come under attack from other perspectives of both right and left. Accordingly, this chapter presents illustrative materials on liberal constitutional theory, both for their own sake and as a point of departure for critical perspectives in later chapters from the right (conservatism, including law-and-economics analyses) and left (feminism and critical race theory). [1]

The very effort to give definitions of the liberal perspective can give rise to many disagreements, but it seems an important place to begin. One common definition of liberalism is used by Duke law and religion professor H. Jefferson Powell in characterizing the notion of philosophical liberalism that has dominated throughout the 20th century: "the tradition of thought and action which originates in the Enlightenment and which regards the individual, understood as an autonomous center of will and reason, as logically and morally prior to any community and all moral commitments." [2] Critical legal studies scholar Mark Tushnet has targeted a similar conception of liberalism in some of his writings. [3] But liberal scholar Richard Fallon of Harvard Law

---

[1] Liberalism remains an extremely strong voice in the legal academy. *See* Deborah Jones Merritt, *Research and Teaching on Law Faculties: An Empirical Exploration,* 73 CHI.[-]KENT L. REV. 765, 780 (1998) (discussing results of a survey of American law professors indicating that only 10 percent characterize themselves as conservative to some degree); James Lingren, *Measuring Diversity* Speech to the National Association of Scholars (Jan. 5, 1997) (reporting that more than 80% of legal academics are registered Democrats).

[2] H. JEFFERSON POWELL, THE MORAL TRADITION OF AMERICAN CONSTITUTIONALISM 6 n.16 (1993).

[3] *See* MARK TUSHNET, RED, WHITE, AND BLUE: A CRITICAL ANALYSIS OF CONSTITUTIONAL LAW

(1988). The concept of philosophical liberalism employed by Professors Powell and Tushnet contrasts with political liberalism. *See, e.g.* Stephen Gardbaum, *Liberalism, Autonomy, and Moral Conflict* 48 STAN. L. REV. 385, 386 (1996) ("Political liberalism explicitly defines itself, in contrast to a second, and more traditional, conception of liberal political theory. This conception, which has recently come to be labeled 'comprehensive,' 'perfectionist,' or 'ethical liberalism,' takes its central task to be that of specifying how the state may fulfill its general duty of enhancing the moral lives of its citizens, while respecting certain values that are constitutive of liberal political practice, such as tolerance, individual freedom, and equality. . ..") (citations omitted); Edward B.

School suggests that Tushnet's definition is defective because it fails to account for "the diversity of the liberal tradition."[4] Moreover, Fallon explains,[5]

> "[l]iberalism" is undoubtedly what philosophers have characterized as an "essentially contestable concept," see, e.g., W. CONNOLLY, THE TERMS OF POLITICAL DISCOURSE 10–44 (2d ed. 1983); Gallie, *Essentially Contested Concepts,* 56 PROC. ARISTOTELIAN SOC. 167, 167–68 (1956), for which no consensus definition exists or can be expected to emerge. Nonetheless, the concept's essential contestability does not exclude that there either are or could be familiarly recognized paradigms of liberalism—authors or works whose status as "liberal" would be acknowledged by virtually everyone. . . .

> Tushnet attempts to insulate himself against refutation by appeal to the works of modern liberals such as [John] Rawls and [Ronald] Dworkin, not by denying their paradigmatic status, but by denying that "the liberal tradition" can be understood by reference to the works of systematic political thinkers. He writes: "It is important to emphasize that the argument of this book is concerned with the liberal tradition, that is, liberalism as lived and experienced in the culture rather than the systematic thought of particular thinkers." . . . But Tushnet's claim to distinguish the liberal tradition from the works of systematic liberal thinkers is deeply problematic. Part of the difficulty is conceptual. It is impossible to establish too sharp a divide between systematic liberal thinkers and liberal culture; identification of what is experienced within the culture as "liberalism" will, directly or indirectly, require reference to those thinkers who are generally regarded within the culture as propounding legal doctrines. Accepting this, Tushnet might wish to argue that he is nonetheless concerned with popular understandings of systematic liberal philosophies and their implications, which might be somewhat different from those philosophies in their more rigorously developed forms. If so, however, Tushnet's research methodology would not support his argument, since he cites very little historical or sociological literature on popular culture or beliefs.

In this chapter, we are primarily concerned with what Professor Fallon refers to as the "recognized paradigms of liberalism."[6] In an essay entitled

---

Foley, *Political Liberalism and Establishment Clause Jurisprudence,* 43 CASE W. RES. L. REV. 963, 963 (1993) (Defining "political liberalism'" as "the idea that the state, insofar as is possible, should remain uncommitted to any of the various religious faiths or other 'comprehensive' philosophies that exist in modern society. . . .") (footnote omitted); Carlos A. Ball, *Moral Foundations for a Discourse on Same-Sex Marriage: Looking Beyond Political Liberalism,* 85 GEO. L.J. 1871, 1875 (1997); (defining political liberalism "as the prioritizing of the right over the good within a paradigm of public reasoning that separates moral values from political discourse"); Nomi Maya Stolzenberg, *A Book of Laughter and Forgetting: Kalman's "Strange Career" and the Marketing of Civic Republicanism,* 111 HARV. L. REV. 1025, 1041 (1998) (referring to Professor Laura Kalman's conception of legal liberalism as linked to political liberalism, which "is defined here in its

conventional sense of opposition to right-wing or conservative policies.") (citations omitted).

[4] Richard H. Fallon, Jr., *What is Republicanism, and Is It Worth Reviving?,* 102 HARV. L. REV. 1695, 1706 (1989).

[5] *Id.* at 1706–07 n.84. Copyright © 1989 by the Harvard Law Review Association. Reprinted with permission.

[6] In the following materials, the terms "legal liberalism" and "liberal legalism" sometimes appear. Some theorists seem to use these terms interchangeably, while others believe that they have very different meanings. For instance, Professor Mike Seidman suggests that "legal liberalism" is that branch of liberalism that depends on law to achieve the neutrality that philosophical liberalism demands, whereas "liberal legalism" is that branch of legal theory that relies on liberal objectives to justify the rule of law.

"Modern American Legal Thought," Stanford Law School Professor Thomas Grey identifies several such paradigms over the last century or so.[7] For example, one important paradigm early in the century was progressive jurisprudence reflected in the writings of Oliver Wendell Holmes, Benjamin Cardozo, and Roscoe Pound. As Professor Grey explains,[8] this jurisprudence

> took its philosophical inspiration from American pragmatism, its politics from the Progressive movement, and much of its vocabulary from the emerging social sciences. It began with Oliver Wendell Holmes's pragmatist critique of the Langdellian vision of the law as an autonomous logical system in which considerations of fairness and utility were relevant. "The life of the law has not been logic; it has been experience," he famously responded and later urged that "[t]he true science of the law consists in the establishment of its postulates from within upon accurately measured social desires instead of tradition." Roscoe Pound and Benjamin Cardozo were the most important of the many jurists who followed Holmes in seeing law as an instrument for the conscious pursuit of social welfare, an instrument whose master term was policy rather than principle, whose master institution was the legislature rather than the courts, and whose servants should devote themselves to social engineering rather than doctrinal geometry.

The paradigm that displaced progressive jurisprudence was legal realism. Like the progressive jurists, legal realists applied the methods of social science to the study of law and were favorably disposed to government regulation of the economy. Unlike the Progressives, Professor Grey explains,[9]

> [t]he Realists shifted the focus of legal study back from legislation to the judicial process, particularly the common law process in private law cases, but with an iconoclastic and revisionist account of what judges did and how they did it. . . .
>
> For the Progressive notion of judges as subordinate legislators, ideally consulting principle in the light of policy to fill in the gaps left between rules laid down by statute and precedent, the Realists substituted the idea of judges as arbitrators, whose social function was to keep the peace by resolving potentially disruptive disputes. Not only did the Realists find the general and distinctively legal concepts and principles found in treatises and Restatements hollow and indeterminate, rhetorical rather than operative in their significance, but they also made the same criticism of the equally general "policies" and "interests" relied on in Progressive legal theory. They believed that the important influences on judicial decisions were the procedures under which they were reached and judges' often unconscious sense of how disputes fit into the web of habitual and customary practice. Like their predecessors, the Realists hoped for progress through social science, but they had in mind progress in the study of the law rather than in the law itself. Judges were not to be the consumers, but rather the objects, of behaviorally oriented social science investigations designed to correlate "stimuli" (the facts of cases) with "nonverbal judicial behavior" (the outcomes of those cases) and to uncover the unconscious roots of the "hunches" leading judges to their decisions. These studies might lead indirectly to improvements in the quality of legal decisions, but only by inducing judges to disregard formal and

---

[7] Thomas Grey, *Modern American Legal Thought,* 106 YALE L.J. 493 (1996) (reviewing Neil Duxbury, *Patterns of American Jurisprudence* (1996)).

[8] *Id.* at 497–98 (citations omitted). Reprinted

by permission of The Yale Law Journal Company and Fred B. Rothman & Company from the Yale Law Journal, vol. 106, pages 493–517.

[9] *Id.* at 500–01 (citations omitted).

systematized abstractions and to go with the unconscious flow of practice-based intuition.

Process-based jurisprudence displaced legal realism and dominated legal thought from World War II until the late 1960s. Professor Grey explains, "Three elements defined the Process approach: focus on the rule of law as a value essential to the preservation of liberal democracy; support for the New Deal and the modern administrative and welfare state; and doctrinal emphasis on jurisdiction and procedure as against substantive law."[10] "The flourishing of Process jurisprudence coincided with the heyday of the Warren Court."[11] Professor Grey explains the impact of the Warren Court's activism on process-based theorists:[12]

> On the Supreme Court's new project of reinterpreting the Constitution with a tilt toward the underdogs, the Process jurists were divided. Most of them followed Felix Frankfurter in rejecting liberal activism as simply the mirror image of the conservative activism of the old Court, equally partisan and no more consistent with the conception of a nonpolitical judiciary dedicated to upholding the rule of law. A minority of Process thinkers took up the suggestion first planted by another old Progressive, Justice Harlan Fiske Stone, shortly before the ascension of the New Deal: these writers argued that the rule of law in a democracy required active judicial correction of the tendency of the majoritarian political system to undervalue the interests of minorities, dissenters, and the downtrodden. This division presaged a more far-reaching break-up: by the late 1960s, the remarkable sway that Progressive jurisprudence had held over postwar American legal thought was about to come to an end.

Over the last three decades, legal scholars' support for the activism of the Warren Court further fragmented. In the following extract, Professor Grey describes this fragmentation and its significance for contemporary American legal thought generally and liberal constitutional theory in particular:[13]

> The intersection of a growing administrative state with the American tradition of adversarial legalism made for enormous growth during the 1960s in the size of the legal profession, and concomitantly in the number of law professors. The influx to law schools of many students (and eventually teachers) with graduate training in other academic subjects stimulated a fashion for interdisciplinary legal scholarship. At the same time, the Warren Court's activism, in conjunction with the liberal agenda of the civil rights and antipoverty movements, led many young lawyers and law professors to believe that reformist courts and movement lawyers could bring about large-scale egalitarian social change. The more ambitious of these hopes were disappointed, creating on the Left a mood of impatient frustration with traditional liberal reformism, and giving birth to a radical legal movement. In the same years, laissez-faire ideas were reinvigorated on the Right, in reaction against two generations of the growth and centralization of state power.
>
> The interplay of these currents gave rise in turn to three tendencies observable in legal thought at the beginning of the 1970s. First, influenced politically by the civil rights movement and intellectually by the revival of rights-based moral and political philosophy,[47] liberal legal theorists shifted the case for judicial activism from the cautious process-based theories of the post-New Deal tradition to a more aggressive and substantive

---

[10] *Id.* at 502.

[11] *Id.* at 504.

[12] *Id.* at 504–05.

[13] *Id.* at 505–07.

[47] Most notably, *see* JOHN RAWLS, A THEORY OF JUSTICE (1971).

approach. The Law and Moral Philosophy movement portrayed judges as practical philosophers whose job was to define and enforce rights as trumps over the policy compromises reached by the ordinary political system of legislation. [48]

Second, just as some liberals impatient with the pace of reform became radicals and gave birth to the New Left, like-minded legal activists became disillusioned with the results of liberal reformist lawyering and founded the Critical Legal Studies movement. The New Left lawyers drew emotional impetus from the radical movement politics of the Vietnam War period, and intellectual sustenance from twentieth-century developments in European Marxist thought, such as Gramsci and the Frankfurt School, that made the critique of liberal capitalist ideology central to the cause of radical social change. Critical Legal Studies accordingly took up the analysis and critique of the ideology of "liberal legalism" in all its versions: process-based, rights-based, and efficiency-based. [49]

Third, many conservative and centrist intellectuals came to believe that the economy was overregulated, and that regulation was often designed more in the interest of organized interest groups, including the professional classes from whom the lawyers and regulators were drawn, than for the benefit of the consuming public in whose name these regulations were imposed. Intellectually, the Law and Economics movement was driven by the work of Ronald Coase and others, who argued that a free market depended for its optimal functioning upon the ability of the legal system to define entitlements so as to minimize information and transaction costs. [50] The more centrist lawyer-economists emphasized changes in regulatory practice that would allow better mimicking of efficient markets, while the more conservative ones focused on arguing for the efficiency of the pre-welfare state common law. [51]

The proliferation of jurisprudential schools did not stop with these three tendencies. The second American women's movement had a great impact upon law and eventually upon legal thought. Some legal feminists sought to advance the cause of women by arguing in the liberal idiom for rights to equal treatment and nondiscrimination, while others argued that women should bring a distinctive and gendered voice to law, emphasizing care and relationships over autonomy and rights. [52] Still others joined the Critical assault on liberal legalism, arguing that it was an ideology sustaining not just capitalism and class privilege but also patriarchy. [53]

---

[48] See e.g. RONALD DWORKIN, TAKING RIGHTS SERIOUSLY 188–91, 198–99 (1977) (arguing that rights are those individual interests based on principle of equal concern and respect that government may not infringe for general utility). The Law and Moral Philosophy school also emerged in more or less conservative-libertarian forms. See e.g. CHARLES FRIED, CONTRACT AS PROMISE (1981) (applying conservative Law and Moral Philosophy arguments to contracts); ROBERT NOZICK, ANARCHY, STATE, AND UTOPIA (1974) (developing philosophical argument for libertarianism); Richard Epstein, A Theory of Strict Liability, 2 J. LEGAL STUD. 151 (1973) (applying conservative Law and Moral Philosophy arguments to torts).

[49] See MARK KELMAN, A GUIDE TO CRITICAL LEGAL STUDIES (1987); THE POLITICS OF LAW (David Kairys ed., rev. ed. 1990).

[50] See R.H. Coase, The Problem of Social Cost, 3 J.L. & ECON. 1 (1960).

[51] Compare GUIDO CALABRESI, THE COSTS OF ACCIDENTS (1970) (arguing for changes in regulatory practice), with Richard Posner, A Theory of Negligence, 1 J. LEGAL STUD. 29 (1972) (arguing for efficiency of pre-welfare state common law).

[52] See DEBORAH L. RHODE, GENDER AND JUSTICE 12–14 (1989) (discussing early liberal feminism); id. at 59 (distinguishing liberal rights-oriented feminism from radical feminism); id. at 308–13 (discussing relational feminism inspired by Carol Gilligan's theory of psychological gender differences).

[53] See e.g. id. at 59–61 (discussing radical feminist critique of liberal, rights-oriented feminism).

The critique of liberal legalism as an ideology has also been extended in recent years by Critical Race Theory to add white supremacy as yet another form of unjust domination protected against radical change by lawyers' theoretical apologetics for the status quo.[54] Some feminists and Critical Race theorists have promoted narrative—fictional and autobiographical—as an important form of legal and scholarly discourse.[55] In this way, their movements have joined with Law and Literature, which, in various modes and from various political perspectives, has argued that literary texts, criticism, and interpretation can enrich the scholarly understanding of law no less than can insights drawn from economics and moral philosophy.[56] Law and Society urges similar interdisciplinary enhancement of law study from social sciences other than economics.[57] Public Choice theory extends the methods of economic analysis from the actors regulated by the legal system to the actors who operate that system, analyzing public life on the assumption that legislators and government officials are seeking to maximize private advantage.[58] Civic Republican theorists argue that preferences and motivations are culturally variable, subject to modification by the way influential social institutions model appropriate behavior, and that law should promote public spirit and cooperation rather than the self-interested autonomy emphasized by classical liberalism.[59]

In this legal world, where each new (and old) theory puts itself forward as the last word on law, it is not surprising that a number of legal intellectuals, mostly of a politically conservative bent, have argued that lawyers should stop theorizing and go back to being lawyers, drawing up rules for the guidance of human affairs, and then trying to see that the rules get applied as written.[60] This neoformalist tendency says, in effect, "none of the above" to the smorgasbord of legal theories offered by academics in recent years.

In contrast, some other recent legal theorists would consciously revive the older pragmatist tendency in American legal thought and would welcome the competing theories in the spirit, "all of the above." Legal pragmatists argue that while the life of the law has indeed not been theory but practice, nevertheless, well informed practice takes account of the insights offered by the various theories. Lawyers can get practical help from theories if modest and critically minded theorists point out where each would-be grand theory fails to make good its claim to supply the truth in jurisprudence, while recasting these theories as perspectives on law, each of which may have something useful to say in context when we understand its limitations.[61]

---

[54] *See* CRITICAL RACE THEORY (Kimberlé Crenshaw et al. eds., 1995).

[55] For a review of this literature, *see* Kathryn Abrams, *Hearing the Call of Stories,* 79 CAL. L. REV. 971 (1991).

[56] *See e.g.* JAMES B. WHITE, JUSTICE AS TRANSLATION (1990).

[57] *See* LAWRENCE M. FRIEDMAN, LAW AND SOCIETY 95–110 (1977).

[58] See DANIEL A. FARBER & PHILIP A. FRICKEY, LAW AND PUBLIC CHOICE (1991).

[59] *See e.g.* Frank I. Michelman, *The Supreme Court, 1985 Term—Foreword: Traces of Self-Government,* 100 HARV. L. REV. 4 (1986).

[60] *See* ROBERT H. BORK, THE TEMPTING OF AMERICA (1990); RICHARD A. EPSTEIN, SIMPLE RULES FOR A COMPLEX WORLD (1995); Charles Fried, *The Artificial Reason of the Law or: What Lawyers Know,* 60 TEX. L. REV. 35 (1981); Antonin Scalia, *The Rule of Law as a Law of Rules,* 56 U. CHI. L. REV. 1175 (1989). All of these writers show to varying degrees the direct or indirect influence of the ideas about law found in FRIEDRICH A. HAYEK, THE CONSTITUTION OF LIBERTY (1960).

[61] *See* PRAGMATISM IN LAW AND SOCIETY (Michael Brint & William Weaver eds., 1991) (surveying views on legal pragmatism of scholars from various disciplines).

§ 8.02 Liberal Theory's Turn to History

Subsequent to the fragmentation of liberal theory that Professor Grey describes in the previous section, more than a few (self-described or popularly perceived) liberal scholars have turned to history. The next three sections illustrate the different uses to which such scholars have used history to solve the ongoing challenge of the countermajoritarian difficulty (no doubt intensified by the Court's activist decision in *Roe v. Wade*) or to support significant social reform or enduring constitutional change by means other than constitutional adjudication. The first subsection reviews the controversy over one of the most important turns to history made by liberal scholars in the 1990s—the so-called republican revival to which Professor Grey refers in the final extract in the first section. The second subsection describes some prominent theorists' attempts to construct theories of constitutional change based on history. The third subsection considers the controversy generated by liberal scholars' reliance on history (particularly original understanding) in defense of President Clinton in his impeachment proceedings.

[A] The Turn to History to Support Judicial Activism

The fragmentation of liberalism did not by any means bring to an end some liberals' efforts to find new ways to support judicial activism embodied by the Warren Court or the Court's decision affirming abortion rights in *Roe v. Wade*. One such liberal is Laura Kalman, a professor of history at the University of California at Santa Barbara. Professor Kalman defends legal liberalism, which she defines as "the potential of courts, particularly the Supreme Court, to bring about 'those specific social reforms that affect large groups of people such as blacks, or workers, or women, or partisans of a particular persuasion; in other words, policy change with nationwide impact.' "[14] In her book *The Strange Career of Legal Liberalism*, she tells the story of "how law professors have kept the faith in what has been called 'the cult of the Court,' . . . in the ability of the courts to change society for what judges believe is the better."[15] Like Professor Grey, she perceives liberal theorists as splintering in the 1970s, but she views the major cause as their division over the legitimacy of the Court's recognition of abortion rights in *Roe v. Wade*. *Roe* divided liberal scholars who could not agree on whether it reflected the Court's return to the substantive due process of *Lochner* or could be explained on different, less controversial, neutral grounds. For Professor Kalman, history holds the promise, particularly as exemplified by the republican revival, to restore respect for the judicial activism of the Warren and Burger Courts in such cases as *Roe*. Republican revivalists stressed the Constitution's grounding in classic republican theory, which, in contrast to classic liberal thinking, subordinated the interests of any given individual to the public good or the community's welfare and emphasized the importance of individual growth through involvement with and participation in civic affairs. In the following extract, Vanderbilt Law School Professor Barry Friedman depicts and then critiques the affinity that Professor Kalman demonstrates for the republican revival. Barry

---

[14] LAURA KALMAN, THE STRANGE CAREER OF LEGAL LIBERALISM 2 (quoting GERALD ROSENBERG, THE HOLLOW HOPE: CAN COURTS BRING ABOUT SOCIAL CHANGE? 4 (1991)).

[15] L. KALMAN, *supra* note 14, at 4.

Friedman, *The Turn to History,* 72 N.Y.U. L. REV. 928, 943–46 (1997)
(reviewing LAURA KALMAN, THE STRANGE CAREER OF LEGAL LIBERALISM
(1996)): [16]

Most of Kalman's attention, however, is directed not at originalism but
at the republican revival. It is here that she draws some of her weaker
conclusions. Kalman is undoubtedly accurate in her description of republicanism, and her discussion of historians' difficulties with the republican
revival is cogent and informative. Yet she reaches dubious conclusions
about the impetus to republicanism, and gets trapped in the very mistake
neorepublican scholars have made, thinking that using history as a tactic
can solve the problems of judicial review.

First, Kalman works too hard to make the probably incorrect point that
neorepublicanism was a reaction to originalism, missing republicanism's
real relationship to contemporary political events. Conservatives' use of
history in promoting originalist interpretation, Kalman seems to reason,
led the left to "fight fire with fire." "We will go back," the neorepublicans
might have said, "and show that the Constitution was really about
something very different than you originalists think." But this explanation is contradicted by other evidence Kalman offers that neorepublicans
cared little for their historical predecessors except as a pedigree, as well
as by her candid admission that "there was no historical pedigree" for
neorepublicanism. [71]

Whether or not neorepublicanism was a response to originalism, republican scholars read very much like a reaction to Reagan-era politics. The
motivating forces seem to have been a disenchantment with liberalism
and a concern with the conservative Supreme Court. Neorepublicans
disfavor liberalism's self-centered focus on rights at the expense of
responsibilities and community. [73] And some neorepublicans join other
frustrated liberals in seeking to de-emphasize a conservative judiciary by
sidestepping a court-centered jurisprudence in favor of dialogue and
deliberation among the population at large. [74] It is not too much to

---

[16] Copyright © 1997 by the New York University Law Review. Reprinted with permission.

[71] [LAURA KALMAN, THE STRANGE CAREER
OF LEGAL LIBERALISM 175 (1996)] ("By mooring
their vision in the Founding, law professors
believed they could make a more powerful case"
for whatever vision of the social order they
wished to promote; *see also id.* at 210 (quoting
Cass Sunstein, *The Idea of a Useable Past,* 95
COLUM. L. REV. 601, 606 (1995), to effect that
"though 'there is a freestanding, nonhistorical
argument for deliberative democracy as a central political ideal,' constitutional lawyers' argument in favor of it 'draws substantial support
from historical understandings' ").

[73] One of the most forceful examples of this
argument is MARY ANN GLENDON, RIGHTS
TALK: THE IMPOVERISHMENT OF POLITICAL DIS-
COURSE 76–144 (1991) (tracing evolution of cur-
rent rights dialectic; *see also* MICHAEL J. SAN-
DEL, DEMOCRACY'S DISCONTENT 28–32 (1996);
MICHAEL J. SANDEL, LIBERALISM AND THE LIM-
ITS OF JUSTICE 59–65 (1982); Suzanna Sherry,

*Civic Virtue and the Feminine Voice in Consti-
tutional Adjudication,* 72 VA. L. REV. 543,
574–79 (1986) (arguing that influx of women
into public sphere will tip balance away from
liberalism toward communitarian values of
classical paradigm). Kalman aptly catches the
tension between liberalism's focus on rights
and republicanism.

[74] *See e.g.* CASS R. SUNSTEIN, THE PARTIAL
CONSTITUTION 145–53 (1993) (arguing that
Congress, not courts, should be the principal
vehicle for interpretation and enforcement of
the Fourteenth Amendment). Although it is
difficult to know whether to put the republican
hat on any specific scholar, included among
those who would de-emphasize the role of the
judiciary are: GIRARDEAU A. SPANN, RACE
AGAINST THE COURT 161–71 (1993) (arguing
that Supreme Court functions to perpetuate
subordination of racial minorities); ROBIN
WEST, PROGRESSIVE CONSTITUTIONALISM 190–
210 (1994) (distinguishing moral from legal
questions, and calling for increased citizen
participation in debate on moral issues); Robert
M. Cover, *Foreword: Nomos and Narrative,* 97

suppose that the neorepublicans (former liberals all), frustrated with a failed ideology and a Supreme Court turning to the right, sought new solutions in republicanism. This interpretation, at any rate, seems far more consistent with neorepublican writings than Kalman's account of republicanism as a response to originalism.

Second, and more important, Kalman fails to focus attention on the fact that the neorepublican turn to history does no better a job than originalism in addressing concerns about judicial legitimacy. The very same problems that haunt originalism also haunt republicanism. At the level of a broad understanding of the Constitution, it is as difficult to argue that the Founders intended a republican Constitution as it is to argue that historian Charles Beard was necessarily right about the foundation of the Constitution in the economic self-interest of its framers, or for any other approach. This Kalman clearly recognizes. But the same is true at the level of constitutional interpretation required to resolve specific constitutional problems. To say that the Founders were republican, and that republicanism emphasizes community and deliberation, still fails to provide us with determinate answers about how the Founders would have resolved difficult questions regarding pornography, education, or (worse yet) the constitutionality of recent telecommunications legislation. History is every bit as indeterminate in the hands of neorepublicanism as it is in the hands of originalists.

Moreover, history creates as many problems for neorepublicanism as it solves, a fact Kalman also recognizes. Neorepublicanism is related to classical republicanism in only the most general of ways. Classical republicanism rested on homogeneity of the body politic and the suppression of difference. " 'It was not the civic humanists to whom women, blacks, Jews, and the marginalized groups of modern times have been able to turn to for solutions.' " Or, as Kalman quotes Gordon S. Wood, "even in 1776 republicanism 'possessed a decidedly reactionary tone.' " Kalman herself is dubious at times of whether republicanism really will do better than liberalism at protecting the values she holds dear.

[B] Liberal Theories of Popular Sovereignty and Constitutional Change

Two prominent scholars, Bruce Ackerman and Akhil Amar of Yale Law School, have each relied heavily on history to construct ambitious theories that posit that the people of the United States rather than the courts may act as the primary agents or facilitators of enduring constitutional change outside of the formal processes for amending the Constitution set forth in Article V. Professor Ackerman sets forth major elements of his theory in the first two volumes of his projected three-volume work, entitled *We the People.*[17] In the

HARV. L. REV. 4, 25–26, 28, 43 (1983) (asserting that certain insular communities create law "as fully as does [a] judge"); Mark Tushnet, *Policy Distortion and Democratic Debilitation: Comparative Illumination of the Countermajoritarian Difficulty,* 94 MICH. L. REV. 245, 249 n.14 (1995) (calling for broader distribution of constitutional authority). Kalman joins me in reading Frank Michelman as not of one mind on the subject. . . .

In neo-neo versions of republicanism, liberalism is again finding favor, as the neo-neorepublicans seek to rescue what was good about liberalism and merge it with republicanism. *See e.g.* Cass R. Sunstein, *Beyond the Republican Revival,* 97 YALE L.J. 1539, 1566–71 (1988) ("Republican thought, understood in a certain way, is a prominent aspect of the liberal tradition.") . . .

[17] BRUCE A. ACKERMAN: WE THE PEOPLE: VOLUME 1, FOUNDATIONS (1991); VOLUME 2, TRANSFORMATIONS (1998).

first volume, he reinterpreted the Founding period. He suggested that the constitutional system created by the founders allows for two kinds of lawmaking—ordinary and higher. Ordinary lawmaking is reflected in the day-to-day operations of government, while higher lawmaking is a much rarer phenomenon in which the people acting in concert with national political leaders render lasting judgments about the need for constitutional change. For Professor Ackerman, there have been three moments in our history when such judgments have been rendered enduring—the Founding, Reconstruction, and the New Deal. In his second volume, Professor Ackerman explains the phases through which these judgments have to pass in order to become enduring. Once an event such as the New Deal has passed through the requisite phases to become identifiable as a constitutional moment, it should then bind courts to the same extent as formal constitutional amendments.

In two books,[18] Professor Amar sets out to demonstrate, among other things, that the Founders meant to empower popular majorities to sit in constant judgment over their government and, when appropriate, to undertake remedial action in their name. He explains that the most important strain in the first ten amendments was majoritarian, reflecting throughout the texts of these amendments an evident desire of the framers to empower popular majorities in each state to be the primary defenders and expositors of the rights set forth therein. Thus, of the many amendments proposed by James Madison, the very first declared that "the people have an indubitable, unalienable, and indefensible right to reform or change their Government."[19] Though this amendment did not make the final cut, its radical essence, Amar contends, is preserved in the First Amendment right of peaceable assembly and in the broad language of the Ninth and Tenth Amendments, which speak of the rights and powers "retained" and "reserved" by the people. Taken together with the Preamble's dramatic opening phrases—"We the people of the United States . . . do ordain and establish this Constitution"—these texts suggest to Amar that what the popular sovereign has made, it may "disassemble at will."[20]

---

[18] AKHIL REED AMAR, THE BILL OF RIGHTS: CREATION AND RECONSTRUCTION (1998); AKHIL REED AMAR & ALAN HIRSCH, FOR THE PEOPLE: WHAT THE CONSTITUTION REALLY SAYS ABOUT YOUR RIGHTS (1998).

[19] A. AMAR, THE BILL OF RIGHTS, *supra* note 18, at 36.

[20] *Id.* Professor Amar suggests in his second book, co-written with journalist Alan Hirsch, that liberals and conservatives have made a major mistake in regarding all constitutional rights as "individualistic in nature." A. Amar & A. Hirsch, *For the People supra* note 18, at xi. Instead, they maintain that the constant invocation of "the people" in the Bill of Rights points to a now all-but-forgotten 18th century ideal of virtuous, vigilant citizenship. The paramount concern of this "Republican tradition" was to ensure that the people remained firmly in control in the face of a potentially "self-

dealing" government. For Amar and Hirsch, this historical context sheds new light on Article V, which they, like Professor Ackerman, do not interpret as restricting amendment of the Constitution by other, nonspecified means. For them (as for Ackerman), the significant fact is that Article V nowhere declares itself the only method for changing our fundamental law. *Id.* at 5. What this means is that a simple majority of the American people, acting outside Congress and the state legislatures, enjoys the "inalienable legal right" to amend the Constitution. *Id.* at 7. Conditions may be placed on this right in order to promote proper deliberation, but fear of rash or oppressive measures should not stand in the way of upholding the people's "first principle." *Id.* For too long, the authors contend, the people's "constitutional muscles" have been allowed to "atrophy through disuse." *Id.* at 32.

He explains further that the libertarian, individual rights-protecting strain in American constitutional law originated with the Radical Republicans and the post-Civil War Amendments. He shows how the originally collective pro-state power Bill of Rights was reconceptualized and recast as an individual rights-protecting federal barrier against abuses by the states of their powers. One important consequence of this transformation was that the framers of the Fourteenth Amendment had in mind protecting not only the newly freed slaves and their descendants from abusive state governments but also others who occupied roughly analogous positions, including women and children.

One might be tempted to think that liberal theorists have warmly received either Professor Ackerman's or Amar's theory, because the former has attempted to reinforce the constitutional underpinnings of many of the New Deal and the Warren Court's rulings on behalf of minorities and the poor while the latter has constructed historical foundations for using the Fourteenth Amendment to protect women and minorities from hostile state governments. To the contrary, liberal scholars have been among the harshest critics of these theories. In particular, a number of liberal scholars have leveled several charges against these theories for the primary purpose of establishing, as one of the most prominent constitutional theorists in the nation, Professor Laurence Tribe of Harvard Law School, has suggested, "that constitutional interpretation is, after all, less free-form an exercise than it would be if methods like theirs were to take hold."[21] First, several legal scholars have questioned whether or the extent to which the framers shared the views attributed to them by Professors Ackerman and Amar that Article V does not set forth the exclusive means for amending the Constitution.[22] Second, to the extent that Professor Amar relies on the same history as republican revivalists do, he is subject to the same criticisms that have been directed against their historiography.[23] Third, legal scholars have taken issue with various aspects of Professor Ackerman's accounts of the Founding, Reconstruction, and the New Deal.[24] Fourth, several scholars maintain that Ackerman's theory fails

---

[21] Laurence H. Tribe, *Taking Text and Structure Seriously: Reflections on Free-Form Method in Constitutional Interpretation*, 108 HARV. L. REV. 1221, 1227 (1995). Because both Professor Ackerman's and Amar's theories of constitutional change have been developing for more than a decade, the theories were subjected to criticism before they appeared in book form.

[22] *See e.g.* Jack N. Rakove, *The Super-Legality of the Constitution, or a Federalist Critique of Bruce Ackerman's Neo-Federalism*, 108 YALE L.J. 1931 (1999); Cass R. Sunstein, *Originalism for Liberals*, THE NEW REPUBLIC, Sept. 28, 1998 (reviewing AKHIL REED AMAR, THE BILL OF RIGHTS (1998), and A. AMAR & A. HIRSCH, FOR THE PEOPLE (1998)); Henry Monaghan, *We the People(s), Original Understanding, and Constitutional Amendment*, 96 COLUM. L. REV. 121, 165–73 (1996); Suzanna Sherry, *The Ghost of Liberalism Past* (Book Review),

105 HARV. L. REV. 918, 928 (1992); Michael J. Klarman, *Constitutional Fact / Constitutional Fiction: A Critique of Bruce Ackerman's Theory of Constitutional Moments*, 44 STAN. L. REV. 759, 777–85 (1992).

[23] *See e.g.* Fallon, *supra* note 4, at 1704–33.

[24] *See e.g.* BARRY CUSHMAN, RETHINKING THE NEW DEAL COURT: THE STRUCTURE OF A CONSTITUTIONAL REVOLUTION (1998); Eric Foner, *The Strange Career of the Reconstruction Amendments*, 108 YALE L.J. 2003 (1999); Michael Les Benedict, *Constitutional History and Constitutional Theory: Reflections on Ackerman, Reconstruction, and the Transformation of the American Constitution*, 108 YALE L.J. 2011 (1999); Rogers M. Smith, *Legitimating Reconstruction: The Limits of Legalism*, 108 YALE L.J. 2039 (1999); William E. Leuchtenberg, *When the People Spoke, What Did They Say?: The Election of 1936 and the Ackerman Thesis*, 108 YALE L.J. 2077 (1999); Stephen M. Griffin, *Constitutional Theory Transformed*,

to provide a compelling justification for present and future generations to abide by past generations' constitutional commitments.[25] Fifth, some critics from the left and right suggest that Ackerman's criteria for determining constitutional change are too malleable.[26] Moreover, Professor Tribe suggests that Professors Ackerman's and Amar's construction of Article V cannot be squared with basic fidelity to or respect for the constitutional text. They both suggest that the text of Article V provides some support for their theories, because Article V does not state explicitly that it is the "only" means for effecting enduring constitutional change. For them, the absence of the qualifier "only" does not foreclose construing Article V as allowing rather than precluding other means for amending the Constitution. In a comment directed at Professsor Amar's theory but equally applicable to Professor Ackerman's construction of Article V, Professor Tribe suggests that

> once one attaches significance to the absence of "only" in a constitutional provision, the meaning of that provision will vary with the placement of the missing "only." Professor Amar notes that Article V "emphatically does not say that it is the only way to revise the Constitution." Although he acknowledges that for provisions such as Article V, it is common to "read the enumeration of one mode . . . as impliedly precluding any other modes," Professor Amar abandons the spirit of this more common approach by latching onto an "alternative way of understanding the implied exclusivity of Article V: it enumerates the only mode(s) by which ordinary Government . . . can change the Constitution . . . Under this alternative view, Article V nowhere prevents the People themselves' from changing their Constitution." Although he presents his construction of Article V as true to the interpretive principle of "implied exclusivity," Professor Amar has simply focused on the "only" absence that supports his argument best. Like Professor Ackerman, he has mistaken a gap in the constitutional map for a hole in constitutional space.[27]

---

108 YALE L.J. 2115 (1999); Laura Kalman, *Law, Politics, and the New Deal*, 108 YALE L.J. 2165 (1999); Walter Dean Burnham, *Constitutional Moments and Punctuated Equilibria: A Political Scientist Confronts Bruce Ackerman's We the People*, 108 YALE L.J. 2237 (1999); William E. Forbath, *Constitutional Change and the Politics of History*, 108 YALE L.J. 1917 (1999); Sanford Levinson, *Transitions*, 108 YALE L.J. 2215 (1999); Klarman, *supra* note 22, at 769–71, 776–85; Sherry, *supra* note 22, at 924–25. For Professor Ackerman's response to these critiques, *see* Bruce A. Ackerman, *Revolution on a Human Scale*, 108 YALE L.J. 2279 (1999).

[25] Klarman, *supra* note 22, at 765–66; Frank I. Michelman, *Constitutional Fidelity/Democratic Agency*, 65 FORDHAM L. REV. 1537, 1538–42 (1997); Sherry, *supra* note 22, at 933.

[26] Joanne B. Freeman, *The Election of 1800:*

A Study in the Logic of Political Change, 108 YALE L.J. 1959 (1999); Tribe, *supra* note 21, at 1286 n.216; Michael McConnell, *The Forgotten Constitutional Moment*, 11 CONST. COMMENTARY 115, 122–40 (1994).

[27] Tribe, *supra* note 21, at 1245 (citations omitted). Copyright © 1995 by the Harvard Law Review Association. Reprinted with permission. Professor Tribe's references to "gaps" and "holes" derive from his efforts to analogize construing multi-sided shapes to constitutional interpretation. For Tribe, the crucial thing to understand is that these shapes as well as the Constitution are *all* multi-dimensional objects, such that making sense of them requires understanding the things that are there and those that are not readily apparent as having significance only by virtue of the relationship of those things to their immediate context as well as to the entirety of the entity of which they are parts.

[C] The Liberal Turn to History in the Clinton Impeachment Proceedings

In 1998 and 1999, many liberal academics turned to history in yet another important forum—President Clinton's impeachment proceedings. Liberal defenders of the President made two historical arguments to try to stop the House from impeaching and later to keep the Senate from removing the President from office.[28] First, many argued that the President's misconduct did not constitute an impeachable offense, because the original understanding of the impeachment clauses indicated that the framers generally conceived that a requisite element of an impeachable offense was a nexus between an official's misconduct and the official's duties and there was no such nexus in the President's case.[29] The major exception to this requirement would be private misconduct (such as murder) that was so outrageous or extreme as to leave Congress little choice but to impeach and remove the offending official. Second, many academic defenders of the President argued that historical practices in the realm of impeachment confirmed that such a nexus was a required element of an impeachable offense.[30] Moreover, some suggested that the House Judiciary Committee's failure to approve an impeachment article against President Nixon based on income tax fraud constituted a precedent for not impeaching President Clinton for trying to conceal an illicit sexual relationship, something that seemed no worse than Nixon's private misconduct.[31]

---

[28] It is important to note that academics and others who opposed the impeachment proceedings also made textual and structural arguments. First, they based their textual argument on Article II, section 4, which provides, "The President and all civil Officers of the United States, shall be removed from Office on Impeachment for and Conviction of, Treason, Bribery, and other high Crimes or Misdemeanors." The President's defenders argued that the modifiers "other high" suggested that the only misconduct that could qualify as legitimately impeachable "Crimes or Misdemeanors" had to be on a par or on the same level of magnitude as "treason" or "bribery." Because the President's misconduct was not in their view on such a par, it did not constitute "other high Crimes or Misdemeanors." See e.g. Special Hearing on the Background and History of Impeachment, Before the House Subcommittee on the Constitution, Committee on the Judiciary, U.S. House of Representatives, Nov. 9, 1998, at 226–27 (prepared statement of Professor Laurence H. Tribe, Harvard Law School). Second, a major structural argument made by many of the President's defenders was that a president required a higher threshold for removal than a judge (some of whom had been removed for misconduct arguably similar to that which the President had allegedly committed). The reason for requiring a higher threshold for presidential removal is that because there is only one president who presides over the executive branch and there are many federal judges no single one of whom presides over the federal judiciary, impeaching a president is likely to have a much greater destabilizing impact on the executive branch than impeaching a single judge would have on the federal judiciary. See e.g. id. at 88–89 (prepared statement of Professor Cass R. Sunstein, University of Chicago Law School).

[29] See e.g. id. at 206–08 (prepared statement of Professor Dan Pollitt, University of North Carolina Law School); id. at 225–28 (prepared statement of Professor Laurence H. Tribe, Harvard Law School); id. at 234–35 (prepared statement of Professor Susan Low Bloch, Georgetown University National Law Center); id. at 248–50 (prepared statement of Professor Jack N. Rakove, Stanford University). See also id. at 374–83 (letter opposing the President's impeachment signed by 430 law professors).

[30] See e.g. id. at 87–89 (prepared statement of Professor Cass R. Sunstein, University of Chicago Law School); id. at 374–83 (letter opposing President Clinton's impeachment signed by 430 law professors).

[31] See id. at 115 (prepared statement of Father Robert Drinan, Georgetown University National Law Center).

The responses to these arguments were directed not just at the merits of the arguments themselves but at the methodologies employed by liberal academics, who had been presumed to be hostile to original understanding (if not also to an imperial presidency). In the following extract, John O. McGinnis, a conservative law professor at Cardozo Law School, takes liberal academics to task primarily for what he regards as their hypocritical use of original understanding in defending the President: [32]

Momentous public issues, like impeachment, have at least this virtue: They promote political accountability by forcing citizens to take positions that will be remembered. Such public reasoning carries with it the risk of public exposure. During President Clinton's impeachment, certain feminists became poster girls for hypocrisy because their support for Clinton conflicted with their previous positions, such as their attacks on Clarence Thomas. But there is a second kind of exposure that can be equally important. Under outside scrutiny, some groups—particularly intellectuals—forsake the style of reasoning they apply regularly in the seclusion of their own salons. This divergence between private and public intellectual persona can reveal the frailty of the ideas by which such groups make an academic living.

As a law professor who testified before the House Judiciary Committee on the subject of impeachment, I had firsthand knowledge of the incongruity of most law professors' approach to this issue. Of course, I was not surprised that my colleagues almost universally opposed the impeachment of the president. Just as it was said in the late nineteenth century that the Anglican Church was the Conservative Party at prayer, our universities today are the Democratic party at play. Indeed, the more than 6 to 1 statistical imbalance in the legal academy between Democrats and Republicans may not fully capture the vigor of its commitment to this president because law professors are most passionate on the subjects of abortion on demand and racial and ethnic preferences—the two issues on which Clinton is most reliably left-wing.

What was curious about my colleagues' presentations was not their bottom line but their methodology. In their academic writings, most professors of constitutional law deploy a signature theory of constitutional interpretation of their own devising, usually some iteration of what are amusingly called "non-interpretative" theories of interpretation. For modern constitutional theorists, the current meaning of the Constitution must be divined through liberal moral theory, or generated by a close study of watershed elections, or grasped by "translating" the Framers' commands to a new code appropriate to our era.

For instance, Laurence Tribe, one of those who argued against impeachment at the hearing, defends *Roe v. Wade* in his constitutional law treatise on the grounds that the Constitution must be construed to protect fundamental rights even if these rights are not enumerated in the Constitution. He then contends that the right to an abortion is fundamental on the basis of a farrago of value judgments also nowhere implied by the Constitution, such as the claim that legal restrictions on abortion "subordinate women to men." Ronald Dworkin, perhaps the most celebrated legal theorist alive today and a signer of the law professors' letter opposing impeachment, is able to discover abortion rights in the Constitution even without appeal to unenumerated rights. For him, the Constitution consists of a set of moral principles so broad as to permit the Supreme

---

[32] John O. McGinnis, *Impeachable Defenses,* POLICY REVIEW 27–31 (June & July 1999).

Court to set itself up as a commission of moral inquisition on all legislation. To condemn the constitutionality of abortion regulations, he musters moral judgments similar to those of Professor Tribe—judgments that are incontestable only in the sense that an overwhelming majority in the academy would never dare question them.

In contrast to the popularity of "non-interpretative" theories, like those of Dworkin or Tribe, the legal academy almost universally derides originalism—the view that the Constitution should be interpreted according to its original meaning—as a dead hand constraining social progress. For instance, to an originalist the Constitution itself suggests that capital punishment must be permissible under at least some circumstances, because it provides that, "No one shall be held to answer for a capital crime unless on a presentment or indictment of a Grand Jury" and that, "no one shall be deprived of life, liberty or property without due process of law." Dworkin, however, argues that the Eighth Amendment can still prohibit capital punishment because the ban on "cruel and unusual punishment" reflects our evolving standards of decency. According to the professor, the content of these new standards can be intuited by judges and professors even if their intuitions conflict with those of the overwhelming majority of people, who support the death penalty.

The disdain for originalism carries over from the constitutional questions involving rights to those involving the structure of the government. Many of those who signed the letter opposing impeachment have also argued that the Supreme Court was correct to have discarded the original understanding of federalism. For instance, Professor Lawrence Lessig of Harvard, yet another signer, has argued that federalism must be "translated" so as to be compatible with a more centralized state, which, in his view, is necessary to regulate modern society.

In their writings on impeachment, however, law professors became, *mirabile dictu* originalists themselves. Without so much as an explanation, let alone an apology, for their transformation, they wove their arguments almost exclusively from text and history.

Of course, being rusty at the mere carpentry of legal analysis, they often misused the most elementary of tools of the originalist method. The professors misconstrued language. For instance, their letter against impeachment argued that the phrase "high Crimes and Misdemeanors" was wholly or largely directed to acts committed in a public capacity, because the adjoining words in the clause governing impeachment, "Bribery" and "Treason," defined acts necessarily committed in the public capacity. This was obviously an error of interpretation. If an executive branch official passed money to influence a judge for a private matter, his act would nevertheless constitute bribery. As for treason, tell the Rosenbergs that it is a crime that can only be committed in a public capacity.

The professors also failed to consider very pertinent evidence from the era of the Framing about the gravity with which perjury was regarded. John Jay, the first chief justice of the United States, said of perjury flatly, "there is no crime more extensively pernicious to society" because it undermines the system of justice at the heart of a civic republic.

As hypocrisy is the tribute that vice pays to virtue, so a faulty reading of text and feeble historical research became the tribute that these liberal law professors paid to originalism. But *why* did such professors, in their testimony and op-eds and endless media appearances, remain faithful to originalist methodology at all, when they ridicule it in their scholarship?

Since it was clearly not by choice, it must have been a decision forced by circumstance. If they had placed their arguments about impeachment in the context of their own often conflicting theories of constitutional interpretation, they themselves would have been ridiculed by members of Congress, because their theories would have been so obviously at odds with common sense. Impeachment was unlike academic debates and even judicial proceedings in one salient and salutary respect: The public was actually paying some attention; therefore, arguments that flew in the face of our common pool of reasoning would have been heavily penalized.

The impeachment hearings are not an isolated example of legal theorists abandoning their own theories in public forums. For instance, Bruce Ackerman, the Yale constitutional theorist, has long contended that the Constitution can be amended outside of the formal process spelled out in the document. In the professor's view, we can dispense with the rusty process of requiring two-thirds majorities in the Congress and ratification by three-fifths of the states. Instead, we can amend by arriving at a revolutionary "constitutional moment," at which time Congress and the president act in a way that was previously unconstitutional and their action is subsequently ratified by their reelection.

In the *Harvard Law Review,* Ackerman contended that the North American Free Trade Agreement (Nafta) could be given effect by ordinary legislation instead of requiring ratification by two-thirds of the Senate, because the treaty ratification requirement had been made a dead letter by a previous "constitutional moment" earlier in this century. Appearing before Congress, however, he did not advance under his own academic coat of arms but made instead a weak textual argument on behalf of Nafta's constitutionality. The reason for his reticence is clear: Many senators and reporters would have recognized that Professor Ackerman's endorsement of ad hoc populist revisions of our founding document discards constitutional restraints when they are most needed—in moments of popular passion. The whole point of a Constitution is, in the memorable words of Justice David Brewer, to have "Philip sober control Philip drunk."

The impeachment-hearing conversion of law professors has many lessons. The most obvious is that, despite the consensus against originalism in the legal academy, it reigns supreme in the public mind. The Constitution is a recipe for government, and the common man, unschooled in the intricacies of theory, understands that to follow a recipe you need to understand it according to the meaning it had to those who formulated it. Otherwise you may get an utterly different dish—one prepared to the perhaps eccentric taste of the cooks. One further argument intuitively understood is that originalism is the only possible default rule for interpretation. Without originalism, our law professors could have spent the entire debate in fruitless disagreement about which of their many "non-interpretative" theories to choose.

But there are also larger lessons about the ability of public attention to act as a counterweight to the bizarre flights of fancy that are now pandemic in the legal academy. Recently one prominent left-wing scholar denied that conservatives face discrimination in the legal academy because they are conservatives. Instead, he contended that conservatives were disfavored because they keep working on the boring theory of originalism in constitutional law and textualism in statutory interpretation rather than working to formulate new, "cutting-edge" theories.

This professor was inadvertently revealing what motivates many legal academics—the taste for novelty rather than the love of truth. It is of no consequence to those ensconced in tenure that each novel theory has itself been shown wanting. Indeed, these flaws present an opportunity for further critique and yet another parlor game. The public may not be experts but they recognize that more is at stake in legal analysis than the opportunity to amuse and dazzle your friends. Many of the theories offered in the academy are so patently dangerous to legal regularity that they dare not speak their name in public.

In a recent book,[33] Judge Richard Posner takes an equally harsh view of the argumentation employed by both the President's defenders and critics. According to Judge Posner, their argumentation revealed the inability of various academic disciplines to build consensus on the proper resolution of moral or political disputes. He explains that legal academics are practitioners of a "soft" field rather than a "hard" field (such as physics or chemistry), in which "agreement on the methods for resolving disagreement enables consensus to be forged despite the differing political agendas of the practitioners. The scholarly output of . . . a [hard] field need not be either interesting or important, but it will tend to be objective, or at least to lack a discernible political infection. A soft field, in contrast, is permeable to political disagreement."[34] Thus, the fatal problem for liberal commentators such as Ronald Dworkin and conservatives such as Robert Bork is that their respective commentaries revealed "unbridgeable differences in values that have their origin in temperament, upbringing, and life experiences rather than in reasoning to divergent conclusions from shared premises."[35]

To illustrate how many liberal law professors distorted the constitutional standards for impeachment in an effort to defend the President, Judge Posner critiques the letter signed by more than 400 law professors submitted in November 1998 to the House Judiciary Committee in opposition to the President's impeachment. At the outset of the letter, the signatories indicated that they wrote "neither as Democrats nor as Republicans" but rather because they jointly believed that members of "Congress would violate their constitutional responsibilities if they sought to impeach and remove the President for misconduct, even criminal misconduct, that fell short of the high constitutional standard required for impeachment."[36] The letter emphasized that "other high Crimes or Misdemeanors" consisted of misconduct that was on a par with treason and bribery, and that "the critical, distinctive feature of treason and bribery is grossly derelict exercise of official power (or, in the case of bribery to obtain or retain an office, gross criminality in the pursuit of official power)."[37] But none of the President's misconduct, in the signatories' view, involved the exercise, much less the abuse, of official power. Nor did the President's misconduct constitute an act of "unspeakable heinousness" that, like murder, would merit the perpetrator's removal from office.[38]

Judge Posner takes the signatories to task for not having been more critical of the President, who, by the time the letter had been submitted, had been shown (in Judge Posner's opinion) beyond a reasonable doubt to be guilty of various crimes (such as perjury and obstruction of justice), as detailed in the report submitted to the House by Independent Counsel Kenneth Starr. Moreover, Judge Posner "draw[s] attention to the sheer number of signatories.

---

[33] RICHARD A. POSNER, AN AFFAIR OF STATE: THE INVESTIGATION, IMPEACHMENT, AND TRIAL OF PRESIDENT CLINTON (1999).

[34] Id. at 240.

[35] Id.

[36] Special Hearing on the Background and History of Impeachment, supra note 28, at 374.

[37] Id. at 375.

[38] Id.

Many, probably most, are not experts on constitutional law; and one wonders how many of them had actually studied either the facts of Clinton's conduct (the Starr Report alone is more than 200 pages) or the law of impeachment. An unkind critic might describe the signing by intellectuals of petitions, open letters, and full-page ads as a form of herd behavior (the 'herd of independent minds') by the animal that likes to see its name in print."[39] He speculates that it is probable that "many of the signatories of the . . . letter know little about the law of perjury or its importance to the litigation process and don't want to take the time to find out more. But then one might expect the professors of criminal law, criminal procedure, and civil procedure to have sought to correct the misleading impression created by the . . . letter by writing a letter of their own to the House Judiciary Committee, which they have not done, emphasizing the gravity of the President's crimes."[40]

§ 8.03 Beyond Liberalism

Some of the sharpest attacks on liberalism have not come from the right but from the left. These criticisms have taken many forms and gone in many directions (as is further discussed in the subsequent chapters on feminism and critical race theory). In this section, we examine the implications of some of the criticisms of liberalism not explored in later chapters. Perhaps the most prominent of these is the critique of liberalism from the perspective of critical legal studies—a radical progressive movement founded in the 1970s that challenged many of the fundamental assumptions on which liberalism is based. The nature of this critique is best illustrated in the work of Mark Tushnet of Georgetown University Law Center, who is by far the most prolific CLS writer on constitutional theory.

An important phase of Professor Tushnet's scholarship is reflected in his book RED, WHITE, AND BLUE: A CRITICAL ANALYSIS OF CONSTITUTIONAL LAW (1988), which collected and updated many of the articles he had written during the 1980s. In that book, he explained the two components of his comprehensive critique of liberal constitutional theory. First, he used an "external" critique to show each liberal theory's "content as too limited," that is, each theory tends not to preclude enough unprincipled judicial review.[41] Second, he applied an "internal" critique to establish "the rather limited . . . maximum coherent content" of each liberal grand theory given its premises.[42] According to Tushnet, these two critiques revealed that each of the "grand" liberal theories of constitutional law (for example, original intent, representation-reinforcement, and moral philosophy) and antiformalist approaches (such as balancing, dialogue, and public values) suppressed competing or contradictory principles and suffered from moral incoherence, logical inconsistency, ineffectiveness, and a significant potential for manipulation to preserve political, economic, and social inequities.

The inevitable question raised by Tushnet's critique[43] is with what would Tushnet replace liberalism. Some CLS scholars have resisted the temptation

---

[39] R. Posner, *supra* note 33, at 242.

[40] *Id.*

[41] M. Tushnet, *supra* note 3, at 179.

[42] *Id.*

[43] Lest the reader come away with the im-

to answer this question. After all, people who question basic premises of the existing social order should perhaps not be faulted if they spend much of their time trying to show what is wrong with it, why it does not work the way it purportedly should, and why it ought to be altered, rather than saying how judges within the very social order under question ought to do their jobs.[44] (One would not normally expect, say, someone who thought that bullfighting was immoral and should be abolished, to offer theories about the best way of being a matador.) Still, disputes about fundamental norms will arise in any social order, and some means of resolving those disputes will be essential. The criticism of failure to sketch an alternative that can be compared with existing approaches, therefore, is not entirely out of place.

By 1996, Professor Tushnet had sketched more than one possible alternative to liberalism.[45] In that year, he and his Georgetown colleague Louis M. Seidman, published the book, REMNANTS OF BELIEF,[46] in which they expressed their "skeptical commitment" to the value of constitutional argument as a device that allows us to "reach[] beyond ourselves and appeal[] to universal values."[47] They remained skeptically committed because of their continued reverence for and hope for a return of something like the "glory days" of New Deal and Great Society liberalism[48] as well as its judicial embodiment—the Warren Court—which "restored the good name of active judicial review."[49] Along these lines, Tushnet and Seidman, who came of age in the 1960s, embrace reform proposals that "satisfy liberal nostalgia for the lost youth of constitutional argument."[50] They trumpet the "promise" of the narrative

---

pression that Professor Tushnet is the only prominent CLS constitutional theorist, Dean Paul Brest of the Stanford Law School is often cited as at least a quasi-Crit. His views are well represented in his article, *The Misconceived Quest for the Original Understanding*, 60 B.U. L. REV. 204 (1980). For a discussion of this article, see the excerpt from Professor Farber's overview of the originalism debate in Chapter 4.

[44] *See e.g.* M. Tushnet, *supra* note 3, at 313 (Professor Tushnet suggests that "the liberal tradition makes constitutional theory both necessary and impossible. It is necessary because it provides the restraints that the liberal tradition requires us to place on those in power, legislators and judges as well. It is impossible because no available approach to constitutional law can effectively restrain both legislators and judges: If we restrain the judges we leave legislators unconstrained; if we restrain the legislators we let the judges do what they want.").

[45] *See e.g. id.* at 315–16 (suggesting that he could not offer "an alternative synthesis to [his] critique of competing theories" but only could sketch "some elements of a republic conception"); *The Dilemmas of Liberal Constitutionalism,* 42 OHIO ST. L.J. 411, 424 (1981) (answer-

ing the question of what he would do as a judge by suggesting that he would make "an explicitly political judgment: which result is, in the circumstances now existing, likely to advance the cause of socialism? Having decided that, I would write an opinion in some currently favored version of Grand Theory. For example, I happen to like the political obstacles theory, probably because it has a neat air of scientism and realism about it. So I would write a political obstacles opinion. That is why my answer should be uninteresting; I am not in a position to do what my theory suggests, I make no special claims to political insight, and, most important, the whole point of the approach is to insist that there are no general answers, but only tentative ones based on the exact conjuncture of events when the question is asked. The answer I give today would not necessarily be the one I would give were I a judge, for that fact itself would signal that political circumstances had changed drastically.")

[46] LOUIS M. SEIDMAN & MARK V. TUSHNET, REMNANTS OF BELIEF: CONTEMPORARY CONSTITUTIONAL ISSUES (1996).

[47] *Id.* at 200–01.

[48] *Id.* at 176.

[49] *Id.* at 43.

[50] *Id.* at 191.

jurisprudence popular in critical race theory and feminism and implore law professors to "maintain sympathy and understanding for the positions they oppose."[51] By calling upon constitutional scholars to "maintain[] a sense of political community" with their opponents,[52] Tushnet and Seidman hope that intrinsically politicized constitutional discourse may be conducted with a more explicit, honest focus on public policy tradeoffs.

In a review of Tushnet's and Seidman's book, Professor Steven Calabresi of Northwestern University Law School examines the merits of their claim that constitutional theory has lost its way. His review begins with a summary of the contemporary problems in constitutional doctrine that Tushnet and Seidman attribute to New Deal constitutionalism. Steven G. Calabresi, *The Crisis in Constitutional Theory*, 83 VA. L. REV. 247, 248–51 (1997):[53]

> Professors Seidman and Tushnet identify three critical and interrelated difficulties that they think the constitutionalism of the New Deal has bequeathed to those of us who study the Constitution today.
>
> First, they argue that a core element of New Deal thought was to see government choice everywhere, both in decisions to intervene *and in decisions not to intervene.* Professors Seidman and Tushnet identify this principle with *Miller v. Schoene,*[11] the Supreme Court's famous 1928 nuisance case in which the Court upheld a Virginia statute confiscating without compensation cedar trees infected with cedar rust that threatened to infect nearby apple orchards. They argue that Justice Harlan Fiske Stone's opinion in that case recognized that doing nothing (and allowing the infected cedar trees to destroy the apple orchard) would have been nonetheless a government choice.[12] Relying on *Miller* and on the 1911 decision by the New York Court of Appeals in *Ives v. South Buffalo Railway Co.,*[13] Professors Seidman and Tushnet contend that the New Deal left us with a constitutional culture where government was seen everywhere, even in the ordinary protection of pure private property rights.
>
> The significance of the constitutional crisis of 1937 for Professors Seidman and Tushnet, then, is that it constitutionalized the notion that government inaction was just as much a choice as government action in a world where private common law rights of property, contract, torts and family law were themselves recognized as being nothing more and nothing less than the creations of government. They develop this point further in their discussion of state action paradox in chapter three—the second troubling legacy we have inherited in their view from the New Deal era. Using the Supreme Court's famous *DeShaney v. Winnebago County Department of Social Services*[15] decision as an example, Professors Seidman and Tushnet contend that in the wake of the New Deal the case is difficult to resolve because a state government's decision to leave a child with his biological parents is as much state action as a decision to remove him due to the risk of child abuse. In the *DeShaney* case, a battery of social service workers failed to remove young Joshua DeShaney from his father's custody until after severe physical abuse had rendered the child permanently brain damaged. The Supreme Court rejected a lawsuit brought

---

[51] *Id.* at 195–96.

[52] *Id.* at 196.

[11] 276 U.S. 272 (1928).

[12] *Id.* at 279.

[13] 94 N.E. 431 (N.Y. 1911) (finding workmen's compensation statute that displaced the common law requirement of fault in industrial accidents inconsistent with constitutionally mandated background of property law).

[15] 489 U.S. 189 (1989).

by the child's mother, holding that there was no state action because the abuse was perpetrated by the child's father and not by government officials.[16] Professors Seidman and Tushnet disagree and, going well beyond the dissenting arguments of Justices Brennan and Blackmun, they contend that it was government action in the first place that "allocated" the child to his divorced biological father. They believe a "central element of the New Deal revolution was the systematic dismantling of the public-private distinction," and, accordingly, they contend that the old dichotomy between feasance and nonfeasance collapsed as the Supreme Court came to understand that government inaction was really a kind of government action. This realization, reflected in the seminal *Miller v. Schoene* opinion with its recognition that doing nothing is nonetheless a choice, leaves us with a paradoxical state action doctrine. The doctrine is paradoxical because it recognizes no public-private distinction that limits legislative power (at least in the realm of economic matters), yet does recognize such a distinction as a constraint on judicial power—at least sometimes—as in the *DeShaney* case.

Professors Seidman and Tushnet are troubled by this inconsistency. They point out, correctly, that the Equal Protection Clause of the Fourteenth Amendment created some "positive" rights to government protection from private violence for African Americans. Given this, and given the collapse of the public-private distinction as a limit on legislative power over economic matters, they question our selective retention of the doctrine as a restraint on courts in cases like *DeShaney* where private violence is occurring. At the same time, they acknowledge that much of our modern constitutional doctrine would collapse in the absence of a public-private distinction. *Roe v. Wade* for example, is allegedly founded on a right to privacy with respect to certain intimate matters of sexuality, reproductive freedom and bodily integrity. This privacy doctrine would collapse, as Professors Seidman and Tushnet acknowledge, in the absence of some kind of public-private distinction.

The third problem bequeathed to us by the New Deal era is connected to the previous two. It is the problem of determining the appropriate "baseline" in cases where there is argument about whether the Constitution has been violated because someone has been unconstitutionally burdened. In many such cases one side will contend that the government is simply denying someone a benefit to which they were never entitled in the first place. The other side will, however, see the same government action as an unconstitutional burden or condition. The resolution of the case will thus turn on a theory of defining the appropriate baseline. The government's action will be either a burden or a benefit depending on the legitimate ex ante baseline distribution.

Professors Seidman and Tushnet argue that the New Deal's central purpose was to shift baselines through government intervention that rejected old natural rights arguments and replaced them with "a pragmatic, policy-management approach that asked whether a particular distribution of resources best served the country's needs." Continuing, they contend that this "revolution in legal ideology should have solved the conditional-offer problem. Once it was understood that all baselines were created by government decision, there was no longer a need to worry about whether a particular action constituted an offer or a threat."

Unfortunately, Professors Seidman and Tushnet conclude that the New Dealers also were interested in creating new natural baselines of their own predicated on social justice and the bare-boned constitutional textualism of Justices like Hugo Black. But textual rights can only provide

---

[16] *Id.* at 194–98.

protection for individuals if one has a stable conception of legitimate baseline distributions. Since the New Deal left us with only a very muddled understanding of legitimate baseline distributions, constitutional textualism is necessarily a muddle today as well.

After identifying the basic legacies of New Deal constitutionalism, Tushnet and Seidman proceed, as Professor Calabresi explains, to consider how these legacies have undermined constitutional doctrine in four areas of constitutional law that have divided the Supreme Court (and theorists)—racial equality, symbolized by the decision in *Washington v. Davis*;[54] First Amendment decisions on pornography and campaign finance regulation; the Court's death penalty jurisprudence; and the Court's federalism and separation of powers doctrines, which they criticize as unworkable and result-oriented. The academic commentaries on the doctrine in these different areas has not produced consensus on understanding either the problems in those areas or the solutions to those problems. Instead, as Professors Tushnet and Seidman suggest, we have been left with a "choice between constitutional theories that rest on controversial value judgments and constitutional theories that steer clear of such judgments."[55] The problem with theories of the first type is that they are not acceptable to people who have different or conflicting values than those reflected in or driving the theories, while theories of the second type lack values that might attract support or interest. "In either event, these theories will not succeed in bridging disagreement over the things we care about the most."[56] The best hope for the future is for all theorists to engage in a constructive dialogue in which the participants show respect for each other's arguments and acknowledge, wherever possible, shared premises, such as the undesirability of unprincipled judicial activism.

Professor Calabresi identifies three major problems with the book. First, he argues that "Professors Seidman and Tushnet do not make a remotely persuasive historical or jurisprudential case that the New Deal actually effected the kind of constitutional revolution that they claim it accomplished. This book contains very little history and very little discussion of Supreme Court case law from the period between 1937 and the emergence of the Vinson Court. . . . By my count, only three of the forty-six cases cited and discussed in this book were decided during the New Deal period. In contrast, thirty-two of the cases cited and discussed date from the modern Burger Court or Rehnquist Court era."[57] Such "disproportion," in Professor Calabresi's opinion, "is really quite surprising," given the authors' "controversial and sweeping claims . . . that the New Deal abolished the state action requirement, abolished the public-private distinction even with respect to liberty rights, legitimized the use of the Constitution to enforce positive rights, and diminished greatly our ability to rely on background baseline distributions of common law entitlements. Applying this constitutionalism, they endorse with varying degrees of enthusiasm the notion that it is state action to 'assign' biological parents the right to raise their own children and that judicially mandated affirmative action, pornography regulation and campaign finance

---

[54] 426 U.S. 229, 96 S. Ct. 2040, 48 L. Ed. 2d 597 (1976).

[55] L. Seidman & M. Tushnet, *supra* note 46, at 188.

[56] *Id.* at 189.

[57] Stephen G. Calabresi, *The Crisis in Constitutional Theory,* 83 VA. L. REV. 247, 254 (1997).

laws may be constitutionally required. These are truly astounding and counterintuitive conclusions to even hint at in the absence of a sustained discussion—indeed in the absence of virtually any discussion of the New Deal Court's actual case law."[58]

Moreover, Professor Calabresi maintains that the New Deal era cases that are analyzed in the book are "susceptible to much narrower interpretations than those suggested by Professors Seidman and Tushnet."[59] For example, he believes *Miller v. Schoene,* 276 U.S. 272, 48 S. Ct. 246, 72 L. Ed. 568 (1928) "is easily understood as a modern application of traditional nuisance law principles. The infected cedar trees in that case were deemed to pose an immediate threat to the apple orchards. As such, they were a nuisance, and the apple orchard owners had a right to have the nuisance abated."[60]

Of even greater importance, Professor Calabresi argues, the Court's activism on behalf of economic rights (for example, in the takings area)[61] and on behalf of state autonomy threatened by the expansion of federal power (in the commerce clause area)[62] "mark[] the final end of New Deal constitutionalism . . . For decades now the Court has been marching in the exact opposite direction from the one that Professors Seidman and Tushnet favor. Negative liberties, baseline entitlements and the public-private distinction are stamped all over the Court's emerging case law, and the trend is accelerating even with the arrival of the new Clinton Justices . . . Not only is the Court refusing to embrace the positive social rights jurisprudence that Professors Tushnet and Seidman wrongly attribute to the New Deal, it is . . . rejecting the much more limited but still revolutionary doctrinal changes that the New Deal did usher in."[63] The Court's rejection of some of the more radical elements of New Deal constitutionalism suggests to Professor Calabresi that "there is no likelihood for the foreseeable future that any member of the Supreme Court will write an opinion in a case like *DeShaney* like the opinion that Professors Seidman and Tushnet say . . . ought to have [been] written."[64]

In the remainder of his review, Professor Calabresi sets forth his other main critiques of Professors Seidman's and Tushnet's arguments in REMNANTS OF BELIEF. Calabresi, 83 VA. L. REV. at 261–66:

> My second critique of this book concerns the authors' misperception of the limits on the judicial role. In many places, the authors seem to hold out a faint though dwindling hope that the United States Supreme Court can actually act under some circumstances as a force for radical social change. They acknowledge that change may often be difficult to achieve legislatively, and they are skeptical that this Court is ever likely to do as much as they want done, but, they hold out hope nonetheless. They conclude with a skeptical view that leaves them simultaneously doubting and hoping that constitutional law and rhetoric could be revived as a transformative and unifying force in American society.
>
> It is important to be clear that the kind of radical constitutional and social change that Professors Seidman and Tushnet hope for greatly

---

[58] *Id.*

[59] *Id.* at 255.

[60] *Id.*

[61] *See e.g.* Nollan v. California Coastal Comm'n, 483 U.S. 825, 107 S. Ct. 3141, 97 L. Ed. 2d 677 (1987).

[62] *See e.g.* United States v. Lopez, 514 U.S. 549, 115 S. Ct. 1624, 131 L. Ed. 2d 626 (1995).

[63] Calabresi, *supra* note 57, at 260.

[64] *Id.* at 260–61.

exceeds anything that is currently the subject of political debate in this country. When politicians argue nowadays about judges legislating from the bench, the argument is usually about the legitimacy of judicially imposed protections for abortion rights, gay rights, or the rights of secular individuals to be free from religious speech and symbolism. No one in the mainstream of American politics today even imagines the judicial legislation of "positive" constitutional rights of the kind Professors Seidman and Tushnet contemplate. The use of the courts as engines for radical social change in this country has hitherto been limited to the sphere of expanding—illegitimately, in my view—negative constitutional liberties. No one in the political realm—or in the judiciary itself—has ever advocated anything that remotely resembles the kind of judicially imposed social change that Professors Seidman and Tushnet imply is possible.

There is, I think, a very good reason for that. The ideas that Professors Seidman and Tushnet advocate have only very limited support in the political institutions of the American government. Recent trends, as reflected in the repeal of a sixty-year New Deal era welfare entitlement, suggest that, to the extent there is a trend, the era of positive entitlements from government is receding, not advancing. Under these circumstances judicial imposition of very radical social change would only be conceivable if the nature of the federal courts was such that one could plausibly imagine the existence of a huge "policy-making" space between the judiciary and the political branches of the government. But there is absolutely no reason whatsoever to imagine that a "policy-making" space as huge as the one that Professors Seidman and Tushnet contemplate could ever come to exist.

The federal courts have never historically been as out of sync with the political branches as the authors' thesis would require here. There is a good reason for this. Federal judges are confirmed by the Senate after presidential nomination and after a process of intensive scrutiny by interest groups, the press, and the FBI and Justice Department. This process is highly adversarial and political, and it resembles nothing so much as an indirect election to high office. With the Supreme Court, the process of indirect election is especially brutal. With rare exceptions, only the blandest and most unthreatening individuals survive to pass through this gauntlet.

In theory those who are confirmed have life tenure and can thus break free to do whatever they would like. In practice, there are countless external constraints on the federal judiciary, even aside from the lifetime habits of caution that must be internalized by those who would climb to the top. First, it takes five votes on the Supreme Court to win even a single case and coalitions of Justices can be hard to hold together over time. Second, when one judicial faction starts to get close to five votes, the political process often reacts and prevents the appointment of additional Justices who would cement a majority for any positions that deviate in more than a trivial way from what a majority of the general public wants. Third, even radical Supreme Court majority decisions require lower federal court and state court support for their implementation. When that support is lacking, as to some extent it was for illegitimate reasons after *Brown v. Board of Education* [72] the Supreme Court's initiative cannot be implemented. Lastly, the Justices are enmeshed in media, governmental, legal and other social networks that wear down judicial values that deviate too sharply from the mainstream. For all of these reasons, it is extremely unlikely that judges or Supreme Court Justices would ever have an opinion about something as important as positive constitutional

---

[72] 347 U.S. 483 (1954).

rights unless that position were also shared by a majority of senators and by most presidents.

These points were made in a more comprehensive fashion many decades ago by Yale Political Science Professor Robert Dahl. [73] After reviewing the history, Professor Dahl recalled only one extended divergence in views between the Court and Congress over a matter of national policy in American history. That divergence—over the child labor issue—was minor in comparison to the kind of divergence that would have to happen for the Seidman-Tushnet thesis to prove true. There is simply no historical or political science reason for thinking that transformative social change of the kind the authors hope for could ever come out of the Supreme Court. . . .

My final critique of this book grows out of its description of constitutional discourse and of the problem that legal commentators now allegedly face in the wake of the New Deal. First, I disagree with the book's thesis that constitutional discourse is now unusually divisive and confused because of the New Deal revolution. Implicit in this thesis is the notion that once upon a time there was a golden age of constitutional law when everyone agreed upon judicial philosophy, baseline assumption or the limits on the judicial role.

This notion, however, is obviously false. No such golden age ever occurred. From the decision in *Chisholm v. Georgia* [76] to the Marshall Court era to the decision in *Dred Scott v. Sandford* [77] to the decision in *Lochner v. New York* [78] to the New Deal crisis to *Brown v. Board of Education* and *Roe v. Wade,* the history of the Supreme Court has been one long story of constant controversy and public disagreement. Constitutional argument and conflict is a venerable American tradition. The constitutional opinions of Supreme Court Justices do not unite us as a people; rather, they give us something to argue and disagree about.

If anything, the cacophony of American constitutional discourse over the last two hundred years suggests that it is not constitutional rhetoric that unites us; it is our collective, social ability to see ourselves and our views in the Constitution when they are not there that unites us. Professor Henry Monaghan has regretted what he described as our tendency to idealize and romanticize the Constitution. [79] This tendency is no doubt exacerbated by the fact that most views with any significant political support in American society usually get reflected in the constitutional opinions and rhetoric of at least one Supreme Court Justice. Other less politically popular views often get picked up and popularized in constitutional form by some prominent law professor. The end result is that the constitutional reflection of the whole range of our political disagreements is usually available to all citizens whether they are moderate Democrats, moderate Republicans, social conservatives, social liberals, economic libertarians, or Marxists.

The Constitution then unites us not because it draws us together in overcoming our political differences. It unites us because all of us seem to be able to see in it some reflection of ourselves and of our views, even when they are not there. This Rorschach-like quality of constitutional discourse may serve a social purpose by permitting everyone, even marginal outsiders, to perceive themselves as belonging to the polity in

---

[73] Robert A. Dahl, *Decision-Making in a Democracy: The Supreme Court as a National Policy-Maker,* 6 J. Pub. L. 279 (1957).

[76] 2 U.S. (2 Dall.) 419 (1793).

[77] 60 U.S. (19 How.) 393 (1857).

[78] 198 U.S. 45 (1905).

[79] Henry P. Monaghan, *Our Perfect Constitution* 56 N.Y.U. L. Rev. 353 (1981).

a way that they would not do in the absence of constitutional law. This assuredly was not the reason the Framers wrote down and gave us a written Constitution, though it is the reason they gave us a short and very general text. It may, however, be one reason why the Constitution continues to fascinate us and command our loyalties. Perhaps it particularly explains the fascination of the Constitution for law professors. Maybe law professors are to an unusual degree narcissists who just enjoy looking at something that is easily turned into a reflection of oneself?

The question persists, however, as to just how socially useful is the whole enterprise of turning the Constitution into a reflection of oneself. Admittedly, it is fun, but is there any redeeming social or intellectual value in the whole enterprise? If there is, does that value depend on there being a reasonable chance that some future Supreme Court will buy aspects of one's pet constitutional theory? Or is it enough to say that merely spinning the theory makes the theorist and his readers feel good? What, in short, should be the purpose of constitutional theory properly conceived?

I have no doubt that advocacy constitutional scholarship serves important social purposes whether it is confined to one concrete issue or whether it is allowed to range more broadly. Such scholarship is of the most value when it helps an emerging constitutional consensus take shape after a period of major change. From time to time, new national majority coalitions come to dominate the Supreme Court giving the Justices and scholars who speak in constitutional rhetoric for those new coalitions an important role in building transitions and in maintaining continuity from the old to the new. They can help legitimize change and also tame it. The social value of this kind of constitutional rhetoric is clear, although its intellectual value is much more doubtful.

Conversely, other scholars and Justices may perform a socially valuable role by forging a new jurisprudence of dissent. Such a jurisprudence can be valuable both as an alternative paradigm to the majority paradigm should the latter fail and as a point of challenge to the majority paradigm which will help keep the majority "honest." Such a dissenting jurisprudence may also be of value socially but not intellectually, given that doctrinal manipulation of a constitutional system with multiple sources of authority poses little intellectual challenge. Moreover, dissenting constitutional arguments (like majority constitutional arguments) may matter intensely for the outcome of one case or one legal issue where different accounts of that case or issue do or do not fit into the reigning constitutional paradigms and can be outcome determinative.

But what about the social value of radical constitutional scholarship or theorizing? What social value is there to radically libertarian, Christian or Marxist constitutional theories? These are theories that are very unlikely ever to be adopted in their entirety by any American Supreme Court, at least at any time soon. It seems to me that these theories may have some social value both as prods to more majoritarian theories and as rallying points for small social minorities who want to feel a sense of social belonging and kinship with their fellow citizens. The value of these theories to constitutional law may roughly parallel the value of third parties to our political process. In both cases, competing radical paradigms are offered which may sometimes sway the mainstream paradigms and which may, even more rarely, occasionally displace the mainstream paradigms. Here too the social but not the intellectual value of constitutional scholarship seems clear.

By now one might well be inclined to ask two additional questions: First, is there any kind of constitutional scholarship that is intellectually valuable as well as socially valuable; and second, why do I agree with Professors Seidman and Tushnet that we are currently experiencing a crisis in our constitutional theorizing?

. . . I think there is a kind of constitutional scholarship that is intellectually valuable: the positive analysis and study of the behavior of our governmental institutions, structures and rules to understand both how they actually work and under what circumstances they seem to work especially well. The Supreme Court and the inferior federal courts are among the primary objects of this study, but at least as much attention should be given to Congress, the executive branch, the various instrumentalities of the state governments, our political parties, the media, and many other relevant private and quasi-private social institutions.

. . .

Why then do I agree with Professors Seidman and Tushnet that constitutional theory is now in a state of crisis? To some extent this is simply a matter of personal observation and conversation. Law professors, judges, lawyers and law students with whom I talk see less value in constitutional scholarship today than they did twenty-five years ago, or than they see today in other forms of writing by legal academics. I think this is just a fact which Professors Seidman and Tushnet are right to note, but which they are wrong to attribute to the post-New Deal crisis that they say is at fault.

No, I think the real explanation for the loss in prestige of constitutional scholarship is that it has become a heavily normative body of advocacy scholarship targeted at the federal courts with the goal of influencing them to do things that they are extremely unlikely to do in the current political and social climate. One risk of writing things that continually lobby for outcomes from an institution that will unlikely be provided by that institution is that people will eventually stop reading and stop listening. I think even much of the best of our current constitutional theorizing may be rapidly approaching that danger point. We may be on the verge of living with a body of constitutional theory that has no practical relevance, no explanatory power, no ability to provide guidance for altering future behavior, and that serves no apparent purpose other than to give small social groups and viewpoints a sense of belonging.

Recently, in a book entitled TAKING THE CONSTITUTION AWAY FROM THE COURTS,[65] Professor Tushnet turned his attention not only to the challenge posed by Professor Calabresi to examine more closely the constitutional decisionmaking of political actors but also to the question whether the time had come to abandon the institution of judicial review altogether. For Tushnet, these questions are related. The major theme of the book is Tushnet's explanation of the reasons for his proposal to abandon judicial review. He suggests replacing the "elitist" approach of judicial review, established by Chief Justice Marshall's opinion in *Marbury v. Madison* with what he calls "populist constitutional law."[66] Under Tushnet's scheme, the judiciary would still solve ordinary legal disputes, but the Constitution would become a creature of the people's representatives, its meaning no more or less than "what a majority of Congress says it is." Tushnet knows his proposal will be greeted as heresy by liberals, but he is convinced that their devotion to judicial review is misplaced.[67] After all, even those rulings that liberals most revere

---

[65] MARK V. TUSHNET, TAKING THE CONSTITUTION AWAY FROM THE COURTS (1999).

[66] *Id.* at 186.

[67] In particular, Professor Tushnet believes

have made little difference by themselves. Segregation in the south yielded in the end not to the decision in *Brown v. Board of Education* but to the civil-rights legislation of the 1960s; and *Roe v. Wade* though overturning abortion laws throughout the states, was decided as it was only because it reflected the "latent" wishes of a majority of Americans.[68] "Looking at judicial review over the course of U.S. history," Tushnet writes, the courts have generally been "in line with what the dominant national political coalition wants."[69]

More fundamentally, Tushnet finds something perverse in giving a small, isolated group of jurists the authority to decide the most controversial issues faced by a democratic society. In such cases, he asserts, the Court usually relies on its "all-things-considered" judgment, weighing today's needs against the demands of history and precedent. Professor Tushnet rejects the notion that there is anything that uniquely qualifies the Court to undertake this task.

At the end of his book, Professor Tushnet suggests that the people and their elected representatives can do at least as good a job at protecting the fundamental guarantees of what Professor Tushnet refers to as "the thin Constitution"[70] as the Court ever did or could do. He argues that this "populist" vision of the Constitution is sounder and posits the possibility of more principled constitutional decisionmaking than either liberal or conservative theory allows. MARK V. TUSHNET, TAKING THE CONSTITUTION AWAY FROM THE COURTS 186–87 (1999):[71]

> Populist constitutional law returns constitutional law to the people, acting through politics. Just as judges can, the people can give wrong answers to important questions. Populist constitutional law offers no guarantees that we will end up with progressive political results. But, of course, neither does elitist constitutional law.
>
> Contemporary constitutional discourse is torn between two poles. Liberals have an impulse to treat all political issues as ultimately constitutional. If an issue is important enough, liberals think, surely the Constitution tells us what to do about it. The criterion of *importance* allows liberals to assert that they reserve a domain for politics. Unfortunately, applying that criterion simply brings out contemporary liberalism's limits. The defense budget is important in a colloquial sense, but it is not *fundamental* in the special constitutional sense that liberals use. But why not? Because liberals either really do not think it that important, or because they believe that courts will not try to regulate the defense budget. For liberals, however, judicial reluctance is a contingent historical fact: They would constitutionalize the defense budget if they could persuade enough judges that controlling the defense budget was really important.
>
> Mark Graber has argued, against liberal constitutional theorists, that their willingness to develop ingenious constitutional arguments supporting a woman's right to choose with respect to abortion must be coupled

---

that the impetus for liberals' resistance to his proposal is not just their misplaced faith in the institution of judicial review but also their basic mistrust of popular majorities. *See id.* at 177–81.

[68] *Id.* at 147.

[69] *Id.* at 153.

[70] Professor Tushnet explains that the "thin Constitution" is the core principle of the Declaration of Independence—"the principle that all people were created equal, the principle that all had inalienable rights." *Id.* at 11.

[71] Copyright © 1999 by Princeton University Press. Reprinted by permission of Princeton University Press.

with their unwillingness to develop constitutional arguments supporting poor people's rights to the material goods essential for minimal well-being.[23] Graber shows that liberal constitutional theory has the *intellectual* resources sufficient for the latter task, but its adherents apparently lack the *political* will to make the effort.

The boundary liberals draw between the Constitution and politics either exposes contemporary liberalism's limits or ultimately dissolves. Liberals leave no domain for a principled, constitutional politics.

Contemporary conservatives have the same problem, although it arises in a different way. If liberals have an impulse to constitutionalize everything, conservatives have an impulse to deconstitutionalize everything. The heart of contemporary conservative constitutional discourse is advocacy of judicial restraint and opposition to judicial activism. True, conservatives leave room for judicial review in the service of the original understandings of the Constitution's provisions. They have rarely done well in explaining to people who do not share their prior political commitments exactly what those understandings were and, more important, how we ought to apply those understandings in the different circumstances of contemporary life.

The central rhetorical move of contemporary conservative constitutional discourse is this: "The Constitution does not say anything about X—abortion, the right to die, or whatever. It therefore leaves it up to our democratically elected legislatures to decide what to do about X."[26] When pushed, conservatives might even give up on restrictive definitions of X, and would go along with saying, "The Constitution does not say anything about affirmative action either." The conservative position leaves no room for a principled politics in either version.

For both liberals and conservatives, then, we have a principled Constitution, where courts rule, and unprincipled politics, where the mere preferences of democratic majorities rule. The only disagreement is where to draw the line (and, to some liberals, whether there is any space left for politics at all).

Populist constitutional law is different. It creates space for a politics oriented by the Declaration's principles by taking constitutional law away from the courts. Such a politics actually can have real bite, but no one can guarantee that it will produce specific results.

In a review of Professor Tushnet's book,[72] Chief Judge Richard Posner assesses the merits of the arguments of Tushnet and other "skeptics" (including Jack Balkin, Michael Klarman, Richard Parker, Robert Bork, and Sandy Levinson) against judicial supremacy or preserving judicial review. He suggests that while it is highly unlikely the Court would ever agree to abandon the practice or that an amendment would be enacted that would outlaw it, the arguments used by Tushnet and others against judicial review are

---

[23] Graber, [*The Clintonification of American Law: Abortion, Welfare, and Liberal Constitutional Theory*, 58 OHIO STATE L.J. 731 (1997)].

[26] For a dramatically contrary illustration, see Justice Scalia's opinion for the Court in Printz v. United States, 117 S. Ct. 2365 (1997), which held unconstitutional a provision in the Brady Handgun Violence Prevention Act. Justice Scalia's opinion stated early on, "Because there is no constitutional text speaking to this precise question, the answer . . . must be sought in historical understanding and practice, in the structure of the Constitution, and in the jurisprudence of this Court." Had the case raised a question about abortion rights, the sentence would surely have ended, "we have nothing further to say about the claim."

[72] RICHARD A. POSNER, APPEAL AND CONSENT, THE NEW REPUBLIC, Aug. 16, 1999, at 36.

important to examine in order to determine whether the arguments have sufficient merit to lead courts to become more "hesitant, at the very least, to exercise the power of judicial review."[73] Based on his review of the arguments made by Tushnet against judicial review (including that there are times, such as during the impeachment proceedings, when the Court is not involved but people and Congress still take the Constitution seriously) and those traditionally made in favor of it (such as that the Court, unlike legislators in the course of ordinary lawmaking, operates more insulated from public pressure and is able to undertake more deliberate study of the issues before it), Judge Posner concludes that it is "inconclusive" whether judicial review is ultimately a good or bad thing for society.[74] Moreover, he suggests there are clear cases (such as *Roe v. Wade, Baker v. Carr,* and *Griswold v. Connecticut*) in which, contrary to Tushnet's assertion, judicial review has made a difference—those cases involving laws that "would have been enacted, at the same time and the same form, had there been no power of judicial review, and—such is the inertia of legislative power—they would have lasted longer, in some cases much longer, had the Court not exercised [its] power to strike them down."[75] There are also cases in which it is unclear whether the absence of judicial review would have made a difference—"those in which legislation was passed in the teeth of the Constitution . . . We do not know whether in the absence of judicial review Congress would still have passed such constitutionally questionable laws."[76] There are still other cases, decided during "periods of real threat to constitutional values, [when] the Court tends to take a back seat, and . . . other times—the present time, for example, its constitutional interventions tend simply to impede efforts to experiment with solutions to social problems," such as the prohibitions against hate speech and internet indecency.[77] "The experiments may be wrong, but we will never know if they are snuffed out before the results are known."[78] Another important question to ask before abandoning judicial review is "in cases in which judicial review has made a difference . . . whether these cases, taken all in all, have made the nation better off in some sense on which most people agree."[79] Judge Posner admits that answering this question is a "daunting task," but insists it should be explored before deciding to abandon the institution of judicial review.[80] Nevertheless, Judge Posner concludes that "[t]he great value of the work of the skeptics is not that they have 'proved' that judicial review is a bad thing on balance, or that their writings will inspire a movement to amend the Constitution to abrogate that power. It is that they have undermined the complacent belief that judicial review is unequivocally a good thing. They have challenged the believers to make a better case; and if the believers fail to do so, the result may be to make the judiciary more sensitive to the dangers to society of throwing its weight around in the name of judicial review . . ."[81]

---

[73] *Id.*

[74] *Id.* at 37.

[75] *Id.*

[76] *Id.* at 38.

[77] *Id.*

[78] *Id.*

[79] *Id.*

[80] *Id.*

[81] *Id.*

§ 8.04   Conclusion

Lest one think that the critiques of liberal constitutional theory have leveled it, one should recognize that more than a few liberal theorists still view the New Deal Court and especially the Warren Court as embodying the ideal of constitutional adjudication. One such scholar is Mark Graber, a political scientist at the University of Maryland. In the final excerpt from TAKING THE CONSTITUTION AWAY FROM THE COURTS, Professor Tushnet refers to Professor Graber's critique of liberal theorists for defending abortion but not welfare rights. In the final reading for this chapter, consider the likely reception of Professor Graber's "clarion call" at the end of his article for liberal theorists to reconsider the need for judicial activism on behalf of welfare rights. Mark A. Graber, *The Clintonification of American Law: Abortion, Welfare, and Liberal Constitutional Theory*, 58 OHIO ST. L.J. 731, 813–18 (1997):[82]

Many leading constitutional theorists advocate doctrines that would require elected officials to take a second look at constitutionally question-able practices. Constitutional errors, in this view, frequently result from the pressures inherent in the legislative process rather than from malevo-lence or interpretive mistakes. Dean (now Judge) Guido Calabresi points out that "[l]egislators often act hastily or thoughtlessly with respect to fundamental rights because of panic or crises or because, more often, they are simply pressed for time."[445] The constitutional harms that result from these legislative failings can be mitigated, however, if courts assume that elected officials have authorized some action that may trench on constitutional liberties only when that authorization is clearly stated on the face of the legislation under constitutional attack. Sandy Levinson, in 1989, suggested that the courts use the Ninth Amendment to require legislatures to take a second look at any government practice that may violate what the Court believes to be fundamental human rights.[447] Judicial review in these instances does not proclaim to the world that elected officials have made a constitutional mistake. Legislators retain the power to reenact the constitutionally controversial policy, as long as they do so explicitly. These commentators simply insist that given the importance of the values at stake, courts should make certain that legislative action is based on a more deliberate and self-conscious weigh-ing of important constitutional considerations than appears to have taken place previously.

This Article suggests that liberal constitutional theorists should take a similar second look at their present constitutional commitments. Dworkin, Tribe, and other pro-choice constitutionalists may have good justifications for emphasizing abortion rights at the expense of welfare rights. The problem is that too little public debate has taken place over the present priorities of liberal theory. Some constitutional commentators may be "act[ing] hastily or thoughtlessly with respect to fundamental [welfare] rights," particularly in light of the reasons that might warrant a greater liberal concern with the constitutional rights of poor people. Liberals committed to a "republic of reasons"[451] owe impoverished citizens a more convincing explanation of why the Constitution contains a judicially enforceable right to abortion, but no judicially enforceable

---

[445] Calabresi, [*Foreword: Antidiscrimina-tion and Constitutional Accountability (What the Bork-Brennan Debate Ignores)*, 105 HARV. L. REV. 80, 103–04 (1991)].

[447] *See* Sanford Levinson, *Constitutional Rhetoric and the Ninth Amendment*, 64 CHI.-KENT L. REV. 131, 157–59 (1988) . . .

[451] Sunstein, [THE PARTIAL CONSTITUTION 17 (1993)].

right to welfare, survival income, or basic necessities. At the very least, liberal constitutional theorists should detail at greater length whether they really believe that abortion has stronger textual, historical, or precedential foundations (before and after 1970) than welfare rights, whether they believe that tactical considerations presently compel liberals to concentrate on abortion rather than welfare, or whether, at bottom, they believe that abortion rights are more fundamental than welfare rights.

This second look may result in more explicit, superior justifications for present liberal priorities. A fuller exegesis might demonstrate that abortion rights have deeper roots than welfare rights in the American constitutional tradition or that sound institutional reasons warrant federal judicial protection for abortion rights but not welfare rights. Some liberal constitutional theorists may even confess that they have rejected the philosophical tenets underlying the Great Society, that although they think abortion is a fundamental human right, they believe that no person in an affluent society has a fundamental human right to basic necessities. This understanding of human rights may be terribly mistaken. Still, such a moral distinction between abortion and welfare rights would provide a principled justification for the present commitments of liberal constitutional theory.

Liberal theorists who take a second look at their constitutional priorities may also conclude that welfare rights are at least as fundamental as abortion rights. No liberal philosopher thinks that abortion rights are more important than welfare rights. Welfare rights are at least as well grounded in the American constitutional tradition as abortion rights. Judicial enforcement of a right to livelihood would not require different constitutional remedies than those liberals presently favor in other areas of constitutional law. Recent precedent does provide far stronger constitutional grounds for abortion rights than welfare rights. Constitutional theorists, however, should not adjust their more fundamental principles to correspond with what they believe are erroneously decided cases. Adherence to stare decisis is particularly unwarranted when the mistaken rulings violate constitutional integrity by privileging rights that advance elite interests at the expense of equally valid constitutional rights that further the life prospects of less fortunate persons. Scholars who believe the Constitution protects welfare rights should feel no more constrained by such recent precedent as *Dandridge* and *Rodriguez* than the Supreme Court in *Brown* felt constrained by *Plessy v. Ferguson* [456] and *Gong Lum v. Rice.* [457] Given the recent run of judicial decisions adverse to welfare rights, liberal constitutional commentators might urge the Supreme Court to develop a more supportive line of precedent before explicitly declaring a constitutional right to welfare. The Hughes, Stone, and Vinson Courts, after all, first established a more supportive line of precedent before ruling that separate was not constitutionally equal. [458] A truly liberal constitutional theory, however, would not use present judicial hostility as an excuse for abandoning work on the foundations of an American constitutional universe in which all persons are guaranteed meaningful access to basic necessities.

The American law of fundamental constitutional rights is fast approaching a normatively unstable impasse. On the one hand, the Supreme Court is protecting a fundamental right to abortion and is not likely to

---

[456] 163 U.S. 537 (1896), *overruled by Brown v. Board of Educ.,* 347 U.S. 483 (1954).

[457] 275 U.S. 78 (1927) (holding that Asian-Americans are not constitutionally entitled to attend a white-only school).

[458] *See* McLaurin v. Oklahoma State Regents for Higher Educ., 339 U.S. 637 (1950); Sweatt v. Painter, 339 U.S. 629 (1950); Sipuel v. Board of Regents, 332 U.S. 631 (1948); Missouri ex rel. Gaines v. Canada, 305 U.S. 337 (1938).

abandon that protection in the foreseeable future. On the other hand, the justices in every area of law not closely associated with gender or the sexual revolution seem increasingly unwilling to recognize any fundamental right not specifically grounded in constitutional history or the constitutional text.[459] Chief Justice Rehnquist, Justice O'Connor, Justice Scalia, and, somewhat surprisingly, Justice Ginsberg, in 1994, explicitly asserted that they would be "reluctant to expand the concept of substantive due process because the guideposts for responsible decisionmaking in this unchartered area are scarce and open-ended."[460] "The protection of substantive due process," the Court continued, "has for the most part been accorded to matters relating to marriage, family, procreation, and the right to bodily integrity."[461] In short, liberal theories of constitutional interpretation presently seem good only for the family of cases closely associated with *Roe*. American law evaluates other claims of fundamental constitutional rights using far more conservative methods of constitutional interpretation.[462]

This status quo violates constitutional integrity. If, properly interpreted, the Constitution does not protect any fundamental right that lacks specific constitutional roots, then the judiciary should move to *Roe* or provide some other grounding for the constitutionality of legal abortion.[463] If, however, *Roe* was correctly decided, then the fundamental rights reasoning of that decision cannot consistently be confined only to the constitutional law of privacy. Constitutional commentators and authorities living in a constitutional universe that considers *Roe* to be a valid precedent must ask what other fundamental rights can be justified using the same constitutional modalities that justify judicial solicitude for abortion rights. Liberals who believe welfare rights enjoy the same philosophical and historical support as abortion rights, therefore, should forthwith develop constitutional theories in which rights to basic necessities play as central a role as abortion rights.

This normatively unstable status quo, unfortunately, may be a political equilibrium point. In a political universe where money talks louder than

---

[459] *See* Albright v. Oliver, 510 U.S. 266 (1994) (finding no constitutional right to be free from malicious prosecution); Reno v. Flores, 507 U.S. 292 (1993) (holding that children of aliens have no constitutional right to have the state determine whether they would be better off in public or private custody); Collins v. City of Shaker Heights, 503 U.S. 115 (1992) (holding that government employees have no constitutional right to be warned about potentially fatal hazards in their workplace); Michael H. v. Gerald D., 491 U.S. 110 (1989) (holding that a natural father has no constitutional right to visit a child born to a mother married at the time to another man); DeShaney v. Winnebago County Dep't of Soc. Servs., 489 U.S. 189 (1989) (holding that children have no constitutional right to be protected against private violence, even when government officials are aware or should be aware that child abuse is taking place).

[460] *Albright*, 510 U.S. at 271–72 (quoting *Collins*, 503 U.S. at 125).

[461] *Id.* at 272.

[462] *See Michael H.*, 491 U.S. at 121 30; *Collins*, 503 U.S. at 124–30; *Reno*, 507 U.S. at 301–05; *Albright*, 510 U.S. at 271–75; *see also* Raoul Berger, *Liberty and the Constitution* 29 GA. L. REV. 585, 593–94 (1995) (discussing how "the Court . . . is putting the brakes on fresh claims of rights unknown to the law").

[463] Claims that bans on abortion violate the equal protection rights of women are likely to prove equally problematic. The persons responsible for the Fourteenth Amendment did not intend to prohibit laws discriminating against women. *See* Earl M. Maltz, *The Constitution and Nonracial Discrimination: Alienage, Sex, and the Framers' Ideal of Equality* 7 CONST. COMMENTARY 251, 266–82 (1990). Moreover, flat bans on abortion do not violate equal protection in a traditional sense because such measures do not give men legal rights denied to women. Thus, feminists who oppose welfare rights must explain why equal protection should be interpreted liberally in gender cases, but strictly construed when poor people claim violations of constitutional equality.

needs, the polity is likely to recognize those rights that affluent Republicans and affluent Democrats recognize, fight over those rights that affluent Republicans and affluent Democrats fight over, and exhibit little interest in those rights that fail to interest either affluent Republicans or affluent Democrats. Pro-choice concerns (other than funding) may thrive in this political culture because elites of all political persuasions tend to exhibit strong support for abortion on demand. Welfare rights are likely to receive little political attention because such issues do not appeal to politically crucial voters or investors. Constitutional theorists probably can do little to challenge this dreary political climate. Nonetheless, by convincing liberal lawyers that a commitment to *Roe* need not entail a commitment to a judicially enforceable right to basic necessities, Dworkin, Tribe, and other pro-choice constitutionalists provide a liberal veneer to a profoundly discriminatory regime.

Law review essays that cannot change the world dramatically may nevertheless influence legal consciousness. A greater focus on the rights of poor people might persuade existing and potential liberal federal justices that their support for abortion rights entails support for rights to basic necessities. Eisenhower justices, appointed to the Court because they supported the result in *Brown* [467] proved willing to support numerous other claims that they believed had equally valid constitutional foundations. Perhaps future justices appointed because they support *Roe* will prove more sympathetic to the equally valid constitutional rights of the poor.

Constitutional theories concerned with the rights of impoverished Americans might also inspire a second look at the too common practice in much contemporary legal literature of establishing authority by declaring victim status. [468] Hierarchies exist in the legal academy as they do elsewhere. "Untouchables" in the law professorate, however, enjoy privileges that the overwhelming majority of persons on this planet cannot even dream of. Elite law professors who pose as "outsiders" risk confusing the interests of the least high-and-mighty with those who are truly low-and-powerless. Liberal abortion policies and bans on hate speech or pornography, in their writings, tend to replace food and shelter as basic needs. These priorities may be shared by upwardly mobile law students, but probably seem perverse to those persons who clean law offices and restrooms for a fraction of the pay that first year lawyers and academics command. A constitutional theory that focused on the rights of persons who live in the streets and beg for scraps of garbage to eat might remind us that—contrary to what we sometimes read in our journals—law professors, law students, and even political scientists are not the wretched of the earth.

---

[467] *See* Michael A. Kahn, *Shattering the Myth About President Eisenhower's Supreme Court Appointments*, 22 PRESIDENTIAL STUD. Q. 47, 47 (1992) (using "a discussion of each of Eisenhower's five appointments to the Supreme Court" to demonstrate how "Eisenhower [or, more accurately, the Eisenhower Justice Department] clearly and undeniably attempted to influence the Supreme Court in the direction of entrenching *Brown*").

[468] For a good collection of some leading works of so-called "outsider scholarship," see MARI J. MATSUDA ET AL., WORDS THAT WOUND: CRITICAL RACE THEORY, ASSAULTIVE SPEECH, AND THE FIRST AMENDMENT (1993).

§ 8.05 Bibliography

[A] Commentaries on the Liberal Activism of the Warren Court

Charles Black, *The Unfinished Business of the Warren Court,* 46 WASH. L. REV. 3 (1970).

Archibald Cox, THE WARREN COURT: CONSTITUTIONAL DECISION AS AN INSTRUMENT OF REFORM (1968).

Owen Fiss, *Dombrowski,* 86 YALE L.J. 1103 (1977).

Frank M. Johnson, Jr., *In Defense of Judicial Activism,* 28 EMORY L.J. 901 (1979).

Douglas Laycock, *Federal Interference With State Prosecutions: The Cases Dombrowski Forgot,* 46 U. CHI. L. REV. 636 (1979).

Suzanna Sherry, *All the Supreme Court Really Needs to Know It Learned from the Warren Court,* 50 VAND. L. REV. 459 (1997) (with comments by Rebecca Brown and Barry Friedman).

J. Skelly Wright, *Professor Bickel, the Scholarly Tradition, and the Supreme Court,* 84 HARV. L. REV. 769 (1971).

J. Skelly Wright, *The Judicial Right and the Rhetoric of Restraint: A Defense of Judicial Activism in an Age of Conservative Judge,* 14 HASTINGS CONST. L.Q. 487 (1987).

[B] Commentaries on the Liberalism of the Burger Court

THE COUNTER-REVOLUTION THAT WASN'T (V. Blasi ed., 1983).

Robert Nagel, *On Complaining About the Burger Court* (Book Review), 84 COLUM. L. REV. 2068 (1984).

Gene R. Nichol, Jr., *An Activism of Ambivalence* (Book Review), 98 HARV. L. REV. 315 (1984).

[C] Commentaries on Liberalism's Turn to History

Barry Friedman & Scott B. Smith, *The Sedimentary Constitution* 147 U. PA. L. REV. 1 (1997).

Stephen Griffin, *Legal Liberalism at Yale* (reviewing Laura Kalman, THE STRANGE CAREER OF LEGAL LIBERALISM (1996)), 14 CONST. COMM. 535 (1997).

Stephen Griffin, AMERICAN CONSTITUTIONALISM: FROM THEORY TO POLITICS (1996).

Nomi Maya Stolzenberg, *A Book of Laughter and Forgetting: Kalman's "Strange Career" and the Marketing of Civic Republicanism* (reviewing Kalman, THE STRANGE CAREER OF LEGAL LIBERALISM (1996)), 111 HARV. L. REV. 1025 (1998).

[D] Commentaries on the Status and Future of Liberal Constitutional Adjudication, Politics, and Theory

Sotorios A. Barber, THE CONSTITUTION OF JUDICIAL POWER (1993).

Stephen Gardbaum, *Liberalism, Autonomy, and Moral Conflict,* 48 STAN. L. REV. 385 (1996).

Linda R. Hirshman, *The Virtue of Liberality in American Communal Life,* 88 MICH. L. REV. 983 (1990).

Stephen Holmes, PASSIONS AND CONSTRAINT: ON THE THEORY OF LIBERAL DEMOCRACY (1995).

LAW AND LIBERALISM IN THE 1980s (V. Blasi ed. 1991) (with essays by J. Skelly Wright, Anthony Lewis, Abram Chayes, Charles L. Black, Jr., Sanford H. Kadish, Cass R. Sunstein, and Anthony Lester).

Thomas K. Lindsay, *Defending Liberalism* (Book Review of Holmes, PASSIONS AND CONSTRAINT: ON THE THEORY OF LIBERAL DEMOCRACY (1995), 82 IOWA L. REV. 943 (1997).

Stephen Macedo, LIBERAL VIRTUES: CITIZENSHIP, VIRTUE, AND COMMUNITY IN LIBERAL CONSTITUTIONALISM (1990).

Frank I. Michelman, *Super Liberal: Romance, Community, and Tradition in William J. Brennan, Jr.'s Constitutional Thought,* 77 VA. L. REV. 1261 (1991).

Dan Ortiz, *Categorical Community,* 51 STAN. L. REV. 769 (1999).

H. Jefferson Powell, THE MORAL TRADITION IN AMERICAN CONSTITUTIONALISM: A THEOLOGICAL INTERPRETATION (1993).

John Rawls, POLITICAL LIBERALISM (1993).

Michael Sandel, *Political Liberalism* (reviewing Rawls, POLITICAL LIBERALISM (1993)), 107 HARV. L. REV. 1765 (1994).

Pierre Schlag, *The Empty Circles of Liberal Justification,* 96 MICH. L. REV. 1 (1997).

Cass R. Sunstein, THE PARTIAL CONSTITUTION (1993).

Cynthia V. Ward, *The Limits of "Liberal Republicanism": Why Group-Based Remedies and Republican Citizenship Don't Mix,* 91 COLUM. L. REV. 581 (1991).

Robin West, *The Ideal of Liberty: A Comment on* Michael H. v. Gerald D., 139 U. PA. L. REV. 1373 (1991); *The Supreme Court, 1989 Term— Foreword: Taking Freedom Seriously,* 104 HARV. L. REV. 43 (1990); *Progressive and Conservative Constitutionalism,* 88 MICH. L. REV. 641 (1990).

Steven L. Winter, *Indeterminacy and Incommensurability in Constitutional Law,* 78 Calif. L. Rev. 1441 (1990).

Michael Zuckert, *The New Rawls and Constitutional Theory: Does it Really Taste that Much Better?,* 11 CONST. COMMENTARY 227 (1994).

[E] Beyond Liberalism

Andrew Altman, CRITICAL LEGAL STUDIES: A LIBERAL CRITIQUE (1993).

Stephen Carter, *Constitutional Adjudication and the Indeterminate Text: A Preliminary Defense of an Imperfect Muddle,* 94 YALE L.J. 821 (1985).

Neal Devins, *The Interactive Constitution: An Essay on Clothing Emperors and Searching for Constitutional Truth* (reviewing Tushnet & Seidman, REMNANTS OF BELIEF (1996)), 85 GEO. L.J. 691 (1997).

Stephen Feldman, *The Persistence of Power and the Struggle for Dialogic Standards in Postmodern Constitutional Jurisprudence: Michelman, Habermas, and Civic Republicanism,* 81 GEO. L.J. 2243 (1993).

James E. Fleming & Linda C. McClain, *In Search of a Substantive Republic,* 76 TEX. L. REV. 509 (1997).

Michael J. Klarman, *The Puzzling Resistence to Process-Based Theories,* 77 VA. L. REV. 747 (1991).

Richard Parker, "HERE THE PEOPLE RULE": A CONSTITUTIONAL POPULIST MANIFESTO (1994).

Eric J. Segall, *The Skeptic's Constitution* (reviewing Tushnet & Seidman, REMNANTS OF BELIEF (1996), 44 UCLA L. REV. 1467 (1997).

Kenneth Ward, *The Allure and Danger of Community Values: A Criticism of Liberal Republican Constitutional Theory,* 24 HASTINGS CONST. L.Q. 171 (1996).

Robin West, PROGRESSIVE CONSTITUTIONALISM (1994).

Chapter 9

Conservative Constitutional Theory

§ 9.01 Introduction

This chapter presents materials that reflect a spectrum of views within conservative constitutional theory, which has gained much prominence in recent years. Like the term "liberalism," the term "conservatism" is used in both political and philosophical senses, and the author's intended usage is often ascertainable only from the context in which the term is used. These materials illustrate the large divisions within conservative ranks, which may not have received as much notice as they deserve. The emergence of divisions is a commonplace event after seemingly united coalitions gain power, and there may be a strong analogy here to the disagreements that arose within the liberal camp after the constitutional revolution of the late 1930s. Political liberals then had been critical of the economic activism of conservative Supreme Court Justices; all of President Franklin Roosevelt's appointees agreed on the constitutionality of New Deal economic measures. But they soon diverged in areas involving civil liberties, with some, like Justice Frankfurter, holding to judicial restraint and tending to remain deferential to the actions of the political branches and of state governments; others, like Justices Black and Douglas, found justification for a more active judicial role in cases involving Bill of Rights and similar claims.[1]

The conservative movement today seems to contain at least as many conflicting strains as old New Deal liberalism, and indeed may have less common ground in matters of constitutional theory. The strands in conservative thought are generally reflected in the degree to which conservative law professors and judges defer to each of the following in their constitutional interpretation: the plain language of the text of the Constitution or of a statute; the original intention of the document's framers; the decisions of the other branches of the federal government and of state governments; and judicial precedents. Other conservatives stress economic reasoning while still others emphasize "natural law" approaches. Some find themselves criticized even by their fellow conservatives for "moral skepticism." In addition, although one's general view on a methodological issue may be clear—such as tending to favor judicial restraint—the legacy of liberal precedents can make the application of that approach problematic: given a general conservative inclination to favor stability and respect precedent, would it be questionable activism now to overrule a liberal activist decision, such as *Miranda v. Arizona*[2] or *Roe v. Wade*?[3]

---

[1] *See, e.g.,* Melvin I. Urofsky, *Conflict Among the Brethren: Felix Frankfurter, William O. Douglas and the Clash of Personalities and Philosophies on the United States Supreme Court,* 1988 DUKE L.J. 71.

[2] 384 U.S. 436, 86 S. Ct. 1602, 16 L. Ed. 2d 694 (1966).

[3] 410 U.S. 113, 93 S. Ct. 705, 35 L. Ed. 2d 147 (1973).

The nature of the divisions within conservative constitutional theory poses several questions. In addition to identifying what seems to be the main themes, students should think about whether these theorists really have anything major in common. On *any* of the large issues of constitutional theory and method, do the readings in this chapter reflect a high degree of consensus among conservatives? Or do the readings indicate that these theorists lack even the sort of single rallying point that New Deal liberals had—namely, deferential approaches in economic regulation cases? It may be possible to identify some areas in which most conservatives would share leanings, such as a pro-prosecution orientation in criminal cases,[4] skepticism about sweeping egalitarian claims,[5] vigorous enforcement of separation of powers,[6] and pro-state positions on questions of federalism.[7] But these alignments may be contingent and less regular than one might expect,[8] and may not reflect broad

---

[4] *See, e.g.,* Payne v. Tennessee, 501 U.S. 808, 829–830, 111 S. Ct. 2597, 115 L. Ed. 2d 720 (1991) (in which Chief Justice Rehnquist and Justices O'Connor, Kennedy, and Souter joined in overruling two previous decisions in which the Court had barred the admission of victim impact statements in the sentencing phase of capital murder trials), *overruling* Booth v. Maryland, 482 U.S. 496, 107 S. Ct. 2529, 96 L. Ed. 2d 440 (1987), and South Carolina v. Gathers, 490 U.S. 805, 109 S. Ct. 2207, 104 L. Ed. 2d 876 (1989).

[5] *See, e.g.,* Adarand Constructors, Inc. v. Pena, 515 U.S. 200, 238–239, 115 S. Ct. 2097, 132 L. Ed. 2d 158 (1995) (striking down federal affirmative action program under strict scrutiny review); Bowers v. Hardwick, 478 U.S. 186, 195–196, 106 S. Ct. 2841, 92 L. Ed. 2d 140 (1986) (holding that there is no fundamental right for consenting adults to engage in homosexual sodomy); San Antonio v. Rodriguez, 411 U.S. 1, 58–59, 93 S. Ct. 1278, 36 L. Ed. 2d 16 (1973) (holding that there is no fundamental right to education).

[6] *See, e.g.,* Metropolitan Washington Airports Auth. v. Citizens for the Abatement of Aircraft Noise, 501 U.S. 252, 277, 111 S. Ct. 2298, 115 L. Ed. 2d 236 (1991) (striking down as violative of separation of powers the creation of a Board of Review partially composed of members of Congress with executive-like veto power over the decisions of the Metropolitan Washington Airports Authority); INS v. Chadha, 462 U.S. 919, 959, 103 S. Ct. 2764, 77 L. Ed. 2d 317 (1983) (treating a one-House veto of an INS administrative law judge's order suspending Chadha's deportation as an exercise of legislative authority, and finding it invalid because it failed to comport with the bicameral and presentment requirements for the enactment of statutes); Bowsher v. Synar, 478 U.S. 714, 736, 106 S. Ct. 3181, 92 L. Ed. 2d 583

(1986) (holding that Congress may not delegate executive functions to an official—the Comptroller General—over whom Congress has removal power).

[7] *See, e.g.,* Coleman v. Thompson, 501 U.S. 722, 726, 111 S. Ct. 2546, 115 L. Ed. 2d 640 (1991) (O'Connor, J., joined by Chief Justice Rehnquist and Justices White, Scalia, Kennedy, and Souter) (beginning opinion that holds day-late filing of notice of appeal in state court to bar federal court consideration of merits of death row prisoner's petition by stating, "This is a case about federalism."). *See also* College Sav. Bank v. Florida Prepaid Postsecondary Educ. Expense Bd., 527 U.S. 666, 119 S. Ct. 2219, 144 L. Ed. 2d 605 (1999) (holding that a state may not be regarded as having implicitly or constructively waived its 11th amendment sovereign immunity by participating in a federally regulated marketplace like any private business); Seminole Tribe v. Florida, 517 U.S. 44, 76, 116 S. Ct. 1114, 134 L. Ed. 2d 252 (1996) (holding that Congress' power to regulate interstate commerce does not entitle it to abrogate states' sovereign immunity under the 11th amendment).

[8] *See, e.g.,* Saenz v. Roe, 526 U.S. 489, 119 S. Ct. 1518, 143 L. Ed. 2d 689 (1999) (Justices Scalia, Kennedy, O'Connor, and Souter joining Justices Breyer, Stevens, and Ginsburg, in striking down as violating the Privileges or Immunities Clause of the Fourteenth Amendment a California law that limited the maximum welfare benefits for new residents); Texas v. Johnson, 491 U.S. 397, 420, 109 S. Ct. 2533, 105 L. Ed. 2d 342 (1989) (Justices Scalia and Kennedy joining Justices Brennan, Marshall, and Blackmun, in striking down on First Amendment grounds a Texas statute criminalizing flag-burning); Maryland v. Craig, 497 U.S. 836, 860, 110 S. Ct. 3157, 111 L. Ed. 2d 666 (1990) (Scalia, J., dissenting) (Justice

agreement about method. As students read the following materials, they should consider what, if anything, is distinctive about conservative constitutional theory? (Outside the judicial area, of course, most modern conservative theorists tend to agree on emphasizing market approaches to economic matters, but they diverge on whether the courts should defer when legislatures adopt regulatory measures that are subject to strong question under the tenets of market-oriented economic analyses.)

§ 9.02 The Many Faces of Judicial Restraint on the Rehnquist Court

The belief that judges should generally defer to decisions by the elected branches of government is commonly viewed as one of the basic tenets of modern conservative judges and scholars. Yet, according to Professor Michael Stokes Paulsen, this belief has not served as "a true unifying principle" for the Rehnquist Court.[9] Instead, he argues, the Court's "conservative justices, to the extent they are consistent in their respective jurisprudential views, tend to defer to fundamentally different sources of authority."[10] His survey of the performances of the conservative justices in 1993 indicated that Justice Scalia had "the most developed, intellectually compelling, consistent, and forcefully applied judicial philosophy of any current justice."[11] The distinctive features of Justice Scalia's approach to constitutional adjudication were his attachment to "clear rules as to the[] priority" of "all available sources of legal meaning."[12] For Justice Scalia, "[e]vidence of the framers' or Congress' intent may not trump a clear textual command or a critical structural principle necessarily implicit in the text. While Scalia will defer to judgments of the federal political branches and of the states, neither may prevail over a document's text or structure, or over reliable evidence of its historical meaning."[13]

Professor Paulsen concludes that the focus of the debate among constitutional theorists should not be on the differences between liberal and conservative judges but rather "the identity of legal conservatism. The debate is among 'interpretivist' conservatives who accord primacy to the text, history, and structure of the document being interpreted, 'majoritarians' who vindicate legislative choices, and 'incrementalist' conservatives who are committed to gradualist approaches to change in the state of the law, giving due weight to stare decisis and 'settled doctrine.'"[14] He explains that the disagreements among these different conservatives is not over whether they should defer to particular sources of authority or to the other branches of the federal and state governments but rather "which of these sources takes priority and [how to] apply[] that hierarchy in a consistent, principled manner."[15]

Scalia arguing on behalf of himself and Justices Brennan, Marshall, and Blackmun that Maryland's procedure for criminal child abuse cases violated the Sixth Amendment's confrontation clause by not allowing for direct confrontation in a courtroom between the criminal defendant and the child accusing him of abuse).

[9] Michael Stokes Paulsen, *The Many Faces*

of Judicial Restraint, 1993 PUB. INT. L. REV. 3, 4.

[10] *Id.*

[11] *Id.* at 8.

[12] *Id.*

[13] *Id.* at 10.

[14] *Id.* at 21.

[15] *Id.*

In 1998, Kathleen Sullivan, then a law professor and now Dean of Stanford Law School, suggested that the apparent failure of the Rehnquist Court to render predictably conservative outcomes in many cases is attributable to several factors in addition to the conservative justices' different prioritizations of sources of constitutional decision. At the time of her analysis, the Court had seven Republican and two Democratic appointees. Kathleen Sullivan, *The Jurisprudence of the Rehnquist Court,* 22 NOVA L. REV. 743 (1998):[16]

Popular discourse about the Supreme Court often seeks to characterize its direction in political terms. Yet the Rehnquist Court, while it has undoubtedly turned rightward, has never turned as starkly rightward as predicted in such accounts, even though Presidents Reagan and Bush between them filled five seats on the current Court. To be sure, President Clinton—with two appointments of his own in the last five years—has had the chance to counterbalance the Reagan-Bush nominations. But both before and after Clinton's appointments, it was evident that Justices who were expected to be "conservative" sometimes voted for "liberal" or "moderate" results.

Why might this be so? One explanation might be that court-packing is simply harder than it looks, and a president's ability to predict the judicial orientation of his nominees is inherently prone to error. . . .

But three other explanations seem more powerful than presidential miscalculation alone. This essay seeks to explore those explanations. First, the institutional structure of the Court may constrain or systematically moderate ideological tendencies. Second, a Justice's jurisprudential commitments may limit his or her expression of ideological orientation. Finally, the very concept of conservative judicial ideology is quite complex, and thus an apparently "liberal" result sometimes represents simply the dominance of one strand of conservatism over others. These institutional, jurisprudential, and ideological factors might help explain the surprising moderation of Justices predicted to be conservative.

Without doubt, the Rehnquist Court has taken positions consistent with conservative politics in a variety of constitutional areas since 1980. The Court has narrowed pregnant women's rights against state regulation of abortion and rejected the claim that consensual homosexual sex is protected by the same conception of liberty that had earlier protected access to abortion and contraception. The Court has likewise declined to extend such liberty rights to physician-assisted suicide. The Court has been increasingly willing to invalidate race-based affirmative action programs, even when implemented by the federal government. In an analogous line of cases, the Court has struck down several state attempts to create majority-minority electoral districts. The Court has made it more difficult for challengers to prove that a school district is continuing to violate the requirements of *Brown v. Board of Education.* For the first time in sixty years, the Court has sought to restrain federal power in relation to the power of the states by striking down a congressional assertion of power under the Commerce Clause. Similarly, the Court has struck down congressional efforts to "commandeer" state legislative or executive action. Perhaps nowhere has the Court's conservative trend been more apparent than in the area of criminal justice. Hence, it is difficult to dispute that Presidents Reagan and Bush had considerable success in moving the Court to the political right.

The Court, however, has also issued a number of decisions disappointing conservative advocates. For instance, the Court did not, as many had predicted, overrule *Roe v. Wade*. Nor did it eliminate Establishment Clause restrictions on school prayer. The Court declined to allow the states or Congress to criminalize flag burning. And, notwithstanding other harbingers of an antifederalist revival, the Court forbade state voters from imposing term limits on their federal legislators—albeit narrowly and over a bitter dissent. Some recent decisions extending the Equal Protection Clause drew a cacophony of conservative opposition—for example, a decision barring the exclusion of women from an all-male public academy and a decision barring a state from precluding all claims of discrimination based on homosexual orientation. The Court granted free access to state appeals courts for indigent parents attempting to retain rights of relationship to their children, thus reviving a long-dormant strand of fundamental rights analysis in equal protection law. Finally, the Rehnquist Court has consistently interpreted the Free Speech Clause to forbid government prescriptions of orthodoxy, protecting groups as divergent as leftist flag burners and white supremacist cross burners.

Even in decisions reaching conservative results, the Court has articulated doctrines that stop short of their apparent logical conclusion. For example, in the affirmative action cases, the Court has stopped short of establishing outright color blindness as a constitutional norm, intimating that race-based affirmative action might be upheld on somewhat weaker justifications than would be required of policies discriminating against racial minorities.[25] In cases imposing federalism-based limits on congressional power, the Court has barred congressional acts requiring states to enact or enforce specified policies but allowed similar results to be accomplished by imposing regulatory conditions on federal funding that states find irresistible as a practical matter. And, in free speech challenges, the Court has sometimes split the difference between the speech claim and the government. For example, the Court has struck down a hate speech law while upholding a hate crime penalty enhancement statute, upheld some but not all regulations of anti-abortion protestors, and permitted public airport terminals to ban the solicitation of funds but not the sale or distribution of literature. Such decisions give greater latitude to speakers than might have been expected given the Court's starting assumptions—for example, that regulations designed to protect access to abortion clinics are content neutral and that airports are not latter-day public forums.

---

[25] While subjecting race-based preferences to strict scrutiny, the Court sought to "dispel the notion that strict scrutiny [in this context] is 'strict in theory, but fatal in fact.'" *Adarand Constructors, Inc. v. Pena*, 515 U.S. 200, 237 (1995) (quoting *Fullilove v. Klutznick*, 448 U.S. 448, 507 (1980)). Under such strict but not fatal scrutiny, governments might permissibly adopt race preferences that are narrowly tailored to redress specifically identified past discrimination—even if that discrimination was not committed intentionally by the state, or the scope of the redress is not limited to the individual victims of adjudicable discrimination. For example, a city or state might use race-conscious procurement policies where it had merely been a "'passive participant' in a system of racial exclusion practiced by elements of the local construction industry," rather than a deliberate practitioner of racial exclusion itself. *City of Richmond v. J.A. Croson Co.*, 488 U.S. 469, 492 (1989) (O'Connor, J., joined by Rehnquist, C.J. and White, J.). And, "[i]n the extreme case, some form of narrowly tailored racial preference might be necessary to break down patterns of deliberate exclusion," *id.* at 509, whether or not such preferences were limited to making particular victims of adjudicable discrimination whole. Indeed, Justice Scalia concurred separately in both *Croson* and *Adarand* to emphasize his disagreement with the Court to the extent it authorized race-conscious measures extending beyond remediation for identified victims of discrimination—the only sort of remediation he would regard as consistent with a constitutional norm of color blindness. *Id.* at 526 (Scalia, J., concurring in the judgment). . . .

In short, the Rehnquist Court has not simply followed but in some cases has defied and in other cases stopped short of the outcomes that might have been predicted by the election returns. These results typically depended on votes of at least one of the five Reagan-Bush nominees, necessarily so in the seven years since Justice Thomas' appointment, and in some cases received the support of several. The following sections explore the role of institutional factors, jurisprudential considerations, and ideological complexity in helping to explain such votes.

Two features of the Court's institutional situation in relation to the other branches suggest reasons why conservative Justices might vote moderate or liberal. The first and most distinctive institutional feature of the Supreme Court is its relative insulation from political pressures. Politics may play an inevitable role in the nomination and confirmation process, but constitutional guarantees of lifetime tenure and protection from salary cuts afford the Justices considerable opportunity to change their minds. Thus, a Justice's opinions, over time, may cease to bear much resemblance to his or her political profile at the time of nomination and appointment. Assuming that Justices sometimes diverge from their predicted political profile while in office, is there any structural reason to suppose that the shift will be in a "liberal" rather than a "conservative" direction? To be sure, there are counterexamples. President Kennedy's only appointee, Justice Byron White, arguably grew more conservative during his long tenure on the bench,[33] except for his nearly parliamentary willingness to defer to the (usually Democratic) Congress. But it is at least plausible to suppose that insulation from political majorities typically creates a structural incentive to articulate and protect the interests of political minorities, if only through repeat exposure to such claims and a desire to distinguish the work of the judiciary from that of the political branches. This tendency will often, though not always, appear politically "liberal."[35]

A second and independent institutional explanation arises from the Justices' concern to protect the Supreme Court's credibility. The Supreme Court cannot tax, nor does it possess armed forces to back up its decisions. Lacking power of sword or purse, the Court depends on the power of its legitimacy. At first glance, the legitimacy problem seems more likely to generate conservative decisions than liberal ones. After all, the Court's legitimacy would appear most threatened when the Court protects the interests of a small minority over the intense opposition of the majority.

However, the Court's need to preserve its legitimacy might motivate unexpectedly liberal decisions in some situations because its reputation depends on the perception that its legal pronouncements transcend ordinary politics. Conservative Justices might favor results that appear liberal in the short run in order to diffuse any suspicion that they are caving in to political pressure from their conservative sponsors and their allies. One way of doing this is to abide by stare decisis and entrench

---

[33] For example, Justice White concurred in the judgment in *Griswold v. Connecticut,* 381 U.S. 479, 502–03 (1965), invalidating a prohibition of contraceptive use on substantive due process grounds, but found no similar Constitutional warrant for protecting access to abortion, *see Roe v. Wade,* 410 U.S. 113, 221 (1973) (White, J., dissenting), or consensual adult sexual conduct, *see Bowers v. Hardwick,* 478 U.S. 186, 191 (1986) (White, J.).

[35] If a challenged policy is itself "liberal," then counter-majoritarian decisionmaking will appear "conservative." The Court's recent affirmative action and race-based districting cases provide an illustration. The Court invalidated popularly enacted programs in order to protect individual members of the racial majority. Another example might be the Court's recent federalism decisions, where it has struck down acts of Congress in the name of divided government.

earlier liberal decisions even if they would not be reached again as an initial matter.

The pivotal joint opinion of Justices Sandra Day O'Connor, Anthony Kennedy, and David Souter in *Planned Parenthood v. Casey,* for example, declined to overrule *Roe v. Wade* in part on the ground that the Court ought not overturn settled law in the face of vehement public controversy over abortion, lest it appear to be doing politics rather than law. Likewise, the Court's recent decisions invalidating most affirmative action programs, but holding out the possibility that some such programs might be justified by remedial or distributive concerns expressed in earlier cases, might be read as seeking to avoid a perception that the Court interprets the Constitution in light of the latest public opinion polls. Similarly, in the area of federal-state relations, Justice Kennedy strikingly defied any preconceived label as a rigid antifederalist by casting the decisive vote in a single Term both to invalidate a federal gun-possession statute as exceeding Commerce Clause authority,[43] and to invalidate state-imposed term limits on members of Congress as exceeding state authority.[44]

A second explanation of why conservative Justices might vote moderate or liberal is that they have a jurisprudential orientation that moderates or constrains any ideological tendencies they might have. Justices' jurisprudential tendencies tend to follow one of two general approaches to fashioning legal directives. One approach employs bright-line rules, while the other utilizes flexible standards. Rules, generally speaking, bind a legal decision-maker in a fairly determinate manner by capturing underlying principles or policies in ways that then operate independently. What gives a rule its force is that judges will follow it in fairly rote fashion even where a particularized application of the background principle might arguably yield a different result. Standards, on the other hand, allow judges to apply the background principle more directly to a fact situation.

To take a simple example; suppose you wished to ensure safe driving on a highway. You might set a rule: "drive no faster than fifty-five miles per hour." Alternatively, you might set a standard of reasonableness: "drive safely for the highway conditions."

What are the comparative advantages of each approach? Rules constrain the discretion of the decision-maker who applies them and typically require the determination of only very limited issues of fact. For example, under the fifty-five miles per hour rule, a police officer only needs to determine at what speed the car was traveling. The fifty-five miles per hour rule also prevents two police officers from treating identical situations differently, whereas under the "reasonableness" standard, one driver might be ticketed while the other drives away free. Thus, the advantages of rules include certainty, predictability, formal fairness, clear notice to those they govern, and economy in the process of decision-making.

Standards, by contrast, require consideration of more facts. Under the "drive safely for the conditions" standard, for example, a police officer must take into account the time of day, the weather, the volume of traffic, and so forth. Standards thus give more discretion to the decision-maker in deciding particular cases. Though less predictable and more time-consuming to apply than rules, those who favor standards would say that

---

[43] United States v. Lopez, 514 U.S. 549, 580 (1995).

[44] United States Term Limits, Inc. v. Thornton, 514 U.S. 779, 838 (1995). Justice Kennedy argued that the Court ought both to stop the states from "invad[ing] the sphere of federal sovereignty," and to hold the federal government "within the boundaries of its own power when it intrudes upon matters reserved to the [s]tates." *Id.* at 841 (Kennedy, J., concurring).

they are more substantively fair and accurate than rules in capturing the relevant policy concern. For example, while the fifty-five miles per hour rule might prohibit a driver from reaching a safe sixty miles per hour on an empty straightaway under sunny skies but permit a driver to travel a treacherous fifty miles per hour on a rain-slicked curve at rush hour, the "drive safely" standard might correct such anomalous outcomes. Advocates of standards also approve their flexibility and capacity to evolve in their application over time with changing mores or circumstances.

Constitutional doctrines, like traffic rules, may be expressed in the form of either rules or standards. Approaches that use categorical, formal, bright-line tests are rule-like. For example, consider holdings that obscenity is unprotected speech, or that the legislature may not wield executive power, or vice versa. Almost as rule-like in practice are tests that use strong presumptions to decide cases once a threshold classification has been made. When the Court employs strict scrutiny—such as to review infringements of fundamental rights, content based suppression of speech, or suspect classifications—it is nearly impossible for the government to prove the law constitutional. Conversely, when the Court employs rationality review—for example, to review challenges to socioeconomic legislation—the Court typically defers to the judgments of the other branches so that it is difficult, if not nearly impossible, for the challenger to win. This two-tiered system of scrutiny limits judicial discretion because once the Court has sorted a challenged law into the appropriate tier, it is confined to the resulting decisional rule, as are the lower courts in deciding analogous cases.

By contrast, constitutional tests that employ balancing, intermediate scrutiny, or functional analysis operate as standards. Consider the Court's express use of intermediate scrutiny to evaluate laws that classify individuals based on gender, [57] as well as facially neutral laws with a disproportionate adverse effect on interstate commerce, [58] and facially neutral laws with a substantial adverse impact on speech or expressive conduct. [59] Intermediate scrutiny, like standard-based reasoning generally, asks how strong the government's interest is in relation to the constitutional policy at stake.

Functional analyses of separation of powers challenges provide another example of standard-like reasoning. Whereas formal approaches would condemn any trespass by one branch into another's powers, a functional approach invalidates only those trespasses that go too far. [60] These overtly balancing modes of analysis gives judges considerably greater discretion than the stark extremes of strict or rational review.

The Court deviates from rules to standards, if more informally, whenever it weakens the presumption traditionally embodied in strict scrutiny or rationality review. For example, applying "strict but not fatal" review to race-based affirmative action invites governments employing such measures to try to justify them in court. Conversely, applying aggressive

---

[57] *See, e.g.,* United States v. Virginia, 116 S. Ct. 2264, 2274 (1996) (inquiring whether the government can offer an "exceedingly persuasive justification").

[58] *See, e.g.,* Pike v. Bruce Church, Inc., 397 U.S. 137, 142 (1970) (inquiring whether the burden on interstate commerce is "clearly excessive in relation to the putative local benefits").

[59] *See, e.g.,* United States v. O'Brien, 391 U.S. 367, 382–86 (1968) (rejecting a facial and as-applied challenge to a law criminalizing the burning of a draft card and establishing the modern Court's test for analyzing content-neutral laws as inquiring whether the law closely fits a substantial government interest).

[60] *See, e.g.,* Morrison v. Olson, 487 U.S. 654, 691–93 (1988) (upholding independent counsel statute because it did not "unduly trammel on executive authority," or "unduly interfere with the role of the Executive Branch").

rationality review to invalidate laws found to reflect irrational animus—for example, the prohibition on gay rights claims struck down in *Romer v. Evans*—invites claimants to challenge measures ranging beyond traditionally suspect classifications. Either way, the two-tier approach collapses into de facto balancing.

A preference for constitutional standards over constitutional rules will tend to register as political moderation because, generally speaking, rules are more effective than standards at effecting sharp and lasting changes in constitutional interpretation. Standards allow the Court to decide cases narrowly: for example, this waiting period is not on its face an undue burden, this wholesale preclusion of gay antidiscrimination claims is unjustified, this particular district was drawn with excessive attention to racial demographics. The use of standards tends to moderate sharp swings between ideological poles; standards allow future courts more discretion to distinguish prior cases and decide cases in fact-specific fashion, and thus to afford more solace and spin opportunities to the losers.

Of the five Justices Presidents Reagan and Bush appointed to the Court, only two (Justices Antonin Scalia and Clarence Thomas) turned out to favor rules; the other three (Justices O'Connor, Kennedy, and Souter) have tended to favor standards.[67] The latter group's preference for standards in deciding constitutional cases furnishes one explanation for unexpectedly moderate or liberal decisions.

To take a few examples, consider first the issue of race-based affirmative action. Four Justices, including Justices Scalia and Thomas, would favor a rule that the Constitution should be color blind, and that no race-conscious measures should ever be permissible, whether aimed at subordinating or benefitting racial minorities. On the other hand, four Justices would apparently defer to many race-conscious measures designed to benefit minorities while still striking down race-conscious measures that are designed to disadvantage minorities, believing that they can perceive the difference between a no trespassing sign and a welcome mat. Between these two camps stands Justice O'Connor—the key swing vote on this issue—who would permit some limited race-conscious measures where they are shown to be closely tied to remedying past discrimination, relatively broadly defined.[68] Justice Kennedy's opinion for the Court in *Miller v. Johnson*[69] does something similar in asking whether race is the "predominant" factor in how electoral district boundaries are drawn, rather than in precluding racial considerations altogether. By saying that race-conscious measures are sometimes, if rarely, permissible, such standards and race-based distinguishing plans [sic] give governments the latitude to defend some affirmative action plans and lower courts the wiggle room to uphold them.

To take another example, consider the First Amendment's bar on establishment of religion. As many as four Justices at any given time, led by Justice Scalia, have argued for a narrow rule that only sectarian

---

[67] *See* Antonin Scalia, *The Rule of Law as a Law of Rules,* 56 U. Chi. L. Rev. 1175, 1176 (1989); *Morrison v. Olson,* 487 U.S. 654, 733 (1988) (Scalia, J., dissenting) (arguing that "[a] government of laws means a government of rules" and that the majority's functional analysis of separation of powers was "ungoverned by rule, and hence ungoverned by law").

[68] . . . . While agreeing that all racial clas-

sifications are subject to strict scrutiny, Justice O'Connor's view is that strict scrutiny here is no longer "fatal in fact" collapses a rule into something like a standard; affirmative action plans are evaluated by how starkly they consider race (is race merely a factor or is it dispositive?) and how closely tied they are to remedying discrimination.

[69] 515 U.S. 900 (1995).

preferences and outright coercion of faith ought to count as forbidden establishment. Justice O'Connor, however, has led a slim majority of the Court to maintain a broader and more flexible standard, holding that the Establishment Clause also forbids any government action that a reasonable observer would interpret as government "endorsement" of religion. This standard is highly fact-intensive and susceptible to shifting outcomes. For example, a publicly sponsored Christmas creche might be permissible if surrounded by reindeer and a talking wishing well in a shopping district, but not if standing alone on a courthouse staircase. This standard permits courts to invalidate more public religious expression than they would under Justice Scalia's rule. . . .

As a final example, compare two approaches the Rehnquist Court has taken to separation of powers issues. In *Morrison v. Olson,* the Court took a highly flexible balancing approach in upholding the independent counsel statute by a vote of 8-1. The majority opinion by Chief Justice Rehnquist reasoned that granting authority to prosecute high-level Executive officers to appointees whom the President does not select and may not remove at will does not trench too far upon the Executive power, even if prosecution is inherently executive in nature. A scathing dissent by Justice Scalia objected to this brand of prudentialism in structural matters, arguing that the issue should be the nature and not the degree of the infringement. By contrast, last Term, in *Printz v. United States,*[83] the Court invalidated, by a vote of 5-4, a federal requirement that local law enforcement officers perform background checks on handgun purchasers to ensure their conformity to federal standards. The Court reasoned that structural principles of federalism forbade any conscription of state or local officers in administering federal law, however trivial the burden or desirable the end. Writing this time for the majority, Justice Scalia flatly stated that any " 'balancing' analysis is inappropriate," and that "no comparative assessment of the various interests" could overcome the affront to state sovereignty embodied in such a law. Plainly, the *Morrison* standard afforded the government more leeway for structural innovation than the *Printz* rule, and against the political backdrop at the time, appeared unexpectedly politically moderate.[86]

The embrace of standards over rules thus leads conservative Justices to reach results that, in a period when the Court is moving rightward, appear more moderate or liberal than would a rule fashioned from a similar ideological starting point. This observation gives rise to an antecedent question: Why do some Justices favor rules and others favor standards? Why any particular Justice is drawn to either disposition is perhaps ultimately a psychological, biographical, or even aesthetic question. But to the extent the choice is conscious and articulate, it is likely to follow from different conceptions of the judicial role. Like the institutional considerations discussed above . . . , the choice of rules or standards might be understood as a strategy for maintaining the Court's legitimacy. Each camp might claim that its method facilitates greater judicial modesty than the other.

Specifically, those who favor rules, like positivists and codifiers of earlier generations, seek to limit the exercise of discretion in judicial decision-making, and thus favor the reduction of constitutional propositions as much as possible to claims of fact, not value. They suspect that the context-specific application of standards will lead judges inappropriately to impose their own values. Those who favor standards, in contrast,

---

[83] 117 S. Ct. 2365 (1997).

[86] Whether endorsement of independent counsels is understood as politically liberal or conservative at any time period, of course, depends to some extent on the political affiliation of such counsels' targets.

see their role in constitutional interpretation as akin to that of common law judges, requiring reference to the accretion of past history, precedent, and collective wisdom in order to constrain the inevitable exercise of some contemporary discretionary judgment. Justices who favor a common law approach to constitutional interpretation believe that they will be disciplined from imposing their own values by our traditions, social practices, shared understandings, and the process of reasoned elaboration from such starting points. They believe that it is more arrogant to assert the philosophical or interpretive certainty required by announcement of a single inflexible rule.[90]

Those who choose standards over rules might believe that such a choice, in addition to embodying judicial restraint, promotes judicial legitimacy in several other ways. It might, as a type of alternative constitutional dispute resolution, help to defuse sharp ideological conflict by giving something to each side. Relatedly, it might take steps toward a desired constitutional end-state while minimizing the expressive injury to the losers.[91] Finally, it might seem to facilitate democratic debate and resolution of the matters it leaves unresolved, placing conflict over values more squarely in the hands of the people than of judges. Whatever its jurisprudential or institutional motivation, the choice of standards over rules will register on the political spectrum as unexpectedly moderate or liberal during a period of general rightward shift.

A third reason why conservative Justices might appear to vote moderate or liberal is that the . . . concept of constitutional conservatism is quite complex. A judicial conservative might be thought to favor, at least to some degree, any of the following: 1) originalism; 2) textualism; 3) judicial restraint (deference to legislatures); 4) libertarianism (deregulation); 5) states' rights (decentralization); 6) traditionalism; 7) stare decisis; 8) capitalism; and 9) law and order. These different strands of judicial conservatism may sometimes pull in competing directions, both among Justices, and even within a single Justice across an array of cases. And when one strand trumps others, the outcome of the case may appear surprisingly moderate or liberal.

Such tensions are easy to identify in divided decisions by the Rehnquist Court. For example, adherence to the original meaning of the Constitution may trump deference to the government for [the] sake of law and order. Justices Scalia and Thomas, typically the Court's staunchest advocates of originalism, have sometimes voted with criminal defendants and against the government where they thought that the framers must have meant to forbid modern practices, such as videotaped testimony in child sexual abuse cases or unannounced drug raids.

Original meaning may be at odds with traditionalism. For example, Justice Thomas voted to sustain a First Amendment right to distribute anonymous election leaflets, reasoning that the framers themselves had engaged in anonymous debates over the Constitution, signing their writings with a variety of pseudonyms from "Publius" to the "Federal

---

[90] For an example of such a critique, see *Rosenberger v. Rector and Visitors of the Univ. of Va.,* 515 U.S. 819, 852 (1995) (O'Connor, J., concurring) ("When bedrock principles collide, they test the limits of categorical obstinacy and expose the flaws and dangers of a Grand Unified Theory that may turn out to be neither grand nor unified.").

[91] For example, the *Casey* decision over-

ruled several post-*Roe* decisions, see *Planned Parenthood v. Casey,* 505 U.S. 833, 881–87 (1992) (upholding waiting period requirements that prior decisions had struck down), even while leaving *Roe*'s Constitutional bar to criminal prohibition intact, with the net effect that abortion must be permitted but could be discouraged. Thus an opinion that reaffirmed the right to abortion at the same time constricted the scope of that right as a practical matter.

Farmer." Justice Scalia, dissenting, found the originalist record ambiguous and would have deferred instead to the long tradition and current legislative practice in nearly all states of requiring identifying information in election literature.

Stare decisis may be at odds with any of the other strands of conservatism. The decisive joint opinion in *Casey,* for example, embraced a strong if limited respect for stare decisis, reaffirming *Roe*'s central holding without regard to whether it was correct as an original matter.[97] The dissenters, in contrast, saw stare decisis as far too weak to overcome the lack of clear textual or originalist authority for invalidating popularly enacted abortion regulation. . . .

Some opinions would seem to represent a triumph of libertarianism over textual or originalist literalism or judicial restraint. For example, all the Justices except Chief Justice Rehnquist recently proved willing to invalidate, as an unreasonable search and seizure, state-mandated drug testing for political candidates. In others, strict adherence to text and original meaning may yield to some combination of stare decisis, traditionalism, and a robust view of property rights. For example, Justice Scalia, who typically favors textualist and originalist readings, exemplified this when he wrote an opinion for the Court in *Lucas v. South Carolina Coastal Council,* calling for strict review under the Takings Clause of regulations that sharply diminish property values—even though the Takings Clause says nothing about regulation of property whose title is not transferred to the state, and even though the framers did not envision applying the Takings Clause to such regulations.

These examples could be multiplied indefinitely, but suffice to illustrate that any effort to carry out a program of judicial "conservatism" in constitutional interpretation involves a simultaneous equation with multiple variables. Even a single Justice pegged as a conservative may be pulled in different directions. The outcome of a case, therefore, depends not only upon a Justice's default weighing of these variables, but on the relative strength of each particular ideological pull in the differing circumstances of each case. To complicate matters still further, Justices may agree on a variable but disagree strenuously over its application. For example, consider the dueling originalism that has led the majority and dissent to disagree vigorously as to whether the framers did or did not intend that Congress might employ state officials to administer federal programs, or whether the framers did or did not intend that the Establishment Clause bar only that aid to religion which preferred one sect over others.

Finally, constitutional rights sometimes may undergo what might be called "ideological drift." That is, rights once thought of as having liberal provenance are embraced by conservatives even as liberal attachment to them falters. There is no better recent example than freedom of speech.[105] Free speech rights were traditionally asserted in this century

---

[97] Stare decisis, or respect for precedent, carries varying degrees of weight among the five Justices appointed by Presidents Reagan and Bush. Justices O'Connor, Kennedy, and Souter give considerable respect to at least the core of prior precedents. Justices Scalia and Thomas are more willing to overturn "unsound" precedents. . . .

[105] For another example, consider the shift from left to right on the political spectrum of the view that the Fourteenth Amendment's guarantee of equal protection is a guarantee of formal equality that bars all official use of race as a classification. Today, many conservatives use a principle once urged in the civil rights movement to reject affirmative action and aggressive interpretations of the Voting Rights Act, while many liberals eschew formal equality claims in favor of a view of the Equal Protection Clause as an antisubordination principle under which benign racial classifications should not be treated the same as invidious ones.

by anarchists, socialists, syndicalists, and communists, and closer to our own time by the pioneers of racial civil rights and opponents of the war in Vietnam. But left-wing support is not always forthcoming when free speech claims are asserted by racist cross-burners, anti-abortion demonstrators, large corporate advertisers, or donors of large sums to political campaigns. In the latter sort of case, liberals often favor government regulation designed to ensure racial dignity, reproductive privacy, or greater equality in the marketplace of ideas, and conservative groups take up the banner of free speech libertarian opposition.

In such circumstances, popular views of the political valence of decisions may lag behind the ideological drift, leading to the perception that conservative Justices have voted "liberal" on free speech, and vice versa. For example, in a recent abortion clinic protest case, the traditionally liberal Justice Stevens voted to uphold all restrictions on the protestors while the historically conservative Justice Scalia would have struck them all down. [106] Similarly, in a recent campaign finance case, the supposedly conservative Justices Kennedy, Thomas, and Scalia embraced vigorously the free speech rights of political parties while several supposedly liberal Justices expressed willingness to allow wide-ranging government regulation of campaign finance. Because the press has an institutional interest in strong First Amendment protection, such decisions are apt to be reported as "liberal" victories for free speech, even if the credit must go to "conservative" Justices.

This essay has suggested three possible explanations—institutional, jurisprudential and ideological—of why a Court moving generally rightward might nonetheless be characterized occasionally by surprising judicial moderation or even a liberal turn. These factors help show why it is so difficult to capture the work of the Court along a single political vector: "sharp right turn," or "the center holds." There is nothing mutually inconsistent among these accounts. Indeed, they may reinforce one another, as when institutional concerns influence jurisprudential orientation. And these accounts help to refute the view, sometimes expressed in popular commentary, that the moderate judicial behavior of the swing Justices on the Rehnquist Court is incoherent or inexplicable.

§ 9.03 Rule- and Tradition-Based Decision Making

Ernest Young, a conservative scholar who subsequently joined the University of Texas Law School faculty, argues that judicial expression of legal commands as standards rather than rules more closely approximates the classic conservatism of eighteenth century British philosopher-politician Edmund Burke.[17] Ernest Young, *Rediscovering Conservatism: Burkean Political Theory and Constitutional Interpretation,* 72 N.C. L. REV. 619, 681–86 (1995):[18]

Although a preference for formulation of legal directives in the form of rules or standards has, at times, been associated with substantive political positions, Professor Sullivan argues convincingly that this choice ultimately does not consistently correlate with political liberalism or

---

[106] Madsen v. Women's Health Ctr., Inc., 512 U.S. 753, 777 (1994). The majority in *Madsen,* steering between the poles set by Justices Stevens and Scalia, upheld some of the restrictions but not others.

[17] For his understanding of this distinction, Young draws heavily from an earlier article by Dean Sullivan. *See* Kathleen Sullivan, *The Supreme Court, 1991 Term: Foreword—The Justices of Rules and Standards,* 106 HARV. L. REV. 22 (1992).

[18] Copyright © 1994 by the North Carolina Law Review Association. Reprinted with permission.

conservatism. The emergence of Justice Scalia as the primary advocate of rule-based decisionmaking, however, has caused rules to be consistently associated with judicial conservatism. Nonetheless, Burkeans must find this characterization to be precisely backwards; indeed, Burke was one of the most eloquent proponents of a balancing approach to political and social problems:

> The pretended rights of these theorists are all extremes; and in proportion as they are metaphysically true, they are morally and politically false. The rights of men are in a sort of middle, incapable of definition, but not impossible to be discerned. The rights of men in governments . . . are often in balances between differences of good; in compromises sometimes between good and evil, and sometimes between evil and evil. Political reason is a computing principle; adding, subtracting, multiplying, and dividing, morally and not metaphysically or mathematically, true moral denominations.[310]

Professor Sullivan's conclusion that the contrasting positions on rules and standards on the present Court represent "two kinds of judicial conservatism, not one" is thus worth reconsidering in light of the Burkean tradition. Rather than equivocating between the two modes, that tradition comes down firmly on the side of standards.

The first and most clearly anti-conservative aspect of rules is the ambitious rationalism inherent in their formation. Comparing Justice Scalia to the "nineteenth-century legal codifiers facing the messy landscape of the common law," Professor Sullivan observes that Scalia "is likewise optimistic about the possibility that judges can rationalize the chaotic jumble of twentieth-century constitutional precedents and reorder constitutional law around clear interpretive and operative rules." The proponent of rules thus makes the same sort of rationalist assumptions about the rule-maker that the originalist makes about the Framers; neither allows much scope for elaboration and alteration in the light of subsequent experience. Standards, on the other hand, operate with greater humility. Although they may aim at a comparable level of determinacy as rules, standards become determinate through a process of elaboration in the course of individual decisions. Through the gradual method of the common law, particularistic decisions in individual cases gradually add up to a rational pattern of doctrine. Professor Duncan Kennedy explains this process as follows:

> [T]he application of a standard to a particular fact situation will often generate a particular rule much narrower in scope than that standard. One characteristic mode of ordering a subject matter area including a vast number of possible situations is through the combination of a standard with an ever increasing group of particular rules of this kind. The generality of the standard means that there are no gaps: it is possible to find out something about how judges will dispose of cases that have not yet arisen. But no attempt is made to formulate a formally realizable general rule. Rather, case law gradually fills in the area with rules so closely bound to particular facts that they have little or no precedential value.[315]

The structure that emerges from this process will likely lack the simplicity of a general rule, yet it is more likely to conform to the complexities of social reality. Hence, as Professor Greenawalt notes, "Skepticism

---

[310] [Edmund Burke, *Reflections on the Revolution in France* (1791), in 8 THE WRITINGS AND SPEECHES OF EDMUND BURKE 112–13 (Paul Langford ed., Clarendon Press 1989)].

[315] [Duncan Kennedy, *Form and Substance in Private Law Adjudication*, 89 HARV. L. REV. 1685, 1690 (1976).]

about abstract ideas and rapid change, and concentration on particular context, does incline one toward balancing approaches to the resolution of social problems."[316]

Standards also promote a Burkean notion of prudence through their facilitation of compromise. For Burke, "All government, . . . every virtue, and every prudent act, is founded on compromise and barter. We balance inconveniences; we give and take; . . . and we choose rather to be happy citizens than subtle disputants." This preference for moderation is based on a suspicion that absolutist positions can never adequately capture the complexity of real life, as well as a notion of political prudence. Although rules may be used to codify moderate positions, they are more amenable than standards to use by proponents of ideological extremes. Because a standard will be applied with some degree of discretion by decisionmakers of varying political views, the distribution of actual results will tend toward the middle to a greater extent than where decisionmakers are more constrained by a rule that incorporates a particular political position. Because standards allow room for the direct application of background principles in individual fact situations, they rank among "'the arts of compromise,' the'ways of muddling through' that permit us to reach an accommodation between our principles and the complex, murky, and often resistant reality on which these principles operate." And because this accommodation occurs over time through successive applications of the standard in individual cases, standards are a means of "permit[ting] the marginal and evolutionary reconciliation of our principles and practices."

A somewhat more complex set of Burkean arguments revolves around what advocates of rules often list as the primary disadvantage of standards: their incompatibility with the ideal of judicial restraint. Because standards leave considerable discretion to the decisionmaker to give content to the law ex post, partisans of rules tend to see standards as a mask for application of the judge's own preferences, or "the wolf of judicial arrogance in the sheep's clothing of the common law judge." In response to this charge, proponents of standards point to three distinct sources of constraint, each of which rests on fundamentally Burkean assumptions. The first is a belief that, over time, social traditions and practices can meaningfully give content to a given constitutional provision. This response reflects a concern that decisionmaking should be slow and decentralized. Because standard-based adjudication relies on case-by-case application to develop the meaning of legal directives, it inevitably devolves considerable responsibility to the lower courts. This devolution ensures that decisionmaking will be incremental, with individual courts serving as laboratories wherein different resolutions of similar problems can be tested without risking the broad systemic consequences of experimentation by the Supreme Court itself. Moreover, decentralization may have the additional benefit of decreasing political pressure on the Court, both because the pace of change will be slower and because the Court will have the opportunity to examine the effects of innovations before having to pass on them.[323]

A second argument for the constraining effect of standards rests on a belief that "shared understandings embedded like bedrock in the legal culture will inform the line-drawing that the Justices do." This position,

---

[316] [Kent Greenawalt, *Justice Harlan's Conservatism and Alternative Possibilities,* 36 N.Y.S. L. REV. 33, 64 (1991)] . . . .

[323] John O. McGinnis, *The 1991 Supreme Court Term: Review and Outlook,* 1993 PUB. INT. L. REV. 165, 167 ("One method of control-ling the pace of change and deflecting criticism of the Court itself is to decentralize decision making by announcing rules that provide lower courts greater responsibility for making decisions on a case-by-case basis.").

in turn, depends on the assumption that our heterogeneous society retains sufficient "shared understandings" that judges will be able to discern and be guided by a common tradition rather than their own personal values. As Professor Tushnet suggests, this view is more characteristic of conservative social theory than of liberalism; "[c]onservatism," according to Tushnet, "has insisted that consensus and community rather than conflict are the basis of social order," whereas liberalism assumes "that each of us is fundamentally in conflict with the rest."[326] Although Tushnet overstates the case when he concludes that "within the conservative tradition, the imagined consensus means that no decisionmaker, whether legislator or judge, can possibly deviate in any interesting way from the community's views," he is certainly correct in attributing to Burkeans a belief in shared traditions and a greater emphasis on the community vis-à-vis the individual. Reliance on shared understandings is, of course, substantially more problematic in our modern, heterogeneous society than in Burke's eighteenth-century Britain; it may be, however, that the primary area of common ground that remains lies in the tradition of rights developed through constitutional adjudication. Moreover, standards are sufficiently capacious to be tailored to the areas of agreement that exist, while making allowances for diversity. In any event, the opposite preference for rules partakes more of the liberal tradition of individualism, as articulated by John Rawls and Friedrich von Hayek. Moreover, rule-based decisionmaking accommodates the liberal individualist belief in the subjectivity of values by constraining the judge to refer only to facts in making decisions. That this position is now being put forward by Justice Scalia simply emphasizes the extent to which modern American conservatives have adopted the libertarian premises of classical liberalism.

Finally, proponents of standards insist that "the Court's own internal practices of reasoned deliberation—the Justices' very self-conception that they are doing law, not politics—will discipline the tendencies of any personal preferences to guide results." This argument emphasizes the Burkean notion that the judge is a legitimate participant in the enterprise of mixed government, rather than an interloper in a presumptively majoritarian system. Indeed, the case for standards generally assumes that adequate constraints on judicial discretion may be found within the judicial process itself; none of the arguments canvassed above rely on other branches of government to check the development of standards by the courts. Rather, they rest on . . . the essence of a Burkean approach to constitutional interpretation: a faith in the ability of judges to oversee the incremental evolution of our constitutional tradition.

In the remainder of his article, Young evaluates which of the conservative justices on the Rehnquist Court comes closest to a Burkean conservative approach that emphasizes tradition and is "committ[ed] to evolutionary development of constitutional doctrine."[19] Professor Young sees this spirit emerging among the Court's centrist Supreme Court justices, particularly Justice Souter.

Conservative law professor Michael McConnell of the University of Utah College of Law rejects the notion of tradition as an evolving concept that is judicially enforceable. Instead, he concludes, after carefully studying the preconstitutional roots of the conceptions of custom and tradition to which the framers' generation was heir, that tradition for constitutional purposes is a lost conception of the common law that may be altered not by judges but

---

[326] [Mark V. Tushnet, *Conservative Consti-*   (1985)].
tutional Theory, 59 TUL. L. REV. 910, 926   [19] Young, *supra* note 17, at 718.

only by the national legislation through laws made in compliance with the requisite steps set forth in the American Constitution. In particular, he explains that the "written Constitution presupposes an established set of fundamental rights not *created* by the Constitution but *protected or preserved* by it."[20] These rights are "protected" or "preserved" by the structure of the Constitution, which allows "departures from these customary rights only through the process of bicameralism and presentment, which is designed to force deliberation and to make legislative action difficult."[21] This system is designed deliberately to "frustrate[] change," and, in Professor McConnell's judgment, "makes eminent sense. If the common law is the most legitimate and reliable source of law, then a constitutional system that makes legislation more difficult—that requires democratic deliberation and consensus before deviating from the common law—is a sensible procedural safeguard."[22] Indeed, this notion of tradition is consistent with Justice Scalia's "insiste[nce], in his opinion, in *Michael H. v. Gerald D.*,[23] that the purpose of the Due Process Clause (indeed, much of the Constitution) 'is to prevent future generations from lightly casting aside important traditional values—not to enable this Court to invent new ones.' "[24]

§ 9.04 Economic Analysis and Rights

In this section, we explore the two ways in which economics is conceivably relevant to the interpretation of the Constitution. The first is as an important tool of analysis for understanding the Constitution or at least certain parts of it (such as the contracts and takings clauses). The second is the extent to which the Constitution protects certain economic liberties (such as a right to contract).

[A] Economic Analysis of the Constitution

Not surprisingly, with the rise of law and economics approaches, an increasing number of scholars have argued that at least some aspects of the Constitution lend themselves to analysis from economic perspectives. While much of this analysis has tried to interpret parts of the Constitution consistently with various conservative policies, principles, and results, the application of economic reasoning to constitutional problems is not necessarily a uniquely conservative enterprise.

For example, one of the pioneering attempts to read the Constitution as an economic document, Charles Beard's AN ECONOMIC INTERPRETATION OF THE CONSTITUTION OF THE UNITED STATES, has implications that could conflict with some of the conservative analyses previously explored in this chapter. Beard argued that the history of the Constitution showed that "it was an economic document drawn with superb skill by men whose property interests

---

[20] Michael W. McConnell, *Tradition and Constitutionalism before the Constitution*, 1998 ILL. L. REV. 173, 198 (emphasis in original).

[21] *Id.*

[22] *Id.*

[23] 491 U.S. 110, 109 S. Ct. 2333, 105 L. Ed. 2d 91 (1989).

[24] McConnell, *supra* note 20, at 192 (quoting Michael H. v. Gerald D., 491 U.S. 110, 122 n.2 (1989)).

were immediately at stake."[25] In a 1987 symposium evaluating the influence of Beard's book, Professor Jonathan Macey of Cornell Law School observed that this book has inspired not only contemporary law and economics theorists, typified by Judge Richard Posner in the next excerpt, but also many Marxist economists, who "espouse the view that the Constitution structured government to facilitate the retention of wealth by, and the transfer of wealth to, a small minority of persons concerned primarily with their immediate property interests."[26] According to Professor Macey, these latter scholars ultimately read the Constitution as a fundamentally flawed charter that requires radical revision to eliminate the economic disparities that its enforcement inevitably produces.[27]

As another participant in the 1987 symposium on Beard's book, Judge Richard Posner rejected the Beardian and Marxist argument that the Constitution guarantees economic exploitation. Rather, he argued that the Constitution makes economic growth possible and generally provides for efficient governmental decisionmaking (for example, through separation of powers). While Posner acknowledged that there are parts of the Constitution that are not "efficiency enhancing," he argued both that economic analysis can provide a basis for criticism of judge-made constitutional doctrines and that some constitutional provisions "seem to have an implicit economic logic," suiting them for use by economic approaches that can lead to welfare-enhancing doctrines. Richard Posner, *The Constitution as an Economic Document,* 56 GEO. WASH. L. REV. 4, 16–18 (1987):[28]

> [An example of a] judge-made constitutional doctrine[] that seem[s] to rest, in part anyway, on bad economic thinking [is] the presumption that due process of law in repossessing property obtained on credit requires a hearing before rather than after repossession[, which] is defended by asserting that property rights will be impaired without such a hearing . . . . In truth, requiring "predeprivation" hearings in credit-sale cases will just raise interest rates, to the detriment of the class ostensibly protected by additional procedural safeguards . . . .
>
> A more modest function of economic analysis in relation to noneconomic doctrines is to remind the courts that all legal doctrines have costs. By displaying those costs, whether analytically or quantitatively, the economist can place warranted pressure on the supporters of the doctrines to

---

[25] C. BEARD, AN ECONOMIC INTERPRETATION OF THE CONSTITUTION OF THE UNITED STATES 188 (1913). *See also id.* at 63 (arguing that the Constitution was enacted because "[l]arge and important groups of economic interests were adversely affected by the system of government under the Articles of Confederation, namely, those of public securities, shipping and manufacturing, money at interest; in short, capital as opposed to land.").

[26] Jonathan Macey, *Competing Economic Views of the Constitution,* 56 GEO. WASH. L. REV. 50, 52 (1987).

[27] Professor Macey himself rejects the theory that he claims law and economics theorists and Marxists share: that "the separation of powers, like the system of checks and balances, of which

it is a part, [w]as a vehicle designed by the Framers to effectuate interest group domination of daily political life." *Id.* at 53. Macey contends that this particular view was mistaken because "[t]he separation of powers and the system of checks and balances thwart rather than facilitate the political effectiveness of special interest group coalitions." *Id.* Macey explains that he views the Constitution as "a public-regarding document expressly designed to impede the welfare-reducing wealth transfers" both Marxists and law and economics theorists believe are promoted through separation of powers. *Id.*

[28] Copyright © 1987 by the George Washington Law Review. Reprinted by permission of the George Washington Law Review.

establish the existence of offsetting benefits. For example, the exclusionary rule leads to overdeterrence of police searches. The resulting costs to the legal process, and to the community (in the form of a higher crime rate, because criminal investigations are made more cumbersome and uncertain), cannot easily be justified if there exists—and there does—an alternative sanction, the tort suit, which if properly configured would provide a deterrent more likely to approximate the optimum.

A number of provisions of the Constitution seem to have an implicit economic logic. This is perhaps clearest with respect to the "negative" or "dormant" commerce clause, which is to say the interpretation of the commerce clause as forbidding states to erect barriers to interstate commerce unless Congress authorizes them. When so interpreted, the commerce clause becomes a charter of free trade—a subject of detailed economic analysis since Adam Smith—and, relatedly, an element of an efficient federalism. By preserving the sovereignty of the states the Framers of the Constitution created a danger that, like independent nations, states might be pressured by interest groups to establish trade barriers. This would be of no concern if competition among states were perfect, for that would imply that any consumer or supplier in a state who was harmed by such a barrier would move immediately and costlessly to another state; the trade barrier would be ineffective. But as mentioned earlier, interstate competition is not perfect; there are significant immobilities . . . . The "negative" commerce clause is one device (and the privileges and immunities clause in Article IV is another—and one better grounded in the text and history of the Constitution)[21] for preventing states from abusing their "market power" and thus for ensuring that the federal principle is used to promote rather than retard interstate competition aimed at optimizing the cost and quality of governmental services.

The takings clause of the Fifth Amendment also seems founded on economic considerations—and so indeed does the Fourth Amendment (and not just the exclusionary rule that has been grafted onto it by the courts). In forbidding only *unreasonable* searches and seizures, the Fourth Amendment requires courts to balance the costs, to privacy and property, of searches and seizures against the benefits in reducing the incidence of crime, and therefore to use an essentially economic calculus in applying the amendment to specific conduct. In so arguing, I do not mean to suggest that any time a legal doctrine requires judgments of more and less, as almost any doctrine that speaks in terms of reasonableness does, it is economic in character. All rational activity involves a balancing of pros and cons, and while economics is in its broadest sense the science of rational choice, it does not follow that every rational choice is in an interesting sense economic. Moreover, the things balanced might not be monetizable even in principle, or might be weighted in a manner remote from utilitarian or economic calculation. It is an empty form of economic analysis of law that is content to attach the economic label to every balancing test in law. However, . . . economics does more than identify the interests to be balanced. It teaches that the exclusionary rule leads to overdeterrence by creating a sanction that costs more to society than the social (not private) cost of an illegal search to the criminal defendant, and it teaches that, other things being equal, the graver the crime being investigated the lower should be the level of probable cause that the police need establish in order to be authorized to conduct a search. These are not truisms; they are nonobvious implications of economic analysis.

In response, Professor Sanford Levinson argued that economic analyses can support liberal positions as well as conservative ones on such issues as the

---

[21] *See* Eule, *Laying the Dormant Commerce Clause to Rest,* 91 YALE L.J. 425, 446–55 (1982).

Fourth Amendment exclusionary rule and tort alternatives.[29] Levinson concluded, however, that economic reasoning is useful for helping "to explain the decisions made by governmental actors, including judges."[30]

Shortly thereafter, Judge Posner acknowledged the limits of economic reasoning for guiding constitutional interpretation. He suggested that economic analysis is only part of a broader theory of legal pragmatism.[31] He explained that economic reasoning "works well only where there is at least moderate agreement on ends."[32] In contrast, "[o]ne value of pragmatism is its recognition that there are areas of discourse where lack of common ends precludes rational resolution; and here the pragmatic counsel (or one pragmatic counsel) to the legal system is to muddle through, preserve avenues of change, do not roil needlessly the political waters."[33]

Whereas economic reasoning constitutes only a portion of Judge Posner's pragmatic outlook, it is the central means by which two other law professors, A.C. Pritchard and Todd J. Zywicki, try to clarify how judges should go about using tradition as a source of constitutional decision.[34] They regard American Constitutionalism as having two efficiency goals—enabling "majorities to precommit themselves against imposing costs on minorities by enshrining certain overwhelmingly accepted principles in a governing document" and "allowing the people to restrain government actors from imposing agency costs on the citizenry by limiting the means by which government can act."[35] Tradition is a legitimate source of constitutional decision, because it "serves the efficiency purposes of constitutionalism by helping to identify those rules that are supported by a broad societal consensus and have been tested over time. Those rules are most appropriate for incorporation into the constitutional scheme as precommitments or devices to reduce agency costs."[36] The challenge in their view, is to find an "efficiency-based model for choosing among different traditions."[37] Such a model would avoid elevating inefficient traditions to constitutional status (i.e., norms that have "not been subject to repeated and decentralized testing and feedback because they rely on a centralized law-giver)."[38] Instead, the two professors propose that the appropriate model for guiding judicial recourse to tradition as a source of constitutional decision is efficient traditions, which "arise from the repeated interactions of many individuals across many generations testing, amending, and reaffirming those traditions."[39]

Zwyicki and Pritchard use two modes of economic reasoning—public choice theory[40] and the spontaneous order theory of Friedrich Hayek[41] –to analyze

---

[29] Sanford Levinson, *Some Reflections on the Posnerian Constitution,* 56 GEO. WASH. L. REV. 39 (1987).

[30] *Id.* at 49.

[31] Judge Posner suggests that an essential aspect of pragmatism is its focus on which possible resolutions of a problem are likely to have the best consequence, all things considered. *See* Richard A. Posner, *What Has Pragmatism to Offer Law?,* 63 SO. CAL. L. REV. 1653, 1664 et seq. (1990).

[32] *Id.* at 1668.

[33] *Id.*

[34] A.C. Pritchard & Todd J. Zwyicki, *Finding the Constitution: An Economic Analysis of Tradition's Role in Constitutional Interpretation,* 77 N.C. L. REV. 409 (1999).

[35] *Id.* at 412.

[36] *Id* at 412–413.

[37] *Id.* at 413.

[38] *Id.*

[39] *Id.*

[40] *Id.* at 477–89.

[41] *See infra* note 42.

whether the federal government or states are better able or situated to produce efficient traditions. For the authors, the federal government represents a centralized, hierarchical order, while states represent Hayek's conception of a spontaneous order, which is a decentralized system in which "law is created by and reflects norms and principles developed outside the legal system through voluntary interaction."[42]

Pritchard and Zwyicki use public choice theory to critique the efficiency of traditions that emerge from either the lawmaking of Congress or the precedents of the Supreme Court. The national lawmaking process is so infused with rent-seeking and rational ignorance that the traditions based on legislation or consensus that emerge from it are unlikely to be efficient; therefore, traditions emerging from that process are not a reliable source of norms facilitating the public good. To the contrary, such traditions are likely to help private interest groups gain goods for themselves because of their undue influence in the political process. Such traditions are thus poor candidates for incorporation into the Constitution, because they are not representative of society's preferences (particularly over time) and do not promote the public welfare.

According to Pritchard & Zwyicki, Supreme Court precedent also does not produce efficient traditions. The reason is that the Court is not subject to any competition. Instead, interest groups appeal to the three incentives that motivate justices: "(1) ideological voting; (2) their reputation and status; and (3) the power of the judiciary."[43] Supreme Court justices will respond to each of these appeals. For example, they will seek to advance their status by advancing the values of the professional class of which they are members— lawyers. Moreover, the same interest groups that make legislation inefficient will wield influence in the confirmation process, leading to the appointments of judges who are disposed to the creation of inefficient law. Thus, Supreme Court precedent is not likely to enhance the development of efficient traditions.

Building on Hayek's theory of spontaneous order, the authors suggest that traditions from "decentralized" ordering are more likely to enhance the constitutional precommitments necessary to allow for the development of legal rules that "best reflect[] the community's prevailing preferences and expectations."[44] The most important advantage of decentralized orders is jurisdictional competition. Efficient social norms are more likely to emerge from competing jurisdictions because capital and people can leave jurisdictions that impose inefficient norms. Thus, state constitutional traditions may provide useful sources of tradition for federal constitutional law because states compete with one another.

Based on their conception of the legal order that is likeliest to produce efficient norms (i.e., decentralized ones), the authors propose a rule for

---

[42] *Id.* at 457. The authors suggest within such a system " 'the judge draws his authority from an ability to discover a law that exists independently of the will of particular political authorities or the judge, embedded in the customs and expectations of the society in which the judge operates.' ") (citation omitted). *Id. See also* 1 FRIEDRICH A. HAYEK, LAW, LEGISLATION, AND LIBERTY: RULES & ORDER 100–01 (1973).

[43] Pritchard & Zwyicki, *supra* note 34, at 494.

[44] *Id.* at 458.

incorporating traditions from decentralized processes into the constitutional order. For example, they argue that where the scope of enumerated rights in the Constitution is ambiguous, federal judges should "look to the tradition found in state court decisions under the common law. State constitutional decisions would also be relevant when state constitutions have a provision analogous to a federal right."[45] This approach will allow for the incorporation of efficient traditions into the federal Constitution. If the Court were to follow this approach, it would in effect "reenact[] the methods used by the Framers of the Constitution and of the Bill of Rights by looking to state constitutions and the common law for the substantive principles of the federal Constitution."[46] Moreover, such an approach might be necessary to keep precommitments of the Constitution updated, because the constitutional amendment process suffers from the defects of a centralized legislative process.[47]

Pritchard and Zwyicki suggest that the Court should follow a similar course when applying unenumerated rights against the federal government. This course allows the Court to "find[] the law in preexisting consensus."[48] If the Court were to follow this course, "it would be the most efficient institution, if not the only institution, for translating that consensus into constitutional principle."[49] This approach would generate new, beneficial precommitments that will restrain the federal government. Nevertheless, the authors conclude their article on a cautionary note that invalidating state laws on the basis of unenumerated rights would be a mistake because it might impede the jurisdictional competition among the states.

In a reply, Professor John McGinnis offers a few gentle criticisms of Pritchard's and Zwyicki's arguments. First, he questions the authors' "almost blanket condemnation of top-down, hierarchical order."[50] Such condemnation ignores the fact that after the New Deal the United States has a mixed constitutional order of centralized and decentralized decisionmaking. Consequently, it is unrealistic to believe that the latter is not shaped or influenced by the former. Moreover the "production of inefficient traditions through centralized legislative power has increased and the conditions for the creation of efficient traditions have deteriorated. If this is a correct description of the real obstacles to the creation of efficient traditions in the United States, Professors Pritchard and Zwyicki's major proposal will not remove them. We no longer have a system for creating good centralized traditions, and incorporating even a few good state traditions into the federal system will not move us toward a system for decentralized tradition creation."[51] Second, McGinnis questions whether jurisdictional competition will in fact produce efficient traditions. "The federal government plays a role in almost every aspect of social policy. This fact may distort the traditions that emerge from states."[52] Third, he questions whether "state constitutional or common law traditions should be used to help interpret the Constitution where it is ambiguous."[53]

---

[45] Id. at 502.

[46] Id. (citations omitted).

[47] See id. at 514–15.

[48] Id. at 515.

[49] Id.

[50] John O. McGinnis, In Praise of the Effi-

ciency of Decentralized Traditions and Their Preconditions, 77 N.C. L. Rev. 523, 526 (1999).

[51] Id. at 529.

[52] Id.

[53] Id. at 530.

Such an interpretive assumption has many disadvantages, including but not limited to the fact that "incorporating such traditions will make it harder to change those traditions once they have ceased to be optimal;"[54] "incorporating predominant state traditions into federal law could create efficiency losses because predominant state traditions may not be efficient for all states;"[55] and using state court constitutional and common law decisions would "undermine the efficiencies that federalism creates by sustaining different bundles of rights that appeal to individuals with different preferences."[56] Lastly, McGinnis questions whether Pritchard's and Zwyicki's proposed methodology would preclude judges from "making up [their] own rules under the guise of discover[ing]" tradition.[57] "Statements about particular traditions emerging from different state courts will never be identical or labeled in the same manner. It will also often be unclear to what extent the traditions referenced in state cases contribute to a legal holding or are merely dicta. Ascertaining whether a particular tradition is recognized as a constitutional right by a majority of states thus will require substantial discretionary judgment."[58]

Pritchard and Zwyicki offer three responses to McGinnis' critique.[59] First, they suggest that the New Deal has not impeded the production of efficient traditions in the states, because the federal government is adequately constrained from impeding unduly on state autonomy because of both the Constitution's structural constraints on the federal government and the constraints set forth in the Bill of Rights. Second, Pritchard and Zwyicki suggest that McGinnis' faith in Article V as the only legitimate means of constitutional change is misplaced. They suggest that the original scheme set forth in Article V for formal constitutional change no longer works, in part because of the dominance of interest groups in the federal political process. It is inferior to the decentralized orders exemplified by the states for effectuating constitutional change in the form of tradition: "Special interests and politicians have no single place they can go to secure their desired changes. Power is decentralized and fragmentary. Thus, a spontaneous order system of constitutional change is more likely to generate constitutionally-efficient change than a centralized, designed order."[60] Third, they defend their proposed model for defining tradition as consistent with the original understanding, which indicates that "the Framers looked to state common law and state constitutions in drafting the Bill of Rights."[61] They suggest that their proposal does not allow for undue judicial discretion in defining unenumerated rights, because efficient traditions supply judges with "an external and neutral rule of decision."[62]

[B] Economic and Libertarian Activism

In the previous sections in this chapter, we have focused on the methodologies that are commonly associated with conservative constitutional theory. In

---

[54] Id.

[55] Id. at 531.

[56] Id.

[57] Id. at 532.

[58] Id.

[59] Pritchard & Zwyicki, Constitutions and Spontaneous Orders: A Response to Professor McGinnis, 77 N.C. L. REV. 537 (1999).

[60] Id. at 546.

[61] Id. at 547.

[62] Id. at 550.

this section, we examine conservative theorists' divisions over the extent to which the Constitution protects economic rights or interests.

The Cato Institute, a "libertarian" think-tank, co-published the book, ECONOMIC LIBERTIES AND THE JUDICIARY (J. Dorn & H. Manne eds. 1987), which features a classic exchange in which then-D.C. Circuit Judge Antonin Scalia and Professor Richard Epstein express contrasting views on the constitutional protections for economic interests. We begin with then-Judge Scalia's views, followed by those of Professor Epstein.

Scalia, *Economic Affairs as Human Affairs,* in Dorn & Manne at 31–37:[63]

My concern in this essay . . . is not economic liberty in general, but economic liberty and the judiciary. One must approach this topic with the realization that the courts are (in most contexts, at least) hardly disparaging of economic rights and liberties . . . . [T]he vast bulk of the courts' civil business consists of the vindication of economic rights between private individuals and against the government. Indeed, even the vast bulk of noncriminal "civil rights" cases are really cases involving economic disputes. The legal basis for the plaintiff's claim may be sex discrimination, but what she is really complaining about is that someone did her out of a job . . . .

. . . [T]he point is that we, the judiciary, do a lot of protecting of economic rights and liberties. The problem that some see is that this protection in the federal courts runs only by and large against the executive branch and not against the Congress. We will ensure that the executive does not impose any constraints upon economic activity which Congress has not authorized; and that where constraints *are* authorized the executive follows statutorily prescribed procedures and that the executive (and, much more rarely, Congress in its prescriptions) follows constitutionally required procedures. But we will never (well, hardly ever) decree that the substance of the congressionally authorized constraint is unlawful. That is to say, we do not provide a *constitutionalized* protection except insofar as matters of process, as opposed to substantive economic rights, are concerned.

There are those who urge reversal of this practice. The main vehicle available . . . is the due process clause of the Fifth and Fourteenth Amendments, which provides that no person shall be deprived of "life, liberty, or property, without due process of law." Although one might suppose that a reference to "process" places limitations only upon the *manner* in which a thing may be done, and not upon the *doing* of it, since at least the late 1800s the federal courts have in fact interpreted these clauses to prohibit the *substance* of certain governmental action, no matter what fair and legitimate procedures attend that substance. Thus, there has come to develop a judicial vocabulary which refers (seemingly redundantly) to "procedural due process" on the one hand, and (seemingly paradoxically) to "substantive due process" on the other hand. Until the mid-1930s, substantive due process rights were extended not merely to what we would now term "civil rights"—for example, the freedom to teach one's child a foreign language if one wishes—but also to a broad range of economic rights—for example, the right to work twelve hours a day if one wishes. Since that time, application of the concept has been consistently expanded in the civil rights field (*Roe v. Wade* is the most

---

[63] Copyright © 1990 by Antonin Scalia and the Cato Institute. Reprinted with permission of the author and the Cato Institute.

controversial recent extension) but entirely eliminated in the field of economic rights. Some urge that it should be resuscitated.

. . . The Supreme Court decisions rejecting substantive due process in the economic field are clear, unequivocal and current . . . . [I]n my view the position the Supreme Court has arrived at is good—or at least that the suggestion that it change its position is even worse.

. . . [M]y position is not based on the proposition that economic rights are unimportant. Nor do I necessarily quarrel with the specific nature of the particular economic rights that the most sagacious of the proponents of substantive due process would bring within the protection of the Constitution; were I a legislator, I might well vote for them. Rather, my skepticism arises from misgivings about, first, the effect of such expansion on the behavior of courts in other areas quite separate from economic liberty, and second, the ability of the courts to limit their constitutionalizing to those elements of economic liberty that are sensible. I will say a few words about each.

First, the effect of constitutionalizing substantive economic guarantees on the behavior of the courts in other areas: There is an inevitable connection between judges' ability and willingness to craft substantive due process guarantees in the economic field and their ability and willingness to do it elsewhere . . . . In the long run, and perhaps even in the short run, the reinforcement of mistaken and unconstitutional perceptions of the role of the courts in our system far outweighs whatever evils may have accrued from undue judicial abstention in the economic field.

The response to my concern, I suppose, is that the connection I assert between judicial intervention in the economic realm and in other realms can simply not be shown to exist. We have substantive due process aplenty in the field of civil liberties, even while it has been obliterated in the economic field. My rejoinder is simply an abiding faith that logic will out . . . . So I must believe that as bad as some feel judicial "activism" has gotten without substantive due process in the economic field, *absent* that momento of judicial humility it might have gotten even worse. And I have little hope that judicial and lawyerly attitudes can be coaxed back to a more restricted view of the courts' role in a democratic society at the same time that we are charging forward on an entirely new front.

Though it is something of an oversimplification, I do not think it unfair to say that this issue presents the moment of truth for many conservatives who have been criticizing the courts in recent years. They must decide whether they really believe, as they have been saying, that the courts are doing too much, or whether they are actually nursing only the less principled grievance that the courts have not been doing what *they* want.

The second reason for my skepticism is the absence of any reason to believe that the courts would limit their constitutionalizing of economic rights to those rights that are sensible . . . . Is there much reason to believe that the courts, if they undertook the task, would do a good job? If economic sophistication is the touchstone, it suffices to observe that these are the folks who developed three-quarters of a century of counterproductive law under the Sherman Act . . . .

But, the proponents of constitutionalized economic rights will object, we do not propose an open-ended, unlimited charter to the courts to create economic rights, but would tie the content of those rights to the text of the Constitution and, where the text is itself somewhat open-ended (the due process clause, for example), to established (if recently forgotten)

constitutional traditions. As a theoretical matter, that could be done—
though it is infinitely more difficult today than it was fifty years ago.
Because of the courts' long retirement from the field of constitutional
economics, and because of judicial and legislative developments in other
fields, the social consensus as to what are the limited, "core" economic
rights does not exist today as it perhaps once did. But even if it is
theoretically possible for the courts to mark out limits to their intervention, it is hard to be confident that they would do so. We may find
ourselves burdened with judicially prescribed economic liberties that are
worse than the pre-existing economic bondage. What would you think,
for example, of a substantive-due-process, constitutionally guaranteed,
economic right of every worker to "just and favourable remuneration ensuring for himself and his family an existence worthy of human dignity?"
Many think this a precept of natural law; why not of the Constitution?
A sort of constitutionally prescribed (and thus judicially determined)
minimum wage. Lest it be thought fanciful, I have taken the formulation
of this right verbatim from Article 23 of the United Nations' Universal
Declaration of Human Rights.

Finally, let me suggest that the call for creating (or, if you prefer,
"reestablishing") economic constitutional guarantees mistakes the nature
and effect of the constitutionalizing process . . . .

Most of the constitutionalizing of civil rights that the courts have
effected in recent years has been at the margins of well-established and
deeply held social beliefs. Even *Brown v. Board of Education,* as significant a step as it might have seemed, was only an elaboration of the
consequences of the nation's deep belief in the equality of all persons
before the law. Where the Court has tried to go further than that (the
unsuccessful attempt to eliminate the death penalty, to take one of the
currently less controversial examples), the results have been precarious.
Unless I have been on the bench so long that I no longer have any feel
for popular sentiment, I do not detect the sort of national commitment
to most of the economic liberties generally discussed that would enable
even an activist court to constitutionalize them. That lack of sentiment
may be regrettable, but to seek to develop it by enshrining the unaccepted
principles in the Constitution is to place the cart before the horse.

Epstein, *Judicial Review: Reckoning on Two Kinds of Error,* in Dorn &
Manne at pp. 39–42, 44–46:[64]

Scalia's position represents the mainstream of American constitutional
theory today. My purpose is to take issue with the conventional wisdom.
I hope to persuade Scalia to take upon himself, and to pursue energetically, the tasks that our Constitution assigns to him and to other federal
judges . . . .

In my view, Scalia has addressed only one side of a two-sided problem.
He has pointed out the weaknesses of judicial action. But he has not paid
sufficient attention to the errors and dangers in unchanneled legislative
behavior. The only way to reach a balanced, informed judgment on the
intrinsic desirability of judicial control of economic liberties is to consider
the *relative* shortcomings of the two institutions—judicial and legislative—that compete for the crown of final authority. The constitutionality
of legislation restricting economic liberties cannot be decided solely by
appealing to an initial presumption in favor of judicial restraint. Instead,

---

[64] Copyright © 1987 by Richard Epstein and
the Cato Institute. Reprinted with permission
of the author and the Cato Institute.

the imperfections of the judicial system must be matched with the imperfections of the political branches of government.

What are the problems with legislation? When we put someone in charge of the collective purse or the police force, we in effect give him a spigot that allows him to tap into other people's property, money, and liberty. The legislator that casts a vote on an appropriations bill is spending not only his own wealth, but everyone else's. When the power of coalition, the power of factions, the power of artifice and strategy come into play, it often turns out that legislatures reach results that (in the long as well as the short run) are far from the social optimum.

. . .

The theory of constitutionalism, as I understand it, tries to find a way to minimize the sum of the abuses that stem from legislative greed on the one hand, and judicial incompetence on the other. There is, by and large, no third alternative to this sorry state of affairs. What I fear is wrong with Scalia's statement of the argument is this: By focusing exclusively on the defects he finds in the judicial part of the process, he tends to ignore the powerful defects that pervade the legislative part of the process. Our Constitution reflects a general distrust toward the political process of government—a high degree of risk aversion. That is why it wisely spreads the powers of government among different institutions through a system of checks and balances. To provide no (or at least no effective) check on the legislature's power to regulate economic liberties is to concentrate power in ways that are inconsistent with the need to diversify risk. To allow courts to strike down legislation, but never to pass it, helps to control political abuse without undermining the distinctive features of the separate branches of government. Once we realize that all human institutions (being peopled by people) are prey to error, the only thing we can hope to do is to minimize those errors so that the productive activities of society can go forward as little hampered as possible.

Thus far I have been discussing general political theory: How is it that one would want to organize a constitution? But we do not have to talk about constitutions in the round and in the abstract. We have an actual constitution, and since it is a written one, we can check to see how it handles the particular problem of protecting economic liberties.

. . . [O]ur Constitution . . . contains many broad and powerful clauses designed to limit the jurisdiction of both federal and state governments. These include the eminent domain clause (which always bound the federal government and since the Civil War amendments has bound the states as well), the contracts clause, the privileges and immunities clause found both in the original Constitution and the Fourteenth Amendment, the equal protection clause, and due process.

These provisions are not curlicues on the margins of the document; they are not without force or consequence. They are provisions designed to preserve definite boundaries between public and private ordering. Take the question of minimum wages. The principle of freedom of contract— that parties should be free to set wage terms as they see fit—is, given the contracts clause, on a collision course with that sort of legislative regulation of the economy . . . . Many of the particular provisions of the Constitution are designed to deal with the very kinds of questions that political theory indicates to be sources of our enormous uneasiness and distrust of the legislative process.

. . .

. . . [J]udicial deference in the protection of economic rights has enormous costs. The moment courts allow all private rights to become unstable and subject to collective (legislative) determination, all of the general productive activities of society will have to take on a new form. People will no longer be able to plan private arrangements secure in the knowledge of their social protection. Instead, they will take the same attitude toward domestic investment that they take toward foreign investment. Assuming that their enterprise will be confiscated within a certain number of years, domestic investors will make only those investments with a high rate of return and short payout period, so that when they see confiscation coming, they will be able to run. To be sure, the probability of expropriation is greater in many foreign contracts than it is in the United States. But given our record of price controls and selective industry regulation, it is clear that the once great protections we enjoyed have been compromised, and for no desirable social goal.

I submit that this is not what we want legislatures to do. It is wrongheaded to argue that, because an auditor cannot hope to correct every abuse in the Defense Department's procurement policies, he should therefore refuse to go after the $5,000 coffee pot—or that because a judge cannot hope to correct every infringement of economic liberties, he should therefore refuse to go after large-lot zoning restrictions. There are many blatantly inappropriate statutes that cry out for a quick and easy kill. Striking them down puts no particular strain on the judiciary. To invalidate a statute, a judge need not make complex factual determinations or continually supervise large branches of the federal government. He need not take over school boards, try to run prisons or mental hospitals, or demand that Congress appropriate funds. He need only say that, in certain circumstances, the government cannot do something—period— while in other circumstances, it can, but must pay those people on whom it imposes a disproportionate burden.

Government exists, after all, because the market's ability to organize forced exchanges is limited. We need to collect taxes, to impose regulations, to assign rights and liabilities through a centralized process, but only for limited public purposes. Our guiding principle should derive from our Lockean tradition—a tradition that speaks about justice and natural rights, a tradition that understands the importance of the autonomy of the person, and respects it in religion, in speech, and in ordinary day-to-day affairs. When government wishes to encroach on those rights in order to discharge its collective functions, it must give all the individuals on whom it imposes its obligations a fair equivalent in exchange. It may be that it is not always possible to measure that equivalence. Possibly we cannot achieve the goal of full compensation and simultaneously provide the collective goods. I am prepared to debate at great length where the proper margins are with respect to the application of this general principle. What I am not prepared to say is that we can organize our society on the belief that the question I just posed is not worth asking. Consequently, when the government announces that it has provided a comparable benefit, courts should not take its word on faith, when everything in the record points indubitably to the opposite conclusion.

When one compares the original Constitution with the present state of judicial interpretation, the real issue becomes not how to protect the status quo, but what kinds of incremental adjustments should be made in order to shift the balance back toward the original design. On this question, we can say two things. First, at the very least, we do not want to remove what feeble protection still remains for economic liberties. Any further judicial abdication in this area will only invite further legislative intrigue and more irresponsible legislation . . . . Second, since courts are bound to some extent by a larger social reality, we cannot pretend that the New Deal never happened. Rather, we must strive to regain sight of the proper objectives of constitutional government and the proper distribution of powers between the legislatures and the courts, so as to come up with the kinds of incremental adjustments that might help us to restore the proper constitutional balance.

Judicial restraint is fine when it keeps courts from intervening in areas where they have no business intervening. But the world always has two kinds of errors: the error of commission (type I) and the error of omission (type II). In the context of our discussion, type I error refers to the probability of judicial intervention to protect economic rights when such intervention is not justified by constitutional provisions. And type II error refers to the probability of forgoing judicial intervention to protect economic liberties when such intervention is justified. This second type of error—the failure to intervene when there is strong textual authority and constitutional theory—cannot be ignored.

What Scalia has, in effect, argued for is to minimize type I error. We run our system by being most afraid of intervention where it is not appropriate. My view is that we should minimize both types of error. One only has to read the opinions of the Supreme Court on economic liberties and property rights to realize that these opinions are intellectually incoherent and that some movement in the direction of judicial activism is clearly indicated. The only sensible disagreement is over the nature, the intensity, and the duration of the shift.

Subsequently, Justice Scalia and Professor Epstein have had many opportunities to amplify their views on economic liberties. For example, Justice Scalia has participated in several controversial opinions that have revitalized the Takings Clause of the Fifth Amendment[65] (applied to the states via the Due Process Clause of the Fourteenth Amendment). For many scholars (both liberal and conservative), the critical question has been how to reconcile *Justice* Scalia's positions with those expressed by *then-Judge* Scalia in the essay above.

Among the most frequently debated cases are *Nollan v. California Coastal Commission,*[66] *Lucas v. South Carolina Coast Council,*[67] and *Dolan v. City of Tigard.*[68] First, in *Nollan,* the Court considered the constitutionality of a coastal commission's decision to condition a couple's right to rebuild their beach home on the couple's granting an easement allowing people to cross the beach near the house. In an opinion by Justice Scalia, the Court held that the condition constituted a per se taking.[69] Quoting from an earlier case, Justice Scalia observed that "where governmental action results in a 'permanent physical occupation' of the property, by the government itself or by others, . . . our cases uniformly have found a taking to the extent of the occupation, without regard to whether the action achieves an important public benefit or has only minimal economic impact on the owner.'"[70] He explained

---

[65] In pertinent part, the Fifth Amendment provides, "[N]or shall private property be taken for public use, without just compensation."

[66] 483 U.S. 825, 107 S. Ct. 3141, 97 L. Ed. 2d 677 (1987).

[67] 505 U.S. 1003, 112 S. Ct. 2886, 120 L. Ed. 2d 798 (1992).

[68] 512 U.S. 374, 114 S. Ct. 2309, 129 L. Ed. 2d 304 (1994).

[69] Justice Scalia was joined by Chief Justice Rehnquist and Justices Powell, White, and O'Connor. The dissenters were Justices Brennan, Marshall, Blackmun, and Stevens.

[70] *Id.* at 832 (quoting Loretto v. Teleprompter Manhattan CATV Corp., 458 U.S. 419, 433, 102 S. Ct. 3164, 73 L. Ed. 2d 868 (1982)).

that the Court "think[s] a 'permanent physical occupation' has occurred, for purposes of that rule, where individuals are given a permanent and continuous right to pass to and fro, so that the real property may continuously be traversed, even though no particular individual is permitted to station himself permanently upon the premises."[71] In response to an objection voiced in the dissent of Justice Brennan, Justice Scalia conceded that land-use regulations do not effect a taking if it "'substantially advance[s] legitimate state interests,'"[72] but he suggested there was not a sufficiently close "nexus" between the condition imposed by commission and its stated purpose, which was to facilitate "the public's ability to see the beach."[73] In the absence of such a nexus, the condition was tantamount to "'an out-and-out plan of extortion.'"[74] Indeed, the Court found that the fit between means and ends in this case was so loose that "this case does not meet even the most untailored standards."[75]

The dissenters charged that the majority demanded an unreasonably tight fit between means and ends, indeed one that was not consistent with the Court's traditional approach in this area. For example, in a dissent joined by Justice Marshall, Justice Brennan argued that the Court demanded a "degree of exactitude that is inconsistent with our standard for reviewing the rationality of a State's exercise of its police power for the welfare of its citizens."[76] The standard analysis, he suggested, would have been more like the traditional rational basis test, which the state had easily satisfied in this case. Justice Blackmun complained in a lone dissent that "[t]he close nexus between benefits and burdens that the Court now imposes on permit conditions creates an anomaly in the ordinary requirement that a State's exercise of its police power need be no more than rationally based."[77] In a dissent joined by Justice Blackmun, Justice Stevens complained that the majority's and other dissenters' tests for determining when a taking occurred were "vague" and thus did not give sufficiently clear guidance to lawmakers for determining how to fashion land-use regulations without violating the Takings Clause.[78]

In the next major Takings Clause decision, the Court in *Lucas* held that South Carolina had violated the Takings Clause by prohibiting construction of any permanent habitable structures on certain ocean-front property. In his opinion for the Court,[79] Justice Scalia based this holding on the view that the Takings Clause requires just compensation "when the owner of real property has been [required by the government] to sacrifice all economically beneficial uses in the name of the common good, that is, to leave his property economically idle."[80]

In reaching the latter conclusion, Justice Scalia rejected all early American experience, prior to and after the passage of the Bill of Rights, and any case

---

[71] *Nollan,* 483 U.S. at 832 (citations omitted).

[72] *Id.* at 834.

[73] *Id.* at 836.

[74] *Id.* at 837.

[75] *Id.*

[76] *Id.* at 843 (Brennan, J., dissenting).

[77] *Id.* at 866 (Blackmun, J., dissenting).

[78] *Id.* at 867 (Stevens, J., dissenting).

[79] In *Lucas,* Justice Scalia's opinion was joined by Chief Justice Rehnquist and Justices White, O'Connor, and Thomas. Justice Kennedy wrote a separate opinion concurring in the judgment.

[80] *Lucas,* 505 U.S. at 1019 (footnote omitted).

law prior to 1897 as "entirely irrelevant" in determining "the historical compact recorded in the Takings Clause."[81] Instead, Justice Scalia relied primarily on a line of post-1922 precedents that rejected the Court's earlier understanding that a "taking" consists "only [of] a 'direct appropriation' of property."[82] Justice Scalia explained that his deviation from earlier understandings of the Takings Clause was "consistent with our 'takings' jurisprudence, which has traditionally been guided by the understandings of our citizens regarding the content of, and the State's power over, the 'bundle of rights' that they acquire when they obtain title to property."[83]

In his dissent, Justice Blackmun took issue with Justice Scalia's conception of tradition.[84] He criticized Justice Scalia for not having any "clear and accepted 'historical compact' or 'understanding of our citizens'" supporting his decision.[85] Moreover, he chastised Justice Scalia for regarding "history as a grab-bag of principles, to be adopted where they support the Court's theory, and ignored where they do not."[86]

In *Dolan*, the Court struck down as violating the Takings Clause a city's decision to condition the approval of a woman's building permit on the dedication of a portion of her property for flood control and traffic improvements. In his opinion for the Court, Chief Justice Rehnquist explained that the land-use regulation at issue in this case did not pass muster under the "well-settled doctrine of 'unconstitutional conditions,'" which provides that "the government may not require a person to give up a constitutional right— here the right to receive just compensation when property is taken for public use—in exchange for the discretionary benefit conferred by the government where the benefit sought has little or no relationship to the property."[87] The Chief Justice clarified that the requisite nexus that must exist between the government's interest and the condition imposed was not the functional equivalent of the traditional rational basis test. Instead, "We think a term such as 'rough proportionality' best encapsulates what we hold to be the requirement of the Fifth Amendment. No precise mathematical calculation is required, but the city must make some sort of individualized determination that the required dedication is related both in nature and extent to the impact of the proposed development."[88] Nevertheless, the Court found that the city failed to make the requisite showing.

In a dissent joined by Justices Breyer and Ginsburg, Justice Stevens criticized, among other things, the Court's "'rough proportionality'" test as "run[ning] contrary to the traditional treatment of these cases . . ."[89] Justice Stevens suggests that at most the relevant case law (consisting of roughly a dozen state cases from which the majority derives its "'rough proportionality'" principle) "lend support to the Court's reaffirmation of Nollan's reasonable nexus requirement."[90]

---

[81] *Id.* at 1029 n.15.

[82] *Id.* at 1014 (citation omitted).

[83] *Id.* at 1028.

[84] Justices Stevens also dissented separately, while Justice Souter took the unusual step of filing a statement. In the statement, Justice Souter objected to the Court's decision on the ground that the case was not ripe for decision.

[85] *Id.* at 1062 (Blackmun, J., dissenting) (citations omitted).

[86] *Id.*

[87] *Dolan*, 512 U.S. at 386 (citations omitted).

[88] *Id.* at 392.

[89] *Id.* at 397 (Stevens, J., dissenting).

[90] *Id.* at 399.

For many conservative and liberal constitutional scholars, the Court's most recent Takings Clause decisions evaluate the constitutionality of land use regulations on the basis of a review demanding a relatively tight nexus between means and ends that is not unlike the relatively tight fit between means and ends that the *Lochner* Court insisted economic regulations generally must satisfy. The question for these scholars is whether any such similarity is a good or bad thing or perhaps mistaken or overstated.

As one could infer from the prior extract by Professor Epstein, he could be expected to support the outcomes in the Court's recent Taking's Clause cases, and he does. In 1995, he suggested that the central rationale of the Takings Clause was reflected in the basic proposition declared by Blackstone that when the state outrightly dispossesses someone of his property, " 'All that the legislature does is to oblige the owner to alienate his possessions for a reasonable price.' "[91] Professor Epstein then considered whether this same principle applies in cases in which there has not been outright dispossession of someone's private property but rather the government has passed a regulation that destroys or significantly diminishes its economic value. In Professor Epstein's view,

> the answer is that so long as the political risks associated with such behavior are identical to those of outright dispossession, then the legal response should be the same. Therefore, what is distinctive about these cases is not that they are beyond constitutional scrutiny, but that they are more likely to benefit and bind alike, so that compensation will be implicit in the legislative scheme itself.
>
> One can freely acknowledge that Blackstone did not see how or why his principle extended to those forms of government regulation. Yet it is equally important to recognize that even our Supreme Court, while no champion of the Takings Clause, does not immunize all regulators from takings challenges. Thus *Lucas v. South Carolina Coastal Council . . .* reaffirmed that regulation amounted to a compensable taking whenever it deprived its owner of "all economically beneficial uses" of the land. Nothing in Blackstone blocks this result, nor the further insistence that partial restrictions on land use should in principle be compensable as well.[92]

Conservative scholar Richard Levy addresses the tension between the Court's activism on behalf of some economic rights (such as the right not to have property taken away with just compensation) and general deference post-New Deal to economic regulations. He traces the origins of this tension to the New Deal Court. He believes "[t]he erosion of common-law baselines in the post-New Deal period facilitated the development of liberal jurisprudence but left the liberal Court without any well-defined baselines. The conservative Court's recent efforts to reinvigorate economic rights have failed in part because its high-profile commitment to judicial restraint prevented the reassertion of common-law baselines or the development of a workable alternative."[93] In

---

[91] Richard A. Epstein, *History Lean: The Reconciliation of Private Property and Representative Government,* 95 COLUM. L. REV. 591, 595 (1995) (quoting 1 William Blackstone, COMMENTARIES *135).

[92] *Id.* at 596 (footnote and citation omitted). Copyright © 1995 by Richard A. Epstein and the Columbia Law Review. Reprinted with the permission of the author and the Columbia Law Review.

[93] Richard E. Levy, *Escaping Lochner's Shadow: Toward a Coherent Jurisprudence of Economic Rights,* 73 N.C. L. REV. 329, 390 (1995).

cases arising under the Takings Clause, the Court fashioned an "expectations-based approach that emphasized the unfairness of frustrating justifiable reliance on the preexisting legal recognition of a given interest."[94] While the advantage of this approach is that it allows the Court to "externalize the creation of property or contract rights,"[95] he regards it as circular, because "if the creation of an entitlement is a function of the government's decision to accord a particular interest [privileged] status by virtue of positive law, the government could freely decide not to create any entitlements."[96] Thus, the expectations model "collapses into a baselineless world unless there is some external referent that limits the government's ability to structure the background law so as to define rights away."[97]

To resolve the incoherence of the Court's approach to takings (and other areas implicating economic rights or interests), Professor Levy suggests a three-pronged analysis, based on constitutional text, history, precedent, and structure. First, "the Court's substantive due process analysis could incorporate a 'proportionality principle' requiring government decisions to be sustained by public purposes proportional to their adverse impact on [economic rights]."[98] Second, he proposes that "equal protection analysis of nonsuspect classifications should employ a form of rational-basis-with-bite review that is designed to protect against [the] failures" of the political process to protect economic interests adequately.[99] Third, he argues that the Takings and Contracts Clauses "should be limited in light of their historical purposes; only measures directed toward relieving contractual obligations should violate the Contracts Clause, and the concept of regulatory takings should be abandoned altogether."[100]

Professor Levy suggests that "none of the rationales" used by the Court to justify the concept of regulatory takings "provides a persuasive foundation for" it.[101] The first rationale is "that property is a bundle of rights and that any diminution of that bundle takes property."[102] The most serious flaw in this rationale is that it "would convert every regulatory measure into a taking, and cripple the government."[103] Professor Levy finds nothing in the text or history of the Constitution to justify such an outcome.

The second rationale is "the unfairness of singling out a few property owners to bear the costs of government action that benefits society as a whole."[104] Professor Levy regards this rationale as flawed, because it "reflects political-process concerns that are poorly addressed in modern regulatory takings doctrine."[105] He explains, "Because there is no way to determine objectively whether a given distribution of costs and benefits is 'fair,' the crucial question is whether there is reason to believe that the political process has failed to afford reasonable protection to those who bear the costs."[106] Professor Levy can find no reason to support such a belief.

---

[94] Id. at 405.

[95] Id.

[96] Id. at 411.

[97] Id.

[98] Id. at 421.

[99] Id. at 421–22.

[100] Id. at 422.

[101] Id. at 432.

[102] Id.

[103] Id.

[104] Id.

[105] Id. at 433.

[106] Id. (citation omitted).

The third rationale is that regulation that " 'goes too far' " may be seen as analogous to physical appropriations, at least in terms of its effects on property owners."[107] Professor Levy argues that this rationale does not apply to cases in which regulations have not completely destroyed the economic value of private property. Moreover, while "[t]otal destruction of property interests recognized at common law often may be inconsistent with constitutional principles,"[108] "there are some governmental or societal purposes of sufficient magnitude to warrant destruction of property interests without compensation."[109] He suggests that the best means for determining whether the government has acted pursuant to such purposes in any given case is to balance the "individual economic interests" at stake "against the legitimate needs of the state."[110]

Like Professor Levy, Professor Molly McUsic explores the implications that the Court has "equipped itself with the doctrinal tools needed to provide the same level of protection of property under the Takings Clause that the *Lochner* Court afforded under the Due Process Clause."[111] She does so, however, from a liberal perspective. First, she is confident that the Court's Takings Clause jurisprudence does not represent a return to *Lochner*. She explains that "[r]ather than protecting market value, as the *Lochner*-era Court did, th[e Rehnquist] Court has instead protected what it considers 'fundamental' or 'core' property interests: interests centered around the right to control land. The Court has found per se or nearly per se takings when there is interference with the right to exclude, to control property disposition, or to develop land, but not when regulation merely limits prices, reduces profits, or decreases market value."[112] She concludes, however, that some of the spirit of Lochner is apparent in the Court's Takings Clause jurisprudence. For, she explains,

> [t]he similarity between the Court's current jurisprudence and the *Lochner* jurisprudence lies not in the amount or type of legislation at risk but the proportion of redistributive legislation put at risk. The *Lochner*-era jurisprudence targeted the major redistributive initiatives of liberal majorities in the late 1800s and early 1900s, primarily labor legislation, the regulation of prices, graduated taxes, and restrictions on entry into business. The Court's [Takings] jurisprudence targets the far more limited liberal agenda of the last twenty years . . . The fresh redistributive efforts of this era are embodied in laws such as environmental regulations, local and land use regulations, and tenant protection laws—the very laws under constitutional attack in the takings doctrine.[113]

§ 9.05 The Relationship Between "Natural Law" and Conservatism

Illustrating the multiplicity of approaches among conservative theorists, some stress not economic analysis but "natural law" approaches rooted in long

---

[107] *Id.* at 432 (citation omitted).

[108] *Id.* at 435 (citation omitted).

[109] *Id.*

[110] *Id.* at 433.

[111] Molly S. McUsic, *The Ghost of Lochner: Modern Takings Doctrine and its Impact on Economic Legislation,* 76 B.U. L. Rev. 605,

607–08 (1996).

[112] *Id.* at 608.

[113] *Id.* at 609. From Volume 76:4, Boston University Law Review (1996) 605–667. Copyright © 1996 Trustees of Boston University. Forum of original publication. Boston University bears no responsibility for any errors which have occurred in reproducing this article.

tradition and in some cases religious teachings. The relevance of natural law is, however, a source of disagreement for many scholars. Though the liberal theorist Thomas Grey speaks of a modern analogue to earlier natural law ideas, others are concerned with natural law itself. For example, Professor Harry Jaffa explained that some conservative theorists who considered themselves originalists (such as Judge Bork) failed to appreciate "that the original intentions of the framers (or ratifiers) of the Constitution . . . were indissolubly connected with the philosophy of natural rights and natural law expressed in the Declaration of Independence."[114] To appreciate the framers' enterprise, one needs to understand, like Madison, that the Declaration of Independence is "the repository of the principles of the Constitution."[115] While the principle of majority rule was one of these principles, it was by no means the only or dominant one. Indeed, a fundamental concern of the framers was containing the tyranny of the majority. Consequently, it is important to determine whether "a legislature is exercising a power that has not been granted to it by the people."[116] If so, the legislature is violating the fundamental compact embodied in the Constitution. As Professor Jaffa asks rhetorically, "What in the world does the proposition 'that all men are created equal' mean, except that (in the words of the Massachusetts Bill of Rights) 'The body politic is [a social compact] formed by a voluntary association of individuals'? How in the world can the 'just powers of government' be derived from the 'consent of the governed' except by an actual or implied contractual relationship defining and limiting the powers of government?"[117] Thus, judicial review entails determining whether government has exercised a power not granted by this compact.

The preceding comments from Professor Jaffa raise the question whether his approach would politicize constitutional law in much the same way that conservatives see liberals as having done, thus depriving conservatives of principled ground to object to liberal judicial activism. One may be at least as likely to read in one's personal views when purporting to determine the content of natural law as when attempting to discern social mores. Even so, Professor Jaffa's "natural law" perspective on constitutional theory received a rather surprising endorsement in an article by then-Chairman of the Equal Employment Opportunity Commission and now-Justice Clarence Thomas.[118] Thomas saw "the fundamental rights of the American regime—those of life, liberty, and property—as inalienable ones, given to man by his Creator," that "did not simply come from a piece of paper."[119] He argued that the "higher law political philosophy of the Founding Fathers" is "far from being a license for unlimited government and a roving judiciary. Rather, natural rights and natural law arguments are the best defense of liberty and of limited government."[120] "Rather than being a justification for the worst type of judicial

---

[114] Harry Jaffa, *Judge Bork's Mistake*, NAT'L REV., March 4, 1988, at 38, 40. This essay summarized the "natural law" view that Professor Jaffa had developed in a longer article, *What Were the "Original Intentions" of the Framers of the Constitution of the United States?*, 10 U. PUGET SOUND L. REV. 351 (1987).

[115] *Id.*

[116] *Id.*

[117] *Id.*

[118] Clarence Thomas, *The Higher Law Background of the Privileges or Immunities Clause of the Fourteenth Amendment*, 12 HARV. J. L. & PUB. POL'Y 63 (1989).

[119] *Id.* at 68 (footnote omitted).

[120] *Id.* at 63.

activism, higher law is the only alternative to the willfulness of both run-amok majorities and run-amok judges."[121]

Then-Chairman Thomas asserted that his outlook was consistent with conservative ideals and critiques of liberal policymaking and constitutional decisionmaking. Consequently, his article became the focus of heated debate in his confirmation hearings to become an Associate Justice,[122] when Thomas explained that his "interest in exploring natural law and natural rights was purely in the context of political theory." He testified that he saw no "role for the use of natural law in constitutional adjudication." He also said that he did not think natural law "has an appropriate role directly in constitutional adjudication" except possibly "to the extent that it is the background in our Declaration [of Independence and] part of the history and tradition of our country, and . . . informed some of the early litigation . . . with respect to the Fourteenth Amendment."[123]

One important question raised by Justice Thomas' remarks about natural law is to what extent, if any, natural law has played a role in his decisionmaking on the Supreme Court. In a comprehensive analysis of Justice Thomas' first five years on the Court, Scott Gerber concludes that the clearest illustration of Justice Thomas' reliance on or reference to the framers' views on natural law is in cases in which "the relationship between the Declaration of Independence and the Constitution" arises.[124] Gerber cites as an example Justice Thomas' concurrence in *Adarand Constructors Inc. v. Pena,* in which the justice argued that " '[t]here can be no doubt that the paternalism that appears to lie at the heart of this [affirmative action] program is at war with the principle of inherent equality that underlies and infuses our Constitution.' "[125] In support of the latter proposition, Justice Thomas quotes the following famous line from the Declaration of Independence: " 'We hold these truths to be self-evident, that all men are created equal, that they are endowed by their Creator with certain inalienable rights, that among these are Life, Liberty, and the pursuit of Happiness.' "[126]

Subsequent to the controversy over Justice Thomas' views on natural law and their possible relevance to his decisionmaking on the Court, many

---

[121] *Id.* at 64.

[122] For commentaries from various perspectives on the Thomas confirmation hearings, see *Gender, Race and the Politics of Supreme Court Appointments: The Impact of the Anita Hill/ Clarence Thomas Hearings,* 65 S. CAL. L. REV. 1279–1582 (1992). For one liberal scholar's critique of then-Chairman Thomas' views on natural law, see Laurence Tribe, *Clarence Thomas and 'Natural Law,'* NEW YORK TIMES, July 15, 1991, at section A, page 15, col. 1. For responses to Tribe's article, see Douglas W. Kmiec, *Natural Law, Unnatural Concern,* CHICAGO TRIBUNE, July 30, 1991, at page 15, zone C; Michael W. McConnell, *Trashing Natural Law,* NEW YORK TIMES, Aug. 16, 1991, at section A, page 23, col. 1; Michael Moore, *Perspectives on the Supreme Court; Unnatural Brawl*

Over Natural Law: What Clarence Thomas' Critics Object to Are His Values, Not His Natural-Law Views, LOS ANGELES TIMES, Sept. 3, 1991, at part B, page 5, col. 3.

[123] Unpublished transcript of U.S. Senate Judiciary Committee Hearing on the Nomination of Judge Clarence Thomas to the Supreme Court, Sept. 10, 1991 (on file with authors).

[124] SCOTT DOUGLAS GERBER, FIRST PRINCIPLES: THE JURISPRUDENCE OF CLARENCE THOMAS 42 (1999).

[125] *Id.* at 42 (quoting *Adarand,* 515 U.S. 200, 240, 115 S. Ct. 2097, 132 L. Ed. 2d 158 (1995) (Thomas, J., concurring in part and concurring in the judgment).

[126] S. Gerber, *supra* note 124, at 42 (citation to the Declaration of Independence omitted in the original).

scholars began to explore (1) what the framers meant when they referred to natural law and natural rights and (2) whether there is a conception of natural law or natural rights that is judicially enforceable. The following extract contains George Washington University Law Professor Philip Hamburger's summary of his answer to the first question, including his conclusion that modern scholars have largely misconstrued the relevance of natural law to the framers. Philip A. Hamburger, *Natural Law, Natural Rights, and the American Constitution,* 102 YALE L.J. 907, 955–59 (1993):[127]

Natural liberty and natural law were ideas that informed American perceptions of the rights protected by their written constitutions. This is not to say that framers and ratifiers regularly paused during their deliberations to specify the detailed theoretical assumptions examined here, or that they did not also have other theoretical assumptions; rather, it suggests that they and other Americans tended to discuss rights, particularly those guaranteed by written constitutions, in the context of their contemporary theoretical analysis of natural rights. . . .

[T]he constitutional implications of the natural rights analysis were striking, for the eighteenth-century American analysis of natural rights did not suggest the existence of expansive rights without substantial restrictions. When Americans said that certain rights were natural and pre-existed civil government, they were not thereby indicating that these rights were unlimited. On the contrary, Americans distinguished between natural rights and acquired rights; they assumed that, in the state of nature, natural rights were subject to the implications of natural law; and they assumed that under civil government natural rights were subject to civil laws. Moreover, natural law could be understood to suggest very imprecisely whether a civil law denied or abridged a natural right—a question that carried particular significance if the natural right was enumerated in a constitution.

By examining the American analysis of these limits on the extent of natural rights, we can learn not only about the circumscribed definition of natural rights, but also about the way Americans reconciled their claims of natural rights and natural law with their relatively restrictive civil laws. Contrary to the assumptions of many modern scholars, natural rights and natural law typically were considered compatible with the notion of a written constitution. Americans usually assumed that the people sacrificed some of their natural rights—that is, some of their natural freedom—in order to preserve the remainder, and these Americans understood written constitutions to be documents in which the extent of the sacrifice was recorded. Natural law was not a residual source of constitutional rights but rather was the reasoning that implied the necessity of sacrificing natural liberty to government in a written constitution. Americans tended to assume that natural rights and natural law were ideas that explained and justified written constitutions.

No less important, the natural law constraints on natural rights explained how natural rights could be regulated without being infringed. We frequently differentiate "mere regulation" from other restrictions, and we often assume that we must do so with little historical guidance about the definition of "mere regulation." Far from being indifferent to this problem, however, early Americans often took for granted a solution based on natural law. If, in the state of nature, the liberty of individuals was subject to natural law, then civil laws in accordance with natural law did

[127] Reprinted by permission of The Yale Law Journal Company and Fred B. Rothman & Company from The Yale Law Journal, vol. 102, pages 907–960.

not abridge or deny any natural rights. Thus, natural law provided a theoretical explanation of how the laws of civil government could regulate natural rights without infringing or diminishing them.

Most dramatically, the account of natural liberty presented here can help us understand what might otherwise appear to be contradictions or paradoxes in constitutional law. For example, Jefferson said both that natural rights were sacrificed to civil society and that no natural rights were sacrificed to civil society. Theophilus Parsons similarly seemed to contradict himself. In the Massachusetts ratification convention, when Parsons sought to assure his fellow delegates about the extent of Congressional power, he pointed out that Congress could not infringe any natural right not already restrained by the Massachusetts legislature: "Is there a single natural right we enjoy, uncontrolled by our own legislature, that Congress can infringe? Not one." By implication, the natural rights that Congress *could* infringe were rights that in any case were subject to control by the government of Massachusetts. Shortly afterward, however, he argued that "no power was given to Congress to infringe on any one of the natural rights of the people." Are we to suppose that a man almost as systematic and elegant in his law as in his mathematics was being so obviously sloppy or inconsistent? As has been seen, not only Jefferson and Parsons but also many other Americans talked about different types of natural right: physical freedom and noninjurious freedom—more precisely, the liberty natural law restrained and the liberty it defined.

Among the constitutional paradoxes in need of explanation are those involving particular natural rights enumerated in the Bill of Rights, such as the freedom of speech and press; and here, as earlier, the freedom of speech and press is the illustration upon which this Article focuses. How could eighteenth-century Americans profess a right of freedom of speech and press and yet not reject as unconstitutional the hiring and firing of public employees for their political opinions? How could they assert the right of free speech and press while accepting the various laws relating to seditious libel, personal defamation, and obscenity? Eighteenth-century Americans recognized that an individual in the state of nature had a freedom to say and publish what he pleased. Yet they also assumed that natural rights were distinct from acquired rights—that rights existing in the state of nature were different from those existing only under civil government—and that therefore the freedom of speech and press did not include, for example, a right to retain government employment. Moreover, Americans assumed that, already in the state of nature, natural law restricted an individual's freedom to say and publish what he pleased and defined the individual's noninjurious or, more broadly, moral natural right of speech and press. Consequently, civil laws that reflected the natural law limitations neither abridged the physical right nor denied the moral right to speak or publish . . . .

Conservative law professor Randy Barnett largely agrees with Professor Hamburger's characterizations of the framers' conceptions of natural law.[128] Unlike Professor Hamburger, Professor Barnett argues that the framers' conceptions of natural rights were incorporated into the Constitution in judicially enforceable ways. His argument has several steps. First, Professor Barnett explains that "for constitutional processes to be legitimate they must include procedures to assure that lawful commands are justified and of such

---

[128] Randy E. Barnett, *A Law Professor's Guide to Natural Law and Rights,* 20 HARV. J. LAW & PUB. POL'Y 655, 658 n.8 (1997).

a nature as to bind in conscience."[129] The governing principle for determining which commands are legitimate is the framers' "belief that enactments should not violate the inherent or natural rights of those to whom it is directed. That this was their belief—and that this belief is reflected in the words of the Ninth Amendment—is conceded even by those who would contest the appropriateness of judicial intervention to ensure that laws have this rights-respecting quality."[130] Based on his historical research, Barnett regards the natural rights retained by the people as "the set of concepts that define the moral space within which persons must be free to make their own choices and live their own lives. They are rights insofar as they entail enforceable claims on other persons (including [government]). And they are natural insofar as their necessity depends upon the (contingent) nature of persons and the social and physical world in which persons reside."[131] He distinguishes this conception of natural rights from natural law—the latter is a "method of addressing the legitimacy of individual conduct,"[132] while the former asks "what moral 'space' or 'jurisdiction' each person requires in order to pursue the good life in society with others."[133]

Given Barnett's conception of natural rights, he next considers why we should be bound by the framers' belief that legislation that violates natural rights is beyond the government's power. The answer suggested by Barnett is that we should be bound by their intentions for three reasons. First, many people "today purport to be governed" by the Constitution "when they issue supposedly binding commands to us."[134] Second, "we are bound in conscience to obey these commands only if the lawmaking processes established and regulated by [the constitutional] text provide assurances that our rights have not been violated."[135] Third, "if the Constitution provides effective protection of rights, then the lawful commands of constitutional authorities may be justified and binding and, if not, then we obey solely to avoid punishment."[136]

The next step in Barnett's analysis requires answering why courts should be bound by the framers' intentions that government is limited by certain rights not spelled out explicitly in the Constitution, such as natural rights. His answer is that "the 'best' interpretation of the U.S. Constitution is one that takes the natural or background rights of a person into account when evaluating the legitimacy of any governmental regulation of a person's rightful exercise of his or her liberty. For unless we do, the enterprise which the Constitution establishes and regulates will have failed in its essential function of providing justified laws that bind in conscience."[137]

The final question considered by Barnett is, to what extent do laws that infringe people's natural rights "bind in conscience those whose liberty is being regulated?"[138] He rejects the notion that natural rights require absolute protection, because "then no government action would withstand scrutiny."[139]

---

[129] Randy E. Barnett, *Getting Normative: The Role of Natural Rights in Constitutional Adjudication,* 12 CONST. COMM. 93, 105 (1995).

[130] *Id.*

[131] *Id.*

[132] *Id.* at 107.

[133] *Id.* at 108 (citation omitted).

[134] *Id.* at 110.

[135] *Id.*

[136] *Id.* at 110.

[137] *Id.* at 112.

[138] *Id.*

[139] *Id.*

Instead, "the fact that the rights retained by the people are inalienable (as I contend) means that, when their regulation is shown to be authorized, necessary, and proper, persons still retain their rights and may insist that a particular type of regulation cease when it has ceased to be necessary."[140] In practice, this principle gives rise to what Barnett characterizes as a "presumption of liberty"[141] that requires "a burden should be placed on those who seek to restrict liberty to justify their actions, rather than on the citizen to justify her freedom. In our constitutional scheme, this can be accomplished by linking state law determinations of rightful conduct with state and federal scrutiny of legislative and executive restrictions of such conduct."[142]

§ 9.06   Conclusion: The Transparency of Constitutional Argumentation?

Whereas the last chapter included some conservative critiques of liberal scholars' arguments on the propriety of removing President Clinton, it is fitting to include some critiques of conservatives' arguments on the same subject. For example, University of Virginia law professor Michael Klarman condemns liberals and conservatives for allowing their politics to drive their constitutional arguments during the Clinton impeachment proceedings.[143] We include below the portion of his critique of conservatives' arguments in the proceedings. Michael J. Klarman, *Constitutional Fetishism and the Clinton Impeachment Debate*, 85 VA. L. REV. 631, 635–37 (1999):[144]

> [T]he Republicans' principal constitutional arguments were every bit as unpersuasive. Some House members claimed during the impeachment debates that the Constitution denied them discretion not to impeach the president if he was found to have committed "high crimes and misdemeanors." This is hard to fathom. The relevant constitutional text provides that "The President . . . shall be removed from Office on Impeachment for, and Conviction of, . . . high Crimes and Misdemeanors."[16] This language seems to suggest that a *conviction* requires removal from office; it does not indicate that the House lacks discretion not to impeach if a "high crime or misdemeanor" has been committed. Nor is it obvious why, as a policy matter, one would wish to deprive the House of discretion in this regard. Prosecutors ordinarily are vested with enormous discretion over which crimes to prosecute.
>
> Equally strained was the argument advanced by numerous Republican Senators that once the House impeached the president, the Senate had no choice but to conduct a trial on that impeachment. Article 1, § 6 says

---

[140] *Id.* at 113.

[141] *Id.*

[142] *Id.* at 121.

[143] Judge Posner argues that the "formalism" of President "Clinton's attackers" blinded them to the practical consequences of their "mantra" that "no man is above the law, no felony should go unpunished, prosecutorial excess should not mitigate a defendant's punishment, but instead should result in two punishments (of the defendant and the prosecutor), and expediency should have no weight in the decision whether"

to remove the President. RICHARD A. POSNER, AN AFFAIR OF STATE: THE INVESTIGATION, IMPEACHMENT, AND TRIAL OF PRESIDENT CLINTON 171 (1999). These arguments alienated the public, which took the position "that pragmatic considerations should bear heavily on the decision whether to remove a President from office." *Id.* at 230.

[144] Copyright © 1999 by the Virginia Law Review Association. Reprinted with permission.

[16] U.S. Const., art. II, § 4.

that "The Senate shall have the sole Power to try all Impeachments."[18] It says nothing about the Senate being required to conduct a trial whenever the House impeaches. It may be that a proper regard for the judgment of a coordinate legislative branch should counsel senators against readily dismissing impeachments without trial. But does the Constitution *forbid* the Senate from doing so if a majority deems that course appropriate? Of course not. It is unsurprising that few if any Democrats were convinced by this fanciful constitutional argument. Nor was there any basis for the claim asserted by numerous Republicans that the Constitution proscribed Democratic attempts to terminate the trial without an up-or-down vote on the articles of impeachment. The Constitution says nothing whatsoever about the Senate's being compelled to carry an impeachment trial through to its bitter end, notwithstanding an indisputable showing on an early motion to dismiss that the requisite supermajority for conviction is lacking.

One of the most important constitutional debates surrounding impeachment was the viability of alternatives short of removal from office. Specifically, voluminous debate transpired regarding the constitutionality of censure and findings of fact. It is difficult to believe that any of this argument persuaded anyone, since the Constitution simply does not answer these questions. Two intersecting constitutional provisions supply the relevant text. Article I, § 7 provides that "Judgment in Cases of Impeachment *shall not extend further than* to removal from Office, and disqualification to hold and enjoy any Office of honor, Trust, or Profit under the United States; . . ."[145] Article II, § 4 says that "The President . . . shall be removed from Office on Impeachment for, and Conviction of, Treason, Bribery, or other high Crimes and Misdemeanors."[146] The former provision seems to leave open the possibility of punishments that do not go as far as removal from office, such as censure. The latter seems to require removal from office for all impeachment convictions. Some commentators have argued that the best way to reconcile the two provisions is to require removal from office for conviction of "Treason, Bribery, or other high Crimes and Misdemeanors" but to allow lesser punishments for lesser offenses. Others have responded that a better reconciliation of the two clauses treats the first as limiting additional punishments beyond removal rather than as inviting alternative punishments short of removal. Neither textual interpretation seems obviously superior to the alternative. More importantly, though, the Constitution plainly says nothing about what Congress can do with regard to a president who has not been convicted on an impeachment. Specifically, the Constitution is silent on the subjects of censure and findings of fact in the course of an impeachment trial. One can argue, of course, that because the Constitution does not specifically authorize Congress to censure the president, it lacks the power to do so. But one might respond with equal plausibility that because the Constitution does not specifically bar Congress from censuring the president, it has the power to do so. A censure resolution that carries no legal consequences is plausibly an exception to the Article I notion that Congress can act only via enumerated powers; Congress passes such resolutions all of the time.

Professor Klarman concedes that politics will inevitably have some impact on the outcomes of constitutional disputes (such as the Clinton impeachment proceedings) in which the conventional sources of constitutional decision provide little guidance. Under such circumstances, he counsels that we should

---

[18] U.S. Const., art. I, Section 3, cl. 6.   [146] *Id.*, art. II, § 4.

[145] U.S. CONST., art. I, § 7 (emphasis added).

all remain quite sensitive to the consequences of such politically-charged debate. He identifies two harmful effects. *Id.* at 651–54:

> While, virtually all the constitutional arguments surrounding impeachment were unpersuasive, they still may have had two deleterious consequences. First, debating impeachment questions in constitutional terms enabled politicians to evade responsibility for their actions. This happened on both sides of the aisle. Democrats should have concentrated on the argument that the president's transgressions were not sufficiently serious to render the country better off by abbreviating his term of office. Instead, they mainly argued that the Constitution did not permit his removal because his misdeeds failed to satisfy the Framers' conception of "high crimes and misdemeanors." That argument was a distraction. Whether or not the Framers in 1787 would have deemed Clinton's behavior impeachable, he should have been removed from office if most people in 1999 deemed his conduct sufficiently egregious. Democrats should not have been permitted to avoid confronting that issue by pleading that the Framers had resolved it for them.
>
> Conversely, Republicans should have stuck with the argument that the president's conduct was sufficiently serious to justify his removal, rather than contending that the Constitution deprived representatives of discretion not to impeach him if he had committed high crimes and misdemeanors, or Senators of discretion not to try him once the House had impeached him, or either house of discretion to adopt a lesser sanction such as censure. The Constitution forbids none of these things, and politicians insisting that it does were simply evading responsibility for their actions. All that the Constitution required of congressmen was a judgment on this straightforward question—were the president's misdeeds sufficiently serious to warrant removing him from office, judged not by an originalist standard of 1787 but by the standards of today?
>
> In answering that question, one might be forgiven for thinking that the views of the American public should have been highly relevant, if not dispositive. It is here that we see the second insidious consequence of the pervasive constitutionalization of the impeachment debate. A large component of American constitutional law is the protection of minority rights and certain basic structural safeguards from majoritarian tampering. For example, popular majorities are not permitted, simply by virtue of their majority status, to impose racial segregation on public schools or to authorize the federal government to exceed its enumerated powers. Advocates of President Clinton's impeachment and removal traded on this antimajoritarian aspect of constitutionalism. Claiming the moral high ground, they invoked the "minority rights" conception of constitutionalism to justify ignoring opinion polls and congressional election results that revealed a substantial majority of Americans opposing the president's removal from office. Yet sometimes the Constitution does require that we follow the election returns. Popular majorities do get to elect representatives and senators, and with the slight complication of the electoral college, presidents as well. If Republicans after the 1992 presidential election had tried to block Clinton's assumption of office, arguing that they were following the moral high ground by ignoring the election returns, their actions rightly would have been perceived as revolutionary rather than praiseworthy. This is because one's entitlement to hold office in a democratic system is based, generally speaking, on majority support.
>
> The pressing question in the Clinton controversy was whether impeachment is more like issues where we protect minority rights from majoritarian oppression or issues where we award popular majorities the fruits of their electoral triumphs. By invoking constitutional rhetoric, Republicans implicitly tapped into the antimajoritarian strand of constitutional

law—the safeguarding of minority rights from majoritarian oppression. Yet it is difficult to fathom arguments for why impeachment is an issue upon which minorities warrant protection from majoritarian decisionmaking. If popular majorities get to elect a president, it is hard to see why they should be ignored on the question of whether he remains fit to hold office. In a democratic society, how can it make sense to remove from office a popularly-elected president whose transgressions are not deemed sufficiently serious to justify removal by roughly two-thirds of the electorate? Republicans never offered an argument for why this was a reasonable way to approach impeachment. Their use of constitutional rhetoric enabled them to avoid explaining why the public sentiment that plainly opposed their objectives was irrelevant.

Professor Klarman concludes that the vagueness of the constitutional standard for impeachment made inevitable the infusion of politics into the President's impeachment proceedings. He explains, "standards inevitably require the exercise of discretion, and discretion invites the interpreter to apply his or her own values. The critical question in the impeachment context is whether or not such discretion is a good thing."[147] In practice, this means that "presidents will be removable from office either when the objectionable conduct meets a threshold standard and the impeaching party has a two-thirds majority in the Senate or when the conduct is sufficiently egregious that bipartisan support for impeachment exists."[148] Otherwise, partisanship is likely to dominate the proceedings. If students agree with Professor Klarman's analysis, they should consider its implications for courts, particularly what constraints if any will preclude politics from dominating judicial decisionmaking. If students disagree with Professor Klarman, they should consider what went wrong in President Clinton's impeachment proceedings, and is it something either judicial review or altering the constitutional procedures for impeachment could fix?

§ 9.07 Bibliography

[A] The Many Faces of Judicial Restraint and Conservatism on the Rehnquist Court

Robert Bork, *Styles in Constitutional Theory,* 26 S. TEX. L. REV. 383 (1985)

Richard A. Brisbin, JUSTICE ANTONIN SCALIA AND THE CONSERVATIVE REVIVAL (1997)

Erwin Chemerinsky, *Is the Rehnquist Court Really that Conservative? An Analysis of the 1991-92 Term,* 26 CREIGHTON L. REV. 987 (1993)

Stephen E. Gottlieb, *The Philosophical Gulf on the Rehnquist Court,* 29 RUTGERS L. REV. 1 (1997)

Nadine Strossen, *The Current Assault on Constitutional Rights and Liberties: Origins and Approaches,* 99 W. VA. L. REV. 769 (1997)

Christopher Wolfe, JUDICIAL ACTIVISM: A BULWARK OF FREEDOM OR PRECARIOUS SECURITY? (1997)

---

[147] Michael J. Klarman, *Constitutional Fetishism and the Clinton Impeachment Debate,* 85 VA. L. REV. 631, 658 (1999). [148] *Id.*

[B] Rule- and Tradition-Based Constitutional Decision Making

Raoul Berger, *Reflections on Constitutional Interpretation,* 1997 B.Y.U. L. REV. 517 (1997); *Constitutional Interpretation and Activist Fantasies,* 82 KY. L.J. 1 (1993)

Thomas W. Merrill, *Bork v. Burke,* 19 HARV. J.L. & PUB. POL'Y 509 (1996)

Antonin Scalia, A MATTER OF INTERPRETATION: FEDERAL COURTS AND THE LAW (1997) (with commentaries by Gordon S. Wood, Laurence H. Tribe, Mary Ann Glendon, and Ronald Dworkin)

David A. Schultz & Christopher E. Smith, THE JURISPRUDENTIAL VISION OF JUSTICE ANTONIN SCALIA (1996)

Cass R. Sunstein, *Justice Scalia's Democratic Formalism* (reviewing Scalia, A MATTER OF INTERPRETATION: FEDERAL COURTS AND THE LAW (1997)), 107 YALE L.J. 529 (1997)

[C] Economic Analysis and Rights

[1] Economic and Libertarian Activism

Richard Epstein, TAKINGS: PRIVATE PROPERTY AND THE POWER OF EMINENT DOMAIN (1985); *The Proper Scope of the Commerce Power,* 73 VA. L. REV. 1387 (1987)

LIBERTY, PROPERTY, AND THE FUTURE OF CONSTITUTIONAL DEVELOPMENT (Ellen Frankel Paul & Howard Dickman eds.) (with articles by James M. Buchanan, Mark Tushnet, William H. Riker, Lino A. Graglia, Stephen Macedo, Frank Michelman, Richard A. Epstein, R. Shep Melnick, Thomas R. Haggard, and Leo Troy)

Stephen Macedo, THE NEW RIGHT V. THE CONSTITUTION (1987) (with postscript by Gary McDowell)

Earl Maltz, *The Prospects for a Revival of Conservative Activism in Constitutional Jurisprudence,* 24 GA. L. REV. 629 (1990)

Bernard Siegan, ECONOMIC LIBERTIES AND THE CONSTITUTION (1980); *Propter Honoris Respectum: Separation of Powers and Economic Liberties,* 70 NOTRE DAME L. REV. 415 (1995)

Federalist Society Symposium, *Constitutional Protections of Economic Activity: How They Promote Individual Freedom,* 11 GEO. MASON U. L. REV. 1 (1988) (with articles by Henry G. Manne, Richard A. Epstein, Gary Lawson, Roger Pilon, Mark Kelman, Gale Norton, Akhil R. Amar, Frank H. Easterbrook, Julian N. Eule, Charles McCurdy, Kenneth W. Starr, Manuel S. Klausner, Robert Pitofsky, Christopher D. Stone, Douglas H. Ginsburg, Kate Stith, Wm. Craig Stubblebine, Leonard D. Liggio, Kenneth S. Abraham, Robert C. Ellickson, and T. Kenneth Cribb)

[2] Commentaries on Economic Analyses of the Constitution

David W. Barnes & Lynn A. Stout, THE ECONOMICS OF CONSTITUTIONAL LAW AND PUBLIC CHOICE (1992)

Michael Conant, THE CONSTITUTION AND THE ECONOMY (1991)

James Rolph Edwards, REGULATION, THE CONSTITUTION, AND THE ECONOMY: THE REGULATORY ROAD TO SERFDOM (1998)

Daniel Farber & Phil Frickey, *The Jurisprudence of Public Choice,* 65 TEX. L. REV. 873 (1987)

Mark Kelman, *On Democracy-Bashing: A Skeptical Look at the Theoretical and "Empirical" Practice of the Public Choice Movement,* 74 VA. L. REV. 199 (1988)

Charles Koch, Jr., *Cooperative Surplus: The Efficiency Justification for Active Government,* 31 WM. & MARY L. REV. 431 (1990)

Richard Pildes, *Why Rights Are Not Trumps: Social Meanings, Expressive Harms, and Constitutionalism,* 27 J. LEGAL STUD. 725 (1998)

Richard Pildes with Elizabeth Anderson, *Slinging Arrows at Democracy: Social Choice Theory, Value Pluralism, and Democratic Politics,* 90 COLUM. L. REV. 2121 (1990)

Richard Posner, THE ECONOMICS OF JUSTICE (1981); *Against Constitutional Theory,* 73 N.Y.U. L. REV. 1 (1998)

PUBLIC CHOICE AND PUBLIC LAW: READINGS AND COMMENTARY (Maxwell Stearns, ed.) (1997)

[D] Conservatism and "Natural Law"

John Finnis, *Liberalism and Natural Law Theory,* 45 MER. L. REV. 687 (1994)

Harry V. Jaffa, ORIGINAL INTENT AND THE FRAMERS OF THE CONSTITUTION: A DISPUTED QUESTION (1994)

Kirk A. Kennedy, *Reaffirming the Natural Law Jurisprudence of Justice Clarence Thomas,* 9 REG. U.L. REV. 33 (1997)

Russell Kirk, *Natural Law and the Constitution of the United States,* 69 NOTRE DAME L. REV. 1035 (1994)

Lewis Lehrman, *The Declaration of Independence and the Right to Life,* The American Spectator, Apr. 1987, at 21

Frederick Schauer, *Constitutional Positivism,* 25 CONN. L. REV. 797 (1993) (with commentaries by Robin West, Sanford Levinson, Randy Barnett, J.M. Balkin, Steven Winter, and Jeremy Paul)

Anthony J. Sebok, *The Insatiable Constitution,* 70 S. CAL. L. REV. 417 (1997)

Symposium, *Natural Law vs. Natural Rights: What Are They and How Do They Differ?,* 20 HARV. J. L. & PUB. POL'Y 627 (1997) (with articles by Douglas W. Kmiec, Randy Barnett, Richard Tuck, and Michael P. Zuckert)

Symposium on Natural Law, 4 S. CAL. INTERDISC. L. REV. 455 (1995) (with articles by Schyler M. Moore, R. George Wright, David M. Adams, Thomas B. McAfee, Charles R. Kesler, Russell Hittinger, Steven D.

Smith, Ronald R. Garet, Michael H. Hoffheimer, Lino A. Graglia, and Harry V. Jaffa)

Symposium, PERSPECTIVES ON NATURAL LAW, 61 U. Cin. L. Rev. 1 (1992) (articles by Raoul Berger, Stephen Macedo, Calvin Massey, Thomas McAfee, and Suzanna Sherry)

Symposium, *The Reemergence of Natural Law Jurisprudence in Decisional Law*, 26 U.C. DAVIS L. REV. 503 (1993)

Clarence Thomas, *Toward a "Plain Reading" of the Constitution—The Declaration of Independence in Constitutional Interpretation*, 30 Howard L.J. 691 (1987); *Why Black Americans Should Look to Conservative Policies*, HERITAGE FOUNDATION REPORTS: THE HERITAGE LECTURES, June 18, 1987

[E] Critical Commentaries on Conservative Constitutional Theory

Sotirios Barber, THE CONSTITUTION OF JUDICIAL POWER (1993); *The New Right Assault on Moral Inquiry in Constitutional Law*, 54 GEO. WASH. L. REV. 253 (1986)

David P. Bryden, *Is the Rehnquist Court Conservative?*, 109 THE PUBLIC INTEREST 73 (1992)

David Chang, *Discriminatory Impact, Affirmative Action, and Innocent Victims: Judicial Conservatism or Conservative Justices?*, 91 COLUM. L. REV. 790 (1991)

Erwin Chemerinsky, *The Supreme Court, 1988 Term—Foreword: The Vanishing Constitution*, 103 HARV. L. REV. 43 (1989)

Commentaries on Justice Harlan as a Judicial Conservative, Centennial Conference in Honor of Justice John Marshall Harlan, 36 N.Y.L.S. L. REV. 3–73 (1991) (with articles by James L. Oakes, Bruce Ackerman, Charles Fried, Kent Greenawalt, and Gerald Gunther)

George Kannar, *The Constitutional Catechism of Justice Scalia*, 99 YALE L.J. 1297 (1990)

David Kairys, WITH LIBERTY AND JUSTICE FOR SOME: A CRITIQUE OF THE CONSERVATIVE SUPREME COURT (1993)

Bernard Schwartz, THE NEW RIGHT AND THE CONSTITUTION: TURNING BACK THE LEGAL CLOCK (1990)

Nadine Strossen, *Justice Harlan and the Bill of Rights: A Model for How a Classic Conservative Court Would Enforce the Bill of Rights*, 36 N.Y.L.S. L. REV. 133 (1991)

Mark Tushnet, *Conservative Constitutional Theory*, 59 TUL. L. REV. 910 (1985)

Chapter 10

Feminist Legal Theory

§ 10.01 Introduction and Overview

The term "feminist legal theory" encompasses various schools of thought premised on the belief that sex and gender significantly affect the manner in which a legal system functions. In this context, the term "sex" typically refers to physical differences that exist between men and women, while the term "gender" typically refers to social or cultural beliefs about distinctions between men and women. This Section provides an overview of feminist legal theory, its relevance to constitutional law, and four schools of thought into which it is commonly organized. Sections 10.02 through 10.05 of this Chapter discuss examples of legal scholarship that are identified with each school of thought. Section 10.06 concludes by describing emerging trends in feminist legal theory.

Feminist legal theory in the United States has roots in the nineteenth century women's rights movement, which included among its goals women's suffrage, the ability of married women to make contracts and own property, and the right of women to use birth control. Although the women's rights movement dates back to at least the 1848 Seneca Falls women's convention, the Reconstruction-era exclusion of women from the constitutional equality and suffrage protections of the fourteenth and fifteenth amendments energized an independent feminist movement built on the realization that the democratic principles of universal liberty and equality would not be extended to women without fundamental changes in the basic assumptions of American culture.[1] In the twentieth century, feminist legal theory has drawn on feminist theory from other disciplines—including philosophy, history, sociology, art, anthropology, psychology, psychiatry and literary theory—in suggesting that women possess unique perspectives on a wide range of issues that are essential to the proper functioning of the American legal system.[2] Nevertheless, most feminists believe that women's perspectives on these issues are often discounted or totally overlooked.

Perhaps the most significant feature of contemporary feminist legal theory is its effort to make women's perspectives an integral part of legal discourse. Philosophy Professor Patricia Smith is one of many feminists who have described the elimination of "patriarchy" as the essence of feminist jurisprudence.

Feminist theory recognizes that throughout history and even today, public discourse has been almost exclusively conducted by men from (quite naturally) the perspective of men. That is, the nature of women has been

---

[1] See ERIC FONER, RECONSTRUCTION: AMERICA'S UNFINISHED REVOLUTION 255–56, 313, 447–48, 472–73 (1988).

[2] See Suzanna Sherry, *Civic Virtue and the Feminine Voice in Constitutional Adjudication*, 72 VA. L. REV. 543, 579–84 (1986).

formulated by men, and the interests of women have been determined by men. Historically, women have never been allowed to represent themselves. They have always been represented by men, but this representation has hardly been accurate or fair. Even though it claims to represent all human beings, the fact is that public discourse has left out, silenced, misrepresented, disadvantaged, and subordinated women throughout all of history, relegating them to a single role and reserving the rest of life for men. . . .

. . . Not even all feminists hold a single perspective, and not all women, of course, are feminists. But all feminism does begin with one presumption, namely, that a patriarchal world is not good for women. Virtually everyone agrees that the world is, in fact, patriarchal; that is, human societies have always been organized in a hierarchical structure that subordinates women to men. This is simply the observation of a social fact. Until recently it was virtually impossible to imagine the world any other way, and even now a great many men and women think that patriarchy is good, natural, or inevitable. Feminists think that patriarchy (the subjugation of women) is not good, not ordained by nature, and not inevitable.

The rejection of patriarchy is the one point on which all feminists agree. It is also apparently a distinguishing feature of feminism as a school of thought, as no other school of thought focuses on the critique of institutions and attitudes as patriarchal. Only feminism analyzes the patriarchal origin, nature, and effects of human attitudes, concepts, relations, and institutions and criticizes them on that ground. So we might take as a reasonable working definition that feminist jurisprudence is the analysis and critique of law as a patriarchal institution.[3]

Feminist legal theory is particularly relevant to constitutional theory, because the Constitution addresses many issues that affect the interests of women. The equal protection clause is central to disputes about gender discrimination, affirmative action and sexual orientation; substantive due process, privacy and liberty provisions affect women's rights to abortion, other reproductive freedoms, and freedom from spousal abuse; and the first amendment is implicated by efforts to regulate pornography, hate speech and sexual harassment. In fact, the Constitution itself may be a suspect document from a feminist perspective. Professor Mary E. Becker, has argued that the Bill of Rights, although drafted largely in gender neutral terms, does more to protect the interests of male owners of property than to protect the interests of women and other marginalized groups.[4] She notes that the Constitution disadvantages women in ways that are both direct and subtle. Some provisions directly benefit men more than women, such as the fourth amendment guarantee of security in one's home, which does not protect women from spousal abuse. Other provisions subtly impede legislative reforms that would benefit women, such as the second amendment impediments to gun control legislation—legislation that is favored by most women.[5] Other provisions impede women's effective political participation, such as the first amendment's protection of political spending, which "constitutionaliz[es] the right of the rich

---

[3] Patricia Smith, *Introduction: Feminist Jurisprudence and the Nature of Law*, in FEMINIST JURISPRUDENCE 3 (Patricia Smith ed., 1993). Copyright © 1993 by Oxford University Press, Inc. Used by permission of Oxford University Press, Inc.

[4] *See* Mary E. Becker, *The Politics of Women's Wrongs and the Bill of "Rights": A Bicentennial Perspective*, 59 U. CHI. L. REV. 453 (1992).

[5] *See id.* at 453–58.

to participate in the political process more effectively than the poor. And women are, of course, disproportionately poor."[6] Because the Bill of Rights "incorporates a public-private split with only negative rights under a limited government . . . women's activities and concerns—from economic rights to religion—seem beyond the proper scope of government."[7] In discussing the countermajoritarian structure of our constitutional government, Professor Becker concludes, "We should see it as a problem of democracy that, to date, women have not exercised their share of governmental power. [O]ther governmental structures and electoral systems may be more democratic."[8]

Feminist legal theory has responded to the law's marginalization of women's perspectives, in part, by advocating the incorporation of nontraditional methods of analysis into legal discourse. Professor Katharine T. Bartlett has described three analytical techniques produced by the feminist movement that she believes can enhance the sensitivity of the legal system to women's perspectives.

> In addition to these conventional methods of doing law, however, feminists use other methods. These methods, though not all unique to feminists, attempt to reveal features of a legal issue which more traditional methods tend to overlook or suppress. One method, asking the woman question, is designed to expose how the substance of law may silently and without justification submerge the perspectives of women and other excluded groups. [For example, in rape cases, why does the defense of consent focus on what the defendant "reasonably" thought the woman wanted and not on what the woman "reasonably" thought she conveyed to the defendant?] Another method, feminist practical reasoning, expands traditional notions of legal relevance to make legal decisionmaking more sensitive to the features of a case not already reflected in legal doctrine. [For example, it can do this by de-emphasizing abstract rules or principles, and focusing on factual context, multiple perspectives, contradictions, and inconsistencies in order to arrive at solutions to disputes that are pragmatic and creative.] A third method, consciousness-raising, offers a means of testing the validity of accepted legal principles through the lens of the personal experience of those directly affected by those principles. [For example, by sharing personal experiences with other women, some of those experiences can be validated and used as the basis for developing theories of oppression to challenge dominant versions of social reality, and those theories can in turn be refined in a trial-and-error manner through the incorporation of yet additional experiences.] . . .[9]

Not all feminists agree about all aspects of feminist legal theory. Rightly or wrongly, it has now become common to divide feminist legal theory into several distinct schools of thought, although the schools of thought are nonexhaustive and membership can be overlapping. A fairly standard organization utilizes four general categories: liberal or equality feminism; cultural or difference or relational feminism; radical or dominance feminism; and postmodern or intersectionality or diversity feminism. Professor Nancy Levit of the University of Missouri-Kansas City School of Law describes these schools of feminist thought and the prevailing view of men that she associates with

---

[6] *See id.* at 455.

[7] *See id.* at 456.

[8] *See id.* at 458; *see also id.* at 517.

[9] Katharine T. Bartlett, *Feminist Legal*

Methods, 103 HARV. L. REV. 829, 836–37 (1990); *see also id.* at 837–67. Copyright © 1990 by the Harvard Law Review Association. Reprinted with permission.

each school. NANCY LEVIT, THE GENDER LINE: MEN, WOMEN AND THE LAW 189–95 (1998).[10]

Liberal Feminism or Equal Treatment Theory: Men as Objects of Analysis

Feminist legal theory has evolved through stages into several different camps. The equal treatment theorists, or liberal feminists, were the first wave of feminist legal theorists. These theorists argued for the abolition of all gender-based classifications. The hallowed building block of liberalism, that all men are created equal, was recast to include women. The goals of liberal feminism were assimilationist in nature: making legal claims that would ensure women received the same rights, opportunities, and treatment as men. Thus, liberal feminists demanded equal pay, employment, education, and political opportunities.

Equal treatment theory viewed men as the benchmark, the norm. Male experiences were an accepted and unquestioned reference point. As theorists emphasized the need for women to achieve equal opportunities, the obvious focus was on the opportunities, rights, and powers men possessed that women did not. Most references to the treatment of men were descriptions of past and present conditions, rather than evaluations of whether those norms were good or bad.

The model of formal equality was reinforced by court decisions. A significant number of the more prominent early cases seeking equal treatment for women were constructed as challenges to gender classifications that burdened men, thereby stigmatizing women as incapable of shouldering those same burdens. Often these cases entailed strategic choices on the part of feminists to attack gender-based classifications using male plaintiffs. As director of the American Civil Liberties Union's Women's Rights Project (WRP), Ruth Bader Ginsburg developed the strategy of proceeding with cases featuring male plaintiffs to press for formal equality for women: "Her briefs consistently characterized sex stereotypes as double-edged. She argued that rigid sex roles limited opportunities for freedom of choice and restricted personal development for members of both sexes."[57] However, it is clear from the cases taken and arguments made that male plaintiffs were being used by women instrumentally, principally to advance women's rights. . .

This litigation strategy did create a standard that was user-friendly to both sexes in the sense that it was gender-blind. Although the initial rubric was gender-neutral, its application in some cases has not yielded gender neutral results, and instead has served to reinforce traditional role expectations.

Equal treatment theory was necessary to eradicate the worst forms of disparity in treatment of women. Liberal feminism was justly concerned with women's systematic and intentional exclusion from educational and vocational opportunities. These early feminists focused on basic disparities in the treatment of women, and approached the resolution of those disparities from a rhetoric of equality for women. Equal treatment theorists were primarily interested in opposing stereotypes of women as needing special protection. Even though these theorists made arguments about the dual disadvantages of gender stereotypes, they did not spin out the systematic implications of a wide variety of rules and laws that perpetuated gender role stereotypes that harmed men as well.

---

[57] [David Cole, *Strategies of Difference: Litigating for Women's Rights in a Man's World*, 2 LAW & INEQ. J. 33 (1984)], at 54.

Cultural Feminism or Difference Theory: Men as Other

The second wave of modern feminists were the difference theorists, also referred to as cultural or relational feminists or special treatment theorists. These scholars would agree with liberal feminism's insistence on gender neutral laws for most issues. However, they maintain that formal equality, particularly with regard to reproduction and child raising, denies important social and biological differences between women and men. They critique equal treatment theory for providing equality of opportunity only to the extent that women are the same as men, but not for accommodating the ways women are different from men. In their view, equal treatment theory will ultimately fail to arrive at gender equity due to fundamental differences between men and women.

The difference theorists call for acknowledgment of the differences between the sexes, and recognition of the biological or social and cultural construction of gender roles. Some of them advocate the need for preferential treatment in the areas of reproduction and child rearing, while others more moderately support accommodation only for actual childbearing.

A central claim of difference theory is that women have distinctive methods of acquiring knowledge and making moral decisions. Women and men typically display different emotional and cognitive patterns, different social skills or characteristics, possibly stemming from innate physiological traits or from different life experiences. Women operate with an ethic of care and are concerned about relationships and collaborative resolution of issues. Men reason toward an ethic of rights; they prize autonomous individualism and attempt to resolve issues with hierarchical and objective methods. Women speak in a "different voice": whereas men are aggressive and competitive, women are sensitive, empathetic, and nurturing.[65] Men are given identity in difference theory only through their differences from women.

In legal theory, cultural feminists argue that the differences between women and men justify different legal treatment on a range of issues. In the area of maternity leave, for example, difference theory necessitated the recognition that notions of formal equality could operate to the detriment of women. Furthermore, at the institutional level, cultural feminists suggest that when women's experiences and methods of reasoning are brought to bear on legal issues, they shape and alter not only traditional outcomes, but also the processes by which those outcomes are reached, in fundamental ways.

Margaret Jane Radin and Robin West have argued that by demonstrating traits that, through biology or acculturation, are predominantly possessed and employed by women, difference theory was not only important empirical work, but was a necessary form of political legitimation for women.[69] Moreover, difference theory was an important form of compensatory scholarship, since it socially validated women's experiences, which, for many years, simply did not count.

At a minimum, cultural feminism focuses on gender similarities and differences. In emphasizing capacities possessed distinctly or predominantly by women, the theory highlights differences between men and women. At the extreme, this has led some theorists toward a wholesale exclusion of men on a number of levels. First, on the theoretical level,

---

[65] [CAROL GILLIGAN, IN A DIFFERENT VOICE: PSYCHOLOGICAL THEORY and WOMEN'S DEVELOPMENT 17–23 (1982)].

[69] *See* Margaret Jane Radin, *Reply: Please*

Be Careful with Cultural Feminism, 45 STAN. L. REV. 1567, 1568 (1993); [Robin West, *Jurisprudence and Gender,* 55 U. CHI. L. REV. 1 (1988)], at 3.

the focus of analysis is women, rather than people. Second, difference theory, with its construction of the dichotomous categories of women and men, excludes those who do not fit neatly into either category. The essentialism of difference theory does not admit that there may be gradations of differences—that gender may be a continuum. Third, in significant respects, a number of cultural feminists may be interpreted as promoting the separatist philosophy that men cannot be reconciled with or included in feminism. Robin West, for example, argues that [the "economic man" constructed by the legal economists is] "incapable of empathic knowledge regarding the subjective well-being of others."[70] Christine Littleton concurs, stating that "women's experience [is] a necessary prerequisite for doing feminism" and maintaining that "men who wanted to use the label 'feminist' would have to spend a significant number of years living as women to qualify."[71]

In the social sciences more than in law, these gender differences have been interpreted as an indication of women's moral superiority. A number of theorists writing about the sociology of consciousness have suggested that women are epistemologically privileged. Certain characteristics (female) are celebrated, while others (male) are not. The contention of some standpoint epistemologists is that the underprivileged position of persistent oppression creates an ability in women to discern reality more objectively than men. They also contend that because women's nurturing or caring faculties are better developed, they are able to do different, and perhaps more exploratory, research than men. Some theorists make the stronger argument that feminist ethics should be privileged over masculinist values, and that the application of feminine ideology creates better social outcomes.

Arguments about the superiority of the feminine difference are one response to the marginalization experienced by women for centuries. Some of these arguments may have functioned correctively by adding the omitted accomplishments and contributions of women. Even the stronger argument that women hold a privileged epistemological status may have been a necessary step in claiming legitimacy for gender differences or in reversing an established hierarchy so that it could be examined, but such an argument comes with a price. On the level of discourse, this framework meant that dialogue was a competition. The form of the argument—that women's ethics should prevail over men's—sets up a discourse that is at best competitive, at worst combative. Whose values should prevail?

Dominance Theory or Radical Feminism: Men as Oppressors

A third group of feminist legal theorists analyze the inequality in power relations between women and men. Instead of focusing on gender differences, dominance theorists, or radical feminists, emphasize women's subordination. They describe how men's cultural and sexual domination structures social and legal relations between the sexes. They assert that legal concepts, crafted by men, operate to control patterns of behavior between men and women. Dominance theorists call attention to the fact that the male norm in law and society is universal and unchallenged.

Dominance theory dwells less on the individual experiences of women and is much more concerned with the class-based oppression of women. These theorists call attention to the social institutions and practices that promote gender inequality as well as the oppression of women. They cite

---

[70] Robin West, *Economic Man and Literary Woman: One Contrast,* 39 MERCER L. REV. 867, 869 (1988). [*Cf. id.* at 867 n.2 (some men may be capable of empathy).]

[71] Christine Littleton, *The Difference Method Makes,* 41 STAN. L. REV. 751, 784 n.72 (1989).

pornography, prostitution, sexual harassment, restrictions on abortion, and inadequate responses to violence against women as examples of social phenomena that contribute to the oppression of women: "Pornography, in the feminist view, is a form of forced sex, a practice of sexual politics, an institution of gender inequality."[78] Radical feminism argues for dramatic social transformation and redress of the power imbalance.

Dominance theory may tend to promote a circumscribed view of both men and women by representing men negatively and portraying women as the victims of centuries of male oppression. Under this theory, men subordinate, ignore, invade, harass, vilify, use, and torture women. They are, quite literally, the bad guys. The essential social relations between men and women are those of domination and submission: male domination and female victimization. Gender is constructed as social position and political prowess. Sexuality is the practice of subjugation. As Robin West capsulizes it, radical feminists believe that "the important difference between men and women is that women get fucked and men fuck: 'women,' definitionally, are 'those from whom sex is taken.' "[79]

Importantly, not even the "good guys" are exempt from this description, for all men are potentially bad. Dominance theory opens the door to an essentialist position for the viewing of men as a uniform collective: none are better, some are worse, and all are guilty. Note that radical feminists are not the only ones to blame men: "To be blunt, it is almost impossible not to blind oneself to the violence in the world of which you are an indirect if not direct beneficiary, and most men do indeed benefit, at least in the short run, from the sexual violence from which many women fear or suffer."[82]

In addition to viewing men as the perpetrators, dominance theory views gender discourse as a finite-sum game in which there must be winners and losers. For dominance theorists, gender equates with and is defined by power. They argue that gender equality can come only through a shift in power: "Equality means someone loses power . . . . The mathematics are simple: taking power from exploiters extends and multiplies the rights of those they have been exploiting."[83] If women can attain equality only by "taking power from those who have it," that is, men, this sets up a fundamental antagonism between the sexes.

Postmodern Feminism: Men Omitted

Much of modern feminist legal scholarship has moved beyond the sameness-difference-dominance debate, although a number of ideas from cultural feminism are being adopted and implemented as mainstream social practice. A principal current focus of feminist exploration in law is postmodern feminism. Feminists influenced by postmodernism emphasize that there is no monolithic female experience, but many experiences that vary according to a woman's race, class, ethnicity, and culture. Femininity is socially constructed, and knowledge, rather than consisting of objective, timeless truths, is situational and constructed from a confluence of multiple perspectives.

Another insight of postmodern feminism is that abstract theorizing should give way to pragmatic, contextual solutions. An important facet

---

[78] *See, e.g.,* Catharine A. MacKinnon, *Not a Moral Issue,* 2 YALE L. & POL'Y REV. 321, 325 (1984).

[79] West, *supra* note [69], at 13.

[82] Robin West, *Feminism, Critical Social Theory and Law,* 1989 U. CHI. LEGAL F. 59, 63.

. . .

[83] ANDREA DWORKIN & CATHARINE A. MACKINNON, PORNOGRAPHY AND CIVIL RIGHTS: A NEW DAY FOR WOMEN'S EQUALITY 22–23 (1988).

of postmodernism generally, and postmodern feminism in particular, is that discourse, perhaps especially legal discourse, constructs social understanding. Some authors suggest that to prevent gender hierarchies from self-reproducing, postmodern feminist theory must focus on the structural conditions perpetuating patriarchy.

Postmodern feminism is concerned with the dilemma of essentialism: how feminists can remain unified on gender issues and yet recognize that feminists are shaped as much, if not more, by characteristics of race, class, and ethnicity. Feminists drawing on postmodernism want to avoid unitary truths and acknowledge multiple identities.

In struggling with the "no woman, many women" concept, much of postmodern feminism simply omits men. Of course, the postmodern perspective that women's identities are shaped by their cultural and social situations necessarily includes their interactions with men. The postmodern exploration of this subject considers the social construction of gender differences and the self. Nevertheless, the idea that many incarnations of women exist is a woman-centered theory—the focus is on women. Even postmodern feminist ideas about the cultural composition of gender concentrate primarily on women. Thus, the reason for the omission of men from postmodern feminism is not that men are irrelevant or that they are evil, but principally that the concentration is on a different subject: woman or women.

§ 10.02   Liberal Feminism

Liberal feminism shares the commitment to individual autonomy that is characteristic of liberal constitutional theory in general.[11] As a result, liberal feminists believe that women should have the same social, political and economic choices that men possess, and they favor the elimination of formal barriers to equality of opportunity. For this reason, liberal feminists are also frequently referred to as "equality" feminists. The proposed equal rights amendment, which fell three states short of ratification in the decade between 1972 and 1982, captures the essence of liberal feminist thought.[12] Liberal feminists choose to emphasize the ways in which men and women are the same rather than the ways in which they are different, in the hope that this will facilitate the breakdown of gender-based distinctions that presently limit the access of women to equal opportunities. Liberal feminists are reluctant to endorse special treatment that is based on presumed differences between men and women for fear that special treatment will simply reinforce the prevailing view that women are different from, and inferior to, men. Liberal feminists tend to focus on legal "rights" as the preferred mechanism for securing nondiscriminatory treatment, and on conventional objectivity grounded in logical principles as the preferred mode of legal discourse. In addition, liberal feminism is often deemed "assimilationist" because it does not challenge either

---

[11] Liberal constitutional theory is discussed in Chapter 8. For a general introductory discussion of liberal feminism see FEMINIST LEGAL THEORY: READINGS IN LAW AND GENDER 5 (Katharine T. Bartlett & Rosanne Kennedy eds., 1991); MARTHA CHAMALLAS, INTRODUCTION TO FEMINIST LEGAL THEORY 24–25, 31–46 (1999); NANCY LEVIT, THE GENDER LINE: MEN, WOMEN AND THE LAW 189–91 (1998); Smith, *supra* note 3, at 4.

[12] Section 1 of the proposed equal rights amendment stated simply: "Equality of rights under the law shall not be denied or abridged by the United States or by any State on account of sex."

existing legal structures or the basic premises of legal liberalism. Rather, liberal feminism seeks incremental reform through the inclusion of women in the protections that existing legal rules and standards make available to men. For this reason, liberal feminism is sometimes accused of accepting male behavior as the norm against which equal treatment is to be assessed.

One of the most controversial aspects of liberal feminism concerns how best to deal with biological reproductive differences that exist between men and women. In an employment context, for example, special treatment for pregnant women or women in their childbearing years could harm women by requiring them to lose pay and seniority when they took pregnancy or child care leave, or by excluding women from job opportunities available to men when exposure to toxic substances might threaten women's fertility. Alternatively, special treatment could benefit women by giving them compensated pregnancy or child care leave without loss of seniority, even though such leave was not available to male employees. Some feminists argue that biological reproductive differences can appropriately serve as a basis for according women special treatment, because they reflect "real" differences that exist between men and women. Georgetown University Law Professor Wendy W. Williams describes the "special treatment" model and then explains why she believes an "equal treatment" model better advances the goal of gender equality. Wendy W. Williams, *Equality's Riddle: Pregnancy and the Equal Treatment/Special Treatment Debate*, 13 N.Y.U. Rev. L. & Soc. Change 325, 325–28, 352–56, 358–59, 364–65, 367–68, 369–70 (1984–85).[13]

The legal battle for gender equality gave birth, in the early 1970's, to a riddle. Faced with the pervasive and profound effect of employer responses to women's reproductive function on their status and opportunity in the paid workforce, feminist litigators asked how laws or rules based on a capacity unique to women—the capacity to become pregnant and give birth—could be susceptible to challenge under any equality doctrine the courts of this country might realistically be persuaded to employ. In response to that question, the proponents of gender equality developed a theory which has been used with moderate success in scores of cases challenging pregnancy rules under Title VII and, for a time, under the equal protection clause as well. Most of these cases have arisen in the employment context; courts have been asked to compare an employer's treatment of pregnancy to its treatment of other physical conditions with similar workplace consequences. The approach has been, in the words of the 1978 Pregnancy Discrimination Act (PDA), to require that "women affected by pregnancy, childbirth or related medical conditions . . . be treated the same for all employment related purposes . . . as other persons not so affected but similar in their ability or inability to work."

Today, commentators have raised questions about the wisdom and propriety of this "equal treatment" approach to pregnancy rules and laws. In Professor Ann Scales's version of the critique, she states her basic assumption as follows:

> The only differences between the sexes which apparently cannot be ignored are *in utero* pregnancy, and breastfeeding, the one function in the childrearing process which only women can perform. In observing that these are the capabilities which *really* differentiate

women from men, it is crucial that we overcome any aversion to describing these functions as "unique." Uniqueness is a "trap" only in terms of an analysis, such as that generated in *Geduldig v. Aiello*, which assumes that maleness is the norm. "Unique" does not mean uniquely handicapped. [3]

Linda Krieger and Patricia Cooney, in their extension of the Scales position, add:

> It is likely that to both the Supreme Court and the American public, the distinctions between the condition of pregnancy, of a potential child developing within a woman's body, and any medical condition faced by a man, would leap out with much greater force and vigor than the similarities. The liberal [equal treatment] model, however, relies completely on the acceptance of the analogy. It fails to focus on the effect of the very *real* sex difference of pregnancy on the relative positions of men and women in society and on the goal of assuring equality of opportunity and effect within a heterogeneous "society of equals." [4]

Thus, at least superficially, the dispute centers on whether pregnancy should be viewed as comparable to other physical conditions or as unique and special. On a deeper level, the dispute is about whether pregnancy "naturally" makes women unequal and thus requires special legislative accommodation to it in order to equalize the sexes, or whether pregnancy can or should be visualized as one human experience which in many contexts, most notably the workplace, creates needs and problems similar to those arising from causes other than pregnancy, and which can be handled adequately on the same basis as are other physical conditions of employees. On the deepest level, the debate may reflect a demand by special treatment advocates that the law recognize and honor a separate identity which women themselves consider special and important and, on the equal treatment side, a commitment to a vision of the human condition which seeks to uncover commonalty rather than difference. The critics believe that the "equal treatment model" precludes recognition of pregnancy's uniqueness, and thus creates for women a Procrustean bed— pregnancy will be treated as if it were comparable to male conditions when it is not, thus forcing pregnant women into a workplace structure designed for men. Such a result, they believe, denies women's special experience and does not adequately respond to the realities of women's lives.

The proponents of the equal treatment model are also concerned with ensuring that workplace pregnancy rules do not create structural barriers to the full participation of women in the workforce. Unlike the critics, however, they are prepared to view pregnancy as just one of the physical conditions that affect workplace participation for men and women. From their perspective, the objective is to readjust the general rules for dealing with illness and disability to ensure that the rules can fairly account for the whole range of workplace disabilities that confront employed people. Pregnancy creates not "special" needs, but rather exemplifies typical basic needs. If these particular typical needs are not met, then pregnant workers simply become part of a larger class of male and female workers, for whom the basic fringe benefit structure is inadequate. The solution, in that view, is to solve the underlying problem of inadequate fringe benefits rather than to respond with measures designed especially for pregnant workers.

---

[3] Scales, *Towards a Feminist Jurisprudence*, 56 IND. L.J. 375, 435 (1981).

[4] Krieger & Cooney, *The Miller–Wohl Controversy: Equal Treatment, Positive Action and the Meaning of Women's Equality*, 13 GOLDEN GATE U. L. REV. 513, 541–42 (1983).

. . .

For equal treatment advocates, the approach is part of a larger strategy to get the law out of the business of reinforcing traditional, sex-based family roles and to alter the workplace so as to keep it in step with the increased participation by women.

The workplace pregnancy rules evident at the beginning of the 1970's were not simply a random collection of malevolent or irrational impediments for wage earning women. They were not a byproduct of ignorance or inadvertence. Rather, they formed a coherent structure which reflected women's predominant pattern of workforce behavior and reified a particular set of values and objectives about women, work and family.

At the core was an ideology defining men's "natural" function as family breadwinners and women's "natural" function as childbearers and rearers. A woman worker's pregnancy was a signal (as her marriage had been decades earlier) of her impending assumption of her primary role. Workplace rules accordingly treated her as terminating her workplace participation. If she defied the presumption and sought to continue her workforce attachment, she met with numerous obstacles. If she avoided outright termination, then she faced mandatory leaves that had nothing to do with her desire or capacity to work. She was not guaranteed the right to return, she was denied sick leave or disability, she lost seniority, and she became ineligible for unemployment insurance. Moreover, her medical coverage for expenses associated with pregnancy was reduced or nonexistent. All of this underscored for her a lesson that pregnancy is not a workplace but a family issue. Employer and state would not recognize her as a worker again until the pregnancy and the infancy of her child were behind her.

Today's feminists from the outset rejected the separate spheres ideology which assigned men to the workplace and women to the home. The crucial functions of the traditional family arrangement—financial support, housework and childrearing—should not, they asserted, be assigned by sex. To the extent that laws and rules force the traditional preassignment and inhibit choice, they should be replaced by laws and rules that make no assumptions about the sex of the family childrearer or wage earner, but simply address those functions directly. Moreover, the workplace should be restructured to respond to the reality that all adult members of a household in which there are children are frequently in the workforce and that co-breadwinner parents might choose or need to share childrearing functions. Equally importantly, a significant number of families today contain only one parent, who must perform both wage earning and childrearing functions.

Accommodation to parental needs and obligations should penetrate to the core of the workplace rather than remain a peripheral "women's issue." Treating parenthood as a non-issue structurally marginalizes women as workforce participants. Women's increasingly pervasive workforce attachment means that pregnancy should no longer be treated as a private problem of marginal workers best handled by the old exclusionary methods. Justice Rehnquist notwithstanding, it will not do to treat women as "real" workers entitled to the full panoply of benefits only until they become pregnant.

Today the workplace remains unacceptably tailored to the old sex-based allocation of childrearing duties. The basic structures still assume that the "real" workers are men whose "personal lives" do not and should not create obstacles to long, uninterrupted hours of work over an adult lifetime. The majority of women are still in a secondary, segregated, marginal workforce, engaged in the dual careers of worker and mother, in jobs where turnover is assumed and provides minimum disruption.

The "equal treatment" model is designed to discourage employers and the state from creating or maintaining rules that force people to structure their family relationships upon traditional sex-based lines and from refusing to respond to pregnancy as within the normal range of events which temporarily affect workers.

Maternity leave, when available, was traditionally an unpaid leave for a woman beginning during pregnancy and extending some months after childbirth. It was typically a package that included not only pregnancy but also infant care, on the assumption that the woman who became pregnant would inevitably be the primary caretaker of the child. The "equal treatment" model separates pregnancy and childrearing and insists that each be independently analyzed.

The separation has important implications. When the childrearing function is considered separately from pregnancy, it becomes apparent that parents of either sex might undertake that responsibility. To grant childrearing leave to mothers only would be, under this analysis, to discriminate against fathers. Employers who provide leaves for childrearing must therefore substitute "parental" for "maternal" leaves. This separation of early childrearing from pregnancy thus serves the objective of prohibiting workplace rules that discourage families from opting for an egalitarian or nontraditional assignment of parental roles and from ordering their lives in a way that best meets their economic and personal needs. Further, it explicitly rejects stereotypes about motherhood and fatherhood, undermining the view that holds the mother naturally and inevitably responsible, and the father exempt from responsibility, for the nurturing of young children. Finally, it may reduce the vulnerability of working single mothers by making childrearing obligations something that the employer must expect that any parent, male or female, may experience.

The separation of childbearing and childrearing also promotes reanalysis of pregnancy in the workplace context. Much of the disadvantageous treatment of pregnant wage earners by employers was based not on the pregnancy itself but on predictions concerning the future behavior of the pregnant woman when her child was born or on views about what her behavior should be. When shorn of its implications about future behavior by the separation of childbearing and childrearing, pregnancy can be analyzed as a purely physical event. As such, it is susceptible to a functional analysis which compares the way it affects the pregnant worker to how other physical conditions affect other workers. Under a functional analysis, it becomes possible to argue that pregnancy, when not disabling, should not be a basis for termination or forced leave any more than any other nondisabling condition should be, and that when pregnancy does become disabling, the benefits appropriate for other workers should be extended to pregnant workers as well.

. . .

There may indeed be instances where special pregnancy rules are neither over-nor underinclusive and are free of sex role stereotypes. In the abstract, at least, one could posit that rules singling out pregnancy, because of its functional implications, may, to a greater degree than male-female distinctions in general, be justified. While, in the employment context, examples are scarce, where they exist, they would appropriately fall within the bona fide occupational qualification exception to Title VII and would be permitted.

. . .

Nonetheless, if the equal treatment approach were limited to the integration of pregnancy into the pattern of existing provisions for job security and economic benefits, Ann Scales would have good reason to protest that the incorporationist vision cannot fully be implemented through that approach. An existing system of protections and benefits, she might point out, is structured to respond to the needs and characteristics of the typical male worker. Even if such protections and benefits are extended to women workers (and this might be especially true for those who become pregnant), they will not necessarily deliver equivalent advantages to women. Schemes set up on a male model are likely to be misconfigured from a woman's perspective. To grasp this point one need only envision what workplace rules would look like if the entire workforce were composed of women of childbearing years. The present scheme of things is thus unlikely to account for the needs and characteristics of women workers to the same extent that it accounts for the needs and characteristics of men.

But the "equal treatment" feminists do not contend only that women who are pregnant must be treated the same as other workers in analogous situations. They also assert that apparently neutral rules that have a disproportionate effect on women, whether because of pregnancy or some other class-based characteristic, may violate Title VII.

The disparate effects theory is fundamentally "incorporationist" in the Scales sense. It permits, in effect, a challenge to "neutral" rules based on a male prototype. It goes beyond assessment of discrimination against individuals to identify the group effects of particular rules. When those effects are substantial, this approach imposes a burden upon the employer to justify its rule or policy. Where the rule or policy cannot meet the standard of justification, it is invalidated—not just for the group upon whom it places a disproportionate burden, but for all affected workers. The employer is left to pursue its objectives in some way that avoids the untoward effects. In short, its replacement rule must be truly, not simply formally, neutral. The tendency of the disparate effects theory is thus to require employers' policies to account for the needs and characteristics of both sexes.

. . .

Krieger and Cooney's view leads them to assert that pregnancy is a difference which must be "accommodated," in the manner that Title VII requires employer accommodation to religious practices, or federal regulations require accommodation to employee handicaps. However, the Supreme Court has interpreted accommodation requirements very narrowly. It has little sympathy for provisions which make employers go out of their way for the atypical worker. This result seems predictable. Special "favors" for such workers are viewed as an imposition unconnected to the employer's business needs and interests. In contrast, provisions for the "typical" worker are more easily seen as necessary or desirable responses to the nature of the workforce which may increase employee loyalty and productivity. Moreover, the special treatment approach for women will always embroil its proponents in a debate about whether they are getting more or not enough. Finally, such provisions are a double-edged sword for their beneficiaries because they impose upon employers special costs and obligations in connection with pregnant workers, rendering them less desirable employees and creating an incentive to discriminate against them. By contrast, the equal treatment approach, premised squarely on an androgynous rather than a male prototype and reaching for an incorporationist rather than accommodationist vision, seeks to avoid these consequences by requiring a fundamental reorganization of the way the presence of pregnant working women in the workplace is understood. The vision is not, as is Krieger and Cooney's, a workplace based on a male definition of employee, with special accommodation to women's differences from men, but rather a redefinition of what a typical employee is that encompasses both sexes.

Not only is Krieger and Cooney's underlying conceptualization of the pregnancy problem different from that of the equal treatment feminists, but the interpretation of Title VII through which Krieger and Cooney seek to effectuate their accommodationist view is unsound. They urge that "accommodation" is to be achieved through an interpretation of the disparate effects doctrine that permits special pregnancy rules or laws to be upheld where they were instituted to overcome the adverse impact of workplace structures on women. However, disparate effects doctrine has not traditionally been, and should not be, put to such a use. Its purpose is to force the evaluation of neutral rules that are shown to have a disproportionate effect. The remedy when such an effect is shown is neither the construction of a dual system in which the rule continues in effect for one group but not the other, nor the formulation of special rules for the adversely affected classes. Instead, the remedy is reformulation or elimination of the rule for everyone.

. . .

Andrew Weissman goes even further than Krieger and Cooney. He contends that the PDA should be interpreted to provide that employers who have no disability plan at all violate Title VII by failing to create special rules for pregnancy disabilities. Congress, he thinks, intended that pregnancy be accorded *different* treatment in order to "rectif[y] the natural asymmetry of the sexes."[169] He urges that women, like the hand-icapped, need special accommodation in order to participate in the workforce on an equal basis; failure of the employer to provide special provisions violates the PDA. As with Krieger and Cooney, his vision implicitly accepts men as the norm and seeks to make special provision for women insofar as they are not like men.

The equal treatment feminists reject the fundamental assumption that men should be treated as the prototype. An androgynous prototype requires sex neutral schemes that take into account the normal range of human characteristics—including pregnancy. Weissman's approach, like that of Krieger and Cooney, constitutes a fine tuning of the old order. More than the provision of identical services may seem necessary when services are geared to the male norm. But inherent in such an approach is the continued definition of women as "other." Dual standards have always been the law's response to the sexes. The equal treatment feminists seek a more radical transformation.

Some feminists have tried to formulate hybrid legal standards to mediate the special treatment/equal treatment debate. For example, Professor Herma Hill Kay favors gender equality, and she opposes the view that biological reproductive differences between men and women create "separate spheres" of public and private life for which men and women are respectively better suited. However, she does believe that biological reproductive differences can legitimately serve as the basis for "episodic" differential treatment of men and women when the reproductive activity of women places them at a temporary

---

[169] Note, *Sexual Equality Under the Pregnancy Discrimination Act,* 83 COLUM. L. REV. 690, 717 (1983).

disadvantage that men do not suffer as a result of their reproductive activity.[14] She believes that the concept of equality is not offended when men and pregnant women are treated differently in an employment context, as long as the differential treatment is narrowly tailored to the differential consequences that *reproductive activity*—as opposed to gender—has for men and women.[15] Similarly, Professor Sylvia Law endorses the goal of gender equality, but she believes that equal treatment may at times require special consideration of biological reproductive differences. She would subject to strict judicial scrutiny laws governing reproductive biology to ensure that they do not perpetuate the *oppression* of women in the absence of a compelling state purpose. Under this test, for example, she would permit laws granting women employees pregnancy leave, as long as those laws did not empirically seem likely to perpetuate the oppression of women.[16]

Professor Christine A. Littleton offers a restructured conception of equality itself that she believes can incorporate both biological and cultural differences between men and women. She believes that both the "symmetrical" model of equality favored by Wendy Williams, and the "asymmetrical" models favored by Herma Hill Kay and Sylvia Law are "phallocentric" in that they acquiesce in a male construction of what constitutes equal treatment.[17] Like the cultural feminists discussed in the next Section, Littleton believes that there are important biological and cultural differences between men and women. However, rather than modify existing institutions so that they can "accommodate" the ways in which women are different, she believes that the culture should "accept" gender differences by identifying "gendered complements" in the culture and ensuring that they are accorded equal treatment.[18] For example, both mothers and soldiers serve similar social functions that entail a lot of unpleasant but important work involving danger and potential death. Under Littleton's restructured conception of equality, the gender differences between those two roles should be made costless by ensuring that mothers receive pay, prestige and job reentry preferences that are comparable to what is currently accorded veterans.[19]

Law and economics advocate Judge Richard A. Posner has suggested that the liberal feminist conception of equality entails an inappropriate subsidy for women. He believes that the market can best determine how to deal with biological differences between men and women. Men and women employees sometimes impose differential costs on employers. Women take time off for pregnancy and childrearing purposes, and their pension costs are higher because they live longer. Similarly, men are less careful about safety than women and have higher job injury costs. Employers should, therefore, be able to reflect these cost differences in the compensation and benefit packages that they make available to men and women employees. If employers were required to subsidize women for costs that were not imposed by men, the requirement would be discriminatory. Posner states that this view does not adopt as an

---

[14] *See* Herma Hill Kay, *Equality and Difference,* 1 BERKELEY WOMEN'S L.J. 1, 1–2 (1985).

[15] *See id.* at 21–27.

[16] *See* Sylvia A. Law, *Rethinking Sex and the Consititution,* 132 U. PA. L. REV. 955, 1008–09, 1031–33 (1984).

[17] *See* Christine A. Littleton, *Restructuring Sexual Equality,* 75 CAL. L. REV. 1279, 1292–97 (1987).

[18] *See id.*

[19] *See id.* at 1323–32.

arbitrary benchmark the costs imposed by male workers, but rather treats all employee costs as equally relevant to compensation. Moreover, to the extent that natural differences are determining social outcomes they are doing so equally for men and for women. Similarly, to the extent that individual differences are being subordinated to group membership, they are being equally subordinated for both men and women. Finally, special benefits for women would discourage employers from hiring, promoting and retaining women in a way that would ultimately work to the disadvantage of women.[20]

§ 10.03   Cultural Feminism

Cultural feminism emerged during the 1980s as a response to perceived deficiencies in the liberal, equality feminism that had characterized the legal feminist movement in the 1970s.[21] By assuming that men and women were essentially the same, liberal feminism ran the risk of reinforcing hidden male biases in the legal system, even though a primary goal of feminist legal theory was to unmask male bias through techniques such as asking the "woman question." For example, when liberal feminists succeeded in establishing parity in terms of employment, between pregnancy and temporary disabilities suffered by men, women remained disadvantaged by employers who denied disability benefits to all of their nonprofessional employees—employees who tended disproportionately to be women. As a cultural matter, it remained obvious that mothers did not possess the same opportunities as fathers to have both families and jobs. More generally, the equal treatment model seemed to accept the view of pregnancy as a *disability*, rather than viewing it as a positive *ability* that contributed to the culture in ways that were as valuable as the contributions that men made.

Cultural feminism sought to compensate for the perceived difficulties of liberal feminism by emphasizing that women make distinctive contributions to the larger "culture" that are as valuable as the contributions made by men. Due to its de-emphasis of equality, and its positive emphasis on ways in which women are different from men, cultural feminism is often referred to as "difference" feminism. In addition, cultural feminism is sometimes referred to as "different voice" or "relational" feminism because of its association with the work of Harvard developmental psychologist Carol Gilligan, who believes that men and women tend to follow different paths of moral development. Gilligan argues that men often adhere to an *ethic of justice*, which emphasizes logical reasoning based on abstract rules, universal principles and a hierarchical conception of individual rights, whereas women often speak in a *different voice*. Women are more inclined than men to adhere to an *ethic of care*, which focuses on the preservation of relationships, favors context and particularity over abstract rules, and prefers pragmatic accommodation to the trumping force of universal principles and hierarchical rights.[22] Relational feminists

---

[20] *See* Richard A. Posner, *Conservative Feminism,* 1989 U. CHI. LEGAL F. 191, 195–98.

[21] For a general introductory discussion of cultural feminism see Bartlett & Kennedy, *supra* note 11, at 5–6, CHAMALLAS, *supra* note 11, at 47–53, 62–68; LEVIT, *supra* note 11, at 191–93; Smith, *supra* note 3, at 7–8.

[22] *See* CAROL GILLIGAN, IN A DIFFERENT VOICE: PSYCHOLOGICAL THEORY AND WOMEN'S DEVELOPMENT (1982).

believe that the distinctive moral development of women gives rise to a greater capacity for nurturing values, including love, patience, sympathy and concern for others. They further believe that the legal system will be improved if the male ethic of justice, which dominates current legal discourse, is supplemented by the female ethic of care.

Professor Suzanna Sherry of the University of Minnesota Law School argues that key elements of the modern feminine perspective coincide with the now-abandoned theory of republicanism that was originally envisioned by the framers. In so doing, she distinguishes between "femin*ist*" and "femin*ine*" perspectives. For her, feminist perspectives are largely political, but the feminine perspective on which she focuses consists of a less political, more psychological set of insights that are derived in part from Gilligan's work on the distinctive moral development of women. Suzanna Sherry, *Civic Virtue and the Feminine Voice in Constitutional Adjudication,* 72 VA. L. REV. 543, 544–49, 580–86, 587, 590–92, 615–16 (1986).[23]

Let us imagine two contrasting (and somewhat idealized) paradigms of political and moral philosophy. The "modern" paradigm is individualist. The underlying theme of this atomistic vision is autonomy and separation. Individuals are seen as distinct units: the individualist paradigm denies the possibility of intersubjective conceptions of self. Thus, relationships among individuals, including the communities they form, are secondary. As Michael Sandel describes it: "[W]hat separates us is in some important sense prior to what connects us—epistemologically prior as well as morally prior. We are distinct individuals first, and *then* we form relationships and engage in co-operative arrangements with others; hence the priority of plurality over unity."

The modern response to this basic human separateness can, in the context of epistemological and moral theory, take either of two forms. The more common is adoption of an essentially pluralistic and non-teleological view of human nature. This view holds that there is no unitary end toward which humans aspire, no transcendent concept of the good life. "[T]he variety and heterogeneity of human goods is such that their pursuit cannot be reconciled in any single moral order.". . .

If there is no human *telos* and no unitary moral order, the mechanism for mediating among competing individual interests must necessarily be abstract and universalizable, for it must be applicable to myriad individuals in unforeseeable circumstances. It cannot be contextual, for a contextual resolution of different interests presupposes an identifiable hierarchy of human values (e.g., one's rights "as a person" are more important than one's rights "as a woman"). Belief in such a hierarchy—or at least the utilization of such a hierarchy to resolve differences within a society—is incompatible with the pluralistic basis of the modern tradition. Moreover, a concern with context is also incompatible with the atomistic perspective of modernism: "[I]f individuals are distinct and not essentially connected with one another, then morality can be expected to concern itself not with the particularity of relationships among people, but with abstractly characterizable features of interactions among individuals whose natures are taken as given."

The modern paradigm must therefore encompass a system of abstract rules that recognizes both the priority of the individual and the likelihood that diversity will engender dispute. The modern political tradition has supplied just such a system. The concept of individual rights contains all the features required by an individualist political philosophy. Rights are abstract and universal, and are expected to resolve disputes without attending to the concrete attributes of the particular individuals involved. A rights-based theory does not require a unitary human *telos,* but instead allows each individual to develop and progress toward realization of his own values. Rights are the perfect mediating mechanism for a collection of individuals whose aims are essentially in conflict.

The alternative modern response to the separateness of individuals is to seek an abstract mediating principle at the level of describing human nature itself: to identify and justify abstract, transcendent human values. These values are epistemologically rational in that they are derived by intellectual means alone, and they are characteristically modern insofar as they are intentionally divorced from the contexts in which humans live. This transcendental method of avoiding contextual decisionmaking can derive its description of human nature from an abstract idealization of a universal human *telos,* from a contractarianism rationally deduced from humanity in the state of nature, or from thin air.

The modern paradigm thus reflects an infrastructure of independent, autonomous individuals, tied together by nothing more than the necessity of society. The particular characteristics of those individuals are irrelevant; and thus the modern tradition has had to develop a transcendental approach to conflicts between individuals, focusing on the abstract rights of each rather than on the relationship between them.

The "classical" paradigm stands in radical contrast to the modern perspective. The central theme is connection rather than autonomy. The classical paradigm recognizes an intersubjective vision of self, insofar as "selves must be beings that exist in communities," and self-knowledge is a communal project. Relationships among individuals are more important than the discrete, abstract individuals themselves. Thomas Jefferson, one of the last adherents of the classical paradigm, described perfectly the contrast between the modern focus on individuals and the classical emphasis on relations among individuals:

> Self-interest, or rather self-love, or *egoism,* has been more plausibly substituted as the basis of morality. But I consider our relations with others as constituting the boundaries of morality. With ourselves we stand on the ground of identity, not of relation, which last, requiring two subjects, excludes self-love confined to a single one. To ourselves, in strict language, we can owe no duties, obligation requiring also two parties. Self-love, therefore, is no part of morality.

The classical tradition "entails the affirmation that *homo* is naturally a citizen and most fully himself when living in a *vivere civile.*"

Moreover, because humans are perceived fundamentally as members of a unitary community, it is possible to construct a shared *telos.* The community chooses and shapes its own aspirations from among competing visions of the good life, not by a mechanism of mediation, nor by abstract philosophizing, but by a conscious selection and ordering of values. The enduring values thus chosen are the product neither of mere interest calculus nor of rational thought divorced from reality, but rather an artistic or creative weaving of rational thought, intuition, and tradition. The classical paradigm is thus teleological, both in the generic sense of being goal-based and in the more specialized Aristotelian sense of envisioning a human end. This is not to suggest an Aristotelian *telos* that transcends history and society. It is instead to suggest an immanent *telos:*

one defined in the context of the historically bound community that aspires to it. The *telos* provides a context in which disputes can be resolved in individual cases, and there is less need to resort to a doctrine of abstract rights.

The modern and classical traditions thus exhibit three characteristic differences. First, modernism is atomistic where classicalism is holistic. In the modern paradigm, society is a collection of individuals; in the classical view, individuals are bits of society. Second, modernism is *either* pluralistic and thus necessarily nonteleological *or* transcendently teleological, while classicalism is unitarily but contextually (immanently) teleological. To describe fully a classical moral or political philosophy one must identify an immanent human *telos;* to describe a modern philosophy is to deny that such a *telos* exists. Third, modernism is abstract and therefore rule-based where classicalism is contextual. A theory of rights is only necessary—indeed only coherent—in the modern paradigm.

. . .

New studies in a variety of academic disciplines suggest that women in fact may have a unique perspective, a world-view that differs in significant respects from that of men. Feminist scholars in such diverse fields as philosophy, history, sociology, art, and anthropology have identified peculiarly feminine perspectives in those disciplines. Recent work in psychology and in literary theory is particularly illuminating. Psychological studies suggest that women's moral development and concept of self may differ from those of men. Feminist literary theory suggests that women's writing differs from men's in ways that reflect a radically different perspective. Despite the independence of the research and the differences in both topics of investigation and terms of description, the feminine perspective identified in each of these fields is, at its core, a single, common approach. That approach is captured in the tension between women's primary concern with intimacy or connection and men's primary focus on separation or autonomy.[168]

This difference between men and women may influence the manner in which they think about, write about, and practice their disciplines. Thus, it is probable that women's unique perspective on law and jurisprudence, as a function of their different world-view, extends well beyond areas traditionally seen as affecting women, and in fact encompasses all legal issues. Just as women's writing on all subjects—not just on intimacy, domesticity, or women's place in society—reflects a different cast, women's views on the law in general may provide insights and approaches that are less natural to, and therefore less available to, male lawyers and judges.

This different approach to the law makes women a potentially innovative force in the legal community. Because women have been excluded from the mainstream of legal authority and legal change, the legal system, like moral, political, and philosophical discourse, has become "a set of

---

[168] The most persuasive explanation for the differences between men and women is based on differences between boys' and girls' development of an ego or sense of self. Ego development occurs while the child is still quite young and is therefore significantly influenced by the child's primary caretaker. Because, in general, girls are raised by a primary caretaker of the same gender and boys are raised by a primary caretaker of the opposite gender, girls reaffirm their early attachments while boys repudiate them. Thus, women come to see themselves as fundamentally connected and men see themselves as fundamentally detached. *See* N. CHODOROW, [THE REPRODUCTION OF MOTHERING: PSYCHOANALYSIS AND THE SOCIOLOGY OF GENDER 166–68 (1978)]; C. GILLIGAN, [IN A DIFFERENT VOICE: PSYCHOLOGICAL THEORY AND WOMEN'S DEVELOPMENT 5–23 (1982).] . . .

cultural and symbolic forms that view human experience from the distorted and one-sided perspective of a single gender." This is not to suggest merely that the legal structure ignores or minimizes significant gender differences, but rather that because women have been excluded from shaping our legal structure in general, that structure reflects a distorted view of the tension between autonomy and connection and between the individual and society.

What sort of distortion has the masculine paradigm introduced into our legal system? Feminist scholars identify three primary dichotomies between men's and women's thinking: while women emphasize connection, subjectivity, and responsibility, men emphasize autonomy, objectivity, and rights. Although the parallels between the feminine perspective and classical paradigm, or between the masculine perspective and modern paradigm, are not precisely congruent, the similarities are too strong to ignore.

Recall the introductory description of the characteristic differences between the classical and modern paradigms. The contrast between women's emphasis on connections among individuals, and men's on individual autonomy, is almost exactly parallel to that between classical holism and modern atomism. Women's preference for a subjective approach, and men's for an objective approach, recall the dichotomy between contextuality and abstraction. Finally, the male emphasis on rights matches the modern paradigm's reliance on an abstract, rule-based method for mediating between competing interests in a pluralist society; the feminine ethic of caring and responsibility suggests instead the classical tendency to define human existence in terms of relationships to others and to favor contextual societal values and individual virtues. The remainder of this Section explores these similarities in detail.

A brief caveat is in order. First, I am not contending that gender-based differences are universal, only that they are likely enough that the historical exclusion of women from the shaping of the legal system has had a profound impact, which cannot be reversed—or, to a large extent, even recognized—until women begin to participate in that enterprise. Second, I am not limiting my analysis to a feminist perspective: feminists have a particular political agenda that may or may not be shared by all women (and is shared by some men). Rather, this is an analysis of a feminine perspective that encompasses aspects of personality and relationship to the world that have nothing to do with one's political preferences. Finally, I am not suggesting that the feminine perspective is any better than the masculine perspective, just that it is different. The incorporation of a new perspective need not imply a hierarchical ranking; I am arguing merely that the law has been distorted by its one-sided focus and that the feminine perspective described here represents a move toward correcting that distortion. In particular, the feminine perspective is a natural reflection of the classical paradigm, and its integration is likely to remove the particular distortions of modern liberalism.

Like the classical paradigm, the feminine perspective views individuals primarily as interconnected members of a community. Nancy Chodorow and Carol Gilligan, in groundbreaking studies on the development of self and morality, have concluded that women tend to have a more intersubjective sense of self than men and that the feminine perspective is therefore more other-directed. Other studies tend to confirm this finding. The essential difference between the male and female perspectives mirrors the fundamental difference between the modern and classical paradigms: "[t]he basic feminine sense of self is connected to the world, the basic masculine sense of self is separate." Women thus tend to see others as extensions of themselves rather than as outsiders or competitors.

Gilligan suggests that Kohlberg's description of a morally mature person—a "rational individual aware of values and rights prior to social contracts" who adopts "universal principles of justice," including "respect for the dignity of human beings as individual persons"—instead describes a masculine morality. That masculine perspective embodies the individualism inherent in the modern paradigm. The parallel between the classical paradigm and feminine morality, by contrast, is clearly illustrated by Gilligan's quotation of a typical female response to a moral dilemma:

By yourself, there is little sense to things. It is like the sound of one hand clapping, the sound of one man or one woman, there is something lacking. *It is the collective that is important to me,* and that collective is based on certain guiding principles, one of which is that *everybody belongs to it,* and that you all come from it. You have to love someone else, because while you may not like them, you are inseparable from them. In a way, it is like loving your right hand. *They are part of you; that other person is part of that giant collection of people that you are connected to.*

Women's emphasis on connection also suggests that the cliche that women are more cooperative and less competitive than men may have some basis in fact. Historically, women have tended to achieve their goals communally; from quilting bees to consciousness-raising sessions, women have banded together rather than striving individually. There are analogous differences between the organization and ideology underlying women's traditional dominion, the family, and men's traditional arena, the marketplace: as Frances Olsen notes, the market is based on an individualist ethic and the family on an altruistic ethic.

. . .

Scholarship in literature and psychology also suggests that women are more contextual and men more abstract. Piaget, for example, found that girls playing children's games tend to treat the rules of the game as less fixed and more flexible than do boys and that girls are more likely to stop a game altogether—thus preserving friendships—if a dispute arises. For boys, development and application of fixed, abstract rules is almost as important as the object of the game itself. Again, Kohlberg's description of moral development (i.e., the development of the masculine perspective) stresses a progression from context-bound judgments to abstract moral principles. Women, on the other hand, in responding to moral dilemmas, tend instead to look to circumstances rather than to abstractions: the right moral response depends on the context. [190]

Until recently, the archetypal developmental continuum of individual moral sensibility was believed to be an orderly progression from self-centeredness through other-centeredness to the development of logical, independent, universal principles—rights—that depend neither on one's own needs nor on what others believe is right. Although this progression mirrors male moral development, it fails to reflect the moral growth pattern of women.

Gender-based differences in moral structure, long seen as evidence of women's moral immaturity, may in fact be evidence of a feminine morality that differs in its emphasis from that of males. In her study of moral development, Carol Gilligan found that women tend to view a moral problem as "a problem of care and responsibility in relationships rather than as one of rights and rules." When faced with the moral dilemma of whether a man should steal a drug he cannot afford to save his dying

[190] See C. GILLIGAN, *supra* note [168], at
38.

wife, Gilligan found that, while men struggle with the conflicting rights of the parties, women focus on the druggist's "moral obligation to show compassion," "not on the conflict of rights but on the failure of response." Although men and women may agree that the man ought to steal the drug, men justify it in terms of a resolution between conflicting rights of husband and druggist, and women in terms of the need for more compassion by the druggist in the face of the husband's compassion for his wife. Whether personal or political, the moral structure of "mature" males reflects a paradigm of independent rights, while that of females emphasizes relational responsibilities.

Gilligan's work suggests that moral development from the conventional level may take either of two directions: progression toward a contextual moral theory (expanding on Aristotelian notions of what is right or good but placing human *teloi* in context) *or* progression toward an abstract moral theory (emphasizing rights as a form of trump). Recognition of alternative routes of moral development may shed new light on the failure of Jeffersonian republicanism and the ultimate triumph of liberalism. The classical paradigm, especially in its republican form, may be an example of the conventional level on the verge of its masculine successor. The republican vision represented an incomplete or immature ideology, but its maturation might have taken either of two paths: development of a mature virtue-based ideology or rejection of virtue in favor of rights. The former reflects a feminine vision, the latter a masculine perspective. Because the feminine paradigm has been conspicuously absent from the shaping of moral or political traditions, the development of the nation's ideology has paralleled individual moral development in the male pattern, not the female pattern.

The preceding argument suggests that the Constitution, especially in light of subsequent interpretations in the liberal tradition, is a quintessentially masculine document. Calls for a more classical interpretation are unlikely to succeed as long as the interpreters are exclusively male. But the interpreters are no longer exclusively male. Justice O'Connor's four years on the Supreme Court provide an excellent opportunity to test the thesis that a feminine perspective might result in a feminine jurisprudence and to sketch the contours of one version of that jurisprudence. If the thesis is correct, O'Connor's jurisprudence should differ in characteristically feminine or classical ways from the jurisprudence of her brethren. The remainder of this article will explore the feminine aspects of her jurisprudence. In particular, it will focus on differences between Justices O'Connor and Rehnquist: because they are otherwise ideologically similar, and because they so often vote together, their disagreements are significant. This pattern of disagreement is highly suggestive of the operation of a uniquely feminine perspective.

[Professor Sherry then discusses Justice O'Connor's opinions in a series of establishment clause and equal protection cases to support her claim that Justice O'Connor has been influenced by a feminine perspective.]

. . .

[R]ecognition of Justice O'Connor's unique perspective, and the unique perspective of women in general, might aid us in ameliorating the distortions of an overly individualist liberal paradigm. Insufficient attention to connection promotes naked self-interest at the expense of altruism, impoverishes our self-perception, and stunts our capacity for growth. Merely communicating a feminine emphasis on connection may be enlightening: "Teaching is not always a matter of either arguing or providing evidence . . . It is sometimes rather a matter of imparting a way of looking at things."

Professor Robin West argues that the distinctiveness of women's perspectives is ultimately traceable to biological differences between men and women. Prevailing liberal theory rests on a "separation thesis" that defines the essence of humanness as the realization that one individual is separate from others. This gives rise to the individual rights emphasis of legal discourse, which West characterizes as "essentially and irretrievably masculine" because it wholly disregards the essence of what it means to be a woman. Women are not "essentially separate" from other human beings, but rather are "essentially connected" to other human beings during pregnancy, heterosexual intercourse, menstruation (representing the potential for pregnancy) and breast-feeding. This "connection thesis" is what gives women their distinctive capacity for the relational virtues recognized by cultural feminism.[24]

Professor West has also cautioned that adherence to the ethic of care is not alone sufficient to realize the full potential of cultural feminism. Rather the female ethic of care should be combined with the male ethic of justice because neither can be complete without the contribution of the other. The male *ethic of justice* (typically associated with universal rules, consistency, reason, rights, the public sphere, and masculine virtues) and the female *ethic of care* (typically associated with particularity, context, affect, relationship, the private sphere, and femininity) are not oppositional, contradictory or even complementary. Rather, they are interdependent in that each is a necessary condition of the other. Justice must be caring if it is to be just, and caring must be just if it is to be caring.[25] More specifically, Professor West states:

> What I have argued so far is that the zealous pursuit of justice, or of some attribute of justice—be it institutional consistency, personal integrity, or impartiality—when unconstrained by the demands of an ethic of care, will fail as a matter of justice as well as a matter of care. On the other hand, the zealous pursuit of some attribute of care—nurturance, compassion, or particularity—when unconstrained by the demands of an ethic of justice, will fail as a matter of care no less than as a matter of justice. . .
>
>   . . .
>
> Put affirmatively, an integrated conception of judging requires that justice be caring, and that the caring in our public and private lives—lives to a considerable degree affected by, if not determined by, the decisions of judges—be just. Let me depart from images and illustrations, and try to say analytically why this might be so. First, legal justice, as is widely acknowledged, requires that judges treat "like cases alike.". . . But if judges are to *do* that—if judges are to identify "likes" and treat them "alike"—they must be able to understand the shared qualities of certain experiences which on their surface may appear to be quite different indeed. That perception—the perception of a deeply shared commonality in the face of surface differences—is a type of understanding that is *of necessity* empathic. Thus, to take an example, if justice *demands* recognition of gay and lesbian marriages, it does so because of the *similarity*—the sameness—of the yearnings for intimacy, commitment, and public recognition experienced by both gays and lesbians and heterosexuals at that poignant moment of intersection of the public world with intimate lives, which is so central to the ritual of a marriage. And if justice demands

---

[24] Robin West, *Jurisprudence and Gender,* 55 U. Chi. L. Rev. 1, 1–4 (1988).

[25] Robin West, Caring for Justice 23–25, 88–93 (1997).

such a recognition, it demands judicial decisions that rule accordingly when faced with challenges to the constitutionality of state laws forbidding such marriages. Such a justice, however, will never be forthcoming unless and until judges involved in adjudicating claims of these sorts exercise their empathic, caring ability to understand the quite private lives of gay and lesbian citizens. That ability will in turn not be exercised, because it will not even be tapped, so long as societal perceptions or claims of "difference" are allowed to trump empathically, and caringly, acquired understandings of a deeper commonality.

. . .

On the other side of the equation, our relationships of care must be just if they are to be caring, and judicial decisions which create, legitimate, or provide incentives for the construction or maintenance of such relationships must carry the burden of this requirement. To take some obvious examples, the relationship of master and slave is highly particular, concrete, and even, in a perverse sense, "total," whole, or holistic. As Mark Tushnet has argued, it is far more particular, concrete, and whole, in a number of ways, than that of employer and wage laborer. But it is also manifestly unjust—it is incompatible with both the mandate of consistency and the scales of justice—and because of that it is uncaring, no matter how much the particular parties may protest to the contrary. The same is true of relationships of husband and wife where the husband has the legal entitlement to rape his wife at will. Judicial decisions which legitimate, legalize, or encourage legal regimes in which such relationships are tolerated or valorized are accordingly themselves unjust.[26]

Professor West emphasizes that proper implementation of the interrelated ethics of care and justice requires a judge to empathize with those whose perspectives the judge does not naturally share. This ability to empathize may be facilitated by the form of narrative jurisprudence that is associated with both feminist legal theory and critical race theory.[27] Professor Patricia J. Williams has become known for her use of narrative to depict aspects of the legal and larger culture from the special perspective arising from the intersection of race, gender and class.[28] West says that Patricia Williams is particularly effective at this precisely because she does not attempt to link her narratives directly to particular legal arguments or principles, but rather permits the narratives to create an "open space" for understanding new perspectives by "dislodging" settled understandings.[29]

Professor Carrie Menkel-Meadow has considered what concrete effects the inclusion of women's perspectives may have on the operation of the legal system as increasing numbers of women lawyers, judges and legislators become involved in the legal system. Using both legal and social science research, she suggests that the inclusion of female perspectives has changed and will continue to change legally relevant categories (such as "consent" in rape cases), to create new legal categories (such as sexual harassment), and to change the nature of legal fact finding (women may perceive and give

[26] *Id.* at 88–91. Copyright © 1997 by New York University. Reprinted with permission.

[27] Narrative jurisprudence and critical race theory are discussed more fully in Chapter 11, Section 11.04.

[28] *See, e.g.,* PATRICIA J. WILLIAMS, THE ROOSTER'S EGG (1995); PATRICIA J. WILLIAMS, THE ALCHEMY OF RACE AND RIGHTS (1991); *see also* Chapter 11, Section 11.04 (containing an example of a narrative by Professor Williams).

[29] *See* West, *supra* note 25 at 215.

significance to facts that men will simply overlook). In addition, the adjudicatory emphasis in legal practice may shift from adversary litigation to mediation and other cooperative forms of alternate dispute resolution as the ethic of care begins to have more influence on legal discourse. [30]

Not all feminists endorse the distinctive gender perspective described by Gilligan and invoked by cultural feminists. Professor Joan C. Williams fears the danger that such a view poses for reinforcing counterproductive gender stereotypes concerning the domesticity of women. [31] She "reject[s] Gilligan's core claim that women are focused on relationships while men are not," finding the claim to represent an "inaccurate and potentially destructive" view that "serves to perpetuate our traditional blindness to the ways in which men are nurturing and women are competitive and power-seeking." [32] Although Joan Williams believes that there are important differences between women and men, she disputes the West claim that gender differences are biologically linked. Rather, she believes that gender differences "such as the feminization of poverty stem in substantial part from a wage-labor system premised on an ideal worker with no family responsibilities." [33] Accordingly, Joan Williams would prefer to challenge the gendered structure of wage labor itself rather than "celebrate a woman's culture that encourages women to 'choose' economic marginalization and celebrate that choice as a badge of virtue." [34]

Professors Pamela S. Karlan and Daniel R. Ortiz believe that the ethic of care, which is central to relational feminism, is "somewhat dangerous and misguided," [35] because it "stands in some tension with women's felt needs" [36] —particularly the need for reproductive freedom. They argue that a woman's right to abortion is easier to justify in terms of the liberal autonomy underpinnings of traditional morality than under the alternative moral perspective derived from Gilligan's work. In fact, the emphasis in relational feminism on the connection between mother and fetus during pregnancy makes the relational model hostile to abortion. Moreover, the modifications that have to be made to relational feminism in order to recognize a right to reproductive freedom end up depriving the model of its distinctiveness by simply incorporating liberal conceptions of autonomy and equality. Although this causes Karlan and Ortiz to disapprove of the prominence often accorded relational feminism, they do believe that relational feminism has successfully demonstrated the difficulties inherent in liberal rights theory, and that future developments in feminist theory should be rooted in a feminist politics that recognizes the actual needs, experiences and oppression of women. [37]

---

[30] See Carrie Menkel–Meadow, *Portia Redux: Another Look at Gender, Feminism, and Legal Ethics,* 2 VA. J. Soc. POL'Y & L. 75, 90–97, 106–14 (1994); Carrie Menkel–Meadow, *Exploring a Research Agenda of the Feminization of the Legal Profession: Theories of Gender and Social Change,* 14 L. & Soc. INQUIRY 289, 315–17 (1989); Carrie Menkel–Meadow, *Portia in a Different Voice: Speculations on a Woman's Lawyering Process,* 1 BERKELEY WOMEN'S L.J. 39, 52–55 (1985).

[31] See Joan C. Williams, *Deconstructing Gender,* 87 MICH. L. REV. 797, 798–802 (1989).

[32] See id. at 802.

[33] See id. at 801.

[34] See id.

[35] See Pamela S. Karlan & Daniel R. Ortiz, *In a Diffident Voice: Relational Feminism, Abortion Rights and the Feminist Legal Agenda,* 87 Nw. U. L. REV. 858, 860 (1993).

[36] See id.

[37] See id. at 858–62, 885–96.

§ 10.04   Radical Feminism

Radical feminism is less concerned with the sameness/difference debate that distinguishes liberal from cultural feminism than it is with confronting the causes of women's oppression directly.[38] Radical feminism is considered "radical" in part for its view that gender—including the cultural significance of biological differences—is "socially constructed" rather than natural. Because gender is socially constructed in ways that subordinate the interests of women to the interests of men, the solution to the problem of women's oppression lies in reconceptionalizing or "reconstructing" social roles and institutions. Some radical feminists are Marxists or socialists, who believe that the oppression of women stems from the class-based, capitalist division of the world into public and private spheres, with women relegated to the private sphere that is devalued because of its noneconomic nature.[39] However, the strand of radical feminism that attracts most current attention is premised on the belief that men oppress women primarily through sexual domination. Accordingly, this "dominance" feminism focuses on problems relating to reproductive freedom, pornography, sexual harassment, rape, spousal abuse and the cultural presentation of women as sex objects.

University of Michigan Law Professor Catharine A. MacKinnon is perhaps the best-known so-called radical or dominance feminist. In her view, the legal system disfavors women's interests because it has been structured by men for the appropriation of women's sexuality. She believes that the sameness/difference debate that characterizes the distinction between liberal and cultural feminism misses the point. For her, both approaches—which she refers to collectively as the "difference approach"—are obsessed with the differences between men and women, which causes them to overlook the ways in which men dominate women, particularly by concealing maleness as the standard of gender neutrality.[40] MacKinnon offers her dominance feminism as an alternative to the standard sameness/difference approach of mainstream equality thinking. CATHARINE A. MACKINNON, *Difference and Dominance: On Sex Discrimination, in* FEMINISM UNMODIFIED: DISCOURSES ON LIFE AND LAW 40–45 (1987):[41]

> There is an alternative approach, one that threads its way through existing law and expresses, I think, the reason equality law exists in the first place. It provides a second answer, a dissident answer in law and philosophy, to both the equality question and the gender question. In this approach, an equality question is a question of the distribution of power. Gender is also a question of power, specifically of male supremacy and female subordination. The question of equality, from the standpoint of what it is going to take to get it, is at root a question of hierarchy, which—as power succeeds in constructing social perception and social reality—derivatively becomes a categorical distinction, a difference. Here, on the first day that matters, dominance was achieved, probably by force.

---

[38] For a general introductory discussion of radical feminism see Bartlett & Kennedy, *supra* note 11, at 6, 7; CHAMALLAS, *supra* note 11, at 53–62; LEVIT, *supra* note 11, at 193–94; Smith, *supra* note 3, at 5–6.

[39] *See* SMITH, *supra* note 3, at 5.

[40] *See* CATHARINE A. MACKINNON, *Difference*

and Dominance: On Sex Discrimination, in FEMINISM UNMODIFIED: DISCOURSES ON LIFE AND LAW 32–40 (1987).

[41] Copyright © 1987 by the President and Fellows of Harvard College, and Catharine A. MacKinnon. Reprinted with permission.

By the second day, division along the same lines had to be relatively firmly in place. On the third day, if not sooner, differences were demarcated, together with social systems to exaggerate them in perception and in fact, *because* the systematically differential delivery of benefits and deprivations required making no mistake about who was who. Comparatively speaking, man has been resting ever since. Gender might not even code as difference, might not mean distinction epistemologically, were it not for its consequences for social power.

I call this the dominance approach, and it is the ground I have been standing on in criticizing mainstream law. The goal of this dissident approach is not to make legal categories trace and trap the way things arc. It is not to make rules that fit reality. It is critical of reality. Its task is not to formulate abstract standards that will produce determinate outcomes in particular cases. Its project is more substantive, more jurisprudential than formulaic, which is why it is difficult for the mainstream discourse to dignify it as an approach to doctrine or to imagine it as a rule of law at all. It proposes to expose that which women have had little choice but to be confined to, in order to change it.

The dominance approach centers on the most sex-differential abuses of women as a gender, abuses that sex equality law in its difference garb could not confront. It is based on a reality about which little of a systematic nature was known before 1970, a reality that calls for a new conception of the problem of sex inequality. This new information includes not only the extent and intractability of sex segregation into poverty, which has been known before, but the range of issues termed violence against women, which has not been. It combines women's material desperation, through being relegated to categories of jobs that pay nil, with the massive amount of rape and attempted rape—44 percent of all women—about which virtually nothing is done; the sexual assault of children—38 percent of girls and 10 percent of boys—which is apparently endemic to the patriarchal family; the battery of women that is systematic in one quarter to one third of our homes; prostitution, women's fundamental economic condition, what we do when all else fails, and for many women in this country, all else fails often; and pornography, an industry that traffics in female flesh, making sex inequality into sex to the tune of eight billion dollars a year in profits largely to organized crime.

These experiences have been silenced out of the difference definition of sex equality largely because they happen almost exclusively to women. Understand: for this reason, they are considered *not* to raise sex equality issues. Because this treatment is done almost uniquely to women, it is implicitly treated as a difference, the sex difference, when in fact it is the socially situated subjection of women. The whole point of women's social relegation to inferiority as a gender is that for the most part these things aren't done to men. Men are not paid half of what women are paid for doing the same work on the basis of their equal difference. Everything they touch does not turn valueless because they touched it. When they are hit, a person has been assaulted. When they are sexually violated, it is not simply tolerated or found entertaining or defended as the necessary structure of the family, the price of civilization, or a constitutional right.

. . .

This second approach—which is not abstract, which is at odds with socially imposed reality and therefore does not look like a standard according to the standard for standards—became the implicit model for racial justice applied by the courts during the sixties. It has since eroded with the erosion of judicial commitment to racial equality. It was based

on the realization that the condition of Blacks in particular was not fundamentally a matter of rational or irrational differentiation on the basis of
race but was fundamentally a matter of white supremacy, under which
racial differences became invidious as a consequence. To consider gender
in this way, observe again that men are as different from women as
women are from men, but socially the sexes are not equally powerful. To
be on the top of a hierarchy is certainly different from being on the bottom,
but that is an obfuscatingly neutralized way of putting it, as a hierarchy
is a great deal more than that. If gender were merely a question of difference, sex inequality would be a problem of mere sexism, of mistaken
differentiation, of inaccurate categorization of individuals. This is what
the difference approach thinks it is and is therefore sensitive to. But if
gender is an inequality first, constructed as a socially relevant differentiation in order to keep that inequality in place, then sex inequality questions
are questions of systematic dominance, of male supremacy, which is not
at all abstract and is anything but a mistake.

If differentiation into classifications, in itself, is discrimination, as it
is in difference doctrine, the use of law to change group-based social
inequalities becomes problematic, even contradictory. This is because the
group whose situation is to be changed must necessarily be legally
identified and delineated, yet to do so is considered in fundamental
tension with the guarantee against legally sanctioned inequality. If
differentiation is discrimination, affirmative action, and any legal change
in social inequality, is discrimination—but the existing social differentia-
tions which constitute the inequality are not? This is only to say that,
in the view that equates differentiation with discrimination, changing an
unequal status quo is discrimination, but allowing it to exist is not.

Looking at the difference approach and the dominance approach from
each other's point of view clarifies some otherwise confusing tensions in
sex equality debates. From the point of view of the dominance approach,
it becomes clear that the difference approach adopts the point of view of
male supremacy on the status of the sexes. Simply by treating the status
quo as "the standard," it invisibly and uncritically accepts the arrangements under male supremacy. In this sense, the difference approach is
masculinist, although it can be expressed in a female voice. The dominance approach, in that it sees the inequalities of the social world from
the standpoint of the subordination of women to men, is feminist.

If you look through the lens of the difference approach at the world as
the dominance approach imagines it—that is, if you try to see real inequality through a lens that has difficulty seeing an inequality as an
inequality if it also appears as a difference—you see demands for change
in the distribution of power as demands for special protection. This is
because the only tools that the difference paradigm offers to comprehend
disparity equate the recognition of a gender line with an admission of lack
of entitlement to equality under law. Since equality questions are primarily confronted in this approach as matters of empirical fit—that is, as
matters of accurately shaping legal rules (implicitly modeled on the
standard men set) to the way the world is (also implicitly modeled on the
standard men set)—any existing differences must be negated to merit
equal treatment. For ethnicity as well as for gender, it is basic to
mainstream discrimination doctrine to preclude any true diversity among
equals or true equality within diversity.

To the difference approach, it further follows that any attempt to change
the way the world actually is looks like a moral question requiring a
separate judgment of how things ought to be. This approach imagines
asking the following disinterested question that can be answered neu-
trally as to groups: against the weight of empirical difference, should we

treat some as the equals of others, even when they may not be entitled to it because they are not up to standard? Because this construction of the problem is part of what the dominance approach unmasks, it does not arise with the dominance approach, which therefore does not see its own foundations as moral. If sex inequalities are approached as matters of imposed status, which are in need of change if a legal mandate of equality means anything at all, the question whether women should be treated unequally means simply whether women should be treated as less. When it is exposed as a naked power question, there is no separable question of what ought to be. The only real question is what is and is not a gender question. Once no amount of difference justifies treating women as subhuman, eliminating that is what equality law is for. In this shift of paradigms, equality propositions become no longer propositions of good and evil, but of power and powerlessness, no more disinterested in their origins or neutral in their arrival at conclusions than are the problems they address.

There came a time in Black people's movement for equality in this country when slavery stopped being a question of how it could be justified and became a question of how it could be ended. Racial disparities surely existed, or racism would have been harmless, but at that point—a point not yet reached for issues of sex—no amount of group difference mattered anymore. This is the same point at which a group's characteristics, including empirical attributes, become constitutive of the fully human, rather than being defined as exceptions to or as distinct from the fully human. To one-sidedly measure one group's differences against a standard set by the other incarnates partial standards. The moment when one's particular qualities become part of the standard by which humanity is measured is a millennial moment.

To summarize the argument: seeing sex equality questions as matters of reasonable or unreasonable classification is part of the way male dominance is expressed in law. If you follow my shift in perspective from gender as difference to gender as dominance, gender changes from a distinction that is presumptively valid to a detriment that is presumptively suspect. The difference approach tries to map reality; the dominance approach tries to challenge and change it. In the dominance approach, sex discrimination stops being a question of morality and starts being a question of politics.

You can tell if sameness is your standard for equality if my critique of hierarchy looks like a request for special protection in disguise. It's not. It envisions a change that would make possible a simple equal chance for the first time. To define the reality of sex as difference and the warrant of equality as sameness is wrong on both counts. Sex, in nature, is not a bipolarity; it is a continuum. In society it is made into a bipolarity. Once this is done, to require that one be the same as those who set the standard—those which one is already socially defined as different from— simply means that sex equality is conceptually designed never to be achieved. Those who most need equal treatment will be the least similar, socially, to those whose situation sets the standard as against which one's entitlement to be equally treated is measured. Doctrinally speaking, the deepest problems of sex inequality will not find women "similarly situated" to men. Far less will practices of sex inequality require that acts be intentionally discriminatory. All that is required is that the status quo be maintained. As a strategy for maintaining social power first structure reality unequally, then require that entitlement to alter it be grounded on a lack of distinction in situation; first structure perception so that different equals inferior, then require that discrimination be activated by evil minds who *know* they are treating equals as less.

I say, give women equal power in social life. Let what we say matter, then we will discourse on questions of morality. Take your foot off our necks, then we will hear in what tongue women speak. So long as sex equality is limited by sex difference, whether you like it or don't like it, whether you value it or seek to negate it, whether you stake it out as a grounds for feminism or occupy it as the terrain of misogyny, women will be born, degraded, and die. We would settle for that equal protection of the laws under which one would be born, live, and die, in a country where protection is not a dirty word and equality is not a special privilege.

Professor MacKinnon's views are controversial among feminists. Professor Katharine T. Bartlett believes that MacKinnon has brilliant and devastating insights concerning the subtle and ironic ways in which women are oppressed in the male world. However, Bartlett also finds inconsistencies and internal contradictions in MacKinnon's work. MacKinnon seems to view women as both unshakable in their experiential knowledge of oppression and easily duped by men into tolerating that oppression. Similarly, sexual harassment is deemed so pervasive that it cannot easily be recognized as discrimination in the male world, and yet so pervasive that it must be recognized as real. Bartlett believes that MacKinnon has missed an opportunity to explore the paradoxical nature of male dominance by not confronting the inconsistencies in her own observations. Perhaps, the conditions that perpetuate oppression can also be used to end it. MacKinnon also fails to show concern for how women should use power if they ever succeed in extracting it from men. MacKinnon views the cultural feminist depiction of women derived from Gilligan's work as the mere endorsement of characteristics that men have ascribed to women for the benefit of men. However, the ethic of care described in Gilligan's work may serve as a starting point for reconstructing values and determining how social power can better be exercised in a more caring culture. [42]

A highly visible outgrowth of dominance feminism was the model antipornography ordinance that MacKinnon drafted with feminist writer and theorist Andrea Dworkin. The ordinance was adopted by the city councils in Indianapolis and Minneapolis, although the Minneapolis ordinance was ultimately vetoed by the Mayor. MacKinnon and Dworkin, and the cities that passed their laws, focused on pornography because their evidence showed that it harmed women, and because they viewed pornography as a mechanism for the social construction of sexuality that was predicated on and promoted sexual violence, harassment and discrimination. The ordinance created a civil rights cause of action for pornography as a form of discrimination against women on the basis of sex. Pornography was defined to include presentations of women as "sexual objects who enjoy pain or humiliation; or . . . sexual objects for domination, conquest, violation, exploitation, possession, or use, or through postures or positions of servility or submission or display."[43] Some feminists opposed the

[42] See Katharine T. Bartlett, *MacKinnon's Feminism: Power on Whose Terms?* 75 CAL. L. REV. 1559, 1559–70 (1988) (Book Review).

[43] See American Booksellers Ass'n v. Hudnut, 771 F.2d 323, 324 (7th Cir. 1985). The court quoted the ordinance as follows:

"Pornography" under the ordinance is the "graphic sexually explicit subordina-tion of women, whether in pictures or in words, that also includes one or more of the following:

(1) Women are presented as sexual objects who enjoy pain or humiliation; or

(2) Women are presented as sexual objects who experience sexual pleasure in being raped; or

model ordinance, arguing that it paternalistically presumed that individual women were unable to determine what forms of sex they found pleasurable. A federal court of appeals invalidated the Indiana ordinance on first amendment grounds in *American Booksellers Ass'n v. Hudnut*.[44] However, the Supreme Court of Canada has upheld a Canadian definition of pornography on the basis that pornography causes the harm that MacKinnon and Dworkin documented.[45] In her 1993 book ONLY WORDS, MacKinnon argued that the first amendment should not be used to protect pornography, harassment or hate speech, because of the direct harms they caused, because of their active role in constructing social inequality, and because pornography did not promote the discovery of truth, but rather reinforced male sexual dominance over women.[46]

§ 10.05 Postmodern Feminism

Postmodern feminism reflects the extreme skepticism about representations of reality—and the loss of faith in rationalism as a means of acquiring knowledge about reality—that is characteristic of postmodernism in general.[47] Since the critical legal studies movement spearheaded the introduction of postmodern ideas into American jurisprudence in the 1970s, postmodern feminists have focused on the manipulability of language, the hidden hierarchies in seemingly neutral and objective concepts, and the oppressive potential of liberal rights discourse in their efforts to uncover the mechanisms that the legal system has used to disadvantage women. Because of their early association with critical legal studies, postmodern feminists have sometimes been referred to as "fem-crits."[48] They have also been referred to as "French feminists" because of their reliance on the critical insights and techniques of French and other continental theorists to expose hidden power relationships in the law, and to "deconstruct" legal standards by exposing internal contradictions that assertedly undermine the coherence of those standards.

---

(3) Women are presented as sexual objects tied up or cut up or mutilated or bruised or physically hurt, or as dismembered or truncated or fragmented or severed into body parts; or

(4) Women are presented as being penetrated by objects or animals; or

(5) Women are presented in scenarios of degradation, injury, abasement, torture, shown as filthy or inferior, bleeding, bruised, or hurt in a context that makes these conditions sexual; or

(6) Women are presented as sexual objects for domination, conquest, violation, exploitation, possession, or use, or through postures or positions of servility or submission or display."

Indianapolis Code § 16-3(q). The statute provides that the "use of men, children, or transsexuals in the place of women in paragraphs (1) through (6) above shall also constitute pornography under this section."

Id. at 324.

[44] 771 F.2d 323 (7th Cir. 1985), *aff'd mem.,* 475 U.S. 1001 (1986).

[45] *See* Regina v. Butler, 89 D.L.R. 4th (S.C.C. 1992). The MacKinnon/Dworkin antipornography ordinance is discussed in CHAMALLAS, *supra* note 11, at 59–62.

[46] *See* CATHARINE A. MACKINNON, ONLY WORDS (1993).

[47] *See* HANS BERTENS, THE IDEA OF THE POSTMODERN 3–11 (1996). For a general introductory discussion of postmodern feminism see Bartlett & Kennedy, *supra* note 11, at 6, 8–10; CHAMALLAS, *supra* note 11, at 72–78, 85–112; LEVIT, *supra* note 11, at 194–95; Smith, *supra* note 3, at 6–7.

[48] Critical legal studies is discussed more fully in Chapter 11, Section 11.02.

Today, postmodern feminists are "antiessentialist" or "post-essentialist" in their belief that cultural "truths" about the nature of women are socially constructed rather than transcendent. Like many other feminists, they reject the view that prevailing male norms are in any sense "natural," and they tend to reject "grand theories" about unitary causes of women's oppression as overly male and overly rational. Instead, they tend to favor phenomenological accounts of "reality" that are concrete, contextual and rooted in the felt experiences of women. Postmodern feminists believe that the oppression of women should be combated not by giving special treatment to women in order to compensate for their "difference" from men, but rather by changing the ways in which we think about the nature of men, women, and the concept of equality itself. Many postmodern feminists have also criticized white, middle-class, heterosexual women for "essentializing" their own experiences and ignoring alternate perspectives that stem from the intersection of gender with race, class and sexual orientation. These "intersectionality" concerns have caused such feminists to emphasize diversity as a means of expanding perspectives and reducing the oppression of women.

The early stages of postmodern feminism focused on the post-realist, critical legal studies challenge to rationalism and rights. Professor Frances Olsen, has argued that law is incapable of being either principled, rational or objective. Rather, law is a form of political ideology that is presently oppressive to women. Professor Olsen believes that liberal thought gave rise to a series of sexualized, hierarchical dualisms that structure our legal thought: rational/ irrational; active/passive; thought/feeling; reason/emotion; culture/nature; power/sensitivity; objective/subjective; abstract/contextualized; principled/ personalized. The first half of each pair is considered male and superior, and the second half is considered female and inferior. The claim that law is principled, rational and objective tends to be associated with the male half of the dualisms. Like the dualisms themselves, however, law has no essence or immutable nature. Law is not principled because legal rules are too specific to have generalizable content, and legal principles are too vague and indeterminate to resolve particular cases. Law is not rational because the legal system always contains competing claims of rights that can generate contradictory outcomes that are equally rational. Finally, law is not objective because the indeterminacy of law can be ameliorated only through recourse to policy preferences, which are themselves necessarily subjective.[49] Professor Olsen has also written a widely cited article about the differential gender treatment mandated by many statutory rape laws, which she uses to illustrate what she perceives to be the failures and disutilities of liberal rights theory.[50]

Some feminists reject the relevance of postmodern indeterminacy and challenges to rationalism. Professor Catharine A. MacKinnon states, "The objective world is not a reflection of women's subjectivity . . . [W]omen know the male world is out there because it hits them in the face. No matter how they think about it, try to think it out of existence or into a different shape,

---

[49] See Frances Olsen, *Feminism and Critical Legal Theory: An American Perspective*, 18 INT'L J. SOC. OF L. 199–200, 208–11 (1990).

[50] See Frances Olsen, *Statutory Rape: A Femi-* nist Critique of Rights Analysis, 63 TEX. L. REV. 387 (1984). The critical legal studies critique of rights is discussed more fully in Chapter 11, Section 11.02.

it remains independently real. . . . It has all the indeterminacy of a bridge abutment hit at sixty miles per hour."[51] A criticism that feminists and others often direct at critical legal theory is that it is better at deconstructing current social structures and hierarchies than it is at reconstructing alternatives that will improve the social situation of women. For example, Professor Drucilla Cornell rejects the nihilistic inclinations of deconstruction and favors, teleological and communitarian approaches to legal interpretation rooted in Hegelian "dialogism."[52] Professor Deborah Rhode argues that postmodern feminists are placed in the paradoxical position of asserting the existence of gender oppression without being able to document the existence of such oppression because of their rejection of universalism. She does, however, discuss strategies that feminist politics can use to make positive contributions to the feminist movement and to avoid being mired in mere critique.[53]

Professor Patricia J. Williams has argued that the critique of rights offered by critical legal theory ignores the positive benefits for marginalized groups that have been derived from rights discourse. Analytical indeterminacy may make reified rights a dispensable luxury for empowered white males, but from the perspective of a disempowered black female, rights rhetoric has value. "The vocabulary of rights speaks to an establishment that values the guise of stability, and from whom social change for the better must come (whether it is given, taken, or smuggled). Change argued for in the sheep's clothing of stability ('rights') can be effective, even as it destabilizes certain other establishment values (segregation). The subtlety of rights' real instability thus does not render unstable their persona of stability."[54] For Williams, rights rhetoric is a "political mechanism" that conveys to marginalized groups a sense of respect and dignity accorded those who are part of a community.[55] Despite their manipulablity, rights "feel new" and "deliciously empowering" in the mouths of disempowered people.[56]

In recent years, postmodern feminism has focused on the problem of "essentialism." Law Professor Angela P. Harris of the University of California at Berkeley has criticized the tendency of white, middle-class, heterosexual feminists to "essentialize" their conception of women, arguing that such gender essentialism suppresses the perspectives of marginalized women. Angela P. Harris, *Race and Essentialism in Feminist Legal Theory*, 42 STAN. L. REV. 581, 585, 586–89, 605–07, 608–09, 610, 612–13, 615 (1990):[57]

> In this article, I discuss some of the writings of feminist legal theorists Catharine MacKinnon and Robin West. I argue that their work, though powerful and brilliant in many ways, relies on what I call gender essentialism—the notion that a unitary, "essential" women's experience can be isolated and described independently of race, class, sexual orientation, and other realities of experience. The result of this tendency toward

---

[51] CATHARINE A. MACKINNON, TOWARD A FEMINIST THEORY OF THE STATE 123 (1989).

[52] *See* Drucilla Cornell, *Toward a Modern/ Postmodern Reconstruction of Ethics,* 133 U. PA. L. REV. 291, 291–99 (1985).

[53] *See* Deborah Rhode, *Feminist Critical Theories,* 42 STAN. L. REV. 617, 617–20, 635–38 (1990).

[54] *See* PATRICIA J. WILLIAMS, *The Pain of Word Bondage, in* THE ALCHEMY OF RACE AND RIGHTS 146, 149 (1991).

[55] *See id.* at 152–53.

[56] *See id.* at 164.

[57] Copyright © 1990 by the Board of Trustees of Leland Stanford Junior University. Reprinted with permission.

gender essentialism, I argue, is not only that some voices are silenced in order to privilege others (for this is an inevitable result of categorization, which is necessary both for human communication and political movement), but that the voices that are silenced turn out to be the same voices silenced by the mainstream legal voice of "We the People"—among them, the voices of black women.

This result troubles me for two reasons. First, the obvious one: As a black woman, in my opinion the experience of black women is too often ignored both in feminist theory and in legal theory, and gender essentialism in feminist legal theory does nothing to address this problem. A second and less obvious reason for my criticism of gender essentialism is that, in my view, contemporary legal theory needs less abstraction and not simply a different sort of abstraction. To be fully subversive, the methodology of feminist legal theory should challenge not only law's content but its tendency to privilege the abstract and unitary voice, and this gender essentialism also fails to do.

. . .

The need for multiple consciousness in [the] feminist movement—a social movement encompassing law, literature, and everything in between—has long been apparent. Since the beginning of the feminist movement in the United States, black women have been arguing that their experience calls into question the notion of a unitary "women's experience." In the first wave of the feminist movement [the women's suffrage movement], black women's realization that the white leaders of the suffrage movement intended to take neither issues of racial oppression nor black women themselves seriously was instrumental in destroying or preventing political alliances between black and white women within the movement. In the second wave [the contemporary feminist movement], black women are again speaking loudly and persistently, and at many levels our voices have begun to be heard. Feminists have adopted the notion of multiple consciousness as appropriate to describe a world in which people are not oppressed only or primarily on the basis of gender, but on the bases of race, class, sexual orientation, and other categories in inextricable webs. Moreover, multiple consciousness is implicit in the precepts of feminism itself . . . . If a unitary "women's experience" or "feminism" must be distilled, feminists must ignore many women's voices.

In feminist legal theory, however, the move away from univocal toward multivocal theories of women's experience and feminism has been slower than in other areas . . . . And in feminist legal theory, as in the dominant culture, it is mostly white, straight, and socioeconomically privileged people who claim to speak for all of us. Not surprisingly, the story they tell about "women," despite its claim to universality, seems to black women to be peculiar to women who are white, straight, and socioeconomically privileged. . .

. . .

The notion that there is a monolithic "women's experience" that can be described independent of other facets of experience like race, class, and sexual orientation is one I refer to in this essay as "gender essentialism." A corollary to gender essentialism is "racial essentialism"—the belief that there is a monolithic "Black Experience," or "Chicano Experience." The source of gender and racial essentialism (and all other essentialisms, for the list of categories could be infinitely multiplied) is . . . the voice that claims to speak for all. The result of essentialism is to reduce the lives of people who experience multiple forms of oppression to addition problems: "racism + sexism = straight black women's experience," or "racism

+ sexism + homophobia = black lesbian experience." Thus, in an essentialist world, black women's experience will always be forcibly fragmented before being subjected to analysis, as those who are "only interested in race" and those who are "only interested in gender" take their separate slices of our lives.

Moreover, feminist essentialism paves the way for unconscious racism . . . . In a racist society like this one, the storytellers are usually white, and so "woman" turns out to be "white woman."

[Professor Harris then discusses why she views Catharine MacKinnon's dominance feminism and Robin West's cultural feminist "connection thesis" as essentialist in their suppression of the voices of black women.]

. . .

If gender essentialism is such a terrible thing, why do two smart and politically committed feminists like Catharine MacKinnon and Robin West rely on it? . . .

First, as a matter of intellectual convenience, essentialism is easy. Particularly for white feminists—and most of the people doing academic feminist theory in this country at this time are white—essentialism means not having to do as much work, not having to try and learn about the lives of black women, with all the risks and discomfort that that effort entails. Essentialism is also intellectually easy because the dominant culture is essentialist—because it is difficult to find materials on the lives of black women, because there is as yet no academic infrastructure of work by and/or about black women or black feminist theory.

Second, and more important, essentialism represents emotional safety. Especially for women who have relinquished privilege or had it taken away from them in their struggle against gender oppression, the feminist movement comes to be an emotional and spiritual home, a place to feel safe, a place that must be kept harmonious and free of difference . . . . Many women, perhaps especially white women who have rejected or been rejected by their homes of origin, hope and expect that the women's movement will be a new home—and home is a place of comfort, not conflict.

Third, feminist essentialism offers women not only intellectual and emotional comfort, but the opportunity to play all-too-familiar power games both among themselves and with men. Feminist essentialism provides multiple arenas for power struggle which cross-cut one another in complex ways. The gameswomanship is palpable at any reasonably diverse gathering of feminists with a political agenda. The participants are busy constructing hierarchies of oppression, using their own suffering (and consequent innocence) to win the right to define "women's experience" or to demand particular political concessions for their interest group. White women stress women's commonality, which enables them to control the group's agenda; black women make reference to 200 years of slavery and argue that their needs should come first. Eventually, as the group seems ready to splinter into mutually suspicious and self-righteous factions, someone reminds the group that after all, women are women and we are all oppressed by men, and solidarity reappears through the threat of a common enemy. These are the strategies of zero-sum games; and feminist essentialism, by purveying the notion that there is only one "women's experience," perpetuates these games.

Finally, as Martha Minow has pointed out, "Cognitively, we need simplifying categories, and the unifying category of 'woman' helps to organize experience, even at the cost of denying some of it."[118] Abandoning mental categories completely would leave us . . . autistic . . . terrorized by the sheer weight and particularity of experience. No categories at all, moreover, would leave nothing of a women's movement, save perhaps a tepid kind of "I've got my oppression, you've got yours" approach . . . . The problem of avoiding essentialism while preserving "women" as a meaningful political and practical concept has thus often been posed as a dilemma. The argument sometimes seems to be that we must choose: use the traditional categories or none at all.

. . .

Black women experience not a single inner self (much less one that is essentially gendered), but many selves. This sense of a multiplicitous self is not unique to black women, but black women have expressed this sense in ways that are striking, poignant, and potentially useful to feminist theory. bell hooks describes her experience in a creative writing program at a predominantly white college, where she was encouraged to find "her voice," as frustrating to her sense of multiplicity.

It seemed that many black students found our situations problematic precisely because our sense of self, and by definition our voice, was not unilateral, monologist, or static but rather multidimensional. We were as at home in dialect as we were in standard English. Individuals who speak languages other than English, who speak patois as well as standard English, find it a necessary aspect of self-affirmation not to feel compelled to choose one voice over another, not to claim one as more authentic, but rather to construct social realities that celebrate, acknowledge, and affirm differences, variety.[125]

This experience of multiplicity is also a sense of self-contradiction, of containing the oppressor within oneself. In her article *On Being the Object of Property*,[126] Patricia Williams writes about herself writing about her great-great-grandmother, "picking through the ruins for my roots." What she finds is a paradox: She must claim for herself "a heritage the weft of whose genesis is [her] own disinheritance." Williams's great-great-grandmother, Sophie, was a slave, and at the age of about eleven was impregnated by her owner, a white lawyer named Austin Miller. Their daughter Mary, Williams's great-grandmother, was taken away from Sophie and raised as a house servant.

. . .

A post-essentialist feminism can benefit not only from the abandonment of the quest for a unitary self, but also from Martha Minow's realization that difference—and therefore identity—is always relational, not inherent.[136] Zora Neale Hurston's work is a good illustration of this notion.

In an essay written for a white audience, *How It Feels to Be Colored Me*, Hurston argues that her color is not an inherent part of her being, but a response to her surroundings. She recalls the day she "became colored"—the day she left her home in an all-black community to go to school: "I left Eatonville, the town of the oleanders, as Zora. When I disembarked from the river-boat at Jacksonville, she was no more. It seemed that I had suffered a sea change. I was not Zora of Orange County

---

[118] Martha Minow, *Feminist Reason: Getting It and Losing It*, 38 J. LEGAL EDUC. 47, 51 (1998).

[125] B. HOOKS, TALKING BACK [: THINKING FEMINIST, THINKING BLACK 11–12 (1989)].

[126] 14 SIGNS 5, [5–7] (1988).

[136] [Martha Minow, *The Supreme Court 1986 Term—Forward: Justice Engendered*, 101 HARV. L. REV. 10, 34–38 (1987)].

any more, I was now a little colored girl." But even as an adult, Hurston insists, her colored self is always situational: "I do not always feel colored. Even now I often achieve the unconscious Zora of Eatonville before the Hegira. I feel most colored when I am thrown against a sharp white background."[139]

. . .

To be compatible with this conception of the self, feminist theorizing about "women" must similarly be strategic and contingent, focusing on relationships, not essences. One result will be that men will cease to be a faceless Other and reappear as potential allies in political struggle. Another will be that women will be able to acknowledge their differences without threatening feminism itself. In the process, as feminists begin to attack racism and classism and homophobia, feminism will change from being only about "women as women" (modified women need not apply), to being about all kinds of oppression based on seemingly inherent and unalterable characteristics. We need not wait for a unified theory of oppression; that theory can be feminism.

. . .

Finally, black women can help [the] feminist movement move beyond its fascination with essentialism through the recognition that wholeness of the self and commonality with others are asserted (if never completely achieved) through creative action, not realized in shared victimization. Feminist theory at present, especially feminist legal theory, tends to focus on women as passive victims . . .

This story of woman as victim is meant to encourage solidarity by emphasizing women's shared oppression, thus denying or minimizing difference, and to further the notion of an essential woman—she who is victimized. But, as bell hooks has succinctly noted, the notion that women's commonality lies in their shared victimization by men "directly reflects male supremacist thinking. Sexist ideology teaches women that to be female is to be a victim."[154] Moreover, the story of woman as passive victim denies the ability of women to shape their own lives, whether for better or worse. It also may thwart their abilities . . . . [R]eluctant to look farther than commonality for fear of jeopardizing the comfort of shared experience, women who rely on their victimization to define themselves may be reluctant to let it go and create their own self-definitions.

At the individual level, black women have had to learn to construct themselves in a society that denied them full selves . . . . [Identity is] a construction, not an essence—something made of fragments of experience, not discovered in one's body or unveiled after male domination is eliminated.

. . .

Finally, on a collective level this emphasis on will and creativity reminds us that bridges between women are built, not found. The discovery of shared suffering is a connection more illusory than real; what will truly bring and keep us together is the use of effort and imagination to root out and examine our differences, for only the recognition of women's differences can ultimately bring [the] feminist movement to strength. This is hard work, and painful work; but it is also radical work, real work . . .

---

[139] ZORA NEALE HURSTON, *How It Feels to Be Colored Me, in* I LOVE MYSELF WHEN I AM LAUGHING . . . AND THEN AGAIN WHEN I AM LOOKING MEAN AND IMPRESSIVE 152 (A. Walker ed., 1979).

[154] BELL HOOKS, FEMINIST THEORY: FROM MARGIN TO CENTER 45 (1984).

In their book GENDER AND LAW, Professors Harris and Katharine T. Bartlett isolate seven different types of gender essentialism that they find to be potentially problematic.[58] Other anti-essentialist feminists have recognized dangers of marginalization similar to those described by Professor Harris. Professor Kimberlé Crenshaw has used the term "intersectionality" to describe the position of women who are members of multiple marginalized groups, and whose interests are therefore likely to be overlooked when gender or some other characteristic is essentialized.[59] For example, the separate spheres phenomenon that is common in feminist jurisprudence recognizes the attribution of characteristics such as dependence and passivity to women. However, this phenomenon fails to recognize that such traits are culturally associated with white women and not with black women. As a result, the separate spheres insight does less to help illuminate the oppression of black women than to describe the oppression of white women.[60] Similarly, antidiscrimination laws that prohibit discrimination on the basis of race or gender overlook discrimination based on the intersection of race *and* gender. Therefore, an employer who likes both women and blacks, but dislikes black women, is free to discriminate against black women because the intersection of race and gender is not a category for which discrimination is prohibited.[61] In addition, the intersection of race and gender not recognized in traditional identity politics raises concerns for black women threatened by rape and domestic violence that are not shared by white women suffering similar threats.[62] Crenshaw emphasizes that experiences of racism can be shaped by gender and experiences of sexism can be shaped by race.[63]

Professor Patricia A. Cain has offered an anti-essentialist analysis, similar to the Harris analysis, that stresses the omission of lesbian perspectives from the work of feminists including MacKinnon and West.[64] MacKinnon wrongly assumed that heterosexual and lesbian experiences were similarly dominated by men, thereby "silencing" those lesbians who experience non-subordinated sex with other women. West's "connection thesis" assumes that the essential aspects of a woman's character derive from heterosexual connections and mother-child connections, thereby ignoring the lesbian connections that women have with other women.[65] Cain believes that both sexism and "heterosexism" are bad, particularly when practice by feminists who are otherwise opposed to ignoring marginalized perspectives. Cain cites Adrienne Rich for the proposition that heterosexuality should be viewed from the new perspective of the "lesbian possibility." However, feminist essentializing that renders

---

[58] *See* KATHARINE T. BARTLETT & ANGELA P. HARRIS, GENDER AND LAW: THEORY, DOCTRINE, COMMENTARY 1007–09 (2d ed. 1998).

[59] *See* Kimberlé Crenshaw, *Demarginalizing the Intersection of Race and Sex: A Black Feminist Critique of Antidiscrimination Doctrine, Feminist Theory and Antiracist Politics,* 1989 U. CHI. LEGAL F. 139, 139–40.

[60] *See id.* at 149–56, 166–67.

[61] *See. id.* at 141–43, 150–51; *see also* Richard Delgado & Jean Stefancic, *Critical Race Theory: Past, Present, and Future, in* LEGAL THEORY AT THE END OF THE MILLENNIUM 467,

473–74 (Michael D. A. Freeman ed., 1998) (Series: CURRENT LEGAL PROBLEMS, vol. 51, Oxford University Press, 1998).

[62] *See* Kimberlé Crenshaw, *Mapping the Margins: Intersectionality, Identity Politics, and Violence Against Women of Color,* 43 STAN. L. REV. 1241, 1241–45 (1991).

[63] *See* Kimberlé Crenshaw, *Race, Gender and Sexual Harassment,* 65 S. CAL. L. REV. 1467, 1468 (1992).

[64] *See* Patricia A. Cain, *Feminist Jurisprudence: Grounding the Theories,* 4 BERKELEY WOMEN'S L.J. 191 (1989–90).

[65] *See id.* at 199–203.

the lesbian experience invisible makes it impossible for women meaningfully to "choose" between lesbian and heterosexual experiences, rather than merely adopting a heterosexual orientation by default.[66]

The postmodern depiction of contextual identity that emerges from the work of anti-essentialist feminists suggests the importance of diversity to the concept of justice. Legal theories that encompass rather than disregard non-dominant perspectives are arguably better than legal theories that simply reinforce existing power relationships. That is the view advanced by Professor Martha Minow in her work on "difference." She argues that the law can better handle the "dilemma of difference" by recognizing that differences are relational rather than objective. She believes that law should be "engendered," meaning that legal discourse should be aware of its own partial perspective so that it can better empathize with the interests of marginalized groups.[67] Minow stresses:

> We need settings in which to engage in the clash of realities that breaks us out of settled and complacent meanings and creates opportunities for insight and growth. This is the special burden and opportunity for the Court: to enact and preside over the dialogue through which we remake the normative endowment that shapes current understandings.

> When the Court performs these roles, it engenders justice. Justice is engendered when judges admit the limitations of their own viewpoints, when judges reach beyond those limits by trying to see from contrasting perspectives, and when people seek to exercise power to nurture differences, not to assign and control them. Rather than securing an illusory universality and objectivity, law is a medium through which particular people can engage in the continuous work of making justice. The law "is part of a distinctive manner of imagining the real." Legal decisions engrave upon our culture the stories we tell to and about ourselves, the meanings that constitute the traditions we invent. Searching for words to describe realities too multiple and complex to be contained by their language, litigants and judges struggle over what will be revealed and what will be concealed in the inevitable partiality of human judgment. Through deliberate attention to our own partiality, we can begin to acknowledge the dangers of pretended impartiality. By taking difference into account, we can overcome our pretended indifference to difference, and people our worlds with those who can surprise and enrich one another. As we make audible, in official arenas, the struggles over which version of reality will secure power, we disrupt the silence of one perspective, imposed as if universal. Admitting the partiality of the perspective that temporarily gains official endorsement may embolden resistance to announced rules. But only by admitting that rules are resistible—and by justifying to the governed their calls for adherence—can justice be done in a democracy. "[I]t is only through the variety of relations constructed by the plurality of beings that truth can be known and community constructed." Then we constitute ourselves as members of conflicting communities with enough reciprocal regard to talk across differences. We engender mutual regard for pain we know and pain we do not understand.[68]

---

[66] See id. at 208–09; see also Adrienne Rich, *Compulsory Heterosexuality and Lesbian Existence*, 5 SIGNS 631, 638 (1980) ("Heterosexuality has been forcibly and subliminally imposed on women," and lesbians have been marginalized from mainstream feminism).

[67] See Martha Minow, *The Supreme Court, 1986 Term—Foreword: Justice Engendered*, 101 HARV. L. REV. 10, 10–17 (1987).

[68] Id. at 94–95. Copyright © 1987 by the Harvard Law Review Association. Reprinted with permission.

Professor Katharine T. Bartlett has also argued in favor of extending perspectives, both as a means of increasing empathy with marginalized groups and as a means of responding to postmodern skepticism about the nature of "truth." She has developed a concept of "positionality" that attempts to mediate the tension between postmodernism and women's perspectives that are experienced as authentic. "Positionality is a sta..ce from which a number of apparently inconsistent feminist 'truths' make sense. The political stance acknowledges the existence of empirical truths, values and knowledge, and also their contingency. It thereby provides a basis for feminist commitment and political action, but views these commitments as provisional and subject to further critical evaluation and revision." Bartlett believes that knowledge can be increased by expanding one's perspective through social relationships, so that the experience of truth can grow in ways that are not "ultimate or objective" but are nevertheless "important and non-arbitrary."[69] Professor Mari Matsuda has developed a concept of "multiple consciousness," which she believes permits marginalized groups such as women and racial minorities to shift perspectives between viewpoints of the dominant and marginalized cultures. This, in turn, permits a single person to experience simultaneous understanding of conflicting perspectives—an experience that Matsuda claims can produce genius, or madness, or both.[70]

§ 10.06 Conclusion

In the three decades since it was first recognized as an independent theoretical discipline, feminist legal theory has evolved through a liberal equality stage, a cultural difference stage, a radical dominance stage, and a postmodern anti-essentialist stage. Throughout all of its developmental stages, ultimate equality has been at least a tacit goal of feminist legal theory. Now, however, equality may once again be emerging as an explicit goal, although the revival is not uncontroversial. Some contemporary feminists have advanced revisionist conceptions of liberalism to support political positions that are quite different from the positions espoused by traditional liberal feminists.

In her book entitled INTRODUCTION TO FEMINIST LEGAL THEORY, Professor Martha Chamallas writes:

> The present period is also marked by particularly trenchant critiques of feminism, coming not only from writers who disagree with most feminist aims but also from self-declared feminists who believe that the direction of feminist scholarship in the last decade has undermined women's quest for equality. Some of the younger feminist critics entered the debate at a time when liberal feminism was under intense scrutiny. They longed for simpler times when the feminist agenda was unitary, focused on equality, and not so clearly linked to politics of race and sexual orientation. One purpose of this book is to provide just enough context and history to the study of feminist legal theory to encourage a new

---

[69] See Bartlett, *supra* note 9, at 880–85.

[70] See Mari J. Matsuda, *When the First Quail Calls: Multiple Consciousness as Jurispruden-* *tial Method,* 11 WOMEN'S RTS. L. REP. 7, 8–10 (1992).

generation of feminists to take a broader and more complex view of the movement and its influence on law.[71]

Chamallas discusses three sources of opposition to feminist legal thought. One comes from opponents of feminism—typically men—who root their opposition in sociobiological or economic theories. They claim that women are so different from men that it would be improper to accord women the special treatment they need to achieve the equal outcomes favored by many feminists.[72] The second source of opposition comes from socially conservative, right-wing women, such as those associated with the Independent Women's Forum, who disapprove of the progressive political outcomes favored by many feminists, including gender integration of the military and an emphasis on equal pay for women.[73] The third source of opposition comes from a new equality-based movement. It is perhaps the most interesting for purposes of constitutional theory because it emanates from women who call themselves feminists, and because it seeks to root itself in legal liberalism.[74]

Among the neo-liberal feminists whom Chamallas discusses are Katie Roiphe, whose book THE MORNING AFTER: SEX, FEAR AND FEMINISM, characterizes established feminism as "victim feminism" because it depicts women as innocent, fragile, vulnerable and sexless. Roiphe objects to the feminist attention given to rape and sexual harassment because it suggests that women lack the agency to protect their own interests. Roiphe's emphasis on individual responsibility is rooted in traditional liberal theory.[75] Chamallas also discusses Cathy Young's article *The New Madonna/Whore Syndrome: Feminism, Sexuality, and Sexual Harassment*, which opposes the use of a "reasonable woman" standard in sexual harassment cases as "protective feminism." Young also objects to Justice Ginsburg's desire to use law to eliminate gender-based disparate treatment, believing that women have the power to liberate themselves if feminists will only get out of the way.[76]

Not all sympathy for a revival of equality feminism is politically conservative. Professor Nancy Levit has argued that feminism has now evolved to the point where it must include men and masculinity within its scope, because men are also harmed by socially constructed stereotypes of maleness and masculinity.[77] Men are coerced by cultural expectations to be breadwinners, risk-takers, independent, competitive and emotionally tough. This construction of masculinity is "one of patriarchy's chief methods of reproduction."[78] Levit argues that gender roles should be socially reconstructed in a way that will benefit both men and women. "If we are to move beyond gender wars, it is absolutely crucial to recognize that *the oppression of men and women are intertwined*."[79] Levit asserts that "feminism has stalled in an important way

---

[71] CHAMALLAS, *supra* note 11, at 29. Copyright © 1999 by Martha Chamallas. Reprinted with permission of Martha Chamallas and Aspen Law & Business.

[72] *See id.* at 117–23.

[73] *See id.* at 128–33.

[74] *See id.* at 124–28.

[75] *See id.* at 124–26 (discussing KATIE ROIPHE,

THE MORNING AFTER: SEX, FEAR AND FEMINISM (1993)).

[76] *See id.* at 126–27 (discussing Cathy Young, *The New Madonna/Whore Syndrome: Feminism, Sexuality, and Sexual Harassment*, 38 N.Y.L. SCH. L. REV. 257 (1993)).

[77] *See* LEVIT, *supra* note 11, at 1–14.

[78] *See id.* at 9.

[79] *See id.* at 13.

by not reaching far enough. The hope is to advance the cause of feminism by pointing out the more universal harms of gender role stereotyping of men. This book was largely impelled by the lessons of feminist theory itself—not to allow issues to remain silenced and to "question everything."[80]

Professor Tracy E. Higgins has suggested another way in which feminism has yet to be fully developed—a way that implicates central issues in constitutional theory. She argues that feminist legal theory has failed to contribute as much as it could to the debate over democracy, constitutionalism, and judicial review.[81] Mainstream constitutional theory is concerned with the countermajoritarian difficulty that emerges from the conflict between democratic sovereignty and respect for individual rights. However, mainstream constitutional theory presupposes a high level of autonomy on the part of individuals in their roles both as possessors of individual rights and as citizen participants in democratic self-governance. This autonomy is necessary for individuals meaningfully to determine how they wish to exercise the individual rights that they possess free from majoritarian control. Moreover, this autonomy is also necessary for the proper functioning of democratic sovereignty. Without such autonomy, the process of democratic self-governance will not be reliable, because individuals as citizens will not be able to express and aggregate their collective preferences in a way that provides the consent to governmental policymaking that is necessary for democratic legitimacy.[82]

Feminist legal theory has focused extensively on the limited agency that women possess as a result of women's unequal treatment in the culture. Not only external constraints imposed by discriminatory treatment, but also internal constraints imposed by women's own internalization of the social construction of gender, limit the ability of women to ascertain and implement their preferences.[83] However, feminist legal theory has also stressed a political agenda that legal feminists wish to advance in the name of women as a group. And the existence of such an agenda risks essentializing women, and overlooking the individual perspectives derived from consciousness-raising and attention to women's actual experiences that feminism seeks to liberate from a patriarchal culture. Professor Higgins suggests that the tension in feminist legal theory between respect for women's actual experiences and the promotion of an agenda for women collectively is analogous to the countermajoritarian tension in mainstream constitutional law between individual rights and democratic sovereignty. She also believes that the method that legal feminists have used to mediate this tension within feminist legal theory can be usefully applied to the countermajoritarian tension in mainstream constitutional law.[84]

Professor Higgins argues that the concept of limited or partial agency developed by legal feminists to describe the constraints imposed on women in a patriarchal society can also be applied to the concept of autonomous individuality that is so central to liberal constitutional theory. Once the liberal individual is recognized to possess only the restricted free agency that is possible within the confines of external constraint and social construction, the

---

[80] See id. at 14.

[81] See Tracy E. Higgins, *Democracy and Feminism*, 110 HARV. L. REV. 1657, 1657–61 (1997).

[82] See id. at 1661–70.

[83] See id. at 1670–84.

[84] See id. at 1684–94.

countermajoritarian dilemma in mainstream constitutional theory is transformed. Concepts such as governmental neutrality and deference to private preferences cease to be appealing. Because private power can interfere with the formation of individual preferences through the process of social construction, the traditional negative-rights orientation of constitutionalism appears too limited. Neither the public/private distinction nor the concept of governmental neutrality continue to make much sense, because "equal protection" may require government intervention to reshape preferences that have been socially constructed through the use of private power. Moreover, the aggregation of private preferences necessary to the consensual legitimacy of democratic self-governance may require similar government intervention. What is needed then is a theory of constitutionalism, including a theory of judicial review, that helps to determine when governmental intervention and departures from the "neutrality" embedded in the status quo are warranted. Professor Higgins argues that feminist legal theory can use its insights into limited agency and hidden inequality to help develop such a theory. She suggests, for example, that dominance theory might prove useful in this endeavor because of its expertise in recognizing subtle and pervasive forms of cultural subordination that can undermine equality. However, because questions of subordination can be complex, she believes that the formulation of anti-subordination policies would evolve primarily through a deliberative democratic process conducted by the political branches, with judicial review serving only a limited role.[85] The work of Professor Higgins suggests that feminist legal theory can have jurisprudential value that reaches even beyond the issue of equality for women. Its value may extend to fundamental issues of constitutional theory concerning judicial review and democratic self-governance as well.

In light of the various strands of feminist legal theory described above, is it best to view men and women as fundamentally the same or as fundamentally different for purposes of constitutional law? If men and women are fundamentally different from each other, are those differences "real" or "socially constructed?" Does the distinction between real and socially constructed differences matter? Is feminist legal theory correct that the culture is "patriarchal," in the sense that the perspectives of men matter more than the perspectives of women? If so, is that realistically ever likely to change?

§ 10.07 Bibliography

Kathryn Abrams, *Sex Wars Redux: Agency and Coercion in Feminist Legal Theory*, 95 COLUM. L. REV. 304 (1995); *Hearing the Call of Stories*, 79 CAL. L. REV. 971 (1991); *Ideology and Women's Choices*, 24 GA. L. REV. 761 (1990)

Anita L. Allen, *Tribe's Judicial Feminism*, 44 STAN. L. REV. 179 (1991) (reviewing Laurence H. Tribe, ABORTION: THE CLASH OF ABSOLUTES (1990)); UNEASY ACCESS: PRIVACY FOR WOMEN IN A FREE SOCIETY (1988)

---

[85] *See id.* at 1694–1703.

Regina Austin, *Sapphire Bound*, 1989 WIS. L. REV. 539

Judith A. Baer, *How Is Law Male? A Feminist Perspective on Constitutional Interpretation*, in FEMINIST JURISPRUDENCE: THE DIFFERENCE DEBATE 147 (Leslie Friedman Goldstein ed., 1992)

Mary Becker, *Conservative Free Speech and the Uneasy Case for Judicial Review*, 64 U. COLO. L. REV. 975 (1993); *Obscuring the Struggle: Sex Discrimination, Social Security, and Stone, Seidman, Sunstein, and Tushnet's Constitutional Law*, 89 COLUM. L. REV. 264 (1989)

Paulette Caldwell, *A Hair Piece: Perspectives on the Intersection of Race and Gender*, 1991 DUKE L.J. 365

Ruth Colker, *Anti-Subordination Above All: Sex, Race, and Equal Protection*, 61 N.Y.U. L. REV. 1003 (1986)

Drucilla Cornell, *Sexual Difference, the Feminine, and Equivalency: A Critique of MacKinnon's* Toward a Feminist Theory of the State, 100 YALE L.J. 2247 (1991)

Andrea Dworkin, *Against the Male Flood: Censorship, Pornography and Equality*, 8 HARV. WOMEN'S L.J. 1 (1985)

Cynthia Farina, *Conceiving Due Process*, 2 YALE J.L. & FEMINISM 189 (1991)

Feminist Jurisprudence Symposium, 24 GA. L. REV. 759–1044 (1990) (with articles by Kathryn Abrams, Patricia A. Cain, Ann E. Freedman, James M. O'Fallon and Cheyney C. Ryan, Judith Resnik, Nadine Taub, Carol Weisbrod, and Robert A. Williams, Jr.)

Ann Freedman, *Sex Equality, Sex Differences, and the Supreme Court*, 92 YALE L.J. 913 (1983)

Mary Joe Frug, *A Postmodern Feminist Legal Manifesto (An Unfinished Draft)*, 105 HARV. L. REV. 1045 (1992) (with responses by Barbara Johnson, Ruth Colker, and Martha Minow)

Leslie Friedman Goldstein, *Can This Marriage Be Saved? Feminist Public Policy and Feminist Jurisprudence*, in FEMINIST JURISPRUDENCE: THE DIFFERENCE DEBATE 11 (Leslie Friedman Goldstein ed., 1992)

Trina Grillo & Stephanie M. Wildman, *Obscuring the Importance of Race: The Implication of Making Comparisons between Racism & Sexism (Or Other Isms)*, 1991 DUKE L.J. 397

Janet E. Halley, *The Politics of the Closet: Towards Equal Protection for Gay, Lesbian, and Bisexual Identity*, 36 UCLA L. REV. 915 (1989)

Tracy Higgins, *"By Reason of Their Sex": Feminist Theory, Postmodernism, and Justice*, 80 CORNELL L. REV. 1536 (1995)

bel hooks, *Ending Female Sexual Oppression*, in FEMINIST THEORY: FROM MARGIN TO CENTER 147–56 (1984)

Kenneth Karst, *Woman's Constitution*, 1984 DUKE L.J. 447

Catharine MacKinnon, *Pornography as Defamation and Discrimination*, 71 B.U. L. REV. 793 (1991); *Reflections on Sex Equality Under Law*, 100 YALE L.J. 1281 (1991)

Linda C. McLain, *"Atomistic Man" Revisited: Liberalism, Connection, and Feminist Jurisprudence*, 65 S. CAL. L. REV. 1171 (1992)

Carrie Menkel-Meadow, *Feminist Legal Theory, Critical Legal Studies, and Legal Education or "The Fem-Crits Go to Law School,"* 38 J. LEGAL EDUC. 61 (1988)

Martha Minow, MAKING ALL THE DIFFERENCE (1990); CONFLICTS IN FEMINISM (1990)

Camille Paglia, VAMPS AND TRAMPS: NEW ESSAYS (1994); SEX, ART AND AMERICAN CULTURE (1992); SEXUAL PERSONAE: ART AND DECADENCE FROM NEFERTITI TO EMILY DICKINSON (1990)

Deborah Rhode, *The No-Problem Problem: Feminist Challenges and Cultural Change*, 100 YALE L.J. 1731 (1991); JUSTICE AND GENDER: SEX DISCRIMINATION AND THE LAW (1990)

Dorothy E. Roberts, *Punishing Drug Addicts Who Have Babies: Women of Color, Equality and the Right of Privacy*, 104 HARV. L. REV. 1419 (1991)

Ann C. Scales, *The Emergence of Feminist Jurisprudence: An Essay*, 95 YALE L. J. 1373 (1986)

Judy Scales-Trent, *Commonalities: On Being Black and White, Different and the Same*, 2 YALE J.L. & FEMINISM, 305 (1990); *Black Women and the Constitution: Finding Our Place, Asserting Our Rights*, 24 HARV. C.R.-C.L. L. REV. 9 (1989)

Elizabeth Schneider, *Feminization and the False Dichotomy of Victimization and Agency*, 38 N.Y.L. SCH. L. REV. 387 (1993); *The Dialectic of Rights and Politics: Perspectives from the Women's Movement*, 61 N.Y.U. L. REV. 589 (1986)

Suzanna Sherry, *The Forgotten Victims*, 63 U. COLO. L. REV. 375 (1992)

Christina Hoff Sommers, WHO STOLE FEMINISM? HOW WOMEN HAVE BETRAYED WOMEN (1994)

Elizabeth V. Spellman, INESSENTIAL WOMAN: PROBLEMS OF EXCLUSION IN FEMINIST THOUGHT (1988)

Nadine Strossen, *A Feminist Critique of "The" Feminist Critique of Pornography*, 79 VA. L. REV. 1099 (1993)

Cass Sunstein, *Neutrality in Constitutional Law (With Special Reference to Pornography, Abortion, and Surrogacy)*, 92 COLUM. L. REV. 1 (1992)

Robin West, *Equality Theory, Marital Rape and the Promise of the Fourteenth Amendment*, 42 FLA. L. REV. 45 (1990); *Progressive and Conservative Constitutionalism: Reconstructing the Fourteenth Amendment*, 88 MICH. L. REV. 641 (1990); *Law, Literature, and the Celebration of Authority*, 83 NW. U. L. REV. 977 (1989); *The Difference in Women's Hedonic Lives: A Phenomenological Critique of Feminist Legal Theory*, 3 WISC. WOMEN'S L.J. 81 (1987)

Joan C. Williams, *Dissolving the Sameness/Difference Debate: A Post-Modern Path Beyond Essentialism in Feminist and Critical Race Theory*, 1991 DUKE L.J. 296

Susan H. Williams, *Feminist Legal Epistemology*, 8 BERKELEY WOMEN'S L.J. 63 (1993)

Wendy Williams, *The Equality Crisis: Some Reflections on Culture, Courts, and Feminism*, 7 WOMEN'S RIGHTS L. REP. 175 (1983)

Chapter 11

Critical Race Theory

§ 11.01 Introduction and Overview

The term "critical race theory" refers to a range of legal theories that are premised on the belief that race, ethnicity and other identifying characteristics of marginalized "outgroups" are central to the operation of the legal system. Critical race theory grew out of the belief that blacks and other racial and ethnic minorities were being treated unfairly by the legal system and by white dominated social institutions. As an outgrowth of the critical legal studies movement, critical race theory has developed several postmodern analytical techniques designed to reveal a racial tilt built into the legal system that affirmatively contributes to the social oppression of racial minorities. Outgroups including blacks, Latinos, Asians, minority feminists and people with nontraditional sexual orientations now use critical race methodologies as part of identity politics. This section provides an overview of critical race theory, briefly describing its history, goals and primary methodologies. Sections 11.02 through 11.05 discuss particular methodologies of critical race theory that have generated controversy. Section 11.06 concludes by describing the combination of pessimism and persistence that seems to mark the future of critical race theory.

Four prominent critical race scholars have written a book about hate speech, the *Introduction* to which provides a concise description of the history and main tenets of critical race theory. In their book entitled WORDS THAT WOUND, Georgetown University Law Professors Mari J. Matsuda, and Charles R. Lawrence III, along with University of Colorado Law Professor Richard Delgado, and Columbia University Law Professor Kimberlé Williams Crenshaw offer the following preamble to critical race theory. MARI J. MATSUDA ET AL., *Introduction, in* WORDS THAT WOUND: CRITICAL RACE THEORY, ASSAULTIVE SPEECH, AND THE FIRST AMENDMENT 3–7 (1993):[1]

---

[1] Copyright © 1993 by Mari J. Matsuda, Charles R. Lawrence III, Richard Delgado and Kimberlé Williams Crenshaw. Reprinted by permission of Westview Press, a member of Perseus Books, L.L.C. (One of the authors suggested modifications to this excerpt which are noted by brackets and ellipses.) For other general introductions to critical race theory see John O. Calmore, *Critical Race Theory, Archie Shepp, and Fire Music: Securing an Authentic Intellectual Life in a Multicultural World*, 65 S. CAL. L. REV. 2129, 2160–94 (1992); Kimberlé Crenshaw et al., *Introduction, in* CRITICAL RACE THEORY: THE KEY WRITINGS THAT FORMED THE MOVEMENT xii–xxxii (Kimberlé Crenshaw et al. eds., 1995); Richard Delgado, *Introduction, in* CRITICAL RACE THEORY: THE CUTTING EDGE xiii–xvi (Richard Delgado ed., 1995); Richard Delgado & Jean Stefancic, *Critical Race Theory: Past, Present, and Future, in* LEGAL THEORY AT THE END OF THE MILLENNIUM 467, 467–91 (Michael D. A. Freeman ed., 1998) [hereinafter *"Past, Present and Future"*] (Series: CURRENT LEGAL PROBLEMS, vol. 51, Oxford University Press, 1998); Richard Delgado, *Critical Race Theory*, 19 SAGE RACE RELATIONS ABSTRACTS 3 (1994) (British publication) [hereinafter *"Sage Abstract"*]. For an annotated bibliography of critical race theory scholarship see Richard Delgado & Jean Stefancic, *Critical Race Theory: An Annotated*

Critical race theory cannot be understood as an abstract set of ideas or principles. Among its basic theoretical themes is that of privileging contextual and historical descriptions over transhistorical or purely abstract ones. It is therefore important to understand the origins of this genre in relation to the particulars of history. Critical race theory developed gradually. . . . [, beginning] in the late 1970s. The civil rights movement of the1960s had stalled, and many of its gains were being rolled back. It became apparent to many who were active in the civil rights movement that dominant conceptions of race, racism, and equality were increasingly incapable of providing . . . meaningful . . . racial justice. Individual law teachers and students committed to racial justice began to meet, to talk, to write, and to engage in political action in an effort to confront . . . dominant societal and institutional forces that maintained the structures of racism while professing the goal of dismantling racial discrimination.

. . .

Kimberlé Crenshaw places the social origins of what was to become critical race theory at a student boycott and alternative course organized in 1981 at the Harvard Law School. The primary objective of the protest was to persuade the administration to increase the number of tenured professors of color on the faculty. The departure of Derrick Bell, Harvard's first African-American professor, to assume the deanship of the law school at the University of Oregon had left Harvard Law School with only two professors of color. Students demanded that the law school begin [addressing] this situation by hiring a person of color to teach "Race Racism and American Law," a course that had been regularly taught by Bell, who was also the author of a ground-breaking text on the subject. When it became apparent that the administration was not prepared to meet their demand, students organized an alternative course [, inviting leading] academics and practitioners of color . . . each week to lecture and lead discussion on a chapter from Bell's book.

This course served as one of several catalysts for the development of critical race theory . . . . It [also] brought together in a common enterprise many of the legal scholars who were beginning to teach and write about race with activist students who were soon to enter the ranks of teaching. . . .

. . .

Some of us sought intellectual community in what was then the dominant progressive movement in the law schools, critical legal studies. . . .

. . .

Even within this enclave on the left we sometimes experienced alienation, marginalization, and inattention to the agendas and a misunderstanding of the issues we considered central to the work of combating

Bibliography, 79 VA. L. REV. 461 (1993); *see also* Delgado, *Sage Abstract, supra,* at 24–28 (unannotated bibliography).

For collections of critical race theory articles see CRITICAL RACE THEORY: THE CUTTING EDGE (Richard Delgado ed., 1995); CRITICAL RACE THEORY: THE KEY WRITINGS THAT FORMED THE MOVEMENT (Kimberlé Crenshaw et al. eds., 1995); *see also* CRITICAL RACE FEMINISM: A READER (Adrien Katherine Wing ed., 1997); CRITICAL WHITE STUDIES: LOOKING BEHIND THE MIRROR (Richard Delgado & Jean Stefancic eds., 1997); THE LATINO/A CONDITION: A CRITICAL READER (Richard Delgado & Jean Stefancic eds., 1998). For an annotated bibliography of critical race theory scholarship see Richard Delgado & Jean Stefancic, *Critical Race Theory: An Annotated Bibliography,* 79 VA. L. REV. 461 (1993); *See also* Delgado, *Sage Abstract, supra,* at 24-28 (unannotated bibliography).

racism. Scholars of color . . . began to ask their white colleagues to examine their own racism and to develop oppositional critiques not just to dominant conceptions of race and racism but to the treatment of race within the left as well.

. . .

New forms of scholarship began to emerge. We used personal histories, parables, chronicles, dreams, stories, poetry, fiction, and revisionist histories to convey our message. We called for greater attention to questions of audience—for whom were we writing and why? None of these methods was unique to our work, but . . .[our frequent use of them] as a part of a race-centered enterprise indicated the emergence of a genre or movement. . . .[having] the following defining elements:

1. Critical race theory recognizes that racism is endemic to American life. Thus, the question for us is not so much whether or how racial discrimination can be eliminated while maintaining the integrity of other interests implicated in the status quo such as federalism, privacy, traditional values, or established property interests. Instead we ask how these traditional interests and values serve as vessels of racial subordination.

2. Critical race theory expresses skepticism toward dominant legal claims of neutrality, objectivity, color blindness, and meritocracy. These claims are central to an ideology of equal opportunity that presents race as an immutable characteristic devoid of social meaning and tells an ahistorical, abstracted story of racial inequality as a series of randomly occurring, intentional, and individualized acts.

3. Critical race theory challenges ahistoricism and insists on a contextual/ historical analysis of the law. Current inequalities and social/institutional practices are linked to earlier periods in which the intent and cultural meaning of such practices were clear. More important, as critical race theorists we adopt a stance that presumes that racism has contributed to all contemporary manifestations of group advantage and disadvantage along racial lines, including differences in income, imprisonment, health, housing, education, political representation, and military service. Our history calls for this presumption.

4. Critical race theory insists on recognition of the experiential knowledge of people of color and our communities of origin in analyzing law and society. This knowledge is gained from critical reflection on the lived experience of racism and from critical reflection upon active political practice toward the elimination of racism.

5. Critical race theory is interdisciplinary and eclectic. It borrows from several traditions, including liberalism, law and society, feminism, Marxism, poststructuralism, critical legal theory, pragmatism, and nationalism. This eclecticism allows critical race theory to examine and incorporate those aspects of a methodology or theory that effectively enable our voice and advance the cause of racial justice even as we maintain a critical posture.

6. Critical race theory works toward the end of eliminating racial oppression as part of the broader goal of ending all forms of oppression. Racial oppression is experienced by many in tandem with oppression on grounds of gender, class, or sexual orientation. Critical race theory measures progress by a yardstick that looks to fundamental social transformation. The interests of all people of color necessarily require not just adjustments within the established hierarchies,

but a challenge to hierarchy itself. This recognition of intersecting forms of subordination requires multiple consciousness and political practices that address the varied ways in which people experience subordination.

Critical race theory is characterized perhaps most strongly by its belief in race consciousness as a necessary element in any analysis that seeks to explain the operation of cultural institutions in the United States. Some white liberal constitutional scholars—such as Professors T. Alexander Aleinikoff and David A. Strauss—have rejected the "myth of colorblindness," and have questioned the view that race-neutrality constitutes a desirable or even a coherent aspirational objective for contemporary constitutional law.[2] Moreover, the early work of Professor Derrick Bell—a founding member of the critical race theory movement—posits that school desegregation efforts tend to advantage liberal civil rights leaders more than black school children,[3] and that blacks are likely to benefit from civil rights initiatives only when black interests happen to coincide with the interests of whites.[4] In addition, Professor Alan David Freeman—a white radical who, before his death, was a founding member of the critical legal studies movement—argued that existing antidiscrimination law was so poorly conceived that it actually legitimized racial discrimination.[5] Critical race theory, however, has taken these insights about race consciousness, white dominance, and legitimation a considerable step further. Many critical race theorists believe that racial oppression is not only a *definitional* component of American culture, but that it is probably a *permanent* component as well. In addition, the analytical methodologies of critical race theory have been viewed by some as so radical that they threaten the very conventions of Western Enlightenment reason.[6]

Critical race theory fights against the prevailing perspectives of constitutional law. Professor Jerome McCristal Culp, Jr. has emphasized that the Constitution was framed by whites who had a very particular racial perspective, and that the Constitution itself adopts that white perspective. Culp believes that black legal scholarship should adopt a black perspective that questions the naturalness and neutrality of the prevailing white perspective—although it can be difficult for blacks to step completely outside of the prevailing white paradigm.[7] One thing that critical race theorists can do, therefore, is continually to ask the "race question" in order to illuminate the

---

[2] *See, e.g.,* T. Alexander Aleinikoff, *The Constitution in Context: The Continuing Significance of Racism,* 63 COLO. L. REV. 325 (1992); T. Alexander Aleinikoff, *A Case for Race-Consciousness,* 91 COLUM. L. REV. 1060 (1991); David A. Strauss, *The Myth of Colorblindness,* 1986 SUP. CT. REV. 99.

[3] *See* Derrick Bell, *Serving Two Masters: Integration Ideals and Client Interests in School Desegregation Litigation,* 85 YALE L.J. 470 (1976).

[4] *See* Derrick A. Bell, Jr., *Brown v. Board of Education and the Interest Convergence Di-*

lemma, 93 HARV. L. REV. 518 (1980).

[5] *See* Alan David Freeman, *Legitimizing Racial Discrimination through Antidiscrimination Law: A Critical Review of Supreme Court Doctrine,* 62 MINN. L. REV. 1049 (1978).

[6] *See* DANIEL A. FARBER & SUZANNA SHERRY, BEYOND ALL REASON: THE RADICAL ASSAULT ON TRUTH IN AMERICAN LAW (1997). The Farber & Sherry objections to critical race theory are discussed in Section 11.05 of this Chapter.

[7] *See* Jerome McCristal Culp, Jr., *Toward A Black Legal Scholarship: Race and Original Understandings,* 1991 DUKE L.J. 39, 67–97.

ways in which seemingly neutral rules adversely affect the interests of racial minorities.[8]

Professor John O. Calmore has invoked a form of oppositional jazz known as "fire music" to convey metaphorically the *feel* of critical race theory. The fire music of the turbulent 1960s was a different style of jazz than the jazz played by white musicians. It rejected the canons of European culture, and it was devalued by mainstream jazz critics. But the fire music was authentic. Its roots were in black ghetto culture—a culture that was unable to be assimilated into mainstream white society. It embodied the black experience of oppression, and it reflected the black nationalism that was emerging during the period. The fire music was raspy; it was militant; and it was revolutionary. The fire music was distinctively black, because whites had not lived the experiences necessary to play it. The fire music was produced by black musicians who did not define themselves in relation to whites. The fire music was blacks just being themselves. Calmore believes that, in terms of its genesis and its reception, critical race theory is like the fire music.[9]

§ 11.02 Critique of Liberalism

Critical race theory is a descendent of the critical legal studies movement of the 1970s and 80s. Accordingly, critical race theory squarely rejects the tenets of legal liberalism, finding the liberal insistence on race neutrality as an aspirational objective to be one of the causes of racial oppression.[10] Critical race theory is also skeptical of "racialism"—the view that law *reflects* the racial prejudices of the culture at large—insisting that the legal system affirmatively *participates* in the creation of racism rather than merely reflecting it. Critical race theory also adopts an ambivalent stance on the utility of rights, accepting the view that liberal conceptions of rights are too indeterminate to be reliable, but asserting that rights can nevertheless play a useful role in liberatory strategies. This Section describes the critique of liberalism as articulated by Professors Kimberlé Crenshaw, Neil Gotanda, Gary Peller, and Kendall Thomas. It then discusses the criticism that critical race theory has received from Professor Randall Kennedy.

Four prominent members of the critical race movement are Columbia Law Professor Kimberlé Crenshaw, Western State Law Professor Neil Gotanda, Georgetown Law Professor Gary Peller, and Columbia Law Professor Kendall Thomas. In the jointly-authored *Introduction* to their collection of critical race writings entitled CRITICAL RACE THEORY, they describe the relationship between critical race theory and critical legal studies, as well as the critique of liberalism that has become an integral component of critical race theory. Kimberlé Crenshaw et al., *Introduction, in* CRITICAL RACE THEORY: THE KEY WRITINGS THAT FORMED THE MOVEMENT xi-xxxii (Kimberlé Crenshaw, et al. eds., 1995):[11]

---

[8] *See* Jerome McCristal Culp, Jr., *Neutrality, The Race Question, and the 1991 Civil Rights Act: The "Impossibility" of Permanent Reform,* 45 RUTGERS L. REV. 965, 971–83 (1993).

[9] *See* Calmore, *supra* note 1, at 2129–59.

[10] Legal liberalism is discussed in Chapter 8.

[11] Copyright © 1995 by The New Press. Reprinted with permission.

The aspect of our work which most markedly distinguishes it from conventional liberal and conservative legal scholarship about race and inequality is a deep dissatisfaction with traditional civil rights discourse. As several of the authors in this collection demonstrate, the reigning contemporary American ideologies about race were built in the sixties and seventies around an implicit social compact. This compact held that racial power and racial justice would be understood in very particular ways. Racial justice was embraced in the American mainstream in terms that excluded radical or fundamental challenges to status quo institutional practices in American society by treating the exercise of racial power as rare and aberrational rather than as systemic and ingrained. The construction of "racism" from what Alan Freeman terms the "perpetrator perspective" restrictively conceived racism as an intentional, albeit irrational, deviation by a conscious wrongdoer from otherwise neutral, rational, and just ways of distributing jobs, power, prestige, and wealth. The adoption of this perspective allowed a broad cultural mainstream both explicitly to acknowledge the fact of racism and, simultaneously, to insist on its irregular occurrence and limited significance. As Freeman concludes, liberal race reform thus served to legitimize the basic myths of American meritocracy.

. . .

In constitutional law, for example, it was well settled that government-sanctioned racial discrimination was prohibited, and that legally enforced segregation constituted such discrimination. That victory was secured in *Brown v. Board of Education* and its progeny. In the language of the Fourteenth Amendment, race is a "suspect classification" which demands judicial strict scrutiny. "Race relations" thus represent an exception to the general deference that mainstream constitutional theory accords democratically elected institutions. Racial classifications violate the equal protection clause unless they both serve a compelling governmental interest and further, are no broader than necessary to achieve that goal. Within the conceptual boundaries of these legal doctrines, mainstream scholars debated whether discrimination should be defined only as intentional government action . . . or whether the tort-like "de facto" test should be used when government actions had predictable, racially skewed results . . . or whether the racial categories implicit in affirmative action policy should be legally equivalent to those used to burden people of color and therefore also be subject to strict scrutiny . . . and then whether remedying past social discrimination was a sufficiently compelling and determinate goal to survive strict scrutiny . . . and so on.

In all these debates we identified, of course, with the liberals against the intent requirement established in *Washington v. Davis,* the affirmative action limitations of *Bakke* (and later *Croson*), the curtailment of the "state action" doctrine resulting in the limitation of sites where constitutional antidiscrimination norms would apply, and so on. Yet the whole discourse seemed to assume away the fundamental problem of racial subordination whose examination was at the center of the work so many of us had spent our college years pursuing in Afro-American studies departments, community mobilizations, student activism, and the like.

The fact that affirmative action was seen as such a "dilemma" or a "necessary evil" was one symptom of the ultimately conservative character of even "liberal" mainstream race discourse. More generally, though, liberals and conservatives seemed to see the issues of race and law from within the same structure of analysis—namely, a policy that legal rationality could identify and eradicate the biases of race-consciousness in social decision-making. Liberals and conservatives as a general matter differed over the degree to which racial bias was a fact of American life:

liberals argued that bias was widespread where conservatives insisted it was not; liberals supported a disparate effects test for identifying discrimination, where conservatives advocated a more restricted intent requirement; liberals wanted an expanded state action requirement, whereas conservatives wanted a narrow one. The respective visions of the two factions differed only in scope: they defined and constructed "racism" the same way, as the opposite of color-blindness.

. . .

At the same time that these events were unfolding, a predominantly white left emerged on the law school scene in the late seventies, a development which played a central role in the genesis of Critical Race Theory. Organized by a collection of neo-Marxist intellectuals, former New Left activists, ex-counter-culturalists, and other varieties of oppositionists in law schools, the Conference on Critical Legal Studies [CLS] established itself as a network of openly leftist law teachers, students, and practitioners committed to exposing and challenging the ways American law served to legitimize an oppressive social order. Like the later experience of Critical Race writers vis-a-vis race scholarship, "crits" found themselves frustrated with the presuppositions of the conventional scholarly legal discourse: they opposed not only conservative legal work but also the dominant liberal varieties. Crits contended that liberal and conservative legal scholarship operated in the narrow ideological channel within which law was understood as qualitatively different from politics. The faith of liberal lawyers in the gradual reform of American law through the victory of the superior rationality of progressive ideas depended on a belief in the central ideological myth of the law/politics distinction, namely, that legal institutions employ a rational, apolitical, and neutral discourse with which to mediate the exercise of social power. This, in essence, is the role of law as understood by liberal political theory. Yet politics was embedded in the very doctrinal categories with which law organized and represented social reality. Thus the deeply political character of law was obscured in one way by the obsession of mainstream legal scholarship with technical discussions about standing, jurisdiction and procedure; and the political character of judicial decision-making was denied in another way through the reigning assumptions that legal decision-making was—or could be determined by preexisting legal rules, standards, and policies, all of which were applied according to professional craft standards encapsulated in the idea of "reasoned elaboration." Law was, in the conventional wisdom, distinguished from politics because politics was open-ended, subjective, discretionary, and ideological, whereas law was determinate, objective, bounded, and neutral.

This conception of law as rational, apolitical, and technical operated as an institutional regulative principle, defining what was legitimate and illegitimate to pursue in legal scholarship, and symbolically defining the professional, businesslike culture of day-to-day life in mainstream law schools. This generally centrist legal culture characterized the entire postwar period in legal education, with virtually no organized dissent. Its intellectual and ideological premises had not been seriously challenged since the Legal Realist movement of the twenties and thirties—a body of scholarship that mainstream scholars ritually honored for the critique of the "formalism" of turn-of-the-century legal discourse but marginalized as having "gone too far" in its critique of the very possibility of a rule of law. Writing during the so-called liberty of contract period (characterized by the Supreme Court's invalidation of labor reform legislation on the grounds that it violated the "liberty" of workers and owners to contract with each other over terms of employment) the legal realists set out to show that the purportedly neutral and objective legal interpretation of the period was really based on politics, on what Oliver Wendell Holmes called the "hidden and often inarticulate judgments of social policy."

The crits unearthed much of the Legal Realist work that mainstream legal scholars had ignored for decades, and they found the intellectual and theoretical basis for launching a full-scale critique of the role of law in helping to rationalize an unjust social order. While the Realist critique of American law's pretensions to neutrality and rationality was geared toward the right-wing libertarianism of an "Old Order" of jurists, crits redirected it at the depoliticized and technocratic assumptions of legal education and scholarship in the seventies. Moreover, in the sixties tradition from which many of them had come, they extended the intellectual and ideological conflict they engendered to the law school culture to which it was linked.

. . .

Critical Race Theory emerged in the interstices of this political and institutional dynamic. Critical Race Theory thus represents an attempt to inhabit and expand the space between two very different intellectual and ideological formations. Critical Race Theory sought to stage a simultaneous encounter with the exhausted vision of reformist civil rights scholarship, on the one hand, and the emergent critique of left legal scholarship on the other. . . .

[Tensions emerged between white adherents to critical legal studies and critical race theorists. One source of tension was the belief that the critical legal studies movement had itself marginalized the importance of race within the movement, much as it had accused mainstream legal institutions of doing within the society at large.]

Another point of conflict and difference between white crits and scholars of color revolved around the widely debated critique of rights. According to other scholars of color . . . another dimension of the failure of CLS to reflect the lived experience of people of color could be glimpsed in the CLS critique of rights. Crits tended to view the idea of legal "rights" as one of the ways that law helps to legitimize the social world by representing it as rationally mediated by the rule of law. Crits also saw legal rights— like those against racial discrimination—as indeterminate and capable of contradictory meanings, and as embodying an alienated way of thinking about social relations.

Crits of color agreed to varying degrees with some dimensions of the critique—for instance, that rights discourse was indeterminate. Yet we sharply differed with critics over the normative implications of this observation. To the emerging race crits, rights discourse held a social and transformative value in the context of racial subordination that transcended the narrower question of whether reliance on rights could alone bring about any determinate results. Race crits realized that the very notion of a subordinate people exercising rights was an important dimension of Black empowerment during the civil rights movement, significant not simply because of the occasional legal victories that were garnered, but because of the transformative dimension of African-Americans reimagining themselves as full, rights-bearing citizens within the American political imagination. We wanted to acknowledge the centrality of rights discourse even as we recognized that the use of rights language was not without risks. The debate that ensued in light of this different orientation engendered an important CRT theme: the absolute centrality of history and context in any attempt to theorize the relationship between race and legal discourse.

A third ideological difference emerged in a series of critiques of early attempts by scholars of color to articulate how law reflects and produces racial power. . . . Although the terms of the debate were not fully clear, and at the time, there were few key words or concepts on which our analysis could then focus, we have come to articulate the central criticism by crits to be that of "racialism." By racialism, we refer to theoretical accounts of racial power that explain legal and political decisions which are adverse to people of color as mere reflections of underlying white interest. To phrase this critical model in more contemporary terms, we might say that racialism is to power what essentialism is to identity—a narrow, and frequently unsatisfying theory in which complex phenomena are reduced to and presented as a simple reflection of some underlying "facts." Specifically, the "sin" of racialism is that it presumes that racial interests or racial identity exists somewhere outside of or prior to law and is merely reflected in subsequent legal decisions adverse to nonwhites.

Such an approach struck crits as far too instrumental to be a useful account of race and power. During the eighties, crits had been debating the issue of "instrumentalist" and "irrationalist" accounts of law; most agreed with the problematic character of what came to be called "vulgar Marxism." Briefly stated, in traditional Marxist analysis, law appears as merely an instrument of class interests that are rooted outside of law in some "concrete social reality." In sum, law is merely an "ideological reflection" of some class interest rooted elsewhere. Many critics—echoing the late sixties New Left—sought to distinguish themselves from these "instrumentalist" accounts on the grounds that they embodied a con-stricted view of the range and sites of the production of social power, and hence of politics. By defining class in terms of one's position in the material production process, and viewing law and all other "superstruc-tural" phenomena as merely reflections of interests rooted in social class identification, vulgar Marxism, crits argued, ignored the ways that law and other merely "superstructural" arenas helped to constitute the very interests that law was supposed merely to reflect. Crits such as Freeman, Duncan Kennedy, and Karl Klare (to name a few) developed non-instrumentalist accounts of law and its relationship to power that focused on legal discourse as a crucial site for the production of ideology and the perpetuation of social power. . . .

. . . To critics of racialism, prevailing theorizations of race and law seemed to represent law as an instrumental reflection of racial interests in much the same way that vulgar Marxists saw the legal arena as reflecting class interests. Just as the white left had learned, by the eighties, that a one-dimensional class account was too simplistic for legal analysis, they interpreted racialist accounts as analogous to class reductionism.

. . .

Drawing on these premises, we began to think of our project as uncovering how law was a constitutive element of race itself: in other words, how law *constructed* race. Racial power, in our view, was not simply—or even primarily—a product of biased decision-making on the part of judges, but instead, the sum total of the pervasive ways in which law shapes and is shaped by "race relations" across the social plane. Laws produced racial power not simply through narrowing the scope of, say, antidiscrimination remedies, nor through racially-biased decision-making, but instead, through myriad legal rules, many of them having nothing to do with rules against discrimination, that continued to repro-duce the structures and practices of racial domination. . . .

. . .

. . . It was obvious to many of us that although race was, to use the term, socially constructed (the idea of biological race is "false"), race was nonetheless "real" in the sense that there is a material dimension and weight to the experience of being "raced" in American society, a materiality that in significant ways has been produced and sustained by law. Thus, we understood our project as an effort to construct a race-conscious and at the same time anti-essentialist account of the processes by which law participates in "race-ing" American society.

. . .

As this volume goes to press, the U.S. Supreme Court has issued a series of decisions which effectively repeal the ideological "settlement" struck during the civil rights era. . . .

Reading these decisions, one cannot help but notice the degree to which they deploy traditional liberal racial principles. The current Court has effectively conscripted liberal theories of race and racism to wage a conservative attack on governmental efforts to address the persistence of societal-wide racial discrimination. This harsh reality confirms the need for a critical theory of racial power and an image of racial justice which rejects classical liberal visions of race as well as conservative visions of equal citizenship.

We believe that core concepts from Critical Race Theory can be productively used to expose the irreducibly political character of the current Court's general hostility toward policies which would take race into account in redressing historic and contemporary patterns of racial discrimination. We might, for example, draw on Critical Race Theory's deconstruction of colorblindness to show that the current Supreme Court's expressed hostility toward race-consciousness must be deemed a form of race-consciousness in and of itself. As Neil Gotanda has cogently argued, one cannot heed the newly installed constitutional rule that forbids race-conscious approaches to racial discrimination without always first taking race into account. Similarly, Critical Race Theory helps us understand how race-consciousness implicitly informs the current Court's paradoxical insistence that the norm of color-blindness requires a voting rights regime which effectively deprives racial minorities of political advantages that are accorded to other organized social interests.

Critical Race Theory indicates how and why the contemporary "jurisprudence of color-blindness" is not only the expression of a particular color-consciousness, but the product of a deeply politicized choice. The current Court would have us believe that these decisions are the product of an ineluctable legal logic. Critical Race Theory tells us rather that the Court's rulings with respect to race may more plausibly be deemed a result of a tactical political choice among competing doctrinal possibilities, any one of which could have been legally defensible. The appeal to color-blindness can thus be said to serve as part of an ideological strategy by which the current Court obscures its active role in sustaining hierarchies of racial power. We believe that Critical Race Theory offers a valuable conceptual compass for mapping the doctrinal mystifications which the current Court has developed to camouflage its conservative agenda.

Professor Crenshaw has written a frequently-cited article entitled *Race, Reform, and Retrenchment: Transformation and Legitimation in Antidiscrimination Law,* that further develops the theme that liberal constitutional discourse is implicated in the perpetuation of racial oppression.[12] She argues that both the neoconservative New Right and the critical legal studies New

---

12 *See* Kimberlé Williams Crenshaw, *Race, Reform, and Retrenchment: Transformation and* *Legitimation in Antidiscrimination Law,* 101 HARV. L. REV. 1331 (1988).

Left have flawed visions of civil rights. The New Right views civil rights as a special interest movement that deviates from race-neutrality, but it ignores the tacit role that race consciousness plays in the existing order. The New Left understands the flaws inherent in liberal discourse, but it ignores the ideological role that racism plays in legal hegemony.[13] Crenshaw believes that, "History has shown that the most valuable political asset of the black community has been its ability to assert a collective identity and to name its collective political reality. Liberal reform discourse must not be allowed to undermine the black collective identity."[14]

Professor Charles R. Lawrence III, has stressed the role that *unconscious*-ness racism plays in the perpetuation of racial oppression under the liberal model. In *The Id, The Ego, and Equal Protection: Reckoning with Unconscious Racism,* he argues that racial prejudice in contemporary culture is pervasive enough to constitute a public health problem, but much racism is transmitted in subtle ways that reinforce the view that racial minorities are inferior.[15] Because the Supreme Court has read the equal protection clause to prohibit only conscious "intentional" discrimination, unconscious discrimination has been placed by the Court beyond the reach of constitutional redress.[16] Professor Lawrence has also argued that white supremacy is omnipresent in the culture, and that the Supreme Court's focus on individual harms must be replaced by a transformative focus on group-level injustices if white supremacy is ever to be overcome.[17] Professor Girardeau A. Spann has argued that a preoccupation with liberalism has actually caused the Supreme Court to become a "veiled majoritarian" institution, whose cultural function is not to protect minority interests at all, but rather to sacrifice minority interests for majoritarian gain. Spann believes that minorities are likely to do better through self-reliance and participation in "pure politics" than by relying on counterproductive Supreme Court protection.[18]

Several critical race scholars have expressed dissatisfaction with the way that the critical legal studies movement both discounted the importance of racism as an oppressive ideology in legal discourse, and discounted the importance of rights rhetoric in the gains that racial minorities have been able to achieve. Some of these writings are collected in a symposium entitled *Minority Critiques of the Critical Legal Studies Movement.*[19] That symposium contains a commonly cited article by Professor Mari J. Matsuda, entitled *Looking to the Bottom: Critical Legal Studies and Reparations,* in which she argues that oppressed minorities speak with a distinctive voice that should

---

[13] See id. at 1332–36.

[14] See id. at 1336.

[15] See Charles R. Lawrence III, *The Id, The Ego, and Equal Protection: Reckoning with Unconscious Racism,* 39 STAN. L. REV. 317 (1987).

[16] See id. at 317–28.

[17] See Charles R. Lawrence III, *Race, Multiculturalism, and the Jurisprudence of Transformation,* 47 STAN. L. REV. 819 (1995).

[18] See GIRARDEAU A. SPANN, RACE AGAINST THE COURT: THE SUPREME COURT AND MINORI-TIES IN CONTEMPORARY AMERICA (1993); Girardeau A. Spann, *Pure Politics,* 88 MICH. L. REV. 1971 (1990).

[19] See Symposium *Minority Critiques of the Critical Legal Studies Movement,* 22 HARV. C.R.-C.L. L. REV. 297 (1987) (containing articles by Jose A. Bracamonte, Mari J. Matsuda, Patricia Williams & Harlon Dalton); see also Responses to the Minority Critiques of the Critical Legal Studies Movement, 23 HARV. C.R.-C.L. L. REV. 295–413 (1988) (containing articles by Alan Freeman, Morton J. Horwitz, and Richard Delgado).

be considered rather than silenced by the legal system—and by leftist scholars—in seeking to achieve racial justice.[20] Another commonly cited article in the symposium is an article entitled *Alchemical Notes: Reconstructed Ideals from Deconstructed Rights,* by Professor Patricia J. Williams—one of the most highly regarded narrative writers associated with critical race theory—which questions the critical legal studies rejection of rights rhetoric.[21] Professor Richard Delgado wrote an article entitled *The Ethereal Scholar: Does Critical Legal Studies Have What Minorities Want?,* arguing that the legal informality favored by critical legal studies is inconsistent with the need for structure in the legal system to contain the effects of racism.[22] In two other articles whose titles include the phrase *The Imperial Scholar,* Professor Delgado has argued that mainstream legal scholarship is dominated by a cadre of white professors who cite each other's work but tend to ignore minority scholarship.[23] Professor Derrick Bell was one of the first to express the views that white scholars were dominating academic debates about affirmative action, and that the distinctive minority voice was being excluded from the debate.[24]

Not all minority scholars are sympathetic to the critique of liberalism embodied in critical race theory. Professor Randall Kennedy, a black Professor at the Harvard Law School, has focused on the writings of Professors Bell, Delgado and Matsuda in criticizing critical race theory. In his article entitled *Racial Critiques of Legal Academia,* Professor Kennedy states:

> . . . [T]he Bell/Delgado/Matsuda line of racial critiques . . . exemplify the tone and substance of much of the literature published over the past decade that uses the prism of race to examine the organization of the professoriat and the evaluation of scholarship. The writings by Professors Derrick Bell, Richard Delgado, and Mari Matsuda have placed on scholarly agendas questions that have heretofore received little or no attention, questions that explore the nature and consequences of racial conflict within legal academia. Prior to the racial critiques, some of the most provocative studies of the history and sociology of legal academia emerged from the legal realist and CLS movements. Like certain proponents of legal realism and current advocates of CLS, proponents of racial critiques are insurgent scholars seeking to transform society, including, of course, the law schools. Unlike previous academic rebels, however, the proponents of racial critiques tap as their primary sources of emotional and intellectual sustenance an impatient demand that all areas of legal scholarship show an appreciation for the far-reaching ways in which race relations have impinged upon every aspect of our culture and a resolute insistence upon reforming all ideas, practices, and institutions that impose or perpetuate white racist hegemony. Thus inspired, they have

---

[20] *See* Mari J. Matsuda, *Looking to the Bottom: Critical Legal Studies and Reparations,* 22 HARV. C.R.-C.L. L. REV. 323 (1987).

[21] *See* Patricia J. Williams, *Alchemical Notes: Reconstructing Ideals from Deconstructed Rights,* 22 HARV. C.R.-C.L. L. REV. 401 (1987).

[22] *See* Richard Delgado, *The Ethereal Scholar: Does Critical Legal Studies Have What Minorities Want?,* 22 HARV. C.R.-C.L. L. REV. 301 (1987).

[23] *See* Richard Delgado, *The Imperial Scholar Revisited: How to Marginalize Outsider Writing,* 140 U. PA. L. REV. 1349 (1992); Richard Delgado, *Comment: The Imperial Scholar: Reflections on a Review of Civil Rights,* 132 U. PA. L. REV. 561 (1984).

[24] *See* DERRICK BELL, *Minority Admissions as a White Debate, in* RACE, RACISM AND AMERICAN LAW § 7.12.1, at 445–48 (2d ed. 1980); Derrick Bell, Bakke, *Minority Admissions, and the Usual Practice of Racial Remedies,* 67 CAL. L. REV. 1, 4 n.2 (1979).

succeeded in making "the race question" a burning issue for a substantial number of persons in legal academia.

At the same time, the writings of Bell, Delgado, and Matsuda reveal significant deficiencies—the most general of which is a tendency to evade or suppress complications that render their conclusions problematic. Stated bluntly, they fail to support persuasively their claims of racial exclusion or their claims that legal academic scholars of color produce a racially distinctive brand of valuable scholarship. My criticism of the Bell/Delgado/Matsuda line of racial critiques extends farther, however, than their descriptions of the current state of legal academia. I also take issue with their politics of argumentation and with some of the normative premises underlying their writings. More specifically . . . I challenge: (1) the argument that, on intellectual grounds, white academics are entitled to less "standing" to participate in race-relations law discourse than academics of color; (2) the argument that, on intellectual grounds, the minority status of academics of color should serve as a positive credential for purposes of evaluating their work; (3) explanations that assign responsibility for the current position of scholars of color overwhelmingly to the influence of prejudiced decisions by white academics.[25]

Kennedy argued that the perceived exclusion of minority scholars from American law schools was not supported by credible evidence, and that critical race theorists had failed to offer any adequate substitute for the current academic selection criteria. They had also failed to identify works of minority scholarship that deserved more recognition than those works had received. Kennedy also challenged the claim that minorities spoke with a distinctive voice, arguing that such a view homogenized the minority experiences and minimized the heterogeneity of opinions held by people of color.[26] Kennedy expressed concern that his work might be used to frustrate efforts at achieving racial justice, but he concluded that remaining silent would pose a more serious threat to informed debate about race relations.[27] Kennedy's article was controversial, and it generated numerous responses—many of which suggested that critical race theory emanated from an understanding of racial oppression that was radically different from Kennedy's own understanding.[28]

§ 11.03　Social Construction

In addition to its critique of liberalism, critical race theory is committed to the view that race is socially constructed rather than biologically determined. Ethnic Studies Professor Michael Omi was inspired to study legal definitions of race by a 1985 Louisiana case involving Susie Guillory Phipps. At the age of 43, in an effort to obtain a passport, Ms. Phipps requested a copy of her birth certificate. Although she had always considered herself to be white—as had each of her two husbands—she was stunned and dismayed to learn that

---

[25] See Randall Kennedy, *Racial Critiques of Legal Academia,* 102 HARV. L. REV. 1745, 1747–49 (1989). Copyright © 1989 by the Harvard Law Review Association. Reprinted with permission.

[26] See id. at 1760–87.

[27] See id. at 1810–19.

[28] See Colloquy, *Responses to Randall Ken-*nedy's Racial Critiques of Legal Academia, 103 HARV. L. REV. 1844 (1990) (containing articles by Milner Ball, Robin Barnes, Richard Delgado, and Leslie Espinoza); see also Richard Delgado, *When a Story is Just a Story: Does Voice Really Matter,* 76 VA. L. REV. 95 (1990); Alex M. Johnson, *Racial Critique of Legal Academia: A Reply in Favor of Context,* 43 STAN L. REV. 137 (1990).

her birth certificate classified her as "colored." Under Louisiana's legal principle of *hypodescent*—sometimes referred to as the "one-drop of blood" rule—Ms. Phipps was black because her great-great-great-great grandmother had been a black slave. Ms. Phipps sued to have her racial designation changed, but she lost.[29] Critical race theory posits that the racial categories we use in law and other aspects of social life do not reflect scientific divisions between members of the species, but rather are the result of social, political and historical forces. Professor john a. powell has argued that the term "race" operates as a verb before it acquires significance as a noun. Outgroups are "raced" by dominant groups through the association of character traits with identifiable group characteristics. The characteristics of the dominant group are then viewed as natural, invisible norms against which the outgroups are unfavorably measured to justify their subordination.[30] In this Section, Professor Ian F. Haney López elaborates the view that race is socially constructed rather than biologically determined.

In an article entitled *The Social Construction of Race,* Professor Ian F. Haney López of the University of California at Berkeley School of Law argues that race has no biological basis, but rather is a cultural invention. Ian F. Haney López, *The Social Construction of Race: Some Observations on Illusion, Fabrication, and Choice,* 29 HARV. C.R.-C.L. L. REV. 1, 3–7, 11–18, 27–28, 61-62 (1994):[31]

. . . Race dominates our personal lives. It manifests itself in our speech, dance, neighbors, and friends—"our very ways of talking, walking, eating and dreaming are ineluctably shaped by notions of race." Race determines our economic prospects. The race-conscious market screens and selects us for manual jobs and professional careers, red-lines financing for real estate, green-lines our access to insurance, and even raises the price of that car we need to buy. Race permeates our politics. It alters electoral boundaries, shapes the disbursement of local, state, and federal funds, fuels the creation and collapse of political alliances, and twists the conduct of law enforcement. In short, race mediates every aspect of our lives.

. . .

Despite the pervasive influence of race in our lives and in U.S. law, a review of opinions and articles by judges and legal academics reveals a startling fact: few seem to know what race is and is not. Today most judges and scholars accept the common wisdom concerning race, without pausing to examine the fallacies and fictions on which ideas of race depend. In U.S. society, "a kind of 'racial etiquette' exists, a set of interpretive codes and racial meanings which operate in the interactions of daily life. . . . Race becomes 'common sense'—a way of comprehending, explaining and acting in the world." This social etiquette of common ignorance is readily apparent in the legal discourse of race. Rehnquist-Court Justices take this approach, speaking disingenuously of the peril posed by racial remediation to "a society where race is irrelevant," while nevertheless failing to offer an account of race that would bear the weight of their cynical assertions. Arguably, critical race theorists, those legal scholars whose

---

[29] *See* Michael Omi, *Racial Identity and the State: The Dilemmas of Classification,* 15 LAW & INEQ. 7, 7–9 (1997).

[30] *See* john a. powell, *The "Racing" of American Society: Race Functioning as a Verb Before Signifying as a Noun,* 15 LAW & INEQ. 99,

103–12 (1997).

[31] Copyright © 1994 by the President and Fellows of Harvard College and the Harvard Civil Rights Civil Liberties Law Review. Reprinted with permission.

work seems most closely bound together by their emphasis on the centrality of race, follow the same approach when they powerfully decry the permanence of racism and persuasively argue for race consciousness, yet do so without explicitly suggesting what race might be. Race may be America's single most confounding problem, but the confounding problem of race is that few people seem to know what race is.

. . .

In this Article, I define a "race" as a vast group of people loosely bound together by historically contingent, socially significant elements of their morphology and/or ancestry. I argue that race must be understood as a sui generis social phenomenon in which contested systems of meaning serve as the connections between physical features, races, and personal characteristics. In other words, social meanings connect our faces to our souls. Race is neither an essence nor an illusion, but rather an ongoing, contradictory, self-reinforcing process subject to the macro forces of social and political struggle and the micro effects of daily decisions. As used in this Article, the referents of terms like Black, White, Asian, and Latino are social groups, not genetically distinct branches of humankind.

. . .

There are no genetic characteristics possessed by all Blacks but not by non-Blacks; similarly, there is no gene or cluster of genes common to all Whites but not to non-Whites. One's race is not determined by a single gene or gene cluster, as is, for example, sickle cell anemia. Nor are races marked by important differences in gene frequencies, the rates of appearance of certain gene types. The data compiled by various scientists demonstrates, contrary to popular opinion, that intra-group differences exceed inter-group differences. That is, greater genetic variation exists within the populations typically labeled Black and White than between these populations. This finding refutes the supposition that racial divisions reflect fundamental genetic differences.

. . .

The notion that humankind can be divided along White, Black, and Yellow lines reveals the social rather than the scientific origin of race. The idea that there exist three races, and that these races are "Caucasoid," "Negroid," and "Mongoloid," is rooted in the European imagination of the Middle Ages, which encompassed only Europe, Africa, and the Near East. This view, reflected in medieval art, found its clearest modern expression in Count Arthur de Gobineau's Essay on the Inequality of Races, published in France in 1853–55. The peoples of the American continents, the Indian subcontinent, East Asia, Southeast Asia, and Oceania—living outside the imagination of Europe and Count Gobineau— are excluded from the three major races for social and political reasons, not for scientific ones. Nevertheless, the history of science has long been the history of failed efforts to justify these social beliefs. Along the way, various minds tried to fashion practical human typologies along the following physical axes: skin color, hair texture, facial angle, jaw size, cranial capacity, brain mass, frontal lobe mass, brain surface fissures and convolutions, and even body lice. As one scholar notes, "[t]he nineteenth century was a period of exhaustive and—as it turned out—futile search for criteria to define and describe race differences."

To appreciate the difficulties of constructing races solely by reference to physical characteristics, consider the attempt to define race by skin color. On the basis of white skin, for example, one can define a race that includes most of the peoples of Western Europe. However, this grouping is threatened by the subtle gradations of skin color as one moves south or east, and becomes untenable when the fair-skinned peoples of Northern China and Japan are considered. . . . [R]ace is not a function of skin color alone. If it were, some now secure in their White status would have to be excluded, and others firmly characterized as non-Whites would need to be included. . . .

Attempts to define racial categories by physical attributes ultimately failed. By 1871, some leading intellectuals had recognized that even using the word "race" "was virtually a confession of ignorance or evil intent." The genetic studies of the last few decades have only added more nails to the coffin of biological race. Evidence shows that those features usually coded to race, for example, stature, skin color, hair texture, and facial structure, do not correlate strongly with genetic variation. Populations that resemble each other might be genetically quite distinct. . . . People who look alike do not necessarily share a common genetic heritage, and people who share a similar genetic background do not necessarily look alike.

The rejection of race in science is now almost complete. In the end, we should embrace historian Barbara Fields's succinct conclusion with respect to the plausibility of biological races: "Anyone who continues to believe in race as a physical attribute of individuals, despite the now commonplace disclaimers of biologists and geneticists, might as well also believe that Santa Claus, the Easter Bunny and the tooth fairy are real, and that the earth stands still while the sun moves."

. . .

Unfortunately, few in this society seem prepared to fully relinquish their subscription to notions of biological race. This is . . . true of Congress and the Supreme Court. Congress' anachronistic understanding of race is exemplified by a 1988 statute that explains that "the term 'racial group' means a set of individuals whose identity as such is distinctive in terms of physical characteristics or biological descent." The Supreme Court, although purporting to sever race from biology, also seems incapable of doing so. In *Saint Francis College v. Al-Khazraji,* the Court determined that an Arab could recover damages for racial discrimination under 42 U.S.C. § 1981. Writing for the Court, Justice White appeared to abandon biological notions of race in favor of a sociopolitical conception, explaining:

> It is said that genetically homogenous populations do not exist and traits are not discontinuous between populations; therefore, a population can only be described in terms of relative frequencies of various traits. Clear-cut categories do not exist. The particular traits which have generally been chosen to characterize races have been criticized as having little biological significance. It has been found that differences between individuals of the same race are often greater than the differences between the "average" individuals of different races. These observations have led some, but not all, scientists to conclude that racial classifications are for the most part sociopolitical, rather than biological, in nature.[69]

Despite this seeming rejection of biological race, Justice White continued: "The Court of Appeals was thus quite right in holding that § 1981, 'at a minimum,' reaches discrimination against an individual 'because he or she is genetically part of an ethnically and physiognomically distinctive subgrouping of homo sapiens.' "[70] By adopting the lower court's language

---

[69] [Francis College v. Al-Khazraji, 481 U.S.   [70] *Id.* at 613.
604 (1987)], at 610 n.4.

of genetics and distinctive subgroupings, Justice White demonstrates the Court's continued reliance on blood as a metonym for race. In *Metro Broadcasting v. FCC*, Justice Scalia again reveals the Court's understanding of race as a matter of blood. During oral argument, Scalia attacked the argument that granting minorities broadcasting licenses would enhance diversity by blasting "the policy as a matter of 'blood,'" at one point charging that the policy reduced to a question of 'blood . . . blood, not background and environment.'"

If an inability to fully free oneself of biologically tainted racial beliefs plagues most people, [Anthony] Appiah frees himself of this malaise by insistently proclaiming that "there are no races." Subtitling his article "The Illusion of Race," Appiah's intention is to repudiate all notions of race, not just those based on biology. In this endeavor, he shares the company of Henry Louis Gates, whom he quotes with approval for the argument "that 'races,' put simply, do not exist, and that to claim that they do, for whatever misguided reason, is to stand on dangerous ground." Appiah also quotes Tzvetan Todorov, agreeing that " 'races' do not exist."

. . .

This Article responds by arguing that races exist as powerful social phenomena. . . .

. . .

Race must be viewed as a social construction. That is, human interaction rather than natural differentiation must be seen as the source and continued basis for racial categorization. The process by which racial meanings arise has been labeled racial formation. In this formulation, race is not a determinant or a residue of some other social phenomenon, but rather stands on its own as an amalgamation of competing societal forces. Racial formation includes both the rise of racial groups and their constant reification in social thought. I draw upon this theory, but use the term "racial fabrication" in order to highlight four important facets of the social construction of race. First, humans rather than abstract social forces produce races. Second, as human constructs, races constitute an integral part of a whole social fabric that includes gender and class relations. Third, the meaning-systems surrounding race change quickly rather than slowly. Finally, races are constructed relationally, against one another, rather than in isolation. Fabrication implies the workings of human hands, and suggests the possible intention to deceive. More than the industrial term "formation," which carries connotations of neutral constructions and processes indifferent to individual intervention, referring to the fabrication of races emphasizes the human element and evokes the plastic and inconstant character of race. . . .

. . .

. . . Biological race is an illusion.

Social race, however, is not, and it is here that . . . race should be measured. . . . Walking down the street, our minds consistently rely on pervasive social mythologies to assign races to the other pedestrians. The absence of any physical basis to race does not entail the conclusion that race is wholly an hallucination. Race has its genesis and maintains its vigorous strength in the realm of social beliefs.

. . .

[Haney López here makes reference to *Hudgins v. Wright*, an 1806 Virginia case in which Hannah Wright secures the release of her family from slavery because the court finds that her straight hair establishes that she is a free Indian rather than a black slave.] This is the promise of choice at its brightest: by choosing to resist racial constructions, we may emancipate ourselves and our children. Unfortunately, uncoerced choice in the arena of U.S. race relations is rare, perhaps nonexistent. Two facets of this case demonstrate the darkened potential of choice. First, the women's freedom ultimately turned on Hannah's long straight hair, not on their decision to resist. Without the legal presumptions that favored their features, presumptions that were in a sense the concrete embodiments of the social context, they would have remained slaves. Furthermore, these women challenged their race, not the status ascribed to it. By arguing that they were Indian and not Black, free rather than enslaved, the women lent unfortunate legitimacy to the legal and social presumptions in favor of Black slavery. The context and consequences of the Wrights' actions confirm that choices are made in a harsh racist social setting that may facilitate but more likely will forestall freedom; and that in our decisions to resist, we may shatter but more probably will inadvertently strengthen the racial structures around us. Nevertheless, race is not an inescapable physical fact. Rather, it is a social construction that, however perilously, remains subject to contestation at the hands of individuals and communities alike.

In his book WHITE BY LAW: THE LEGAL CONSTRUCTION OF RACE, Haney López emphasizes that *whiteness* is also a social construction.[32] Unlike most other racial constructions, however, whiteness is typically accorded a privileged status in American culture. Moreover, the legal system does not merely reflect this social privilege, but actively participates in the construction of whiteness as a privileged status. Haney López analyzes a number of state and federal naturalization cases in which courts attempted to determine who was "white" for purposes of deciding whether aliens could be naturalized under statutes that, from 1790 to 1952, made white identity a prerequisite to naturalization. Without a scientific basis for race to fall back on, the racial prerequisite cases reached inconsistent results, and the courts tended to incorporate popular racial prejudices into their definitions of whiteness.[33]

Professor George Martinez argues that whiteness has always had a privileged status, and that courts sometimes treat Mexican Americans as white and sometimes as non-white, depending on which characterization best serves the interests of whites.[34] Professor Gerald Torres and Kathryn Milun argue that, when the Mashpee Indians brought suit in federal court to enforce certain treaty rights against the United States government, a federal court rejected their claim on standing grounds by actually defining the Tribe out of existence. Using white rather than Indian conceptions of Indian identity, the Court held that the Tribe had ceased to exist due to intermarriage and departures from the reservation.[35]

The case for white privilege is sometimes illustrated by focusing on statistical differences that exist between whites and others in the allocation of societal resources, or on current "reverse discrimination" opposition to affirmative action that is rooted in the view that whites are "entitled" to benefits that

---

[32] *See* IAN F. HANEY LÓPEZ, WHITE BY LAW: THE LEGAL CONSTRUCTION OF RACE (1996).

[33] *See id.* at 1–36, 197–202.

[34] George A. Martinez, *Mexican-Americans and Whiteness, in* CRITICAL WHITE STUDIES,

supra note 1, at 210–13.

[35] *See* Gerald Torres & Kathryn Milun, *Translating* Yonnondio *by Precedent and Evidence: The Mashpee Indian Case*, 1990 DUKE L.J. 625.

are being given to racial minorities.[36] However, Haney López chose to illustrate the value that whiteness plays in American culture by reporting a story told by Andrew Hacker in his book Two Nations: Black and White, Separate, Hostile, Unequal. When white college students were asked how much compensation they thought they would be entitled to if they were suddenly to wake up with black physical features, they asked for $50 million–$1 million per year for having to be black for the rest of their lives.[37]

Professor Cheryl I. Harris has argued that race is not only socially constructed in a way that accords privileged status to whiteness, but that whiteness is treated in law as a *property* right. The law gave whites the ability to appropriate Native American lands as white real property; to acquire black slaves as chattels; and to use black women's bodies as the means of production for new items of black property. However, whiteness was the shield that protected whites from having their real property appropriated or their bodies commodified as chattels. Because the law used race to define legal status, to regulate the right to possess things of value, and to govern expectations about social treatment, whiteness itself served the function traditionally accorded the concept of property. *Plessy v. Ferguson*, 163 U.S. 537, 165 S. Ct. 1138, 41 L. Ed. 256 (1896), recognized a white property right to be segregated from blacks—a property right in white supremacy—and *Brown v. Board of Education*, 347 U.S. 483, 74 S. Ct. 686, 95 L. Ed. 873 (1954), dismantled formal segregation only to replace it with a white property right to continued de facto segregation.[38] In recent times, affirmative action has been rejected on grounds that essentially view whites as having vested property rights that cannot be divested in order to redistribute white resources to minorities.[39]

Professor Anthony Paul Farley has used a sexual metaphor to describe what he views as the social construction of race and white privilege. In what he terms "a friendly postmodern challenge to Critical Legal Studies and Critical Race Theory,"[40] Farley suggests that race relations in the United States can best be understood as a quest for sado-masochistic pleasure. Whites take pleasure in the humiliation of racial groups that they have placed in a subordinate position, in much the same way that sadists take pleasure in humiliating those whom they have sexually subordinated. Subordinated minorities take pleasure in the detachment and humiliation that is produced by their subordination, in much the same way that masochists take pleasure in their sexual subordination. The pleasure of each reinforces the pleasure of the other to perpetuate the subordinating relationship. Farley believes that the appreciation by racial minorities of their total submission to white racial dominance may give rise to a new liberatory consciousness.[41]

Many critical race theorists understand the dilemma in which the social construction thesis places them. If race is merely a social construct, how can

---

[36] See, e.g., Charles R. Lawrence III & Mari J. Matsuda, We Won't Go Back: Making the Case for Affirmative Action 1–8, 46, 59–66, 69–74 (1997).

[37] See Haney López, *supra* note 32, at 198–99 (citing Andrew Hacker, Two Nations: Black and White, Separate, Hostile, Unequal 32 (1992)).

[38] See Cheryl Harris, *Whiteness as Property*, 106 Harv. L. Rev. 1707, 1710–57 (1993).

[39] See id. at 1766–77.

[40] See Anthony Paul Farley, *The Black Body As Fetish Object*, 76 Or. L. Rev. 457, 460 (1997).

[41] See id.

their claims about racism be anything more than another social construct? Haney López, anticipating this difficulty, refused to concede that race was merely an illusion.[42] The postmodern leanings of many critical race theorists permit them to argue that race can be both socially constructed and real. Professor Crenshaw states that it is important to avoid "[o]ne version of anti-essentialism, embodying what might be called the vulgarized social construction thesis, [which] is that since all categories are socially constructed, there is no such thing as say, Blacks or women, and thus it makes no sense to continue reproducing those categories by organizing around them."[43] She adds that, "In *Metro Broadcasting, Inc. v. FCC,* the Court conservatives, in rhetoric that oozes vulgar constructionist smugness, proclaimed that any set-aside designed to increase the voices of minorities on the air waves was itself based on a racist assumption that skin color is in some way connected to the likely content of one's broadcast."[44] She concludes that, "to say that a category such as race or gender is socially constructed is not to say that that category has no significance in our world. On the contrary, a large and continuing project for subordinated people—and indeed, one of the projects for which postmodern theories have been very helpful—is thinking about the way power has clustered around certain categories and is exercised against others."[45]

Professor Neil Gotanda has identified four ways in which race has been socially constructed in American culture, and five ways in which the Supreme Court has used these constructions of race to promote white supremacy through the rhetoric of colorblindness. Professor Gotanda argues that the social construction of race makes the aspirational goal of colorblindness normatively unattractive. It both camouflages the ways in which race is used to allocate social power, and it discounts the value of racial diversity in American culture. Gotanda suggests that, rather than repress the significance of racial differences through colorblind constitutionalism, race should be accorded the pluralistic deference that we accord religion in constitutional law. Just as the establishment and free exercise clauses of the first amendment seek to promote respect for religious liberty without permitting religious domination, the Constitution should be understood to value, rather than eliminate, racial differences.[46] Professor Gotanda concludes:

> By returning to strict scrutiny as the sole equal protection principle for racial judicial review, the color-blind constitutionalists would have the Supreme Court risk perpetuating racism and undermining its own legitimacy. This article invokes a parallel between the modern civil rights movement and the "first" Reconstruction; the Supreme Court's civil rights decisions of 1989 are the equivalent of the Compromise of 1877, which ended the first Reconstruction.[271] By fixating on formal race and

---

[42] *See* Ian F. Haney López, *The Social Construction of Race: Some Observations on Illusion, Fabrication, and Choice,* 29 HARV. C.R.-C.L. L. REV. 1, 7 (1994).

[43] *See* Kimberlé Crenshaw, *Mapping the Margins: Intersectionality, Identity Politics and Violence Against Women of Color,* 43 STAN. L. REV. 1241, 1296 (1991).

[44] *See id.*

[45] *See id.* at 1296–97.

[46] *See* Neil Gotanda, *A Critique of "Our Constitution Is Color-Blind,"* 44 STAN. L. REV. 1, 3–7 (1991).

[271] This is the standard historical reading of the Hayes-Tilden compromise in which an agreement to withdraw federal troops from the South was part of the agreement which elected Rutherford B. Hayes president. *See generally* ERIC FONER, RECONSTRUCTION: AMERICA'S UNFINISHED REVOLUTION, 1863–1877 (1988).

ignoring the reality of racial subordination, the Court, in this second post-Reconstruction era, risks establishing a new equivalent of *Plessy v. Ferguson*. There is, however, a second parallel for the Court. The greater danger for the current Court is that it will face the loss of legitimacy which confronted the Taney Court after *Dred Scott*.

The United States is entering a period of cultural diversity more extensive than any in its history. In the past, white racial hegemony went essentially unchallenged. The Court today faces a far more complex set of issues. Whatever the validity in 1896 of Justice Harlan's comment in *Plessy*-that "our Constitution is . . . color-blind"—the concept is inadequate to deal with today's racially stratified, culturally diverse, and economically divided nation. The Court must either develop new perspectives on race and culture, or run the risk of losing legitimacy and relevance in a crucial arena of social concern.[47]

§ 11.04 Narrative

The use of narrative, or legal storytelling, as a supplement to traditional doctrinal analysis is a technique that has come to be associated with critical race theory and feminist legal theory. Consistent with the social construction thesis, and with postmodern skepticism about the utility of reason as the exclusive means for acquiring knowledge, many critical race theorists believe that narrative is a useful means of conveying insights about the legal system and the culture at large. Professor Richard Delgado points out that standard accounts of social reality—which can be found in judicial opinions and other social texts—seem natural and neutral, but they can also be viewed as mere narratives that emanate from the dominate, white male perspective. Those dominant stories can then be contested by "counterstories," emanating from outgroup perspectives, in a way that permits the dominant perspectives to be recognized as contingent and ideological rather than ahistorical and universal.[48] Like literature, good narratives can convey ideas through non-syllogistic means. Professor Gerald Lopez believes that "stories and storytelling de-emphasize the logical and resurrect the emotive and intuitive."[49] Professor Carrie Menkel-Meadow believes that stories can teach us to learn law in more empathetic ways.[50] Professor William N. Eskridge believes that narrative has the potential to inspire social transformation through the inclusion of previously excluded outgroup perspectives.[51] Professor Jerome McCristal Culp, Jr. believes that narrative can usefully illustrate the flavor of white cultural supremacy,[52] but cautions that whites will find conventional

---

[47] Gotanda, *supra* note 46, at 68. Copyright © 1991 by the Board of Trustees of Leland Stanford Junior University. Reprinted with permission.

[48] *See* Richard Delgado, *Storytelling for Oppositionists and Others: A Plea for Narrative*, 87 MICH. L. REV. 2411, 2411–16 (1989); *see also* Thomas Ross, *The Richmond Narratives*, 68 TEX. L. REV. 381 (1989) (using Supreme Court opinions in City of Richmond v. J.A. Croson Co., 488 U.S. 469 (1989), to document claim that judicial opinions can be read as narratives in a way that reveals their ideological underpin-

nings and exposes the hidden capacity of law to do violence).

[49] *See* Gerald Lopez, *Lay Lawyering*, 32 UCLA L. REV. 1, 10 (1984).

[50] *See* Carrie Menkel-Meadow, *The Power of Narrative in Empathetic Learning: Post-Modernism and the Stories of Law*, 2 UCLA WOMEN'S L.J. 287, 304–07 (1992).

[51] *See* William N. Eskridge, Jr., *Gaylegal Narratives*, 46 STAN. L. REV. 607, 607–11 (1994).

[52] *See* Jerome McCristal Culp, Jr., *The Michael Jackson Pill: Equality, Race, and Culture*, 92 MICH. L. REV. 2613 (1994).

narratives more easy to accept than transformative narratives.[53] This Section reproduces a brief legal narrative by Professor Patricia J. Williams, and then describes some of the criticisms that have been directed at the narrative technique.

The widespread use of legal narrative by critical race theorists began with the 1985 publication by Professor Derrick Bell of *The Civil Rights Chronicles* in the HARVARD LAW REVIEW. The *Chronicles* are dialogues between Bell and his fictional heroine Geneva Crenshaw discussing black frustrations with the state of race relations in the United States.[54] Since then, many critical race theorists have used the narrative technique to convey their insights about race, gender and class in contemporary culture. Among the most prolific are Professors Bell,[55] Delgado[56] and Patricia J. Williams.[57] In the introductory chapter of her book THE ALCHEMY OF RACE AND RIGHTS, Columbia Law Professor Williams has written a narrative entitled *The Brass Ring and the Deep Blue Sea,* describing her goals in writing narrative. PATRICIA J. WIL-LIAMS, *The Brass Ring and the Deep Blue Sea (some parables about learning to think like a lawyer), in* THE ALCHEMY OF RACE AND RIGHTS: DIARY OF A LAW PROFESSOR 3-14 (1991):[58]

> Since subject position is everything in my analysis of the law, you deserve to know that it's a bad morning. I am very depressed. It always takes a while to sort out what's wrong, but it usually starts with some kind of perfectly irrational thought such as: I *hate* being a lawyer. This particular morning I'm sitting up in bed reading about redhibitory vices. A redhibitory vice is a defect in merchandise which, if existing at the time of purchase, gives rise to a claim allowing the buyer to return the thing and to get back part or all of the purchase price. The case I'm reading is an 1835 decision from Louisiana, involving the redhibitory vice of craziness:
>
> > The plaintiff alleged that he purchased of the defendant a slave named Kate, for which he paid $500, and in two or three days after it was discovered the slave was crazy, and run away, and that the vices were known to the defendant . . .
>
> > It was contended [by the seller] that Kate was not crazy but only stupid, and stupidity is not madness; but on the contrary, an apparent defect, against which the defendant did not warrant . . .

---

[53] *See* Jerome McCristal Culp, Jr., *You Can Take Them to Water but You Can't Make Them Drink: Black Legal Scholarship and White Legal Scholars,* 1992 U. ILL. L. REV. 1021.

[54] *See* Derrick Bell, *The Supreme Court, 1984 Term—Foreword: The Civil Rights Chronicles,* 99 HARV. L. REV. 4 (1985).

[55] *See, e.g.,* DERRICK BELL, AFROLANTIC LEGACIES (1998); DERRICK BELL, GOSPEL CHOIRS: PSALMS OF SURVIVAL IN AN ALIEN LAND CALLED HOME (1997); DERRICK BELL, FACES AT THE BOTTOM OF THE WELL: THE PERMANENCE OF RACISM (1992); DERRICK BELL, AND WE ARE NOT SAVED: THE ELUSIVE QUEST FOR RACIAL JUSTICE (1987); Bell *supra* note 54.

[56] *See, e.g.,* RICHARD DELGADO, WHEN EQUALITY ENDS: STORIES OF RACE AND RESISTANCE (1999); RICHARD DELGADO, THE COMING RACE

WAR?: AND OTHER APOCALYPTIC TALES OF AMERICA AFTER AFFIRMATIVE ACTION AND WELFARE (1997); RICHARD DELGADO, THE RODRIGO CHRONICLES: CONVERSATIONS ABOUT AMERICA AND RACE (1995).

[57] PATRICIA J. WILLIAMS, THE ROOSTER'S EGG: ON THE PERSISTENCE OF PREJUDICE (1996); PATRICIA J. WILLIAMS, THE ALCHEMY OF RACE AND RIGHTS: DIARY OF A LAW PROFESSOR (1991).

[58] Copyright © 1991 by the President and Fellows of Harvard College. Reprinted with permission of the Harvard University Press. Professor Carrie Menkel-Meadow has written a review of THE ALCHEMY OF RACE AND RIGHTS that describes in an accessible way many of the subtle postmodern attributes of Professor Williams' narrative scholarship. *See* Menkel-Meadow, *supra* note 50.

> The code has declared, that a sale may be avoided on account of any vice or defect, which renders the thing either absolutely useless, or its use so inconvenient and imperfect, that it must be supposed the buyer would not have purchased with a knowledge of the vice. We are satisfied that the slave in question was wholly, and perhaps worse than, useless. [1]

As I said, this is the sort of morning when I hate being a lawyer, a teacher, and just about everything else in my life. It's all I can do to feed the cats. I let my hair stream wildly and the eyes roll back in my head.

So you should know that this is one of those mornings when I refuse to compose myself properly; you should know you are dealing with someone who is writing this in an old terry bathrobe with a little fringe of blue and white tassel dangling from the hem, trying to decide if she is stupid or crazy.

Whenever I'm in a mood like this, it helps to get it out on paper, so I sit down to write even when I'm afraid I may produce a death-poem. Sometimes I can just write fast from the heart until I'm healed. Sometimes I look at my computer keyboard and I am paralyzed, inadequate— all those letters of the alphabet, full of random signification. I feel like a monkey. Those mornings, and this is one, I need a little extra push to get me started, and if I turn on the television, almost any story will do. I switch channels through a sea of news programs with the coopting, carnivorous eagerness of catharsis.

Conditions are bad, very bad, all over the world. The newscasters tell me that everyone is afraid of black men these days, even black women. Black people are being jailed in huge numbers, and the infant-mortality rate is staggering. Courts have authorized the custody removal of children at birth from mothers who are drug-addicted. Drugs bring pleasure to the biological catastrophe of having been born in the fearsome, loathsome packaging of an "other" body. Editorials talk about the efficiency of apartheid. Bigger better prisons. Spy satellites. Personnel carriers in Harlem. Door-to-door searches. State-sanctioned castration. Some neutral market thing devouring the resources of the earth at a terminally reckless rate. The Ku Klux Klan and the Aryan Brotherhood are the major unions among prison guards. Eastern Europe wants more freedom in the form of telephone-answering machines and video cassettes. AIDS spreads and spreads and spreads, among black and brown communities in particular. Subsistence farmers and indigenous people are dying all over the world, their ways and knowledge devoured and lost forever. According to the most authoritative scientists, the greenhouse effect is supposed to raise the temperature of the earth by two or three degrees over the next millennium. The winter of 1989 was five, ten, sometimes fifteen degrees above normal, all over the earth. It is the spring of 1990, and we are all worried about the summer to come.

I don't know how to find something to write about in the panic of this deadly world. There is more in the news than even my depression can consume.

Then I see it. A concise, modular, yet totally engaging item on the "MacNeil/Lehrer News Hour": Harvard Law School cannot find one black woman on the entire planet who is good enough to teach there, because we're all too stupid. (Well, that's not precisely what was said. It was more like they couldn't find anyone smart enough. To be fair, what Associate

---

[1] Icar v. Suars, 7 Louisiana Rep. 517 (1835).

Dean Louis Kaplow actually said was that Harvard would have to "lower its standards," which of course Harvard simply cannot do.[2]

So now you know: it is this news item, as I sit propped up in bed with my laptop computer balanced on my knees, clad in my robe with the torn fringe of terry bluebells, that finally pushes me over the edge and into the deep rabbit hole of this book.

When I dust myself off, I am sitting with my sister at my parents' kitchen table. Grown now, she and I are at home for Christmas. We chat, catching up on each other's lives. My sister tells me how her house is haunted by rabbits. I tell her how I'm trying to write a book on law and liberation.

"The previous owner had hundreds of them," she says. "You can hear them dancing in the dining room after midnight."

"It will be a book about the jurisprudence of rights," I respond. "I will attempt to apply so-called critical thought to legal studies. I believe that critical theory has valuable insights to contribute to debates about the ethics of law and the meaning of rights; yet many of those insights have been buried in relatively arcane vocabulary and abstraction. My book will concern itself with the interplay of commerce and constitutional protections and will be organized around discussion of three basic jurisprudential forces: autonomy, community, and order. My chapters will address such issues as surrogate motherhood and ownership; neighborhood and homelessness; racially motivated violence and disownedness. I will try to write, moreover, in a way that bridges the traditional gap between theory and praxis. It is not my goal merely to simplify; I hope that the result will be a text that is multilayered—that encompasses the straightforwardness of real life and reveals complexity of meaning."

"But what's the book *about*?" my sister asks, thumping her leg against the chair impatiently.

"Howard Beach, polar bears, and food stamps," I snap back. "I am interested in the way in which legal language flattens and confines in absolutes the complexity of meaning inherent in any given problem; I am trying to challenge the usual limits of commercial discourse by using an intentionally double-voiced and relational, rather than a traditionally legal black-letter, vocabulary. For example, I am a commercial lawyer as well as a teacher of contract and property law. I am also black and female, a status that one of my former employers described as being 'at oxymoronic odds' with that of commercial lawyer. While I certainly took issue with that particular characterization, it is true that my attempts to write in my own voice have placed me in the center of a snarl of social tensions and crossed boundaries. On the one hand, my writing has been staked out as the exclusive interdisciplinary property of constitutional law, contract, African-American history, feminist jurisprudence, political science, and rhetoric. At the same time, my work has been described as a 'sophisticated frontal assault' on laissez-faire's most sacred sanctums, as 'new-age performance art,' and as 'anecdotal individualism.' In other words, to speak as black, female, *and* commercial lawyer has rendered me simultaneously universal, trendy, and marginal. I think, moreover, that there is a paradigm at work, in the persistent perceptions of me as inherent contradiction: a paradigm of larger social perceptions that divide

---

[2] "MacNeil/Lehrer News Hour" (PBS television broadcast), May 10, 1990. See also Anthony Flint, "Bell at Harvard: A Unique Activism," *Boston Globe,* May 7, 1990, p. 1, describing the resignation of Professor Derrick Bell from the faculty of Harvard Law School "until a black woman was considered for tenure."

public from private, black from white, dispossessed from legitimate. This realization, while extremely personal, inevitably informs my writing on a professional level."

"What's so new," asks my sister, losing interest rapidly, "about a schizophrenic black lady pouring her heart out about food stamps and polar bears?"

I lean closer to her. "Floating signifiers," I whisper. I continue: "Legal writing presumes a methodology that is highly stylized, precedential, and based on deductive reasoning. Most scholarship in law is rather like the 'old math': static, stable, formal—rationalism walled against chaos. My writing is an intentional departure from that. I use a model of inductive empiricism, borrowed from—and parodying—systems analysis, in order to enliven thought about complex social problems. I want to look at legal issues within a framework inscribed not just within the four corners of a document—be it contract or the Constitution—but by the disciplines of psychology, sociology, history, criticism, and philosophy. The advantage of this approach is that it highlights factors that would otherwise go unremarked. For example, *stare decisis* (the judicial practice of deciding cases in a manner limited by prior court decisions in factually analogous situations), rather than remaining a silent, unquestioned 'given,' may be analyzed as a filter to certain types of systemic input. Another advantage is that this sort of analytic technique can serve to describe a community of context for those social actors whose traditional legal status has been the isolation of oxymoron, of oddity, of outsider. I am trying to create a genre of legal writing to fill the gaps of traditional legal scholarship. I would like to write in a way that reveals the intersubjectivity of legal constructions, that forces the reader both to participate in the construction of meaning and to be conscious of that process. Thus, in attempting to fill the gaps in the discourse of commercial exchange, I hope that the gaps in my own writing will be self-consciously filled by the reader, as an act of forced mirroring of meaning-invention. To this end, I exploit all sorts of literary devices, including parody, parable, and poetry."

". . . as in polar bears?" my sister asks eagerly, alert now, ears pricked, nose quivering, hair bristling.

"My, what big teeth you have!" I exclaim, just before the darkness closes over me.

It is my deep belief that theoretical legal understanding and social transformation need not be oxymoronic. I want this book to occupy the gaps between those ends that the sensation of oxymoron marks. What I hope will be filled in is connection; connection between my psyche and the readers', between lived experience and social perception, and between an encompassing historicity and a jurisprudence of generosity.

"Theoretical legal understanding" is characterized, in Anglo-American jurisprudence, by at least three features of thought and rhetoric:

(1) The hypostatization of exclusive categories and definitional polarities, the drawing of bright lines and clear taxonomies that purport to make life simpler in the face of life's complication: rights/needs, moral/immoral, public/private, white/black.

(2) The existence of transcendent, acontextual, universal legal truths or pure procedures. For example, some conservative theorists might insist that the tort of fraud has always existed and that it is part of a universal system of right and wrong. A friend of mine demanded of a professor who made just such an assertion: "Do you mean to say that when the first

white settlers landed on Fiji, they found tortfeasors waiting to be discovered?" Yes, in a manner of speaking, was the professor's response. This habit of universalizing legal taxonomies is very much like a cartoon I once saw, in which a group of prehistoric fish swam glumly underwater, carrying baseball bats tucked beneath their fins, waiting to evolve, looking longingly toward dry land, where a baseball was lying in wait on the shore. The more serious side of this essentialized world view is a worrisome tendency to disparage anything that is nontranscendent (temporal, historical), or contextual (socially constructed), or nonuniversal (specific) as "emotional," "literary," "personal," or just Not True.

(3) The existence of objective, "unmediated" voices by which those transcendent, universal truths find their expression. Judges, lawyers, logicians, and practitioners of empirical methodologies are obvious examples, but the supposed existence of such voices is also given power in romanticized notions of "real people" having "real" experiences—not because real people have experienced what they really experienced, but because their experiences are somehow *made* legitimate—either because they are viewed as empirically legitimate (directly corroborated by consensus, by a community of outsiders) or, more frequently, because those experiences are corroborated by hidden or unspoken models of legitimacy. The Noble Savage as well as the Great White Father, the Good-Hearted Masses, the Real American, the Rational Consumer, and the Arm's-Length Transactor are all versions of this Idealized Other whose gaze provides us either with internalized censure or externalized approval; internalized paralysis or externalized legitimacy; internalized false consciousness or externalized claims of exaggerated authenticity.

The degree to which these three features of legal thought are a force in laws ranging from contracts to crimes, from property to civil liberties, will be a theme throughout the rest of this book. For the moment, however, a smaller example might serve to illustrate the interpretive dynamic of which I am speaking.

A man with whom I used to work once told me that I made too much of my race. "After all," he said, "I don't even think of you as black." Yet sometime later, when another black woman became engaged in an ultimately unsuccessful tenure battle, he confided to me that he wished the school could find more blacks like me. I felt myself slip in and out of shadow, as I became nonblack for purposes of inclusion and black for purposes of exclusion; I felt the boundaries of my very body manipulated, casually inscribed by definitional demarcations that did not refer to me.

The paradox of my being black yet notblack visited me again when, back to back, the same (white) man and then a (black) woman wondered aloud if I "really identified as black." When the white man said this, I was acutely aware that the choice of identifying as black (as opposed to white?) was hardly mine; that as long as I am identified as black by the majority of others, my own identifying as black will almost surely follow as a simple fact of human interdependency. When the black woman told me the very same thing, I took it to heart as a signpost of self-denial; as possible evidence within myself of that brand of social distress and alienation to which blacks and oppressed people are so peculiarly subject; and as a call for unity in a society that too often helps us turn against ourselves.

I heard the same words from each, and it made no difference to me. I heard the same words from each, but differently: one characterized me as more of something I am not, white; the other called for me to be more conscious of something I am, black. I heard the same-different words addressed to me, a perceived white-male-socialized black woman, as a challenge to mutually exclusive categorization, as an overlapping of black and female and right and male and private and wrong and white and public, and so on and so forth.

That life is complicated is a fact of great analytic importance. Law too often seeks to avoid this truth by making up its own breed of narrower, simpler, but hypnotically powerful rhetorical truths. Acknowledging, challenging, playing with these *as* rhetorical gestures is, it seems to me, necessary for any conception of justice. Such acknowledgment complicates the supposed purity of gender, race, voice, boundary; it allows us to acknowledge the utility of such categorizations for certain purposes and the necessity of their breakdown on other occasions. It complicates definitions in its shift, in its expansion and contraction according to circumstance, in its room for the possibility of creatively mated taxonomies and their wildly unpredictable offspring.

I think, though, that one of the most important results of reconceptualizing from "objective truth" to rhetorical event will be a more nuanced sense of legal and social responsibility. This will be so because much of what is spoken in so-called objective, unmediated voices is in fact mired in hidden subjectivities and unexamined claims that make property of others beyond the self, all the while denying such connections. I remember A., a colleague, once stating that he didn't like a book he had just read because he had another friend who was a literary critic and he *imagined* that this critical friend would say a host of negative things about the book. A. disclaimed his own subjectivity, displacing it onto a larger-than-life literary critic; he created an authority who was imaginary but whose rhetorical objectivity was as smooth and convincing as the slice of a knife. In psychobabble, this is known as "not taking responsibility." In racial contexts, it is related to the familiar offensiveness of people who will say, "Our maid is black and *she* says that blacks want . . ."; such statements both universalize the lone black voice and disguise, enhance, and "objectify" the authority of the individual white speaker. As a legal tool, however, it is an extremely common device by which not just subject positioning is obscured, but by which agency and responsibility are hopelessly befuddled.

The propagated mask of the imagined literary critic, the language club of hyperauthenticity, the myth of a purely objective perspective, the godlike image of generalized, legitimating others—these are too often reified in law as "impersonal" rules and "neutral" principles, presumed to be inanimate, unemotional, unbiased, unmanipulated, and higher than ourselves. Laws like masks, frozen against the vicissitudes of life; rights as solid as rocks; principles like baseballs waiting on dry land for us to crawl up out of the mud and claim them.

This semester I have been teaching a course entitled Women and Notions of Property. I have been focusing on the semantic power and property of individualistic gendered perspectives, gender in this instance having less to do with the biology of male and female than with the semiotics of power relations, of dominance and submission, of assertion and deference, of big and little; as well as on gender issues specifically based in biology, such as reproductive rights and the complicated ability of women in particular to live freely in the territory of their own bodies. An example of the stories we discuss is the following, used to illustrate the rhetoric of power relations whose examination, I tell my students, is at the heart of the course.

Walking down Fifth Avenue in New York not long ago, I came up behind a couple and their young son. The child, about four or five years old, had evidently been complaining about big dogs. The mother was saying, "But why are you afraid of big dogs?" "Because they're big," he responded with eminent good sense. "But what's the difference between a big dog and a little dog?" the father persisted. "They're *big*," said the child. "But there's really no difference," said the mother, pointing to a large slathering wolfhound with narrow eyes and the calculated amble of a gangster, and then to a beribboned Pekinese the size of a roller skate, who was flouncing along just ahead of us all, in that little fox-trotty step that keep Pekinese from ever being taken seriously. "See?" said the father. "If you look really closely you'll see there's no difference at all. They're all just dogs."

And I thought: Talk about your iron-clad canon. Talk about a static, unyielding, totally uncompromising point of reference. These people must be lawyers. Where else do people learn so well the idiocies of High Objectivity? How else do people learn to capitulate so uncritically to a norm that refuses to allow for difference? How else do grown-ups sink so deeply into the authoritarianism of their own world view that they can universalize their relative bigness so completely that they obliterate the subject positioning of their child's relative smallness? (To say nothing of the position of the slathering wolfhound, from whose own narrow perspective I dare say the little boy must have looked exactly like a lamb chop.)

I used this story in my class because I think it illustrates a paradigm of thought by which children are taught not to see what they see; by which blacks are reassured that there is no real inequality in the world, just their own bad dreams; and by which women are taught not to experience what they experience, in deference to men's ways of knowing. The story also illustrates the possibility of a collective perspective or social positioning that would give rise to a claim for the legal interests of groups. In a historical moment when individual rights have become the basis for any remedy, too often group interests are defeated by, for example, finding the one four-year-old who has wrestled whole packs of wolfhounds fearlessly to the ground; using that individual experience to attack the validity of there ever being any generalizable four-year-old fear of wolfhounds; and then recasting the general group experience as a fragmented series of specific, isolated events rather than a pervasive social phenomenon ("You have every right to think that that wolfhound has the ability to bite off your head, but that's just your point of view").

My students, most of whom signed up expecting to experience that crisp, refreshing, clear-headed sensation that "thinking like a lawyer" purportedly endows, are confused by this and all the stories I tell them in my class on Women and Notions of Property. They are confused enough by the idea of property alone, overwhelmed by the thought of dogs and women as academic subjects, and paralyzed by the idea that property might have a gender and that gender might be a matter of words.

But I haven't been able to straighten things out for them because I'm confused too. I have arrived at a point where everything I have ever learned is running around and around in my head; and little bits of law and pieces of everyday life fly out of my mouth in weird combinations. Who can blame the students for being confused? On the other hand, everyday life is a confusing bit of business. And so my students plot my disintegration, in the shadowy shelter of ivy-covered archways and in the margins of their notebooks. . . .

Not everyone likes critical race narratives. Some dispute the literary value of narrative; some dispute the claim that racial minorities and other outgroups can speak with a distinctive voice; and some question the value of storytelling as legal scholarship. In an article entitled *The Degradation of Constitutional*

Discourse,[59] Professor Mark Tushnet has argued that critical race and feminist narratives sometimes contain "flawed stories"[60] that suffer from "missteps in literary style,"[61] making them, "in the end, failures of integrity and judgment."[62] In discussing the narratives of Patricia Williams, Tushnet suggests that a tone of self-righteousness can often be found in her narratives. Such a tone can cause readers to be skeptical of the author's veracity, and can accordingly limit the literary effectiveness of the author's work.[63] In a reply article entitled *The Discourse of Constitutional Degradation,* Professor Gary Peller argues that—despite Tushnet's prior association with the critical legal studies movement—Tushnet's criticisms ultimately rest on hostility to critical race theory and its successful use of narrative.[64]

In his *Racial Critique of Legal Academia,*[65] Professor Randall Kennedy is skeptical of the claim that critical race theorists represent minority perspectives that are presently missing from academic debates. He argues that:

> Certain racial critiques display this mode of thought when they assert that the racial background of a minority scholar should be seen as an intellectual credential because the experiences associated with it create a distinctive scholarly "voice" that is of value insofar as we prize intellectual diversity.
>
> . . .
>
> . . . I simply do not want race-conscious decisionmaking to be naturalized into our general pattern of academic evaluation. I do not want race-conscious decisionmaking to lose its status as a deviant mode of judging people or the work they produce. I do not want race-conscious decisionmaking to be assimilated into our conception of meritocracy. It is true, as I have noted, that there are many nonracial and ameritocratic considerations that frequently enter into evaluations of a scholar's work. The proper response to that reality, however, is not to scrap the meritocratic ideal. The proper response is to abjure *all* practices that exploit the trappings of meritocracy to advance interests—friendships, the reputation of one's school, career ambitions, ideological affiliations—that have nothing to do with the intellectual characteristics of the subject being judged.[66]

Professors Daniel A. Farber and Suzanna Sherry have similarly questioned the critical race theory claim that narratives present a distinctive minority perspective. In their article *Telling Stories Out of School: An Essay on Legal Narratives,*[67] Farber and Sherry concede that outgroup narratives may enlarge the perspectives of readers possessing mainstream values derived from mainstream experiences. However, they believe that narratives should not only satisfy standards of truthfulness and typicality, but they should also satisfy traditional standards of scholarly rigor. Farber and Sherry reject the

---

[59] See Mark Tushnet, *The Degradation of Constitutional Discourse,* 81 GEO. L.J. 251 (1992).

[60] See *id.* at 251.

[61] See *id.* at 252.

[62] See *id.* at 251.

[63] See *id.* at 258–60, 266–77.

[64] See Gary Peller, *The Discourse of Constitutional Degradation,* 81 GEO. L.J. 313, 313–16

(1992); *see also* Mark Tushnet, *Reply,* 81 GEO. L.J. 343 (1992).

[65] See Kennedy *supra* note 25.

[66] See *id.* at 1801, 1807. Copyright © 1989 by the Harvard Law Review Association. Reprinted with permission.

[67] See Daniel A. Farber & Suzanna Sherry, *Telling Stories Out of School: An Essay on Legal Narratives,* 45 STAN. L. REV. 807 (1993).

critical race theory claim that prevailing standards are more likely to reflect the dominant ideology than to reflect neutral conceptions of merit. Accordingly, they reject the claim that narrative should be judged by its own set of special standards. Instead, they favor use of the same standards that govern conventional legal scholarship. Although literature might properly be assessed against a purely aesthetic standard, in a law school environment, good scholarship should contain more than mere narrative; it should contain an analytical component. Mere emotive appeal is not sufficient to qualify as good scholarship. Good scholarship invites a response, but bare narrative may operate as a conversation-stopping invocation of privileged authority.[68] They conclude their article in the following manner:

> In this article, we have tried to take legal storytelling seriously, yet without simply acceding to the storytellers' views about scholarship. Although we have not found sufficient evidence to support strong versions of the "different voice" thesis, we do find weaker versions credible; we also conclude that legal stories, particularly those "from the bottom," can play a useful role in legal scholarship. Unlike some advocates of storytelling, however, we see no reason to retreat from conventional standards of truthfulness and typicality in assessing stories. Nor do we see any reason to abandon the expectation that legal scholarship contain reason and analysis, as well as narrative. A legal story without analysis is much like a judicial opinion with "Findings of Fact" but no "Conclusions of Law."
>
> We suspect that these conclusions will please no one. Arch-traditionalists will believe that, in the name of "practical reason," we have jettisoned intellectual rigor by giving any credence at all to legal storytelling. Advocates of legal storytelling will find us guilty of an illicit attempt to apply white male standards to their outsider jurisprudence: yet another effort by the establishment to domesticate and thereby neutralize a new radical movement. And scholars in the middle—those who like us believe in being open-minded but not empty-headed in response to new ideas—may have the most wounding critique of all: that we have merely stated the obvious. Our consolation is that, serious as these criticisms may be, they cannot all be correct.[69]

Professor Anne Coughlin has made similar criticisms of narrative scholarship, focusing on the use of autobiographical stories in critical race narratives. She suggests that such use of autobiography will not have the transformative effect that critical race theorists hope for.[70] Farber and Sherry proved to be prophetic. Supporters of legal narrative published responses to the Farber, Sherry and Coughlin critiques of narrative scholarship, which essentially accused Farber, Sherry and Coughlin of adopting a white, male, heterosexual perspective on the value of legal narratives, and of ignoring the value of alternate perspectives.[71]

---

[68] See id. at 830–55.

[69] See id. at 854–55. Copyright © 1993 by the Board of Trustees of Leland Stanford Junior University. Reprinted with permission.

[70] See Anne M. Coughlin, Regulating the Self: Autobiographical Performances in Outsider Scholarship, 81 VA. L. REV. 1229, 1229–34 (1995).

[71] See, e.g., Jerome McCristal Culp, Jr., Tell-ing a Black Legal Story: Privilege, Authenticity, "Blunders," and Transformation in Outsider Narratives, 82 VA. L. REV. 69, 90–91 (1996) (the critique of narrative adopted by Sherry & Farber, and the critique of autobiography adopted by Coughlin, reflect anger at the erosion of white male hegemony resulting from the increasing popularity of outsider narratives); Richard Delgado, On Telling Stories in School: A Reply to Farber and Sherry, 46 VAND. L. REV. 665, 665–67, 670–71, 673–76 (1993) (because

§ 11.05 Identity Politics

The critical race theory premise that race *matters* is consistent with a belief in the importance of identity politics. Although the term "identity politics" is sometimes used in a pejorative manner—in the same way that "political correctness" is often used as a pejorative term—identity politics literally describes two important features of critical race theory that emanate from its critique of liberalism. The focus on group "identity" reflects the view that social power tends to be allocated according to group membership rather than according to individual merit, and "politics" reflects the view that social power is allocated in accordance with ideological preferences rather than in accordance with apolitical neutral standards. The pejorative connotations sometimes attributed to identity politics in part reflect conservative disagreement with the leftist political goals of critical race theorists. However, those connotations may also reflect a fear that identity politics will lead to balkanization based on race, gender, ethnicity, sexual orientation or other traits that serve a group-definitional function. Although critical race theorists are cultural pluralists, most tend to favor a form of "multiculturalism" in which diversity and group identity will be respected rather than eradicated through coerced assimilation. Others, more strongly associated with traditional conceptions of "nationalism," are skeptical of the claim that multiculturalism can exist without some form of cultural imperialism. They fear that common understandings of multiculturalism fail to capture the manner in which cultural power inevitably constructs the background structures of our social interactions. In this Section, Professor John O. Calmore describes the form of multiculturalism to which he aspires. Then, Professors Farber and Sherry describe why they believe that the critical race theory preference for multiculturalism, and the tenets of critical race theory on which that preference rests, threaten Western conceptions of Enlightenment reason.

Professor John O. Calmore, of the University of North Carolina School of Law, describes himself as a long-standing integrationist. However, in his article entitled *Random Notes of an Integration Warrior,* he explains that the racial integration he favors encompasses a particular vision of multiculturalism that precludes assimilation into the dominant culture. John O. Calmore, *Random Notes of an Integration Warrior,* 81 MINN. L. REV. 1441, 1470-78 (1997) (*in Dismantling the Master's House: Essays in Memory of Trina Grillo*):[72]

> When I envision a multicultural future that reflects a more just society,
> I "colorize" whites and include them in the transformative process. I want

Farber & Sherry accept majoritarian stories, they fail to see the value of outsider counterstories); Eskridge, *supra* note 51, at 609–11, 644–46 (Farber & Sherry ignore the value of gay and lesbian perspectives); Alex M. Johnson, Jr., *Defending the Use of Narrative and Giving Content to the Voice of Color: Rejecting the Imposition of Process Theory in Legal Scholarship,* 79 IOWA L. REV. 803, 803–09, 822–30 (1994) (Farber & Sherry attempt to legitimate narrative by subjecting it to traditional stan-

dards that deprive it of its distinctive value); Reginald Leamon Robinson, *Race, Myth and Narrative in the Social Construction of the Black Self,* 40 HOW. L.J. 1, 135–44 (1996) (Farber & Sherry reinforce traditional white male paradigm).

[72] Copyright © 1997 by the Minnesota Law Review. Reprinted with permission. John O. Calmore is the Reef C. Ivey II Research Professor of Law at the University of North Carolina School of Law.

whites to buy into this adventure, but I do not want to change places with them, respectively, as powerholder and subject. I want them to reimagine the content of their character, more than change the color of their skin. As Ruth Frankenberg points out, "whiteness does have content inasmuch as it generates norms, ways of understanding history, ways of thinking about the self and other, and even ways of thinking about the notion of culture." It is this sense of whiteness that whites must reformulate.

Multiculturalism stems from the earlier push of "cultural pluralism" dating back to the work of Horace Kalen in 1915 and came somewhat into vogue under its own name in the 1970s. Since the late 1980s, multiculturalism has asserted itself as a principal framework for analyzing relations among diverse groups. The working viability of the concept, however, continues to be hampered by its many ambiguities and contested meanings. . . . For these reasons, among others, the notion of multiculturalism simultaneously sparks a good deal of interest, ambivalence, and rejection.

. . .

. . . I am trying to bring multiculturalism home—to claim it, to share in it, and to live with it in connective and constructive ways. An initial step is to trace the genealogy of multiculturalism and appreciate it as a historical reaction to the dictates of monoculturalism. As an ideology and set of normative values, monoculturalism persists even as the empirical and demographic description of the nation contradicts it.

Monoculturalism is both an intellectual ideology and a set of institutional practices, steadfastly linking power and politics to the dictates of one, centered, dominant culture to which all subordinated subjects must adapt. The history of monoculturalism is wedded to the melting-pot assimilationism that required European immigrants to relinquish their "un-American" values and to adopt in their place America's core set of cultural and political values. As David Theo Goldberg points out, this meant accepting core values that represented the class and racial culture that constituted the prevailing hegemony. The melting-pot process forced one to renounce one's subjectivity, giving up one's self in name, in culture, in ethnicity, and to the degree possible, in color. Moreover, until the 1940s, assimilation did not take into account blacks (then known as Negroes) because dominant society deemed us to be unmeltable, "inherently inassimilable." After World War II, as the institutional exclusion and segregation of blacks became more subject to viable political and legal challenge, equal treatment was equated, at least formally, with that accorded to European ethnic groups under the dictates of an assimilationist monoculturalism. Black assimilation became unproblematic, at least theoretically. After all, as Nathan Glazer and Daniel Moynihan wrote in 1963, "[T]he Negro is so much an American, the distinctive product of America. He bears no foreign values and culture that he feels the need to guard from the surrounding environment."

The homogenous, hegemonic creed of America thus translated its particularistic core into values represented as neutral and universal. In Goldberg's view, "The language of ethno-racial relations and harmony served the interests of those with power; those, that is, who continued to define what the acceptable core monocultural values were." Moreover, as the name suggests, monoculturalism has always extended beyond merely legitimating the universalized presuppositions and terms—the rules of the game—of the nation's single culture. It also denies any possible cultural value to expressions that were incompatible with the core. Cultural expressions that were compatible were misappropriated and melted down, fused into the core.

With gains brought about from the civil rights movement, monocultur-alism's force diminished somewhat under the qualified weight of integra-tion and equal opportunity. At the margins and in private circles, room was made for cultural distinctiveness. Blacks asserted themselves in rebuttal to Glazer's claim that we had no distinct values and culture to protect and guard against the crush of assimilationist dictates.

. . .

As my earlier discussion of integration as a form of sociological passing indicates, the African American involvement with assimilation is prob-lematic in many ways that are less salient for European ethnic groups. I believe the jury is still out on how effectively Asians, Pacific Islander, and Latino groups will fare under the dictates of assimilation. In benign form, assimilation merely presents a road map for newcomers and marginalized individuals who wish to benefit from the existing economic and political mainstream. It guides one to interesting and rewarding em-ployment opportunities, good neighborhoods and home ownership, finan-cial security, good schools, and the various bundle of benefits that are reserved for America's middle class. It represents a way to realize the American Dream. But assimilation in this benign form really masks a bolder, not-so-benign expression of "assimilationism," which Christopher Newfield and Avery Gordon refer to as "a specific ideology that sets the fundamental conditions for full economic and social citizenship in the United States." It is this ideological expression of assimilation I challenge, a challenge that aligns me with a critical multiculturalism.

According to Newfield and Gordon, assimilationism has three main features, all challenged by critical multiculturalism: (1) it demands that one adhere to core principles and behaviors, marginalizing those who do not; (2) it opposes race consciousness; and (3) it repudiates the distinc-tively cultural equity of diverse groups.

In the 1970s, a significant number of people of color sought to articulate and endorse cultural pluralism even as the assimilationist mainstream opportunity structure began to invite our participation. The proposition was not just empirically difficult, but conceptually as well, because core assimilationism also, paradoxically, paid lip service to pluralism. As Newfield and Gordon point out:

> Assimilationist pluralists continually insist on conformity to [the] core, even as they profess their belief in plurality. This assimilation-ist-pluralist position is contradictory, and yet it forms a pillar of the American Creed, standing next to its fellow pillars "democracy" and "free enterprise" and transforming these into elements of the core political culture.[126]

The pressures of assimilationism to adapt are unrelenting. Moreover, its explanations for and justifications of status-quo America are compel-ling to most members of the national community. It pretends to value diversity and promote equal opportunity, but it also seeks to impose a "single explanatory system or view of reality [that purports to] account for all the phenomena of life." Thus, its primary objective is to subsume diverse groups into a single whole at the center, with pluralism lightly tolerated at the margins.

In opposing assimilationism, even while assimilating, those of us who press for enhanced equality and social justice cannot be deterred by others

---

[126] [Christopher Newfield & Avery F. Gor-don, *Multiculturalism's Unfinished Business,* in MAPPING MULTICULTURALISM 76 (Avery F.   Gordon & Christopher Newfield eds., 1996)], at 81.

who characterize us as threats to social harmony. We cannot let our individual upward mobility dissuade us from challenging "unjust ground rules" merely because that mobility may be contingent on obeying those rules. We cannot buy into standards that our social group—colored people—had no share in formulating and little stake in implementing. We must disrupt the operation of these standards and destroy their masquerade as inclusive, neutral, and unifying when they are, in truth, themselves racial and divisive. As Newfield and Gordon conclude, "Assimilationism is the general operating system for everybody's software of cultural interaction. And it is an immensely powerful opponent of all kinds of equity movements in American life." As an integration warrior, I am fighting more against assimilationism than I am fighting for integration. It is just difficult, however, because I am fighting from within integrated settings, having necessarily assimilated to a degree. But I have been doing it for the last thirty years and I am committed to do so for another thirty if I am able.

. . .

Progressives who act from a critical feminist, "queer," or race-critical standpoint, must be insurgent, critical multiculturalists. Our position demands it, because the assimilationist ideology seeks to suppress our claims for a more inclusionary and just society. Moreover, monocultural-ism sets the stage for sexism, heterosexism, and racism. For those of us who occupy cultural borderlands, our values, interests, and life experi-ences are reduced to "annoying exceptions rather than central areas for inquiry." We must react to monoculturalism and its handmaiden, as-similationism, by reclaiming our status on the borderlands and position-ing it center stage. As Peter McLaren states, "We must create new narratives—new 'border narratives'—in order to reauthor the discourses of oppression in politically subversive ways as well as create sites of possibility and enablement."

The ultimate task is to move beyond assimilationism and integration-ism and separatism. These represent a three-strikes phenomenon. Throughout our history, a significant number of African Americans have swung at all three. At this point, many of us are genuine "players," but we are standing at the plate fouling off the third strike (in whichever form it is thrown). What we must seek instead is what Goldberg terms "incorporation." The principle of incorporation "involves the dual transfor-mations that take place in the dominant values and in those of the insurgent group as the latter insists on more complete incorporations into the body politic and the former grudgingly gives way." It rejects the mere extension of dominant values and protections to the formerly outsider marginalized and subordinated groups. This is, in legal terms, a recogni-tion that equality before the law is necessary but not sufficient to ensure justice in society and equality in fact. It will require us to press for a reinterpretation of America's common ground, shared values, and rules of the game.

Critical race theorists recognize the danger that multiculturalism may merely mask majoritarian cultural dominance in ways that perpetuate the subordination of racial minorities. Professor Gary Peller has argued that "integrationism," which characterizes the current liberal posture toward race relations in the United States, successfully marginalized the more progressive black "nationalism" of Malcolm X and the Black Panthers during the 1960s and early 1970s. Integrationism did this by rhetorically equating the race consciousness on which nationalism is based with the race consciousness of reactionary white racism that liberals condemn. In his article entitled *Race*

Consciousness, Peller highlights the hegemonic power of the dominant culture by demonstrating how even radical versions of nationalism can be domesticated and absorbed into the milder forms of integrationism favored by white liberals.[73] Perhaps in recognition of such cultural power, theorists like Calmore have been sympathetic to black residential communities,[74] and theorists like Derrick Bell have been sympathetic to black schools, as preferable alternatives to assimilationist integration.[75]

Critical race theorists also recognize that identity politics poses the danger of "essentialism"—the practice of viewing all members of an identity group as alike, in a way that overlooks sub-group and individual differences. Professor Crenshaw argues that successful identity politics and coalition building must take account of "intersectionality"—the view that members of multiple marginalized groups (*e.g.* poor black women or gay Asian men) have distinct problems and interests that are not encompassed by a focus on only one of their identity groups.[76] Professor Francisco Valdes has cautioned that, while the "outsider jurisprudence"[77] of critical race theory has transformed legal scholarship, the androcentric, Afrocentric and heterocentric inclinations of critical race theory (*i.e.* the focus on straight, black males) pose a danger of marginalizing other outgroups in the way that blacks themselves were marginalized by the critical legal studies movement.[78] Valdes hopes that "post-identity" politics in a "post-postmodern" legal culture will transcend the "Black/White paradigm"—the focus on white discrimination against blacks, which overlooks the importance of discrimination against other people of color.[79] He also hopes that outsider scholars will learn to identify with each other "despite differences of race, sex, class and sexuality"[80] in a way that can transcend the "sameness/difference dilemma."[81]

Not surprisingly, the identity politics and multiculturalism associated with critical race theory have generated controversy. One of the best known challenges to critical race theory has come from Farber and Sherry. In their book BEYOND ALL REASON, Farber and Sherry not only confront the critical race theory endorsement of multiculturalism, but they argue that the postmodern and narrative techniques of critical race scholarship are inconsistent with Western Enlightenment conceptions of reason. Their book has itself generated controversy, because of its suggestion that radical multiculturalism may be anti-Semitic and racist. What follows is an excerpt from the *Introduction* to their book, which summarizes their argument. DANIEL A. FARBER &

---

[73] *See* Gary Peller, *Race Consciousness*, 1990 DUKE L.J. 758, 758–63, 783–86, 818–20.

[74] *See, e.g.,* John O. Calmore, *Race/ism Lost and Found: The Fair Housing Act at Thirty,* 52 MIAMI L. REV. 1067 1067–74, 1102–20 (1998); John O. Calmore, *Racialized Space and the Culture of Segregation: "Hewing a Stone of Hope from a Mountain of Despair,"* 143 U. PA. L. REV. 1233, 1234–40 (1995).

[75] *See, e.g.,* Derrick Bell, *Neither Separate Schools Nor Mixed Schools: The Chronicle of the Sacrificed Black Schoolchildren, in* AND WE ARE NOT SAVED, *supra* note 55, at 102–22; Bell, *supra* note 3, at 471–72, 477–93.

[76] *See* Crenshaw, *supra* note 43, at 1296–99. The concepts of essentialism and intersectionality are discussed more fully in Chapter 10, Section 10.05.

[77] *See* Francisco Valdes, *Foreword—Latina/o Ethnicities, Critical Race Theory, and Post-Identity Politics in Postmodern Legal Culture: From Practices to Possibilities,* 9 LA RAZA L.J. 1, 4 (1996).

[78] *See id.* at 1–4.

[79] *See id.* at 4–7.

[80] *See id.* at 9.

[81] *See id.* at 7–12.

Suzanna Sherry, *Introduction, in* Beyond All Reason: The Radical Assault on Truth in American Law 5-12 (1997): [82]

Over the past few years, a group of legal academics has been making startling claims about the nature of reality and its implications for law. Although these scholars are social constructionists, not all social constructionists are allied with this camp, nor do they all make such radical claims. To distinguish the subjects of this book from other scholars, we label them *radical multiculturalists*. Largely politically progressive, radical multiculturalism includes adherents of a broad assortment of theories, including critical race theory, radical feminism, and legal writing about gays and lesbians, often called "gaylegal" theory. It also includes the occasional iconoclast at the other end of the political spectrum who uses postmodern theories to support recognizing creationism as a valid alternative to evolution. This motley group is united primarily by their rejection of the aspiration to universalism and objectivity that is the fruit of the European Enlightenment. Reality, they suggest, is subjective and socially constructed.

. . . [T]hese radical multiculturalists believe in particular that western ideas and institutions are socially constructed to serve the interests of the powerful, especially straight, white men. This leads them to attack such core concepts as truth, merit, and the rule of law. Catharine MacKinnon, the well-known feminist theorist, says that traditional standards of merit for jobs and school admissions are merely "affirmative action for white males," reflecting what white males value about themselves. This theme has been repeated by a number of other feminists and critical race theorists. . . . Others attack the concepts of reason and objective truth, condemning them as components of white male domination. They prefer the more subjective "ways of knowing" supposedly favored by women and minorities, such as storytelling. . . . As to the rule of law, it is an article of faith that legal rules are indeterminate and serve only to disguise the law's white male bias. In short, radical multiculturalism includes a broad-based attack on the Enlightenment foundations of democracy.

Not surprisingly, this movement has encountered resistance in the legal academy. Both law and the academic world have long been viewed as bastions of objective, reasoned argument within a broader world that relies less on reason and more on political power or manipulative rhetoric. Universities increasingly have come to be treasured as enclaves of reason in an unreasoning world, evolving from their beginnings as gentlemen's finishing schools to become scholarly communities dedicated to the proposition that "reason could grasp the essentials of human activity." . . . The conventional view is thus that, within the university, persuasion takes place "on the basis of reason and evidence," not "social standing, physical strength, or the raw vehemence of argument."

. . .

So what's wrong with radical multiculturalism and its rejection of the Enlightenment? The standard answers are that it is impractical and that it necessarily deconstructs itself. Camille Paglia notes wittily that "if there were no facts, surgeons couldn't operate, buildings would collapse, and airplanes couldn't get off the ground." Physicist Alan Sokal invites those who believe that "the laws of physics are mere social conventions"

---

[82] Copyright © 1997 by Oxford University Press, Inc. Used by permission of Oxford University Press, Inc.

to "try transgressing those conventions" from the windows of his twenty-first floor apartment. But these types of "facts" aren't the main target of the radical multiculturalists. As far as we know, they obey the same laws of physics as the rest of us.

As for radical multiculturalism deconstructing itself, we are certainly not the first to ask: If there is no such thing as objective truth or knowledge, why should we bother listening to what the (powerless) radical multiculturalists have to say? After all, if reason and knowledge are only the belief systems favored by the powerful, whoever is in power will make his own belief the definition of reality, so it becomes difficult to find a basis for the powerless to criticize social arrangements. This is a significant philosophical problem for radical multiculturalists; but having philosophical problems does not necessarily distinguish radical multiculturalism from any other jurisprudential approach. . . . All jurisprudential theories have unresolved philosophical problems—that's what makes jurisprudence interesting.

In any event, we are constitutional law professors, not philosophers or literary theorists. We will therefore address neither of these frequently noted flaws of social constructionism. Instead, we propose to examine the legal and societal implications of radical multiculturalist legal theories. Where do the radical multiculturalists' beliefs take them? In particular, we explore whether their beliefs serve or instead undermine the radicals' own progressive goals. We share their goals of increasing both social justice and individual freedom and improving the quality of public discourse. But these goals are not necessarily well served by radical multiculturalism. Indeed, we contend that the radicals' attachment to social constructionism and related doctrines hinders rather than furthers attainment of all these goals.

. . .

[Radical multiculturalism] fails on its own terms because it cannot support the kind of world that it seeks to create or maintain. For example, we argue that although radical multiculturalism attempts to promote equality, its conception of equality is fatally flawed because of its inherently anti-Semitic and racist implications. It's not that the radicals necessarily have anti-Semitic or racist feelings themselves. Instead, they are toying with an ideology that in the end is a fundamental misfit with their own values. We might call this attempt to grapple with social constructionism on its own terms a *normative critique*.

Because we take the use of the labels "anti-Semitism" and "racism" seriously, we should pause for a moment to explain our meaning. We do not accuse radical multiculturalists of harboring even covert animosity toward Jews or Asians. We nevertheless view their theories as anti-Semitic and racist in implication. Although anti-Semitism was traditionally based on religious aversion, modern anti-Semitism more often takes the form of rejection of Jewish success, and radical multiculturalism falls into this latter category.

In the end, radical multiculturalists cannot answer an important question without invoking disturbingly anti-Semitic and racist explanations: If there is no such thing as objective merit, what explains the success of Jews and Asian Americans, both of whom, like blacks, have been victims of discrimination by white gentile America?. . . .

The radical theories inescapably imply that Jews and Asians enjoy an unfair share of wealth and status. Thus, the necessary normative implication of the radical theory is that steps should be taken to redress the balance more in favor of white gentiles. In addition, the radicals cannot

easily explain Jewish and Asian success. Although benign explanations
for this success are available, they are logically inconsistent with radical
multiculturalism; consequently, the radicals would be forced to explain
Jewish and Asian success by deploying theories that parallel historic
forms of anti-Semitism. In short, if the radical multiculturalists are not
personally anti-Semitic or anti-Asian, it is only because they have failed
to work fully through the logic of their own theories.

Their theories also play into the historic dynamics of prejudice against
Jews and similarly successful minority groups. Because of their relative
success and their group identities, Jews, Chinese, and other groups have
always been attacked by the "have nots" (not to mention some of the
"haves"). These attacks are generic reactions against the success of
minority groups—reactions that existed long before the radical multiculturalists. The Enlightenment idea of merit provided a partial defense to
these basic social antagonisms. Even though the radical multiculturalists
may care nothing about Jews one way or the other, their theories have
the potential to expose Jews to the traditional attacks by removing the
shield of Enlightenment values. Particularly given the role of anti-
Semitism and anti-Asian sentiment in some minority communities, the
radicals are unwittingly supplying ammunition to less scrupulous group
leaders.

We are confident that radical multiculturalists do not have any personal
resentment toward Jews or Asians. But most people today would consider
a theory racist if it implied that blacks are inherently inferior mentally.
They would consider a theory sexist if it implied that women are incapable
of pursuing professional careers. And they would attach these labels
regardless of whether the holders of the theories had any personal anger
toward blacks or women. By the same token, we consider radical multiculturalism anti-Semitic and anti-Asian.

Obviously, radical multiculturalists do not dislike Jews or Asians, nor
is their goal to deprive them of their success. How, then, did they get to
this point? How could they have failed to notice the pitfalls of their theory?
The answers are deeply embedded in their world view. Although the anti-
Semitism and racism claims may be the most serious of our charges
against radical multiculturalism, we believe that radical multiculturalism
suffers from additional grave flaws. In particular, it is corrosive to public
discussion of racial and gender issues. It also encourages an evasive
attitude toward historical reality. As a result, radical multiculturalists
have adopted a position whose disturbing implications are not easily
disclaimed.

In the first part of the book, we explore the tenets of radical
multiculturalism. . . .

We then turn, in the second part of the book, to a three-pronged critique
of radical multiculturalism. First, in our view, the radical attack on merit
has implications that should appall the radicals themselves as well as
others. If merit is nothing but a mask for white male privilege, then it
becomes difficult to defend the fact that Jews and Asians are quite
disproportionately successful. If their success cannot be justified as fairly
earned, it can only be attributed to a heightened degree of entanglement
with white male privilege. In short, we believe that radical multiculturalism implies that Jews and Asian Americans are unjustly favored in the
distribution of social goods. These anti-Semitic and racist implications of
radical multiculturalism are unavoidable, and lead us to condemn radical
multiculturalism itself as unacceptable.

Second, radical multiculturalism leads to disturbing distortions in scholarship and public discourse. Because they reject objectivity as a norm,

the radicals are content to rely on personal stories as a basis for formulating views of social problems. These stories are often atypical or distorted by self-interest, yet any criticism of the stories is inevitably seen as a personal attack on the storyteller. More generally, because radical multiculturalists refuse to separate the speaker from the message, they can become sidetracked from discussing the merits of the message itself into bitter disputes about the speaker's authenticity and her right to speak on behalf of an oppressed group. Criticisms of radical multiculturalism are seen as pandering to the power structure if they come from women or minorities, or as sexist and racist if they come from white men. This makes dialogue difficult at best.

Third, the radical multiculturalist attack on the concept of objective truth has other disturbing consequences. Besides leading the radicals on occasion to a nonchalant mishandling of evidence, it also provides no defense against even the most outrageous distortions of history, such as Holocaust denial. On less dramatic issues, it licenses the radicals to ignore uncomfortable facts about our present racial and gender situation. When the facts do not fit your preconceptions, it is handy to have a theory that says facts can be dismissed as social constructs.

In the last chapter, we try to clear up some loose ends. We show how the various tenets of radical multiculturalism fit together and reinforce each other. We also explore the mechanisms that allow the radicals to abandon common sense and adhere to a set of basically implausible beliefs. One factor is the distortion of discourse mentioned above, which helps them to brush off criticism. Other factors include a reliance on misleading or inaccurate "stock stories" that reinforce their view of society, and a self-sealing ideology that resists punctures by evidence or logic. In combination, these factors encourage a somewhat paranoid style of thought, which sees the covert influence of white male power behind every text, event, or institution, and which interprets any criticism or disagreement as a political power play. Finally, although we believe that radical multiculturalism is itself a dead end, we believe that progressive legal scholars have other valuable insights, and in the "Conclusion" we discuss the prospects for constructive dialogue between them and mainstream scholars.

§ 11.06   Conclusion

Consistent with its postmodern heritage, critical race theory sometimes adopts positions that are in logical tension with each other. As Section 11.02 discussed, critical race theorists accept the doctrinal indeterminacy thesis inherent in the critical legal studies critique of rights. Nevertheless, critical race theorists also believe that rights rhetoric continues to serve a useful function in the minority quest for racial justice. As Section 11.03 discussed, critical race theorists believe in radical theories of social construction. Nevertheless, critical race theorists also believe that race is a "real" social category that justifies an insistence on race consciousness in analyzing the operation of social structures. As Section 11.05 discusses, critical race theorists are acutely aware of the dangers of "essentializing" race. Nevertheless, critical race theorists also favor forms of identity politics that stress the importance of "intersectionalities" and nonassimilationist multiculturalism. Although postmodernism tolerates logical tension better than legal liberalism and other traditional schools of constitutional theory, there is one additional logical tension in critical race theory that is nevertheless striking. Many critical race theorists are profoundly pessimistic about the possibility of ever achieving racial justice in the United States. Nevertheless, critical race theorists resist despair, and continue to struggle for racial justice, often placing special emphasis on pragmatism. This Section discusses that juxtaposition of pessimism and praxis, which seems to mark the future of critical race theory.

Professor Derrick Bell has captured the pessimism of many critical race theorists about the prospects for racial justice in the title of his book, FACES AT THE BOTTOM OF THE WELL: THE PERMANENCE OF RACISM (1992).[83] In the epigraph to his book, Bell writes:

> Black people are the magical faces at the bottom of society's well. Even the poorest whites, those who must live their lives only a few levels above, gain their self-esteem by gazing down on us. Surely, they must know that their deliverance depends on letting down their ropes. Only by working together is escape possible. Over time, many reach out, but most simply watch, mesmerized into maintaining their unspoken commitment to keep us where we are, at whatever cost to them or us.[84]

Professor Crenshaw has argued that white racism is not a deviation from some nondiscriminatory norm, but rather is a persistent form of ideology that is necessary for whites to justify the racial inequalities that they continually inflict.[85] Professor Culp has argued that it will be hard to change the racial status quo because whites no longer believe that discrimination is a problem, and whites have become tired of dealing with the whining of racial minorities.[86] Professor Linda Greene has become pessimistic about the possibility of achieving racial equality within the existing legal framework.[87] Professor Roy L. Brooks has argued that integration has failed many black Americans and that a strategy of "limited separation" may constitute the only way to improve the social condition of blacks.[88] Professor Delgado and Jean Stefancic have argued that, due to the re-emergence of "rampant conservatism," the type of racism that is practiced today "is no longer subtle or unconscious, but rather of the blatant, in-your-face variety, much like the 1940s or 1950s."[89]

In his book THE RODRIGO CHRONICLES[90] —a series of fictional dialogues about race relations in the United States between two civil rights activists, one of whom is young and impetuous, and the other of whom is aging and experienced—Professor Delgado paints a bleak picture of the possibilities for the legal system to remedy racial injustice. In the Chapter entitled *Rodrigo's Fourth Chronicle: Neutrality and Stasis in Antidiscrimination Law,* Delgado has his young reformer explain to his older activist why the concept of neutrality in antidiscrimination law is destined to be applied in ways that will perpetuate racial subordination. Not only will ambiguities in the concept

---

[83] See BELL, FACES AT THE BOTTOM OF THE WELL, *supra* note 55. Copyright © 1992 by Basic Books, Inc. Reprinted with permission of Perseus Books Group.

[84] See id. at v.

[85] See Crenshaw, *supra* note 12, at 1369–81.

[86] See Jerome McCristal Culp, Jr., *Water Buffalo and Diversity: Naming Names and Reclaiming the Racial Discourse,* 26 CONN. L. REV. 209, 210–20 (1993); *see also* Culp, *supra* note 8, at 971–83.

[87] See Linda Greene, *Race in the Twenty-First Century: Equality Through Law?,* 64 TUL. L. REV. 1515, 1539–41 (1990).

[88] See ROY L. BROOKS, INTEGRATION OR SEPARATION: A STRATEGY FOR RACIAL EQUALITY 1–3, 199–214, 282–86 (1996).

[89] See Delgado & Stefancic, *Past, Present and Future, supra* note 1, at 489-90.

[90] See DELGADO, THE RODRIGO CHRONICLES, *supra* note 56.

of neutrality inevitably be resolved against the background of white rather than minority value systems, but the vertical and horizontal myopia built into the way that the legal system frames legally cognizable events will inevitably disable the legal system from viewing purportedly neutral criteria in a way that permits their discriminatory character to be ascertained.[91]

Professor Bell is even more pessimistic in FACES AT THE BOTTOM OF THE WELL. In the story entitled *Racism's Secret Bonding,* Bell suggests that whites share an unstated bond through which they tacitly understand that the function of blacks in the United States is to serve as a buffer between powerful and powerless whites. Blacks are indispensable scapegoats whose presence as victims of discrimination is necessary to prevent class warfare among whites, and to prevent the type of balkanization that has now been revived in Eastern Europe. For that reason, neither social programs designed to help blacks, nor educational programs designed to teach whites about the harms inflicted by discrimination are likely to improve the social condition of blacks. Moreover, black appeals to the conscience of whites are destined to provoke both rejection and retaliation, as if they were the prophecies of Jeremiah.[92] Indispensability notwithstanding, Bell carried this idea one step further in his story *The Space Traders,* where aliens from outer space offered the United States gold, the elimination of pollution, and a safe energy source if the United States would turn over to the space traders all of the blacks living in the United States. After due deliberation, which included a constitutional amendment designed to eliminate any legal difficulties, the United States agreed. Blacks were delivered-up to the space traders for an unknown fate. They left the United States in chains, as their forebears had arrived.[93]

Professor Anthony Paul Farley—a young critical race scholar reminiscent of Delgado's fictional Rodrigo—is perhaps the most pessimistic. In an article entitled *Thirteen Stories*[94] he writes:

> The stories that follow—and I might have called them essays—are written in flight from the American progress narrative. . . . There are no boards over the well. We are falling. We have been falling. We are the fallen. It never ends.
>
> I do not have a project. I do not want any more American Progress—white over black to white over black to white over black. I am not going to fall for any more up-from-slavery stories. I want to shatter the Dream. I want to play with the fragments of the narrative. You may find yourself and me by the thirteenth story. Perhaps we will, together, escape the Promised Land.[95]

Despite the bleak predictions of many critical race theorists concerning the future of racial justice in the United States, critical race theorists have not surrendered to despair. Ironically, although critical race theory is rather

---

[91] *See* RICHARD DELGADO, *Rodrigo's Fourth Chronicle: Neutrality and Stasis in Antidiscrimination Law, in* THE RODRIGO CHRONICLES, *supra* note 56, at 58–82.

[92] DERRICK BELL, *Racism's Secret Bonding, in* FACES AT THE BOTTOM OF THE WELL, *supra* note 55, at 147–57.

[93] *See* DERRICK BELL, *The Space Traders, in*

FACES AT THE BOTTOM OF THE WELL, *supra* note 55, at 158–94.

[94] *See* ANTHONY PAUL FARLEY, *Thirteen Stories,* 15 TOURO L. REV. 543 (1999). Copyright © 1999 by the Touro Law Review and Anthony Paul Farley. Reprinted with permission.

[95] *See id.* at 549.

abstract in its critique of liberalism and its focus on social construction, many
critical race theorists have emphasized the need for pragmatic activism to
make the best of a difficult situation. Professor Calmore seems resigned to
the continued existence of "hypersegregation," but he nevertheless favors
grass roots efforts to eliminate poverty, reduce systemic injustices toward
people of color, and ameliorate intergroup conflict in polarized inner-city
communities.[96] In the midst of the current anti-affirmative action backlash,
Professor Alex M. Johnson has advocated the use of racial quotas to increase
the admission of qualified blacks to colleges and professional schools, arguing
that the use of such quotas is necessary to eliminate the existence of a
permanent black underclass.[97] Professor Paul Butler has argued that, in appropriate criminal cases, black jurors have a "moral responsibility" to use jury
nullification to "emancipate" black criminal defendants where the defendants
are being prosecuted for conduct that is a natural outgrowth of racial
oppression. This allows black jurors, rather than white lawmakers and
prosecutors, to determine who should be removed from black communities.[98]
In one of his most recent CHRONICLES, Professor Delgado expresses the fear
that critical race theory has become fixated on the critique of liberalism and
should instead focus on pragmatic efforts to counteract the re-emergence of
rampant conservatism and the rollback of civil rights gains.[99]

Some responses to the perceived permanence of racism are less pragmatic
and more abstract—perhaps even utopian. A premise of Professor Delgado's
RODRIGO CHRONICLES seems to be that the younger generation of critical race
scholars will provide the skepticism, persistence and creativity needed to somehow invent a way out of the Nation's enduring problem of racial inequality.[100]
Even Farley holds out hope that, when blacks fully appreciate the hopeless-
ness of their social position, they may develop a new liberatory consciousness.[101] Professor Spann has argued that, if race—like reality—is socially
constructed, minorities may possess the power to imagine their way out of
racial oppression.[102] Professor Bell relates a real—as opposed to fictional—
incident in the *Preface* to FACES AT THE BOTTOM OF THE WELL, suggesting that
persistence in the face of pessimism may be definitional in the identity of
oppressed minorities. The incident occurred in the summer of 1964:

> . . . It was a quiet, heat-hushed evening in Harmony, a small black
> community near the Mississippi Delta. Some Harmony residents, in the
> face of increasing white hostility, were organizing to ensure implementa-
> tion of a court order mandating desegregation of their schools the next
> September. Walking with her up a dusty, unpaved road toward her
> modest home, I asked one of the organizers, Mrs. Biona MacDonald, where
> she and the other black families found the courage to continue working
> for civil rights in the face of intimidation that included blacks losing their

---

[96] *See* Calmore, *Racialized Space, supra* note
74, at 1254–73.

[97] *See* Alex M. Johnson, Jr., *Defending the
Use of Quotas in Affirmative Action: Attacking
Racism in the Nineties,* 1992 U. ILL. L. REV.
1043, 1043–46, 1071–73.

[98] *See* Paul Butler, *Racially Biased Jury
Nullification: Black Power in the Criminal
Justice System,* 105 YALE L.J. 677, 677–80

(1995).

[99] *See* DELGADO, *Rodrigo's Notebook: Race,
Resistance and the End of Equality, in* WHEN
EQUALITY ENDS, *supra* note 56, at 230–32.

[100] *See* DELGADO, THE RODRIGO CHRONICLES,
supra note 56, at xvii–xix, 52–57.

[101] *See supra* note 40, and accompanying text.

[102] *See* SPANN, RACE AGAINST THE COURT, *supra* note 18, at 170–71.

jobs, the local banks trying to foreclose on the mortgages of those active in the civil rights movement, and shots fired through their windows late at night.

Mrs. MacDonald looked at me and said slowly, seriously, "I can't speak for everyone, but as for me, I am an old woman. I live to harass white folks."[103]

Does the future of race relations seem as bleak as many critical race theorists seem to think it is? Has the liberal goal of colorblindness become obsolete? Is race inevitable, or artificial, or both? Is identity politics the only realistic strategy for racial minorities—and for the white majority—to pursue in the future? In this regard, did you wonder about the race or gender of the commentators whose work you considered in other chapters of this book? Should you have? Many black leaders, including the late federal judge and legal academic A. Leon Higginbotham, Jr., have argued that conservative black Supreme Court Justice Clarence Thomas has turned his back on the needs of racial minorities and has opposed the very types of civil rights and affirmative action measures that enabled him to become a supreme court justice.[104] Are such criticisms warranted, or do they instead illustrate dangers of the race consciousness on which critical race theory rests?

§ 11.07　Bibliography

Larry Alexander, *What We Do, and Why We Do It,* 45 STAN. L. REV. 1885, 1895–96 (1993)

Jane B. Baron, *Resistance to Stories,* 67 S. CAL. L. REV. 255 (1994)

Derrick Bell, CONFRONTING AUTHORITY: REFLECTIONS OF AN ARDENT PROTESTER (1994); RACE, RACISM, AND AMERICAN LAW (3d ed. 1992); *Racial Realism—After We're Gone: Prudent Speculations on America in a Post-Racial Epoch,* 34 ST. LOUIS U. L.J. 393 (1990); *Property Rights in Whiteness—Their Legal Legacy, Their Economic Costs,* 33 VILL. L. REV. 767 (1988); *White Superiority in America: Its Legal Legacy, Its Economic Costs,* 33 VAND. L. REV. 767 (1988); Bakke, *Minority Admissions, and the Usual Price of Racial Remedies,* 67 CALIF. L. REV. 1 (1979)

Roy L. Brooks, RETHINKING THE AMERICAN RACE PROBLEM (1990)

John O. Calmore, *Exploring Michael Omi's "Messy" Real World of Race: An Essay for "Naked People Longing to Swim Free,"* 15 LAW & INEQ. 25 (1997)

Stephen Carter, REFLECTIONS OF AN AFFIRMATIVE ACTION BABY (1991)

Robert S. Chang, *Toward an Asian American Legal Scholarship: Critical Race Theory, Post-Structuralism, and Narrative Space,* 81 CAL. L. REV. 1244 (1993)

---

[103] DERRICK BELL, *Preface,* in FACES AT THE BOTTOM OF THE WELL, *supra* note 55, at xi–xii. Copyright © 1992 by Basic Books, Inc. Reprinted with permission of Perseus Books Group.

[104] *See* A. Leon Higginbotham, Jr., *Justice*

Clarence Thomas in Retrospect, 45 HASTINGS L.J. 1405 (1994); A. Leon Higginbotham, Jr., *An Open Letter to Justice Clarence Thomas From a Federal Judicial Colleague,* 140 U. PA. L. REV. 1005 (1992).

Anthony E. Cook, *Reflections on Postmodernism,* 26 New Eng. L. Rev. 751 (1992); *Beyond Critical Legal Studies: The Reconstructive Theology of Dr. Martin Luther King Jr.,* 103 Harv. L. Rev. 985 (1990)

Kimberlé Williams Crenshaw, *Beyond Racism and Misogyny: Black Feminism and 2 Live Crew, in* Matsuda, et al., Words that Wound: Critical Race Theory, Assaultive Speech and the First Amendment 111 (1993)

Jerome McCristal Culp, Jr., *Black People in White Face: Assimilation, Culture, and the* Brown *Case,* 36 Wm. & Mary L. R.ev. 665 (1995); *Colorblind Remedies and the Intersectionality of Oppression: Policy Arguments Masquerading as Moral Claims,* 69 N.Y.U. L. Rev. 162 (1994); *Posner on Duncan Kennedy and Racial Difference: White Authority in the Legal Academy,* 41 Duke L. J. 1095 (1992)

Harlon Dalton, *Storytelling On Its Own Terms, in* Law's Stories: Narrative and Rhetoric in the Law 59 (Peter Brooks & Paul Gewirtz eds., 1996); Racial Healing: Confronting the Fear between Blacks and Whites (1995); *The Clouded Prism,* 22 Harv. C.R.-C.L. L. Rev. 435 (1987)

Peggy Cooper Davis, Neglected Stories (1997); *Neglected Stories and the Lawfulness of* Roe v. Wade, 28 Harv. C.R.-C.L. L. Rev. 299 (1993); *Law as Microaggression,* 98 Yale L.J. 1559 (1989)

Richard Delgado, *Rodrigo's Tenth Chronicle: Merit and Affirmative Action,* 83 Geo. L.J. 1711 (1995); *Zero-Based Racial Politics and an Infinity-Based Response: Will Endless Talking Cure America's Racial Ills?,* 80 Geo. L.J. 1879 (1992); *Brewer's Plea: Critical Thoughts on Common Cause,* 44 Vand. L. Rev. 1 (1991); *Zero-Based Racial Politics: An Evaluation of Three Best-Case Arguments on Behalf of the Nonwhite Underclass,* 78 Geo. L.J. 1929 (1990); *Derrick Bell and the Ideology of Racial Reform: Will We Ever Be Saved?* (Book Review), 97 Yale L.J. 923 (1988); *Words that Wound: A Tort Action for Racial Insults, Epithets and Name Calling,* 17 Harv. C.R.-C.L. L. Rev. 133 (1982)

Richard Delgado & Jean Stefancic, Must We Defend Nazis?: Hate Speech, Pornography, and the New First Amendment (1996); *Images of the Outsider in American Law and Culture: Can Free Expression Remedy Systemic Social Ills,* 77 Cornell L. Rev. 1258 (1992); *Norms and Narratives: Can Judges Avoid Serious Moral Error?,* 69 Tex. L. Rev. 1929 (1991); *Why Do We Tell the Same Stories?: Law Reform, Critical Librarianship, and the Triple Helix Dilemma,* 42 Stan. L. Rev. 207 (1989)

Selena Dong, *"Too Many Asians": The Challenge of Fighting Discrimination Against Asian Americans and Preserving Affirmative Action,* 47 Stan. L. Rev. 1027 (1995)

Daniel A. Farber & Suzanna Sherry, *The 200,000 Cards of Dimitri Yurasov: Further Reflections on Scholarship and Truth,* 46 Stan. L. Rev. 647 (1994)

Anthony Paul Farley, *All Flesh Shall See It Together,* 19 Chicano-Latino L. Rev. 163 (1998)

Stephen M. Feldman, *Whose Common Good? Racism in the Political Community*, 80 GEO. L.J. 1835 (1992)

Ronald J. Fiscus, THE CONSTITUTIONAL LOGIC OF AFFIRMATIVE ACTION: MAKING THE CASE FOR QUOTAS (1992)

A Forum on Derrick Bell's Civil Rights Chronicles, 34 ST. LOUIS L.J. 393–484 (1990) (featuring article by Derrick Bell and responses by Leland Ware, Robin D. Barnes, Michael A. Olivas, Michael A. Middleton, Barbara Luck Graham, Daniel J. Monti, R. Randall Rainey, S.J.)

Henry Louis Gates, Jr., *Let Them Talk,* NEW REPUBLIC, Sep. 20 & 27, 1993, at 37-49 (reviewing MARI J. MATSUDA ET AL., WORDS THAT WOUND: CRITICAL RACE THEORY, ASSAULTIVE SPEECH, AND THE FIRST AMENDMENT (1993))

Linda S. Greene, *"Breaking Forms,"* 44 STAN. L. REV. 909 (1992)

Lani Guinier, *Groups, Representation and Race-Conscious Districting: A Case of the Emperor's Clothes,* 71 TEX. L. REV. 1589 (1993); *No Two Seats: The Elusive Quest for Political Equality,* 77 VA. L. REV. 1413 (1991); *The Triumph of Tokenism: The Voting Rights Act and the Theory of Black Electoral Success,* 89 MICH. L. REV. 1077 (1991)

Lisa C. Ikemoto, *Traces of the Mater Narrative in the Story of African American/Korean American Conflict: How We Constructed "Los Angeles,"* 66 S. CAL. L. REV. 1581 (1993)

Alex M. Johnson, Jr., *Bid Whist, Tonk, and United States v. Fordice: Why Integrationsim Fails African-Americans Again,* 81 CAL. L. REV. 1401 (1993)

Duncan Kennedy, *A Cultural Pluralist Case for Affirmative Action in Legal Academia,* 1990 DUKE L.J. 705

Randall Kennedy, *Martin Luther King's Constitution: A Legal History of the Montgomery Bus Boycott,* 98 YALE L.J. 999 (1989); *Persuasion and Distrust: A Comment on the Affirmative Action Debate,* 99 HARV. L. REV. 1327 (1986); *Race Relations Law and the Tradition of Celebration: The Case of Professor Schmidt,* 86 COLUM. L. REV. 1622 (1986)

Charles R. Lawrence, III, *The Word and the River: Pedagogy as Scholarship or Struggle,* S. CAL. L. REV. 2231 (1992); *If He Hollers Let Him Go: Regulating Racist Speech on Campus,* 1990 DUKE L.J. 431

Jayne Chong-Soon Lee, *Navigating the Topology of Race,* 46 STAN. L. REV. 747 (1994)

Nancy Levit, *Critical of Race Theory: Race, Reason, Merit, and Civility,* 87 GEO. L.J. 795 (1999)

Mari J. Matsuda, *Beside My Sister, Facing the Enemy: Legal Theory Out of Coalition,* 43 STAN. L. REV. 1183 (1991); *Public Response to Racist Speech: Considering the Victim's Story,* 87 MICH. L. REV. 2320 (1989)

Mari J. Matsuda & Charles R. Lawrence III, *Epilogue: Banning Crosses and the R.A.V. Case, in* Matsuda, et al., WORDS THAT WOUND: CRITICAL RACE THEORY, ASSAULTIVE SPEECH AND THE FIRST AMENDMENT 133 (1993)

Angela E. Oh, *Race Relations in Los Angeles: "Divide and Conquer" is Alive and Flourishing*, 66 S. CAL. L. REV. 1647 (1993)

Michael A. Olivas, *The Chronicles, My Grandfather's Stories and Immigration Law: The Slave Traders Chronicle as Racial History*, 34 ST. LOUIS U. L.J. 425 (1990)

Gary Peller, *Notes Toward a Postmodern Nationalism*, 1992 U. ILL. L. REV. 1095

Richard Posner, *The Skin Trade*, NEW REPUBLIC, Oct 13, 1997, at 40 (Book Review of Daniel A. Farber & Suzanna Sherry, BEYOND ALL REASON: THE RADICAL ASSAULT ON TRUTH IN AMERICAN LAW (1997)); *Comment: Duncan Kennedy on Affirmative Action*, 1990 DUKE L.J. 1157; *The DeFunis Case and the Constitutionality of Preferential Treatment of Racial Minorities*, 1974 S. CT. REV. 1

Ronald Suresh Roberts, CLARENCE THOMAS AND THE TOUGH LOVE CROWD: COUNTERFEIT HEROES AND UNHAPPY TRUTHS (1995)

Thomas Ross, *Innocence and Affirmative* Action, 43 VAND. L. REV. 297 (1990)

Joseph William Singer, *Persuasion*, 87 MICH. L. REV. 2442 (1989)

Thomas Sowell, CIVIL RIGHTS: RHETORIC OR REALITY? (1984)

Girardeau A. Spann, *Proposition 209*, 47 DUKE L.J. 187 (1997); *Affirmative Action and Discrimination*, 39 HOWARD L.J. 1 (1995)

Shelby Steele, THE CONTENT OF OUR CHARACTER: A NEW VISION OF RACE IN AMERICA (1990)

Susan Sturm & Lani Guinier, *The Future of Affirmative Action: Reclaiming the Innovative Ideal*, 84 CAL. L. REV. 953 (1996)

Symposium, *The Critique of Normativity*, 139 U. PA. L. REV. 801 (1991) (with articles by Pierre Schlag, Richard Delgado, Steven L. Winter, Frederick Schauer, and Margaret Jane Radin and Frank Michelman; and replies by Pierre Schlag, Steven L. Winter, and Richard Delgado)

Symposium, *Our Private Obsession, Our Public Sin*, 15 LAW & INEQ. 1–125 (1997) (with articles about the social construction of race by Jeffrey H. Rutherford, Michael Omi, John O. Calmore, Nancy A. Denton & john a. powell)

Kendall Thomas, *"Ain't Nothing Like the Real Thing": Black Masculinity, Gay Sexuality, and the Jargon of Authenticity, in* REPRESENTING BLACK MEN 66 (Marcellus Blount & George Cunningham eds., 1996); *Beyond the Privacy Principle*, 92 COLUM. L. REV. 1431 (1992); *Rouge et Noir Reread: A Popular Constitutional History of the Angelo Herndon Case,* 65 S. CAL. L. REV. 2599 (1992)

Joan Williams, *Dissolving the Sameness/Difference Debate: A Post-Modern Path Beyond Essentialism and Critical Race Theory*, 1990 DUKE L.J. 296

Patricia J. Williams, Metro Broadcasting, Inc. v. FCC: *Regrouping in Singular Times*, 104 HARV. L. REV. 525 (1990)

Robert A. Williams, Jr., *Documents of Barbarism: The Contemporary Legacy of European Racism and Colonialism in the Narrative Traditions of Federal Indian Law,* 31 ARIZ. L. REV. 237 (1989)

Chapter 12

Interpretation Theory and Postmodernism

§ 12.01 Introduction

Underlying many of the foregoing readings, such as those on the constitutional text, feminism, and critical race theory, is a welter of issues about legal "interpretation." Scholarly writing in the past few decades has sought to bring to the surface what may be questionable presumptions about approaches to, and the very possibility of, the meaningful interpretation of legal texts. Aspects of the area under discussion are sometimes labeled "hermeneutics," which is "the study of the methodological principles of interpretation and explanation; *specifically:* the study of the general principles of biblical interpretation."[1] That definition highlights two significant points for our purposes: the conventional contrast between ideas about methods of interpretation and the practice of interpretation itself, and the problems of "hermeneutics" in other fields such as religion and literature—from which recent writers about legal interpretation problems have borrowed.

The writers raising these questions in recent times have often been influenced by schools of thought given various labels such as structuralism, poststructuralism, deconstruction, and—most prominently for our purposes— "postmodernism." This last term implies a contrast with modernism, with its still widely shared Enlightenment "commitment to reason, science, ethics, and, more generally, the conviction that these disciplines reflected the existence of an independent reality."[2] But with postmodernity "reason turned on itself,"[3] challenging "the possibility of grounding reason in anything other than actual social practices."[4] The implications of this abstract-sounding questioning are far-reaching: belief systems, including scientific theories—not to mention ideas about what the Constitution "really" means—may be social constructions, not statements about an "objective" reality that exists independently of the observer and statement-maker.[5]

Some of the debate about postmodernist views on objectivity and a reality that exists independently of its observers can be put succinctly, if colloquially, with a story and a challenge. The story is of an exchange among three baseball umpires, the first of whom says, "I call them as I see them." The second umpire, the modernist, responds, "I call them as they are." The postmodernist third umpire trumps with, "They aren't anything until I call them." The challenge, from the skeptic toward postmodernism, defies the postmodernist who

---

[1] WEBSTER'S THIRD NEW INTERNATIONAL DICTIONARY 1059 (1971).

[2] Robert Justin Lipkin, *Can American Constitutional Law Be Postmodern?*, 42 BUFF. L. REV. 317, 327–28 (1994).

[3] *Id.* at 328.

[4] *Id.* at 329 (footnote omitted).

[5] For another application of this idea of the socially constructed nature of concepts that may be assumed to represent external reality, see *supra* Chapter 11, § 11.03, on critical race theory's "view that race is socially constructed rather than biologically determined."

claims that theories are just social constructions to jump off the Empire State Building without a parachute and test the theory of gravity. Saving details for later, we can say that to our knowledge the incidence of postmodernististically inspired test jumps has been nil; to say that a theory is a social construction is not necessarily to denigrate it or deny that it has any—even great—utility. And in the words of a sympathetic expositor, "postmodern theorists themselves operate according to nonpostmodern assumptions, and paradoxically . . . a consistently applied postmodern theory leads full circle to the affirmation of those same commonsense notions prevailing in most people's minds."[6]

§ 12.02 Controversies over Interpretation Theory

The materials that follow present, first, still-classic writings on interpretation theory and its implications for constitutional interpretation; second, following the sequence with which these ideas came to the fore in significant discussions bearing on constitutional theory, come treatments of the possible implications of postmodernism for constitutional adjudication. As the readings on interpretation theory will reflect, there has been considerable controversy not only about approaches to legal interpretation but about the value of this whole line of inquiry for most practical legal applications. Is all this just a tempest in an academic teapot? Or does it appropriately suggest that we too often assume some of the most crucial premises—that our very approaches to interpretation affect results in ways we should recognize and consider openly to the extent we can? For example, some of the writers on these subjects doubt whether objective interpretation is possible. If they are right, that may undermine the very idea of the "rule of law" that is central to much of Western jurisprudence. If "nihilism" about legal texts is appropriate, then perhaps the texts cannot be relied on to bind either judges or other legal actors; and something other than legal norms must be what guides even decisions that purport to be "legal."

Unsurprisingly, "nihilist" questioning has not gone unanswered. One of the major early articles in this controversy was by Professor Owen Fiss of the Yale Law School. In *Objectivity and Interpretation,* 34 STAN. L. REV. 739, 739–50, 762–63 (1982), Fiss argued that the possibility of an "interpretive community," accepting "disciplining rules" as authoritative, can mean that in practice interpreters are constrained (although not wholly bound to particular results in all instances). "Objectivity" is thus possible in the sense that interpretation is at least constrained by a source external to the judge:[7]

> Adjudication is interpretation: Adjudication is the process by which a judge comes to understand and express the meaning of an authoritative legal text and the values embodied in that text.

> Interpretation, whether it be in the law or literary domains, is neither a wholly discretionary nor a wholly mechanical activity. It is a dynamic interaction between reader and text, and meaning the product of that

---

[6] Peter C. Schanck, *Understanding Postmodern Thought and Its Implications for Statutory Interpretation,* 65 S. CAL. L. REV. 2505, 2512 (1992).

[7] Copyright © 1982 by the Trustees of the Leland Stanford Junior University and Owen M. Fiss. Reprinted with permission.

interaction. It is an activity that affords a proper recognition of both the subjective and objective dimensions of human experience; and for that reason, has emerged in recent decades as an attractive method for studying all social activity. The idea of a written text, the standard object of legal or literary interpretation, has been expanded to embrace social action and situations, which are sometimes called text-analogues. . . .

Admittedly, to treat everything as a text might seem to trivialize the idea of a text, but the appeal of the interpretive analogy stems from the fact that interpretation accords a proper place for both the perspective of the scholar and the reality of the object being studied and from the fact that interpretation sees the task of explicating meaning as the most important and most basic intellectual endeavor. This appeal is considerable and, as a consequence, liberties have been taken with the notion of a text and interpretation is now accepted as central to disciplines that were once on the verge of surrendering to the so-called scientific ethos, such as politics and history (though interestingly, not economics—there the surrender to the pretense of science seems complete). . . .

To recover, then, an old and familiar idea, namely, that adjudication is a form of interpretation, would build bridges between law and the humanities and suggest a unity among man's many intellectual endeavors. A proper regard for the distinctive social function of adjudication, and for the conditions that limit the legitimate exercise of the judicial power, will require care in identifying the kinds of texts to be construed and the rules that govern the interpretive process; the judge is to read the legal text, not morality or public opinion, not, if you will, the moral or social texts. But the essential unity between law and the humanities would persist and the judge's vision would be enlarged.

A recognition of the interpretive dimensions of adjudication and the dynamic character of all interpretive activity and its capacity to relate constructively the subjective and objective will also deepen our understanding of law and in fact might even suggest how law is possible. It might enable us to come to terms with a new nihilism, one that doubts the legitimacy of adjudication—a nihilism that appears to me to be unwarranted and unsound, but that is gaining respectability and claiming an increasing number of important and respected legal scholars, particularly in constitutional law. They have turned their backs on adjudication and have begun a romance with politics.

This new nihilism might acknowledge the characterization of adjudication as interpretation, but then would insist that the characterization is a sham. The nihilist would argue that for any text—particularly such a comprehensive text as the Constitution—there are any number of possible meanings, that interpretation consists of choosing one of those meanings, and that in this selection process the judge will inevitably express his own values. All law is masked power. In this regard the new nihilism is reminiscent of the legal realism of the early twentieth century. It too sought to unmask what was claimed to be the true nature of legal doctrine, particularly the doctrine that insulated laissez faire capitalism from the growth of the activist state and the reforms pressed by Progressives and the supporters of the New Deal. It saw law as a projection of the judge's values.

In the decades following the Second World War, particularly in the sixties, at the height of the Warren Court era, a new judicial doctrine arose to replace the doctrine that was associated with laissez faire capitalism and that was ultimately repudiated by the glorious revolution of 1937 and the constitutional victory of the New Deal. It embraced the role of the activist state and saw equality rather than liberty as the central constitutional value. Scholars turned to defending this new doctrine and in so doing sought to rehabilitate the idea of law in the face of the realist legacy. They sought to show that *Brown v. Board of Education* was law, not just politics. . . .

The nihilism of today is largely a reaction to this reconstructive effort of the sixties. It harks back to the realist movement of an earlier era, and coincides with a number of contemporary phenomena—the transfer of the judicial power from the Warren Court to another institution altogether; a social and political culture dominated by the privatization of all ends; and a new movement in literary criticism and maybe even in philosophy called deconstructionism, which expands the idea of text to embrace all the world and at the same time proclaims the freedom of the interpreter.

The nihilism of which I speak fastens on the objective aspiration of the law and sees this as a distinguishing feature of legal interpretation. The judge, the nihilist reminds us, seeks not just a plausible interpretation, but an objectively true one. Judges may not project their preferences or their views of what is right or wrong, or adopt those of the parties, or of the body politic, but rather must say what the Constitution requires. The issue is not whether school desegregation is good or bad, desirable or undesirable, to the judge, the parties, or the public, but whether it is mandated by the Constitution. The law aspires to objectivity, so the nihilist observes, but he concludes that the nature of the constitutional text makes this impossible. The text is capable of any number of possible meanings, and thus it is impossible to speak of one interpretation as true and the other false. It is impossible to speak of law with the objectivity required by the idea of justice.

The nihilist stresses two features of the legal text in explaining why objectivity is impossible. One is the use of general language. The Constitution does not, for example, contain a specific directive about the criteria for assigning students among the public schools, but provides that no state shall "deny to any person within its jurisdiction the equal protection of the laws." There is no further specification of what is meant by "state," "person," "jurisdiction," "protection," "laws," or most importantly, "equal." The potential of "equal" is staggering, and the nihilist is confounded by it. A second feature of the text is its comprehensiveness. The Constitution is a rich and varied text. It contains a multitude of values, some of which potentially conflict with others. It promises equality *and* liberty. In fact, at times it seems to contain almost every conceivable value, especially when one refers to such provisions as the privileges and immunities clause of article IV or the fourteenth amendment, or the provision of the ninth amendment that reserves to the people rights not otherwise enumerated in the Constitution.

In coming to terms with this nihilism, one must begin by acknowledging the generality and comprehensiveness of the constitutional text and also by insisting that in this regard the Constitution is no different from a poem or any legal instrument. Generality and comprehensiveness are features of any text. Though the Constitution may be more general and comprehend more than a sonnet or a contract, it is comparable in this regard to an epic poem or some national statutes. Few, if any, statutes touch as many activities as the Constitution itself (which, after all, establishes the machinery of government) but many, if not most, embody conflicting values and are in that sense comprehensive. It should also be understood that generality and comprehensiveness do not discourage interpretation but are the very qualities that usually provoke it. Interpretation is a process of generating meaning, and one important (and very common) way of both understanding and expressing the meaning of a text is to render it specific and concrete.

There are some legal theorists who would limit legal interpretation to highly specific constitutional clauses. This school, misleadingly called "interpretivism," but more properly called "textual determinism," operates with a most arid and artificial conception of interpretation. For an interpretivist only a specific text can be interpreted. Interpretation is thus confused with execution—the application of a determinate meaning to a situation—and is unproblematic only with regard to clauses like that requiring the President to be at least 35 years old. Most interpretivists, including Justice Black, would recognize the narrowness of such a perspective and want to acknowledge a role for less specific clauses, like freedom of speech; but in truth such provisions are hardly obvious in their meaning and require substantial judicial interpretation to be given their proper effect. Does "speech" embrace movies, flags, picketing, and campaign expenditures? What is meant by "freedom"? Does it, as Isaiah Berlin wondered, pertain exclusively to the absence of restraint, or does it also embrace an affirmative capacity for self-realization?

To endorse active judicial interpretation of specific clauses and to caution against judicial interpretation of the more general and potentially more far-reaching clauses, such as due process and equal protection, represents an attempt at line-drawing that cannot itself be textually justified. It is instead motivated by a desire—resting on the most questionable of premises—to limit the role of constitutional values in American government and the role of the judiciary in expressing those values. And the line itself would be illogical. It would require that small effect be given to the comprehensive constitutional protections while full effect is given to the narrow ones. I reject this attempt at line-drawing because I reject the premises and the result, but it must be emphasized that, for purposes of this essay, the critical question is not whether judicial interpretation of specific clauses, understood in any realistic sense, is legitimate and that of general clauses is not, since, as we saw in the case of the first amendment, both require substantial interpretation. Rather the question is whether *any* judicial interpretation can achieve the measure of objectivity required by the idea of law.

Objectivity in the law connotes standards. It implies that an interpretation can be measured against a set of norms that transcend the particular vantage point of the person offering the interpretation. Objectivity implies that the interpretation can be judged by something other than one's own notions of correctness. It imparts a notion of impersonality. The idea of an objective interpretation does not require that the interpretation be wholly determined by some source external to the judge, but only that it be constrained. To explain the source of constraint in the law, it is necessary to introduce two further concepts: One is the idea of disciplining rules, which constrain the interpreter and constitute the standards by which the correctness of the interpretation is to be judged; the other is the idea of an interpretive community, which recognizes these rules as authoritative.

The idea of objective interpretation accommodates the creative role of the reader. It recognizes that the meaning of a text does not reside in the text, as an object might reside in physical space or as an element might be said to be present in a chemical compound, ready to be extracted if only one knows the correct process; it recognizes a role for the subjective. Indeed, interpretation is defined as the process by which the meaning of a text is understood and expressed, and the acts of understanding and expression necessarily entail strong personal elements. At the same time, the freedom of the interpreter is not absolute. The interpreter is not free to assign any meaning he wishes to the text. He is disciplined by a set of rules that specify the relevance and weight to be assigned to the material (e.g., words, history, intention consequence), as well as by those that define basic concepts and that established the procedural circumstances under which the interpretation must occur.

The disciplining rules may vary from text to text. The rules for the interpretation of a poem differ from those governing the interpretation of legal material; and even within the law, there may be different rules depending on the text—those for contractual interpretation vary from statutory interpretation, and both vary from those used in constitutional interpretation. Though the particular content of disciplining rules varies, their function is the same. They constrain the interpreter, thus transforming the interpretive process from a subjective to an objective one, and they furnish the standards by which the correctness of the interpretation can be judged. These rules are not simply standards or principles held by individual judges, but instead constitute the institution (the profession) in which judges find themselves and through which they act. The disciplining rules operate similarly to the rules of language, which constrain the users of the language, furnish the standards for judging the uses of language, and constitute the language. The disciplining rules of the law may be understood . . . as a professional grammar.

Rules are not rules unless they are authoritative, and that authority can only be conferred by a community. Accordingly, the disciplining rules that govern an interpretive activity must be seen as defining or demarcating an interpretive community consisting of those who recognize the rules as authoritative. This means, above all else, that the objective quality of interpretation is bounded, limited, or relative. It is bounded by the existence of a community that recognizes and adheres to the disciplining rules used by the interpreter and that is defined by its recognition of those rules. The objectivity of the physical world may be more transcendent, less relativistic, though the Kuhnian tradition in the philosophy of science throws considerable doubt on that commonsense understanding; but as revealed by the reference to language, and the analogy I have drawn between the rules of language and the disciplining rules of interpretation, the physical does not exhaust the claim of objectivity, nor does it make this bounded objectivity of interpretation a secondary or parasitic kind of objectivity. Bounded objectivity is the only kind of objectivity to which the law—or any interpretive activity—ever aspires and the only one about which we care. To insist on more, to search for the brooding omnipresence in the sky, is to create a false issue.

. . .

. . . For my purposes, it is sufficient to recognize the distinctive feature of legal interpretation: In law the interpretive community is a reality. It has authority to confer because membership does not depend on agreement. Judges do not belong to an interpretive community as a result of shared views about particular issues or interpretations, but belong by virtue of a commitment to uphold and advance the rule of law itself. They belong by virtue of their office. There can be many schools of literary interpretation, but as Jordan Flyer put it, in legal interpretation there is only one school and attendance is mandatory. All judges define themselves as members of this school and must do so in order to exercise the prerogatives of their office. Even if their personal commitment to the rule of law wavers, the rule continues to act on judges; even if the rule of law fails to persuade, it can coerce. Judges know that if they relinquish their membership in the interpretive community, or deny its authority, they lose their right to speak with the authority of the law.

Nothing I have said denies the possibility of disagreement in legal interpretation. Some disputes may be centered on the correct application of a rule of discipline. For example, a dispute may arise over a rule that requires the interpreter to look to history. Some may claim that the judge has misunderstood the history of the fourteenth amendment or that he is using a level of generality that is inappropriate for constitutional interpretation. They may claim, for example, that the focus should not be on the existence of segregated schools in 1868 or on the willingness of those who drafted and adopted the fourteenth amendment to tolerate segregated schools, but on the framers' desire to eradicate the caste system and the implication of that desire for segregated education today. Disputes of this kind are commonplace, but they pose little threat to the legitimacy of the disciplining rules; they pose only issues of application.

Other disputes may arise, however, and they may involve a challenge to the very authority or existence of a rule. Some judges or lawyers may, for example, deny the relevance of history altogether in constitutional interpretation. Disputes of this type pose a more serious challenge to the idea of objectivity than those over the application of a rule, for such disputes threaten the source of constraint itself. It should be remembered, however, that in the law there are procedures for resolving these disputes—for example, pronouncements by the highest court and perhaps even legislation and constitutional amendments. The presence of such procedures and a hierarchy of authority for resolving disputes that could potentially divide or destroy an interpretive community is one of the distinctive features of legal interpretation. One should also be careful not to exaggerate the impact of such disputes. The authority of a particular rule can be maintained even when it is disputed, provided the disagreement is not too pervasive; the integrity of an interpretive community can be preserved even in the face of a dispute or disagreement as to the authority of some particular disciplining rule. The legal community transcends cliques; some cliques may dissolve over time, others may come to dominate the community.

Just as objectivity is compatible with a measure of disagreement, it should also be stressed that objectivity is compatible with error: An objective interpretation is not necessarily a correct one. *Brown v. Board of Education* and *Plessy v. Ferguson,* one condemning segregation, the other approving it, may both be objective and thus legitimate exercises of the judicial power, though only one is correct. To understand how this is possible, we must first recognize that legal interpretations can be evaluated from two perspectives, one internal, the other external.

From the internal perspective, the standards of evaluation are the disciplining rules themselves, and the authority of the interpretive community is fully acknowledged. The criticism, say, of *Plessy v. Ferguson* might be that the judges did not correctly understand the authoritative rules, or may have misapplied them; the judges may have failed to grasp the constitutional ideal of equality imported into the Constitution by the fourteenth amendment, or incorrectly assumed that the affront to blacks entailed in the Jim Crow system was self-imposed. Though such a criticism argues that the interpretation is mistaken, it might well acknowledge the objective character of the interpretation on the theory, borrowed from Wittgenstein, that misunderstanding is a form of understanding, that a judge could misunderstand or misapply a rule and still be constrained by it. An objective but (legally) incorrect interpretation partakes of the impersonality or sense of constraint implied by the idea of law. Not every mistake in adjudication is an example of lawlessness.

The internal perspective permits another type of criticism in which both the objectivity and the correctness of the decision may be challenged. The charge may be that the judge utterly disregarded well-recognized disciplining rules, such as those requiring the judge to take account of the

intention of the framers of the fourteenth amendment or those rules prohibiting the judge from being influenced by personal animosities or bias.
If these are the bases of criticism of the judicial decision, and arguably
they may have some relevance to *Plessy*, then the claim is that the
interpretation is both wrong and non-objective. I imagine that it is also
possible for an interpretation to be both non-objective and correct, as when
a judge pretty much decides to do what he wishes, that is, once again
utterly disregards the disciplining rules, and yet in this instance gives
the text the same meaning—in a substantive sense—as would a fair and
conscientious judge constrained by all the appropriate rules. Such a
situation does not seem to be of great practical importance, but it once
again illustrates the analytic distinction between objectivity and correctness, even from the wholly internal perspective. Both qualities arise from
the very same rules: Objectivity speaks to the constraining force of the
rules and whether the act of judging is constrained; correctness speaks
to the content of the rules and whether the process of adjudication and
the meaning produced by that process are fully in accord with that
content. From the internal perspective, legitimacy largely turns on
objectivity rather than correctness; judges are allowed to make some
mistakes.

The internal perspective does not exhaust all evaluation of legal
interpretation. Someone who stands outside of the interpretive community and thus disputes the authority of that community and its rules may
provide another viewpoint. A criticism from this so-called external perspective might protest *Plessy* on the basis of some religious or ethical
principle (e.g., denying the relevance of any racial distinction) or on the
grounds of some theory of politics (e.g., condemning the decision because
it will cause social unrest). In that instance, the evaluation is not in terms
of the law; it matters not at all whether the decision is objective. It may
be law, even good law, but it is wrong, whether morally, politically, or
from a religious point of view.

The external critic may accept the pluralism implied by the adjectives
"legal," "moral," "political," and "religious," each denoting different standards of judgment or different spheres of human activity. The external
critic may be able to order his life in a way that acknowledges the validity
of the legal judgment and that at the same time preserves the integrity
of his view, based on non-legal standards, about the correctness of the
decision. He may render unto the law that which is the law's. Conflict
is not a necessity, but it does occur, as it did over the extension of slavery
in the 1850s and over the legalization of abortion in the 1970s. The external critic will then have to establish priorities. He may move to amend
the Constitution or engage in any number of lesser and more problematic
strategies designed to alter the legal standards, such as packing the court
or enacting statutes that curtail jurisdiction. Failing that, he remains free
to insist that the moral, religious, or political principle take precedence
over the legal. He can disobey.

One of the remarkable features of the American legal system is that
it permits such a broad range of responses to the external critic, and that
over time—maybe in some instances over too much time—the legal
system responds to this criticism. The law evolves. There is progress in
the law. An equally remarkable feature of the American system is that
the freedom of the external critic to deny the law, and to insist that his
moral, religious, or political views take precedence over the legal interpretation, is a freedom that is not easily exercised. Endogenous change is
always preferred, even in the realm of the wholly intellectual. The
external critic struggles to work within the law, say, through amendments, appointments, or inducing the Supreme Court to recognize that

it had made a mistake. An exercise of the freedom to deny the law, and to insist that his moral, religious, or political views take precedence, requires the critic to dispute the authority of the Constitution and the community that it defines, and that is a task not lightly engaged. The authority of the law is bounded, true, but as de Tocqueville recognized more than a century ago, in America those bounds are almost without limits. The commitment to the rule of law is nearly universal.

. . .

. . . My defense of adjudication as objective interpretation . . . assumes that the Constitution has some meaning—more specifically, that the text embodies the fundamental public values of our society. I have confronted the nihilism that claims the Constitution means everything; but my defense does not work . . . if it is said that the Constitution has no meaning, for there is no theory of legitimacy that would allow judges to interpret texts that themselves mean nothing. The idea of adjudication requires that there exist constitutional values to interpret, just as much as it requires that there be constraints on the interpretive process. Lacking such a belief, adjudication is not possible, only power.

The roots of this alternative version of nihilism are not clear to me, but its significance is unmistakable. The great public text of modern America, the Constitution, would be drained of meaning. It would be debased. It would no longer be seen as embodying a public morality to be understood and expressed through rational processes like adjudication; it would be reduced to a mere instrument of political organization—distributing political power and establishing the modes by which that power will be exercised. Public values would be defined only as those held by the current winners in the processes prescribed by the Constitution; beyond that, there would be only individual morality, or even worse, only individual interests.

Against the nihilism that scoffs at the idea that the Constitution has any meaning, it is difficult to reason. The issue seems to be one of faith, intuition, or maybe just insight. This form of nihilism seems so thoroughly at odds with the most elemental reading of the text itself and with almost 200 years of constitutional history as to lead me to wonder whether anything can be said in response. On the other hand, I believe it imperative to respond, in word and in deed, for this nihilism calls into question the very point of constitutional adjudication; it threatens our social existence and the nature of public life as we know it in America; and it demeans our lives. It is the deepest and darkest of all nihilisms. It must be combated and can be, though perhaps only by affirming the truth of that which is being denied—the idea that the Constitution embodies a public morality and that a public life founded on that morality can be rich and inspiring.

Acknowledging that he shares many of Fiss's basic values, Professor Sanford Levinson of the University of Texas School of Law regretfully finds that he cannot intellectually accept Fiss's argument. Levinson argues that Fiss's view presumes an "interpretive community" that does not exist and boils down to a strong rhetorical appeal for a particular position. Interpretation therefore lacks even the limited measure of "objectivity" that Fiss claimed was possible. Sanford Levinson, *Law as Literature*, 60 TEX. L. REV. 373, 378–84, 394–96, 399–402 (1982):[8]

Two classic approaches to understanding a written constitution involve emphasizing either the allegedly plain words of the text or the certain meaning to be given those words through historical reconstruction. I think it fair to say that these particular approaches are increasingly without defenders, at least in the academic legal community. . . .

As Richard Rorty has pointed out, however, there are at least two options open to critics who reject the two approaches outlined above but who, nonetheless, remain interested in interpreting the relevant texts. The first option involves the use of an allegedly more sophisticated method to extract the true meaning of the text. Thus Rorty refers to "the kind of textualist who claims to have gotten the secret of the text, to have broken its code," as a "weak" textualist, where the term is seemingly a metaphor for the power of the individual critic. . . . A "weak" textualist "is just doing his best to imitate science—he wants a *method* of criticism and he wants everybody to agree that he has cracked the code. He wants all the comforts of consensus, even if only the consensus of readers of the literary quarterlies" (or law reviews).

Perhaps the best current example of such a "weak" textualist is John Hart Ely, whose *Democracy and Distrust,* however radical some of its criticisms of so-called "interpretivism" purport to be, is merely the latest effort to crack the code of the United States Constitution and discover its true essence. . . . Ely is engaged in a "quest for the ultimate constitutional interpretivism" which would in effect foreclose further debate about the genuine meaning of the Constitution.

. . . Ely is savagely critical of those who seek constitutional meaning in the isolated words of the clauses themselves. . . . Ely looks instead to the overall structure of the Constitution for guidance. If the lines themselves are no longer a plausible source of meaning, there is still a Constitution to be discovered "between the lines," as it were, in the interplay of conceptual structures—states, nation, citizens, republican government—that are undoubtedly present in the constitutional text. Consequently, Ely's structuralism is no less addicted to a search for the "one-and-only truth" about the Constitution than are its discredited competitors. He continues to presuppose what Rorty calls a *"privileged vocabulary,* the vocabulary which gets to the essence of the object" and "expresses the properties which it has in itself as opposed to those we read into it."

No one can read Ely and miss his anger at those who merely read their own views into the Constitution. Indeed, most of Ely's reviewers agree with him at least on this last point, even as they criticize him for reading *his* preferred views into the Constitution. What unites Ely and most of his critics, though, is the continued belief that there is something "in" the Constitution that can be extracted if only we can figure out the best method to mine its meaning.

Against such weak textualists—the decoders, whatever the fanciness of their methods of decoding—Rorty posits "strong" textualists, who reject the whole notion of questing for the essential meanings of a text. "Strong," it should be emphasized, refers to the power of the critic, not the power of the text (or of its author). According to Stanley Fish, one of the leading proponents of this approach, "Interpretation is not the art of construing but the art of constructing. Interpreters do not decode poems; they make them." Fish has argued that "[t]he objectivity of the text is an illusion and, moreover, a dangerous illusion, because it is so physically convincing. The illusion is one of self-sufficiency and completeness. A line of print or a page is so obviously *there.* . . that it seems to be the sole repository of whatever value and meaning we associate with it."

Instead Fish emphasizes the reader's active role and concomitant inability to measure any given interpretation against the "actual" text. He correctly insists that the debate about what it means to read a text is of more than academic interest:

> [D]ifferent notions of what it is to read . . . are finally different notions of what it is to be human. In [one] view, the world, or the world of the text, is already ordered and filled with significances and what the reader is required to do is get them out (hence the question, "What did you get out of that?"). In short, the reader's job is to extract the meanings that formal patterns possess prior to, and independently of, his activities. In my view [on the other hand], these same activities are constitutive of a structure of concerns which is necessarily prior to any examination of meaningful patterns because it is itself the occasion of their coming into being.

As Fish notes, "The difference in the two views is enormous." The first one regards "human beings as passive and disinterested comprehenders of a knowledge external to them (that is, of an *objective* knowledge)."[33] It is worth noting, I believe, that Felix Frankfurter's favorite single word was "disinterested," and that the ideology of the Harvard Law School, from Langdell's time to the days of Hart and Sacks and afterward, can be regarded as centered around the search for a "disinterested," impersonal approach to legal analysis.

The view endorsed by Fish regards "human beings as at every moment creating the experiential spaces into which a personal knowledge flows." Meaning is created rather than discovered, though the source of creative energy is the particular community within which one finds him or herself. . . .

The patron saint of all strong textualists is Nietzsche:

> [W]hatever exists, having somehow come into being, is again and again reinterpreted to new ends, taken over, transformed, and redirected by some power superior to it; all events in the organic world are a subduing, a *becoming master,* and all subduing and becoming master involves a fresh interpretation, an adaptation through which any previous "meaning" and "purpose" are necessarily obscured or even obliterated.

And the argument of Fish . . . and other strong textualists, whether American or continental, is *not* that they prefer to do their thing as an alternative to the more banal work of "truthseekers" . . . but rather that the project of ultimate truth-seeking is based on philosophical error. At the very least it presumes a privileged foundation for measuring the attainment of truth, and it is precisely this foundation that Nietzsche and most of the more radical literary theorists deny. Like Rorty, they do not substitute a new candidate for a winning method of how to recognize literary truth when one sees it; rather, they reject the very search for finality of interpretation.

---

[33] . . . I will quickly concede that courts and other constitutional interpreters operate within constraints. That is the importance of Fish's own distinction between "on-the-wall" and "off-the-wall" arguments; but the point is that whatever constraints exist are not constant over time.

. . .I agree. . . that the alternative to determinacy (certainty) is not an anything-goes indeterminacy. However, especially from the perspective of the losers in a necessarily coercive legal system, a court decision that remains even within the ambit of "on-the-wall" arguments may appear to be arbitrary (though not "whimsical"), given the presence of other available arguments that would have generated more palatable results.

To be sure, none of the radical critics defend the position that any interpretation is just as good as any other. Stanley Fish, for example, notes that he genuinely believes in the validity of any given view that he happens to hold, and he can present reasons for rejecting the views of his opponents on the interpretation of a given text. In this regard Fish seems similar to Ronald Dworkin, who views judging as including the phenomenological experience of feeling oneself to have achieved the uniquely correct solution even to a hard case. But Fish, more candid than Dworkin on this point, admits that his own conviction of rightness will provide no answer at all to anyone who happens to disagree with him, and that there is no way to resolve the dispute. It is at this point that he retreats to his Kuhnian emphasis on communities of understanding and shared conventions. It may be true that these communities will share, at any given moment, a sense of what distinguishes "on the wall" from "off the wall" arguments, but Fish is acutely aware of the contingency of such judgments. They describe only our own temporal sense of what is currently acceptable, rather than anything genuinely mirroring the essential characteristics of the texts being discussed.

. . .

Fiss's notion . . . is very close to Fish's emphasis on the importance of interpretive communities, and both have been influenced by the work of Thomas Kuhn.[85] It is easy enough to see why Fish and I find Kuhn's notions attractive, rooted as they are in the tradition of the sociology of knowledge and its rejection of the correspondence between ideas believed to be true and the external world itself. It is harder to understand Fiss's embrace of Kuhn, given that the key element in Fiss's program is his defense of the objective truthfulness of claims about public and constitutional values.[87] The notions of "truth according to the conventions of my community" and "objective knowledge as determined by my reference group" differ substantially from notions of unmodified "truth" or "objective knowledge." The former exist within the language of skepticism, including that most virulent form castigated as nihilism. It was Nietzsche, after all, who emphasized the reduction of "truth" to the views of one's own perspective (and who thus went on to assert the possibility of changing our world by adopting different perspectives).

Fiss is aware, of course, that legal adepts argue vigorously among themselves over the meaning of the Constitution; he does not seriously suggest that legal academicians are significantly more in agreement with one another than are professors of literature debating the meaning of a poem or a novel. His most interesting (and dubious) move, however, is to differentiate the lawyer from the literary critic by asserting the significance of the membership of the former in an interpretive community presided over by authoritative courts and judges. The legal system

---

[85] *See* T. KUHN, THE ESSENTIAL TENSION: SELECTED STUDIES IN SCIENTIFIC TRADITION AND CHANGE (1977); T. KUHN [THE STRUCTURE OF SCIENTIFIC REVOLUTIONS (2d ed. 1970).] [Ed. note: Thomas S. Kuhn was a historian and philosopher of science whose influential and controversial book, THE STRUCTURE OF SCIENTIFIC REVOLUTIONS (1962; 3d ed. 1996), discussed such concepts as "paradigm shift" in scientific theories. His emphasis on social and psychological factors in the development of science has been drawn upon by postmodernist thinkers, *see infra,* for the support it lends to the idea that theories are social constructions rather than reflections of external reality.]

[87] In fairness to Fiss, I should note that he does not specifically endorse a correspondence theory of truth and, indeed, he specifically recognizes the participation of a reader-judge in bestowing meaning upon textual materials. "The idea of objective interpretation accommodates *the creative role* of the reader." Fiss, [*Objectivity and Interpretation,* 34 STAN. L. REV. 739, 744 (1982)] (emphasis added). Yet Fiss's article is replete with the tension generated by the joint embrace of creativity and objectivity.

offers procedures that can resolve disputes through, "for example, pronouncements by the highest court and perhaps even legislation and constitutional amendments. The presence of such procedures and a hierarchy of authority resolving disputes that could potentially divide or destroy an interpretive community is one of the distinctive features of legal interpretation." Ultimately, then, the judge is "a combination of literary critic and moral philosopher. But that is only part of the picture. The judge also speaks with the authority of the Pope."

This last assertion is directly relevant to an earlier essay of mine, in which I posited the existence of "protestant" and "catholic" approaches to the Constitution. That Fiss embraces a "catholic" Constitution, in the senses of looking to unwritten norms and accepting the institutional authority of the judiciary, tells us a great deal about him but only a little about the interpretive community. . . .

Fiss's approach to the Constitution, like that of Professor Dworkin, ultimately rests on the premise that there is no genuine conflict among the values that animate the different parts of the public. . . . But . . . the early dispute in our history about the power of Congress to charter the Bank of the United States ". . . demonstrated at the very outset that the Constitution had not displaced rival principles or reconciled them but had become their dialectical arena." This last term may bring to mind either the controversy of the seminar table or warfare in which each side claims adherence to the "true" meaning of the disputed document. It is the latter mode of dispute resolution that is suggested by Justice Black's comment that "the fundamental issues over the extent of federal supremacy had been resolved by war." But surely there is something peculiar about the assertion that fundamental ideological issues are "resolved" by war, even if we concede that political power indeed often comes from the barrels of guns, and even if it is possible to identify clearly the doctrinal position that won or lost a particular battle. . . .

The American wish is that one can avoid having to answer the political question posed by a Harlan County labor song, "Which side are you on?", by responding that one stands by the Constitution and that, in turn, the Constitution itself stands for the proper values. The transformation of political questions into legal questions, first emphasized by de Tocqueville, allows the "adjudication" of disputes. As Fiss notes, however, "The idea of adjudication requires that there exist constitutional values to interpret, just as much as it requires that there be constraints on the interpretive process. Lacking such a belief, adjudication is not possible, only power."

As he portrays the bleakness of a world that rejects belief in the possibility of principled adjudication, Fiss speaks with much of the same eloquence and vigor as does Gerald Graff. It is worth noting that Richard Rorty, whose work has much influenced me, has indicated his own empathy with the attacks of Graff and others on the new literary criticism. What is at stake is a conception of the possibility of a shared moral life. Rorty refers to "the view that, in the end, when all the intellectuals have done all their tricks, morality remains widely shared and available to reflection—something capable of being discovered rather than created, because already implicit in the common consciousness of everyone." Critics with this view "want criticism to bring an antecedent morality to light, enlarge upon it and enrich it," and they consequently "resist the suggestion that there is no common vocabulary in terms of which critics can argue with one another about how well this task has been performed." No one with a democratic sensibility can easily reject the vision of a common discourse described by Rorty and evoked by Fiss.

Empathy, however, does not equal agreement. It would be contradictory to say that the historicist pragmatism celebrated by Rorty is "true," or that philosophy has "disproved" the possibility of true and certain knowledge about the natural world, including its moral component. But those who do not already share Fiss's faith are unlikely, I suspect, to be persuaded by his attack on positions like the one articulated in the present essay. . . . The united interpretive community that is necessary to Fiss's own argument simply does not exist. What one does in the absence of such a community is, of course, a problem of more than merely theoretical import. The decreasing propensity of the body politic to accord the Supreme Court ultimate authority in constitutional interpretation may portend an ever deeper constitutional crisis, especially if any of the jurisdiction-and remedy-limiting bills now before Congress had passed and received presidential signature.

Both Levinson and Fiss refer to Stanley Fish, now Dean of the College of Liberal Arts and Sciences at the University of Illinois at Chicago. Fish began his work as a literary scholar and theorist but has gone on to provoke controversy among legal academics by bringing his ideas about interpretation to bear in debates about legal approaches. In a reply to Fiss's *Objectivity and Interpretation,* Fish argues that Fiss got Fish's notion of the "interpretive community" somewhat wrong. Fiss's view that rules about how to interpret could exercise a constraining force, Fish argues, suffers from a circularity problem: if they are really to constrain, they must have their force independently of being interpreted themselves. Yet that is impossible, for how is an interpreter to know what to make of a rule of interpretation? And once that problem exists, there arises the possibility of disagreement over the rules of interpretation—and there, Fish argues, goes their constraining force.

This description may have made Fish sound as "nihilistic" as Levinson (or as some others' characterizations of Levinson). But Fish would presumably reject the label, for he further contends that the lack of external constraints does not imply the lack of all constraint—far from it. External rules about interpretation are unnecessary, because the very act of interpretation already presumes that the interpreter is "deeply inside" an interpretive context, not rigidly bound but thinking in terms of existing, evolving practice. (For example, the game of baseball is not meaningfully "constrained" by rules external to baseball itself and is always developing, with changes in tactics, practices, and its own rules—will the designated hitter survive? Still, people learn how to play baseball and manage to have games that run without reference to a separate set of rules about how to construe the rules of sporting events. And if there were such a set, one who relied on those external rules but did not know a good deal about baseball already would probably be among the worst of umpires or even of rule-construers.)

One significant implication of Fish's argument is to collapse the distinction between theory and practice. Both the Constitution and ideas about how to interpret it, for example, are "texts" that we can do meaningful things with only by interpreting them. As we shall see, this argument does not satisfy Fiss; he sees Fish's fusion of theory and practice as amounting to the obliteration of the distinction between law and politics, which he is unwilling to accept. But first Fish, from *Fish v. Fiss,* 36 STAN. L. REV. 1325, 1325-47 (1984):[9]

Fiss proposes to recognize the contributions of both text and reader to the determination of meaning by placing between the two a set of "disciplining rules" derived from the specific institutional setting of the interpretive activity. These rules "specify the relevance and weight to be assigned to the material" and define the "basic concepts and . . . procedural circumstances under which the interpretation must occur." They thus act as constraints on the interpreter's freedom and direct him to those meanings in the text that are appropriate to a particular institutional context.

[T]his proposal seems reasonable enough, but ultimately it will not do, and it will not do because the hinge on which Fiss's account turns is not sufficiently fixed to provide the stability he needs. That hinge is the notion of "disciplining rules" that will constrain readers or interpreters and mitigate (if not neutralize) the inherent ambiguity of texts. The claim is that, given a particular situation, the rules tell you what to do and prevent you from simply doing whatever you like.

The trouble is that they don't. If the rules are to function as Fiss would have them function—to "constrain the interpreter"—they themselves must be available or "readable" independently of interpretation; that is, they must directly declare their own significance to any observer, no matter what his perspective. Otherwise they would "constrain" individual interpreters differently, and you would be right back in the original dilemma of a variously interpretable text and an interpretively free reader. . . . Unfortunately, rules *are* texts. They are in need of interpretation and cannot themselves serve as constraints on interpretation.

That at least is my argument, and we can test it by trying to think of some rules. Fiss does not spend much time telling us what the disciplining rules are like, but the general form they would take is clear from what he does say. They would be of at least two kinds, particular and general. A particular rule would be one that "specif[ied] the relevance and weight to be assigned to the material," and would presumably take a form like: "If someone takes the property of another without his consent, count that as larceny." A general rule would be one that defined the "basic concepts and . . . procedural circumstances under which the interpretation must occur," and its form would be something like: "Always consult history" (one of Fiss's examples, in fact). The problem with the particular rule is that there will always be disputes about whether the act is indeed a "taking" or even about what a "taking" is. And even where the fact of taking has been established to everyone's satisfaction, one can still argue that the result should be embezzlement or fraud rather than larceny. The same analysis holds for the more general rules. To say that one must always consult history does not prevent—but provokes—disagreements about exactly what history is, or about whether or not this piece of information counts as history, or (if it does count) about what its factual configurations are.

Fiss himself acknowledges the possibility of such disputes, but says that they "pose only issues of application"; that is to say, they do not affect the "legitimacy of the disciplining rules," which are still doing their disciplining. "The authority of a particular rule can be maintained even when it is disputed . . . .." But how can "it" be maintained *as a constraint*

---

[9] Copyright © 1984 by the Trustees of the Leland Stanford Junior University. Reprinted with permission.

when the dispute is about what "it" is or about what "it" means? Fiss assumes that one first "has" a rule and then interprets it. But if the shape of the rule could be had without interpretation, then the interpretation would be superfluous. And if interpretation is not superfluous to the "reading" of rules (Fiss would agree that it is not) then one only has rules in an interpreted shape. Thus we are back once again to my assertion that a so-called "disciplining rule" cannot be said to act as a constraint on interpretation because it is (in whatever form has been specified for it) the product of an interpretation.

This is true even in those cases where there are no disputes, where there is perfect agreement about what the rule is and what it means. There is a temptation (often irresistible to those on Fiss's side of the street) to assume that such cases of perfect agreement are normative and that interpretation and its troubles enter in only in special circumstances. But agreement is not a function of particularly clear and perspicuous rules; it is a function of the fact that interpretive assumptions and procedures are so widely shared in a community that the rule appears to all in the same (interpreted) shape. And if Fiss were to reply that I am not denying the existence—and authority—of disciplining rules, but merely suggesting a new candidate for them in the "persons" of interpretive assumptions and procedures, I would simply rehearse the argument of the previous paragraphs all over again, pointing out this time that interpretive assumptions and procedures can no more be grasped independently of interpretation than disciplining rules can; thus they cannot be thought of as constraints upon interpretation either.

The difficulty, in short, cannot be merely patched over; it pervades the entire situation in which someone (a judge, a literary critic) faced with the necessity of acting (rendering a judgment, turning out a reading) looks to some rule or set of rules that will tell him what to do. The difficulty becomes clear when the sequence—here I am, I must act, I shall consult the rule—becomes problematic in a way that cannot be remedied. Let us imagine that the President of the United States or some other appropriate official appoints to the bench someone with no previous judicial or legal experience. This person is, however, intelligent, mature, and well-informed. As she arrives to take up her new position she is handed a booklet and told "Here are the rules—go to it!" What would happen? The new judge would soon find that she was unable to read the rules without already having a working knowledge of the practices they were supposed to order, or, to put it somewhat more paradoxically, she would find that she could read the rules that are supposed to tell her what to do only when she already knew what to do. This is so because rules, in law or anywhere else, do not stand in an independent relationship to a field of action on which they can simply be imposed; rather, rules have a circular or mutually interdependent relationship to the field of action in that they make sense only in reference to the very regularities they are thought to bring about. The very ability to read the rules in an informed way presupposes an understanding of the questions that are likely to arise (should liability be shared or strictly assigned?), the kinds of decisions that will have to be made, the possible alternative courses of action (to dismiss, to render a summary judgment), the consequences (for future cases) of deciding one way or another, and the "deep" issues that underlie the issue of record (are we interested in retribution or prevention?). Someone who was without this understanding would immediately begin to ask questions about what a rule *meant,* and in answer would be told about this or that piece of practice in a way that would alert her to what was "going on" in some corner of the institutional field. She would then be able to read the rule because she would be seeing it as already embedded in the context of assumptions and practices that make it intelligible, a context that at once gives rise to it (in the sense that it is a response to needs that can be felt) and is governed by it.

Even that would not be the end of the matter. Practices are not fixed and finite—one could no more get out a list of them than one could get out a list of *the* rules. Sooner or later the new judge would find herself "misapplying" the rules she thought she had learned. In response to further questions she would discover that a situation previously mastered also intersected with a piece of the field of practice of which she had been ignorant; and in the light of this new knowledge she would see that the rule must be differently applied because in a sense it would be a different, though not wholly different, rule.

. . .

. . . A rule can never be made explicit in the sense of demarcating the field of reference independently of interpretation, but a rule can always be received as explicit by someone who hears it within an interpretive pre-understanding of what the field of reference could possibly be.

The moral of the story, then, is not that you could never learn enough to know what to do in every circumstance, but that what you learn cannot finally be reduced to a set of rules. Or, to put the case another way (it amounts to the same thing), insofar as the requisite knowledge *can* be reduced to a set of rules (. . . "Consult history"), it will be to rules whose very intelligibility depends on the practices they supposedly govern. Fiss believes that the rules must exist prior to practice, or else practice will be unprincipled; but . . . practice is already principled, since at every moment it is ordered by an understanding of what it is practice *of* . . . , an understanding that can always be put into the form of rules—rules that will be opaque to the outsider—but is not produced by them.

. . .

. . . In the course of explaining why rules cannot serve as constraints on interpretation, I have explained why rules (in that strong sense) are not necessary; and in the course of explaining why rules are unnecessary, I also have explained why the fear of unbridled interpretation—of interpreters whose determinations of meaning are unconstrained—is baseless. It is this fear that animates Fiss's entire enterprise, but it is a fear that assumes an interpreter who is at least theoretically free to determine meaning in any way he or she likes, and who therefore must be constrained by something *external,* by rules or laws. But on the analysis offered in the preceding paragraphs there can be no such interpreter. To be, as I have put it, "deeply inside" a context is to be already and always thinking (and perceiving) with and within the norms, standards, definitions, routines, and understood goals that both define and are defined by that context.

The point is an important one because it clarifies the relationship between my argument and Fiss's (which is not simply one of opposition, as it is, for example, in the dispute between Fiss and Sanford Levinson). The notion of disciplining rules is crucial to Fiss's account because it represents for him the chief constraint on the process of adjudication; and by taking away the firmness and independence of those rules I may seem to have undermined the process altogether by leaving an undisciplined interpreter confronting a polysemous text, with nothing between them to assure that the assignment of meaning will proceed in one direction rather than another. But these consequences follow only if readers and texts are in need of the constraints that disciplining rules would provide, and the implication of what I have already said is that they are not.

To see why they are not, one must remember that Fiss's account takes the form it does because he begins by assuming two kinds of independence, one good and one bad. The bad kind of independence attaches to readers and texts: Readers are free to choose any meanings they like, and texts contain too many meanings to guarantee a principled choice. The good kind of independence attaches to rules: Because they stand outside of or are prior to a field of interpretive practice, they can guide and control it in appropriate ways. The good kind of independence controls and disciplines the bad. My contention is that by showing why the good kind of independence can never be achieved, I have shown at the same time why the bad kind is never a possibility. Just as rules can be read only in the context of the practice they supposedly order, so are those who have learned to read them constrained by the assumptions and categories of understanding embodied in that same practice. It is these assumptions and categories that have been internalized in the course of training, a process at the end of which the trainee is not only possessed *of* but possessed *by* a knowledge of the ropes, by a tacit knowledge that tells him not so much what to do, but already has him doing it as a condition of perception and even of thought. The person who looks about and sees, without reflection, a field already organized by problems, impending decisions, possible courses of action, goals, consequences, desiderata, etc. is not free to choose or originate his own meanings, because a set of meanings has, in a sense, already chosen him and is working itself out in the actions of perception, interpretation, judgment, etc. he is even now performing. He is, in short, already filled with and constituted by the very meanings that on Fiss's account he is dangerously free to ignore. This amounts finally to no more, or less, than saying that the agent is always and already situated, and that to be situated is not to be looking about for constraints, or happily evading them (in the mode, supposedly, of nihilism), but to be constrained already. To be a judge or a basketball player is not to be able to consult the rules (or, alternatively, to be able to disregard them) but to have become an extension of the "know-how" that gives the rules (if there happen to be any) the meaning they will immediately and obviously have.

Of course, what holds for the rules holds too for every other "text" encountered in a field of practice, including the text with which Fiss is most concerned, the Constitution. Fiss believes that texts present the same liabilities (the liabilities of independence) as interpreters. Interpreters have too many choices; texts have too many meanings. "[F]or any text," he says, "there are any number of possible meanings and the interpreter creates a meaning by choosing one." I have tried to show why this is the wrong account of the position occupied by interpreters, and I shall now show why it is also (and for the same reasons) the wrong account of texts. Although Fiss says that any text has any number of possible meanings, we have already seen that for his system to work there must be at least some texts—i.e., disciplining rules—that have only one meaning, and we have seen too that (1) there are no such texts, and (2) the fact that there are no such texts is not fatal to the goal of principled interpretive behavior. The reason that this fact is not fatal is that there are also no texts that have a plurality of meanings, so that there is never a necessity of having to choose between them.

Now I know that this will seem immediately paradoxical. How can there be at once no texts that have a single meaning and no texts that have many meanings, and how can this impossible state of affairs (even if it could exist) be seen as a *solution* to the problem of interpretation? The answer to this question will emerge once we are no longer in the grip of the assumption that gives rise to the paradox, the assumption that texts "have" properties before they are encountered in situations, which is also the assumption that it is possible to encounter texts in anything but an already situated—that is, interpreted—condition.. . . . [A] sentence does not ask to be read in a particular way because it is a particular kind of sentence; rather, it is only in particular sets of circumstances that sentences are encountered at all, and the properties that sentences display are always a function of those circumstances. Since those circumstances (the conditions within which hearing and reading occur) can change, the properties that sentences display can also change; and it follows that when there is a disagreement about the shape or meaning of a sentence, it is a disagreement between persons who are reading or hearing (and therefore constituting) it according to the assumptions of different circumstances.

Everything that I have said about sentences applies equally, *mutatis mutandis,* to texts. If there are debates about what the Constitution means, it is not because the Constitution "provokes" debate, not because it is a certain *kind* of text, but because for persons reading (constituting) it within the assumption of different circumstances, different meanings will seem obvious and inescapable. By "circumstances" I mean, among other things, the very sense one has of what the Constitution is *for.* Is it an instrument for enforcing the intentions of the Framers? Is it a device for assuring the openness of the political process? Is it a blueprint for the exfoliation of a continually evolving set of fundamental values? Depending on the interpreter's view of what the Constitution is for, he will be inclined to ask different questions, to consider different bodies of information as sources of evidence, to regard different lines of inquiry as relevant or irrelevant, and, finally, to reach different determinations of what the Constitution "plainly" means. Notice, however, that these differences are not infinite; at any one time there are only so many views as to what the Constitution is for; and therefore even those who are proceeding within different views and arguing for different meanings are constrained in their proceedings by the shared (if tacit) knowledge that (1) the number of such views is limited, and (2) they are all views of the *Constitution,* a document whose centrality is assumed by all parties to the debate. (Here is a way in which it does make a kind of sense to say that the Constitution "provokes" debate—not because of any properties it "has," but because the position it occupies in the enterprise is such that specification of its meaning is the business everyone is necessarily in.) Even when the central text of the enterprise is in dispute, all parties to the dispute are already situated within the enterprise, and the ways of disputing and the versions of the Constitution produced by those ways are "enterprise specific." What this means is that the Constitution is never in the condition that occasions the urgency of Fiss's essay—it is never an object waiting around for interpretation; rather, it is always an already-interpreted object, even though the interpretations it has received and the forms it has taken are in conflict with one another.

How are these conflicts to be settled? The answer to this question is that they are always in the process of being settled, and that no transcendent or algorithmic method of interpretation is required to settle them. The means of settling them are political, social, and institutional, in a mix that is itself subject to modification and change. This means, of course, that the *arena* of settling is never purely internal; and indeed the distinction between the internal and the external is in general less firm and stable than Fiss assumes. He makes the point that judgments concerning the law are sometimes made from an "external perspective" by someone who is operating "on the basis of some religious or ethical principle (such as denying the relevance of any racial distinction) or on the grounds of some theory of politics (such as condemning the decision because it will cause social unrest)." In such instances, he concludes, "the

evaluation is not in terms of the law." Well, yes and no. If Fiss means
by this that the evaluation originates from a source that is not part of
the "judicial system," narrowly conceived, then his statement is both true
and trivial; but if he means that an evaluation emanating from some
social, political, religious, or moral concern is not a legal one, then he is
propounding a notion of the law that is as positivistic as it is
impossible. . . .

[I]n fact the entire system is political, and the question at any moment
is: From which point in the system is pressure being applied, and to what
other points? It is no more illegitimate to enact statutes or to make appointments than it is to engage in the slower and less theatrical activity
of amending the Constitution. The processes for executing any of these
courses of action are already in place, and they have been put in place
by political acts. The fact that one rather than another course is taken
reflects the conditions obtaining in the entire system, not a bypassing of
the system or an unwarranted intrusion on proper legal procedure.

Consider, for example, the course of "packing the Court." That phrase,
now laden with pejorative connotations, refers to an attempt by Franklin
Delano Roosevelt to assure that the ethical and social philosophy informing the Court's decisions was similar to his own. Roosevelt made that
attempt not as an anarchist or an outlaw but as a political agent whose
actions were subject to the approval or disapproval of other political
agents, all of whom were operating within a system of constraints that
made it possible for him to do something but not everything. In other
words, "packing the Court" is a possible legal strategy, but it can be
successful only if other parts of the legal system assist it or fail to block
it. The fact that Roosevelt was in fact blocked is not to be explained by
saying that a "lesser" strategy was foiled by a legitimate one, but by
saying that the political forces always at work in the system exist in ever
changing relationships of strength and influence. (It is not the case that
because Roosevelt was unable to do it it can never be done; but it is true
that doing it has been made harder by the fact that he tried and failed.)

At times the disposition of the entire system will be such that the
judiciary can settle constitutional questions by routine procedures and
in accordance with principles that have been long articulated and accepted; at other times the legislature or the executive will feel called upon
to intervene strongly in an attempt to alter those principles and institute
new procedures. The mistake is to think that one state of affairs is
normative and "legal" while the other is extraordinary and "external."
Both are perfectly legal and normative; they simply represent different
proportions of the mix of agencies that participate in the ongoing project
of determining what the Constitution is. The same analysis holds for the
oft-opposed policies of judicial restraint and judicial activism. It is often
assumed that the one indicates a respect for the Constitution while the
other is an unwarranted exercise of interpretive power, as influenced by
social and political views; but in fact, so-called judicial restraint is
exercised by those judges who, for a variety of reasons, decide to leave
in place the socially and politically based interpretations of the activists
of an earlier generation.

It is time, I think, to take stock and look back at the argument as it
has unfolded so far. The first thing to recall is that Fiss's account of
adjudication is inspired by the fear that interpretation will be unprincipled, either because (1) the "interaction" between the reader and the text
is not sufficiently constrained by rules that put limits on the freedom of
the one and the polysemy of the other, or because (2) interpretive
authority is simply a function of the power wielded by those who happen

to occupy dominant positions in certain political or bureaucratic structures. I have argued against the first version of this fear by pointing out that readers and texts are never in a state of independence such that they would need to be "disciplined" by some external rule. Since readers are already and always thinking within the norms, standards, criteria of evidence, purposes, and goals of a shared enterprise, the meanings available to them have been preselected by their professional training; they are thus never in the position of confronting a text that has not already been "given" a meaning by the *interested* perceptions they have developed. More generally, whereas Fiss thinks that readers and texts are in need of constraints, I would say that they *are* structures of constraint, at once components of and agents in the larger structure of a field of practices, practices that are the content of whatever "rules one might identify as belonging to the enterprise. At every point then, I am denying the independence (of both the "good" and "bad" kinds) that leads Fiss first to see a problem and then to propose its solution.

The second version of Fiss's fear—that the law may be nothing but "masked power"—is merely a "bogeyman" reformulation of the first, and it can be disposed of in the same way. By "masked power," Fiss means authority that is not related to any true principle, but that instead represents a "mere" exercise of some official will. . . .

. . .

The opposition between legitimate (virtue-based) and illegitimate (power-based) authority is for Fiss part of a broader opposition between authority of any kind and interpretation:

> It is important to note that the claim of authoritativeness, whether it be predicated on virtue or power, is extrinsic to the process of interpretation. It does not arise from the act of interpretation itself and is sufficient to distinguish the judge from the literary critic or moral philosopher who must rely on intellectual authority alone.

Obviously there is a harmless (and trivial) sense in which what Fiss says is true: Arriving at a judicial decision and subsequently enforcing it are distinct processes, in the sense that the one precedes the other; but to say that one is *extrinsic* to the other is to attribute to both of them an independence and purity that neither could have. That is to say, neither "arises" from the other, since they both "arise" from the same set of institutional imperatives. Interpretation is not an abstract or contextless process, but one that elaborates itself in the service of a specific enterprise, in this case the enterprise of the law; the interpretive "moves" that occur to a judge, for example, occur to him in a shape already informed by a general sense of what the law is *for,* of what its operations are intended to promote and protect. Even when the particulars are the subject of debate, it is that general sense that legitimizes interpretation, because it is the content of interpretation. As we have seen, it is that same general sense that legitimizes (because it is the content of) authority, whether of the virtue-based or power-based variety. To put the matter starkly, interpretation is a form of authority, since it is an extension of the prestige and power of an institution; and authority is a form of interpretation, since it is in its operations an application or "reading" of the principles embodied in that same institution. So while it is possible to distinguish between these two activities on a narrow procedural level (on the level, for example, of temporal precedence), it is not possible to distinguish between them as activities essentially different in kind.

. . .

It may seem that by collapsing so many distinctions—between the intellectual and the institutional, between authority and power, between

virtue and authority—I am undermining the possibility of rational
adjudication; but in fact, everything I have said points to the conclusion
that adjudication does not need these distinctions (any more than it needs
"disciplining rules") to be rational. All it needs is an understanding,
largely tacit, of the enterprise's general purpose; with that in place (and
it could not help but be) everything else follows. Fiss knows this too, but
not in a way that figures strongly in his analysis. He knows, for example,
that "[a] judge quickly learns to read in a way that avoids crises," and
that "[t]he judge must give a remedy"; but he does not recognize such facts
for what they are: the very motor of adjudication and a guarantee of its
orderliness. The judge who has learned to read in a way that avoids crises
is a judge who has learned what it means to be a judge, and has learned
that the maintenance of continuity is a prime judicial obligation because
without continuity the rule of law cannot claim to be stable and rooted
in durable principles. It is not simply that crisis would be disruptive of
the process, but that crisis and disruption are precisely what the process
is supposed to forestall. That is why the judge must give a remedy: not
only because the state, defendant, and plaintiff have a right to one, but
also because every time a remedy is given the message is repeated that
there is always a remedy to be found, and that the law thereby under-
writes and assures the ongoing and orderly operations of society.

. . .

. . . Legal texts might be written in verse or take the form of narratives
or parables (as they have in some cultures); but so long as the underlying
rationales of the enterprise were in place, so long as it was understood
(at a level too deep to require articulation) that judges give remedies and
avoid crises, those texts would be explicated so as to yield the determinate
or settled result the law requires. In both law and literature it is ways
of reading, inseparable from the fact of the institution itself, and not rules
or special kinds of texts that validate and justify the process of rational
interpretation, whether it leads to the rendering of a clear-cut legal
decision or to the demonstration that what is valuable about a poem is
its resolute refusal to decide.

All of which is to say that, while I stand with Fiss in his desire to defend
adjudication in the face of "nihilist" and "subjectivist" arguments, I do not
believe that this defense need take the form of asserting a set of external
constraints, because the necessary constraints are always already in
place. Indeed, I would put the case even more strongly: It is not just that
the dangers Fiss would guard against—the dangers of excessive interpretive freedom, of "masked power," of random or irresponsible activity—
have been neutralized, but that they are *unrealizable,* because the
conditions that would make them the basis of a reasonable fear—the
condition of free subjectivity, of "naturally" indeterminate texts, of
unprincipled authority—could never obtain. . . .

. . . On my analysis, the Constitution cannot be drained of meaning,
because it is not a repository of meaning; rather, meaning is always being
conferred on it by the very political and institutional forces Fiss sees as
threats. Nor can these forces be described as "mere," because their shape
and exercise are constrained by the very principles they supposedly
endanger. And, since the operation of these forces is indeed principled,
the fact that they determine (for a time) what will be thought of as "public
values" is not something to be lamented, but simply a reflection of the
even more basic fact that values derive from the political and social visions
that are always competing with one another for control of the state's
machinery. Moreover, such values are never "individual," since they
always have their source in some conventional system of purposes, goals,
and standards; therefore, the very notion of "merely individual" interests

is empty. In short, if *these* are the fears that animate Fiss's efforts, then there is nothing for him to worry about.

Paradoxically, he need not even be worried by the possibility that his account of adjudication might be wrong. Fiss believes that it is important to get things right because, if we don't, nihilism might triumph. Nihilism must therefore be "combated" in "word and in deed" because it "calls into question the very point of constitutional adjudication." But if I am right, nihilism is impossible; one simply cannot "exalt the . . . subjective dimension of interpretation" or drain texts of meanings, and it is unnecessary to combat something that is not possible. Of course, there may be people who regard themselves as nihilists or subjectivists . . . and who try to instruct others in nihilist ways, but the fact that they intend the impossible does not make them capable of doing it; they would simply be conferring meanings and urging courses of action on the basis of principles they had not fully comprehended. One could of course combat those principles and dispute those meanings; but in doing so one would simply be urging alternative courses of action, not combating nihilism.

Another way of putting this is to say that nothing turns on Fiss's account or, for that matter, on my account either. To be sure, one would rather be right than wrong, but in this case being right or wrong has no consequences for the process we are both trying to describe.[44] Fiss thinks otherwise; he thinks that there are consequences and that they are grave ones: "Viewing adjudication as interpretation helps to stop the slide toward nihilism. It makes law possible." But if the slide toward nihilism is not a realizable danger, the urging of nihilist views cannot accelerate it, and, conversely, the refutation of nihilist views cannot retard it. From either direction, the account one has of adjudication is logically independent of one's ability to engage in it. Your account may be nihilist or (as it is for Fiss) objectivist or (as it is for me) conventionalist, and when all is said and done, adjudication is still either possible or it is not. The empirical evidence is very strong that it is; and it has been my argument that its possibility is a consequence of being situated in a field of practice, of having passed through a professional initiation or course of training and become what the sociologists term a "competent member." Owen Fiss has undergone that training, but I have not; and, therefore, even though I believe that his account of adjudication is wrong and mine is right, anyone who is entering the legal process would be well-advised to consult Fiss rather than Fish.

Briefly, there follow a few extracts from Fiss's reply to Levinson and Fish. Fiss sees himself and Fish as occupying a middle ground between writers like Ely, whom Fiss regards as too deterministic, and Levinson, whose view Fiss sees as too unconstrained. Still, Fiss argues that there remain significant differences between Fish and himself. The reader should consider whether Fiss succeeds in drawing a line between law and politics, or whether he

---

[44] There is a large issue to be considered here, the issue of the consequences of theory in general. It is my position that theory has no consequences, at least on the level claimed for it by its practitioners. Rather than standing in a relationship of precedence and governance to practice, theory is (when it happens to be a feature of an enterprise) a form of practice whose consequences (if there are any) are unpredictable and no different in kind from the consequences of any form of practice. Both those who fear theory and those who identify it with salvation make the mistake of conceiving of it as a special kind of activity, one that stands apart from the practices it would ground and direct. If there were a theory so special, it would have nothing to say to practice at all; and, on the other hand, a theory that does speak meaningfully to practice is simply an item in the landscape of practices.

reflects only a deep wish that there be such a line. Owen Fiss, *Conventionalism*, 58 S. CAL. L. REV. 177, 184–86, 192–97 (1985):[10]

Fish emphasizes practice and I emphasize norms. Compared to my disagreement with those at the ends of the spectrum—Ely . . . at one, Levinson at the other—this difference might seem trivial (and probably accounts for the play on the similarity of our names in Fish's title and the difficulty some may have in remembering who's who). But I believe the difference between us is worth noting: Fish's account of these constraints trivializes the reflective moments of the law and, like Levinson's account (but for different reasons), blurs the distinction between law and politics.

. . . Fish makes two claims about the disciplining rules: first, they will not work, and second, they are unnecessary.

Disciplining rules are, as I have said, to provide constraints. . . . I agree that disciplining rules must be interpreted and like Fish conceive of the interpretive process as a dynamic interaction between the text and the reader; but none of this renders these rules incapable of constraining the interpretive process.

To see this, let us return to *Brown.* The Justices' task was to determine whether segregated schools were consistent with the promise of equality in the fourteenth amendment. This seems like a rather open-ended judgment, one in which the Justices could have said a large number of things or, as Levinson (invoking a notable image of Richard Rorty) might put it, they could have beaten the text into any shape that served their purposes. I maintain, however, that their freedom was in fact bounded by certain disciplining rules, some that required them to pay attention to precedents, others that directed their attention to the purposes of the Civil War and the fourteenth amendment, and still others that precluded them from favoring one side over the other simply because of the race of the parties. Under my view of interpretation, judges faced with an open-ended question (such as whether Jim Crow laws are consistent with equal protection) are increasingly circumscribed in their discretion by more particularized constraints (which direct their attention to the framers' intent, precedent, etc.). The image I have in mind is that of a judge moving toward judgment along a spiral of norms that increasingly constrain.

At any point in the spiral there might be a disagreement over the meaning of a rule (just as there might be disagreement over whether the conditions that make the rule applicable are present). There may, for example, be a dispute as to the level of authorial intent one must look to—whether it be the particularized desires of the framers with regard to segregated schools or, as Dworkin would maintain, their general concept of equality. To resolve this dispute, the disciplining rules must be interpreted, and the process of interpreting those rules must itself be constrained by other norms further along or higher up the spiral. Of course, if the dispute about any norm is so pervasive as to return one to the previous level of constraint, then we have made no progress. The judge is as unconstrained as before we made any mention of disciplining rules.

In my original article I acknowledged the possibility of disputes over a disciplining rule, but then confidently asserted, "The authority of a particular rule can be maintained even when it is disputed. . . ." To this Fish replies, "But how can 'it' be maintained as a constraint when the dispute is about what 'it' is or about what 'it' means?" I would answer:

---

the same way that the Constitution, or a statute, or a common law rule can be "maintained" as a constraint even though there are disputes as to its meaning. Disputes over the meaning of a text deny neither the existence of the text nor that it has a meaning which can inform, guide or constrain intellectual processes.

. . .

In insisting that the disciplining rules will not work, Fish is not making a claim about the pervasiveness of disagreement or of disputes about the meaning of disciplining rules. He is not making a claim about indeterminacy but about contextualization. He notes that disciplining rules, like any text, are always situated within a practice and thus are always interpreted, even where there is perfect agreement as to what they mean. And from this rather straightforward observation Fish concludes that these rules cannot constrain: "[A] so-called 'disciplining rule' cannot be said to act as a constraint on interpretation because it is (in whatever form has been specified for it) the product of one."

I am a conventionalist insofar as I see all texts and agents as situated. I agree with Fish that all disciplining rules, even where there is no dispute as to their meaning, are in need of interpretation and have in fact received that interpretation. Like all texts, disciplining rules are always contextualized and arrive in an "interpreted shape." But that does not reduce (in either a logical or practical sense) the content or meaning of a rule to its various interpretations, nor does it mean that one text (disciplining rules) cannot constrain the interpretation of another text (the Constitution).

. . .

. . . The Constitution for Fish is not the "repository" of a public morality or of any meaning whatsoever. When we speak of a text such as the Constitution and say that it has many meanings, we are, according to Fish, really talking about a situation in which people disagree about the meaning of the text (because they are reading it with different interpretive assumptions, etc.). When we speak of a text with a single meaning, we are talking about a situation of agreement.

I do not believe that this view (which makes the meaning of a text the property of a context rather than a text) in any way follows from the conventionalist tenet—which I believe to be true—that every text is "always and already" embedded in a context and "is always an already interpreted object." Fish simply seems to be taking conventionalism to illogical extremes and confounding a situation (context) with an object located in that situation (the text), or confusing the act of interpretation with the object of interpretation. Moreover, I fail to see what there is to be gained from his strategy of making meaning a property of a context rather than of a text. The theoretical problem we confront, you will recall, is one of constraint: The question is whether there is a need for a concept such as disciplining rules. Fish sought to deny that there is any such need by proclaiming that there are no texts with many meanings, but all he has done is recharacterize the problem of choice and thus the need for constraint. Choices still must be made, though now it is not a choice among several "meanings of a text" (for texts have no meanings), but rather among "different interpretive assumptions" (for example, about the purpose of the text, etc.). The Constitution is, I admit, an "always and already interpreted object," but that does not deny the need to interpret it, to reinterpret it, or to choose among conflicting interpretations.

. . .

Adjudication may be subject to two different attacks. One is based on a moral vision that condemns the institutionalized relationships that are necessarily entailed in adjudication and that begins to point to new institutional forms. Adjudication is condemned because it is evil. A prominent intellectual and political movement of the day, Critical Legal Studies, often aspires to a critique so radical, but it fails in its delivery because it does not explain how we could meet the genuine needs presently served by adjudication and yet avoid the excesses of that institution. There is, however, another, somewhat lesser critique of adjudication also mounted by the Critical Legal Studies movement: This critique claims not so much that adjudication is evil, but that it is incoherent. The theory is that the judge lacks any distinctive legal standards to guide or constrain his or her judgment, and that the judge, by choice and of necessity, draws upon values, viewpoints, etc., that are either personal or rooted in the various social groups to which he or she belongs. This theory is similar to that espoused by Levinson and is encapsulated in the movement's slogan, "law is politics."

Stanley Fish is not, by any stretch of the imagination, a member of the Critical Legal Studies movement. He believes in professionalism, as do most conventionalists. He does not seek to undermine adjudication: He does not claim that it is evil nor even that it is incoherent. Indeed, he probably thinks it is more coherent than I do. The problem, however, is that he offers an account of that institution and answers the question of method in a way that blurs the line between law and politics. His point is not so much to dispute the existence of *legal* norms or standards, but to deny a role for *any* norms or standards. All is practice. But once you enter Fish's normless world, you have lost the basis—other than instinct or "know-how"—for separating good judgments from bad ones, or legal judgments from political ones. All you can say is that there are conflicting interpretations and that "[t]he means of settling [them] are political, social, and institutional, in a mix that is itself subject to modification and change"—which, in my judgment, is not saying much at all.

Under my account, professional norms constrain judges in choosing among the conflicting interpretations and are the standards for assessing the correctness of their decisions. My reference to disciplining rules allows me to see an inner coherence to the law, and to speak about the legal correctness of a decision such as *Brown*. I also envision a role for an external critic of a decision, who stands outside of the law and operates on some other standards, such as those rooted in moral or political principles. Fish insists that this distinction between the internal and external critic is "less firm and less stable" than I suggest. He also belittles the distinction I draw between the various strategies open to a critic of a judicial decision—amending the Constitution as opposed to "packing" the Court or enacting statutes that curtail jurisdiction: "In calling these latter strategies 'lesser' and 'more problematic,' Fiss once again assumes a distinction that cannot finally be maintained. Presumably," Fish continues, "they are 'lesser' and 'more problematic' because they are obviously political; but in fact the entire system is political and the question at any moment is from which point in the system is pressure being applied to what other points."

Too often in the law we transform differences in degree into differences in kind; lawyers tend to see lines where there are only gradations of gray (so my students and friends often remind me). Fish's brand of conventionalism may be a healthy corrective for this tendency, but I cannot help believing that in the end it is a bit too much, and that Fish is destroying distinctions that comport with the way we think and talk about the law and that have served us well. For those in the profession, and maybe even for those outside, it seems terribly important—not just as a psychological matter, but also for purposes of figuring out what you can and cannot do—to know the difference between a "legal" argument, and a "political" one, that is, to know that passing a constitutional amendment is a more "legitimate" response to a detested decision than is "packing" the Court. Of course, all of these distinctions are made in terms of an ongoing "system,"—a certain discourse and set of institutions that we know all too well—and it might be that the "entire system," viewed from some transcendental perspective, is "political." But that seems to be beside the point. We work and live within this world, not at some point of transcendence (as any conventionalist should know). Adjudication is an ongoing institution (or practice) and the purpose of this exercise [is] to identify those features that distinguish it from other institutions and that call forth and justify the special normative discourse that surrounds it.

Let me also note, on perhaps a more technical level, that Fish's assault on the distinction between law and politics does not in any way flow from his views about the contextualized nature of texts or any of the other insights of conventionalism. It simply flows from his unwillingness to allow any place in his system for disciplining rules or any other form of generalized norms. I see them as essential because, for me, adjudication is a process that calls upon judges to choose among conflicting interpretations (or "meanings," or "interpretive assumptions," or whatever) of some authoritative text and because the law assumes that these choices are made pursuant to standards. The distinction between law and politics arises from the fact that the standards for judges are not necessarily the same as those for political actors or moral prophets. The distinction assumes different standards for different actors.

. . .

. . . As Wittgenstein put it, "[D]on't think, but look." As a conventionalist, Fish believes that everything is in place: The judge is situated; the test is situated; so what possible significance could there be to a theoretical dispute about adjudication?

This may be a real problem for Fish (I doubt it), but not for me. I do not believe that everything is in place. It is important to look, but I also believe that it is important to think, and that there is a crucial place in the profession of law for the theoretical. Professional training does try to instill "know how," but that is not all there is to the law. . . . Ideas do matter. Indeed, the interest the profession has shown in Fish's own theoretical work suggests that not all is practice. . . .

Theory informs practice, just as surely as practice informs theory, and in my view Fish's theory threatens two important practices of the profession. One is the value placed on self-conscious reflection—those moments when a judge considers the interpretive choices and identifies and weighs the norms of the profession that are to guide that choice. Fish denies that such moments exist ("a judge always knows in general what to do"), and in that denial both legitimates and invites a certain thoughtlessness. Those who judge by instinct are told not to worry, because that is what they must of necessity do. The others—the great judges—only believe that they are deliberating.

Fish's account also jeopardizes the special pull that the norms of the profession have—and should have—upon the judge. Anything goes. The judge is told by Fish that "the entire system is political" and all that differs is the "point in the system" where the pressure is applied. These words might be taken seriously by some judges (although I have explained why they shouldn't), and if so, they might generate a set of practices that would turn law into politics. Judges who listen to Fish would see no reason for being especially faithful to the norms of the profession and would instead

believe they are entitled to do whatever they think best. The discipline
that is so prized by the law would be gone, and with it much of the law's
special claim for our respect.

§ 12.03 Postmodernism and Constitutional Theory

To put some themes from the foregoing extracts in one broader perspective,
it may be useful to present a brief survey of the controversial concept of
postmodernism, mentioned in the introduction to this chapter. Claiming that
the postmodernist paradigm "has emerged to become as dominant in legal
theory as any paradigm was in the past,"[11] Marquette law professor Peter
Schanck summarizes key concepts. Peter C. Schanck, *Understanding Postmodern Thought and Its Implications for Statutory Interpretation*, 65 S. CAL.
L. REV. 2505, 2508–13, 2515–17 (1992):[12]

. . . [T]here is no single principle on which postmodernism is grounded
or which comprises its essence. Instead, several interrelated concepts do
so, each of which in a sense undergirds the others. Each depends on the
others for its existence and each is a precondition of the others. These
concepts may be summarized as follows: (1) The self is not, and cannot
be, an autonomous, self-generating entity; it is purely a social, cultural,
historical, and linguistic creation. (2) There are no foundational principles
from which other assertions can be derived; hence, certainty as the result
of either empirical verification or deductive reasoning is impossible. (3)
There can be no such thing as knowledge of reality; what we think is
knowledge is always belief and can apply only to the context within which
it is asserted. (4) Because language is socially and culturally constituted,
it is inherently incapable of representing or corresponding to reality;
hence all propositions and all interpretations, even texts, are themselves
social constructions.

. . . Stated in somewhat different terms, the postmodern school of
thought conceives of knowledge as always mediated by our social, cultural,
linguistic, and historical circumstances, and it will thus vary as those
circumstances change. The truth, consequently, can never be transparent
to us; it is and must always be a social construction, one made even more
opaque by the mediation of language, a system of communication inherently incapable of capturing reality. This includes the "truth" about legal
doctrines, legal principles, and legal interpretations: All are social
constructions.

Both in commonsense, everyday understanding and in Western philosophy, including traditional jurisprudence, the bedrock assumption has
been that we are capable of representing reality more or less precisely
and that some knowledge transcends particular perspectives and contexts. This is exactly what postmodern thought rejects. Because, in the
view of postmodernists, knowledge of the world is filtered through the
structures of the socially and culturally derived assumptions that each
of us has accumulated as human beings, and because each of us is
differently situated, there are different perspectives on objects and events
and thus differing content to our knowledge of them. Knowledge is thus
conceived by postmodernists as always contingent, always dependent on
context, and always "local" rather than "universal," as it is so often
assumed to be. This results in the charge that postmodernists are

---

[11] Schanck, *supra* note 6, at 2507.

[12] Copyright © 1992 by the Southern California Law Review, University of Southern California. Reprinted with permission of the Southern California Law Review.

relativists—that is, that postmodernists hold that the content of knowledge varies according to the framework, perspective, and circumstances of the observer—but . . . some postmodern thinkers deny this accusation.

Although understood in this way, postmodern theory seems highly philosophical, even esoteric, it has come under heavy assault in recent years from the mass media and from conservative writers of popular books on higher education. The onslaught began in 1987 with the late Allan Bloom's indirect criticism of postmodern ideas in his best-seller, *The Closing of the American Mind.* In his book Bloom lambastes universities for their lack of faith in the existence of ultimate truths, for advocating relativism in values, and for cowardly capitulating to radical demands during the 1960s. Even more vitriolic, if less scholarly and erudite, attacks have been launched since Bloom's book came out by . . . Roger Kimball[13] . . . and Dinesh D'Souza,[14] among others. Although these books perhaps focus their greatest attention on such current trends in academia as "political correctness," multiculturalism, affirmative action, and restrictions on racist speech, they are also more directly critical than Bloom of postmodern thought. Kimball . . . and D'Souza center their attacks on two of postmodernism's leading proponents, [including] Stanley Fish . . . . Fish's ideas are held up by Kimball and D'Souza as exemplifying everything wrong with higher education, in particular their alleged denial of disinterested scholarship and objective knowledge . . . .

Although those academics who are immersed in postmodern assumptions take for granted such ideas as the social construction of reality, the uncertainty of knowledge, the impossibility of disinterested inquiry, and the indeterminacy of meaning, it is hardly surprising that most people, including many scholars, find these concepts inconceivable, ridiculous, or abhorrent. The average person goes through life believing without hesitation in the certainty of many things. Even within the context of a generally pervasive modern skepticism, in which far fewer propositions are accepted as absolutely true, there is still a vast array of ideas in whose truth people have no doubt. There is thus a large void between most people's common-sense understanding and the assumptions of postmodern-oriented intellectuals . . . .

Notwithstanding its vilification in the popular media, postmodern theory has been accepted almost unanimously by legal theorists in the past decade, especially by radical critical legal studies scholars, feminists, critical race theorists, and civic republicans. It has spread even to the more conservative law and economics theorist Judge Richard Posner (who seems to have moved considerably to the left jurisprudentially in recent years) . . . .

. . .

How is it logically possible for postmodern thinkers to assert ideas [—that our perspectives on the world are culturally and linguistically conditioned, that reality is never transparent to us, and that the content of our knowledge depends on our different situation—] so counterintuitive to our commonsense understandings of "knowledge," "truth," and individual autonomy? Perhaps the best way to begin an explanation is with the concept of the individual self, or "subject," as that concept is termed in philosophical discourse. Postmodernists deny the conventional Western assumption of free will, that each person is an autonomous individual

---

[13] ROGER KIMBALL, TENURED RADICALS: HOW POLITICS HAS CORRUPTED OUR HIGHER EDUCATION (1990).

[14] DINESH D'SOUZA, ILLIBERAL EDUCATION: THE POLITICS OF RACE AND SEX ON CAMPUS (1991).

capable of free and rational choice among alternatives. From the postmodern perspective all thought is based on concepts and ideas previously absorbed from the subject's surroundings. In other words, as much as we may wish that we are solely responsible for our decisions, our thoughts, our desires, and our fantasies, that cannot be the case. Imagine trying to think about something without reference to your foundation of compiled thoughts, assumptions, presuppositions, prejudgments, premises, and constructs with content you did not create. It is, of course, inconceivable. This reservoir of material is, in turn, structured and formed by language. Again, try to imagine thinking about anything without the use of language. Even one's emotions, many of which precede speech, are now conceived in linguistic terms. We are, to some degree, prisoners of the words and patterns of words constructed through the long history of humankind. The meanings associated with these words and structures are themselves shaped throughout the course of history and are, therefore, socially and culturally constituted. The end result is that all of us, as much as we would like to believe otherwise, are entirely formed by our society and culture.

Many postmodernists, in keeping with their seeming wish to employ hyperbole and to scandalize their readers, phrase this concept in terms of the subject being illusory, fictitious, or *nonexistent*. All that means is that there is no such thing as an autonomous self-determining subject, that the self is a construct. Rather than deny the existence of the self, these postmodernists write that the subject is "decentered," "dispersed," or "fragmented." What they mean is that the subject is not fixed but varies from context to context, for the following reasons: (1) People lack identifiable, fixed, autonomous selves; (2) they are socially constituted and thus subject to widely varying and often conflicting social and cultural influences (a person can be at once a woman, an African-American, a lawyer, a Catholic, a wife, a parent, a Democrat, a liberal, ad infinitum); and (3) the language with which their thoughts and utterances are formed is incapable of providing a determinate meaning.

At first glance this antihumanistic rejection, or decentering, of the self appears nihilistic. If we lack free will and are incapable of determining our own selves, no value system or morality can exist independently of our historical and cultural circumstances. We are all either soulless automatons ground out by our societies or free-floating beings subject to no standards. If there are no transcendent values, then Ivan Karamazov in Dostoyevsky's *The Brothers Karamazov* is right that "nothing then would be immoral, everything would be lawful, even cannibalism." We can have no basis for condemning or praising any activity or behavior. As certainly as that conclusion seems to follow from the premise of the nonautonomous subject, there are solidly postmodern reasons for rejecting it . . . .

If the subject is socially, culturally, historically, and linguistically constituted, it *appears* to follow logically that there is no way to evaluate the truth or falsity of any claims made about the nature of things. Persons cannot themselves interrogate their own thoughts or the utterances of others except in terms of already socially and linguistically constituted assumptions. There is thus no neutral, objective standpoint to which we can retire in order to determine the truth value of any assertion. We can, however, evaluate the truth of a proposition from within our own knowledge system; that is to say, there are generally accepted criteria within a particular discourse, reference group, or community for determining whether something is true. This is the basic epistemology, or theory of knowledge, of postmodernism. It . . . constitutes a set of assumptions, sometimes unrecognized, behind much current legal theory.

Finally, to explore the bearing—if any—of postmodernism on constitutional law and constitutional theory: A leading expositor of postmodernist theories in the legal academy has been Professor Jack Balkin of Yale Law School. Emphasizing effects of postmodern culture such as mass "mediazation" (and writing before the rapid emergence of the World Wide Web brought still further major technological change), Balkin raised questions about the impact of cultural and technological developments on the groundings of much constitutional and political theory—and about the relationship between the judiciary and the legal academy. J.M. Balkin, *What Is a Postmodern Constitutionalism?*, 90 MICH. L. REV. 1966, 1966-67, 1976-81, 1982-83, 1984-88 (1992):[15]

I begin with a puzzle. It must certainly strike one as odd that the subject of postmodern constitutional law arises at a time when the actual arbiters of the Constitution—the federal judiciary and in particular the Supreme Court of the United States—appear to be more conservative than they have been for many years, and indeed, are likely to remain so for the foreseeable future. Postmodernism is often associated with what is new, innovative, and on the cutting edge of cultural development. Yet if we were to define the elements of a postmodern constitutional culture, it would be clear that one of the most central features of the present period—if the expression "central" still has any remaining currency in an era of postmodernism—is a judiciary which has no intention of being new or innovative in anything. Its intellectual leader, Justice Scalia, has even called for a constitutional jurisprudence of tradition, coupled with a return to an interpretive theory of plain meanings for statutes and original intention with respect to the Constitution.

. . .

Nevertheless, I think the attempt to see a postmodern constitutional jurisprudence in opposition to the increasingly conservative practice of constitutional law is mistaken. It is understandable why postmodern theorists might wish to identify postmodernism with the progressive, with the new that will eventually replace the old, and deny that title to the work of the Rehnquist Court and the rest of the Reagan judiciary. Yet to treat constitutional law as it is actually practiced by courts as foreign or exceptional to a postmodern era or as the target of an eventual postmodern revolution fails fully to grasp the meaning of postmodernism as a feature of current culture. Moreover, I think that such an attempted marginalization would be ironic coming from those who claim to adopt a postmodern . . . stance. Rather than seeing this political phenomenon as exceptional or aberrational to postmodern constitutional culture, I think we should see it as exemplary of that culture. Postmodern constitutionalism is the constitutionalism of reactionary judges surrounded by a liberal academy that despises or disregards them, and which is despised and disregarded in turn; postmodern constitutional culture is the culture in which the control of constitutional lawmaking apparatus is in the hands of the most conservative forces in mainstream life, while constitutional law as practiced in the legal academy has cast itself adrift, whether out of desperation, disgust, or despair, and engaged itself in spinning gossamer webs of republicanism, deconstruction, dialogism, feminism, or what have you. Postmodern legal culture is the rout of progressive forces, the increasing insularity, self-absorption, and fragmentation of progressive academic writing, and the increasing irrelev[a]nce of that writing to the positive law of the U.S. Constitution.

---

[15] Copyright © 1992 by the Michigan Law Review Association.

How is this possible? What does postmodernism mean if Chief Justice Rehnquist already presides over the postmodern Supreme Court? What is the promise of postmodernism or of postmodern constitutionalism in such an age? . . .

. . . I do not think that the greatest relevance of postmodernism to American constitutional law lies in methods of interpreting the Constitution. Rather, I think constitutional lawyers need to understand postmodernism because they need to understand the cultural changes that have taken place around them in art, politics, technology, and economics. Just as one cannot understand modernism without understanding the Industrial Revolution and the spurt of technological and cultural change that accompanied it, one cannot understand postmodernism without understanding the particular technological and cultural changes in society that have accompanied it. Postmodernity is the era in which the industrial model of mass production is applied to the creation and distribution of symbolic forms. Therefore, we might approach the question of postmodern constitutionalism in the following way: How have changes in technology, communication, and the organization of living and working changed the public's understandings and practice of law, the Constitution, human rights, and democracy? How should the various social actors concerned with the Constitution (lawyers, judges, academics, legislators, citizens) understand the forms and practices of democratic self-government in light of the cultural changes occurring during the postmodern period, and what should they do in response to these changes?

In stating the question this way, I wish specifically to contrast my perspective with the view or assumption that constitutional postmodernism primarily involves questions of how to interpret the Constitution using postmodernist theories of interpretation or insights gained from understanding the "postmodern" or the socially constructed self. These projects may be useful ones. Yet they are only part of the story. To focus on postmodern theories of subjectivity without understanding the cultural and technological basis of change risks turning postmodernism into a sterile form of idealism.

Moreover, my analysis seeks to go beyond the concern with the "social construction of the subject" commonly associated with postmodernism in law. Without further development, there is the danger that such analyses will remain rooted in an overly idealist conception of culture. Shared symbols, values, discourses, or ideas are implicitly assumed to be the "forces" of social construction. But no account is given of how this force operates in practice. In contrast, the analysis presented here is distinctly material in its concerns. It asks how changes in technology and culture create new opportunities for the exercise of power. It seeks to draw closer connections between the material conditions of life and thought by studying the technological re-creation of forms of life.

A postmodern constitutionalism, in my view, must ask how postmodern culture and technology have affected law as an institution: the way that the courts, Congress, and the executive interact with each other, and the way that law is understood, promulgated, argued about, experienced, and assimilated. How is information about constitutional rights distributed and spread? What changes have occurred in the ways in which politics is organized, and in the ways in which laws are debated publicly or within government institutions? How have advances in technology changed the possible forms of power, control, and surveillance? What effect has mediazation wrought on the practice of American democracy? These are the key questions for a postmodern constitutionalist. . . .

The Constitution regulates democratic self-government. Yet democracy as a set of institutional practices has changed greatly since the Second

World War and especially since the 1960s and 1970s. Political action committees have taken advantage of developments in computerization and data processing to manipulate the political process in ways heretofore undreamed of. The past twenty-five years have seen the increasing concentration of media industries into multinational conglomerates. What effects will these changes have on our understanding of free speech and traditional expectations about the press as guardians of democracy? What does the First Amendment mean in an age of increasing economic concentration in media industries, or in an age of organizations specifically devoted to mass distribution of political messages?

Perhaps even more important from the standpoint of postmodernist theory, mediazation has fundamentally changed the terms of public debate. The movement from newspapers to television broadcasting as the major source of public information has changed the nature of information received by the public. It has changed the public's expectations of political behavior and the content and form of political communication. What constitutional analysis should apply to regulation of public elections in the era of the sound bite, the photo opportunity, and the media event? Technological improvements have also made possible sophisticated polling techniques, whose power has made them indispensable to modern political discourse. What effect have these developments had on the democratic nature of public opinion? Has virtually instantaneous polling created a feedback loop of public expectations about expectations that will lead to volatility in public opinion or put in doubt the meaning or the authority of "majority preferences"? Worse yet, has the very concept of a true "public opinion" that is not manufactured or simulated lost its meaning in the postmodern age?

Mediazation has not only affected the form in which information about public affairs is conveyed to the public; it has also had a profound effect on the presentation of the self in public life. Political fortunes can vanish overnight by the slightest slip of the tongue when it is broadcast nationwide. Mediazation has also permitted revelations about politicians to be broadcast quickly and widely in simplified and highly charged symbolic forms. Similarly, the public's expectations about what will or will not be revealed about political life, and hence what aspects of private life are relevant, have surely been affected by the mediazation of politics.

. . . Finally, has mediazation helped to impose increasingly insuperable barriers to entry for challengers to incumbent politicians or for persons without access to considerable wealth? The study of the Constitution has always had to confront structural effects and limitations on self-government and democratic ideals. A postmodernist constitutionalism, then, simply asks whether the technological and cultural features of the present era have altered these structural effects or limitations or added new ones of supervening importance.

The question of mediazation must also be confronted by anyone who seeks to ground democratic theory on any form of dialogism or informed public discourse. Mediaized communication conveys information on a mass scale, but unidirectionally; it arrives instantaneously, but in the form of highly charged symbols and sound bites. Mediazation of political culture thus jeopardizes the kind of neutral dialogism that many contemporary political theorists view as necessary to the success of their projects. Ironically, these philosophical projects do not always consider the extent to which technology has rendered their dreams impossible of attainment, or even worse, wholly irrelevant. Yet no theory of democracy can succeed unless it takes these technological changes in dissemination of information into account. Dialogism may already have died the death of a thousand sound bites.

. . .

. . . In the same way that mass media create the possibility of unidirectional political participation on a mass scale, so too the mediazation of law will create opportunities for manipulation of symbolic forms, commodification and spectacle. If the Bork hearings symbolized a sea change in the confirmation of Supreme Court nominees and a blurring of lines between judicial and political candidates, as many have argued, this is not simply due to the bad faith of Bork's political opponents. Rather, I suggest that it is at least partly due to the technological and cultural changes of the postmodern era, which made mass political organization and mediazation of the confirmation process possible. Opposition to Bork was raised through forms of mass politics that would have been impossible without contemporary quasi-industrial methods of political organization or the use of mass media for distribution of messages. Hence, the Bork nomination, for all the things that it symbolized, may also have symbolized a breakthrough in the mediazation of law. In this way Bork, the pessimistic modernist, was defeated, for good or ill, by forces unleashed by the postmodern era.

. . .

. . . I would argue that . . . a public sphere, in which lawyers, judges, and the legal professoriat engaged in a more or less continual discourse on the growth, restatement, and reform of positive law, existed at least from the end of the nineteenth century. This public sphere continues even today, although the growth of mass media as a method for distribution of legal information (Lexis, Westlaw, and computer satellite broadcast of CLE programs) may also threaten its disintegration. But perhaps an equally important feature of the disintegration of this public sphere of legal discourse is the development of the special status of the legal academic. The legal academy has, for the past twenty-five years at least, become increasingly interdisciplinary. At the same time, it has become increasingly distanced from the work of actual lawyers and judges . . . . [C]onstitutional law is perhaps the best example of how a public sphere of legal discourse that once included practitioners, judges, and academics has largely disintegrated. In constitutional law, we clearly see the fragmentation of legal culture into an increasingly conservative body of judges and an academy that is quite liberal and whose work is increasingly irrelevant to the actual practice of constitutional adjudication. In my view, this is the best explanation of the puzzle I began this essay with. Postmodern legal culture is not necessarily a culture of lawyers and judges who embrace postmodern interpretive theories, but rather a legal culture mimetic of postmodernity: fragmented, decentered, diffused.

As the judiciary becomes increasingly conservative, we witness increasing self-absorption within the legal academy and its increasing isolation from legal practice. Once again, these phenomena occur in differing degrees in different areas of the law, but they are especially pronounced with respect to constitutional scholarship. As a result, a new class of academics arises who have little or no interest in practical political activity, practical law reform, or even practical restatement of the law. Thus, the postmodern period is marked by the creation of a species of legal scholarship known as "legal theory." As a result of the rise of interdisciplinary scholarship, genres of scholarship defined by traditional practice areas (e.g., contracts, torts) are replaced by scholarly genres defined by theoretical allegiances (e.g., law and economics, feminist legal theory), which may cut across traditional doctrinal areas or simply be irrelevant to them . . . .

The flip side of academic alienation from practitioners is academics' increasing lack of respect for the products of judges, legislatures, and administrative agencies. Academics increasingly recognize, or rather assume, the product of these bodies is written by clerks, politically biased, incompetently reasoned, or all three at once. At the same time, they attempt to redescribe law in terms of ideas that have no possible chance of being enacted into legal practice, at least absent a miraculous mass indoctrination of the judiciary. We thus witness the creation of a "shadow constitution" by progressive scholars, in which they declaim what the Constitution really means in the face of the increasing likelihood that it will never mean that in practice.

Finally, a postmodernist constitutionalism must come to grips with the effects of technology on privacy, and, more generally, on autonomy itself. Each of us, whether we recognize it or not, produces traces of her activities in material form, just as an animal leaves a trail in the dust where it travels. These traces are signs, but, equally important, they are material signs. If one were able to capture and reconstruct increasing numbers of a person's material traces, one would have an increasingly full picture of that person—not only of her locations and activities, but even of her thoughts, beliefs, and desires. With the growth of computers, electronic information collection and retrieval systems, mass media, electronic recording equipment and forensic science, it is now possible to organize an incredible number of facts about individuals from the traces they leave behind them . . . . In this way, knowledge, or more correctly information encoded in material form, creates ever new sources of power and ever new possibilities for control in the postmodern age.

These developments pose significant problems for constitutional theory. Both the state and private individuals will have control over the new technologies of information collection and surveillance. What limits should be placed on the ability of public and private organizations to collect, organize, and distribute such information? Traditional First Amendment philosophy has asserted that the best weapon against speech we do not like is still more speech. Does this philosophy continue to make sense in an era of new information and surveillance technologies? Will increased availability of information about the most detailed aspects of our lives lessen the dangers of control through surveillance or data compilation? Or is the problem precisely the opposite—that the availability of the information is itself the problem? Do traditional liberal notions of autonomy continue to make sense in an age where control of information processing increasingly means new forms of control over individuals themselves? Or has the liberal ideal of the free market of ideas now turned in on itself and created a new form of totalitarianism, a prison constructed from access to information rather than from steel bars?

These issues strike at the heart of liberal political philosophy. Privacy is deeply related to notions of individualism and individual autonomy. Each of us has both a public and a private self; the public self we reveal to the world, and the private self we retain control over by withholding it from others. Our ability alternatively to provide or withhold aspects of our private selves preserves and constitutes our autonomy. Exchanges of private information signal intimacy and trust, and their disclosure to third parties is usually thought a sign of betrayal. But the ability to withhold information about the private self is not wholly a natural attribute of existence—it is technologically circumscribed and determined. What will happen to the fabric of intimate relations in a world in which technological advancement increasingly shrinks the domain of the private self? Will traditional assumptions about personal privacy (and hence autonomy) still make sense, or will they have to be reimagined in wholly different ways? And if this is so, what will happen to a constitutional jurisprudence based on eighteenth-century notions of privacy and autonomy that assumed a world without our present technological advances?

. . . If changes in material conditions can so alter or undermine our conceptions of privacy, it is neither our shared ideas nor their social construction that become the key issues, but rather technological change and who has control over its shape and direction.

§ 12.04 Conclusion

Is the gulf between the bench and the constitutional-theory academy as wide and unbridgeable as Balkin seems to believe? And does the acceptance by many theorists of postmodernist premises, which are not widely embraced by those on the bench, necessarily mean that those making constitutional law and those writing about constitutional theory will have little to say to each other, not to mention little regard for each other?

It may help in this connection to consider a distinction between, on the one hand, legal postmodernists' methodology with its apparently radical or nihilistic implications and, on the other hand, what if any implications necessarily follow from postmodernism for one's politics or views on how to do constitutional law. Much of the legal academy is considerably to the left of today's national political center, but the same does not seem to be true of the contemporary Supreme Court. Yet some see Stanley Fish's postmodernistic approach as actually leading to conservative positions,[16] and recall Schanck's contention that "a consistently applied postmodern theory leads full circle to the affirmation of those same commonsense notions prevailing in most people's minds."[17] So one may emerge from immersion in the debates over interpretation theory and postmodernism shorn of certainty about the possibility of determinate answers to hard questions in legal practice and theory—but may one still be persuaded to beliefs in accord with the views of, say, feminists and critical race theorists, or even textualists, originalists, and conservatives?

§ 12.05 Bibliography

J.M. Balkin, *Deconstructive Practice and Legal Theory,* 96 YALE L.J. 743 (1987)

Paul Brest, *Interpretation and Interest,* 34 STAN. L. REV. 765 (1982)

Stephen M. Feldman, *The Supreme Court in a Postmodern World: A Flying Elephant,* 84 MINN L. REV. 673 (2000); *Playing with the Pieces: Postmodernism in the Lawyer's Toolbox,* 85 VA. L. REV. 151 (1999); *The Politics of Postmodern Jurisprudence,* 95 MICH. L. REV. 166 (1996)

Stanley Fish, THERE'S NO SUCH THING AS FREE SPEECH AND IT'S A GOOD THING, TOO (1994); DOING WHAT COMES NATURALLY: CHANGE, RHETORIC, AND THE PRACTICE OF THEORY IN LITERARY AND LEGAL STUDIES (1989); *Don't Know Much About the Middle Ages: Posner on Law and Literature,* 97 YALE L.J. 777 (1988); *Dennis Martinez and the Uses of Theory,* 96 YALE L.J. 1773 (1987)

---

[16] *See* Schanck, *supra* note 6, at 2548-54 (considering criticism by several theorists that Fish's approach is "conservative and unduly supportive of the status quo").

[17] *Id.* at 2512.

Kenney Hegland, *Goodbye to Deconstruction,* 58 S. CAL. L. REV. 1203 (1985)

Interpretation Symposium, 58 S. CAL. L. REV. 1 (1985) (with articles by Christopher D. Stone, Geoffrey Joseph, Mark Poster, Renato Rosaldo, Robert L. Thomas, Ronald R. Garet, David Couzens Hoy, Owen M. Fiss, Paul G. Chevigny, Thomas C. Grey, David Kennedy, Michael S. Moore, Frederick Schauer, Sanford Levinson, Stephen R. Munzer, James W. Nickels, David A.J. Richards, Michael J. Perry, Larry Simon, Robert W. Bennett, Paul Brest, Walter Benn Michaels, Mark V. Tushnet, and Allan C. Hutchinson)

Duncan Kennedy, A CRITIQUE OF ADJUDICATION (FIN DE SIÈCLE) 339–64 (1997)

Law, Truth, and Interpretation: A Symposium on Dennis Patterson's Law and Truth, 50 SMU L. REV. 1563 (1997) (with contributions by Dennis Patterson, George P. Fletcher, David Luban, Jefferson White, George A. Martinez, Charles Altieri, Benjamin C. Zipursky, Leslie Pickering Francis, and Brian Leiter)

Sanford Levinson & Steven Mailloux, INTERPRETING LAW AND LITERATURE: A HERMENEUTIC READER (1988)

Dennis Patterson, LAW AND TRUTH (1996)

Richard Posner, LAW AND LITERATURE: A MISUNDERSTOOD RELATION (1988)

Steven Winter, *Bull Durham and the Uses of Theory,* 42 STAN. L. REV. 639 (1990)

PART IV

Conclusion

Chapter 13

Theory and Its Discontents

§ 13.01 Introduction

Much of this book has focused on efforts to defend or critique unitary or global theories of constitutional interpretation. Though many scholars agree that no theory built around a single unifying principle of constitutional interpretation is free of problems, they do not agree on the consequences of this viewpoint or the appropriate methodologies with which to replace imperfect or incomplete theories. In this chapter, we feature two of the more ambitious and provocative alternatives proposed for replacing defective or problematic unitary or global theories of constitutional interpretation.[1] This focus is not meant to denigrate the importance or popularity of other nonglobal or nonunitary theories of constitutional interpretation. Instead, it is meant to serve two other purposes. First, the focus is designed to underscore the fact that nonglobal or nonunitary theories of interpretation are not necessarily any less ambitious than unitary or global theories to explain constitutional law. Second, the materials in this chapter are designed to allow readers to scrutinize in depth whether the scholars whose theories have been excerpted have been able to achieve their stated objectives, including the avoidance of the problems that they regard as undermining unitary or global theories of interpretation.

The first section contains two extracts by Yale Law School Professor Bruce Ackerman. In the first, he explains his objective, which is to posit the essential elements of constitutional change or "higher lawmaking" that occurs in the absence of a formal constitutional amendment as set forth in Article V. In the second extract, Professor Ackerman explains why the Founding, Reconstruction, and the New Deal each qualify as special transformative moments in which such higher lawmaking occurred. The second section features a lengthy extract by Professor Jed Rubenfeld, in which he explains his conception of the Constitution as setting forth paradigms for restricting governmental action. As background to this discussion, Professor Rubenfeld suggests one possible answer to the provocative question widely debated among scholars about

---

[1] Generally, these alternatives are characterized as anti-formalist, because of their rejection of or opposition to theories that demand rigid adherence to formal criteria for guiding constitutional interpretation. For a brief discussion of these different approaches, *see* Part I, Chapter One: A Brief Historical Overview of the Development of Constitutional Theory.

461

whether it is possible to develop a theory of constitutional interpretation without first clarifying the fidelity required by our written Constitution. The final section contains another extract by Professor Ackerman, in which he addresses another subject widely debated among constitutional scholars about the proper relationship between theory and practice. Professor Ackerman's analysis brings us full circle back to the question of what is the basic purpose of constitutional theory.

§ 13.02 Constitutional Politics, Moments, and Interpretation

Professor Bruce Ackerman's theory of constitutional change has probably generated more controversy than any other nonglobal or nonunitary theory of constitutional interpretation. In the following extract, Professor Ackerman explains the distinctive features of revolutionary reform of the Constitution, a focus of his book, *Transformations*. Bruce A. Ackerman, *Revolution on a Human Scale* 108 YALE L.J. 2279, 2292–95 (1999):[2]

> *Transformations* focuses upon a distinctive kind of lawmaking practice that is obscured by a simple but tenacious dichotomy often used to classify legal change. On this familiar view, some new strict initiative, *X* can become law in one of two ways. Either *X* is enacted in strict compliance with all the rules, principles, and practices regulating legislative and constitutional revision—in which case it counts as an *ordinary* change in municipal law—or it becomes effective despite its breach of these norms, in which case it is part of a *revolutionary* change in the entire legal system.
>
> I have no problem with the idea of ordinary legal change, but I do challenge the implicit notion that all revolutions are sufficiently alike to justify legal analysts putting them into a single conceptual box. Just as one may distinguish revolutions on a human scale from those of the totalizing variety, I propose an analogous distinction when considering a revolution's relationship to the preexisting legal order. Totalizing revolutions aim for nothing less than a complete break with all the rules, principles and practices that previously governed legal change. But revolutions on a human scale may aim for a more discriminating relationship. While they may reject key elements of the preexisting legal mix, they may also seek to retain others unchanged, while adapting yet others into the new system of revolutionary legality they seek to establish. I call this *unconventional adaptation,* and it is my principal aim to emphasize its importance in American constitutional development. Indeed, the Constitution of 1787 would never be higher law today without its repeated unconventional adaptation by later generations of Americans at moments of great crisis.
>
> This thesis is hard to state, let alone evaluate, within the traditional conceptual dichotomy between ordinary and revolutionary legal change. Since both unconventional adaptations and total breaks involve a rejection of at least some of the old elements defining valid legal change, neither counts as an *ordinary* legal revision. As long as we are content with the old dichotomy, both kinds of revolution get thrown into the same conceptual box. Worse yet, legal analysts may easily lose sight of the significance of unconventional adaptation as their attention is arrested by the more melodramatic gestures of the totalizing revolutionary. To

[2] Reprinted by permission of the Yale Law Journal Company and Fred B. Rothman and Company from the Yale Law Journal, vol. 108, pages 2279–2349.

guard against this danger, I propose to replace the received dichotomy with a clarifying trichotomy—ordinary change, unconventional change, and totalizing change.

I do not deny that totalizing legal change is possible. The Bolshevik Revolution of 1917 provides a case in point. Before the Communists seized power in October, the previous provisional government scheduled elections for a Constituent Assembly whose task was the framing of a new constitution. The Bolsheviks allowed these elections to proceed only to find themselves gaining a minority of the seats. It was at this point that the question of total revolution was raised in dramatic fashion: Would the Bolsheviks disband the Constituent Assembly and thereby break their last institutional links to the past?

The question provoked much anxious indecision. Nonetheless, Lenin persuaded his comrades to use the Red Army to disband the assembly and to make a clean break with the existing legal order. Rather than adapting preexisting constitutional ideas and institutions to broaden support and to gain consent, the Bolsheviks took a different path. The new regime's fate would depend on institutions—most notably the Red Army and Communist Party—that had *no* constitutional relationship, however remote, to the old regime.

But this is not what happened in America during each of its great periods of revolutionary reform. While the participants were perfectly aware that they were violating certain basic legal norms, they did not take this point as a license for destroying the entire preexisting system. Instead, they extracted many traditional elements from the mix in their effort to make new higher law in the name of the People. My book's first aim is to follow each generation of revolutionary reformers down this unconventional path, describing how one unconventional adaptation generated others in the ongoing struggle for popular legitimacy, until the entire higher lawmaking system had been reorganized on principles different from those of its predecessors.

While sensitive historical reconstruction of these revolutionary transformations is obviously important, *Transformations* tries for something more, and different. It treats the unconventional adaptations achieved at the Founding, Reconstruction, and New Deal as great constitutional precedents deserving the same kind of careful legal analysis we devote to those established by judges. To be sure, these precedents require us to give the sayings and doings of Presidents, congressional representatives, and other popular leaders the same kind of respectful consideration we typically reserve for the juridical elite. But putting this difference to one side, the book's aim is ultimately similar to that of the standard treatise on constitutional law. Just as the ordinary treatise interprets the constitutional doctrine elaborated by judges over time, *Transformations* interprets the law of higher lawmaking based on the great precedents elaborated by the Founders, Reconstructors, and New Dealers in the name of the People of the United States. Just as the traditional treatise attempts an authoritative statement of the doctrinal baseline for future legal development, *Transformations* makes an identical effort, elaborating the principles and practices that lawyers should use to evaluate future efforts to make higher law in the name of the American People.

As Rogers Smith suggests,[20] there may seem something paradoxical about such an effort: How can there be such a thing as *law* when the

---

[20] *See* Rogers M. Smith, *Legitimating Reconstruction: The Limits of Legalism*, 108 YALE L.J. 2039, 2052–53 (1999). For another effort that erects an overly dichotomous understanding of the relationship between law and revolution, *see* PAUL W. KAHN, THE REIGN OF LAW: MARBURY V. MADISON AND THE CONSTRUCTION OF AMERICA 69–74 (1997).

subject is the revolutionary transformation of the higher lawmaking system itself? The paradoxical quality of this question dissolves once one distinguishes between total breaks and unconventional adaptations. Law does break down in the interpretation of total breaks—since, by hypothesis, there is absolutely nothing linking the lawmaking system before and after the revolutionary breakthrough. But there is no similar paradox involved in the legal attempt to study the prevailing patterns of unconventional adaptation achieved during the Founding, Reconstruction, and New Deal. Despite the revolutionary character of these periods, certain basic continuities manage to maintain themselves. Perhaps, then, we will be in a position to identify the systemic imperatives shaping key decisions to transform some basic principles and practices *but not others*? To be sure, the constitutional meaning of the surviving elements may themselves be transformed as a result of the emergence of new principles and practices. Nonetheless, the reflective study of patterns of legal continuity within the context of revolutionary change may yield insights into the most durable elements of our constitutional language and practice.

Even these elements are not immune from challenge in the future. But before we can assess their claims to our continuing respect, we had better consider more carefully how, and whether, they may be identified.

In the next extract, Professor Ackerman summarizes the phases through which Reconstruction and the New Deal passed in order to qualify as paradigms of special transformative moments in which the public interacted with its national leaders to change the Constitution outside of the formal amendment process of Article V. Bruce A. Ackerman, 2 WE THE PEOPLE: TRANSFORMATIONS 17–26 (1998):[3]

First and foremost, the Republicans challenged the Federalists' view that the states should be an equal partner in the amendment process, with the right to veto any innovation that did not meet with their overwhelming approval. During the debate over slavery, the Presidency served as the principal vehicle for the Republicans' assault on this Federalist premise. Not only did Abraham Lincoln's Emancipation Proclamation shift the constitutional status quo before the Thirteenth Amendment was formally proposed, but Andrew Johnson's role was no less remarkable. President Johnson did not allow the Southern states to suppose that the original Federalist idea of an equal nation-state partnership applied to their consideration of the Emancipation Amendment.

The President fundamentally restructured the conditions under which Southern states would consider the Thirteenth Amendment. These actions violated original Federalist principles, but they fell far short of coercion. They did not, for example, deter Mississippi from formally rejecting the Thirteenth Amendment, but they did suffice to induce other Southern states to give their reluctant consent to this great nationalizing initiative on behalf of universal freedom. Overall, the ratification process is best described as a Presidentially led effort that diminished, but did not eliminate, the role of the states—an artful weave of old Federalist and new Presidential patterns that culminated in Secretary of State Seward's proclamation of December 1865, declaring the Thirteenth Amendment part of our higher law.

This precedent will prove especially important when we encounter the New Deal—which represents yet another quantum leap in the development of the *model of Presidential leadership*. As we turn to the Fourteenth Amendment, our analysis takes a different turn. Johnson refused to throw the Presidency's support behind this amendment's broad-ranging commitment to equal protection for American citizens of all races. Opposing further unconventional actions on the higher lawmaking front, he inaugurated a dramatic struggle with the Reconstruction Congress for the mantle of national leadership. The result was the elaboration of a *model of Congressional leadership* in which the Republicans on Capitol Hill finally gained the acceptance of the President (and the Supreme Court) of their claim that the Fourteenth Amendment was a valid expression of We the People.

The unconventional process evolved in five stages. During most of 1866, Congress and the President struggled to an impasse from their citadels on either end of Pennsylvania Avenue: each challenging the very authority of its antagonist to speak on fundamental matters in the name of We the People.

This first period of point-counterpoint induced both the President and Congress to transform the next regular election into one of the greatest higher lawmaking events of American history. The Congressional leadership proposed the Fourteenth Amendment as the platform on which they called upon the American people to renew their mandate. Andrew Johnson used the Presidency to mobilize the people against the Republicans by electing solid conservatives to Congress who would repudiate the Fourteenth Amendment.

The result was a decisive electoral victory for the party of revolutionary reform. This inaugurated the second stage of the process. The returning Republicans claimed a mandate from the People for the Fourteenth Amendment; the conservatives, led by Johnson, denied that the People had spoken decisively. The President encouraged ten Southern states to exercise the veto seemingly offered them by the Federalist's Article Five. This put Congress in an awkward position, since these Southern governments had been instrumental in giving the Thirteenth Amendment its three-fourths majority. Nonetheless, the Republicans refused to allow Federalist norms to monopolize their lawmaking options. Rather than accept an Article Five veto of the Fourteenth Amendment, they took unconventional action to redeem their mandate from the People.

This tactic inaugurated a third phase, involving an unconventional assault upon dissenting institutions. It began with the enactment of the Reconstruction Act of March 2, 1867, and continued through the impeachment of Andrew Johnson one year later. During this period, Congress claimed a popular mandate to destroy the autonomy of any institution—the Southern governments, the Presidency, and the Supreme Court—that opposed the legitimation of the Fourteenth Amendment. At the same time, the dissenters were under no compulsion to bend their knee before Congressional demands. They were free to resist until the next round of elections in 1868 in the hope that conservatives might gain a decisive victory at the polls.

The dissenters chose the path of resistance until they confronted their moment of truth in March of 1868—when the voters in the South, the conservatives on the Supreme Court, and Andrew Johnson in the White House made some of the pivotal decisions in our history. The central event was the President's impeachment trial, precipitated by Johnson's effort to slow down ratification of the Fourteenth Amendment so that its validity could remain a campaign issue in the upcoming 1868 elections. Would the President continue to resist the Republicans' vision of the Union—and thereby suffer conviction at the hands of the Senate? Or would he try to save his Presidency by negotiating a "switch in time," in which he would accept Congress's authority to override the South's Article Five veto?

The President chose the latter course, inaugurating a fourth stage—the "switch in time." Virtually simultaneous "switches" by the other dissenting institutions also allowed them to preserve their institutional autonomy. As a consequence, a new institutional situation emerged in the months after the impeachment trial. After years of intense struggle, all three branches in Washington, together with the reconstructed governments of the South, were converging on the legitimacy of the Fourteenth Amendment.

With the outlines of the Republican solution emerging from Washington, D.C., the elections of 1868 provided leading Democrats with another opportunity to denounce the constitutional legitimacy of the Fourteenth Amendment. But the Democratic challenge had the very opposite effect from its intended aim. Rather than provoking a further debate over first principles, 1868 served as a consolidating election, making it plain that most Americans wanted to bring the period of turbulent constitutional politics to an end. With Grant replacing Johnson in the White House, and the Republicans in firm control of Congress and the Court, nobody remained in authority to continue agitating public opinion about the constitutional irregularities involved in the enactment of the Civil War amendments. After the consolidating election of 1868, there was no longer a serious question whether the Civil War amendments were legal; the question, instead, was what they meant, and whether Americans would live up to their promise.

To summarize this five-stage process in terms of a simple schema:

Constitutional Impasse → Electoral Mandate → Challenge to Dissenting Institutions → Switch in Time → Consolidating Election

Consider how this schema challenges basic premises of the Federalist model of constitutional change. As we have seen, the Federalists used the division of powers between state and nation as their basic building block in constructing the Founding system: new amendments would be forged through a joint decisionmakng process dominated by popularly elected assemblies on both levels of government. As this system threatened to doom the Fourteenth Amendment, the Republicans adapted a second building block—the separation of powers—to a new constitutional use. For the Federalists, the separation between Congress, President, and Court played no significant role in higher lawmaking; it was simply a mechanism for passing normal legislation within higher-law constraints. But now it became the means by which contending protagonists tested each others' claims to a decisive "mandate" from the People on behalf of rival visions of the Union. The Fourteenth Amendment became higher law only because the Republican Congress emerged victorious from this test. It was the separation of powers, not the division of power, that became the nineteenth century's great engine of higher lawmaking.

One adaptation led to another. The protagonists in the White House and on Capitol Hill were given powerful incentives to impress new plebiscitarian meanings on national elections. The election of 1866 is paradigmatic, with both sides trying to break the impasse by gaining a decisive electoral victory. But the consolidating election of 1868 was hardly less important. In both cases, the election decisively changed the balance of perceived legitimacy, endowing the victors with a new credibility for their claim that the People had given broad and emphatic support for their constitutional solutions.

Putting these two interlocking innovations together, the successful struggle for the Fourteenth Amendment introduces a new nationalistic pattern into our higher lawmaking repertoire—one which supplements, but does not displace, the classical Federalist model. In contrast to its predecessor, the Republican model contemplates a constitutional dynamic dominated by a debate between rival branches of the national government—which, if successful, is culminated by a series of decisive electoral victories by the transformative movement after a sustained period in which its vision is subjected to withering criticism by the more conservative branches.

Having recovered this model, we come to the next question: how are lawyers going to use it? Those heavily invested in the reigning professional narrative may be tempted by a strategy of trivialization: "Granted, there is something fishy about the Fourteenth Amendment. But surely Reconstruction was an exceptional time, full of the passions of Civil War. It was the blood and sacrifice at battles like Gettysburg, not the nationalistic model of constitutional change, that legitimated the *Civil War* amendments. Whatever anomalies may have accompanied these amendments, they are of no relevance to the larger enterprise of constitutional understanding."

This easy answer allows lawyers to make their peace with Reconstruction, but only at a great cost in historical understanding. All that the victory of the Union army established was the failure of secession. It did not establish the terms for reunion, and certainly did not establish that most Americans supported a move beyond the Thirteenth Amendment. As the Republicans well understood, President Johnson was speaking for a large portion of the public when he rejected the Fourteenth Amendment's promise of equal protection to black Americans. The challenge was to organize a constitutional process that came to a decisive conclusion only after both sides were given a fair chance to bring their case to the country and mobilize their supporters for a series of focused electoral struggles.

Here is where the enduring status of the Federalist model became central. Quite simply, if the Republicans had respected the initial Article Five veto of the Fourteenth Amendment, Johnson would have won the struggle over the constitutional meaning of the Civil War. It was only through unconventional innovation that the Republicans finally won legitimacy for their more egalitarian understanding of the Union. Battlefield victories were necessary but not sufficient conditions for the Reconstruction amendments. Change in the higher lawmaking system was also crucial.

Putting the point more broadly, the Republicans' relationship to the Civil War is no different from the Federalists' relation to the Revolutionary War. George Washington, after all, gained his place at the Constitutional Convention by virtue of his wartime triumphs. But the war against England, like the war between the states, only established the military conditions for American independence. The enduring constitutional terms would be determined by the People during the peace that followed.

The parallel with the Federalists goes further. As we shall see, the 1787 Constitution would never have been ratified if the Federalists had played by the established rules. In 1787 as in 1868, unconventional adaptation was a necessary, if not a sufficient, condition for constitutional victory in the name of the People. Why, then, should the professional narrative give pride of place to the Federalist model while ignoring the Republican model?

We ignore these questions only by blinding ourselves to some deep truths about American identity expressed by the Republican model. After the searing experience of Civil War, Americans did become more of a nation. This is made plain by the very first sentence of the Fourteenth Amendment, which expressly affirms that national citizenship is primary and makes state citizenship derivative. The nation-centered character of the Republican model of constitutional change meshes perfectly with this substantive change. A professional narrative that ignores the Republican model would have us pretend that we still lived in the Federalist era, when Americans were still uncertain whether We the People of the *United* States were anything more than a confederation of sovereign states.

I do not deny the continuing importance of the Federalist system. Article Five provides an enduring resource for the American people when they wish to exercise their constituent power through the states. Rather than choosing between Federalism and Republicanism, I want to affirm both aspects of our higher lawmaking legacy.

Finally, the trivializing response goes wrong in suggesting that the Republican achievement is an anomaly in American history. As we shall see, it is the Republican model, more than the Federalist, which permits deeper insights into the dynamics of twentieth-century development.

. . .

I shall be inviting you to reflect upon a series of remarkable parallels between the 1860's and the 1930's. The effort will reveal that the New Deal Democrats' struggle for activist government went through a five-stage process that was broadly similar to the one encountered by the Republicans in their struggle for freedom and equality.

. . .

As in Reconstruction, the separation of powers served as the central engine for constitutional debate and decision during the New Deal. The big difference between the two periods concerns the identity of the leading reformist and conservative branches. After Lincoln was shot, the Presidency turned conservative, and Congress was left alone as the champion of revolutionary reform. In contrast, Roosevelt remained at the helm throughout the New Deal, leaving it up to the Court to defend the conservative view of the Constitution. With this variation, however, the five-phase pattern repeats itself.

Roosevelt's first term marks the first phase of institutional impasse, as the Supreme Court struck down a series of revolutionary reforms. As in 1866, the New Dealers responded by using the next regularly scheduled election as a device to break the constitutional impasse. When they gained a crushing victory in Presidential and Congressional elections of 1936, they claimed a mandate from the People for their activist vision of American government.

A third phase followed, characterized by an unconventional assault on dissenting institutions. Since the leading conservative branch during Reconstruction was the Presidency, the Republicans threatened Johnson with impeachment unless he accepted their constitutional reforms. Since the leading conservative branch in the 1930's was the Court, the President threatened the Justices with court-packing if they continued to defend the principles of laissez-faire constitutionalism. While impeachment and court-packing differ in legal form, their constitutional function was identical: to confront the leading conservative institution with a distinctive, and fundamental, question. Should it continue supporting the older constitutional tradition at the risk of permanent damage to its institutional autonomy?

Just as President Johnson made his "switch in time" in the late 1860's, so did the Court in the 1930's. Both retreats, in turn, allowed the dissenting institution to escape grievous long-term damage. Once the switch was made, conservatives managed to convince the Senate to reject court-packing in the 1930's, just as it had rejected impeachment in the 1860's. This not only enabled the separation of powers to survive. It encouraged the endangered branch to rehabilitate itself over time by playing a constructive role in the emerging constitutional order. As in 1868, so in 1937, all three branches were beginning to converge upon a new constitutional solution.

But this new solution had not yet been woven into the fabric of higher law. While the Supreme Court had supported some key New Deal programs by narrow margins in 1937, a Republican presidential victory in 1940 could have led to a reappraisal of these transitional decisions. As in the case of Reconstruction, the party of constitutional reform required a "consolidating election" before it could definitively set constitutional law on a new course.

Roosevelt's election to an unprecedented third term marked the point of no return. By 1941, the President and the Senate had replaced the last holdover Justices from the Republican era with convinced believers in activist national government. The 5-to-4 decisions of 1937 were now transformed into unanimous judgments that self-consciously swept away the fundamental doctrines of an earlier age.

. . .

The New Deal pattern is, then, best viewed as a variation on historic precedents established during Reconstruction. It was the Reconstruction Republicans, not the New Deal Democrats, who first combined the separation of powers with decisive electoral victories to gain the constitutional authority to speak in the voice of the We the People of the *United States*—a voice distinct from, but no less authentic than, the voice of We the People of the United *States* expressed through the Federalist rules of Article Five. But, of course, it is crucially important to clarify the variations introduced in the 1930s since they mark the parameters of modern constitutional development. I shall be emphasizing three themes.

The first, and most important, involves the Presidency. While Lincoln and Johnson played unprecedented roles in the constitutional emancipation of the slaves, Presidential leadership came to end with Andrew Johnson's defection. In contrast, New Deal Democrats could rely on the Presidency to provide ongoing constitutional leadership.

The Democrats' good fortune gave them more lawmaking options. They did not need to follow the example of the Reconstruction Congress as it destroyed state governments when they vetoed the Fourteenth Amendment. Nor did they need to threaten a hostile President with impeachment. Roosevelt could target the Supreme Court, and codify the New Deal vision, by flooding the bench with new Justices prepared to endorse a revolutionary transformation of traditional doctrine.

This led to a second fundamental change—the self-conscious use of *transformative judicial appointments* as a central tool for constitutional change. Roosevelt introduced this device in his famous court-packing proposal of 1937—which would have given him the right to make six new nominations immediately. When the old Court switch took the political wind out of this radical proposal, President and Congress elaborated a more gradual, but similar, approach. As traditionalist Justices resigned or died, they were systematically replaced by appointees prepared to support and elaborate a transformative vision of constitutional law.

By the early 1940s the stage had been set for a third change: the use of *transformative judicial opinions* to establish the basic contours of constitutional doctrine. These New Deal cases not only rejected leading decisions of the old regime, like *Lochner v. New York* which struck down maximum-hours legislation in the name of "freedom of contract." They transformed *Lochner* into a symbol of an entire constitutional order that had been thoroughly repudiated by the American people. These New Deal opinions have operated as the functional equivalent of formal constitutional amendments, providing a solid foundation for activist intervention in national social and economic life for the past sixty years.

I do not claim that this New Deal jurisprudence is an unchangeable element of our Constitution—but then again, neither is most of the formal text. I do claim that any future transformation of New Deal principles should require a higher lawmaking process comparable to the one led by President Roosevelt in the 1930s.

§ 13.03 Reading the Constitution as Written

Jed Rubenfeld, Professor Ackerman's Yale Law School colleague,[4] has suggested that conventional debates about constitutional theory (which focus on their relative fidelity to the Constitution) are misguided, because they ignore that a theory of constitutional interpretation ultimately is dependent on and must be derived from a political theory of legitimacy. In the following extract, he posits one such theory and explores its implications for interpreting the Constitution.[5]

Why, to take what is at once the simplest and hardest of questions, can't judges apply the unamended text when they render constitutional decisions, if that text seems to them the truer or purer national charter? Why can't judges rule love unconstitutional if that's what it takes to bring the Constitution alive for a contemporary audience? What does it mean to say with certainty that judges cannot do these things? It does not imply a set of premises concerning the nature of interpretation. It implies a set of premises concerning legitimacy: a set of premises concerning the legitimate role of judges in a democratic polity when rendering decisions irreversible through the ordinary political process. In constitutional law, legitimation precedes interpretation.

But if the constraints of legitimacy incumbent on constitutional judges are put in question, as they must be, there can be no answer to this question without asking further what gives constitutional law as such— this past-enacted, historically-given law—legitimate authority in the present? No one can say "a judge who does X with the Constitution acts legitimately" without providing an account of why the Constitution's having any result (whether X or not-X) is legitimate. (It is just the mistake of typical originalists—Raoul Berger and Robert Bork are good examples—to suppose that they can argue about the requirements of legitimacy that apply to judges when engaging in constitutional adjudication without

---

[4] Yale Law Professors Bruce Ackerman's and Akhil Amar's unconventional theories of constitutional change are sometimes referred to as representing a "Yale school" of constitutional law. *See, e.g.*, James E. Fleming, *We the Unconventional American People*, 65 U. CHI. L. REV. 1513, 1540 (1998) (reviewing 2 BRUCE A. ACKERMAN, WE THE PEOPLE: TRANSFORMATIONS

(1998)); Laurence H. Tribe, *Taking Text and Structure Seriously: Reflections on Free-Form Method in Constitutional Interpretation*, 108 HARV. L. REV. 1221, 1246 (1995).

[5] Jed Rubenfeld, *On Fidelity in Constitutional Law*, 65 FORD. L. REV. 1469, 1477–88 (1997). Copyright © 1997 by the Fordham Law Review. Reprinted with permission.

thinking through the legitimacy of constitutional adjudication or constitutional law as such.)

Constitutional interpretation is not to be derived from interpretive theory, nor even from legal theory (jurisprudence), but from political theory: from a theory accounting for the revolutionary place of written constitutionalism in democratic self-government. In the second half of this paper, I summarize one such theory and the implications it would have, if accepted, for constitutional interpretation.

A. The Problem of Time

The chief difficulty in trying to say why or how constitutional law could claim legitimate authority is simple to identify: the difficulty is that no account of political legitimacy could ever yield the conclusion that this aged text (even on the heroic supposition that it represented the legitimate democratic will of America a century or two ago) exerts any legitimate authority over American citizens today. The past is past. It is not a source of legitimate authority in the present.

Or so we have been told, and with considerable confidence. For example, Joseph Raz states, "[t]ake a law made at the beginning of this century. No account of legitimate authority can yield the conclusion that we are now subject to the authority of the long-defunct maker of that law."[12] Raz can make this claim without feeling the embarrassment of offering no argument to prove his negative because he merely states what many take for granted: that political legitimacy, whatever it may be, is a thing of the here and now.

Nor is this a view that came into fashion recently. "[T]he earth belongs in usufruct to the living," wrote Jefferson. "The dead have neither power nor rights over it."[14] A written constitution is, therefore, a scandal, a deviant institution, an offense against nature. "[B]y the law of nature, one generation is to another as one independent nation to another."[15]

The basic problem identified in these positions, past and present (notwithstanding the significant differences among them), is the same. It is the constitutional problem of time. We *here and now* (the implication always seems to be) could govern ourselves by giving ourselves law *here and now* (provided that certain deliberative conditions are met, that we define this "we" appropriately, that we reason properly, or that other stipulated conditions were met). But even if we imagine an American "People" in the most romantic . . . constitutional sense—as inclusive, collective, and participatory as you like—this people would not be self-governing if its governance were governed by law the people gave itself two hundred years ago. Only we here and now have legitimate authority over ourselves here and now.

We should have to go back beyond Jefferson to get to the beginnings of this view. Hobbes, for example, made a similar point:

The Sovereign of a Common-wealth, be it an Assembly or one Man, is not Subject to the Civill Lawes [sic] . . . . For he is free, that can

---

[12] Joseph Raz, *Why We Interpret* (unpublished manuscript on file with the author).

[14] 5 THE WRITINGS OF THOMAS JEFFERSON, 1788–1792, at 116 (1895).

[15] Thomas Jefferson, Letter of Sept. 6, 1789 to James Madison, in THOMAS JEFFERSON: WRITINGS 959, 962 (M. Peterson ed., 1984). *See also* Thomas Paine, *The Rights of Man, in* THE LIFE AND MAJOR WRITINGS OF THOMAS PAINE 251, 251 (P. Foner ed., 1961) ("[E]very age and generation must be free to act for itself, in all cases, as the ages and generations which preceded it.") (emphasis added).

be free when he will: Nor is it possible, for any person to be bound to himself; because he that can bind, can release; and therefore, he that is bound to himself only, is not bound. [17]

No sovereign self can bind himself "to himself." If so, then a written constitution, precisely insofar as it represents an attempt by sovereign people today to make its own present will binding tomorrow, is absurd and contradictory. It violates the very principle of self-government on which the Constitution claims legitimacy in the first place.

What principle? Rousseau stated it in exact if exacting terms: "[T]he general will that should direct the State is not that of a past time but of the present moment, and the true characteristic of sovereignty is that there is always agreement on time, place and effect between the direction of the general will and the use of public force."[19] The operative principle is nothing other than government by the will of the governed—the present, living will of the present, living governed.

B. Superficial Rejoinders

There are familiar, superficial answers to this conundrum. (What conundrum? The conundrum of the Constitution's legitimacy, given its historical givenness and hence its manifestly anti-democratic consequences.) One such answer is that the Constitution escapes the snare of time by the simple expedient of providing for its own amendment. Through Article V, which sets out an amendment procedure available to the people at any moment, the Constitution disclaims "perpetual" authority. It never purported to bind subsequent generations or even the same generation at a later point in time. It does not bind the sovereign, only the politicians. Citizens can amend whenever they choose, and the conundrum thereby disappears.

But citizens cannot amend the Constitution whenever they choose. On the contrary, amendment is very difficult: Article V imposes stringent supermajority requirements and onerous procedural obstacles before it permits amendment. As a result, as a practical matter, constitutional law in America does override popular will on any given day. And that is part of its point. When it comes to certain elemental matters of political power, justice and liberty, we are in fact governed, and designedly so, by reference to a text enacted generations ago and interpreted by a judiciary insulated from popular will.

It might yet be tempting to declare, all the same, that the majority of Americans today do in fact consent to being ruled by the Constitution in this way. Hence there is no true temporal conflict after all. So long as the Constitution retains current popular consent, all the temporal difficulties again disappear.

But this is no answer. Assuming it could overcome the usual weaknesses in arguments from tacit consent, the claim still would not answer the problem of time. By locating legitimate authority in present majority will, it would concede the following: if today's majority genuinely, deliberately wanted to establish a church or enslave a minority, there would be no reason of constitutional principle why this majority should not have its way. But American constitutionalism stands precisely for the principle that there *is* a reason why such a majority should not have its way: it would violate the Constitution. Constitutionalism affirms that there are

[17] Thomas Hobbes, LEVIATHAN pt. 2, ch. 26, at 204 (1965).

[19] Jean-Jacques Rousseau, *On the Social*

Contract, in ON THE SOCIAL CONTRACT 157, 168 (Judith R. Masters trans., 1978).

limits *legitimately and rightfully* imposed on majority will by virtue of the democratic enactment of a text a century or two ago. The problem of time is nothing other than the problem of explaining how the majority today can rightfully and legitimately be bound by—held to, *against its will*—limits on its power enacted generations ago. Invoking current majority consent as the source of the Constitution's legitimacy does not save constitutionalism from the problem of time. It repudiates constitutionalism, implicitly conceding that the problem of time is insuperable.

In other words, if we say that a constitution can escape the problem of time just insofar as it continues to comport with present majority will, we are saying that a constitution remains fully legitimate only to that extent. But a fully legitimate constitution, so defined, could not fully function *as* a constitution. It could, to be sure, impose restraints on local or individual actors who acted contrary to the present will of the national majority. But it could not perform at least one definitive constitutional function: it could impose no restraints on governmental action that accurately represented national majority will. If the Constitution's purchase on legitimacy depends on its conformity with present majority will, the price of attaining this legitimacy would be constitutionalism itself.

The embarrassing conclusion is that constitutional thought in America has never answered Hobbes's conundrum. Constitutional law has no account of its own legitimacy.

C. Democracy as Demography

Constitutionalism's relationship to democratic self-government will never be understood until we rid ourselves root and branch of the premise that democratic self-government consists ideally in government by the will or consent of the present-day governed. This premise, common to virtually all thinking about self-government in the modern era, is what produces a seeming antithesis between constitutionalism and democracy; it is what underlies Bickel's countermajoritarian difficulty, and it is what motivates most of the contemporary schools of constitutional interpretation.[21]

Government by the will of the governed has a certain temporal orientation. It is a present-tense orientation. On this view, we are ideally self-governing if we are governed at each successive moment by nothing but our own will at that moment. I have called this view "speech-modeled" because its present-tense orientation invariably leads it to a rhetoric of popular voice, or dialogue, or speech, when articulating the core of democracy. From this perspective, a constitutional text, handed down to us from the past, necessarily confronts freedom as an external threat, a dead letter that would choke the living voice of the people. It follows, from an interpretive point of view, that constitutional law must take the position either that the "voice of the people" from the moment of ratification somehow remains supreme today (originalism), or that constitutional law must become the vehicle of present popular voice (representation-reinforcement; contemporary-ratification), or perhaps that constitutional law must endeavor to hand down decisions to which citizens would give their consent at some predicted moment (early Bickel; hypothetical-consent models). None of these positions can do justice to written constitutionalism.

---

[21] *See* Jed Rubenfeld, *Reading the Constitution as Spoken*, 104 YALE L.J. 1119, 1127–34 (1995).

There is another conception of self-government we might have, which is temporally extended rather than oriented to the will of the governed at any particular moment. On this alternative view, self-government is a project in which a people attempts to govern itself over time: to live up over time to principles to which it has committed itself in writing, apart from or even contrary to its will at any particular moment—including its will at the present moment, and including its will at the so-called "constitutional moment."

Contrast two images of self-government. In the first, the citizenry gathers in a polis every day—or at regular, frequent intervals—to deliberate on public affairs and ultimately to deliver up the voice of the people (to which governance must then conform). In the second, a people struggles through a time-consuming politics of constitution-making to commit to writing a set of foundational principles to govern the life of the nation for a long period of time. The first image aspires after the Rousseauian ideal of conforming governance as nearly as possible to present will or voice of the governed. The second does not. It aspires rather toward the uniquely human freedom to give one's life a purpose, a meaning, a text: the freedom to write, rather than the freedom of speech.

Man does not achieve liberty by acting on his own will at each successive moment. Animals have such liberty. Man's peculiar relation to time is a condition of his being and his freedom. Of all animals, only man makes history; only man makes himself over time. This condition of human being and human freedom has its own condition: writing. Man alone can write. Man relates to himself over time through writing. Autonomy is always auto-biography: It is self-life-writing—not after the fact, but before and during the fact as well.

This means that freedom is possible for us only over time. A being is free in the human sense when holding itself to a commitment laid down by itself for itself over time, even if this holding happens to run against its desires at any particular moment. Man must commit himself to be free. He must give his life character. Which is to say, he must give it a text.

And this means that for persons to be politically self-governing, they must have more than a politics permitting themselves to give voice to their will. If that were all they had, their political order might be able to deliver law (by making the will of a past moment govern), it might be able to deliver self-rule (by making the will of the present moment govern), or it might be able to deliver justice (by making the perfected will of a predicted moment govern). But it could never do justice to self-government under law. Political legitimacy consists in a confluence of just these three aspirations: law, self-rule, and justice. Speech-modeled self-government relentlessly disjoins them in a competition among past, present, and predicted will.

To be free, a people must attempt the kind of self-government that can be realized only over generations. It must attempt the reins of time.

American constitutionalism broke from the two-thousand year history of democracy by virtue of its effort to exercise the freedom to write: to make a politics of popular authorship (rather than popular voice) the foundational or constitutional politics of the nation. Before late-eighteenth-century America, political theory had sometimes found political liberty to require a democratic constitution, but had never supposed that a democratic constitution had to be formed through a democratic politics. What was genuinely revolutionary in the American Revolution was its creation of a constitutional politics—a democratic politics of constitution-writing.[23]

There is no antithesis between written constitutionalism and democratic self-government. Constitutionalism—that is, written constitutionalism of the American variety—*is* democratic self-government. It is democracy not on the model of popular voice, but on the model of popular authorship or writing. It is democracy as *demo-graphy*. It is self-government over time.

To make good on this picture of self-government, I would have to persuade you that there is such a thing as a people that exists over time and that is properly regarded as the temporally extended subject of self-government. I would also have to persuade you that there is such a thing as a commitment, which is properly regarded as a normative operation irreducible to any act of will. And I would have to tell you more about the difference between voice-modeled democracy and demo-graphic democracy. But I won't try to do any of that here and now. Instead, I want to skip directly to the problem of interpretation. Assuming I could render a compelling account of demo-graphy, what sort of interpretation would follow from it?

. . .

Demo-graphy insists on two essential requirements for constitutional interpretation. First and foremost, interpretation must always respect the revolutionary politics of constitution-writing introduced by American constitutionalism in the late eighteenth century. This means that interpretation must always remain faithful in a determinate, recognizable way to the actions, the achievements, and the text wrought by those who fought for and memorialized our constitutional enactments. At the same time, however—and this is the second requirement of demo-graphic interpretation—interpretation cannot be wholly reduced to the original will or intentions, for then it would have privileged a single moment of democratic will and thereby contradicted its fundamental premise, which is that self-government must never be reduced to government in accordance with the will of the governed at any particular time.

How are these two demands to be satisfied? The answer lies in the use of *paradigm cases*.

Demography insists that the interpretation of a constitutional enactment must always adhere to and take its shape from the original paradigm cases: the core applications that the enactment was originally intended to have. Consider the following example. In 1999, Alabama enacts a statute barring blacks from becoming members of the Bar, from serving on juries, and from owning property. The Supreme Court finds no Fourteenth Amendment violation.

What is wrong with the Supreme Court's interpretation?

Well, one thing we might say is that the Court's interpretation is grotesque as a matter of justice or morality. But we should also be able to say that the Court's decision is grotesque as a matter of interpretation. If the Fourteenth Amendment means anything, we ought to say, it means that such a statute is unconstitutional. But this is so not as a matter of logic, nor as a matter of incontrovertible plain meaning, nor as a matter of the requirements of interpretation as such. It is so as a matter of history. The Fourteenth Amendment has certain paradigm cases, and all

[23] Madison was well aware of the world-historical character of this innovation. *See* THE FEDERALIST No. 38 (James Madison) (Gary Wills ed., 1982).

interpretation of that Amendment must adhere to and take its shape from them.

Adhering to paradigm cases respects the popular politics of constitution-making, but also accounts for the exercise of normative judgment in constitutional law. The judge's task is to extrapolate from the paradigm cases—to formulate principles or rules that capture these paradigm cases within the language of the text committed to writing, and then to apply those principles or rules to every other case, regardless of the original intentions. Thus in the case of the Fourteenth Amendment: what rules or principles does the guarantee of "equal protection" stand for if it prohibits at its core imposing on blacks the kinds of disabilities we have just described? This question can be answered in more than one way. The paradigm cases will rule out many possible interpretations of constitutional provisions, but they will not rule only one in. The place of normative judgment in constitutional interpretation is the place at which a principle is settled upon for a constitutional guarantee: a principle that must capture the provision's paradigm cases and that must, to be successful, offer itself as an account of what made this guarantee worthy of constitutional struggle—an account of what the guarantee means in the life of the nation.

To understand the phrase "what the guarantee means in the life of the nation," think for a moment of a personal (rather than a constitutional) commitment. You are married; perhaps you have had a child. You wonder what obligations are entailed by your commitment(s).

There will be certain right and wrong answers to this question, but there will be many answers neither ruled out nor ruled in. One thing is clear, however: the correct interpretive methodology for you to pursue cannot be to inquire into what you intended, or said to yourself, or would have said to yourself, at the "original" moment. To make a commitment is to engage oneself to something in part outside oneself, and hence the interpretation of a commitment is always interpretation of that to which you committed yourself, rather than an interpretation of your mental state at any particular time. [24] At the same time, however, interpretation of a commitment is not abstract philosophy: The question is not, ultimately, what child-rearing must mean to any rational being, or what child-rearing ought to mean to everyone, but what the meaning of children or family is in your life (even if its meaning might be something quite different in someone else's). Through this activity of interpretation and living-under, you draw together or re-collect your temporally distant experiences. You give your life character; you give it a text.

Constitutional interpretation serves the same function, and it is like-wise not moral philosophy, even while its task, most broadly stated, is to elaborate on the meaning of sweeping constitutional principles. What keeps the interpretation of a constitutional commitment anchored as interpretation of this nation's commitment (rather than what the same guarantee might mean in the life of some other nation) are the paradigm cases. In one particular, however, a judge's interpretation of a constitutional commitment differs fundamentally from your interpretation of a personal commitment. You are free in most cases to repudiate your commitments entirely. But you are also free to rebuild your commitment (as it were) one plank at a time: in this way, without ever repudiating your familial commitments, you might find yourself living three thousand

---

[24] Robert Cover made a very similar point fifteen years ago. *See* Robert Cover, *Nomos and Narrative,* in NARRATIVE, VIOLENCE, AND THE LAW: THE ESSAYS OF Robert Cover 93, 144–46 (M. Minow et al. eds., 1995).

miles away from your family, perhaps calling by telephone once every six months. . . .

Judges have no authority to remake the ship, even if it is done plank by plank, even if it will be stranded otherwise. Judges have the authority neither to repudiate a constitutional commitment, nor to preside (through a process of gradual interpretive substitution) over its transformation into something altogether different from what it was. Judges are bound, in preserving the *identity* of the commitment over time, to preserve something more than just its *continuity* over time. Day can turn to night by infinitesimal degrees, but judges have no authority to sail off into that darkness, not even by a slow, crepuscular passage. So long as interpretation adheres to the paradigm cases, so long as it takes its shape from them, it will remain recognizable as the interpretation of the principles to which the nation committed itself rather than as creations of, or evolutions into, brand new ones.

The paradigm-case method is, however, far from originalism. For example, the protection of women from sex discrimination can easily be derived from the paradigm case of protecting blacks from race discrimination, even if every single framer and ratifier of the Fourteenth Amendment intended that amendment to permit sex discrimination. What the framers intended a constitutional right *to permit* is of no consequence from the point of view of demo-graphy; but what those who fought for a constitutional right intended it to forbid, at its core, is ineradicable.

If these conclusions seem rather predictable and straightforward, I want to say two things. They should be predictable and straightforward: constitutional interpretation should be structured by its history in the way described, and in this country it has been shaped in large, conspicuous ways by the paradigm-case method throughout its development (examples will have to await another occasion). But observe that the current dominant schools of constitutional interpretation fail to arrive at what ought to be predictable and straightforward.

A strict originalism is able (like demo-graphic interpretation) to insist on the unalterability of the paradigm cases, but it must twist and turn in agonies of rationalization if it wants to account for the great departures from original intent—the single example of *Brown v. Board of Education*[27] is sufficient here—that demo-graphic interpretation can wholeheartedly embrace. The "softer" versions of originalism (advocating fidelity to the originally understood "principles" or "purposes"of the framers, even if the framers' specific intentions have to be discarded along the way) may be able to cover cases like *Brown,* but in doing so they lose their hold on the paradigm cases. For if the judge's job is to fulfill the general principles or purposes of the framers, without anchoring these principles or purposes in any specific applications, then, given today's "superior" understanding and changed circumstances, no particular result is secure. (Perhaps a modern judge, having read the *Bell Curve,* will assert that the "equal protection" of different racial groups now requires a paternalistic attitude toward certain of these groups according to their abilities.)

And all the non-originalist versions of judicial review, from processualist to fundamental-values to pure justice-seeking approaches, fail entirely to guarantee the paradigm cases. They could say, of the hypothetical given above, that a court upholding a new set of black codes had not made the Constitution the most just, or the most representative, or the most congruent with current values, and so on. But they could not see that such a

---

[27] 349 U.S. 294 (1955).

court had committed an inexcusable *interpretive* offense preceding all inquiry into whether the result was otherwise justifiable or unjustifiable. And in this blindness, these schools of interpretation fail to give us any adequate criteria to distinguish between interpreting our constitutional commitments and creating brand new ones.

The predicament of modern constitutional interpretation is as follows. An account of constitutional interpretation must be able (1) to distinguish interpreting from rewriting, rooting interpretation somehow in text and history; and yet (2) to explain and incorporate the undeniable role of normative judgment in constitutional law, beyond the letter of the law, and sometimes in defiance of the original intentions. None of the dominant schools of interpretation can negotiate this double demand. Thus originalism satisfies the first, but goes into furious denial when confronted with the second. The situation is just the reverse with the fundamental-values approaches. The reason is that all these schools are speech-modeled, and this double demand is but one manifestation of constitutionalism's simultaneous dedication to legality and justice—twin aspirations that the model of speech must invariably disjoin.

But demography, which joins the aspirations of law and justice into a single project of temporally extended self-government, can negotiate this double demand. The paradigm cases serve always to supply criteria to distinguish interpreting from rewriting, while their under-determinacy (and the concomitant need for interpretation of foundational commitments) always requires normative judgment beyond the letter and original intentions.

Let's not ask judges to hear the "Voice of the People" supposedly expressed at constitutional moments that fail to eventuate in a constitutional text. Let's not look at our judges as chain novelists of constitutional law. Let us rather look at the Constitution as a set of written political commitments whose definitive structure is and always remains given by what those who fought for the constitutional commitment fought most centrally to accomplish. And let us ask our judges to elaborate those commitments, never fearful of finding that these commitments commit us to more than what was originally supposed, so long as they are not held to commit us to less.

NYU Law School Professor Ronald Dworkin responded to Professor Rubenfeld's arguments at the close of the same symposium at which Professor Rubenfeld delivered the preceding paper. After suggesting that Professor Rubenfeld mistakenly had listed him among academics who have not appreciated the need for a theory of interpretation to be grounded in a political theory of legitimacy, Professor Ronald Dworkin explained what he considered to be the logical fallacy inherent in Professor Rubenfeld's argument. Ronald Dworkin, *Reflections on Fidelity*, 65 FORDHAM L. REV. 1799, 1811–15 (1997):[6]

Any general theory of interpretation, he says, is radically incomplete because it is itself an interpretation, and therefore it presupposes a theory of what makes an interpretation of anything a good one. But it cannot presuppose itself in that capacity, because that would beg the question. So it must presuppose a different and therefore rival theory of interpretation as more securely grounded than itself, which is a concession of its own infirmity. "This other mode of interpretation," he says, "that should have been ruled out but instead turns out to have been presupposed, makes it impossible to claim that the interpretive theory dictates a specific methodology for constitutional law."

We can quickly see that something is wrong with this argument. Since a theory can't justify itself by pressing the snake of a rival theory to its own bosom, but can only destroy itself in that way, the argument, if valid, would prove not that we have too many eligible theories of interpretation, but none at all. We might start, in seeing what has gone wrong, with an essential distinction between two questions. When is it sensible to ask for an external justification for a theoretical claim—a justification, that is, that does not presuppose the truth of part of what is being justified? When this is sensible, with respect to some theoretical claim, can an external justification actually be supplied? The first is a complex and disputed question of epistemology, but it seems plausible to say, as many philosophers do, that an entire domain of supposed knowledge or belief, like science as a whole or a comprehensive moral system, cannot have an external justification and does not need one. (As we shall see, Rubenfeld apparently agrees, at least in the case of science.) But someone who defends, not science as a whole, but, for example, a particular proposition of biology can sensibly be asked to provide evidence or argument for it that does not simply assume its truth, and we can indeed reasonably expect someone who offers advice about the right way to conduct some special level or kind of interpretation to argue for that advice in a way that does not assume its cogency.

Rubenfeld apparently thinks that writers who offer accounts of special types of interpretation must fail to meet that reasonable requirement. [For example,] Rubenfeld quotes my own comment in *Law's Empire* that "if a community uses interpretive concepts at all, the concept of interpretation itself will be one of them: a theory of interpretation is an interpretation of the higher-order practice of using interpretive concepts. (So any adequate account of interpretation must hold of itself.)" This, I said, is a necessary condition of a successful account of interpreting a particular kind of concept that plays a particular role in our social and political lives. But I certainly did not count satisfying that necessary condition as a sufficient condition of success; I defended my own account of how interpretive concepts should be interpreted not by appealing to itself, but by calling attention to the structure of social practices (like the practice of arguing about what courtesy actually is or demands) in which people back social claims with arguments trying to show how a practice would go better if their claims were recognized as sound or appropriate within it.

Rubenfeld might say, however, that these latter claims about social practice are themselves constructive interpretations at a higher level, because any explanation of human behavior, whether it takes the form of a philosophical account of translation, or a semantic theory of speech acts, or an account like mine of a social practice, is in the most general sense an interpretation that seeks to make the best sense of human thoughts, acts, practices and institutions, so that the question can therefore always be asked, even at the most general level, why we should try to understand ourselves in *that* way, rather than, for example, by seeing how we can make the least or worst sense of ourselves. We have something to say in answer to that question: we can appeal to an ethical standard of inquiry that connects our investigation of anything with our ethical responsibilities. But that roughly pragmatist conception of inquiry can itself be challenged, and, of course, explanation must come to an end someplace. At that point, according to Rubenfeld's argument, we face his dilemma. Either we just assume the truth of the entire package of ideas we have been defending, including its account of interpretation as making best rather than worst sense of what is interpreted, in which case we have begged the question, or we presuppose a different, rival set of ideas, in which case we have embraced two sets of ideas, not one. He answers, that is, that the demand for external justification must be met no matter how global the scope of the ideas on which that demand is pressed.

In the discussion that followed his paper, I pointed out that if his argument were sound, it would follow that science and mathematics and other apparently well-established domains of thought are also self-defeating. Scientists, for example, claim to have established truths through a complex methodology in which empirical assumptions about the interaction between human brains and the world figure prominently. But these empirical assumptions can themselves be challenged, and it would beg the question to claim to validate them through the very methodology they themselves are said to support. So, if Rubenfeld's thesis were sound, any scientist must be assuming some other, rival, methodology that justifies the premises of the methodology he is trying to defend. He has left us with two scientific methodologies, not one, and we must turn elsewhere (to political theory?) to choose between them. (We can easily construct a parallel argument aimed at the heart of mathematics.)

Rubenfeld replies to my argument in his published text. He says that I am correct about our inability to defend science and mathematics in any but a question-begging way, and that he meant to make the same point in calling his thesis a "Gödelian" one. But he adds the *ad hominem* comment that "math and science stand on a somewhat firmer footing, making somewhat firmer claims on our belief, than does *Law's Empire.*" My aim, of course, was not to challenge these domains as no sounder than my own theories, but on the contrary to rely on their solidity to show the fallacy in Rubenfeld's argument. The following three propositions cannot all be true: (1) A theory suffers from a fatal self-referential contradiction if it cannot defend its most basic claims without begging the question, because it must then assume the truth of a rival account of its own territory; (2) Science, mathematics and other large domains cannot defend their most basic claims without begging the question; (3) Science and mathematics stand on firm footing. Since Rubenfeld says that he accepts (2) and insists on (3), he must abandon (1). A theory may be complete and coherent even though it can appeal to no wholly external support.

But perhaps Rubenfeld's present point is that he meant (1) to hold only for theories that are controversial, as any general account of interpretation is likely to be, and not for domains of thought like mathematics and most of science which are not controversial. But the controversiality of a body of thought cannot affect the logical consequences of its failure to find external support. If that failure is fatal on logical grounds, then science and mathematics do not "stand on firm footing" after all, in spite of the widespread opinion that they do. If that failure is not fatal, so that science and mathematics can stand on a firm footing, then it is not a reason to reject a global but controversial set of ideas that it lacks external support. Any reason to reject it must lie elsewhere, presumably in the greater appeal of a rival set of ideas. That point has special importance to moral theory. A grand and comprehensive system of moral claims cannot claim any non-question-begging support from outside itself, but though we may reject such a system as unfounded or unconvincing, we must not insist that it has therefore already rejected itself.

§ 13.04   Conclusion: The Relationship between Theory and Practice

In this final extract, Professor Ackerman responds to criticisms from Professors Sanford Levinson of the University of Texas Law School and

Stephen Griffin of Tulane Law School that his theory of constitutional change either lacks, or misguidedly aspires to have, a meaningful relationship to the world of practice. In the course of explaining that such a relationship is fundamental to his work, Professor Ackerman considers whether the Clinton impeachment proceedings (in which he participated as an expert witness on behalf of the President) qualify as part of a transformative constitutional moment. In reading this final excerpt, consider the implications of Ackerman's conscious efforts to cultivate a relationship between his scholarly work and practice, particularly with respect to scholars' obligations beyond disclosing their respective politics. Ackerman, *Revolution on a Human Scale,* 108 YALE L.J. at 2340–49:[7]

> [Professors Levinson and Griffin] join the growing group of intellectual anti-intellectuals who would build a high wall of separation between serious legal scholarship, on the one hand, and competent legal practice, on the other.[121] On this view, it is philosophically naive or professionally pretentious (or both) to suppose that theory and practice can or should be linked up in a mutually supportive, and ultimately holistic, approach to constitutional law.
>
> . . .
>
> Professor Levinson suggests that "Ackerman provides no guidance at all as to how one should think during a constitutional moment"—and analyzes my own defense of President Clinton in the recent impeachment affair as a telltale example.[122] Undoubtedly, there is much to criticize in my professional performance, but these personal failings should not obscure the possibility that the framework provided by *Transformations* might serve other practicing constitutionalists as a source of useful guidance—of at least four kinds.
>
> The first is diagnostic. If *Transformations* establishes anything, it is that no constitutional regime lasts forever. One ongoing practical problem, then, is to identify the conditions under which a fundamental challenge to the existing regime is constitutionally legitimate, and when it is not. After all, whenever a politician wins at the polls, he is in the habit of claiming a "mandate from the People" for anything he wants— even so unrevolutionary a President as George Bush had no trouble interpreting his election as a profound popular "mandate" for a reduction in the capital gains tax! Since talk is cheap, the first practical challenge is to distinguish between the banalities of normal politics and the relatively rare occasions on which the constitutional system should begin to take the claim of a mandate from the People seriously. To put the point in terms of Levinson's claim, before one can determine whether *Transformations* can provide practical guidance "during a constitutional moment,"

---

[7] Reprinted by permission of the Yale Law Journal Company and Fred B. Rothman and Company from the Yale Law Journal, vol. 108, pages 2279-2349.

[121] There has been an explosive growth of separationist theories in recent years. Here is a sampler: Paul Kahn, THE CULTURAL STUDY OF LAW: RECONSTRUCTING LEGAL SCHOLARSHIP (1999); Anthony Kronman, THE LOST LAWYER (1993); Pierre Schlag, LAYING DOWN THE LAW: MYSTICISM, FETISHISM, AND THE AMERICAN LE-

GAL MIND (1996); Cass SUNSTEIN, ONE CASE AT A TIME (1999); Roberto Manganbeira Unger, WHAT SHOULD LEGAL ANALYSIS BECOME? (1996); Meir Dan-Cohen, *Listeners and Eavesdroppers: Substantive Legal Theory and Its Audience,* 63 U. COLO. L. REV. 569 (1992); Stanley Fish, *Dennis Martinez and the Uses of Theory,* 96 YALE L.J. 1773 (1987); Charles Fried, *The Artificial Reason of the Law or: What Lawyers Know,* 60 TEX. L. REV. 35 (1981) . . .

[122] Levinson, *Transitions,* 108 YALE L.J. 2215, 2235 (1999).

we must determine whether it can reliably identify such moments in the first place and distinguish them from the to-and-fro of normal politics.

My proposed method involves the use of our most successful past revolutions as paradigm cases for testing the claims of present-day revolutionaries to speak for the People. For example, any reader of *Transformations* will immediately begin to draw analogies between Bill Clinton's recent travails and the impeachment of Andrew Johnson. Despite all the obvious differences, there are striking similarities. As in the 1860s, so in the 1990s, the Republican Party had become an ideological instrument of self-declared "revolutionaries" intent on setting American politics on a radically new course; as in the 1860s, the revolutionaries of the 1990s were not in control of the presidency, but sought to use their power in the House as the springboard for an effort to revolutionize public values and institutional relationships. Newt Gingrich appears as the constitutional heir of Thaddeus Stevens—each seeking to pursue a transformative project to a successful conclusion despite the spirited resistance of a President committed to the defense of the constitutional status quo.

But *Transformations* suggests the existence of salient differences as well. The Republicans of the 1860s had lost the Presidency as the result of an assassin's bullet. When Stevens began to confront Johnson, it was against the background of the Republican electoral victories of 1860 and 1864. In contrast, the Republican revolutionaries who swept into the House after the election of 1994 could not follow through with another large victory in 1996. They could not even gain the presidential nomination for one of their number, and had to settle for Bob Dole—the very paradigm of a normal politician who would react with alarm to any seriously transformative initiative. Even then, the Republican candidate was defeated by Bill Clinton—in no small measure because of the public's negative reaction to the House's confrontational style of politics, exemplified by the extraordinary government shutdown.

In short, while both Gingrich and Stevens were engaged in broadly analogous efforts to renegotiate basic terms in the government's "Contract With America," the two impeachments arose at very different stages in the revolutionary enterprise. Before using impeachment as a weapon in their struggle with President Johnson, the Radical Republicans waited to win the triggering election of 1866. In contrast, the Republican revolutionaries of 1998 proceeded against Clinton despite their electoral setbacks of 1996 and 1998. If you will excuse a lapse into jargon, the House campaign against Clinton represented a belated effort at *signaling* to the People the rise of a transformative politics of revolutionary reform, while the campaign against Johnson represented an effort to *consolidate* the judgment of the People on the Fourteenth Amendment reached after a lengthy series of institutional struggles and electoral victories.

Despite this big difference, neither Stevens nor Gingrich allowed legalistic compunctions to override their fundamental aims. To be sure, the breaches with constitutional principle contemplated by the Gingrich Republicans paled in comparison with those endorsed by their Reconstruction predecessors. But by any other measure, they were very substantial. Given the doubtful constitutional status of the independent prosecutor— emphasized by a Supreme Court justice who is generally admired by the Republican revolutionaries[124] —one would have supposed that conscientious Representatives would have refused to delegate so much of their impeachment power to so doubtful a constitutional authority. Nevertheless, the House allowed the independent counsel, and not its own judiciary

---

[124] *See* Morrison v. Olson, 487 U.S. 654, 697–734 (1988) (Scalia, J., dissenting).

committee, to do most of the heavy lifting. Similarly, given the American People's repudiation of the authority of lameduck Congresses with the enactment of the Twentieth Amendment, one would have supposed that the lameduck House would have waited until it was replaced by its newly elected successor before entertaining such a fateful assault on the Presidency—or that Henry Hyde and his fellow impeachment managers would have waited for a new bill of impeachment before proceeding to a Senate trial.

But nothing of the sort happened. Very much as in the late 1860s, the Gingrich Republicans used constitutionally anomalous institutions—the independent counsel, the lameduck House—to generate a sense of institutional momentum that might create a "bandwagon effect" in the public mind that served to legitimate their behavior, despite the objections of legalistic nit-pickers.

This diagnosis of the evolving situation brings certain normative questions of constitutional process to the fore—leading to a second practical use of my framework. For present purposes, two questions will suffice. The first addresses the situation from the perspective of the Republican revolutionaries: Under what conditions is it constitutionally appropriate to override legalistic compunctions and try to create an unconventional "bandwagon" effect? The second takes up the matter from the vantage of Democratic defenders of the constitutional status quo: Under what conditions should legalistic objections be energetically pressed, and when is it constitutionally appropriate to engage in statesmanlike retreat?

As Professor Levinson notes, I concluded that the Republicans' bandwagon was constitutionally illegitimate, and repeatedly protested against the lameduck impeachment in a variety of public places.[126] In launching my personal campaign in defense of the President, Levinson suggests, I was somehow acting inconsistently with the professed message of *Transformations*: If I hoped to reinvigorate the revolutionary tradition of American constitutionalism by writing the book, why did I come out so loudly in conservative defense of the status quo in defending the President?

Well, for one thing, I deeply oppose the substance of the Gingrich revolution. But even if this were not so, I very much hope I would have come out the same way on the basis of my study of constitutional law. As *Transformations* establishes, American revolutionaries cannot rightly hope for instant gratification simply because they have won control over a single institution of American government. To the contrary, our constitutional system rightly requires them to endure a decade-long period of rigorous institutional testing before they can legitimately claim to revolutionize governing values in the name of We the People.

Apart from my opposition to the merits of their program, I had a serious constitutional problem with the way the Republicans were seeking to advance it. Quite simply, they were trying to do too much too quickly with

---

[126] *See* my testimony before the House Judiciary Committee on December 8, 1998, reprinted in *Testimony Before the House Judiciary Committee*, PS: POLITICAL SCIENCE AND POLITICS, Mar. 1999, at 24. My media campaign on the procedural issues included Bruce Ackerman, *Contest Lame-Duck House Vote*, USA TODAY, Dec. 23, 1998, at 12A; Bruce Ackerman, *Lame-Duck Impeachment? Not So Fast*, N.Y. TIMES, Dec. 8, 1998, at A27; Bruce Ackerman, *This Lame-Duck Impeachment Should Die*, WASH. POST, Dec. 24, 1998, at A17; and Bruce Ackerman, *Without the People, Impeachment Fails*, L.A. TIMES, Nov. 6, 1998, at B9, culminating in a pamphlet, published in mid-January and submitted to all members of the House and Senate with a supporting letter by leading legal scholars.

too little popular support. Instead of allowing the Republicans to use the independent prosecutor and lameduck House to generate a bandwagon effect, the right thing to do was to challenge the constitutional legitimacy of these shortcuts—and call upon the newly elected House of Representatives to do its own homework, and revote articles of impeachment, before proceeding to a trial in the Senate.

It is a matter of public record that the President and his lawyers took my proposal seriously. In the end, however, they decided to waive their constitutional objections to the lameduck impeachment, and move immediately to a trial before the Senate. While I was in ongoing contact with the President's legal staff, I was not privy to their most important deliberations on this strategic decision. But my own guess, for whatever it's worth, is that the President's remarkably high standing in the public opinion polls played a crucial role in his decision to waive his procedural objections.

To see why, consider that the President had nothing to fear from a Senate trial as long as his popular support remained at stratospheric levels—since it was obvious to all concerned that, so long as the President stood at seventy percent in the polls,[128] such a trial would lead to a quick acquittal. In contrast, there were dangers involved in throwing the matter back to the House. At the very least, this threatened to drag out the proceedings for months before the House leadership either pushed through a new bill of impeachment or gave up on the project. At the worst, the President's popularity might sink in the meantime, encouraging the House Republicans to vote out a second impeachment at a moment when the President ran a greater risk of Senate removal. Why not, then, waive the procedural objections, and move quickly to acquittal?

I do not challenge this strategic calculation, but emphasize its paradoxical aspect: If the President had been less popular, it would have been harder for Clinton to predict the outcome of his Senate trial, and it would have made more strategic sense to stop the trial dead in its tracks by challenging the legitimacy of the lameduck impeachment, and force the Republicans to go through a second round of activities in the House.

Easy cases make bad law: The President's popularity led him to create a precedent that may well weaken the Presidency at some future moment. After all, most sitting Presidents do not enjoy the luxury of seventy percent approval ratings. If and when the next resident of the White House is obliged to confront a lameduck impeachment, he or she may well regret Clinton's decision to allow the Republican bandwagon to proceed unchallenged!

To be sure, nothing in *Transformations* led me to anticipate the strategy President Clinton would ultimately select to defend his interests. But it is far too simple to suggest, with Professor Levinson, that *Transformations* did not guide my practical activities on behalf of the President, or that these did not help shape—and in a constructive way?—the President's constitutional understanding of his strategic alternatives.

Thus far, I have been discussing the way in which *Transformations* might serve to guide practical deliberation about matters of constitutional process. But another aspect of Professor Levinson's critique generates a third, and more substantive, use of my framework—as a guide in determining the kind of "high crimes and misdemeanors" that might justify the President's removal from office. As he notes, I opposed a broad

---

[128] *See* Gary C. Jacobson, *Impeachment Politics in the 1998 Congressional Elections,* 114 POL. SCI. Q. 31, 51 (1999) (noting that the first post-impeachment Gallup Poll put Clinton's job approval rating at 73%).

construction of this famous formula on the ground that it would dramatically weaken the Presidency and result in "a massive shift toward a British-style system of parliamentary government." So far as Levinson is concerned, this was precisely the wrong ground to stand on. As an academic pioneer in the exploration of our Constitution's stupidest ideas, Professor Levinson offers his considered opinion that a "fixed-term president, who is impervious, as a practical matter, to removal" is high up on the list—perhaps one of the crowning "stupidities" of our system. Why, then, did I intervene in defense of such a retrograde notion?

If we were writing a constitution on a clean slate, there would be much to be said in favor of Levinson's critique of the American Presidency. Indeed, I have recently written a paper criticizing the export of our presidentialist model abroad for reasons that he might well commend.[131] I also agree with Levinson's claim that we will not get very far by asking about the original intentions of the Framers. In writing about "high crimes and misdemeanors," the Founders envisioned a very different Presidency from the one that has emerged over the last two centuries. Indeed, the Founding vision did not survive Thomas Jefferson, let alone Abraham Lincoln and Franklin Roosevelt.[132] We cannot begin to elaborate modern standards for impeachment by pretending that the Founding vision of the Presidency represents our reality when it has in fact long since been exploded by the constitutional experience of the American people. If we are to decode the meaning of "high crimes and misdemeanors" successfully, nothing less than a profound act of translation is required.[133] We must place these words within the context of the modern Presidency as it has been transformed over time by the American People, not as it emerged from the collective imagination of the Founders.

Up to this point, then, Levinson and I are travelling down a common path: When considered in the abstract, there is much to be said against the idea of an independent Presidency; and the Founders' deliberations shouldn't serve to block critical thought in this area. It is one thing, however, to urge us to move beyond the Founders; it is quite another to ignore the larger lessons of American history. This is the place where Professor Levinson underestimates the potential contribution of *Transformations* to a thoughtful modern elaboration of impeachment standards. My revised professional narrative tells a story that emphasizes the role of the independent Presidency in the practical exercise of popular sovereignty by the American People over the generations. I believe that this historically rooted connection between the Presidency and popular sovereignty should serve as a focus of our inquiry: Would the use of impeachment in cases like the Lewinsky Affair serve to undermine this constitutionally fundamental presidential function?

This is not the place to attempt a final answer. But the question should suffice to rebut the charge that my framework "provides no guidance at all" in guiding final judgment on the merits. At the very least, *Transformations* cautions against an unconsidered weakening of the Presidency in the absence of broad and deep popular support for a reconstruction of its powers.

The first three uses of my framework—diagnostic, processual, and substantive—were available as a guide to conduct during the episode

---

[131] *See* Bruce Ackerman, *Rethinking the Separation of Powers* 113 HARV. L. REV. (forthcoming Jan. 2000).

[132] I discuss the shattering consequences of the Jeffersonian Revolution in a forthcoming book . . . .

[133] *See* Lawrence Lessig, *Fidelity as Translation: Fidelity and Constraint,* 65 FORDHAM L. REV. 1365 (1997); Lawrence Lessig, *Understanding Changed Readings: Fidelity and Theory,* 47 STAN. L. REV. 395 (1995).

itself. The final function deals with its enduring constitutional significance: What is the precedential value of the President's impeachment and acquittal? How should we view the episode as we proceed with our further struggles over the future of the Republic?

Transformations suggests that we should view the episode as a failed constitutional moment—and one that rightly failed because the Republican revolutionaries went too far too fast without remotely gaining the kind of mobilized and sustained support required by the American constitutional tradition. Such an abuse, of course, may well generate more abuses in the coming decades. House Democrats will long remember the days of Newt Gingrich and Henry Hyde—and they will be sorely tempted to exact their pound of flesh the next time they are in control of Congress and a Republican President sits in the White House.

If this happens, I'd be happy to sign on to the President's legal team at my customary rate of $0 an hour. I am a constitutionalist first, a liberal Democrat second: If the next abusive impeachment gets as far as the last one, we will find ourselves trapped in an endless cycle of incivility and recrimination. Constitutionalists of all parties should work together to build a consensus that establishes the Clinton case as a *negative precedent* for future constitutional development. If we fail in constructing such a common understanding, the ensuing cycles of impeachment will make it increasingly impossible for Americans to conduct a decent system of normal politics, let alone a serious and mobilized debate on our constitutional future as a nation.

Professor Griffin attacks the relationship between theory and practice from a different front. Professor Levinson proceeds from the side of practice, telling the thoughtful statesman that he is wasting his time consulting *Transformations* as a source of practical insight. Professor Griffin attacks from the side of legal scholarship. His credo is straightforward: Scholars should seek the truth, and nothing but the truth.[135] We should not be addressing the practical concerns of lawyers or judges or statesmen, but the academic concerns expressed by our fellow scholars in the humanities and social sciences. One citation from Jürgen Habernas or Kenneth Arrow is worth a million cites from Anthony Kennedy's law clerk.

I propose an amendment to Griffin's credo. The legal scholar's rightful aim is not simply to speak the truth, though this is hard enough. It is *to speak the truth to power.* I am unwilling to cut my links to the men and women charged with the task of governing this country according to the Constitution of the United States. They need all the help they can get; if the academy turns its back on them, the quality of their decisions is sure to suffer.

But speaking truth to power generates its own pathologies. The powerful may not listen unless the truthtellers pander to their prejudices. The price of credibility in the world of the powerful may be the sacrifice of truth itself.

It is not a price worth paying, but this is easier said than done. Each legal academic dreams his own dreams of direct influence in the world, and these dreams may prove intoxicating. Perhaps they suggest the need to write a rhetorically powerful law review article that might convince a judge to do justice, but at the cost of accepting a host of legal fictions that do not correspond to the scholar's understanding of truth. Is there

---

[135] *See* Griffin [*Constitutional Theory Transformed,* 108 YALE L.J. 2115, 2156 (1999)].

anything wrong with steaming ahead regardless, and getting the thing published in the *Harvard Law Review?*

I am not a purist, but I agree with Griffin that law reviews contain too much thinly-disguised instrumental advocacy. And too little truth seeking. But I think his remedy—academic purism—is even worse than the disease. I part company in particular when it comes to the longer run, measured in decades, which represents the natural time-horizon for scholarly influence on professional opinion. It is right and proper to hope for such influence; and [] legal scholarship that refuses to direct itself toward this goal is in danger of preciosity and self-indulgence.

Let me make the point in terms of my hopes for *Transformations.* Within the short run of the next decade, I completely agree with Professor Griffin's pessimistic assessment of the chances that my revisionist view of American constitutional development will triumph on the pages of the *United States Reports.* The present generation of judges are the captives of their own legal educations, just like the rest of us, and they have neither the time nor the inclination to undertake the agonizing reappraisal required to move beyond the present interpretive horizon. Within the near term, then, I expect most lawyers and judges to continue adhering to the "restorationist" account of the New Deal that many leading scholars in law, history, and political science have discarded. As cracks in this consensus appear, the judicial debate will orient itself by the light cast by the plurality opinion in *Casey,* with Justice Thomas's dissent in *Lopez* serving as a visible, if not popular, alternative. If I am lucky, *Transformations* will be a distant third in the judicial sweepstakes.

But I am not so despairing of the longer run. There are two ways *Transformations* might ultimately gain professional ascendancy. The first is through the model of elite management. This requires, first, that many younger members of the legal academy come to believe that something like my account is really true; second, that these newly understood truths change the teaching of constitutional law in the nation's classrooms; and third, that the new learning then trickles into the practical life of the profession, incorporating itself slowly into judicial opinions at various levels of the hierarchy—until at long last, it trickles up to the Supremes.

The second path is through a new round of revolutionary renewal. On this scenario, the next cycle of popular mobilization contrasts sharply with the recent movements from the Radical Right. Rather than seeking to restore a narrowly sectarian version of Christian morality, the next generation of Americans prove to be more interested in seeking to redeem, and move beyond, the promises of economic and social justice made during the New Deal and Civil Rights eras. If such a renascent liberalism ever regains the support of the American People, the judges flooding the courts would become much more interested in reinterpreting their relationship to earlier episodes of revolutionary renewal, opening themselves up to whatever truths on such matters have been stored up in the academy.

I am not holding my breath in anticipation of either of these great judicial awakenings. Only a fool actually expects to succeed in speaking truth to power. But only a knave gives up entirely, at least if he is a law professor conscious of his debt to his fellow citizens. What kind of legal order can Americans ever hope to achieve without *anybody* in the academy making the effort to take the courts' ongoing claims to constitutional legitimacy seriously?

§ 13.05 Bibliography

Critiques of and Commentaries on Alternatives to Formal Theories of Constitutional Interpretation

Bruce A. Ackerman, *Constitutional Politics / Constitutional Law*, 99 YALE L.J. 453 (1989); *Storrs Lecture: Discovering the Constitution*, 93 YALE L.J. 1013 (1984)

Matthew D. Adler, *Rights Against Rules: The Moral Structure of American Constitutionalism*, 97 MICH. L. REV. 1 (1998); *Judicial Restraint in the Administrative State: Beyond the Counter-Majoritarian Difficulty*, 145 U. PA. L. REV. 759 (1997)

T. Alexander Aleinikoff, *Constitutional Law in the Age of Balancing*, 96 YALE L.J. 943 (1987)

Akhil Reed Amar, *Intratextualism*, 112 HARV. L. REV. 747 (1999)

J.M. Balkin, *What Is a Postmodern Constitutionalism?*, 90 MICH. L. REV. 1966 (1992)

J.M. Balkin & Sanford Levinson, *The Canons of Constitutional Law*, 111 HARV. L. REV. 963 (1998)

Guido Calabresi, *The Supreme Court, 1990 Term Foreword: Antidiscrimination and Constitutional Accountability (What the Bork-Brennan Debate Ignores)*, 105 HARV. L. REV. 80 (1991)

Barry Cushman, RETHINKING THE NEW DEAL COURT: THE STRUCTURE OF A CONSTITUTIONAL REVOLUTION (1998).

Michael C. Dorf, *Supreme Court 1997 Term—Foreword: The Limits of Socratic Deliberation*, 112 HARV. L. REV. 4 (1998); *Integrating Normative and Descriptive Constitutional Theory: The Case of Original Meaning*, 85 GEO. L.J. 1765 (1997)

Christopher L. Eisgruber, *The Fourteenth Amendment's Constitution*, 69 S. CAL. L. REV. 47 (1995)

Richard H. Fallon, Jr., *How to Choose a Constitutional Theory*, 87 CALIF. L. REV. 535 (1999) (with commentaries by David A. Strauss and Michael C. Dorf)

James E. Fleming, *We the Unconventional American People*, 65 U. CHI. L. REV. 1513 (1998) (reviewing 2 BRUCE A. ACKERMAN, WE THE PEOPLE: TRANSFORMATIONS (1998)); *Constructing the Substantive Constitution*, 72 TEX. L. REV. 211 (1993) (with a response by Cass R. Sunstein)

Michael J. Gerhardt, *Ackermania: The Quest for a Common Law of Higher Lawmaking*, 40 WM. & MARY L. Rev. 1731 (1999) (reviewing 2 BRUCE A. ACKERMAN, 2 WE The PEOPLE: TRANSFORMATIONS (1998))

Stephen Griffin, AMERICAN CONSTITUTIONALISM: FROM THEORY TO POLITICS (1996)

Daniel J. Hulesbosch, *Civics 2000: Process Constitutionalism at Yale*, 97 MICH. L. REV. 1520 (1999) (reviewing 2 Bruce A. Ackerman, WE THE

PEOPLE: TRANSFORMATIONS (1998); Akhil Reed Amar, THE BILL OF RIGHTS: CREATION AND RECONSTRUCTION (1998))

Michael J. Klarman, *Constitutional Fetishism and the Clinton Impeachment Debate*, 85 VA. L. REV. 631 (1999)

Deborah Jones Merritt, *Constitutional Fact and Theory: A Response to Chief Judge Posner*, 97 MICH. L. REV. 1287 (1999)

Henry Paul Monaghan, *We the People, Original Understanding, and Constitutional Amendment*, 96 COLUM. L. REV. 121 (1996)

Richard H. Pildes, *Avoiding Balancing: The Role of Exclusionary Reasons in Constitutional Law*, 45 HAST. L.J. 45 (1994)

Richard A. Posner, AN AFFAIR OF STATE: THE INVESTIGATION, IMPEACHMENT, AND TRIAL OF PRESIDENT CLINTON (1999); *Against Constitutional Theory*, 73 N.Y.U. L. REV. 1 (1998); *This Magic Moment*, THE NEW REPUBLIC, April 6, 1998, at 35

L.A. Powe, Jr., *Ackermania or Uncomfortable Truths?*, 15 CONST. COMM. 547 (1998) (reviewing 2 Bruce A. Ackerman, WE THE PEOPLE: TRANSFORMATIONS (1998))

Lawrence Sager, *The Incorrigible Constitution*, 65 N.Y.U. L. REV. 893 (1990)

Stephen D. Smith, *The Pursuit of Pragmatism*, 100 YALE L.J. 409 (1990)

Symposium: Constitutional Theory and the Practice of Judging, 63 U. COLO. L. REV. 291 (1992) (with articles by Kathleen M. Sullivan, Robert F. Nagel, T. Alexander Aleinikoff, Suzanna Sherry, Richard Delgado, Sanford Levinson, David M. Ebel, Philip Bobbitt, Pierre Schlag, Mark V. Tushnet, William Wayne Justice, and Abner J. Mikva)

Symposium: The Renaissance of Pragmatism in American Legal Thought, 63 S. CAL. L. REV. 1569 (1990) (with articles by Thomas C. Grey, Martha Minow and Elizabeth V. Spelman, Richard A. Posner, Hilary Putnam, Margaret Jane Radin, Catharine Wells, and Cornel West; and comments by Scott Brewer, Mari J. Matsuda, Frank Michelman, Ruth Anna Putnam, Richard Rorty, Joseph William Singer, and Marion Smiley)

Symposium, Voices of the People: Essays on Constitutional Democracy in Memory of Professor Julian N. Eule, 45 UCLA L. REV. 1523 (1998) (with articles by Susan Westerberg Prager, Julian N. Eule as completed by Jonathan D. Varat, Erwin Chemerinsky, Jonathan D. Varat, Kathleen M. Sullivan, Kimberlé Crenshaw & Gary Peller, Frank I. Michelman, Hans A. Linde, and Kenneth L. Karst)

Laurence H. Tribe, AMERICAN CONSTITUTIONAL LAW: PART I (3d ed. 1999); *Taking Text and Structure Seriously: Reflections on Free-Form Method in Constitutional Interpretation*, 108 HARV. L. REV. 1221 (1995)

Appendix

Constitution of the United States Of America

WE THE PEOPLE of the United States, in Order to form a more perfect Union, establish Justice, insure domestic Tranquility, provide for the common defence, promote the general Welfare, and secure the Blessings of Liberty to ourselves and our Posterity, do ordain and establish this Constitution for the United States of America.

ARTICLE I

SECTION 1. All legislative Powers herein granted shall be vested in a Congress of the United States which shall consist of a Senate and House of Representatives.

SECTION 2. [1] The House of Representatives shall be composed of Members chosen every second Year by the People of the several States, and the Electors in each State shall have the Qualifications requisite for Electors of the most numerous Branch of the State Legislature.

[2]No Person shall be a Representative who shall not have attained to the Age of twenty five Years, and been seven Years a Citizen of the United States, and who shall not, when elected, be an Inhabitant of that State in which he shall be chosen.

[3]* [Representatives and direct Taxes shall be apportioned among the several States which may be included within this Union, according to their respective Numbers, which shall be determined by adding to the whole Number of free Persons, including those bound to Service for a Term of Years, and excluding Indians not taxed, three fifths of all other Persons.] The actual Enumeration shall be made within three Years after the first Meeting of the Congress of the United States, and within every subsequent Term of ten Years, in such Manner as they shall by Law direct. The Number of Representatives shall not exceed one for every thirty Thousand, but each State shall have at Least One Representative; and until such enumeration shall be made, the State of New Hampshire shall be entitled to chuse three, Massachusetts eight, Rhode Island and Providence Plantations one, Connecticut five, New York six, New Jersey four, Pennsylvania eight, Delaware one, Maryland six, Virginia ten, North Carolina five, South Carolina five, and Georgia three.

[4]When vacancies happen in the Representation from any State, the Executive Authority thereof shall issue Writs of Election to fill such Vacancies.

[5] The House of Representatives shall chuse their Speaker and other Officers; and shall have the sole Power of Impeachment.

NOTE.—The superior number preceding the paragraphs designates the number of the clause.

* The part included in heavy brackets was repealed by section 2 of amendment XIV.

[1]SECTION 3. ** The Senate of the United States shall be composed of two Senators from each State, [chosen by the Legislature] thereof, for six Years; and each Senator shall have one Vote.

[2]Immediately after they shall be assembled in Consequence of the first Election, they shall be divided as equally as may be into three Classes. The Seats of the Senators of the first Class shall be vacated at the Expiration of the second Year, of the second Class at the Expiration of the fourth Year, and of the third Class at the Expiration of the sixth Year, so that one third may be chosen every second Year; [and if Vacancies happen by Resignation, or otherwise, during the Recess of the Legislature of any State, the Executive thereof may make temporary Appointments until the next Meeting of the Legislature, which shall then fill such Vacancies]. *

[3]No Person shall be a Senator who shall not have attained to the Age of thirty Years, and been nine Years a Citizen of the United States, and who shall not, when elected, be an Inhabitant of that State for which he shall be chosen.

[4]The Vice President of the United States shall be President of the Senate, but shall have no Vote, unless they be equally divided.

[5]The Senate shall chuse their other Officers, and also a President pro tempore, in the absence of the Vice President, or when he shall exercise the Office of President of the United States.

[6]The Senate shall have the sole Power to try all Impeachments. When sitting for that Purpose, they shall be on Oath or Affirmation. When the President of the United States tried, the Chief Justice shall preside: And no Person shall be convicted without the Concurrence of two thirds of the Members present.

[7]Judgment in Cases of Impeachment shall not extend further than to removal from Office, and disqualification to hold and enjoy any Office of honor, Trust or Profit under the United States: but the Party convicted shall nevertheless be liable and subject to Indictment, Trial, Judgment and Punishment, according to Law.

SECTION 4. [1]The Times, Places and Manner of holding Elections for Senators and Representatives, shall be prescribed in each State by the Legislature thereof; but the Congress may at any time by Law make or alter such Regulations, except as to the Places of chusing Senators.

[2] The Congress shall assemble at least once in every Year, and such Meeting shall [be on the first Monday in December,] unless they shall by Law appoint a different Day. **

SECTION 5. [1]Each House shall be the Judge of the Elections, Returns and Qualifications of its own Members, and a Majority of each shall constitute a Quorum to do Business; but a smaller Number may adjourn from day to day, and may be authorized to compel the Attendance of absent Members, in such Manner, and under such Penalties as each House may provide.

** The part included in heavy brackets was changed by section 1 of amendment XVII.

* The part included in heavy brackets was changed by clause 2 of amendment XVII.

** The part included in heavy brackets was changed by section 2 of amendment XX.

[2]Each House may determine the Rules of its Proceedings, punish its Members for disorderly Behavior, and, with the Concurrence of two thirds, expel a Member.

[3]Each House shall keep a Journal of its Proceedings, and from time to time publish the same, excepting such Parts as may in their Judgment require Secrecy; and the Yeas and Nays of the Members of either House on any question shall, at the Desire of one fifth of those Present, be entered on the Journal.

[4]Neither House, during the Session of Congress, shall, without the Consent of the other, adjourn for more than three days, nor to any other Place than that in which the two Houses shall be sitting.

SECTION 6. [1]The Senators and Representatives shall receive a Compensation for their Services, to be ascertained by Law, and paid out of the Treasury of the United States. They shall in all Cases, except Treason, Felony and Breach of the Peace, be privileged from Arrest during their Attendance at the Session of their respective Houses, and in going to and returning from the same; and for any Speech or Debate in either House, they shall not be questioned in any other Place.

[2]No Senator or Representative shall, during the Time for which he was elected, be appointed to any civil Office under the authority of the United States, which shall have been created, or the Emoluments whereof shall have been encreased during such time; and no Person holding any Office under the United States, shall be a Member of either House during his Continuance in Office.

SECTION 7. [1]All Bills for raising Revenue shall originate in the House of Representatives; but the Senate may propose or concur with Amendments as on other Bills.

[2]Every Bill which shall have passed the House of Representatives and the Senate, shall, before it becomes a Law, be presented to the President of the United States; If he approve he shall sign it, but if not he shall return it, with his Objections to the House in which it shall have originated, who shall enter the Objections at large on their Journal, and proceed to reconsider it. If after such Reconsideration two thirds of that House shall agree to pass the Bill, it shall be sent, together with the Objections to the other House, by which it shall likewise be reconsidered, and if approved by two thirds of that House, it shall become a Law. But in all such Cases the Votes of both Houses shall be determined by yeas and Nays, and the Names of the Persons voting for and against the Bill shall be entered on the Journal of each House respectively. If any Bill shall not be returned by the President within ten Days (Sundays excepted) after it shall have been presented to him, the Same shall be a Law,, in like Manner as if he had signed it, unless the Congress by their Adjournment prevents its Return, in which Case it shall not be a Law.

[3]Every Order, Resolution, or Vote to Which the Concurrence of the Senate and House of Representatives may be necessary (except on a question of Adjournment) shall be presented to the President of the United States; and before the Same shall take Effect, shall be approved by him, or being disapproved by him, shall be repassed by two thirds of the Senate and House

of Representatives, according to the Rules and Limitations prescribed in the Case of a Bill.

SECTION 8. [1]The Congress shall have Power To lay and collect Taxes, Duties, Imposts and Excises, to pay the Debts and provide for the common Defence and general Welfare of the United States; but all Duties, Imposts and Excises shall be uniform throughout the United States;

[2]To borrow money on the credit of the United States;

[3]To regulate Commerce with foreign Nations, and among the several States, and with the Indian Tribes;

[4]To establish an uniform Rule of Naturalization, and uniform Laws on the subject of Bankruptcies throughout the United States;

[5]To coin Money, regulate the value thereof, and of foreign Coin, and fix the Standard of Weights and Measures;

[6]To provide the Punishment of counterfeiting the Securities and current Coin of the United States;

[7]To establish Post Offices and post Roads;

[8]To promote the Progress of Science and useful Arts, by securing for limited Times to Authors and Inventors the exclusive Right to their respective Writings and Discoveries;

[9]To constitute Tribunals inferior to the supreme Court;

[10]To define and punish Piracies and Felonies committed on the high Seas, and Offenses against the Law of Nations;

[11]To declare War, grant Letters of Marque and Reprisal, and make Rules concerning Captures on Land and Water;

[12]To raise and support Armies, but no Appropriation of Money to that Use shall be for a longer Term than two Years;

[13]To provide and maintain a Navy;

[14]To make Rules for the Government and Regulation of the land and naval Forces;

[15]To provide for calling forth the Militia to execute the Laws of the Union, suppress Insurrections and repel Invasions;

[16]To provide for organizing, arming, and disciplining, the Militia, and for governing such Part of them as may be employed in the Service of the United States, reserving to the States respectively, the Appointment of the Officers, and the Authority of training the Militia according to the discipline prescribed by Congress;

[17]To exercise exclusive Legislation in all Cases whatsoever, over such District (not exceeding ten Miles square) as may, by Cession of particular States, and the Acceptance of Congress, become the Seat of the Government of the United States, and to exercise like Authority over all Places purchased by the Consent of the Legislature of the State in which the Same shall be, for the Erection of forts, Magazines, Arsenals, dock-yards, and other needful Buildings; And

[18]To make all Laws which shall be necessary and proper for carrying into Execution the foregoing Powers, and all other Powers vested by this Constitution in the Government of the Untied States, or in any Department or Officer thereof.

SECTION 9. [1]The Migration or Importation of such Persons as any of the States now existing shall think proper to admit, shall not be prohibited by the Congress prior to the Year one thousand eight hundred and eight, but a Tax or duty may be imposed on such Importation, not exceeding ten dollars for each Person.

[2]The privilege of the Writ of Habeas Corpus shall not be suspended, unless when in Cases of Rebellion or Invasion the public Safety may require it.

[3]No Bill of Attainder or ex post facto Law shall be passed.

[4]* No Capitation, or other direct, Tax shall be laid, unless in Proportion to the Census or Enumeration herein before directed to be taken.

[5]No Tax or Duty shall be laid on Articles exported from any State.

[6]No Preference shall be given by any Regulation of Commerce or Revenue to the Ports of one State over those of another: nor shall Vessels bound to, or from, one State, be obliged to enter, clear, or pay Duties in another.

[7]No Money shall be drawn from the Treasury, but in Consequence of Appropriations made by Law; and a regular Statement and Account of the Receipts and Expenditures of all public Money shall be published from time to time.

[8]No Title of Nobility shall be granted by the United States: And no Person holding any Office of Profit or Trust under them, shall, without the Consent of the Congress, accept of any present, Emolument, Office, or Title, of any kind whatever, from any King, Prince, or foreign State.

SECTION 10. [1]No State shall enter into any Treaty Alliance, or Confederation; grant Letters of Marque and Reprisal; coin Money; emit Bills of Credit; make any Thing but gold and silver Coin a Tender in Payment of Debts; pass any Bill of Attainder, ex post facto Law, or Law impairing the Obligation of Contracts, or grant any Title of Nobility.

[2]No State shall, without the Consent of the Congress, lay any Imposts or Duties on Imports or Exports, except what may be absolutely necessary for executing its inspection Laws: and the net Produce of all Duties and Imposts, laid by any State on Imports or Exports, shall be for the Use of the Treasury of the United States; and all such Laws shall be subject to the Revision and Controul of the Congress.

[3]No State shall, without the Consent of Congress, lay any Duty of Tonnage, keep Troops, or Ships of War in time of Peace, enter into any Agreement or Compact with another State, or with a foreign Power, or engage in War, unless actually invaded, or in such imminent Danger as will not admit of delay.

---

* See also Amendment XVI.

ARTICLE II

SECTION 1. [1]The executive Power shall be vested in a President of the United States of America. He shall hold his Office during the Term of four Years, and, together with the Vice President, chosen for the same Term, be elected, as follows:

[2] Each State shall appoint, in such Manner as the Legislature thereof may direct, a Number of Electors, equal to the whole Number of Senators and Representatives to which the State may be entitled in the Congress: but no Senator or Representative, or Person holding an Office of Trust or Profit under the United States, shall be appointed an Elector.

** [The Electors shall meet in their respective States, and vote by Ballot for two Persons, of whom one at least shall not be an Inhabitant of the same State with themselves. And they shall make a List of all the Persons voted for, and of the Number of Votes for each; which List they shall sign and certify, and transmit sealed to the Seat of the Government of the United States, directed to the President of the Senate. The President of the Senate shall, in the Presence of the Senate and House of Representatives, open all the Certificates, and the Votes shall then be counted. The Person having the greatest Number of Votes shall be the President, if such Number be a Majority of the whole Number of Electors appointed; and if there be more than one who have such Majority, and have an equal Number of Votes, then the House of Representatives shall immediately chuse by Ballot one of them for President; and if no Person have a Majority, then from the five highest on the List the said House shall in like Manner chuse the President. But in chusing the President, the Votes shall be taken by States, the Representation from each State having one Vote; a quorum for this Purpose shall consist of a Member or Members from two thirds of the States, and a Majority of all the States shall be necessary to a Choice. In every Case, after the Choice of the President, the Person having the greatest Number of Votes of the Electors shall be the Vice President. But if there should remain two or more who have equal Votes, the Senate shall chuse from them by Ballot the Vice President.]

[3]The Congress may determine the Time of chusing the Electors, and the Day on which they shall give their Votes; which Day shall be the same throughout the United States.

[4]No person except a natural born Citizen, or a Citizen of the United States, at the time of the Adoption of this Constitution, shall be eligible to the Office of President; neither shall any Person be eligible to that Office who shall not have attained to the Age of thirty five Years, and been fourteen Years a Resident within the United States.

[5]In case of the removal of the President from Office, or of his Death, Resignation or Inability to discharge the Powers and Duties of the said Office, the Same shall devolve on the Vice President, and the Congress may by Law provide for the Case of Removal, Death, Resignation or Inability, both of the President and Vice President, declaring what Officer shall then act as

---

** This paragraph has been superseded by amendment XII.

President, and such Officer shall act accordingly, until the Disability be removed, or a President shall be elected.

[6]The President shall, at stated Times, receive for his Services, a Compensation, which shall neither be increased nor diminished during the Period for which he shall have been elected, and he shall not receive within that Period any other Emolument from the United States, or any of them.

[7]Before he enter on the Execution of his Office, he shall take the following Oath or Affirmation: "I do solemnly swear (or affirm) that I will faithfully execute the Office of President of the United States, and will to the best of my Ability, preserve, protect and defend the Constitution of the United States."

SECTION 2. [1]The President shall be Commander in Chief of the Army and Navy of the United States, and of the Militia of the several States, when called into the actual Service of the United States; he may require the Opinion, in writing, of the principal Officer in each of the executive Departments, upon any subject relating to the Duties of their respective Offices, and he shall have Power to grant Reprieves and Pardons for Offenses against the United States, except in Cases of Impeachment.

[2]He shall have Power, by and with the Advice and Consent of the Senate, to make Treaties, provided two thirds of the Senators present concur; and he shall nominate, and by and with the Advice and Consent of the Senate, shall appoint Ambassadors, other public Ministers and Consuls, Judges of the supreme Court, and all other Officers of the United States, whose Appointments are not herein otherwise provided for, and which shall be established by Law: but the Congress may by Law vest the Appointment of such inferior Officers, as they think proper, in the President alone, to the Courts of Law, or in the Heads of Departments.

[3]The President shall have Power to fill up all Vacancies that may happen during the Recess of the Senate, by granting Commissions which shall expire at the End of their next Session.

SECTION 3. He shall from time to time give to the Congress Information of the State of the Union, and recommend to their Consideration such Measures as he shall judge necessary and expedient; he may, on extraordinary occasions, convene both Houses, or either of them, and in Case of Disagreement between them, with Respect to the time of Adjournment, he may adjourn them to such Time as he shall think proper; he shall receive Ambassadors and other public Ministers; he shall take Care that the Laws be faithfully executed, and shall Commission all the Officers of the United States.

SECTION 4. The President, Vice President and all civil Officers of the United States, shall be removed from Office on Impeachment for, and Conviction of, Treason, Bribery, or other high Crimes and Misdemeanors.

ARTICLE III

SECTION 1. The judicial Power of the United States, shall be vested in one supreme Court, and in such inferior Courts as the Congress may from time to time ordain and establish. The Judges, both of the supreme and inferior

Courts, shall hold their Offices during good Behaviour, and shall, at stated Times, receive for their Services, a Compensation, which shall not be diminished during their Continuance in Office.

SECTION 2. [1]The Judicial Power shall extend to all Cases, in Law and Equity, arising under this Constitution, the Laws of the United States, and Treaties made, or which shall be made, under their Authority; to all Cases affecting Ambassadors, other public Ministers and Consuls; to all Cases of admiralty and maritime Jurisdiction; to Controversies to which the United States shall be a Party; to Controversies between two or more States; between a State and Citizens of another State;* between Citizens of different States; between Citizens of the same State claiming Lands under Grants of different States, and between a State, or the Citizens thereof, and foreign States, Citizens or Subjects.

[2]In all Cases affecting Ambassadors, other public Ministers and Consuls, and those in which a State shall be a Party, the supreme Court shall have original Jurisdiction. In all the other Cases before mentioned, the supreme Court shall have appellate jurisdiction, both as to Law and Fact, with such Exceptions, and under such Regulations as the Congress shall make.

[3]The trial of all Crimes, except in Cases of Impeachment, shall be by Jury; and such Trial shall be held in State where the said Crimes shall have been committed; but when not committed within any State, the Trial shall be at such Place or Places as the Congress may by Law have directed.

SECTION 3. [1]Treason against the United States, shall consist only in levying War against them, or in adhering to their Enemies, giving them Aid and Comfort. No person shall be convicted of Treason unless on the Testimony of two Witnesses to the same overt Act, or on Confession in open Court.

[2]The Congress shall have Power to declare the Punishment of Treason, but no Attainder of Treason shall work Corruption of Blood, or Forfeiture except during the Life of the Person attainted.

ARTICLE IV

SECTION 1. Full Faith and Credit shall be given in each State to the public Acts, Records, and judicial Proceedings of every other State. And the Congress may by general Laws prescribe the Manner in which such Acts, Records and Proceedings shall be proved, and the Effect thereof.

SECTION 2. [1]The Citizens of each State shall be entitled to all Privileges and Immunities of Citizens in the several States.

[2]A Person charged in any State with Treason, Felony, or other Crime, who shall flee from Justice, and be found in another State, shall on demand of the executive Authority of the State from which he fled, be delivered up, to be removed to the State having Jurisdiction of the Crime.

[3]* [No Person held to Service or Labour in one State, under the Laws thereof, escaping into another, shall, in Consequence of any Law or Regulation

---

* This clause has been affected by amendment XI.   * This clause has been affected by amendment XIII.

therein, be discharged from such Service or Labour, but shall be delivered up on Claim of the Party to whom such Service or Labour may be due.]

SECTION 3. [1]New States may be admitted by the Congress into this Union; but no new State shall be formed or erected within the Jurisdiction of any other State; nor any State be formed by the Junction of two or more States, or Parts of States, without the Consent of the Legislatures of the States concerned as well as of the Congress.

[2]The Congress shall have Power to dispose of and make all needful Rules and Regulations respecting the Territory or other Property belonging to the United States; and nothing in this Constitution shall be so construed as to Prejudice any Claims of the United States, or of any particular State.

SECTION 4. The United States shall guarantee to every State in this Union a Republican Form of Government, and shall protect each of them against Invasion; and on Application of the Legislature, or of the Executive (when the Legislature cannot be convened) against domestic Violence.

ARTICLE V

The Congress, whenever two thirds of both Houses shall deem it necessary, shall propose Amendments to this Constitution, or, on the Application of the Legislatures of two thirds of the several States, shall call a Convention for proposing Amendments, which, in either Case, shall be valid to all Intents and Purposes, as part of this Constitution, when ratified by the Legislatures of three fourths of the several States, or by Conventions in three fourths thereof, as the one or the other Mode of Ratification may be proposed by the Congress; Provided that no Amendment which may be made prior to the Year One thousand eight hundred and eight shall in any Manner affect the first and fourth Clauses in the Ninth Section of the first Article; and that no State, without its Consent, shall be deprived of its equal Suffrage in the Senate.

ARTICLE VI

[1]All Debts contracted and Engagements entered into, before the Adoption of this Constitution, shall be as valid against the United States under this Constitution, as under the Confederation.

[2]This Constitution, and the Laws of the United States which shall be made in Pursuance thereof; and all Treaties made, or which shall be made, under the Authority of the United States, shall be the supreme Law of the Land; and the Judges in every State shall be bound thereby, any Thing in the Constitution or Laws of any State to the Contrary notwithstanding.

[3]The Senators and Representatives before mentioned, and the Members of the several State Legislatures, and all executive and Judicial Officers, both of the United States and of the several States, shall be bound by Oath or Affirmation, to support this Constitution; but no religious Test shall ever be required as a Qualification to any Office or public Trust under the United States.

ARTICLE VII

The Ratification of the Conventions of nine States shall be sufficient for the Establishment of this Constitution between the States so ratifying the Same.

Done in Convention by the Unanimous Consent of the States present the Seventeenth Day of September in the Year of our Lord one thousand seven hundred and Eighty seven and of the Independence of the United States of America the Twelfth.

ARTICLES IN ADDITION TO, AND AMENDMENT OF, THE CONSTITUTION OF THE UNITED STATES OF AMERICA, PROPOSED BY CONGRESS, AND RATIFIED BY THE LEGISLATURES OF THE SEVERAL STATES, PURSUANT TO THE FIFTH ARTICLE OF THE ORIGINAL CONSTITUTION.

AMENDMENT I

Congress shall make no law respecting an establishment of religion, or prohibiting the free exercise thereof; or abridging the freedom of speech, or of the press; or the right of the people peaceably to assemble and to petition the Government for a redress of grievances.

AMENDMENT II

A well regulated Militia, being necessary to the security of a free State, the right of the people to keep and bear Arms, shall not be infringed.

AMENDMENT III

No Soldier shall, in time of peace be quartered in any house, without the consent of the Owner, nor in time of war, but in a manner to be prescribed by law.

AMENDMENT IV

The right of the people to be secure in their persons, houses, papers, and effects, against unreasonable searches and seizures, shall not be violated, and no Warrants shall issue, but upon probable cause, supported by Oath or affirmation and particularly describing the Place to be searched, and the persons or things to be seized.

AMENDMENT V

No person shall be held to answer for a capital, or otherwise infamous crime, unless on a presentment or indictment of a Grand Jury, except in cases arising in the land or naval forces, or in the Militia, when in actual service in time of War or public danger; nor shall any person be subject for the same offence to be twice put in jeopardy of life or limb; nor shall be compelled in any criminal case to be a witness against himself, nor be deprived of life, liberty, or property, without due process of law; nor shall private property be taken for public use, without just compensation.

AMENDMENT VI

In all criminal prosecutions, the accused shall enjoy the right to a speedy and public trial, by an impartial jury of the State and district wherein the crime shall have been committed, which district shall have been previously ascertained by law, and to be informed of the nature and cause of the accusation: to be confronted with the witnesses against him; to have compulsory process for obtaining witnesses in his favor, and to have the Assistance of Counsel for his defence.

AMENDMENT VII

In suits at common law, where the value in controversy shall exceed twenty dollars, the right of trial by jury shall be preserved, and no fact tried by jury, shall be otherwise reexamined in any Court of the United States, than according to the rules of the common law.

AMENDMENT VIII

Excessive bail shall net be required, nor excessive fines imposed, nor cruel and unusual punishments inflicted.

AMENDMENT IX

The enumeration in the Constitution, of certain rights, shall not be construed to deny or disparage others retained by the people.

AMENDMENT X

The powers not delegated to the United States by the Constitution, nor prohibited by it to the States, are reserved to the States respectively, or to the people.

(Ratification of first ten amendments was completed December 15, 1791.)

SECTION 2. The Congress shall have power to enforce this article by appropriate legislation.

(Declared ratified March 30, 1870.)

AMENDMENT XI

The Judicial power of the United States shall not be construed to extend to any suit in law or equity, commenced or prosecuted against one of the United States by Citizens of another State, or by Citizens or Subjects of any Foreign State.

(Declared ratified January 8, 1798.)

AMENDMENT XII

The electors shall meet in their respective states and vote by ballot for President and Vice-President, one of whom, at least, shall not be an inhabitant of the same state with themselves; they shall name in their ballots the person voted for as President, and in distinct ballots the person voted for as Vice-President, and they shall make distinct lists of all persons voted for as President, and of all persons voted for as Vice-President, and of the number of votes for each, which lists they shall sign and certify, and transmit sealed to the seat of the government of the United States, directed to the President the Senate; The President of the Senate shall, in presence of the Senate and House of Representatives, open all the certificates and the votes shall then be counted; The person having the greatest number of votes for President, shall be the President, if such number be a majority of the whole number of Electors appointed; and if no person have such majority, then from the persons having the highest numbers not exceeding three on the list of those voted for as President, the House of Representatives shall choose immediately, by ballot, the President. But in choosing the President, the votes shall be taken by states, the representation from each state having one vote; a quorum for this purpose shall consist of a member or members from two-thirds of the states, and a majority of all the states shall be necessary to a choice. * [And if the House of Representatives shall not choose a President whenever the right of choice shall devolve upon them, before the fourth day of March next following, then the Vice-President shall act as President, as in the case of the death or other constitutional disability of the President.] The person having the greatest number of votes as Vice-President, shall be the Vice-President, if such number be a majority, then from the two highest numbers on the list, the Senate shall choose the Vice-President; a quorum for the purpose shall consist of two-thirds of the whole number of Senators, and a majority of the whole number shall be necessary to a choice. But no person constitutionally ineligible to the office of President shall be eligible to that of Vice-President of the United States.

(Declared ratified September 25, 1804.)

AMENDMENT XIII

SECTION 1. Neither slavery nor involuntary servitude, except as a punishment for crime whereof the party shall have been duly convicted, shall exist within the United States, or any place subject to their jurisdiction.

AMENDMENT XIV

SECTION 1. All persons born or naturalized in the United States, and subject to the jurisdiction thereof, are citizens of the United States and of the State wherein they reside. No, State shall make or enforce any law which shall abridge the privileges or immunities of citizens of the United States; nor shall any State deprive any person of life, liberty, or property, without due process of law; nor deny to any person within its jurisdiction the equal protection of the laws.

SECTION 2. Representatives shall be apportioned among the several States according to their respective numbers, counting the whole number of persons

---

* The part included in heavy brackets has been superseded by section 3 of amendment XX.

in each State, excluding Indians not taxed. But when the right to vote at any election for the choice of electors for President and Vice-President of the United States, Representatives in Congress, the Executive and Judicial officers of a State, or the members of the Legislature thereof, is denied to any of the male inhabitants of such State, being twenty-one years of age, and citizens of the United States, or in any way abridged, except for participation in rebellion, or other crime, the basis of representation therein shall be reduced in the proportion which the number of such male citizens shall bear to the whole number of male citizens twenty-one years of age in such State.

SECTION 3. No person shall be a Senator or Representative in Congress, or elector of President and Vice-President, or hold any office, civil or military, under the United States, or under any State, who, having previously taken an oath, as a member of Congress, or as an officer of the United States, or as a member of any State legislature, or as an executive or judicial officer of any State, to support the Constitution of the United States, shall have engaged in insurrection or rebellion against the same, or given aid or comfort to the enemies thereof. But Congress may by a vote of two-thirds of each House, remove such disability.

SECTION 4. The validity of the public debt of the United States, authorized by law, including debts incurred for payment of pensions and bounties for services in suppressing insurrection or rebellion, shall not be questioned. ut neither the United States nor any State shall assume or pay any debt or obligation incurred in aid of insurrection or rebellion against the United States, or any claim for the loss or emancipation of any slave; but all such debts, obligations and claims shall be held illegal and void.

SECTION 5. The Congress shall have power to enforce, by appropriate legislation, the provisions of this article.

(Declared ratified July 28, 1868.)

AMENDMENT XV

SECTION 1. The right of citizens of the United States to vote shall not be denied or abridged by the United States or by any State on account of race, color, or previous condition of servitude

SECTION 2. The Congress shall have power to enforce this article by appropriate legislation.

(Declared ratified March 30, 1870.)

AMENDMENT XVI

The Congress shall have power to lay and collect taxes on incomes, from whatever source derived, without apportionment among the several States, and without regard to any census or enumeration.

(Declared ratified February 25, 1913.)

AMENDMENT XVII

The Senate of the United States shall be composed of two Senators from each State, elected by the people thereof, for six years; and each Senator shall have one vote. The electors in each State shall have the qualifications requisite for electors of the most numerous branch of the State legislatures.

When vacancies happen in the representation of any State in the Senate, the executive authority of such State shall issue writs of election to fill such vacancies: Provided, That the legislature of any State may empower the executive thereof to make temporary appointments until the people fill the vacancies by election as the legislature may direct.

This amendment shall not be so construed as to affect the election or term of any Senator chosen before it becomes valid as part of the Constitution.

(Declared ratified May 31, 1913.)

AMENDMENT XVIII

[SECTION 1. After one year from the ratification of this article the manufacture, sale, or transportation of intoxicating liquors within, the importation thereof into, or the exportation thereof from the United States and all territory subject to the jurisdiction thereof for beverage purposes is hereby prohibited.

[SECTION 2. The Congress and the several States shall have concurrent power to enforce this article by appropriate legislation.

[SECTION 3. This article shall be inoperative unless it shall have been ratified as an amendment to the Constitution by the legislatures of the several States, as provided in the Constitution, within seven years from the date of the submission hereof to the States by the Congress.] *

AMENDMENT XIX

The right of citizens of the United States to vote shall not be denied or abridged by the United States or by any State on account of sex.

Congress shall have power to enforce this article by appropriate legislation.

(Declared ratified August 26, 1920.)

AMENDMENT XX

SECTION 1. The terms of the President and Vice-President shall end at noon on the 20th day of January, and the terms of Senators and Representative at noon on the 3d day of January, of the years in which such terms would have ended if this article had not been ratified; and the terms of their successors shall then begin.

SECTION 2. The Congress shall assemble at least once in every year, and such meeting shall begin at noon on the 3d day of January, unless they shall by law appoint a different day.

SECTION 3. If, at the time for the beginning of the term of the President, the President elect shall have died, the Vice-President elect shall become

---

* Amendment XVIII was repealed by section 1 of amendment XXI. (Declared ratified January 29, 1919).

President. If a President shall not have been chosen before the time fixed for the beginning of his term, or if the President elect shall have failed to qualify, then the Vice-President elect shall act as President until a President shall have qualified; and the Congress may by law provide for the case wherein neither a President elect nor a Vice-President elect shall have qualified, declaring who shall then act as President, or the manner in which one who is to act shall be selected, and such person shall act accordingly until a President or Vice-President shall have qualified.

SECTION 4. The Congress may by law provide for the case of the death of any of the persons from whom the House of Representatives may choose a President whenever the right of choice shall have devolved upon them and for the case of the death of any of the persons from whom the Senate may choose a Vice-President whenever the right of choice shall have devolved upon them.

SECTION 5. Sections 1 and 2 shall take effect on the 15th day of October following the ratification of this article.

SECTION 6. This article shall be inoperative unless it shall have been ratified as an amendment to the Constitution by the legislatures of three-fourths of the several States within seven years from the date of its submission.

(Declared ratified February 6, 1933.)

AMENDMENT XXI

SECTION 1. The eighteenth article of amendment to the Constitution of the United States is hereby repealed.

SECTION 2. The transportation or importation into any State, Territory, or possession of the United States for delivery or use therein of intoxicating liquors, in violation of the laws thereof, is hereby prohibited.

SECTION 3. This article shall be inoperative unless it shall have been ratified as an amendment to the Constitution by conventions in the several States, as provided in the Constitution, within seven years from the date of the submission hereof to the States by the Congress.

AMENDMENT XXII

SECTION 1. No person shall be elected to the office of the President more than twice, and no person who has held the office of President, or acted as President, for more than two years of a term to which some other person was elected President shall be elected to the office of the President more than once. But this article shall not apply to any person holding the office of President when this Article was proposed by the Congress, and shall not prevent any person who may be holding the office of the President, or acting as President, during the term within which this Article becomes operative from holding the office of President or acting as President during the remainder of

SECTION 2. This article shall be inoperative unless it shall have been ratified as an amendment to the Constitution by the legislatures of three-fourths of the several States within seven years from the date of its submission to the States by the Congress.

(Declared ratified March 1, 1951.)

AMENDMENT XXIII

SECTION 1. The District constituting the seat of Government of the United States shall appoint in such manner as the Congress may direct:

A number of electors of President and Vice President equal to the whole number of Senators and Representatives in Congress to which the District would be entitled if it were a State, but in no event more than the least populous State; they shall be in addition to those appointed by the States, but they shall be considered, for the purposes of the election of President and Vice President, to be electors appointed by a State; and they shall meet in the District and perform such duties as provided by the twelfth article of amendment.

SECTION 2. The Congress shall have power to enforce this article by appropriate legislation.

(Declared ratified April 3, 1961.)

AMENDMENT XXIV

Section 1. The right of citizens of the United States to vote in any primary or other election for President or Vice President, for electors for President or Vice President, or for Senator or Representative in Congress, shall not be denied or abridged by the United States or any State by reason of failure to pay any poll tax or other tax.

SECTION 2. The Congress shall have power to enforce this article by appropriate legislation.

(Declared ratified February 4, 1962.)

AMENDMENT XXV

SECTION 1. In case of the removal of the President from office or of his death or resignation, the Vice President shall become President.

SECTION 2. Whenever there is a vacancy in the office of the Vice President, the President shall nominate a Vice President who shall take office upon confirmation by a majority vote of both Houses of Congress.

SECTION 3. Whenever the President transmits to the President pro tempore of the Senate and the Speaker of the House of Representatives his written declaration that he is unable to discharge the powers and duties of his office, and until he transmits to them a written declaration to the contrary, such powers and duties shall be discharged by the Vice President as Acting President.

SECTION 4. Whenever the Vice President and a majority of either the principal officers of the executive departments or of such other body as Congress may by law provide, transmit to the President pro tempore of the Senate and the Speaker of the House of Representatives their written declaration that the President is unable to discharge the powers and duties of his office, the Vice President shall immediately assume the powers and the duties of the office as Acting President.

Thereafter, when the President transmits to the President pro tempore of the Senate and the Speaker of the House of Representatives his written declaration that no inability exists, he shall resume the powers and duties of this office unless the Vice President and a majority of either the principal officers of the executive department or of such other body as Congress may by law provide, transmit within four days to the President pro tempore of the Senate and the Speaker of the House of Representatives their written declaration that the President is unable to discharge the powers and duties of his office. Thereupon Congress shall decide the issue, assembling within forty-eight hours for that purpose if not in session. If the Congress, within twenty-one days after receipt of the latter written declaration, or, if Congress is not in session, within twenty-one days after Congress is required to assemble, determines by two-thirds vote of both Houses that the President is unable to discharge the powers and duties of his office, the Vice President shall continue to discharge the same as Acting President; otherwise, the President shall resume the powers and duties of his office.

(Declared ratified February 10, 1967.)

AMENDMENT XXVI

SECTION 1. The right of citizens of the United States, who are eighteen years of age or older, to vote shall not be denied or abridged by the United States or by any State on account of age.

SECTION 2. The Congress shall have power to enforce this article by appropriate legislation.

(Declared ratified July 1, 1971.)

AMENDMENT XXVII [1992]

No law varying the Compensation for the services of the Senators and Representatives shall take effect, unless an election of Representatives shall have intervened. *

(Declared ratified May 7, 1992.)

---

* The 27th Amendment was proposed by the First Congress in 1789 as one of twelve amendments, ten of which including those now known as the Bill of Rights were ratified by 1791. Without further action by Congress, efforts at ratification of this amendment resumed in the 1970s; by 1992 thirty-eight states had acted to ratify. The Archivist of the United States certified the amendment's adoption, and Congress by joint resolution declared it validly part of the Constitution. The passage of over two centuries between proposal and ratification raises questions about the effectiveness of the 27th Amendment's adoption, cf. Coleman v. Miller, 307 U.S. 433 (1939), but no challenge has been adjudicated or seems likely.

Table of Readings

Table of Cases

[References are to page numbers and footnotes.]

[References are to page numbers and footnotes.]

[References are to page numbers and footnotes.]

INDEX

[References are to page numbers.]

[References are to page numbers.]

[References are to page numbers.]

[References are to page numbers.]